Mobile Technologies in the Ancient Sahara and Beyond

The ancient Sahara has often been treated as a periphery or barrier, but this agenda-setting book – the final volume of the Trans-Saharan Archaeology series – demonstrates that it was teeming with technological innovations, knowledge transfer and trade from long before the Islamic period. In each chapter, expert authors present important syntheses, and new evidence for technologies from oasis farming and irrigation, animal husbandry and textile weaving, to pottery, glass and metal making by groups inhabiting the Sahara and contiguous zones. Scientific analysis is brought together with anthropology and archaeology. The resultant picture of transformations in technologies between the third millennium BC and the second millennium AD is rich and detailed, including analysis of the relationship between the different materials and techniques discussed, and demonstrating the significance of the Sahara both in its own right and in telling the stories of neighbouring regions.

CHLOË N. DUCKWORTH is a Lecturer in Archaeological Materials Science at Newcastle University, specialising in the archaeology of technology, and particularly in the multidisciplinary investigation of ancient and Medieval glasses, from experimental reconstruction of furnaces and glass objects, to the use of historical texts, to chemical and stylistic analysis.

AURÉLIE CUÉNOD is an Honorary Visiting Fellow at the University of Leicester. Her research has focused on metal production and trade in the pre-Islamic Sahara. She has in particular studied the metalworking evidence from Fazzan in Libya as a member of the Trans-SAHARA Project and participated to field and laboratory research on the metals of southern Morocco for the Middle Draa Project.

DAVID J. MATTINGLY is Professor of Roman Archaeology at the University of Leicester. He has worked in the Sahara for forty years and is the author of many books and articles related to Saharan archaeology, such as *Farming the Desert* (2 vols, 1996), which won the James R. Wiseman book award of the American Institute of Archaeology, and the *Archaeology of Fazzan* series (4 vols, 2003–2013). He was the principal investigator of the European Research Council-funded Trans-SAHARA Project (2011–2017) which created the groundwork for this volume, and he is the overall series editor of *Trans-Saharan Archaeology*, in which this is the final instalment of four volumes.

THE TRANS-SAHARAN ARCHAEOLOGY SERIES

Series editor
D. J. Mattingly

Trade in the Ancient Sahara and Beyond
Edited by D. J. Mattingly, V. Leitch, C. N. Duckworth, A. Cuénod, M. Sterry and F. Cole

Burials, Migration and Identity in the Ancient Sahara and Beyond
Edited by M. C. Gatto, D. J. Mattingly, N. Ray and M. Sterry

Urbanisation and State Formation in the Ancient Sahara and Beyond
Edited by M. Sterry and D. J. Mattingly

Mobile Technologies in the Ancient Sahara and Beyond
Edited by C. N. Duckworth, A. Cuénod and D. J. Mattingly

Mobile Technologies in the Ancient Sahara and Beyond

Edited by

C. N. DUCKWORTH
University of Newcastle upon Tyne

A. CUÉNOD
University of Leicester

D. J. MATTINGLY
University of Leicester

Trans-Saharan Archaeology Volume 4
Series editor:
D. J. Mattingly

European Research Council
Established by the European Commission

Society for Libyan Studies

CAMBRIDGE
UNIVERSITY PRESS

CAMBRIDGE
UNIVERSITY PRESS

University Printing House, Cambridge CB2 8BS, United Kingdom

One Liberty Plaza, 20th Floor, New York, NY 10006, USA

477 Williamstown Road, Port Melbourne, VIC 3207, Australia

314–321, 3rd Floor, Plot 3, Splendor Forum, Jasola District Centre,
New Delhi – 110025, India

79 Anson Road, #06–04/06, Singapore 079906

Cambridge University Press is part of the University of Cambridge.

It furthers the University's mission by disseminating knowledge in the pursuit of
education, learning, and research at the highest international levels of excellence.

www.cambridge.org
Information on this title: www.cambridge.org/9781108830546
DOI: 10.1017/9781108908047

First published 2020

Printed in the United Kingdom by TJ International Ltd, Padstow Cornwall

A catalogue record for this publication is available from the British Library.

Library of Congress Cataloging-in-Publication Data
Names: Duckworth, Chloë N. editor. | Cuénod, Aurélie, 1985– editor. |
Mattingly, D. J., editor.
Title: Mobile technologies in the ancient Sahara and beyond / edited by C.N. Duckworth,
A. Cuénod D.J. Mattingly.
Description: Cambridge, United Kingdom ; New York, NY : Cambridge University Press,
2020. | Series: Trans-saharan archaeology ; 4 | Includes bibliographical references and index.
Identifiers: LCCN 2020022948 (print) | LCCN 2020022949 (ebook) | ISBN 9781108830546
(hardback) | ISBN 9781108908047 (ebook)
Subjects: LCSH: Africa, Sub-Saharan – Antiquities. | Material culture – Africa, Sub-Saharan.
| Technology – Social aspects – Africa, Sub-Saharan. | Textile fabrics, Ancient – Africa,
Sub-Saharan. | Glassware, Ancient – Africa, Sub-Saharan. | Pottery, Ancient – Africa,
Sub-Saharan. | Garamantes (African people). | Africa, North – History.
Classification: LCC DT352.3 .M63 2020 (print) | LCC DT352.3 (ebook) | DDC 966–dc23
LC record available at https://lccn.loc.gov/2020022948
LC ebook record available at https://lccn.loc.gov/2020022949

ISBN 978-1-108-83054-6 Hardback

Contents

Figures

Tables

xii

Contributors

Touatia Amraoui is a CNRS Researcher at Aix-Marseille Université, CCJ, Aix-en-Provence, France.

Aurélie Cuénod is an Honorary Research Fellow in the School of Archaeology and Ancient History, University of Leicester.

Chloë N. Duckworth is Lecturer in Archaeological Science at the Newcastle University.

B. Tyr Fothergill is an Honorary Research Fellow at the De Montfort University, Leicester.

Maria Carmela Gatto is an Honorary Research Fellow in the School of Archaeology and Ancient History, University of Leicester.

Jane Humphris is Director of the British Institute in Eastern Africa.

Veerle Linseele is Senior Policy Advisor at VARIO (Flemish Advisory Council for Innovation and Enterprise).

Mario Liverani is Emeritus Professor at La Sapienza University, Rome, and a Fellow of the Accademia dei Lincei.

Sonja Magnavita is Lecturer at the Institute for Archaeological Research, Rühr-University in Bochum.

David J. Mattingly is Professor of Roman Archaeology in the School of Archaeology and Ancient History, University of Leicester.

Thilo Rehren is A.G. Leventis Professor for Archaeological Sciences and Director of the Science and Technology in Archaeology and Culture Research Center, the Cyprus Institute.

Peter Robertshaw is Emeritus Professor at California State University, San Bernardino.

Caroline Robion-Brunner is a CNRS Researcher at the Université de Toulouse.

Daniela Rosenow is Senior Research Fellow at the German Archaeological Institute, Cairo.

Martin Sterry is an Honorary Research Fellow in the School of Archaeology and Ancient History, University of Leicester.

Silvia Valenzuela Lamas is Principal Researcher ERC-StG ZooMWest, Consejo Superior de Investigaciones Científicas (CSIC), Barcelona.

Andrew Wilson is Professor of Archaeology of the Roman Empire, University of Oxford.

Preface

When I was working on my PhD thesis on the Roman province of Tripolitania (north-west Libya) in the early 1980s, I became intrigued by a desert people who inhabited Fazzan, the area of the Central Sahara to the south of Tripolitania. This was my first introduction to the Garamantes. They were regularly mentioned in the ancient Greek and Roman sources, although seldom in complimentary terms – for the most part being depicted as nomadic and uncouth barbarians.[1] However, some pioneering archaeological work in the 1930s and then again in the 1960s–1970s had revealed their physical traces to be considerably more sophisticated than would be assumed on the basis of the literary stereotypes.[2]

This volume arises out of my subsequent direct engagement across more than 20 years with the archaeology of Fazzan. In 1996, I was given the chance to renew field research in what were effectively the Garamantian heartlands. Following an initial scoping visit that year, I directed the Fazzan Project across six years, carrying out excavations and a survey around the capital of the Garamantes at Garama (Old Jarma), with an emphasis on tracing evidence for their settlements, but also mapping other archaeological features including cemeteries and irrigation systems.[3] A notable result of this work was the clear demonstration of the sophisticated and substantial network of oasis farming settlements that lay at the heart of the Garamantian territory. Rather than being 'nomadic barbarians', the Garamantes now appear to have been predominantly sedentary oasis farmers, living in substantial permanent and complex settlements of mudbrick buildings. That is not to say that the Garamantes did not also incorporate pastoral elements, but simply to highlight the unexpected density and sophistication of sedentary oasis settlements. There is strong

---

[1] See in particular, Mattingly 2003, 79–81; 2011, 34–37 on the concept of 'progressive barbarisation' imposed by ancient authors as a factor of distance from the Mediterranean.

[2] Ayoub 1967; Daniels 1968; 1970; 1971; 1989; Pace *et al.* 1951.

[3] There were five seasons of fieldwork (1997–2001) and a finds study season (2002). The results are now fully published as Mattingly 2003; 2007; 2010; 2013. Funding for the Fazzan Project came primarily from the Society for Libyan Studies, the Leverhulme Trust, the British Academy and the Arts and Humanities Research Council.

evidence to identify the top level of their settlement hierarchy as 'urban' in character and their overall society as an early Saharan state.[4]

My work on the Garamantes has subsequently evolved through a series of further projects. From 2007 to 2011, I directed the Desert Migrations Project, with a particular focus on Garamantian burials and funerary traditions.[5] The increasing availability of high-resolution satellite imagery opened a new avenue of research in 2011, the Peopling the Desert project, which extended research on the Garamantes to another of the major oasis bands in Fazzan, the Murzuq depression.[6]

The Trans-SAHARA Project: State Formation, Migration and Trade in the Central Sahara (1000 BC–AD 1500) (2011–2017) marked a further evolution of this body of work, seeking to place the Garamantes in their Saharan context and to address the wider implications of the results obtained in the earlier work.[7] The project sought to investigate the nature and consequences of the interconnectivity of the Trans-Saharan zone in the pre-Islamic period. The work of the Trans-SAHARA Project was organised around a series of four workgroups, each one supported by early career postdoctoral research associates and each dealing with a discrete group of themes: trade; migration, burial practice and identity; mobile technologies; urbanisation and state formation. As a key element of the work programme, a small conference was held at Leicester for each of the workgroups, to which international scholars working on neighbouring areas of the Trans-Saharan zone were invited. From the outset, these conferences were conceived as offering a chance to engage a group of leading experts in the field in a high-level debate about the implications of the new information on the Garamantes for studies of the wider Trans-Saharan world. Papers were commissioned for an intended series of agenda-setting volumes on Trans-Saharan archaeology and pre-circulated so that the conferences focused entirely on discussion of their content.

One of the major obstacles hindering understanding of the Sahara through history is that the study of the desert and the neighbouring zones of North Africa, the Nile Valley, Sudan and West Africa has tended to be compartmentalised into chronologically or regionally specific

---

[4] Mattingly 2013, 530–34; Mattingly and Sterry 2013.

[5] Five planned seasons of fieldwork were completed by 2011, but the scheduled study season could not take place in 2012 because of the Libyan civil war. Interim reports have been published in *Libyan Studies* from 2007 to 2011, Mattingly *et al.* 2007; 2008; 2009; 2010a; 2010b; 2011. Funding for the Desert Migrations Project came primarily from the Society for Libyan Studies.

[6] Sterry and Mattingly 2011; 2013; Sterry *et al.* 2012. The Peopling the Desert Project was funded by the Leverhulme Trust.

[7] The Trans-SAHARA Project was funded by the European Research Council (grant no. 269418).

investigations. Broader synthesis across the vast Trans-Saharan zone has been lacking. The term 'Trans-Saharan' should be understood in the context of this book as referring to the connected spaces of the Sahara and its eastern, northern and southern peripheries. The Sahara has often been likened to a great sea and no sea can be understood without reference to its adjacent shore-lands. The idea of Trans-Saharan perspectives on historical developments thus shares much in common with recent studies of the Mediterranean, which have stressed the importance of connectivity and supra-regional influences.[8]

This volume, the fourth in a series of four, thus presents some of the key work of the Trans-SAHARA team and an international pool of collaborators on the theme of technology. The recent systematic work on the Garamantes has revealed much new information about their technological capabilities and their engagement with technologies or technological packages developed elsewhere. Several contributions to this volume describe and analyse the main evidence for the technology of the Garamantes, while others present complementary studies on neighbouring regions and later time periods. The volumes in this series are thus unusual edited books in that each one has at its core an extended and detailed presentation of the key results of the Trans-SAHARA research team's work, combined with the comparative perspectives of invited external experts. As the Cambridge University Press reviewers of the volumes have noted, in the interest of promoting debate we also invited critique and contradiction from these external specialists. We think that adds to the special character of the resulting books, integrating new evidence with a broad overview of the state of the field and combining agenda-setting ideas with different perspectives.

The resulting series of publications meets one of the key aims of the Trans-SAHARA Project: to examine from a broad perspective questions of trade, human movement, identity, production and urbanisation on a supra-regional scale. Interaction is central to both the developing historical-archaeological picture of past life in the Sahara, and the integrated methodological perspective offered by the Trans-SAHARA Project, with experts in various materials and regions learning from and sharing with one another.

In the spirit of this interaction, we also held two additional workshops associated with the technology conference. The first of these, spread over two days, brought together experts in the handmade pottery of different

---

[8] Abulafia 2011; Broodbank 2013; Horden and Purcell 2000. See Lichtenberger 2016 for the explicit comparison of Mediterranean and Sahara.

regions of the Sahara and Sahel. Crucially, the attendees brought samples
of pottery with them, allowing comparisons between the techniques and
styles of different regions, as well as discussions of the broader themes and
questions arising from this regional approach. No consensus view emerged
on whether we can discuss these materials from a supra-regional perspective, but the possibility was at least put on the table – as were the pots – for
the first time.[9] The second workshop was a one-day affair, examining the
latest advances in studying the archaeology of metals and glass recycling,
themes of direct relevance to the scientific examination of these materials
in the archaeological record. Recycling affects a whole range of methodological approaches, from geographical provenance studies to concepts of
object biography and what counts as a 'raw material' in different social
contexts. In the course of the workshop, attendees presented and discussed
various methods of studying recycling from an analytical perspective, and
considered some of the current challenges facing archaeometry, including
the use of historical datasets, access to data, and the meaning and contexts
of recycling practice. The workshop brought together various experts
working on recycling from an archaeometric perspective for the first
time.[10] The conversations which were initiated are ongoing, and are
being revisited and developed in other fora.[11]

As we are asking our readers to often step outside their core areas of
knowledge and expertise to engage with material from other parts of the
Trans-Saharan zone, place names and their mapping have exercised us all.
Systems of transliteration and spelling of place names across the Trans-
Saharan region vary enormously and the same site can be presented in
several distinct ways. We have tried to impose a measure of consistency in
the transliteration of names, following the practice I adopted for the

---

[9] Workshop organised by Maria Carmela Gatto (University of Leicester). Participants: Touatia
Amraoui (CNRS-Université Lyon 2), Youssef Bokbot (INSAP), David Edwards (University of
Leicester), Olivier Gosselain (Université Libre de Bruxelles), Anne Haour (University of East
Anglia), Victoria Leitch (University of Leicester), Kevin MacDonald (University College
London), Susan McIntosh (Rice University), Sonja Magnavita (German Archaeological
Institute, Bonn), Carlos Magnavita (Frankfurt) and Anne Mayor (University of Geneva).

[10] Workshop organised by Chloë N. Duckworth and Aurélie Cuénod (University of Leicester).
Participants: Peter Bray (University of Oxford), Simon Chenery (British Geological Survey),
Thomas Fenn (Yale University), Ian Freestone (University College London), Julian Henderson
(University of Nottingham), Caroline Jackson (University of Sheffield), Marianne Mödlinger
(Université Bordeaux Montaigne), Sarah Paynter (English Heritage), Mark Pollard (University
of Oxford), Peter Robertshaw (California State University), Daniela Rosenow (University
College London) and Victoria Sainsbury (University of Oxford).

[11] For example, a workshop led by Peter Bray, entitled 'Recycling Things and Ideas', held at the
21st Annual Meeting of the European Association of Archaeologists, Glasgow,
2–5 September 2015.

Archaeology of Fazzan series. However, for ease of recognition some exceptions have been allowed for sites whose canonical spelling is so well established in the literature. We trust that the maps provided will prove helpful with the identification of places named in the text, but hope that readers will share our sense of being on a journey of discovery as they read the following contributions.

David J. Mattingly

References

Abulafia, D. 2011. *The Great Sea: A Human History of the Mediterranean*. London: Allen Lane.

Ayoub, M.S. 1967. *Excavations in Germa between 1962 to 1966*. Tripoli: Ministry of Education.

Broodbank, C. 2013. *The Making of the Middle Sea: A History of the Mediterranean from the Beginning to the Emergence of the Classical World*. London: Thames and Hudson.

Daniels, C.M. 1968. Garamantian excavations: Zinchecra 1965–67. *Libya Antiqua* 5: 113–94.

Daniels, C.M. 1970. *The Garamantes of Southern Libya*. London: Oleander.

Daniels, C.M. 1971. The Garamantes of Fezzan. In F.F. Gadallah (ed.), *Libya in History*. Benghazi: University of Libya, 261–87.

Daniels, C.M. 1989. Excavation and fieldwork amongst the Garamantes. *Libyan Studies* 20: 45–61.

Horden, P. and Purcell, N. 2000. *The Corrupting Sea: A Study of Mediterranean History*. Oxford: Blackwell.

Lichtenberger, A. 2016. 'Sea without water' – conceptualising the Sahara and the Mediterranean. In M. Dabag, D. Haller, N. Jaspert and A. Lichtenberger (eds), *New Horizons. Mediterranean Research in the 21st Century*, Paderborn: Ferdinand Schoningh, 267–83.

Mattingly, D.J. (ed.) 2003. *The Archaeology of Fazzan. Volume 1, Synthesis*. London: Society for Libyan Studies, Department of Antiquities, London.

Mattingly, D.J. (ed.) 2007. *The Archaeology of Fazzan. Volume 2, Site Gazetteer, Pottery and Other Survey Finds*. London: Society for Libyan Studies, Department of Antiquities.

Mattingly, D.J. (ed.) 2010. *The Archaeology of Fazzan. Volume 3, Excavations Carried out by C.M. Daniels*. London: Society for Libyan Studies, Department of Antiquities.

Mattingly, D.J. 2011. *Imperialism, Power and Identity Experiencing the Roman Empire*. Princeton: Princeton University Press.

Mattingly, D.J. (ed.) 2013. *The Archaeology of Fazzan. Volume 4, Survey and Excavations at Old Jarma (Ancient Garama) Carried out by C.M. Daniels (1962–69) and the Fazzan Project (1997–2001).* London: Society for Libyan Studies, Department of Antiquities.

Mattingly, D.J. and Sterry, M. 2013. The first towns in the Central Sahara. *Antiquity* 87 (366): 503–18.

Mattingly, D.J., Lahr, M., Armitage, S., Barton, H., Dore, J., Drake, N., Foley, R., Merlo, S., Salem, M., Stock, J. and White, K. 2007. Desert migrations: People, environment and culture in the Libyan Sahara. *Libyan Studies* 38: 115–56.

Mattingly, D.J., Dore, J. and Lahr, M. (with contributions by others) 2008. DMP II: 2008 fieldwork on burials and identity in the Wadi al-Ajal. *Libyan Studies* 39: 223–62.

Mattingly, D.J., Lahr, M. and Wilson, A. 2009. DMP V: Investigations in 2009 of cemeteries and related sites on the west side of the Taqallit promontory. *Libyan Studies* 40: 95–131.

Mattingly, D.J., Abduli, H., Aburgheba, H., Ahmed, M., Ali Ahmed Esmaia, M., Baker, S., Cole, F., Fenwick, C., Gonzalez Rodriguez, M., Hobson, M., Khalaf, N., Lahr, M., Leitch, V., Moussa, F., Nikita, E., Parker, D., Radini, A., Ray, N., Savage, T., Sterry, M. and Schörle, K. 2010a. DMP IX: Summary report on the fourth season of excavations of the Burials and Identity team. *Libyan Studies* 41: 89–104.

Mattingly, D.J., Al-Aghab, S., Ahmed, M., Moussa, F., Sterry, M. and Wilson, A.I. 2010b. DMP X: Survey and landscape conservation issues around the Taqallit headland. *Libyan Studies* 41: 105–32.

Mattingly, D.J., Abduli, H., Ahmed, M., Cole, F., Fenwick, C., Gonzalez Rodriguez, M., Fothergill, B.T., Hobson, M., Khalaf, N., Lahr, M., Moussa, F., Nikita, E., Nikolaus, J., Radini, A., Ray, N., Savage, T., Sterry, M. and Wilson, A.I. 2011. DMP XII: Excavations and survey of the so-called Garamantian Royal Cemetery (GSC030–031). *Libyan Studies* 42: 89–102.

Pace, B., Sergi, S. and Caputo, G. 1951. Scavi sahariani. *Monumenti Antichi* 41: 150–549.

Sterry, M. and Mattingly, D.J. 2011. DMP XIII: Reconnaissance survey of archaeological sites in the Murzuq area. *Libyan Studies* 42: 103–16.

Sterry, M. and Mattingly, D.J. 2013. Desert Migrations Project XVII: Further AMS dates for historic settlements from Fazzan, south-west Libya. *Libyan Studies* 44: 127–40.

Sterry, M., Mattingly, D.J. and Higham, T. 2012. Desert Migrations Project XVI: Radiocarbon dates from the Murzuq region, southern Libya. *Libyan Studies* 43: 137–47.

PART I

Introduction

1 | Debating Mobile Technologies

CHLOË N. DUCKWORTH, AURÉLIE CUÉNOD
AND DAVID J. MATTINGLY

Introduction

This volume is the fourth and final volume resulting from a focused programme of research and intensive group discussion of a wide range of topics related to the archaeological (and to a lesser extent, historical and anthropological/ethnographic) analysis of ancient societies in and around the Sahara, from the first millennium BC to the mid-second millennium AD.[1] While the focus of the present volume is technology, there will inevitably be discussion of crossovers and contrasts with the main conclusions from earlier volumes in the series. As explained in the Preface, the Trans-SAHARA Project evolved out of a long-term programme of fieldwork on an ancient people of the Libyan Sahara. Just as they occupied a significant nodal location in the Sahara, the Garamantes are at the centre of this volume, but the scope of debate here extends way beyond the history of a single group.[2] Connections and barriers within the Trans-Saharan region (and the interrelationship between these two aspects) form one focus. In this introduction we present an overview of crucial themes and considerations which cross-cut all or many of the contributions. Fundamentally, this book seeks to explore what defines technology, how technological knowledge spreads and how technological change has happened in Saharan societies.

Following this introductory section, Part II of the volume comprises a series of chapters that broadly relate to technological mobility and transfers. Mario Liverani argues for the importance of technological transfer running along a hyper-arid Middle-Eastern belt that extended both

---

[1] For other volumes in the series, see Gatto *et al.* 2019; Mattingly *et al.* 2017; Sterry and Mattingly 2020.

[2] Mattingly 2003; 2007; 2010; 2013.

west and east of the Nile. Wilson *et al.* provide a detailed case study of foggara irrigation systems, one of the technologies that appear to have moved along Liverani's belt. B. Tyr Fothergill *et al.* take a similar approach to re-evaluating the evidence for the introduction of a range of domesticated animals, but with some chronological and spatial discontinuities highlighted, suggesting that the process of transfer was more complex. Chapters by Touatia Amraoui and Sonja Magnavita have a main focus on textile working in the Maghrib and West Africa, highlighting differences of chronology and technology that are not easy to reconcile with a single model of technological dissemination.

In Part III, three case studies on metallurgy are presented, with Aurélie Cuénod's chapter also serving as an introduction to the section. The bulk of her chapter presents the results from her work on Garamantian metallurgical practices and the compositional signatures of their metals. The following pair of chapters by Jane Humphris and Caroline Robion-Brunner focus on the debate about early ironworking technology in Sudan and West Africa respectively. They reflect on aspects of scale of production and local variability in technology.

Part IV then features three chapters on glassworking technology, with an extensive introduction again in the lead-off chapter by Chloë N. Duckworth. The detailed case study at the heart of her chapter again draws on the significant material she has analysed from Garamantian sites. Peter Robertshaw offers a masterly overview of glass beads, looking at but going beyond the scientific analysis of their provenance and focusing also on their social and commercial power in African societies. The overview by Thilo Rehren and Daniela Rosenow of Egyptian glassmaking across 3,000 years of production provides a benchmark of comparative analytical data.

Part V comprises a single discussion chapter by Maria Carmela Gatto, summarising the discussion and outcomes of the handmade pottery workshop that was held as part of the Mobile Technologies work of the Trans-SAHARA Project. A concluding chapter by the editors completes the volume by returning to some of the questions outlined in this chapter, as well as considering the contribution of the volume for future agendas.

Rather than providing a generalised description of the contributions to this volume one by one, we have attempted in what follows to interweave references to them throughout our discussion of the broad themes. In the next section we set out some issues relating to connectivity within the Trans-Saharan region, before turning to definitions of technology. The technological context of the Saharan world is then introduced, before we examine some more methodological aspects. The contributions of scientific studies are highlighted. In the second half of the chapter we introduce the other side of this volume's framing equation: how technology transfer works in a highly mobile desert world. The final section of the chapter addresses issues that complicate the narratives of technological change (adaptation and micro-invention, cross-craft interactions and interruptions).

The Connecting Sahara

> From southern Tunisia to southern Syria, the desert directly borders the sea. The relationship is not casual; it is intimate, sometimes difficult, and always demanding. So the desert is one of the faces of the Mediterranean.[3]

The very name Sahara is evocative, and conjures up a vast array of images, but it is perhaps fair to say that technology is not usually among them. Trade is certainly a prominent point of reference, epitomised by long camel trains driven by Muslim traders, carrying slaves, gold and salt. Whether the scale of trade and interaction across its vast distances allows us to see the Sahara as a barrier to contact, or a sort of connective tissue akin to Braudel's Mediterranean, has been debated numerous times over the years,[4] but it is generally agreed that the history of the Sahara itself is to a large extent a history of mobility.[5]

In this context, one of the factors that make the primarily oasis-dwelling Garamantes of the Central Sahara so significant is that they managed to build up and in the long term sustain a sedentary lifestyle on a relatively large scale, thanks largely to ingenious management and technological development of below-ground water resources,[6] coupled with involvement in far-reaching trade networks. Garamantian reliance on long-distance contacts must imply a close connection with mobile peoples, who are often less directly visible in the archaeological record.[7] For these nomadic peoples, too, technologies – particularly the use of animals – have been vital components in survival, economic gain and the structure of social life. The possibilities and constraints of changing technologies, and the interplay

---

[3] Braudel 1995, 24.

[4] See Lichtenberger 2016, for a recent discussion of Sahara as a desert sea. See also Lecocq 2015 and Lydon 2015.

[5] For definitions of mobility in a Saharan context, see Gatto *et al.* 2019, 19–22.

[6] See Wilson *et al.*, Chapter 3, this volume.

[7] Sterry and Mattingly 2020, chapters 1 and 2 for a detailed discussion of the mix of sedentary and pastoral elements in Garamantian society.

Table 1.1 *Summary of historical and environmental phasing in the Sahara and beyond*

Date (Millennium BC/AD)	Saharan climate and environment	Technological developments	Maghrib/ Mediterranean	Nile Valley	East Sahara	Central Sahara	West Sahara	Sub-Sahara
8 M BC	Start of Holocene pluvial, high stand of palaeolakes	Hunting and gathering, microlith and fine flaking technology, exploitation of wild animals and plants	Hunter gatherer societies	Hunter gatherer societies	Hunter gatherer societies	Hunter gatherer societies	Hunter gatherer societies	Hunter gatherer societies
7–6.5 M BC	Drought, reduced wadi flows, low stand of palaeolakes	Continuation of hunter gatherer technologies	Hunter gatherer societies	1st animal domestication/ transfers	Hunter gatherer societies	Hunter gatherer societies	Hunter gatherer societies	Hunter gatherer societies
6.5–4 M BC	Last pluvial phase, high stand of palaeolakes	Pastoralism – cattle and ovicaprins Pottery Ground stone tools for food processing Rock art	Pastoral phase	Pastoral phase & 1st agriculture experiments	Pastoral phase	Pastoral phase	Pastoral phase	Hunter gatherer societies
3 M BC	Start of hyper-arid phase	Donkeys Agriculture and arboriculture (Egypt) Nile irrigation Textiles Writing (Egypt)	Pastoral phase, first agricultural experiments	Pharaonic Egypt, Kerma in Sudan	First oases in Egyptian W. Desert	Final Late Pastoral era	Final Late Pastoral era	Pastoral societies – reinforced by Saharan migrants

2 M BC	Hyper-arid	Oasis irrigation (including shaduf well) Horses Chariots Copper metallurgy	Mainly pastoral, some agriculture?	Pharaonic Egypt, Kerma in Sudan	Spread and expansion of oases	Final Late Pastoral, first agricultural experiments?	Tichitt culture	Pastoral societies
1 M BC	Hyper-arid	Agriculture Iron metallurgy Oasis irrigation (including foggara) Mudbricks Camels Writing (Libya)	Early agrarian nucleated settlements (Althiburos) Phoenician emporia Greek colonies	Pharaonic Egypt, Meroitic Sudan	Monumentalisation of oases – e.g. Siwa	First oases in C. Sahara – rise of Garamantes	Still mainly pastoral societies?	Foundation of first urban sites (Jenne-jeno, etc.), agriculture and metallurgy
1 M AD	Hyper-arid	Glassworking Rotary querns Aqueducts and baths, concrete	Roman provinces (Cyrenaica, Africa, Mauretania). Vandal and Byzantine rule, then first Islamic dynasties	Roman Egypt, then Islamic	Urban status of leading oasis centres, high productive capacity	Garamantian heyday and decline, initial Islamic centre at Zuwila	Rise of W. Saharan routes in late 1st M (Sijilmasa)	Urban-scale settlements widespread (Chad, Mali, Senegal). Early proto-states
2 M AD	Hyper-arid	Water wheel Animal well (dalw)	Almoravid and Almohad dynasties	Islamic Egypt	Oasis civilisation continues on reduced scale	Oasis civilisation continues on reduced scale	Boom in oasis civilisation. Almoravid and Almohad dynasties originate in Sahara	Kingdoms of Ghana, Kanim, Songay empire

between technology and the fluctuating environment, are thus crucial elements in charting how human groups developed over time in this large and complex region. By applying a broader definition of technology and moving beyond simplistic evolutionary models of technological progress, as outlined below, we can begin to unravel the complex web of long-distance interchanges and local manipulations which gave rise to, and sustained, Saharan connections over several millennia.

Geography and Historiography

To provide a succinct contextual background for much that follows, Table 1.1 summarises some of the key environmental and historical phases relating to the Saharan zone and its neighbours. The table simplifies both time and technological developments and may appear overly deterministic, but hopefully conveys some sense of the complex linkages and discontinuities between environmental factors and technological and societal developments. In the period that primarily concerns us, the first millennium BC and first millennium AD, the Sahara was already a hyper-arid desert and the localised availability of groundwater was a crucial factor for human communities.[8] The physical realities of life in a desert environment also make long-distance movement a vital component of survival. Even in areas where part of the population is known to have been sedentary, the existence of a symbiotic relationship between sedentary and nomadic pastoralist groups was necessary for the survival of the oasis.[9] The one provided food and managed the access to water, while the other bred pack animals and possessed the navigational skills paramount to conducting trade, providing the surplus of goods which allowed the growth of the oasis. In this sense, we are studying a dynamic and fluid world. The consideration of the vast geographical area described above is a vital component of this. Of course, not every individual within this area travelled a great distance, as the permanent settlements of the Garamantes imply, but the movement of goods and ideas is clearly visible in the archaeological evidence. On the other hand, the vast expanses of rocky plateaus, mountain ranges or sand seas between many settled or navigable areas of the Sahara meant that even for those with access to the appropriate technologies of donkey, mule, horse or camel exploitation, movement was

---

[8] For a discussion of climatic change and the onset of the current hyper arid conditions *c.*5,000 years ago, see Gatto and Zerboni 2015; Mattingly *et al.* 2017, 5–6; Sterry and Mattingly 2020, 8–12.

[9] Scheele 2017.

not free and unlimited. But just as some topographic features present barriers or obstacles to movement, some locations are preferentially suited to support human life in an extremely arid and hostile environment (through the availability there of seasonal pasture, springs, shallow groundwater, etc.). Such *refugia* were likely to become better connected to other parts of the Sahara, some becoming established oasis centres (and to remain so in the face of social and political change).[10]

The first volume in this series, *Trade in the Ancient Sahara and Beyond*, explored the complexity and shifting realities of the network of trails connecting the Sahara in the pre-Islamic period.[11] The availability of water and the topography of the terrain are key, but so is the rise or fall of sites that would have been nodes in this network. By engaging with the archaeological evidence for oasis formation, it is possible to suggest some of the main 'routes' through which goods and people might have travelled the Sahara.[12] These possible axes of communication have been traced on the map shown in Figure 1.1, but it must be noted that these are intended more as a visual aid for the reader and an illustration of the potential for connections; a chronological palimpsest rather than an exact representation of the ancient trails at any given moment. Indeed, although the inherently 'mobile' nature of the Trans-Saharan zone is becoming ever more apparent, detailed studies of what, how and when things moved are compounded by the relative lack of data points in our field: comparative, contemporary sites are rare, so in addition to the general paucity and geographical dispersion of excavated sites, there exists a daunting temporal lag between data points.

This leads us on to some important considerations: how do we trace technological transfer and interaction in the unique situation provided by the Sahara, and – in continuation of a point raised above – how may we address whether we are dealing with technology transfer, imitation (mimesis) or multiple 'inventions' of a given technique or practice?

To an extent, the answer to this question lies in how much faith we place in the ability of archaeological specialists to distinguish the meaningful connections. Behind a broad-brush division between data 'splitters' (who emphasise differences between categories) and 'clumpers' (who emphasise similarities) there lie myriad interesting positions: the polemic between the two serves to mask the complex reality of technology transfer. As made clear by Touatia Amraoui, back-and-forth technological dialogues between

---

[10] Purdue *et al.* 2018a; 2018b.   [11] Mattingly *et al.* 2017.
[12] Explored in detail in Sterry and Mattingly 2020, with detailed listings of all available historic-era radiocarbon dates.

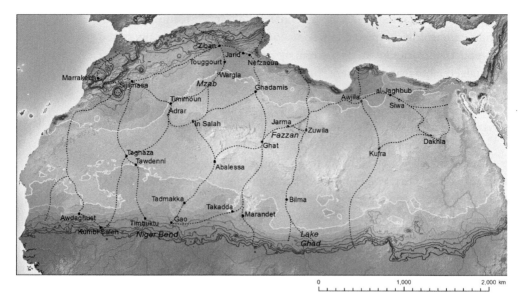

Figure 1.1 Map of key sites and axes of communication across the Sahara over time with indication of rainfall and vegetation (M. Sterry for Trans-SAHARA Project).

neighbouring areas are more difficult to trace in the archaeological record than direct 'transfer' over vast distances, but they form an equally significant window on technological practice, adoption and adaptation.[13]

The volumes in this series have demonstrated that the essential networks of communication, hardwired into social and economic connections, were already well developed within the Sahara in pre-Islamic times.[14] The establishment of oases was a particularly crucial step in that it created a network of fixed population hubs, where food and water was to be found. Although it is undeniable that certain elements of the Saharan networks became more significant in the Islamic era than they had been earlier, basic elements seem to have been laid down in the first millennium BC and the early first millennium AD. The implications of this new paradigm are considerable and studies of technology, as promoted here, will have an important role to play in developing this new agenda. But to do so effectively, we first need to be clear about the models we are using to define technology and technological transfer.

[13] Amraoui, Chapter 4, this volume.
[14] As illustrated in relation to trade: Mattingly *et al.* 2017; burial and identity markers: Gatto *et al.* 2019; oasis formation: Sterry and Mattingly 2020.

While older theories of diffusionism have largely been replaced in general archaeological debate by an emphasis on independent invention and local trajectories of technological development, the Sahara remains a privileged laboratory for reassessing key issues of technological change. We can document significant transformations in technologies between the third millennium BC and the second millennium AD within the environmentally constrained landscapes of the Sahara. As we shall see, there are a number of technological innovations recognisable in the Central Sahara in the first millennium BC that must have originated outside the desert environment and that were introduced through the wider connections and networks of Saharan communities. The classic instance is the oasis agricultural 'package' (date palm, cereals, vines, figs), which clearly indicates connections to Near East or Mediterranean agricultural practices. Similarly, some of the domesticated animals of the Sahara correlate with domesticated stock of Egyptian or Near Eastern origin. Even if we accept the importance of an ultimate eastern origin for some technologies, the precise chronologies and routes of introduction (via the Mediterranean or along desert trails?) remain very uncertain. Moreover, as will become clear, the idea of a predominant series of technological transfers from the east is an oversimplification of the ebb, flow and interchange of mobile technologies, with the danger that it becomes a default assumption before other possibilities are considered. It is also apparent that there are many other questions that we could and should be asking of the available evidence relating to the technological capacity of societies in the broader Trans-Saharan zone (see Fig. 1.2 for a map showing many of the key sites across the Trans-Saharan zone relevant to this volume).

One of the main conclusions of the *Trans-Saharan Archaeology* series is that many of the key transformations of the period 1000 BC–AD 1500 had a significant technological dimension. The oasis centres were clearly vital loci for change and deployment of technologies. Sedentary oasis living depended on specific agricultural knowledge, a package of cultivated crops and irrigation methods suited to different hydrological milieu. Urban sites, although always rare in the Sahara, generally coincide with major oases. Although their establishment has often been seen as the result of external forces, other paths to urbanism are possible. Trade was intimately linked to the development of oases, to the introduction and breeding of appropriate pack animals and to the appearance of craft/manufacturing activity. Similarities in burial technologies and rites across large swathes of the Sahara indicate the existence of a sort of *koine* (cultural commonality), no doubt based on connectivity. Whereas most of these changes were at one time believed not to

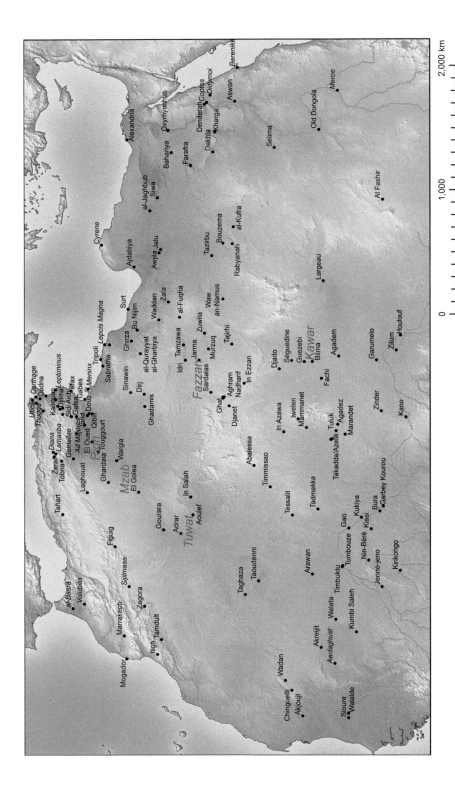

Figure 1.2 Map of the Trans-Saharan zone showing many of the key sites relevant to this volume (M. Sterry for Trans-SAHARA Project).

have appeared until the early Medieval period, the evidence now available plainly indicates that these processes were initiated 1,000–2,000 years earlier, with progressive growth in population, technological competence and capacity, commerce and cultural contacts in the Sahara. This has really significant implications for our understanding of technology transfer and invention – reducing the importance of exogenous actors (Phoenicians, Romans and Arabs) and focusing greater attention on the role of 'Libyan' peoples. Older historical models of technological revolutions in the Sahara, such as the introduction of the camel, need careful reappraisal.[15]

Defining Technology

Technology is a difficult subject to delimit, and it occupies an ambiguous space in modern thought, at once denigrated as the less philosophical cousin of science, and lauded as an essential part of humanity's 'progress'. We can trace a long history of this definition of technological knowledge as something distinct from scientific knowledge, summarised by Aristotle in the definitions of *technē* (art, that is, craft-knowledge) and *epistēmē* (theoretical or scientific knowledge) given in Book VI of the *Nicomachean Ethics*. This Greek/Aristotelian concept of *technē*, from which the English word 'technology' was derived in the seventeenth century (though it was not to come into popular use until the early twentieth), defines it as a sort of 'productive knowledge' and understanding which have, crucially, come about by habit.[16] The distinction between technique/technik and technology which is found in many European languages (including German and French), is less heavily dwelt upon in Anglophone scholarship, so our use of the term technology has to encapsulate both the practice itself – which can be individual or communal – and the external pool or system of knowledge from which this is seen to derive.

Even in English, 'technology' has an abundance of meanings, not all of which are complementary: systems, people, tools; all have been defined as forming a part, or the whole, of technology. As argued by David Edgerton in *The Shock of the Old*, we also tend to exclude older (longer-lived) technologies from our consideration, focusing instead on the latest development in any given period.[17] Defining technology from an archaeological perspective is fraught with yet more problems, not least the difficulty that what constitutes technology, and the perceptions of its practitioners, vary

[15] Bulliet 1975.   [16] Schadewaldt 1979.   [17] Edgerton 2008.

enormously depending on social context, and that the precise nature of this variation is unknown for the vast majority of the human past. As a starting point, we may borrow the following definition from Heather Miller:

> I think of technology in the context of an outwardly expanding, nested set of actions and relationships: from production itself, to the organization of the production process, to the entire cultural system of processes and practices associated with production and consumption . . . I use *technological systems* or just *technology* primarily in the broadest sense, to refer to the active system of interconnections between people and objects during the creation of an object, its distribution, and to some extent its use and disposal. In other words, technology or technological systems can be roughly described as the processes and practices associated with production and consumption, from design to discard.[18]

To a large extent, Miller's definition is the one we follow here, albeit with some alterations. In particular, we would place even more emphasis on the sequence of operations following the primary productive act. For example, in chapters by Duckworth and Robertshaw, we discover that the 'life story' of a glass object cannot necessarily be traced back to a single act of production.[19] High-temperature recycling of glass from several sources would serve to render meaningless the idea of an ultimate provenance of the glass, and the same may be said of metals. From a social perspective, we might argue that the long-term curation and long-distance trade in glass beads renders the question of their original geographical origins only slightly more relevant than that of the geological formation of the sands used in their production. In looking only at the chemically traceable primary production of an object, we are missing perhaps the most crucial parts of its story.

A second consideration is that of maintenance. The maintenance of technological 'systems' can be more labour intensive and costly than their original construction, although we tend to focus primarily on the latter. This point is beautifully illustrated by Wilson *et al.* who highlight the high maintenance costs of the sophisticated irrigation systems (foggaras) in the face of an ever-falling water table.[20]

Finally, a crucial difficulty in delimiting what counts as 'technology' lies in a preoccupation with the ideology of modern science. The anthropological definition of technology emphasises the *effectiveness* of the technological act, and thus excludes magic or religion,[21] but numerous examples demonstrate that these can be an integral part of technological knowledge

---

[18] Miller 2009, 4–5.   [19] Duckworth, Chapter 10; Robertshaw, Chapter 11, this volume.
[20] Wilson *et al.*, Chapter 3, this volume.   [21] Pfaffenberger 1992, 501.

and practice.[22] This is the case even if we adopt a purely functionalist view, as ritual can play a crucial role in the organisation of labour. Furthermore, and as also noted by Pfaffenberger, a vast amount of technological information is learned, stored and transmitted non-verbally, and we must not assume 'that technology is applied science – that it represents the practical use of logically-formulated, linguistically-encoded knowledge'.[23]

Those seeking a clearly delimited characterisation of technology may be frustrated by the lack of exclusivity in the above suggestions. Yet it is important to recognise that we can only offer a general definition; each archaeological case study carries its own context, as demonstrated by the range and variety of contributions to this volume, and although we are seeking to trace links and connections, we also recognise the vast differences that are manifested – sometimes abruptly, at other times gradually – as we move the lens of investigation over geographical space or through time. Added to this are the methodological constraints of examining the various materials and processes under study: each brings its own difficulties and limitations, and while some – such as the spread of foggara technology – lend themselves to tracing long-distance connections in a somewhat traditional, diffusionist manner, others – such as the study of metallic slags and other production remains – are more suited to understanding localised technological practice.

In this context, one might be tempted to ask why we investigate technology as a distinct theme in an archaeological context, rather than treating it as and when it arises. One answer we would give is that technology needs to be explicitly examined in order to avoid implicit assumptions regarding the movement of ideas and people, and the 'development' of a society.

For science, the mid-twentieth century saw a sea change away from positivist, deterministic concepts of the long march of progression,[24] and the social forces acting upon scientific practice were afforded centre stage. As noted by Scharff and Dusek, however, the applications of this understanding to technology have consistently lagged behind, with even current debates often failing to account for the shortcomings of purely positivist approaches to describing technological practice.[25] And in all of this, the great double-edged sword of modern technological advancement and its social and environmental costs looms large, rendering yet more difficult the task of seeing technology from anything but a highly presentist perspective.

---

[22] Budd and Taylor 1995; Oppenheim 1970.   [23] Pfaffenberger 1992, 518.
[24] As encapsulated in Kuhn 1970.   [25] Scharff and Dusek 2014.

The archaeology of technology is strikingly relevant in all this, providing a basis for comparison with the increasingly globalised technological developments of today, and helping to move the focus away from recent history – especially from the late Industrial Revolution onwards, a period which, significantly, also saw the emergence of modern history and archaeology as disciplines.[26] Whether we can ever discuss technological universals in human culture remains in doubt, but we can certainly use the evidence of the past to question our assumptions about the present.

Some of the ideas originally related to technological determinism have been resurrected of late in archaeological theories such as materiality and entanglement,[27] responding to a move away from structuralist approaches which relegated the material world to little more than sign or symbol of the social, and failed to acknowledge the delimiting or enabling factors of materials themselves. Most now acknowledge, however, that 'hard' determinism is ultimately flawed: technology, surely, cannot exist outside of society to the extent that it can be the sole, or even the primary, driver of social change.[28]

Naturally, archaeology brings its own limitations. Bias is unavoidable in the material record, which preserves inorganic so much better than organic materials, and certain technologies are thus consistently more visible than others. This is arguably compounded by the nineteenth-century origins of the discipline, which for much of its history has prioritised tools, weapons and pyrotechnologies over textiles, land management and animal husbandry (unless we are discussing a context in which these are perceived to be especially innovative, and thus significant, such as the onset of the Neolithic). It is also important to recognise at the outset the existence of a strong focus in the history of ancient technology on the great Mediterranean civilisations.[29] Insofar as North Africa is discussed at all in such works, the default assumption is that technology transfer was always from the outside in, although as Cyprian Broodbank has remarked this is potentially a case of absence of evidence more than evidence of absence, given the state of research on the second to first millennia BC across much of the region.[30] This is all the more significant if we recognise that the contextual specifics of technological change within the Sahara were

[26] For example, Roe Smith and Marx 1994.   [27] For example, Hodder 2012.
[28] See, for example, Bulliet 1994, 205–08.   [29] Hodges 1970; Oleson 2008; White 1984.
[30] Broodbank 2013, 36–40 on 'North Africa, the great lacuna'. The maps in Hodges 1970 showing the diffusion of many innovations from the Near East to the Mediterranean exclude Africa (apart from Egypt) and Broodbank's maps of key Bronze Age and Iron Age sites and distributions reflect a continuing gap in knowledge.

different to those at the Mediterranean seaboard, and that the interconnections of the Trans-Saharan world also brought other African civilisations into play. As in other volumes in this series, recentring debate on the Sahara and looking out from there towards neighbouring lands provides a very different viewpoint.

In a book of this sort, it is not feasible to cover all technologies, much as that might be desirable, and what follows is a selective sample of case studies. There are a number of reasons for the particular examples developed here. Of the wide-ranging technologies considered in this book, some – notably glass, metals and various irrigation systems – have been more intensively studied than others. They draw on a deeper literature and are thus afforded more weight here. Irrigation technologies are absolutely crucial to survival in a desert landscape, and their importance is unquestionable. Glass and metals survive well in the archaeological record, and they also travel widely, so they can be studied as both key technologies in their own right, and as proxies for trade and contact in a more general sense. But we also highlight the importance of technologies which have been less frequently studied in a Trans-Saharan context, including animal domestication, textile production, and the techniques for shaping and decorating handmade pottery. A few comments are also provided in this introduction on technologies that are not studied in fuller detail in what follows.

The most thoroughly studied technologies are also the ones that are most heavily burdened by decades of controversies tied into the history of intellectual thought, from the first encounters of Portuguese with African people in the sixteenth century to the present day. As mentioned by Liverani in Chapter 2 and recently reviewed by Killick,[31] the African continent, and Sub-Saharan Africa in particular, has traditionally been seen as devoid of inventiveness for much of its history. Since the end of the colonial era, some scholars, including many African historians and archaeologists, have worked on reversing this view by focusing on African inventions. The study of iron metallurgy is particularly embedded in this narrative and the question of whether or not iron smelting was independently invented on the African continent has been the subject of sometimes acrimonious debate, as summarised by Aurélie Cuénod in Chapter 7.[32] In this climate, suggestions that technologies came to the African continent from outside are frequently considered as 'old-fashioned',[33] or as reviewed

---

[31] Killick 2015; Liverani, Chapter 2, this volume.   [32] See detailed review by Alpern 2005.
[33] Liverani, Chapter 2, this volume.

by Alpern concerning metalworking, simply racist.[34] From this perspective, a volume seeking to examine the Trans-Saharan transfer of technologies may be seen as problematic from the start. Yet, as highlighted by Killick,[35] the controversy comes in the first place from the implied notion that technologies such as metalworking are markers of civilisation, with what qualifies as such a marker generally being defined from a Eurocentric perspective.[36] The second issue he raises is the failure to recognise the difference between invention and innovation. He argues convincingly that although Africa has witnessed many *inventions*, these have only rarely resulted in *innovations*, possibly in part due to low population densities and a lack of literacy. In the context of the Trans-Saharan region, where population densities are indeed very low, it is therefore paramount that we not only study the transfer of successful technologies, but, as discussed in more detail below, that we also seek to recognise those that might have been short-lived, as they present us with interesting information on the context in which they were invented or adopted, and the underlying conditions required for this, including in some cases other pre-existing technologies. This aspect is addressed in several chapters within the volume, in the study of cross-craft interaction and technological packages.

Technology in a Saharan Context

The Trans-Saharan zone is defined as the hypothetical reach of contacts and networks encompassing all parts of the Sahara and the Maghrib, the Mediterranean parts of Libya and Egypt, the Nile Valley down to Sudan and the Sub-Saharan regions and countries from Darfur in the east to Western Sahara and Senegal in the west.[37] Through the various connections within this area at different times, it also tapped into much wider trade and contact zones such as the Indian Ocean and the Middle East.

A strong case can be advanced for the most significant and far-reaching technological transfers within the Trans-Saharan world being those related to agriculture/farming. In this short subsection we shall present a summary of some of the principal strands of technological evidence in relation to farming – crops, tools, animal husbandry and irrigation. The creation of oases within the Sahara depended on the exploitation of groundwater sources through a variety of technological inventions, accompanied by

---

[34] Alpern 2005, 89–93.   [35] Killick 2015.
[36] See also the debate on what 'civilisation' means in Sterry and Mattingly 2020.
[37] Mattingly *et al.* 2017, chapter 1.

the spread of particular cultivars, with all that implies about the transfer of seeds or young plants, as well as propagation techniques, methods of cultivation, harvesting and processing.[38] The transition to agriculture was accomplished not at a climatic optimum, but at some point after catastrophic climatic downturn *c.*5,000 years ago.[39] This transformation thus took place in a hostile and increasingly more challenging landscape, where there was minimal rainfall and oasis life was made possible only by the exploitation of subterranean water sources. The Garamantes of southern Libya once again provide a key case study for framing our debate about the precise chronology and character of this change, with significant implications for other areas within and bordering the Sahara. What follows is a broad picture of the conclusions drawn from the evidence available to date, but it should be borne in mind that the data points are still few and far between for most of the area and time periods under study.[40] While broad changes are discernible, diffusionist theory and concepts of 'agricultural packages' work best where the data are limited. As primary research into these themes advances in the future, it is likely that a more nuanced and complex picture will emerge. Recent research into the spread of agriculture into northern Europe in the Neolithic period, based on extensive datasets, has challenged unitary models relating to migrationism or indigenism, arguing that integrationism (combining repeated cycles of migration and indigenous uptake) offers a better way forward.[41] In a similar way, the spread of agriculture in the Sahara is likely to have involved both migration of some outsiders with technological know-how and the uptake of new ways of life by some elements of the existing pastoral societies. It has long been apparent that consideration of the spread of animal and plant domestication needs to take account of chronological and genetic variation across large spaces, as represented by the Trans-Saharan zone defined in this book.[42]

Botanical Evidence

Botanical and palynological evidence relating to the Garamantes has been well published in recent years and, in consequence, a detailed case study

---

[38] Barker 2007.   [39] Cremaschi 2001; Cremaschi and di Lernia 1998, 243–96.

[40] Even among the editors of this volume there is disagreement over the precise interpretation of the agricultural changes evidenced in the archaeological record.

[41] Gron and Sørensen 2018.

[42] For recent summaries on animal and plant domestication, see di Lernia 2013; Fuller and Hildebrand 2013; Gifford-Gonzalez and Hanotte 2013.

Table 1.2 *Main cultivated plants exploited by the Garamantes*

Cultivated plant	Common name	Major cult	Site	First occurrence	Possible origin
Phoenix datilifera	Date palm	*	Zinkekra	980–670 calBC	Egypt, Mediterranean
Triticum aestivum	Bread wheat	*	Zinkekra	980–670 calBC	Egypt, Mediterranean
Triticum dicoccum	Emmer wheat		Zinkekra	980–670 calBC	Egypt, Mediterranean
Hordeum vulgare	Barley	*	Zinkekra	980–670 calBC	Egypt, Mediterranean
Vitis vinifera	Grape vine	*	Zinkekra	980–670 calBC	Egypt, Mediterranean
Ficus carica	Fig tree	*	Zinkekra	980–670 calBC	Egypt, Mediterranean
Gossypium	Cotton	*	Jarma	416–320 calBC	Sub-Sahara
Sorghum bicolor	Sorghum	*	Jarma	390–110 calBC	Sub-Sahara
Pennisetum glaucum	Pearl millet	*	Jarma	360–40 calBC	Sub-Sahara
Punica granatum	Pomegranate		Jarma	calAD 49–183	Mediterranean
Prunus amydalis	Almond		Jarma	calAD 183–353	Mediterranean
Olea europaea	Olive		Jarma	calAD 183–353	Mediterranean
Pisum sativum	Pea		Jarma	calAD 183–353	Mediterranean
Triticum durum	Durum wheat		Jarma	calAD 183–860	Mediterranean
Vicia faba	Faba bean		Jarma	calAD 353–860	Mediterranean
Lens culinaris	Lentil		Jarma	calAD 860–1093	Mediterranean

has not been included in this book, although a brief summary is offered here.[43] Botanical remains indicate the presence at the Early Garamantian site of Zinkekra early in the first millennium BC of an initial Mediterranean/Nilotic 'agricultural package', ultimately derived from Near Eastern domestication of the date palm, emmer and bread wheat, barley, the fig tree and the grapevine (Table 1.2).[44] There is a second rather later group of imports of probable Mediterranean origin (durum wheat, almond, olive, pomegranate, pulses) that first appear at the Garamantian capital at Jarma in levels dating to the early centuries AD. Chronologically between these two, there is a third group of agricultural innovations, with the introduction of pearl millet, sorghum and cotton. Although not attested in abundance until the early centuries AD, these are persistently present in levels dating to the later first millennium BC.

There were then at least three phases of crop introductions to Garamantian Fazzan. These crops all require significant levels of water to be cultivated successfully and the fairly sudden uptake of cultivation of an

---

[43] Pelling 2008; 2013a; 2013b; Van der Veen 1995; Van der Veen and Westley 2010.
[44] Pelling 2013a; 2013b; Van der Veen 1995; Van der Veen and Westley 2010.

evolved package, rather than a gradual domestication of locally available plants, highlights the fact that this was a technological transfer from outside the region. At any rate, taking account of the fact that Fazzan is 1,000 km from the Mediterranean and over 2,000 km from the Nile, it is apparent that the agriculture first practised in the Central Sahara was dependent on a range of technologies and knowledge whose ultimate origin was external. The clearest hints of where the initial package came from all point to the oases of the Western Egyptian desert, where sedentary settlements and cultivation appear to have commenced during the Old or Middle Kingdom (third to second millennia BC).[45] However, the distance between the suspected source and the Central Sahara strongly suggests that oasis cultivation in the latter area was not the result of a single one-off leap, but rather the end result of a more gradual spread of oasis cultivation into and between a series of pre-existing Saharan *refugia*.[46] Rather than seeking external agents, then, much of the pioneering work of oasis formation almost certainly involved much more local actors. The presence of the cultivated package in the Central Sahara from *c.*1000 BC is in sharp contrast to the contemporary evidence of the natural vegetation, which shows a marked decrease in water availability in the Late Pastoral phase (last millennia BC), comprising predominantly species well adapted to hyper-arid conditions.[47] However, the initial stages of agriculture in the Saharan case study did not preclude further introductions over time. As an immediate argument against a simplistic diffusionist explanation, we should note some further interesting aspects of the Garamantian case study. As noted, we can trace additions to the initial 'agricultural package' by the latter centuries BC (so about 500–700 years after the initial appearance of irrigated agriculture), with the introduction of Sub-Saharan crops like pearl millet, sorghum and cotton added to the cultivated crops in Fazzan.[48] Although there have been suggestions that these crops could have travelled north along the Nile Valley and then reached Fazzan from the east along the oasis trail from the Western Desert, the available chronological indices suggest their presence in the Central Sahara may be earlier than in Egypt and the simpler explanation is that they reached Fazzan directly from the Lake Chad area.[49] This is highly significant as it shows that not all agricultural innovations had the same point of origin. Finally, at the height of Garamantian trading contacts with the Roman Empire in the early centuries AD, additional Mediterranean

---

[45] Sterry and Mattingly 2020, chapters 2–3.   [46] Mattingly *et al.* 2018.
[47] Mercuri *et al.* 1998; Pelling 2013a, 484–86; Van der Veen and Westley 2010, 515–16.
[48] Pelling 2008; 2013a, 478–84; 2013b, 841–52.   [49] Wild *et al.* 2007; 2011.

Table 1.3 *Main cultivated plants exploited at Althiburos*

Cultivated plant	Common name	Major cult	Phase	First occurrence	Origin
Triticum aestivum/ durum	Bread wheat/ durum wheat	*	Alth-EN1	1020–810 calBC	Mediterranean
Triticum dicoccum	Emmer wheat	*	Alth-EN1	1020–810 calBC	Mediterranean
Triticum cf spleta	Spelt wheat		Alth-EN3	1020–810 calBC	Mediterranean
Hordeum vulgare	Barley	*	Alth-EN1	1020–810 calBC	Mediterranean
Panicum miliaceum	Millet	*	Alth-EN1	1020–810 calBC	Mediterranean
Vitis vinifera	Grape vine	*	Alth-EN1	1020–810 calBC	Mediterranean
Ficus carica	Fig tree	*	Alth-EN1	1020–810 calBC	Mediterranean
Lens culinaris	Lentil	*	Alth-EN1	1020–810 calBC	Mediterranean
Vicia faba	Faba bean		Alth-EN1	1020–810 calBC	Mediterranean
Linum cf usitatissimum	Flax		Alth-EN1	1020–810 calBC	Mediterranean
Setaria italica	Foxtail millet		Alth-EN2	910–820 calBC	Mediterranean
Pisum sativum	Pea	*	Alth-EN2	910–820 calBC	Mediterranean
Punica granatum	Pomegranate		Alth-EN2	910–820 calBC	Mediterranean
Olea europaea	Olive	*	Alth-EN3	790–760 calBC	Mediterranean
Secale cereale	Cereal rye		Alth-Med	Medieval	Mediterranean
Avena sativa	Oats		Alth-Med	Medieval	Mediterranean

crops, including a range of pulses not present in the initial agricultural phase, made their appearance.

The agricultural package of the Garamantes is strikingly different to the first steps towards domestication of Saharan plants, evident in the late Neolithic era, when certain grasses appear in fodder deposits in caves in the Akakus mountains.[50] On the other hand, it has some significant differences from other evidence of the adoption of agriculture in the Maghrib in the early first millennium BC, as evidenced at the site of Althiburos in central Tunisia (Table 1.3).[51] The Spanish-Tunisian excavations at Althiburos investigated a deeply stratified sequence extending back to the start of the first millennium BC. The main cultivated crops here were hard wheat (bread/durum), emmer wheat, barley, the vine, fig and a variety of pulses – which from the outset seem to have provided an important element in crop rotation. Olives were also cultivated by the eighth century, if not earlier, along with some additional fruit trees (pomegranates and almonds) and

---

[50] Castelletti *et al.* 1999; Mercuri 1999; Mercuri *et al.* 1998.
[51] López and Cantero 2016; Sanmartí *et al.* 2012.

this early first-millennium package then continued more or less unchanged right through the Roman period and into the Medieval era, when there were some small experiments with additional cereals (oats and rye).

It is not clear when or where agriculture became established in Mediterranean North Africa. Although there are some precocious occurrences in Neolithic contexts in Morocco,[52] it is quite possible that a number of separate areas began to incorporate plant cultivation into their lifestyle in the second millennium BC. At any rate the material at Althiburos predates the main period of establishment of Phoenician emporia on the North African coast, so an endogenous explanation for its spread within the Maghrib now seems probable. The recent Althiburos and Fazzan discoveries make this archaeologically visible from the early first millennium BC, but it is clear from the nature of the crop package involved in both cases that cultivation was already well established in the Maghrib and Sahara – contradicting long-held beliefs that the practice was only introduced by Phoenician, Greek and Roman 'colonists' during the first millennium BC.[53]

The different composition of the two agricultural packages in the early first millennium BC is a strong indicator of a probable separate pathway of technological transfer for these two areas. Broadly, Althiburos is a Mediterranean-adapted package and Fazzan a Saharan one. Although there is some overlap in the range of crops, the differences are also significant, with the date palm, the limited range of cultivated trees and delayed appearance of pulses in Fazzan contrasting with the high presence of pulses and greater development of arboriculture at an earlier date at Althiburos. The extent to which movements of things like crops can be mapped on to population migrations is alluring, but potentially misleading. Recent linguistic studies of the evolution and spread of Saharan and Maghribian linguistic groups, especially those associated with Berber dialects, correlate quite closely with phases of development of Saharan oasis societies and the sedentary agricultural settlements of Numidia like Althiburos.[54] But while 'Berbers' were undoubtedly part of Garamantian society, studies of Garamantian skeletal remains clearly indicate a more mixed population including black Africans in all probability of Saharan and Sub-Saharan origins.[55] Similarly, the material remains on the Early Garamantian site of Zinkekra include lithic tools that associate strongly with the Late Pastoral tradition. This seems to be evidence in favour of the

---

[52] Zapata *et al.* 2013.   [53] Mattingly 2016.   [54] Ehret 2019; Fentress 2019.
[55] Power *et al.* 2019, 148–54.

sort of integrationist and cyclical model of the spread of agriculture in northern Europe advocated by Gron and Sørensen.[56]

Tools for Cultivation and Processing

Changes in cultivation and processing technology are other important markers, such as the ground stone tools used for crop processing, which show significant evolution over time, for example with progressive replacement of saddle querns with rotary querns from the late first/early second century AD onwards.[57] Similarly, the availability and use of metal tools for digging, weeding, pruning and harvesting had important implications. The spread of plough technology in the Maghrib and pre-desert zones is one suggestive case study that also links to the diffusion of domesticated equids.[58] Metal tools are rare finds in the Sahara, probably due to a very high rate of recycling, but the importance of metallurgy in support of agriculture should not be underestimated. As we shall see below, the construction of vast networks of subterranean irrigation channels (foggaras) was facilitated by the availability of metal-tipped digging tools as is evident from marks on the walls of these underground features.[59] There is also important evidence in Roman relief sculpture, for instance at Ghirza in the Libyan pre-desert, of the use of ploughs, metal sickles and digging tools.[60] Metallurgy, especially ironworking, must thus be seen as a crucial accompanying technology for oasis agriculture. Mediterranean/Nile Valley and Sub-Saharan ironworking traditions have often been seen as distinctly separate from one another, leading to complex arguments about the technological implications of supposed independent invention of iron production in West Africa.[61] The realisation that oasis development may serve as a proxy measure for the spread of iron production and ironworking technology thus has implications in that it puts that metallurgy in the Sahara at a date contemporaneous with the main spread in Maghrib and Sub-Sahara.

Animal Husbandry

Some changes in animal husbandry in the Sahara related to sedentary farming communities, such as the spread of the chicken and pig as

---

[56] Gron and Sørensen 2018.   [57] Camps-Fabrer 1966.
[58] Camps 1986; Capot-Rey and Marcais 1953.   [59] Mattingly *et al.* 2010, 116–17.
[60] Brogan and Smith 1984.   [61] Mapunda 2013, for a good summary of the debate.

discussed by Fothergill *et al.*[62] While the uptake of domesticated beasts of burden including camels, horses, mules and donkeys can also be linked to the development of networks of communication across the Trans-Saharan zone, there is some evidence to link their appearance closely with the spread of oasis communities.[63]

It was at one time commonly believed that the camel was introduced into the Sahara only in late antiquity and that this was one of the things that facilitated the expansion of Islam in the Sahara.[64] There is now pretty clear evidence that the camel was present by the late first millennium BC, but that it gained rising importance over time. This should not surprise us, as the availability of groundwater almost certainly became more constrained as non-renewable water tables dried up and the distances between springs and wells within the Sahara increased, while yields of water at the larger wells diminished (or took longer to replenish) with the passing of each caravan. By the end of the first millennium AD, the camel was the pre-eminent beast of burden, but not to the total exclusion of others. More revolutionary in many respects was the earlier introduction of the horse to the Sahara in the second millennium BC.[65] Domesticated horses were so much more than animals for transporting people or things; they quickly transformed the nature of warfare and raiding. The technologies associated with horses were multiple, involving breeding, taming, riding and guiding, lading and fighting. Chariots appeared in Saharan rock art around the same time as horses and testify to other significant technological transfers – wheeled vehicles cannot have been an easy or obvious solution to the difficult terrain in many areas of the Sahara, but on flat gravel plains they will have been terrifyingly effective in chasing down human and animal prey.[66] Even in Medieval and Early Modern times, horses remained a prestige animal among Saharan peoples, despite the significantly greater difficulty in maintaining them with water and fodder.[67]

One of the key conclusions of Chapter 5 concerns the importance of a number of other domesticated species that are less celebrated than horses and camels. Donkeys were a third crucial element in making the Sahara a connected space and potentially the first on the scene. For the most mobile of domesticates, pastoral groups must have been key actors in their

---

[62] Fothergill *et al.*, Chapter 5, this volume.

[63] Holmes 2013; Holmes and Grant 2013; Van der Veen and Westley 2010; cf. also Mattingly *et al.* 2017; Sterry and Mattingly 2020, chapter 2.

[64] Bulliet 1975.   [65] Camps and Gast 1982.

[66] Camps and Chaker 1993; Gauthier and Gauthier 2011.

[67] Daumas 1968; Mattingly *et al.* forthcoming.

adoption and transmission. On the other hand, some domesticated live-stock are fundamentally more suited to sedentary oasis communities (pigs and chickens) and this suggests a close interrelationship between techno-logical developments involving animals and agriculture.

Irrigation Technology

The main focus of Chapter 3 is the irrigation technologies used, in particular focusing on a distinctive type of subterranean channel known as the foggara, although we want to stress at the outset that the connected issues raised above ideally need also to be considered alongside the detail of hydraulic technologies. The Central Saharan region of Fazzan is much better investigated in respect of its earliest irrigation technology than are most other areas.[68] In the absence of more detailed archaeological studies of many oases, the presence or absence of different styles of irrigation work may provide some hints relating to chronology and connections in the different Saharan oasis groups.

Foggara technology was not always suited to the local hydrological conditions and there are large areas of the Sahara where it was not adopted (Fig. 1.3). The pattern of predominant irrigation technology employed across the Sahara is in fact a very complex mosaic. Each irrigation technol-ogy needed to be locally contingent and appropriately adapted to the varied hydrology. For example, oases at locations where natural artesian springs occurred required the development of highly specialised expertise in how to augment the springs with dug artesian wells (an extremely dangerous process even for skilled practitioners).[69]

Another way of thinking about irrigation technology is to focus on the hydraulic resources available and then to consider how these might best be accessed and optimised. A perennial river requires water deviation or lifting systems to exploit – simplified in cases like the Nile by the phenom-enon of annual flood events. An artesian spring requires consolidation of a spring head tank or pool and canalisation systems. A shallow ground-water level can be accessed by the simple technology of the balance well (*shaduf*), but is labour intensive and each well can serve only a limited area of gardens. The advantage of the foggara lies in the ability to provide running water to areas of the landscape that lack natural springs, but the initial start-up costs are very high. An important distinction between well

---

[68] Mattingly *et al.* 2010, 113–17, 128–31; Wilson and Mattingly 2003.
[69] Berbrugger 1862, 44–83.

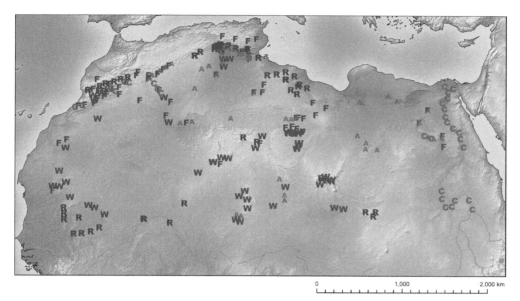

Figure 1.3 Map of the distribution of key irrigation technologies across the Sahara: rainfall runoff (R), springs (A), wells (W), underground irrigation channels/foggaras (F), canals (C) (M. Sterry for Trans-SAHARA Project).

irrigation and spring/foggara irrigation is that the former is often an individual technological project, whereas the scale and complexity of the latter involve communities in their construction and maintenance. Social organisation may thus be a factor in delayed adoption of particular technologies. As we shall see in the case of foggara technology, the peak construction period in the Western Sahara seems to have lagged well behind the precocious development in East and Central Sahara, although its wider uptake may have followed long after its initial introduction.

A final issue of vital significance to technological choices in communal irrigation projects concerns the mechanism employed to divide the water among stakeholders. Two main options existed: volumetric division by a mechanical device or chronological division according to measured units of time. Again the preference for one or the other varied greatly across Saharan oases.[70] For artesian springs, with relatively consistent and predictable flow, timed units seem to have been more favoured, giving access to the water to different sectors of a garden zone in turn. With foggaras, where flow may have been more variable due to fluctuation in the water table or to maintenance issues, the tendency seems to have been more

---

[70] For illustration and discussions, see Laureano 1991, 151–59; Trousset 1986, 164–94.

commonly to split the flow by mechanical means into substreams providing equal volumes of water to all zones of a garden system simultaneously. These differences had technological implications for the way in which gardens were laid out and where sluice gates needed to be provided and who was responsible for their operation. For the earliest oases, such features rarely survive – and the issue is not given great attention in Chapter 3 – but we should note that water division/allocation within oasis gardens was nonetheless an important technological decision.

Scientific Contributions to the Study of Technology

Despite the above arguments in favour of tracing the geographical spread and provenance of technologies, it is also true that we can never fully disentangle ourselves from methodological constraints when considering the interpretation and meaning of archaeological evidence. In one case, however, there is still plenty of scope for increasing our dataset and – hopefully – our understanding: that is, in the generation of archaeometric data for sites in and surrounding the Sahara. We now turn to a consideration of the use of these scientific data in their own right.

Following the scientific revolution in archaeology, which was initiated by the discovery of radiocarbon dating in the late 1940s, modern analytical science has become one of the principal means by which the archaeology of technology is studied. For the technology of animal and plant domestication and husbandry, scientific analysis has focused upon identification of species and the chronicling of their movement(s) and change(s) over time. For the products of pyrotechnology, experimental and ethnographic approaches allow us to reconstruct large parts of the stages of operation by which various materials, tools or objects were made: the so-called *chaîne opératoire*, but for many processes this picture is incomplete without the use of microscopy or chemical analysis. For example, the form into which glasses were worked tells us nothing about the processes by which they were fused from raw ingredients; similarly, in the absence of substantial furnace remains, only the study of metallurgical slag can inform us about the techniques with which metals were extracted from their ores.

As a result, much archaeological interpretation of these materials has been afforded or constrained by the sorts of questions we can ask of their analysis. In addition to chronometric dating methods, a key focus from a relatively early stage in archaeometry has been on the use of scientific analysis to ascertain the geological provenance of materials such as stone, or the raw ingredients used to make metals, ceramics and glass, with more or less success depending on the material analysed.[71] While such studies have significantly developed our understanding of many past phenomena, not least long-distance trade,[72] researchers are increasingly acknowledging that the relationship between artefact composition and provenance is rarely straightforward.

Traditional approaches have sought to establish a direct match between the chemical or isotopic signature of archaeological artefacts and that of the primary materials from which they originated. This task in itself is not as simple as it may seem, as it supposes not only the existence of good reference data for geological materials (to this date still comparatively limited for the African continent), but also that the various sources of raw materials have distinct enough 'fingerprints' for us to be able to distinguish between them. We can cite, for example, the overlap between the lead isotope signatures of ores from Tunisia and those of ores from regions of Greece and Spain to show that this is a complex situation, although one that can be improved by adding other types of archaeological data, particularly relating to the economic context, into the picture.[73]

More often than not, however, the relationship between the material forming the analysed artefact and the source of the raw materials is far from linear. The chapter by Robertshaw illustrates the potential complexities of the life history of the artefacts (in this case, beads) and by extension of the material they are made of.[74] He discusses how the beads can shift in and out of various 'states' (trade commodities, luxury items, etc.) at several points during their 'lifetime'. For copper alloys and glass, which can easily be returned to a liquid state by remelting, this should be extended to consider the material's potential to shift into a state where it is seen as a raw material again at various points in its history. Early Modern accounts of this in Africa include the mention of 'old copper' (scrap metal) by Barth, a European traveller describing the Mediterranean goods traded at Kano (northern Nigeria) in the 1850s,[75] and the fluidity between ingots, ornaments and currencies in many African communities.[76] This shows the importance of escaping from innate cultural assumptions about the technical superiority or greater desirability of, say, Mediterranean or Egyptian goods in Saharan trade. Thus, technology must be considered in many cases as being intimately woven into the life history of a material or

---

[71] See Wilson and Pollard 2001.   [72] Mattingly *et al.* 2017.
[73] Tunisia: Skaggs *et al.* 2012; Greece: Stos-Gale *et al.* 1996, Vavelidis *et al.* 1985; Spain: Stos-Gale *et al.* 1995 (non-exhaustive lists of references for these countries).
[74] Robertshaw, Chapter 11, this volume.   [75] Barth 1858 [1890], 308.   [76] Herbert 1984, 186.

artefact.[77] With it comes the potential for alterations to the material's chemical signature: as discussed by Duckworth, each melting episode can alter the chemistry of a material, due to oxidative losses or contamination, mixing with material from other sources, or dilution by the addition of various alloying elements (metals), colourants or decolourants (glass).[78] Duckworth further argues that, far from the sort of 'blind' mixing models we typically adopt in order to address issues such as recycling, these acts can often include a high degree of human intentionality: for example, we may witness compensation for the loss of alkalis due to reheating, or for unwanted colouring effects due to recycling, with a direct effect upon the chemical make-up of the material, and thus also upon the conclusions drawn by the analysts.

It is thus important that we continue to conduct scientific analysis where possible, but also that it is framed within the appropriate methodological and archaeological contexts. Provided that the right questions are asked of the data, they can be a powerful tool in exploring not only trade, but also technology and life history (including the history of modifications). Indeed, in the current political climate, where work in the field is increasingly difficult, it is potentially our primary tool for advancing research. As exemplified by a number of chapters in the first volume of this series,[79] in a region such as the Trans-Saharan zone where scientific analyses are still generally scarce, even the analysis of a small number of objects can lead to interesting suggestions, the reality and complexity of which will undoubtedly be refined in the future.

A significant category of production waste is that which has the potential of being reused as a raw material. This includes metal or glass offcuts or drips, or malformed glass beads, for example. Indeed, considering the potential of these materials for reuse, their discovery should always prompt the question of why they were abandoned and not simply remelted. Perhaps collection and reuse simply was not worth the time and effort, but other factors might also apply. As an example, the malformed glass beads found at the Malian site of Gao have been interpreted by the excavators as evidence for the working of glass.[80] Yet, if glassworkers were present at Gao, why did they not choose to rework, rather than

---

[77] This theme was discussed at the recycling workshop and has been developed by some of the participants elsewhere (Bray *et al.* 2015).
[78] Duckworth, Chapter 10, this volume.   [79] Cissé 2017; Leitch *et al.* 2017; Magnavita 2017.
[80] Cissé 2017.

discard, the malformed beads?[81] We would like to highlight two possible explanations for this. Peter Robertshaw discusses the town of Purdalpur in India (visited and reported upon by Alok Kanungo) where malformed beads were found not at the place of production, but rather at the house of the tradesman, at which location they were sorted from the 'good' beads.[82] Clearly, this calls for a careful consideration of the spatial association between production and waste. The second potential explanation, noted by Duckworth and discussed extensively elsewhere,[83] is that deliberately discarded materials are more likely to be representative of a 'failed batch' of glass, which has significant consequences for any assumed association between the chemical 'signatures' of production waste and finished items. As detailed below, we believe that the study of these 'failed' episodes of production have the potential to tell us more about the history of technology than we think.

Mobility and Technology Transfer

Underpinning the Trans-SAHARA Project and its associated publications is the movement of things – including people, ideas and material culture – from one place to another. The present volume focuses on the movement of technologies, but technology, like anything else, travels over time and space by a variety of processes. What, then, do we mean when we discuss the idea, not simply of technology, but of 'mobile technologies'?

Technology transfer is not intended as a substitute term for diffusion. Technologies are transferred vertically from one generation to the next, or laterally from one social group to another: either case may or may not include a geographical transition. It is undoubtedly true, however, that for the archaeologist the latter are the easiest mechanisms to trace. This is in part a methodological constraint: as mentioned above, we have relatively few data points, and the chronology of these is broad by comparison with lived experience. Equally difficult to trace, but also considered in this volume, are unsuccessful transfers of technologies and transfers that have been accompanied by a rapid adaptation of the technology. We thus tend to trace the geographical transfer of technologies first, and consider the other complicating factors of our data at a later stage.

---

[81] See Dussubieux 2017.
[82] Robertshaw, Chapter 11, this volume, discussing Kanungo 2004, 143.
[83] Duckworth, Chapter 10, this volume; Duckworth *et al.* 2014; 2016.

Mechanisms of Technological Transfer

Tracing geographical transfer is no mean endeavour, for it is historically apparent that successful technologies can and do spread from one location to the next, at times with startling rapidity; and at others by slow processes, which would have been all but imperceptible at the time. Happily, the way in which a technology is transferred can often be discerned by careful consideration of its material remains. In a basic reading of themes discussed in more detail in Chapter 13, the fabric of a handmade pot is most likely to reflect the location in which it was made; the decorative style may signify the transmission of ideas and the tools or methods employed. Commonalities in the mode of decoration most frequently represent direct contact between groups, or the movement of individuals from one area to another. But these distinctions are rarely clear cut. We can cite as an example the discussions that took place at our 2015 pottery workshop, regarding the presence of roulette decoration on pottery from Fazzan dating from the Garamantian period. While the participants agreed that its presence in the Central Sahara is remarkable and indicates the use of a technique similar to one used in West Africa from a much earlier date,[84] no consensus was reached as to the meaning of this observation. Is this a coincidental occurrence or does it indicate some form of contact between Fazzan and West Africa? Notions of shared aesthetics or repertoire, direct or gradual copying, reinvention based on a limited observation of the original technology and migrations (forced or otherwise) were all put forward,[85] with the identity of the potters and the scale of interactions in the Trans-Saharan zone being at the centre of the discussions, but we are yet to reach any consensus on the matter.

Underpinning discussion of this kind is the consideration of processes by which technologies are learned, although this seems to be an area in which archaeology generally struggles and tends to tap into the much richer anthropological, ethnographic and ethnoarchaeological literature to gain insights on the subject.[86] Several chapters in this volume discuss the highly social character of learning as observed in ethnographic studies. Robertshaw examines how glassmaking can be considered in the framework of 'communities of practice',[87] while Robion-Brunner describes smelting as a collective activity within which rituals and taboos play

---

[84] Gosselain *et al.* 2010; Livingstone Smith 2007 and references therein.

[85] See discussions in Gatto, Chapter 13, this volume.   [86] Killick 2004a, 572–73.

[87] Robertshaw, Chapter 11, this volume; the idea of 'communities of practice' is discussed by Lave and Wenger 1991. See also Haour 2011 for similar considerations in the study of pottery.

a central role, and apprentices learn through the imitation of these rituals.[88] However, as Gosselain demonstrated in a study of pottery decoration and fashioning techniques, not all aspects of a manufacturing process are influenced to the same degree by different groups of people.[89] Those that are less visible on the finished product (in the case of pottery fashioning techniques) tend to be more rooted in the initial learning process and the relationship between experienced artisans and apprentices, and thus are less prone to change. On the other hand, the most 'visible' aspects of the *chaîne opératoire*, such as decoration, are more heavily influenced by a variety of actors (local community, markets) and more easily transmitted through space provided that there is a sufficiently dense (and continuous) network of interaction within which people living in geographically distinct areas can share things and ideas.[90] This highlights the importance of allowing for differential rates and patterns of transmission for different aspects of the *chaîne opératoire* in our study of ancient technologies. It also reiterates the potentially crucial role of the Trans-Saharan trade network and the Saharan market towns such as Jarma in the diffusion of some aspects of technology although this zone.

Corridors and Barriers

In Gosselain's example of the modern spread of roulette decoration, the diffusion seems to have stopped at natural boundaries: the limits of the Sahara, the rainforest and the eastern Rift Valley, rather than being dictated by cultural boundaries. This idea of barriers or end-points, which may prevent the 'diffusion' of a technology from one location to the next, and their converse – corridors – through which technologies move with greater ease, is another key theme in this volume. Mario Liverani suggests that insights might be gained by considering the Sahara as a westwards continuation of arid regions in the Arabian Peninsula and farther afield, in the Near East and Central Asia. This arid belt, within which environmental conditions are broadly comparable, can be seen as a corridor facilitating the transfer of a suite of technologies linked to the sustenance of the oasis. As discussed above, particularly significant was the east to west advance of the foggara, originating in the Near East in the early first millennium BC.[91] The spread of this technology is intimately linked to early Saharan and Trans-Saharan trade, at times contributing to the development of oases as

---

[88] Robion-Brunner, Chapter 9, this volume.   [89] Gosselain 2000.   [90] Gosselain 2000, 200.
[91] Liverani, Chapter 2, this volume.

nodes in this trade; at others facilitated by an early network of trade routes. This vision of a connected Saharan (and Near Eastern) corridor departs markedly from earlier models for the spread of foggara technology, in which the role of various groups of outsiders (Romans, Jews, Persians) was emphasised.[92]

Another example of corridors favourable to the geographical transmission of technologies can be found in the spread of natural draught furnaces to smelt iron in two different zones of Sub-Saharan Africa: the first in West Africa, in the savannah woodland zones from Senegal to Nigeria, the second farther to the south-east between Tanzania and Mozambique. David Killick has argued that this fuel-intensive but low-labour type of smelting was adopted throughout these regions because ironworking had to compete with the labour-intensive swidden agriculture driven by poor soil fertility.[93] Both examples show the favourable spread of innovations responding to specific environmental problems within environmentally similar zones.

The direction of technological transmission is another subject raised by Liverani. He suggests that 'we have to assume – not as a true and proper "law", but as a statistical imbalance – that the general direction of the innovations is determined by a difference in advancement', although he acknowledges the existence of more complexity and exceptions.[94] The danger here (aside from potentially opening the door to qualitative judgements of societies of the type that archaeologists have been striving to avoid in the past few decades) lies in the definition of 'advancement' and the potential for a modern bias of what constitutes a 'better' technological solution. As mentioned above, pre-industrial metalworking in Africa was deeply embedded in the realms of beliefs and rituals, and smelting has often been seen as an analogy for childbirth.[95] As such, considerations of such factors as the yield or quality of the metal produced are unlikely to provide sufficient explanation of the technological choices made by smiths.

As noted already, traditional studies of technological change and transfers have tended to be suffused with the notion of progress and of evolutionary stages that link with social advances. New inventions and innovations are often assumed to have rendered less advanced technology obsolete or marginal.[96] Societies that did not innovate or adopt progressive technology are seen as backwards, technologically stagnated or

---

[92] Goblot 1979; Wilson *et al.*, Chapter 3, this volume.
[93] Killick 2015, 314, 316 and references therein. See also Robion-Brunner, Chapter 9, this volume.
[94] Liverani, Chapter 2, this volume.
[95] Childs and Killick 1993; Herbert 1984, 32–42; Schmidt and Mapunda 1997.   [96] White 1984.

disinterested in notions of economic progress.[97] However, an alternative perspective is that in many societies through history the reality has been rather different, with new tools being added to a 'technology shelf' from which people drew what was appropriate to their needs, means and situation.[98] In this view of past society, technological choices were governed by pragmatism and empirical realities. Knowledge of inventions can be widely spread, at the same time that the practical application of a new technology remains limited. In the event, people tend to invest in what is useful to them and workable in their local context. If camels are shown to be superior to donkeys on long-range Saharan trails, they will tend to replace donkeys over time. Donkeys will not necessarily disappear if they remain a cheaper alternative for local transport or water-raising duties, or where there is terrain to be crossed that camels will find difficult, like mountain passes. It is also evident that the cost-effectiveness of a 'superior' technology may create a threshold that allows alternative technologies to remain current and viable additions. For example, at many Saharan locations a predominant mode of irrigation was supplemented by a secondary form, where that offered an alternative way of augmenting the supply of water (and thus the cultivable area) of the oasis.[99]

As well as looking at how and why technologies were transferred in the Trans-Saharan zone, this volume also touches on those cases in which the spread of technologies was slowed or halted; or, to put it another way, where the choice was made *not* to adopt a particular technology. Several studies have shown the role of geographical barriers (either human or physical) in acting as dividing lines between different technological zones.[100] From a diffusionist perspective, higher population densities lead to increased social interactions, potentially facilitating the geographical spread of technology. One might thus expect technological transfer through the Sahara to be very limited, but this does not seem to be uniformly true. The picture that emerges from the review of technology transfer provided by this volume is still very patchy. While for some technologies (irrigation, animal husbandry) general trends can be traced through the desert, in many cases the data seem insufficient to track technology movement once we reach the limits of the Sahara. Rehren and Rosenow note that little is known about the appearance of glassmaking

---

[97] Finley 1965.
[98] See Greene 1994; 2000; Mattingly 1996 for archaeological applications of the technological shelf idea.
[99] Sterry and Mattingly 2020, 12–17.   [100] Gosselain 2000, 198–200; Killick 2015, 315.

west of the Nile Valley and south of the Mediterranean zone.[101] In a similar way, the work of Jane Humphris has highlighted the difficulty of considering ironworking in Meroe within a Trans-Saharan network, given how few 'nodes' are known in surrounding areas.[102] If sites subjected to archaeological attention are – for a variety of reasons – rare, then sites at which an in-depth examination of production remains is accompanied by a study of cultural context and accurate dating are even more exceptional. Low levels of training and funding for materials analysis and dating are among the reasons for this,[103] but desert conditions are also a factor, as some sites have experienced severe wind deflation meaning that the temporal affinity between datable material and technological remains can be difficult to ascertain.[104] For those technologies which do seem to have been transmitted across the Sahara, it is interesting to consider by what means, in such a sparsely populated landscape, they would have been transferred. The answer here may lie with the highly mobile nomadic pastoral populations. This mobility, rather than a dense settlement pattern, may have created the spatial propinquity necessary for technological transfer. Direct evidence for the role of pastoralists is limited, but certainly worthy of investigation. Examples of their involvement may be suggested in the translocation of animal species and husbandry techniques, as discussed by Fothergill *et al.* in Chapter 5 and potentially also for weaving techniques that may have travelled alongside the wool itself, as discussed by Magnavita in Chapter 6 (though textile production has often been an important component of oasis economies too).[105]

Another factor to be considered in the adoption and/or success of foreign technologies in new areas is the initial investment (private or communal) in both capital and labour.[106] The adoption of foggara irrigation is one example of technology where a substantial initial investment would have been necessary, a clear limiting factor on who could undertake the construction of foggaras in a new area. The perceived risk (ideological, economic or otherwise) of the adoption of a new technology in a given socio-economic context can have a significant impact on whether a group will choose to adopt change or maintain the status quo.[107] Land ownership is also a factor, and different notions of this

---

[101] Rehren and Rosenow, Chapter 12, this volume.   [102] Humphris, Chapter 8, this volume.

[103] Killick 2015, 312.

[104] See for example the debate on the dating of metalworking remains in the Termit massif in Niger: Killick 2004b; McIntosh 1994.

[105] Mattingly and Cole 2017, on the importance of textiles in Trans-Saharan trade.

[106] Van der Veen 2010, 3.   [107] Van der Veen 2010, 3–4.

(particularly between nomadic and settled groups) can play a significant role in the decisions regarding technological change. For example, Robion-Brunner observes that the Kompa Moussekoubou ironworkers did not use the closest available ores sources, suggesting that this might have been due to constraints imposed by a local landholder.[108] In Chapter 3, Wilson *et al.* also consider the influence of land ownership, noting that in the early to mid-twentieth century foggaras were more commonly encountered in regions with a small group of elite landlords able to command a significant body of labour, rather than in regions with many smallholders. This highlights the importance of intensive coopera-tion in the management of water resources. We can also see how the rooting of certain technologies within specific belief systems (as dis-cussed above), social logics or technological traditions may have consti-tuted another kind of cultural barrier. These ideas have been explored by the proponents of a social construction of technology, for whom choices between various technical solutions allowing people to carry out the same task may be influenced, consciously or not, by the preferences or norms of a society.[109] For many of the studies in this volume it is too soon to build a strong case demonstrating that such choices were the reason behind the adoption or not of a certain technology, but suggestions that social logics might be at play are being made where the choice of specific solutions remains to be explained, as for example in the use of human-powered grain mills in North Africa rather than the larger animal-powered ones more common in Italy,[110] or the existence of a multitude of variations on the smelting furnace in a geographically limited area in Dogon Country in Mali.[111] Further collection of information will of course help address such questions, but there is also a crucial need for interdisciplinary dialogues given that, as put by Killick, 'the social inter-pretation of technological acts will always be more credible if it can be shown that the same pattern recurs in different contexts'.[112] By bringing together scholars specialising in the study of different technologies, this volume takes a step towards breaking down the barriers that may hinder the understanding of underlying choices behind the adoption or not of new technologies.

---

[108] Robion-Brunner, Chapter 9, this volume.
[109] Childs and Killick 1993; Gosselain 2000; Lechtman 1977; Lemonnier 1992; 1993.
[110] Amraoui, Chapter 4, this volume.   [111] Robion-Brunner, Chapter 9, this volume.
[112] Killick 2004a, 574. See for example Lechtman 1984 for an example of the value system related to technological choices in both metallurgy and textiles production.

Complexity

The discussions in this volume highlight the fact that technology transfers have rarely been well-defined linear phenomena involving the direct adoption of a completely new foreign technology. Rather they have emerged as complex stories of local adaptations, cross-craft interaction and even failures.

Adaptation and Micro-Inventions

It is frequently through their encountering new environments that technologies are altered and adapted to follow new trajectories. This aspect of technology transfer often signifies a fair degree of intent on the part of the individuals concerned. It also involves another factor that archaeologists are relatively well placed to measure: environmental constraints. The adaptation of technologies to new environments, and the development of technological packages to respond to particular environmental challenges, are key themes in this volume. Amraoui, for example, demonstrates in Chapter 4 how the Roman model of textile fulling tubs was adapted to the North African environment by allowing for a more restricted water supply. We can also cite the obvious necessity to adapt the management strategies of animal species when translocating them to a new environment, and in some cases the possible adaptation of the species themselves. Indeed, in Chapter 5 Fothergill *et al.* suggest that some species translocated to West Africa may have developed trypanotolerance: a resistance to the fly-born ailment called trypanosomiasis.

Adaptations, however, do not necessarily result from being faced with new environments, but can occur at a very local scale, either driven by skilled workers making small improvements to existing techniques or responding to local changes in circumstances.[113] Equally localised technological change can appear as the cumulative result of replication errors.[114] The likelihood for adaptations, whether rapid or incremental, needs to be carefully considered when looking at Trans-Saharan technologies. Given the limited archaeological evidence and especially the poor time resolution available in the region, our ability to recognise technological transfer as such may be compromised if a technology has been substantially adapted in the process.

---

[113] Van der Veen 2010, 7 and references therein.
[114] Charlton *et al.* 2010; Eerkens and Lipo 2005.

Cross-Craft Interactions

The adoption and adaptations of technologies, just like inventions and innovations, do not happen in a vacuum but are necessarily based on a prior accumulation of knowledge. These enabling ideas or technologies are not necessarily to be found within the realms of a single craft, but are usually cross-material and cross-craft.[115] One of the strengths of this book is that we are able to overlap material and subject specialisms with regional foci, with some interesting results. A clear point to emerge is the inter-connectivity of the technologies discussed: we could not have pigs in the Sahara without foggaras, and we could not have foggaras without advanced metallurgy. The spread of literacy and a written script for the Berber language may have in part serviced the needs of trade across vast distances, but it also answered a basic need of complex water-sharing arrangements in oases. The written documentation of water rights at Ghadamis or the Jarid oases are excellent examples of this.[116] Examples of the interconnect-edness of crafts abound in this volume. As well as the links between irrigation technologies, introduction of crops and animal species and changes in tools dedicated to digging, ploughing or grinding,[117] we can site for example the existence of workshops presumably dedicated to jewellery making at Saniat Jibril, near the Garamantian capital, where copper, iron and glass were worked in close proximity to (if not by the same people as) semi-precious stones and ostrich eggshells.[118] Another example is the spinning and weaving of textiles that was linked not only to the spread of animals and crops (and thus irrigation technologies), but also to earlier basketry and matting techniques, the evidence for which is found impressed on pottery.[119] The spread of technological 'packages' shows examples where sets of connected technologies, enabled or made necessary by others, appear seemingly simultaneously (albeit given the limited tem-poral resolution of the archaeological data). The social implications of such packages should be given due weight in any consideration of human movement over the Sahara. Some technologies were more specific in terms of adoption and application to pastoral groups and others to oasis cultivators, but the two broad groups operated within a common over-arching knowledge base. Parallel studies of trade and urbanisation in the Sahara suggest that the connectivity of this zone was far higher in the first

---

[115] For a variety of examples in the Mediterranean World see Rebay-Salisbury *et al.* 2014.
[116] Eldblom 1968; Trousset 1986.   [117] Wilson *et al.*, Chapter 3, this volume.
[118] Cuénod, Chapter 7, this volume; Mattingly 2010, 189–201; Schrüfer-Kolb 2007.
[119] Magnavita, Chapter 6, this volume.

millennium BC and early first millennium AD than generally admitted before.[120] Knowledge, ideas, technology and material culture were widely shared across this network, even if they were not developed everywhere in the exact same way.

However, as highlighted by Robertshaw in Chapter 11, in environments like those found in the Sahara or the Sahel where resources are scarce the coexistence of technologies creates a duality between shared knowledge and competition for resources such as water, labour or fuel. Metallurgy and glass production for example, although sharing pyrotechnological knowledge, are both very hungry in fuel and would also have competed with food preparation. It is interesting to consider how such competition might have resulted in solutions such as a seasonality of activities (unfortunately rather difficult to establish from the archaeological record) or innovative techniques such as the possible use of dung or date stone fuel in Fazzan.[121]

Interruptions, Dead Ends or Untold Stories?

Another theme which we might tentatively draw out as in need of further academic attention is that of technological 'dead ends'. Methodological constraints (archaeological visibility) along with a bias to evolutionary, unidirectional models are largely responsible for an almost unthinking focus on technological evolution or development, which naturally prioritises the successful (that is, long-lived) technologies. Yet the extent to which this reflects the true nature of technological change remains unclear. As argued by Pinch and Bijker, 'The *success* of an artifact is precisely what needs to be expained'.[122] If we are to better understand the past economics and experience of technology, perhaps we should pay more attention to the technological 'failures', such as the foggaras excavated into an unsuitable water table described by Wilson *et al.* in Chapter 3, or the unsuccessful introduction of guinea fowl to Europe noted by Fothergill *et al.* in Chapter 5. A lack of focus on failure may also bias archaeometric approaches. For example, as noted by Duckworth in Chapter 10, we tend to assume that the composition of glass found at a production site is reflective of the

---

[120] Mattingly *et al.* 2017; Sterry and Mattingly 2020.

[121] Cuénod, Chapter 7, and Duckworth, Chapter 10, this volume. See as mentioned above the development of the natural draught furnace in regions of West-Africa as a possible result of the competition in labour due to the high demands of agriculture in the infertile woodlands: Killick 2015, 314.

[122] Pinch and Bijker 2012, 18, emphasis added.

output at that site, despite archaeological and historical evidence that glass was frequently recycled, and that the abandonment of material at a production site may indicate failure of the recipe or selective discard of less useful material.

Another example of the non-linearity of technological development is the possibility of the 'loss' of knowledge (and a possible subsequent 'rediscovery' or 'reinvention') in a certain geographical area of a technology that had previously been successful. In our current knowledge of West African copper metallurgy, for example, there is an intriguing lack of finds of artefacts or waste relating to copper metallurgy in the first half of the first millennium AD, despite clear evidence of production in the first millennium BC (mining in the Akjoujt region of Mauritania in particular) and traces of activities at various sites of Mauritania, Mali or Niger in the second half of the first millennium AD. Unfortunately, since the region remains generally underinvestigated it is difficult to establish whether this is a real interruption or a problem of lack of data or dating issues,[123] but a severe aridification of the region in this period driving the people and herds south and thus potentially reducing the accessibility of the raw material has been suggested as an explanation for this lag.[124] There exist other examples of such interruptions outside of Africa,[125] which serve to remind us of the 'punctuated' and branching nature of technological change.[126] It is precisely the study of the relationship between the complex trajectories of technologies, the physical environment in which they develop and the societies within which they are embedded that can provide the best contributions to our understanding of the human past, and we hope this volume makes a small step in that direction in a geographical area where much still needs to be done.

In the end, the theme that is most apparent in the chapters in this book is that of interconnectivity, both in the archaeological evidence and in the way in which the individuals studying it interact with one another. We frequently discuss interdisciplinarity in archaeology, but when dealing with an area as vast as the Sahara intradisciplinarity is just as important a consideration. Communication between materials specialists and regional specialists is vital. Finally, as demonstrated by our various workshops

---

[123] The dating of the copper exploitation in Mauritania in unfortunately unclear. See original date published in Lambert 1983; and discussion in McIntosh 2020.

[124] McIntosh 2020.

[125] For example, the interruption of the use of wheel-thrown pottery in the East Mediterranean: Roux 2003; 2010.

[126] See Roberts and Radivojević 2015, 302.

and conference discussions, we must learn to learn from one another. For example, a 'big data' approach to metals recycling may be equally valuable in the study of glass. Similarly, the importance given to praxis in the study of potterymaking techniques should arguably be offered a more central place in the study of all technologies, which, after all, are transferred from person to person, and not from object to object.

Reference

Alpern, S.B. 2005. Did they or didn't they invent it? Iron in Sub-Saharan Africa. *History in Africa* 32: 41–94.

Barker, G. 2007. *The Agricultural Revolution in Prehistory: Why Did Foragers Become Farmers?* Oxford: Oxford University Press.

Barth, H. 1858. [1890]. *Travels and Discoveries in North and Central Africa.* London: Ward, Lock and Co.

Berbrugger, A. 1862. *Les puits artesiens des oasis meridionales de l'Algerie.* Paris: Hachette.

Braudel, F. 1995. *The Mediterranean and the Mediterranean World in the Age of Philip II.* Berkeley: California University Press.

Bray, P., Cuénod, A., Gosden, C., Hommel, P., Liu, R. and Pollard, M. 2015. Form and flow: The 'karmic cycle' of copper. *Journal of Archaeological Science* 56: 202–09.

Brogan, O. and Smith, D.J. 1984. *Ghirza. A Libyan Settlement in the Roman Period.* London and Tripoli: Society for Libyan Studies/Department of Antiquities.

Broodbank, C. 2013. *The Making of the Middle Sea. A History of the Mediterranean from the Beginning to the Emergence of the Classical World.* London: Thames and Hudson.

Budd, P. and Taylor, T. 1995. The faerie smith meets the bronze industry: Magic versus science in the interpretation of prehistoric metal-making. *World Archaeology* 27.1: 133–43.

Bulliet, R.W. 1975. *The Camel and the Wheel.* Cambridge, MA: Harvard University Press.

Bulliet, R.W. 1994. Determinism and pre-industrial technology. In M. Roe Smith and L. Marx (eds), *Does Technology Drive History? The Dilemma of Technological Determinism*, Cambridge, MA: The MIT Press, 201–16.

Camps, G. 1986. L'araire berbere. In *Histoire et archéologie de l'Afrique du nord. 3e colloque international Montpellier*, Paris: CNRS, 177–84.

Camps, G. and Chaker, S. 1993. Cheval. *Encyclopédie berbère, 12 (Capsa – Cheval).* Aix-en-Provence: Edisud, 1907–11.

Camps, G. and Gast, M. (eds). 1982. *Les chars préhistoriques du Sahara.* Aix en Provence: Université de Provence.

Camps-Fabrer, H. 1966. *Matière et art mobilier dans la préhistoire nord-africaine et saharienne.* Paris: Mémoires du centre de recherches anthropologiques préhistoriques et ethnographiques.

Capot-Rey, R. and Marcais, P. 1953. La charrue au Sahara. *Travaux de l'Institut de Recherches Sahariennes* 9: 39–69.

Castelletti, L., Castiglioni, E., Cottini, M. and Rottoli, M. 1999. Archaeobotanical analysis of charcoal, wood and seeds. In di Lernia 1999, 131–48.

Charlton, M., Crew, P., Rehren, T. and Shennan, S. 2010. Explaining the evolution of ironmaking recipes: An example from northwest Wales. *Journal of Anthropological Archaeology* 29: 352–67.

Childs, S.T. and Killick, D. 1993. Indigenous African metallurgy: Nature and culture. *Annual Review of Anthropology* 22: 317–37.

Cissé, M. 2017. The Trans-Saharan trade connection with Gao (Mali) during the first millennium AD. In *Mattingly et al.* 2017, 101–30.

Cremaschi, M. 2001. Holocene climatic changes in an archaeological landscape: The case-study of the Wadi Tanezzuft and its drainage basin (SW Fezzan, Libyan Sahara). *Libyan Studies* 32: 5–28.

Cremaschi, M. and di Lernia, S. (eds). 1998. *Wadi Teshuinat. Palaeoenvironment and Prehistory in South-Western Fezzan (Libyan Sahara): Survey and Excavations in the Tadrart Acacus, Erg Uan Kasa, Messak Sattafet and Edeyen of Murzuq, 1990–1995.* Milan: All'Insegna del Giglio.

Daumas, E. 1968. *The Horses of the Sahara* (trans. S. M. Ohlendorf). Austin and London: University of Texas Press.

di Lernia, S. 1999. *The Uan Afuda Cave: Hunter-Gatherer Societies of Central Sahara.* Firenze: All'Insegna del Giglio.

di Lernia, S. 2013. The emergence and spread of herding in Northern Africa: A critical reappraisal. In Mitchell and Lane 2013, 528–40.

Duckworth, C.N., Cuénod, A. and Mattingly, D.J. 2014. Non-destructive µXRF analysis of glass and metal objects from sites in the Libyan pre-desert and Fazzan. *Libyan Studies* 46: 15–34.

Duckworth, C.N., Mattingly, D.J., Chenery, S. and Smith, V.C. 2016. End of the line? Glass bangles, technology, recycling and trade in Islamic North Africa. *Journal of Glass Studies* 58: 135–69.

Dussubieux, L. 2017. Glass beads in the Trans-Saharan trade. In Mattingly *et al.* 2017, 414–32.

Edgerton, D. 2008. *The Shock of the Old: Technology and Global History since 1900.* London: Profile Books.

Eerkens, J.W. and Lipo, C.P. 2005. Cultural transmission, copying errors and the generation of variation in material culture and the archaeological record. *Journal of Anthropological Archaeology* 24: 316–34.

Ehret, C. 2019. Berber peoples in the Sahara and North Africa: Linguistic historical proposals. In Gatto *et al.* 2019, 464–94.

Eldblom, L. 1968. *Structure foncière. Organisation et structure sociale: Une étude comparative sur la vie socio-économique dans les trois oasis libyennes de Ghat, Mourzouk et particulièrement Ghadamès.* Lund: Uniksol.

Fentress, E.W. 2019. The archaeological and genetic correlates of Amazigh linguistics. In Gatto *et al.* 2019, 495–524.

Finley, M.I. 1965. Technical innovation and economic progress in the ancient world. *Economic History Review* 18: 29–45.

Fuller, D. and Hildebrand, E. 2013. Domesticating plants in Africa. In Mitchell and Lane 2013, 507–25.

Gatto, M.C. and Zerboni, A. 2015. Holocene supraregional environmental crises as motor for major sociocultural changes in Northeastern Africa and the Sahara. *African Archaeological Review* 32: 301–33.

Gatto, M., Mattingly, D.J., Ray, N. and Sterry, M. (eds) 2019. *Burials, Migration and Identity in the Ancient Sahara and Beyond.* Trans-Saharan Archaeology, Volume 2. Series editor D.J. Mattingly. Cambridge: Cambridge University Press and the Society for Libyan Studies.

Gauthier, Y. and Gauthier, C. 2011. Des chars et des Tifinagh: Étude aréale et corrélations. *Les Cahiers de l'AARS* 15: 91–118.

Gifford-Gonzalez, D. and Hanotte, O. 2013. Domesticating animals in Africa. In Mitchell and Lane 2013, 491–505.

Goblot, H. 1979. *Les qanats: Une technique d'acquisition de l'eau.* Paris and New York: Industrie et artisanat 9.

Gosselain, O. 2000. Materializing identities: An African perspective. *Journal of Archaeological Method and Theory* 7.3: 187–217.

Gosselain, O., Haour, A., MacDonald, K. and Manning, K. 2010. Introduction. In A. Haour, K. Manning, N. Arazi, O. Gosselain, N.S. Guèye, D. Keita, A. Livingstone Smith, K. MacDonald, A. Mayor, S. McIntosh and R. Vernet (eds), *African Pottery Roulettes Past and Present: Techniques, Identification and Distribution,* Oxford: Oxbow, 1–34.

Greene, K. 1994. Technology and innovation in context: The Roman background to Medieval and later developments. *Journal of Roman Archaeology* 7: 22–33.

Greene, K. 2000. Technological innovation and economic progress in the ancient world: M.I. Finley reconsidered. *Economic History Review* 53: 29–59.

Gron, K.J. and Sørensen, L. 2018. Cultural and economic negotiation: A new perspective on the Neolithic transition of Southern Scandinavia. *Antiquity* 92.364: 958–74.

Haour, A. 2011. Putting pots and people in the Sahelian empires. *Azania* 46.1: 36–48.

Herbert, E.W. 1984. *Red Gold of Africa: Copper in Precolonial History and Culture.* Madison, WI: University of Wisconsin Press.

Hodder, I. 2012. *Entangled: An Archaeology of the Relationships between Humans and Things.* Oxford: Wiley-Blackwell.

Hodges, H. 1970. *Technology in the Ancient World.* London: BCA.

Holmes, M. 2013. Faunal data appendices. In Mattingly 2013, 853–64.

Holmes, M. and Grant, A. 2013. The animal bone assemblage. In Mattingly 2013, 495–501.

Kanungo, A. 2004. Glass beads in ancient India and furnace-wound beads at Purdalpur: An ethnoarchaeological approach. *Asian Perspectives* 43.1: 130–50.

Killick, D. 2004a. Social constructionist approaches to the study of technology. *World Archaeology* 36.4: 571–78.

Killick, D. 2004b. Review essay: What do we know about African iron working? *Journal of African Archaeology* 2.1: 97–112.

Killick, D. 2015. Invention and innovation in African iron-smelting technologies. *Cambridge Archaeological Journal* 25.1: 307–19.

Kuhn, T. 1970. *The Structure of Scientific Revolutions* (2nd edition). Chicago: University of Chicago Press.

Lambert, N. 1983. Nouvelle contribution à l'étude du Chalcolithique de Mauritanie. In N. Echard (ed.), *Métallurgies Africaines: Nouvelles contributions*, Paris: Société des Africanistes (Mémoires de la Société des Africanistes 9), 63–87.

Laureano, P. 1991. *Sahara: Jardin méconnu*. Paris: Larousse.

Lave, J. and Wenger, J. 1991. *Situated Learning: Legitimate Peripheral Participation*. Cambridge: Cambridge University Press.

Lechtman, H. 1977. Style in technology: Some early thoughts. In H. Lechtman and T. Merrill (eds), *Material Culture: Style, Organization and Dynamics of Technology*, St Paul (Minn): West, 3–20.

Lechtman, H. 1984. Andean value systems and the development of prehistoric metallurgy. *Technology and Culture* 25.1: 1–36.

Lecocq, B. 2015. Distant shores: A historiographic view of trans-Saharan space. *Journal of African History* 56.1: 23–36.

Leitch, V., Duckworth, C., Cuénod, A., Mattingly, D.J., Sterry, M. and Cole, F. 2017. Early Saharan trade: The inorganic evidence. In Mattingly *et al.* 2017, 287–340.

Lemonnier, P. 1992. *Elements for an Anthropology of Technology*. Ann Arbor: University of Michigan, Museum of Anthropology.

Lemonnier, P. (ed.) 1993. *Technological Choices: Transformation in Material Cultures since the Neolithic*. London: Routledge.

Lichtenberger, A. 2016. 'Sea without water': Conceptualising the Sahara and the Mediterranean. In M. Dabag, D. Haller, N. Jaspert and A. Lichtenberger (eds), *New Horizons: Mediterranean Research in the 21st Century*, Paderborn: Ferdinand Schoningh, 267–83.

Livingstone Smith, A. 2007. Histoire du décor à la roulette en Afrique subsaharienne. *Journal of African Archaeology* 5.2: 189–216.

López, D. and Cantero, F.J. 2016. L'agriculture et alimentation à partir de l'étude des restes des grains et des fruits. In N. Kallala, J. Sanmarti and C. Belarte (eds), *Althiburos II. L'aire du capitol et la nécropole méridionales: études*, Tarragona: Universitat de Barcelona, 449–89.

Lydon, G. 2015. Saharan oceans and bridges, barriers and divides in Africa's historiographical landscape. *Journal of African History* 56.1: 3–22.

McIntosh, S.K. 1994. Changing perceptions of West Africa's past: Archaeological research since 1988. *Journal of Archaeological Research* 2.2: 165–98

McIntosh, S.K. 2020. Long-distance exchange and urban trajectories in the first millennium AD: Case studies from the Middle Niger and Middle Senegal river valleys. In Sterry and Mattingly 2020, 521–63.

Magnavita, S. 2017. Track and trace: Archaeometric approaches to the study of early Trans-Saharan trade. In Mattingly *et al.* 2017, 393–413.

Mapunda, B.B.B. 2013. The appearance and development of metallurgy south of the Sahara. In Mitchell and Lane 2013, 615–26.

Mattingly, D.J. 1996. Olive presses in Roman Africa: Technical evolution or stagnation? *L'Africa romana* 11: 577–95.

Mattingly, D.J. (ed.) 2003. *The Archaeology of Fazzan. Volume 1, Synthesis.* London: Society for Libyan Studies, Department of Antiquities.

Mattingly, D.J. 2007. *The Archaeology of Fazzan. Volume 2, Site Gazetteer, Pottery and other Survey Finds.* London: Society for Libyan Studies, Department of Antiquities.

Mattingly, D.J. (ed.) 2010. *The Archaeology of Fazzan. Volume 3, Excavations carried out by C.M. Daniels.* London: Society for Libyan Studies, Department of Antiquities.

Mattingly, D.J. (ed.) 2013. *The Archaeology of Fazzan. Volume 4, Survey and Excavations at Old Jarma (Ancient Garama) carried out by C.M. Daniels (1962–69) and the Fazzan Project (1997–2001).* London: Society for Libyan Studies, Department of Antiquities.

Mattingly, D.J. 2016. Who shaped Africa? The origins of agriculture and urbanism in Maghreb and Sahara. In N. Mugnai, J. Nikolaus and N. Ray (eds), *De Africa Romaque. Merging Cultures across North Africa*, London: Society for Libyan Studies, 11–25.

Mattingly, D.J. and Cole, F. 2017. Visible and invisible commodities of trade: The significance of organic materials in Saharan trade. In Mattingly *et al.* 2017, 211–30.

Mattingly, D.J., al-Aghab, S., Ahmed, A., Moussa, F., Sterry, M. and Wilson, A.I. 2010. DMP X: Survey and landscape conservation issues around the Tāqallit headland. *Libyan Studies* 41: 105–32.

Mattingly, D.J., Leitch, V., Duckworth, C.N., Cuenod, A., Sterry, M. and Cole, F. (eds) 2017. *Trade in the Ancient Sahara and Beyond.* Trans-Saharan Archaeology, Volume 1. Series editor D.J. Mattingly. Cambridge: Cambridge University Press and the Society for Libyan Studies.

Mattingly, D.J., Sterry, M., al-Haddad, M. and Bokbot, Y. 2018. Beyond the Garamantes: The early development of Saharan oases. In Purdue *et al.* 2018a, 205–28.

Mattingly, D.J., Sterry, M. and Fothergill, B.T. Forthcoming. Animal traffic in the Sahara. In V. Blanc-Bijon (ed.), *Hommes et animaux au Maghreb, de la Préhistoire au Moyen Age: Explorations d'une relation complexe. XIe Colloque international Histoire et Archéologie de l'Afrique du Nord (Marseille – Aix-en-Provence, 8–11 octobre 2014)*, Aix-en-Provence: Presses universitaires de Provence.

Mercuri, A.M. 1999. Palynological analysis of the early Holocene sequence. In di Lernia 1999, 149–82.

Mercuri, A.M., Trevisan Grandi, G., Mariotti Lippi, M. and Cremaschi, M. 1998. New pollen data from Uan Muhuggiag rockshelter (Libyan Sahara). In Cremaschi and di Lernia 1998, 107–24.

Miller, H.M.-L. 2009. *Archaeological Approaches to Technology*. Walnut Creek, CA: Left Coast Press Inc.

Mitchell, P. and Lane, P. (eds) 2013. *The Oxford Handbook of African Archaeology*. Oxford: Oxford University Press.

Oleson, J.P. (ed.) 2008. *The Oxford Handbook of Engineering and Technology in the Classical World*. Oxford: Oxford University Press.

Oppenheim, A.L. 1970. The cuneiform texts. In A.L. Oppenheim (ed.), *Glass and Glassmaking in Ancient Mesopotamia: An Edition of the Cuneiform Texts which Contain Instructions for Glassmakers with a Catalogue of Surviving Objects*, Corning, NY: The Corning Museum of Glass Press, 2–101.

Pelling, R. 2008. Garamantian agriculture: The plant remains from Jarma, Fazzān. *Libyan Studies* 39: 41–71.

Pelling, R. 2013a. The archaeobotanical remains. In Mattingly 2013, 473–94.

Pelling, R. 2013b. Botanical data appendices. In Mattingly 2013, 841–52.

Pfaffenberger, B. 1992. The social anthropology of technology. *Annual Review of Anthropology* 21: 491–516.

Pinch, T.J. and Bijker, W.E. 2012. The social construction of facts and artifacts: Or how the sociology of science and the sociology of technology might benefit each other. In W.E. Bijker, T.P. Hughes and T.J. Pinch (eds), *The Social Construction of Technological Systems: New Directions in the Sociology and History of Technology*, Cambridge, MA: MIT Press, 17–50.

Power, R., Nikita, E., Mattingly, D.J., Lahr, M.M. and O'Connell, T. 2019. Human mobility and identity: Variation, diet and migration in relation to the Garamantes of Fazzan. In Gatto *et al.* 2019, 134–61.

Purdue, L., Charbonnier, J. and Khalidi, L. (eds) 2018a. *Des refuges aux oasis: Vivre en milieu aride de la Préhistoire à aujourd'hui. XXXVIIIe rencontres internationales d'archéologie et d'histoire d'Antibes*. Antibes: Éditions APDCA.

Purdue, L., Charbonnier, J. and Khalidi, L. 2018b. Introduction: Living in arid environments from prehistoric times to the present day: Approaches to the study of refugia and oases. In Purdue *et al.* 2018a, 9–32.

Rebay-Salisbury, K., Brysbaert, A. and Foxhall, L. (eds) 2014. *Knowledge, Networks and Craft Traditions in the Ancient World: Material Crossovers*. London: Routledge.

Roberts, B.W. and Radivojević, M. 2015. Invention as a process: Pyrotechnologies in early societies. *Cambridge Archaeological Journal* 25.1: 299–306.

Roe Smith, M. and Marx, L. 1994. *Does Technology Drive History? The Dilemma of Technological Determinism*. Cambridge, MA: The MIT Press.

Roux, V. 2003. A dynamic systems framework for studying technological change: Application to the emergence of the potter's wheel in the southern Levant. *Journal of Archaeological Method and Theory* 10: 1–30.

Roux, V. 2010. Technological innovation and developmental trajectories: Social factors as evolutionary forces. In M.J. O'Brien and S.J. Shennan (eds), *Innovation in Cultural Systems. Contributions from Evolutionary Anthropology*, Cambridge (MA): MIT Press, 217–34.

Sanmartí, J., Kallla, N., Belarte, M.C., Ramon, J., Telmini, B.M., Jornet, R. and Miniaoui, S. 2012. Filling gaps in the Protohistory of the eastern Maghreb: The Althiburos Archaeological Project (el Kef, Tunisia). *Journal of African Archaeology* 10.1: 21–44.

Schadewaldt, W. 1979. The concepts of 'nature' and 'technique' according to the Greeks. In C. Mitcham and R. Mackey (eds), *Research in Philosophy and Technology* 2, New York: Free Press, 159–71.

Scharff, R.C. and Dusek, V. 2014. Part II. Philosophy, modern science, and technology. In R.C. Scharff and V. Dusek (eds), *Philosophy of Technology: The Technological Condition, an Anthology* (Second edition), Chichester: Wiley-Blackwell, 89–90.

Scheele, J. 2017. The need for nomads: Camel-herding, raiding, and Saharan trade and settlement. In Mattingly *et al.* 2017, 55–79.

Schmidt, P.R. and Mapunda, B.B. 1997. Ideology and the archaeological record in Africa: Interpreting symbolism in iron smelting technology. *Journal of Anthropological Archaeology* 16.1: 73–102.

Schrüfer-Kolb, I. 2007. Metallurgical and non-metallurgical industrial activities. In Mattingly 2007, 448–62.

Skaggs, S., Norman, N., Garrison, E., Coleman, D. and Bouhlel, S. 2012. Local mining or lead importation in the Roman province of Africa Proconsularis? Lead isotope analysis of curse tablets from Roman Carthage, Tunisia. *Journal of Archaeological Science* 39: 970–83.

Sterry, M. and Mattingly, D.J. (eds) 2020. *Urbanisation and State Formation in the Ancient Sahara and Beyond*, Trans-Saharan Archaeology, Volume 3, series editor D.J. Mattingly, Cambridge: Cambridge University Press and the Society for Libyan Studies.

Stos-Gale, Z., Gale, N.H., Houghton, J. and Speakman, R. 1995. Lead isotope data from the Isotrace Laboratory, Oxford: 'Archaeometry' data base 1, ores from the Western Mediterranean. *Archaeometry* 37.2: 407–15.

Stos-Gale, Z.A., Gale, N.H. and Annetts, N. 1996. Lead isotope data from the Isotrace Laboratory, Oxford: 'Archaeometry' data base 3, ores from the Aegean, part 1. *Archeometry* 38: 381–390.

Trousset, P. 1986. Les oasis présahariennes dans l'antiquité: Partage de l'eau et division du temps. *Antiquités africaines* 22: 161–91.

Van der Veen, M. 1995. Ancient agriculture in Libya: A review of the evidence. *Acta Palaeobotanica* 35.1: 85–98.

Van der Veen, M. 2010. Agricultural innovation: Invention and adoption or change and adaptation. *World Archaeology* 42.1: 1–12.

Van der Veen, M. and Westley, B. 2010. Palaeoeconomic studies. In Mattingly 2010, 488–522.

Vavelidis, M., Bassiakos, I., Begemann, F., Patriarcheas, K., Pernicka, E., Schmitt-Strecker, S. and Wagner, G.A. 1985. Geologie und Erzvorkommen. In G. A. Wagner and G. Weisgerber (eds), *Silber, Blei und Gold auf Sifnos*, Bochum: Deutsches Bergbau-Museum, 59–80.

White, K.D. 1984. *Greek and Roman Technology*. London: Thames and Hudson.

Wild, J.P., Wild, F.C. and Clapham, A.J. 2007. Irrigation and the spread of cotton growing in Roman times. *Archaeological Textiles Newsletter* 44: 16–18.

Wild, J.P., Wild, F.C. and Clapham, A.J. 2011. Roman cotton revisited. In C. A. Giner (ed.), *Purpureae Vestes I. Textiles y tintes del Mediterráneo en época romana*. Valencia: Universitat de Valencia: 143–47.

Wilson, A. and Mattingly, D.J. 2003. Irrigation technologies: Foggaras, wells and field systems. In Mattingly 2003, 234–78.

Wilson, L. and Pollard, A.M. 2001. The provenance hypothesis. In D.R. Brothwell and A.M. Pollard (eds), *Handbook of Archaeological Sciences*, John Wiley & Sons Ltd, 507–17.

Zapata, L., López-Sáez, J.A., Ruis-Alsonso, M., Linstädter, J., Pérez-Jordà, G., Morales, J., Kehl, M. and Peña-Chocarro, L. 2013. Holocene environmental change and human impact in NE Morocco: Palaeo-botanical evidence from Ifri Oudadane. *The Holocene* 23.9: 1286–96.

PART II

Technological Mobility and Transfers

2 | Technological Innovations Transfer through the Hyper-Arid Belt

MARIO LIVERANI

Planning a History of the Sahara

I feel the need to preface this chapter with a personal admission. I wish to state that I am not a professional scholar in the field of Saharan studies.[1] Nonetheless, a ten-year field engagement and my background in broader Near Eastern studies gives me a certain perspective on the debates that are at the heart of this volume.

A traditional image of the Sahara desert is one of an unchanging environment and society, fixed across millennia. It is an image built up of sand dunes, oases and date palms, dromedary caravans and veiled Tuareg. The stereotype is a product of the early colonial period, but is still deep-rooted in popular imagination and continues to exert some (unconscious) influence on scholars dealing with the Medieval and modern history of the area. In addition to being a desert, the Sahara is an African desert, and Africa has traditionally been considered in colonialist thought as belonging to the 'people without history', evolving only thanks to external (basically European) interventions. But scholars devoted to prehistory and to antiquity are well aware that the Sahara, like every other part of the globe, has its own history, and underwent relevant changes through time. The need to write a revised history of the Sahara

---

[1] It is true that I did work in the Libyan Sahara for some ten years (from 1997 to 2006), but this happened because of an academic accident rather than a scientific reason. When the late Professor Fabrizio Mori retired, he did not find anybody but me, in our Department, to entrust with the charge of director for the Italian mission in the Akakus and surrounding area. I took the charge seriously and was able to carry out fieldwork and to produce several publications. But as soon as Savino di Lernia became academically mature enough to ensure a continuity in fundraising, I left to him the direction of the mission and went back to my own field of studies, namely the ancient Near East, and since then I worked mostly on the Assyrian imperial ideology. This means that the ideas that I am trying to uphold in the present chapter go back to some ten years ago.

during antiquity should be apparent, but remains to be accomplished. This book will no doubt mark a notable advancement in this direction. Since the central focus of our discussion here is the kingdom and/or civilisation of the Garamantes (both because they are the best known ancient people in the entire Central/Western Sahara, and because much work in recent decades was carried out by teams from the University of Leicester), this leads me to make two further remarks: for many Classical historians the Garamantes are still to be considered as the extreme (and quite poor or primitive) southern end of 'true' history writing (if not of true civilisation). In the contrary direction, among Africanist archaeologists the Garamantes are apparently considered as 'not African enough' to be included in their general syntheses.[2]

It is not my task to discuss here the great climatic changes occurring in the *longue durée* of geological time (including times when there was no desert at all). Climate is still an important factor in prehistoric and in properly historical times, when even a minor shift in the amount of rainfall made a great difference to the exploitability of the arid lands. I shall just allude here to the results obtained by Mauro Cremaschi and his team, based on the tree rings of the Tassili cypress, results that underscore a relevant (and rather sudden) aridification that occurred in the first centuries AD.[3] Nor is it my task to discuss the great transformation related to the advent of pastoralism, an innovation in which the Saharan peoples were at the vanguard of human progress. All these facts will be better discussed by colleagues properly expert in those fields of research. My intention is to evaluate in general terms the changes occurring in the 'Protohistoric' period, both in the technological innovations and in their social (socio-economic and socio-political) effects. It has been previously suggested that these so-called *siècles obscurs* in Saharan history were in fact a period of major innovations.[4]

This chapter concerns the period *c.*1500 BC to AD 500, which is properly historical in the Mediterranean, Nilotic and Near Eastern regions; and 'proto-historical' in the Sahara, in the sense that it deals with rather complex societies, but with written historical information provided only by external and/or later sources. While the details of a *histoire événementielle* are mostly obscured (just a few 'events' are in fact documented) and the *longue durée* of the environmental conditions pertains to other branches of science, a mid-term history centred on the technological and social changes is possible,

---

[2] Cf. my notes in Liverani 2006, 1003–10.   [3] Cremaschi *et al.* 2006.
[4] McIntosh and McIntosh 1988.

thanks to a combined use of archaeological data (and their scientific treatment) and external written sources, supported by an enlargement of horizons to include the adjacent regions. The major technical innovations that provided the desert with the key elements of its present image came into being during the two millennia defined above.

The External Origin of Innovations

In general terms, and within the period treated here, I have the impression that most technological innovations were first elaborated elsewhere and introduced into the Sahara only in a second stage, to be adapted to the local environment and cultural traditions. The two areas to be considered as strictly contiguous and connected to the Sahara are the Mediterranean basin on one side, and the Near East (especially the Arabian Peninsula) on the other: innovations of southern origin seem to belong mostly to a previous phase than the one here considered. The Mediterranean and Near East, no matter how dissimilar, share two characteristics. Both are much better known (from archaeological research and written documents) than the Sahara, and both were much more complex and advanced in socio-political order and in material culture. The impression of an external origin of Saharan innovations may thus be partly the result of the different level of information available, as much as to a different level of cultural advancement.

I am well aware that the old-fashioned habit of crediting the merit of cultural transfer to the 'givers' and not to the 'receivers', or else of attributing to the first party an active role, to the second a passive role, is now outdated, as is the concentration of attention (and appreciation) on the first introduction of an innovation more than on its later adaptation, transformation and further diffusion. However, we have to qualify the receivers as an active party, and to appreciate the amount of adaptation that any transfer brings about as compared to its original formulation. In our case, we must appreciate the role of the Sahara in adapting to its own environment and to its own cultural traditions and inventions first elaborated elsewhere. While I am well aware that the old 'diffusionist' model was a side effect of the colonialist relations of the past centuries, we should also be well aware that the present 'interactive' view is a side effect of post-colonialism and of neo-capitalist globalisation. Of course, it proves easier to historicise past generations than ourselves. In this sense, the present habit of considering northern contributions as a post-colonial inheritance, and to consider the southern contributions as politically correct, clearly belongs to such a problem. But these theoretical aspects would bring us too far from our more practical topic.

Northern versus Eastern Innovations

As for the south, that is the Sahelo-Sudanese belt, I have the impression that most technical/cultural contributions came into being in a phase when, for well-known climatic reasons, the landscape of the Central Sahara was not too different from that of the present Sahelo-Sudanese belt: a kind of savannah with various species of trees and animals, with perennial lakes and wadis. In such a condition, the question about a movement from south (present Sahel) to north (present Sahara desert) or vice versa seems rather irrelevant, and in any case difficult to solve given the at present limited (and unevenly distributed) availability of archaeological sites at which modern survey and excavation procedures have been adopted. Eventually, when the two belts became properly diversified, trade (salt versus gold and slaves) took place rather than cultural transfer, but this matter has already been treated in a previous volume in this series.[5]

The two major neighbours of the Sahara – the Mediterranean and the Near East – were quite different in terms of environment (climate and landscape) and socio-political organisation. The Mediterranean basin was characterised by a totally different environment and by major developments in the socio-political field. The latter included an interest in setting foot on the north African coast (the true interface between Mediterranean and Sahara), by means of colonies (Greek colonies in Cyrenaica, Phoenician-Punic colonies from Tripolitania to Morocco) mainly for commercial reasons, and eventually (in Roman times) by means of imperial conquest for the aims of direct exploitation and peopling. We might expect, therefore, that Mediterranean innovations that could have had an effect on the Saharan peoples would not belong to the realm of technology, at least in basic food production (considering the totally different environment), but rather to the realm of socio-political organisation and of the administrative tools connected with state management.

On the other hand, the Near East was characterised by a variety of environments, including (but not only) a desert environment quite similar to the Saharan one. The main part of the Arabian Peninsula is a sort of eastwards continuation of the Sahara, interrupted by the Nile Valley

---

[5] Mattingly *et al.* 2017; see Liverani 2000, for my own reconstruction of the basic trade pattern.

(whose role I will examine later on) and by the Red Sea. We should bear in mind that the arid belt continues farther north-east, into Iran and Central Asia. The environment being basically similar, we can expect that those Near Eastern innovations that could be adopted in the Sahara would belong to the basic technologies of environmental exploitation and modification on the one hand and of food production on the other.

In both cases, we have to assume – not as a true and proper 'law', but as a statistical imbalance – that the general direction of the innovations was determined by a difference in advancement. A more complex (in the socio-political realm) and more advanced (in the technological realm) society will probably for the most part disseminate its own features towards less advanced neighbours than the other way round, although there could certainly have been exceptions of various kinds. In practical terms, we can expect that the socio-political organisation of the peoples and states of the Mediterranean would influence the Saharan peoples more than the Saharan peoples could influence Mediterranean political formations. It also follows that we can expect that in terms of basic technology the Sahara received more stimuli from the Near East than Saharan innovations impacted on that area.

In any 'regional system' (I do not like the abused expression of 'world system' when applied to pre-modern times) the interactions are mostly stimulated by differences in available resources (largely dependent on environmental features) and by differences in organisational levels (in politics and economy as well). We can gain positive insights in conceiving the Sahara as a constitutive part of a wider 'regional system' including its neighbouring areas. Of course, regional systems do not exist in reality, they are just 'mental maps' that we build in order to better understand economic and cultural relationships. The most current mental map is built up with a Euro-Mediterranean core and in such a map the Sahara is present as a minor and remote periphery. But in the case of the discussions in this book, we have to locate the Sahara at the centre of our 'mental map' – as a 'simpler core' surrounded by 'more complex peripheries'.

The Construction of the Oasis

In what follows, I summarise the problems and the arguments, often referring to a more detailed and better documented presentation that I published some years ago.[6] The Saharan oasis as we know it from Early

---

[6] Liverani 2006.

Modern times was already described in a famous passage of Pliny,[7] as cultivated in four or five superposed layers: from top to bottom, date palms, then olives, figs, vines, cereals and legumes on the ground – all irrigated by a spring or a well providing water for a fixed radius, exploited by a plurality of families according to a timetable of fixed quotas. All these cultivars, including most cereals and legumes, were still alien in the Central Sahara during Pastoral (late Neolithic) times. The oasis, consisting of date palms and irrigation, is not a 'natural' landscape; it is one made by people, and at a relatively late date. The colonial opinion that the Romans introduced agriculture in the Sahara is obviously untenable, yet we have to try to establish a chronology for the introduction of the various cultivars and also of the irrigation technology. Following the already mentioned passage of Pliny, we shall consider the cultivars from the top layer to the ground.

The date palm had been domesticated in the Gulf area from the fourth millennium. It reached Mesopotamia around 3000 BC, Egypt around 2000 BC, the oases of the Western Desert around 1500 BC[8] and Fazzan around 1000 BC,[9] to become important in the Formative (Zinkekra) and Classic (Aghram Nadharif/Jarma) Garamantian periods.

Figs and olives (whose domestication had started in the Levant during Late Chalcolithic times), had already reached Egypt and the oases of its Western Desert in the Early Kingdom (that is by about 3000 BC), and could have reached Fazzan together with the date palm.

The introduction of grape vines is less sure for the Garamantian period, when it proved perhaps more convenient to import wine from Tripolitania. But its cultivation in Egypt is attested from around 3000 BC, and in the oases of the Western Desert since the second millennium BC, and the production of wine in those oases was intensive in Ptolemaic and Roman times. Therefore, a presence of vines in Fazzan during Garamantian times is not surprising.[10]

Finally, even the cereals cultivated in the Saharan oases, namely barley and emmer (*triticum dicoccum*), were of Near Eastern origin[11] and should have reached Fazzan towards the end of the second millennium BC, during the process of constitution of the nucleated oases. Note that the cultivars of African origin, namely millet and sorghum, had been the object of intensive collection and perhaps incipient cultivation (according the technique of 'décrue agriculture') during Pastoral times, later shifting southwards

---

[7] Pliny, *Natural History* 18.188.   [8] Zohary and Hopf 1994, 157–62.

[9] Cottini and Rottoli 2002.

[10] On figs, olives and vine I refer back to Liverani 2006, 1048–49. Cf. Duckworth *et al.*, Chapter 1, this volume, for citation of evidence from Zinkekra and Jarma.

[11] Zohary and Hopf 1994, 15–85.

following the process of aridification of the Sahara – so that the new 'nucleated oases' had to be colonised anew with cultivars of Oriental origin. Only later, in Roman and above all in Islamic times, were millet and sorghum reintroduced, possibly from India.

As for water availability, Saharan oases had to depend solely on springs or wells reaching the subsoil water table. Only in a second stage was a new technique of underground canalisation (the foggara) introduced. In this case too, the idea expressed during modern colonial times that the Romans had been responsible for their introduction is untenable. An Oriental origin is widely assumed, with a consensus that the foggara derive from the Near Eastern *qanat*,[12] and that their diffusion followed the route from Iran to the Levant, to the Egyptian oases and finally to Fazzan, and later also to the Northern and Western Sahara.[13] The problem is to define better the moment of their original invention and of their introduction in the Sahara. Geographers and historians of the Islamic periods generally support a late date, and even some historians of the Achaemenid empire reject an earlier origin. But the archaeological record supports an origin in the frame of the innovations marking the shift that took place in the Near East from the Bronze to the Iron Age. Bronze Age irrigation systems were on the surface and basically limited to river valleys. In the Early Iron Age, in the frame of the extension of settlements towards hilly and steppe regions, the new technique proved convenient – both in allowing transfer of water beyond hilly reliefs and in lowering the rate of evaporation. The first attested case is in Oman, *c.*1100–600 BC,[14] and then in Urartu and Assyria (eighth century), while in the Levant we have mainly attestations of underground canals in urban contexts. Foggaras reached Egypt and its oases in the Western Desert during the Persian period (if not earlier) since a foggara in the oasis of Kharga is cut by a building of Artaxerxes I.[15] For Fazzan, according to the extensive research of Andrew Wilson and David Mattingly (mainly based on the 'horizontal stratigraphy' of relations between canals and necropoleis), it is sure that the foggara system cannot be later than the Classic Garamantian period (first century BC to fourth century AD) and probably started already during the previous phase (fourth to first century BC). More details and updated information can be found in Chapter 3 of this volume.[16] The idea that the introduction of cotton could be in some way connected to the increase of irrigation is a possibility in need of better evidence.

---

[12] Goblot 1979; Briant 2001.
[13] Wilson and Mattingly 2003; Wilson *et al.*, Chapter 3, this volume.   [14] Boucharlat 2001.
[15] Wuttmann 2001.   [16] Wilson *et al.*, Chapter 3, this volume.

As for the management and division of the water (coming both from springs or canals) by the oasis community, we do not have direct evidence from Fazzan, but the system of fixed shares and time turns, granting to each family an equitable availability, is well attested in Roman times both in the Eastern Sahara (Kharga)[17] and in the borders of the Northern Sahara (Lamasba),[18] and is well described by Pliny. We have to assume that such a system precedes the introduction of the foggara, going back (maybe in a more simple formalisation) to the first organisation of the nucleated oases, because a well can belong (and often belongs) to a single family, but springs belong to the entire oasis community.

The Construction of the Caravan

The typical Saharan caravan is a caravan of dromedaries, but dromedaries were domesticated at a relatively late date, in general terms at the passage (in the Near East) from the Bronze Age to the Iron Age, towards the end of the second millennium. Previously, caravans were made up of donkeys, and their organisation is well known from the detailed documentation of the Old Assyrian trade between Assur and Central Anatolia. In the Sahara during the Pastoral period, when donkeys were already present, we can imagine a network of short-distance displacements rather than a long itinerary crossing the entire desert. The first attestation of a Trans-Saharan route is the one described by Herodotus, going back to the sixth century BC – but we have to imagine a group of pedestrians and presumably donkeys. An important factor is the climatic one: during the Pastoral (and still in the Late Pastoral) period, there were no nucleated oases in the middle of properly desert (hyper-arid) lands, but rather much larger stretches of land with permanent or seasonal watercourses, an environment that could be covered by donkeys. The progressive worsening of climate and the ensuing desertification made donkey caravans no longer suited for Trans-Saharan routes, and dromedaries became the most convenient solution.

Colonial-era scholars advanced the theory that dromedaries were introduced by Romans, first on the coast for agricultural work, and later in the desert for trade caravans (not forgetting war and brigandage).[19] Such a theory is clearly unwarranted. The dromedary had been domesticated in the area of Oman and Emirates since the mid-third millennium BC,[20] to reach the East-Arabian and Syro-Mesopotamian areas in the last quarter of

---

[17] Bousquet 1996; Bousquet and Reddé 1994.   [18] Shaw 1982.   [19] Brogan 1954.
[20] Compagnoni and Tosi 1978.

the second millennium BC, acquiring commercial relevance with the open-ing of the West Arabian route from Yemen to Syria towards the end of the millennium.[21] The passage from the Syro-Arabian to the Saharan area took almost a millennium. We have sure evidence of domesticated dromedaries in the eastern Delta in Ramesside times (thirteenth or twelfth century),[22] and their use had reached Egypt in the seventh–sixth centuries, and Middle Nile Valley in the eighth century[23] and then the oases of the Western Desert in the Saitic and Persian periods. Its spread over the Central Sahara in the fifth–fourth centuries is quite reasonable,[24] although the palaeozoological record is still limited and the dating of the rock engravings rather vague. In summary, caravans of dromedaries (or mixed dromedaries and donkeys) were in use from the fourth century BC, but not much earlier than that.

Northern Political and Administrative Tools

I limit myself here only to briefly hinting at the political-administrative innovations that the Sahara received from the Mediterranean – certainly not because they were less relevant than the technological ones, but because they are better known. As already said, they mostly concern political organisation, and are an obvious response to the presence, along the northern interface already defined, in a first stage (eighth–third centuries BC) of the Greek and Phoenician colonies, and in a later stage (second century BC–fifth century AD) of the Roman Empire and its provincial order. I will quote here the major innovations, in the form of a list, in order to show how different they are from those of eastern origin.

(1) The political organisation into 'ethnic states', based on former ethnic groups but in Roman times endowed with a closer decisional and behavioural unit, and considered as true 'kingdoms'. The process started and was consolidated in the northern area (Numidia, Mauretania, Getulia), but also reached the Central Sahara with the Garamantian kingdom.
(2) Some kind of urbanisation, especially at the northern interface, but also in properly Saharan regions (e.g. Jarma) obviously hampered by the limited extent of the oases and of the agricultural resources.
(3) The organisation and protection of frontiers and of caravan routes by means of castles.[25] Notice that the typical Saharan settlement, a small

---

[21] Bulliet 1990; Köhler-Rollefson 1996; Wapnish 1984. [22] Pusch 1997.
[23] Rowley-Conwy 1988. [24] Demougeot 1960; Shaw 1979.
[25] See in more detail Liverani 2006, 1028–35.

walled village or citadel (for example, Aghram Nadharif), is the combined result of the city and castle models. While the squared shape of the Garamantian castles is of northern derivation, an 'embryonic' frontier was probably present well before the *limes tripolitanus* was established by Septimius Severus *c.*AD 200.

(4) Writing, obviously inspired by Punic and Greek scripts but formalised in a local form (the so-called *tifinagh*), was first elaborated in the Numidian area, but was adopted also by the Garamantian kingdom.[26] We are left mostly with rock inscriptions (that is, with a small-scale celebrative use), but it is reasonable to assume the use of writing also in administrative recording. A recently published inscribed plaque could confirm such a hypothesis.[27]

(5) Monumental buildings and especially monumental burials connected with the existence of royal families and administrative elites. Of course, the monumental burials were a development of the local traditional burials already established during Late Pastoral times, but their new cylindrical shape was an innovation indirectly derived from building techniques of northern origin. Properly monumental burials were limited to the core of the Garamantian kingdom (they are absent in the Wadi Tanzzuft).

The Diachronic Arrangement

Admittedly, the chronology of the innovations and of their adoption by the communities of the Central Sahara remains rather vague, and will probably remain so even with more advanced research. But the main lines seem to be already established. I see two major concentrations. The first concentration marks the passage from the Late Pastoral to the Formative Garamantian phase at the end of the second millennium BC, and concerns the basic arrangement of the oasis as an agricultural (or better, horticultural) unit. The second concentration can be dated around the fourth century BC, is related to a more complex socio-political organisation and includes features concerning irrigation and caravan trade. By Classic Garamantian times, the Saharan oases and caravans had already reached a configuration quite similar to the one better known from Islamic and Early Modern sources – a configuration that allowed Saharan communities to face the serious climatic deterioration that occurred during the first centuries AD.

---

[26] See Camps 1996.   [27] Mattingly 2013, fig. 17.16.

The Reasons for the Eastern Advance

At this point we have to explain better the reasons for the eastern origin (or advance) and its outcome in an east to west movement. This east to west progress requires an explanation since, in the time span under consideration, the culture of the Arabian desert in its strict sense was no more advanced than that of the Sahara, although its neighbouring regions certainly were. We have to notice that the most innovative subregion seems to have been Oman, at the far eastern end of the peninsula, bordering the Gulf and the Indian Ocean and influenced by a monsoonal climate. The area (ancient Magan) was rich in copper mines, the major source of supply for Mesopotamia. Moreover, the area was touched by maritime trade between Lower Mesopotamia and the Indus Valley (ancient Meluhha), a route of transit and interconnection not just for precious stones and craft-made objects but also for cultivars between two of the oldest regions for the domestication of plants, namely the so-called 'Greater Mesopotamia' and the Indian subcontinent. In other words, Oman was in a strategic position for major cultural contacts and disseminations in materials either basic (cultivars) or strategic for those times (metals, semi-precious stones, spices). The export of copper towards Mesopotamia had its counterpart in the presence of Mesopotamian merchants or prospectors (from the Ubaid period) and in a stimulus for a more advanced political organisation.

We have to exercise a good deal of caution, since Oman is archaeologically better explored in comparison to inner Arabia (and also to the Sahara for that matter). Yet, given the present state of knowledge, it seems that the advances of Oman in the technological development of key aspect of desert infrastructures (the arrangement of nucleated oases, domestication of the dromedary, etc.) provide a reasonable historical and environmental explanation. Once oases and caravans (or if you prefer, date palm and dromedary) had proved decisive for a more efficient exploitation in one area, their transfer to similar areas was just a matter of time.

The Role of the Nile Valley

Another critical point to be examined is the role played by Egypt in the entire process under examination. In rather simplified terms we could ask two questions. The first question is: why did Egypt not exert in the Sahara the same positive effects exercised by Mesopotamia in the Arabian Peninsula? To my mind, the reason is that Western Asia was characterised by the coexistence, in close contact, of a plurality of ethnic groups, languages and cultures, and also by a plurality of landscapes (and subsequent ways of life) merging one into the other – an ideal condition for cultural cross-fertilisation. On the contrary, Egypt was much more self-contained and unitary. In the Nile Valley the border between 'desert and sown' is neat, without an intermediate belt (it has been said that you can stand with one foot in the desert and the other in the sown). Moreover, Egypt conceived the foreign peoples and foreign cultural elements as too inferior to be much interested in interacting with them. On a previous occasion I suggested a contraposition between the economic and technological strategy of Egypt, based on 'intensification', versus that of Greater Mesopotamia, based on 'extensification'.[28] In cultural terms extensification means contacts and interrelation, while intensification means self-sufficiency.

The second question is: why did the presence of Egypt, situated in the middle of the east–west corridor for the transfer of innovations, play a role in delaying the process rather than stimulating it? No doubt Egypt extended several features of its own culture in the great oases of the Western Desert, and played a major role in shaping their political organisation. Egypt also organised and used the sequence of the Western Oases in establishing a major trade route towards the south, a privileged direction leading to the sources of various important resources. The same did not apply to the direct line to the west, which was a properly empty and irrelevant area. In fact, the desert between the Egyptian oases and Fazzan comprises one of the most impassable extents of sand of the entire Sahara, and did not encourage transit.

But apart from this technical reason, I think cultural reasons proved more important, so that the process of east–west technological transfer was hampered not by the Libyan Desert but by the Nile Valley. The technologies under consideration were totally alien to, and unusable in, a valley dominated by a great river and its seasonal floods. Consequently, the great valley acted as a sort of barrier, interrupting or delaying the westwards flow of technological innovations.

Further Research: Will It Ever Be Possible?

The various topics touched on in this chapter deserve a much more in-depth analysis, which is obviously impossible given present circumstances. The present state of our knowledge about ancient Saharan societies is still very approximate. Just compare the number of reasonably explored

[28] Liverani 1997.

archaeological sites to the total existing sites: the percentage is very low, and not at all comparable to our archaeological knowledge of the Euro-Mediterranean lands, nor even to those of several Near Eastern regions. We are often forced to formulate our proposals on the basis of just two or three case studies, sometimes on only one. Any new discovery could change our views in a significant way. The ancient written sources are extremely thin and cannot be increased to any substantial degree. But the real question is: will it be ever possible to substantially enlarge the information we have?

Of course, until a few years ago the answer to such a problem would have been that we just have to raise more funds, recruit more people, organise more projects, excavate more sites, survey more regions and so on. But now such an answer is completely outdated; the political and cultural situation has changed. In practical terms, it is now impossible to work in the Sahara. The problem is not just that we need to wait and hope that the present crisis be surmounted. The problem is that the overall conditions are tremendously changed and will remain so for a long time. On the one hand, the Western monopoly of archaeological research in Islamic countries is over, and forever. On the other hand, we have to wait for the local states to be in a condition that is open to (and willing to) resume the protection and recovery of their cultural heritage. They will no longer do that according to Western rules, but according to their own rules. They have to conceive and elaborate their own relationship with their cultural heritage, including pre-Islamic heritage. They have to build their own cultural institutions and train their scholars no longer according to the Western views but according to their own views. This will be a long process – very, very long – and the issues are uncertain. My own generation will not see the end of the process; the younger generation hopefully will. But in the long run, globalisation cannot mean exporting Western values all over the world. Globalisation must mean accepting a compromise between different values; different world views.

References

Boucharlat, R. 2001. Les galeries de captage dans la péninsule d'Oman au premier millénaire avant J.-C. In Briant 2001, 157–83.

Bousquet, B. 1996. *Tell-Douch et sa région (Documents de Fouilles, 31)*. Le Caire: Institut Français d'Archéologie Orientale.

Bousquet, B. and Reddé, M. 1994. Les installations hydrauliques et les parcellaires dans la région de Tell Douch (Égypte) à l'époque romaine. In B. Menu (ed.), *Les problèmes institutionnels de l'eau en Égypte ancienne et dans l'Antiquité méditerranéenne* (Bibliothèque d'Études 110), Le Caire: Institut Français d'Archéologie Orientale, 73–88.

Briant, P. (ed.) 2001. *Irrigation et drainage dans l'Antiquité: qanats et canalisations souterraines en Iran, en Égypte et en Grèce.* Paris: Éditions Recherche sur les Civilisations.

Brogan, O. 1954. The camel in Roman Tripolitania. *Papers of the British School at Rome* 9: 126–31.

Bulliet, R.W. 1990. *The Camel and the Wheel.* Cambridge, MA: Harvard University Press.

Camps, G. 1996. Écriture libyque. *Encyclopédie Berbère* 17: 2564–73.

Compagnoni, B. and Tosi, M. 1978. The camel: Its distribution and state of domestication in the Middle East during the third millennium B.C. In R. H. Meadow and M. Zeder (eds), *Approaches to the Faunal Analysis in the Middle East*, Cambridge, MA: Harvard University Press, 91–103.

Cottini, M. and Rottoli, M. 2002. Some information on archaeobotanical remains. In S. di Lernia and G. Manzi (eds), *Sand, Stones and Bones: The Archaeology of Death in the Wadi Tanezzuft Valley*, Firenze: All'Insegna del Giglio, 169–80.

Cremaschi, M., Pelfini, M. and Santilli, M. 2006. Cupressus dupreziana: A dendroclimatic record for the Middle-late Holocene in the Central Sahara. *The Holocene* 16: 293–303.

Demougeot, E. 1960. Le chameau et l'Afrique du nord romaine. *Annales économies, sociétés, civilisations* 15: 209–47.

Goblot, H. 1979. *Les qanats: une technique d'acquisition de l'eau.* Paris: École des Hautes Études en Sciences Sociales.

Köhler-Rollefson, I. 1996. The one-humped camel in Asia: Origin, utilization, and mechanisms of dispersal. In D.R. Harris (ed.), *The Origins and Spread of Agriculture and Pastoralism in Eurasia*, Washington, DC: Smithsonian Institution Press, 282–94.

Liverani, M. 1997. Comments to J. McCorriston, 'The fiber revolution'. *Current Anthropology* 38: 536–37.

Liverani, M. 2000. The Libyan caravan road in Herodotus IV 181–185. *Journal of the Economic and Social History of the Orient* 43: 496–520.

Liverani, M. 2006. Imperialismo, colonizzazione e progresso tecnico: Il caso del Sahara libico in età romana. *Studi Storici* 47: 1003–57.

McIntosh, R.J. and McIntosh, S.K. 1988. From 'siècles obscurs' to revolutionary centuries in the Middle Niger. *World Archaeology* 20: 141–65.

Mattingly, D.J. (ed.) 2013. *The Archaeology of Fazzan. Volume 4, Survey and Excavations at Old Jarma (Ancient Garama) Carried out by C.M. Daniels (1962–69) and the Fazzan Project (1997–2001).* London: Society for Libyan Studies, Department of Antiquities.

Mattingly, D.J., Leitch, V., Duckworth, C.N., Cuénod, A., Sterry, M. and Cole, F. (eds) 2017. *Trade in the Ancient Sahara and Beyond.* Trans-Saharan

Archaeology, Volume 1. Series editor D.J. Mattingly. Cambridge: Cambridge University Press and the Society for Libyan Studies.

Pusch, E.B. 1997. Ein Dromedar aus der ramessidischen Hauptstadt Altägyptens. *Archaeozoologia* 9: 123–36.

Rowley-Conwy, P. 1988. The camel in the Nile Valley: New radiocarbon accelerator (AMS) Dates from Qasr Ibrim. *Journal of Egyptian Archaeology* 74: 245–48.

Shaw, B.D. 1979. The camel in Roman North Africa and the Sahara: History, biology, and human economy. *Bulletin de l'Institut Fondamental de l'Afrique Noire* 41: 663–721.

Shaw, B.D. 1982. Lamasba: An ancient irrigation community. *Antiquités Africaines* 18: 61–102.

Wapnish, P. 1984. The dromedary and Bactrian camel in Levantine historical settings. In J. Clutton-Brock and C. Grigson (eds), *Early Herders and their Flocks* (BAR International Series), Oxford: British Archaeological Reports, 171–200.

Wilson, A. and Mattingly, D.J. 2003. Irrigation technologies: Foggaras, wells and field systems. In D.J. Mattingly (ed.), *The Archaeology of Fazzan. Volume 1, Synthesis*, London: Society for Libyan Studies, Department of Antiquities, 235–78.

Wuttmann, M. 2001. Les qanāts de 'Ayin-Manâwâr (oasis of Kharga, Égypte). In Briant 2001, 109–35.

Zohary, D. and Hopf, M. 1994. *Domestication of Plants in the Old World*. Oxford: Clarendon Press.

3 | The Diffusion of Irrigation Technologies in the Sahara in Antiquity

Settlement, Trade and Migration

ANDREW WILSON, DAVID J. MATTINGLY
AND MARTIN STERRY

Introduction

This chapter reviews the hydraulic technologies used in the Sahara and the evidence for technological transfers within this region. A first point to make concerns the vast and diverse geography of the Sahara, which results in complex and highly varied hydrological conditions.[1] As a consequence, there has never been a 'one-size-fits-all' technological answer to irrigation. The most basic distinction to be made concerns the availability of surficial waters, as opposed to subsurface sources.[2] For instance, the irrigation of the Nile Valley comprises the earliest agriculture in the Sahara, but was achieved due to quite exceptional hydrological conditions and opportunities. The only other Saharan oases fed by perennial rivers lie at the far western end of the Sahara, where rain and snow melt from the Moroccan Atlas sustain the Wadi Draa and one or two smaller streams, and the Niger and Senegal Rivers mark abrupt frontiers between Sahel and Sahara. However, the vast majority of Saharan oases depend on accessing subsurface waters. Such oases tend to lie in natural depressions, some below sea level, where fossil waters feed lakes and springs, or could be tapped at shallow depths by wells.[3]

The basic forms of irrigation used in the Sahara can thus be summarised as follows:

---

[1] See Capot-Rey 1953; Charbonneau 1955; Gautier 1935; Laureano 1991 for good introductions to the varied topography and hydrology. See also Sterry and Mattingly 2020, 5–19. For discussion on the Roman sources mentioning oases, see Desanges 1980; Trousset 1986; for Islamic sources see Levtzion and Hopkins 2001; Thiry 1995.

[2] For this binary division see Capot-Rey 1953, 308–10; Gautier 1935, 65.

[3] Capot-Rey 1953, 303–32; de Villiers and Hirtle 2002, 90–125; Gautier 1935, 65–93, 108–18.

1. Perennial streams and diversion canals (may include use of water-lifting devices like the Archimedes screw).[4]
2. Periodic streams (wadis) exploited by floodwater farming methods.[5]
3. Artesian springs, bringing water to the surface under pressure along faults and chimneys in geological strata. Natural artesian springs have often been augmented by excavation into an artesian aquifer and the construction of collection basins and distribution channels.[6]
4. Springs from a non-artesian aquifer – generally less prolific and significant than artesian springs and more easily exhausted if involving fossil water.[7]
5. Balance wells (*shaduf* or *khattara*).[8]
6. Animal-operated wells with the self-dumping bucket (*dalw*).[9]
7. Sunken gardens (*bour*) allowing the roots of palms planted within them to reach down to an elevated water table (the classic example is the Suf region in the Great Erg Oriental round al-Wad).[10]
8. The foggara (essentially the same technology as the Persian *qanat* or *falaj* in Oman).[11] This is a gently sloping underground channel, constructed and maintained by a line of shafts, that takes water from a mother well (often dug close to the foot of an escarpment) to the centre of the oasis depression (Fig. 3.1).[12]
9. There is an important variant on the foggara that needs to be recognised as a distinct irrigation technology, where the foggara is used to capitalise on water flows in the alluvium beneath the wadi bed, collecting water to feed small gardens located alongside the wadi, as in parts of the Ahaggar.[13]

Foggaras versus Other Technological Choices

The character and scale of the Saharan variants of the Persian *qanat* are described in detail below, but these underground channels that brought running water from a distance to irrigate oasis gardens are iconic (though

---

[4] Gautier 1935, 65–77.

[5] Barker *et al.* 1996 for the Libyan pre-desert; Gaucher 1948 and Gautier 1935, 76–93, for Saharan wadis susceptible to periodic floods.

[6] Durand and Guyot 1955; Lethielleux 1948, 110–12; Martel 1965, I, 30–33; Nesson 1965; Savornin 1947; 1950; Scarin 1934, 15–19.

[7] Drake *et al.* 2004.   [8] Lethielleux 1948, 6–7; Wilson and Mattingly 2003, 266–67.

[9] Lethielleux 1948, 83–104; Wilson and Mattingly 2003, 267–70.   [10] Capot-Rey 1953, 306–8.

[11] Goblot 1979 is a key starting point for *qanat*/foggara technology and its spread; see also, *inter alia*, Beaumont *et al.* 1989; Briant 2001; Cressey 1958; English 1968.

[12] Wilson and Mattingly 2003, 235–65.   [13] Capot-Rey 1953, 327–29.

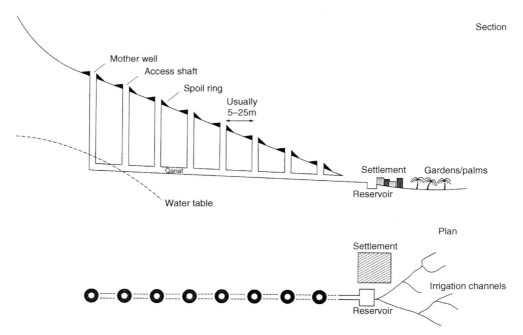

Figure 3.1 Section and plan of a foggara

fast disappearing) monuments of the Sahara.[14] They are most commonly recognisable by their lines of close-spaced construction/maintenance shafts (Figs 3.2 and 3.3a–b). The subsurface channel is often dangerous or impossible to access (Fig. 3.3c) and the features at the delivery end of ancient foggaras are generally poorly preserved, often overlaid by later phases of the oasis (but see Fig. 3.8). The date of foggaras in North Africa has been much debated, with many commentators favouring an Islamic date for their introduction,[15] although some colonial-era researchers wanted to credit the Romans for their introduction.[16] In the Western Saharan oases (like the Tafilalat and Tuwat) they have generally been assumed to be of Medieval or Early Modern date, not least as construction and maintenance continued well into the twentieth century.[17] However, they have now been firmly dated in the Egyptian oases to the mid-first millennium BC.[18] Our work on the Garamantian heartlands has produced much clearer associations between foggaras and Garamantian settlements and cemeteries. As reported below, we also have a late first-millennium

[14] Wilson and Mattingly 2003; Sterry *et al.* forthcoming; Wilson 2006; 2009.
[15] Klitzsch and Baird 1969, 73–80.   [16] Caputo 1937, 309–10; Despois 1946, 59–60.
[17] See further below and Wilson 2009.   [18] Agut-Labordère 2018; Wuttmann *et al.* 2000.

Figure 3.2 Rock-cut foggara shafts in the Taqallit area, Wadi al-Ajal, Fazzan. (a) view of Libyan inscription cut in the mouth of a shaft; (b) Andrew Wilson preparing to descend into a 30-m deep foggara shaft; (c) view up the same rectangular-section shaft, showing metal tool marks on walls; (d) view down the same shaft (photos (a) and (c): A. Wilson; (b) and (d): T. Savage for DMP).

BC radiocarbon (AMS) date from the mudbrick lining of one example (Fig. 3.4). The spread of foggara technology from the Western Desert of Egypt to the Central Sahara during the first millennium BC thus seems assured, and this suggests that we need to shift our default assumptions about its further diffusion westwards from there.[19] As we shall see, though, that does not mean that we should expect it to be taken everywhere at the same rate or at the moment the technology became known in a new area.

The foggara was, as noted above, only one of several irrigation technologies used in the Sahara, and not the earliest among those. We should not consider these different forms of hydraulic technology in an evolutionary sequence, looking for progressively more sophisticated techniques over time. Rather, we

[19] Wilson 2005; 2006; 2009; cf. de Angeli 2013.

Figure 3.3 A foggara in the north-western Tafilalat, Morocco. a) conical spoil mounds around the line of vertical shafts; b) view up the roughly circular shaft; c) view of the channel cut through a friable sub-stratum (all photos: D. Mattingly).

need to recognise that they are technologies that were developed in particular hydrological contexts to solve problems specific to each milieu. Technological choices would generally be appropriate to the effective exploitation of the local hydrological conditions, informed by empirical observation and experimentation. In other words, those trying to create or augment an oasis would work from the visible and the known in the first instance. Where they existed in the Sahara, seasonal or perennial streams and lakes and natural springs were the most obvious places to start. Clues to an elevated

Figure 3.4 Mudbrick lining of foggara shaft (ELH013) at al-Hatiya (Wadi al-Ajal, Fazzan); organic material from one of the mudbricks produced an AMS date of 391–206 calBC (photo: A. Wilson).

groundwater table include stands of vegetation in parts of the landscape, or the presence of spring mounds (phreatophytic mounds), although the only way to find out how close to the surface the water lay or to assess its quality would be to dig a well.

Surface Water from Rivers and Wadis

The optimum way to irrigate the oases of the Sahara varied across the vastly differing landscapes and could also change over the course of time as water resources became depleted or exhausted. The most important limitation is mechanical and in any situation having access to free-flowing water is to be preferred to the necessity of lifting water mechanically. Where perennial rivers existed these will have been targets for diversion and canalisation. It is logical to consider locations where there was the potential to extract water from such perennial surface features as being the most obvious locations for early experimentation with hydraulic technologies. The River Nile with its annual flood is the most obvious example and we know that by the third millennium BC irrigated agriculture of lands alongside the river was already well established.[20] The Wadi Draa is the only perennial river that runs into the Sahara from the north and it is still exploited today by means of diversion dams feeding irrigation canals and gardens that run alongside the main river channels.[21] There are also a number of locations in the Sahara where periodic flash floods in wadis are exploited by diversion dams or help replenish an elevated water table in the wadi bed that supports stands of palms and other trees (as in the Wadi Gir, Wadi Saura and the Ahaggar).[22] The oases along the Roman frontier in southern Algeria and southern Tunisia (Wadi Jedi, Ziban, Nemencha and so on) and those of the Mzab also augment groundwater with seasonal floodwater.[23]

Springs

Natural springs in the Sahara were already well-known locations and following the climatic downturn around 5,000 years ago these will have been key *refugia*. These will have been crucial to pastoral groups before the creation of the first artificial oases there.[24] They were for this reason locations that were also favoured for early oasis development. Where there were vigorous artesian springs, the major effort will have been invested in capturing and maximising their delivery and distribution networks. Complex systems were developed for allocating shares of the precious water, whether by units of time or through splitting the flow into measured fractions.[25] Artesian springs are particularly significant because of the enhanced flow from such pressurised water sources. But natural

[20] Gautier 1935, 72–76.   [21] Capot-Rey 1953, 310–14; Riser 1996.
[22] Capot-Rey 1953, 314–18; Gautier 1935, 76–93.
[23] Capot-Rey 1953, Carte VII; Estorges 1964.
[24] See Purdue *et al.* 2018 for definition and discussion of *refugia*.
[25] Trousset 1986 provides one of the best studies of irrigation arrangements in the southern Tunisian oases; see also Eldblom 1968 for Ghadamis.

artesian wells are rare and human augmentation of such sources can be difficult and dangerous if, as is often the case, the pressurised water reserve is at some depth. Prior to modern deep-drilling equipment, the digging of new artesian wells adjacent to natural springs was both costly and hit and miss. In the Wadi Righ oasis belt in southern Algeria, a social group of specialist artesian well diggers evolved.[26] Paradoxically, one of the chief hazards in digging such wells was that the enterprise might encounter a higher perched water table of non-artesian nature, which would effectively flood the shaft before the pressurised artesian waters were reached.[27] In many cases, the relative inaccessibility of the artesian waters for human augmentation has constrained the growth potential of spring-fed oases until the modern era or obliged the oasis farmers to supplement the artesian spring waters with non-artesian groundwater employing different technology (Ghadamis is a good example on both counts).[28] Many oasis areas reveal the contemporaneous use of different hydraulic technologies to exploit different water sources.[29]

Wells

Where there were no springs, but relatively elevated groundwater, mechanical means had to be found for accessing water by wells or foggaras. As regards wells, broadly, the deeper the water table the more difficult and costly the process of raising water. In Fazzan undoubtedly, and probably in many other areas too, the earliest water-lifting device was the *shaduf* (or *khattara* in Arabic, except in Morocco where the word has been applied to the foggara), a swing beam with a bucket on one end and a counterweight on the other. Its advantage was that it allowed the operator to pull *downwards* on the bucket to immerse it in the water, using the stronger back and leg muscles, to raise the counterweight; on releasing the rope, the counterweight raised the container of water which the operator simply tipped into a receiving container or channel. It was a relatively simple machine with

[26] Berbrugger 1862, 66–80. These remarkable well-diggers had developed the ability to work underwater for up to five minutes.

[27] See Berbrugger 1862 for a detailed account of the perils and difficulties of creating new artesian wells around the natural springhead pools (*bahar*) in the Wadi Righ.

[28] See Eldblom 1968 for Ghadamis. In contrast, the Wadi ash-Shati in northern Fazzan is an oasis zone where the initial development in Garamantian times appears to have been limited, but the eventual augmentation of the artesian springs by humanly created artesian wells led to this being the most populous area in Fazzan by the early modern period, Scarin 1934; 1937; cf. Despois 1946.

[29] See for example Cornet 1952 on the Gourara.

a low lift and a fairly low output. The *shaduf* was used in ancient Mesopotamia, and was known in Ancient Egypt from the later second millennium BC, as shown by a wall painting from the tomb of Ipy, at Deir el-Medinah, *c.*1240 BC.[30] It proved a remarkably effective and long-lasting, low-cost water-lifting device: it was common in the Classical and Roman Mediterranean;[31] in the nineteenth century AD its use was widespread, from Britain to the Sahara; and in the late twentieth century it was still in use in rural Romania, Egypt, Fazzan and parts of Sub-Saharan Africa.[32]

In Fazzan, we have evidence from tenth- to early seventh-century BC levels at the Garamantian-defended promontory settlement of Zinkekra for the cultivation of crops that would have required irrigation.[33] As this is shortly after the failure of the natural springs that flowed from the base of the southern escarpment of the Wadi al-Ajal, which dried up around the end of the second millennium BC[34] but well before any evidence of the introduction of the foggara to the region, we assume that the irrigated agriculture of this period depended on *shadufs* mounted over shallow wells in the centre of the wadi, where the depth to water would have been between one and three metres. There was a very high water table in the centre of the valley, where the Garamantian capital at Jarma was located, and some springs there feeding a small lake may also have been exploited in early agriculture.

It is likely that the *shaduf* remained in use alongside the foggara after the latter had been introduced to Fazzan, in areas unsuited to foggara irrigation, or after foggaras had failed. The Garamantian landscape of fortified villages to the east of Murzuq, investigated in 2011, consists of field systems clustered around fortified *qsur*; each field has a well, visible as a circular depression.[35] These probably originated as *shaduf* wells where the depth to the water was shallow, even if they were later deepened. Even in the mid-twentieth century the use of *shaduf* wells in Fazzan continued in the eastern Wadi ash-Shati, the Murzuq region, the Hufra, the Wadi Hikma, and around ash-Sharqiyat, where the depth to the water table was very shallow.[36]

Important evidence for the use of the *shaduf* in Medieval Fazzan is provided by al-Idrisi, writing in the twelfth century, who says of Jarma and Tsawa: 'There one drinks water from wells. Palm trees, millet and

---

[30] Oleson 1984; 2000.
[31] Oleson 1984, 56–47, 127–71; 2000, 225–29; Malouta and Wilson 2013, 278–80.
[32] Despois 1960; Wilson 2003, 126. Romania: Wilson 2002, figure I.1; Chad: Mirti *et al.* 1999.
[33] Van der Veen and Westley 2010.   [34] Drake *et al.* 2004.   [35] Sterry *et al.* 2011.
[36] Lethielleux 1948, 6–7, 27, 105.

barley grow there, which one waters by means of a machine which bears the name of *indjafa*, and which the inhabitants of the Maghrib call *khattara*.'[37] Although in Morocco the word *khattara* now means foggara or *qanat*, the normal meaning of the word in Fazzan and the Maghrib is a *shaduf* well,[38] and that this is the meaning that Idrisi had in mind is confirmed by his use of the word *ala*, 'machine', to describe it, and his stress on the supply from wells.[39] We can therefore conclude that by the twelfth century, in the heartland of Fazzan around Jarma in the central Wadi al-Ajal and Tsawa to the west of Murzuq, irrigation by foggaras had ceased and that the dominant mode of agriculture relied on the *shaduf* well. Moreover, the fact that the *shaduf* in Fazzan was called by a Berber name, *indjafa*, seems to confirm the idea of a pre-Arab introduction to the region that we have just argued on archaeological grounds.[40]

Outside the Nile Valley and the coastal strip of Roman North Africa, the animal-driven water wheel or *saqqiya* does not seem to have taken hold. This was originally a Hellenistic invention that spread in the Roman period and continued in use in parts of Tunisia and Egypt until the late twentieth century.[41] Instead, throughout much of North Africa and parts of the Sahara in the post-Roman period the main competitor to the *shaduf* was the *dalw* or *sanya*. This device consisted of a funnel-shaped leather bag (*dalw*) with a wide mouth and narrow tubular tail, let down over a pulley into a well, and drawn up by an animal (usually a donkey or a camel) walking down an inclined ramp. As the bag reached the top of its lift, the ropes were arranged so as to jerk the tail down, discharging the water from the bag into a trough at the top of the well. The *dalw* required a greater capital investment than the simpler *shaduf*, which was the machine of the poor, but it could lift water from greater depths. There has been very little work on the archaeology and early history of this machine, which remains obscure, but we can attempt a sketch here. There is a possible reference in the fourth-century BC author Ktesias of Knidos, who writes of cattle irrigating royal gardens at Susa who would lift exactly 100 buckets per day, but no more, a reference which irrespective of its truth value makes no sense in the context of a rotary machine.[42] More promising is a passage in the *De rebus bellicis* (c.AD 370), which refers to softening calf-skins by the 'Arabian process', since the Arabs

---

[37] Al-Idrisi, from the French translation by Dozy and De Goeje 1866, 42.
[38] Colin 1932, 35–39; Despois 1960, 1232; Lethielleux 1948, 93.
[39] Wilson and Mattingly 2003, 277; Wilson 2003, 126 n. 53.   [40] Wilson 2003, 126.
[41] Wilson 2003.
[42] *Persica* frag. 34a (in Aelian, *De natura animalium* 7.1) and 34b (in Plutarch, *Moralia* 974e); Oleson 1984, n. 23, 39–41; see discussion in Wilson 2003, 126–27.

have developed the art of softening leather 'because they draw water from wells in leather bags'.[43] The connection with Arabia is underlined by the fact that although the device was only barely known to Classical authors, pre-Islamic Arabic poetry uses the pulley and other constituent parts of the *dalw* well as a metaphor for cosmic imagery, implying that it was an entirely familiar part of common experience in Arabia by the sixth century AD.[44] The first author has therefore suggested that the widespread distribution of the *dalw* well across North Africa and parts of the Sahara is due to the Arab expansion into North Africa with the Islamic conquest.[45] This idea would be consistent with the fact that in the eleventh century AD al-Bakri evidently refers to the *dalw* well when he says that around Zuwila, in Fazzan, 'There are palm groves and cultivated areas which are irrigated by means of camels'.[46] By the twentieth century and probably much earlier the *dalw* well, with its higher lift and greater output, was the dominant irrigation technology throughout Fazzan, except in the regions where there was a shallow depth to water, in the Wadi Hikma and around Tsawa, where the simpler and cheaper *shaduf* was still used; and al-Bakri's comment suggests that this switch had taken place by the eleventh century.

The balance well was not viewed as simpler and less desirable technology than the more complicated animal-drawn *dalw* wells, which were costlier to construct and operate. The simple balance well was ideally suited to the needs of raising water from a depth of a metre or so and continued to be employed, wherever such favourable conditions existed, into the twentieth century. The wider dissemination of the *dalw* well in the Sahara in Islamic times can be seen in this light as a forced response to declining water tables, rather than as a technological advance per se, although it did allow the expansion of oasis cultivation in some areas where water had always lain beyond the lifting range of the balance well.

Foggaras and Technological Choices

The foggara was extremely labour intensive to construct, but transformed a groundwater source into the equivalent of a spring. The choice of

---

[43] De Rebus Bellicis 16.2: *vitulinis pellibus Arabica arte mollitis cura propter aquam de puteis follibus hauriendam.*

[44] Jamil 1999, esp. 19–25, 28.

[45] Wilson 2003, 126–27, 140. Interestingly, it would also be a continuation into Islamic times of the Trans-Nile technological transfer corridor postulated by Liverani, Chapter 2, this volume.

[46] Al-Bakri 10.16; Wilson and Mattingly 2003, 272.

technology was above all specific to the place and its hydrological potential, and we might expect the distribution map of irrigation types to respect such distinctions (Fig 1.3). However, one of the interesting aspects of the overall distribution of the foggara is that it seems to have been adapted to a variety of different hydrological conditions. Where used alongside spring-fed irrigation methods, we might see its adoption as symptomatic of a desire, or need, to enhance the irrigated area, perhaps to support a larger population.

The main descriptive part of this chapter will review the evidence for the occurrence of foggara technology across the Sahara, presenting dating indications where available. The final section of the chapter will then compare the overall diffusion of the foggara with what we know of other irrigation technologies, following up a classic study by Capot-Rey.[47] We shall revisit the debates about their spread and chronology, as well as evidence reflecting on the decline and abandonment of foggara systems in some regions.

Chronological and Geographical Distribution of Foggaras

The following account follows a broadly east to west transect across the Northern Sahara, finishing with the sparser evidence from the Southern Sahara.[48]

Egypt's Western Desert

The earliest foggaras known in the Sahara are those found in Egypt's Western Desert. The oldest reliably dated foggaras come from Ain Manawir in the Dush area of the Kharga Oasis. Here excavators were able to link the digging of a complex of 22 foggaras to a settlement that developed in the fifth century BC. A house containing a cache of ostraca dated between 436 and 388 BC was built over the spoil rings of one of the foggaras and acts as a *terminus ante quem* for the creation of the system, while the earliest associated ceramic material dates to the fifth century and it is unlikely that these foggaras date any earlier.[49] More ostraca dating 465–398 BC have been recovered from the Temple of Osiris and include a series of contracts dated between 443 and 393 BC which detail the

---

[47] Capot-Rey 1953, 303–67.

[48] The accounts may most usefully be read alongside the relevant chapters in Sterry and Mattingly 2020, dealing with the overall archaeological evidence for each oasis grouping.

[49] Agut-Labordère 2018; Wuttmann 2001, 124–30.

distribution rights from at least 20 different foggaras.[50] On this evidence it can be concluded that the adoption of foggara technology in the Kharga Oasis post-dates the Persian takeover of Egypt, and probably reflects the introduction of this technology from Persia or from parts of the Arabian Peninsula under Persian control.[51] Foggaras continued to be used in the Kharga Oasis until at least the sixth century AD, by which time five groups had been dug in the area of Dush and three more in North Kharga where they can be associated with Roman fortified sites.[52]

Less is known of irrigation in the Dakhla oases, beyond a number of major springs. There are numerous canals visible that are widely considered to be of Roman origin. Some may have been covered channels, and Fakhry refers tantalisingly to ancient foggaras in the Dakhla oasis region, but without further details.[53]

The foggara systems of Farafra have been investigated by De Angeli since 2007.[54] Full publication of the research is still awaited, but foggaras have been identified at 12 locations. In most cases these are single foggaras or pairs of foggaras with no evidence of the groups or strips of foggaras found in the other parts of the Western Desert.[55]

Among the gardens of al-Hays in southern Bahariya there are at least seven groups of foggaras totalling more than 20 km of channels.[56] These are generally less than 1 km in length and like those found elsewhere in Egypt they present in a variety of forms on the surface from small shafts to large spoil rings and occasionally as holes or collapsed channels. Two shafts have been excavated measuring 1.3×0.55 m in cross-section and 7–8 m in depth.[57] The small groups in al-Hays are particularly interesting for the extent of criss-crossing and tributaries, with foggaras regularly running perpendicular to each other. This implies frequent restructuring of the system as the water table dropped. Dospěl and Suková argue that the foggaras were required to support the increased number of Roman-period settlements and that their exhaustion was linked to the widespread abandonment of the oasis in late antiquity.[58]

---

[50] Agut-Labordère 2018; Chauveau 1996; 2001; Gonon 2018; Wuttmann *et al.* 1998, 442–44; Wuttmann 2001.

[51] Bousquet 1996; Wuttmann *et al.* 2000; cf. Wilson 2006; De Angeli 2013.

[52] Bousquet 1996; Wuttmann 2001; Schacht 2003.   [53] Fakhry 1942, 83.

[54] De Angeli 2013; Buongarzone and De Angeli 2011.   [55] De Angeli 2013, 279–80.

[56] Dospěl and Suková 2013 identify four groups; in the same volume Bárta and Brůna 2013, 12 have five groups marked although they refer to them using a local name of Manawar. Satellite reconnaissance has spotted two more groups.

[57] Bárta and Brůna 2013, 25.

[58] Dospěl and Suková 2013, 9–10. Nineteenth-century travellers recorded the oasis as only thinly occupied.

In the northern part of Bahriya there are three groups of foggaras, one group to the west of Bawiti and two to the east. In the western group the mid-eighth- to seventh-century BC settlement of Qasr'Allam is cut by a foggara, while in the same group, the third-century AD fort of Qaret el Toub sits atop some shafts of another channel.[59] However, Pantalacci and Denoix considered that this system was in use for a long time and into the Islamic period.[60] The other two groups have not been fully explored, but there are probably at least 20 km of channels in this region.[61]

Two further mentions of foggaras have been made for the Mediterranean cities of Marsa Matruh and Cyrene.[62] These are both aqueducts with underground sections, rather than true foggaras, but it is relevant to show that the technology for constructing gently sloping water-bearing tunnels was being adopted on the northern fringe of the Sahara throughout the Roman period, as well as in the oases.

Fazzan and al-Jufra

Hundreds of foggaras are known from Fazzan and al-Jufra forming the oldest of the three major concentrations in the Central and West Sahara (alongside the Gourara-Tuwat-Tidikelt group and the Tafilalat group, see below). The work of the Fazzan and Desert Migration Projects has established that the foggara irrigation systems in Fazzan were constructed and operational in the Garamantian period (*c*.500 BC–AD 600). First, there is a strong spatial relationship between areas of settlement and the output points of foggaras, especially in the Jarma to Ubari region. Second, tombs and a settlement with Roman pottery (ARS) have been identified overlying foggara spoil rings in two locations (ITF002 and FJJ001). A foggara originally thought to underlie a tomb (TAG006.T2) was shown by excavation to be later, but the tomb gave a *terminus post quem* of 382–204 calBC.[63] Third, we have a direct date on one of the foggaras at al-Hatiya. Here there is a group of 13 foggaras that run south-west to north-east into an area of Garamantian settlements and cemeteries (ELH001–002, ELH005–006, ELH008). In one of the most easterly of the foggaras a mudbrick lining was visible around some shafts (Fig. 3.4). One of these shafts was partly excavated in 2009 and although no ceramics were found, several dried plant fibres were extracted from the matrix of a mudbrick. These have given a radiocarbon date of 391–206 calBC (at 95.4 per cent confidence).[64]

---

[59] Pantalacci and Denoix 2008, 315.   [60] Pantalacci and Denoix 2008, 315.
[61] De Angeli 2013, 277–78   [62] For example, Walpole 1932; English 1968.
[63] See Sterry and Mattingly 2020.   [64] OxA-26746, 2243±26 BP.

Another foggara shaft in the Taqallit area has a Libyan inscription carved in its inner surface and examples of other Libyan inscriptions have been found around a number of foggaras in this sector (Fig. 3.2a).[65] The cemeteries and settlements at the end of the channels in the al-Hatiya and Taqallit areas have been intensively fieldwalked and datable ceramics from the latter centuries BC to the fourth century AD as well as industrial residues were collected.[66] The spatial association of these sites suggests that the foggara systems were in use in this part of the wadi for at least 500 years, but no more than 800.

In the al-Jufra oases, between Fazzan and the Mediterranean, there are three distinct groups of foggaras located 5 km and 15 km to the south-east of Waddan and 5 km to the south of Hun.[67] The group closest to Waddan has been almost entirely destroyed by modern agricultural expansion, but consists of at least three foggaras leading into a natural depression. The second Waddan group is the most extensive in the al-Jufra with foggaras running south–north along a 12 km front. At the northern end the foggaras stop at the edge of a dry-wadi channel that forms a natural dip. There are substantial remains of settlement, gardens and reservoirs at the outlets of the foggaras. All parts of this system are in immediate danger of destruction from agricultural projects that have been laid out over them. Like the previous group, the Hun foggaras run south–north into a low depression along a front of 2.5 km. The group is clearly visible on Corona imagery (from the 1970s), but by 2004 almost the entirety had been destroyed. Two short sections under 300 m in length remain in fields that have not yet been developed. Several other ancient town-sized settlements are known around Waddan and Hun that appear to demonstrate a chronological sequence.[68] Given the distance from the modern oasis and the different settlement morphology we would suggest that the foggara groups are likely to date between 500 BC and AD 500, but obtaining dating material is an important priority for the archaeology of this oasis.

Between al-Jufra and the Wadi al-Ajal there are two tiny oases at al-Fuqha and Umm al-Abid. No fieldwork has been undertaken at either, but in the former foggaras are mentioned by Scarin,[69] and remote sensing has identified a handful of small foggaras. These run *c.*100 m down the sides of wadis on the south side of the crater and *sabkha* that forms the oasis. A hill fort of possible Protohistoric date (500–1 BC?) lies in the centre of this area

[65] Wilson and Mattingly 2003, 264–65.   [66] See Cuénod, Chapter 7, this volume.
[67] Rayne *et al.* 2017, 34–37.   [68] Mattingly *et al.* 2018, 220–21.
[69] Scarin 1938, 81–82 (though his text is ambiguous).

of channels. Due to a lack of modern or Medieval development, Umm al-Abid has one of the best preserved foggara and field systems in Libya, which was commented on by nineteenth-century travellers.[70] What appears to be a Late Garamantian *qasr* overlies one foggara and a second *qasr* sits at the outlet of another foggara. Apart from a colonial fort there is little evidence for any later settlement and again a date somewhere in the range 500 BC–AD 500 would be consistent with the visible remains.

At Zala, Scarin described seeing four foggaras which tapped into springs and were possibly still flowing in the early twentieth century. These were constructed with rectangular wells with a drop in relief of 20 m and of some length, but he does not indicate where in the oasis they were located. These were also mentioned by Ward in 1968, but are yet to be identified on satellite imagery and may have been destroyed.[71]

In contrast to other parts of south-west Libya, there are many artesian springs along the edge of the Wadi ash-Shati and a high groundwater table. This means that settlement (past or present) does not sit in the lowest part of the wadi and the region is not well suited to foggaras. However, fieldwork by Daniels and remote sensing by Merlo have established the presence of foggaras in two locations: on the eastern side of the Wadi Dabdab (five channels) and to the west of the Wadi Ziqzah (five channels; the longest survives for 800 m). Both are areas with no springs and a lower water table.[72] Merlo *et al.* have noted the destruction from agricultural expansion in this area and it is difficult to ascertain whether these are the majority of the original number, or a surviving minority. The lack of associated features – settlements or cemeteries – currently makes it impossible to date these foggaras; however, the clear evidence of recuts, tributaries and rerouting suggests that they were in use for a long period of time.

South of the Ubari Sand Sea, in the Wadi al-Ajal, are the largest and longest foggaras in Libya. A combination of aerial photographs from 1958 and satellite imagery taken between 2003 and 2014, supplemented by ground surveys, has allowed these to be mapped in great detail. Around 700 km of foggaras in approximately 700 channels have now been traced.[73] However, we would estimate that the original total would have amounted to more than 1,000 km prior to their destruction and truncation by

---

[70] For example, Hugh Clapperton in 1822 (Bruce-Lockhart and Wright 2000, 286), and Gustav Nachtigal (1974, 61, cf. 107 and 216).

[71] Scarin 1938; Ward 1968, 35.

[72] Daniels only made a fleeting visit, but his fieldwork is described in Mattingly 2007, 290, including a photograph of one of the channels. Merlo *et al.* 2013, 154–55.

[73] Cf. an estimate of 550 channels in Wilson and Mattingly 2003, 241; the best maps of the overall distributions along the Wadi are in Mattingly 2007.

agricultural, urban and other developments. These foggaras typically form dense clusters of 5–20 channels over a span of a few kilometres and in many locations these can be linked to groups of Garamantian settlements.[74] In the western half of the wadi the foggaras are longer, deeper and probably carried more water. The longest channels run for up to 8 km, but a more typical length is 2–4 km. The eastern half are all under 1.8 km reflecting the narrower width of the wadi with many channels less than 1 km in length. Our modelling suggests that in the Proto-urban and Classic Garamantian periods settlement was generally denser in the western part of the Wadi, but in the Late Garamantian period it was more evenly distributed between west and east.[75] It is tempting to think that this may relate to the exhaustion of water sources starting in the west and gradually moving east, but this also probably relates to changing patterns of movement and trade in the later period.[76]

South of the Wadi al-Ajal there are several clusters of foggaras.[77] At Ghuddwa there is a small group of foggaras that feed into a low depression within which lies a series of mudbrick *qsur* and settlement features. These appear very likely to be of second- to sixth-century AD date. Further west along the same valley, the Wadi an-Nashw'a, there are three clusters of probable foggaras (*c.*40 in total) that have been identified from a mixture of aerial photographs and satellite images. These can be no more than a few metres deep and in many cases may have been open channels (or covered with organic materials) rather than true foggaras. To the north of these foggaras are a number of *qsur* and nucleated cemeteries. More substantial are those in the far south-west of the depression where there are at least six channels running for 1.5 km south-west to north-east. Although there is little clear sign of settlement there are many Garamantian cemeteries nearby and the Late Garamantian to Medieval town of Qasr ash-Sharraba lies only 4 km to the north-east. Close to Qasr Mara to the north of Sharraba there is a pair of foggaras on an almost flat plateau that run almost perpendicular to each other, forming a cross. They appear to flow towards the east, and Daniels collected Roman-period imported amphorae and other coarsewares from the site.

Closer to Murzuq, a group of foggaras has been noted running into fields set on *sabkha* next to two *qsur* (UTB002 and UTB004). Similar small foggaras are found running into two other areas of *sabkha* to the north-

---

[74] For example TMT002, EDS008, EDS009, TAG008, ELH13, GSC32/33/36. See Mattingly 2007 for details.

[75] Mattingly 2013, 525–29.   [76] Mattingly *et al.* 2015; Mattingly *et al.* 2017.

[77] Despois 1946, 56; cf. Daniels 1973, 37.

east of Murzuq, and each group passes close to probably associated *qsur*, being sites of morphologically Late Garamantian type. As with those of the Wadi an-Nashw'a some of these may have been open channels for part or all of their length. The most easterly group runs for almost 3 km with shafts clearly visible at the southern end; as the channels approach the Garamantian settlement cluster of HHG006–8 they become visible only as lines of bushes. One channel flows into the ditch of HHG006 before continuing to the south-east. The chronological relationship is not clear, although the channel was surely not cut after the abandonment of the *qasr*. Elements of the associated field system follow the line of the foggaras (or vice versa) and it seems most likely that the settlement, foggaras and fields were contemporary (although all elements were subject to rebuilding and realignments). Three ^{14}C dates have been taken from mudbricks used in the construction of the *qsur* giving dates of calAD 76–254, 139–341 and 398–535.[78] There are no foggaras in the eastern end of the Murzuq depression which has a substantially higher water table making it 'swampier' and perhaps not settled until the Medieval period.

East of the Murzuq depression, the northern side of the Wadi ash-Sharqiyat has four distinct clusters of foggaras, each of which feeds into an area of *sabkha* that is still the focus of a modern settlement. The most prominent of these is the Medieval capital of Zuwila, but the foggaras flow away from the main nucleus of the settlement and we interpret these to be of Garamantian date.[79] Two other groups, at Umm al-Aranib (10 foggaras) and al-Bdayir (15 foggaras), feed into areas of field systems that lie close to the modern villages, and these may be of Garamantian or just possibly Medieval date. Another cluster of about 20 foggaras on the southern side of the Wadi ash-Sharqiyat, at Tirbu, are most likely to be of Garamantian date.

Two further possible groups of foggaras have been identified from satellite imagery further south again at Ghat and Tajirhi. Those at Ghat (Wadi Tannzuft) are severely truncated to only a few hundred metres with no associated remains making it difficult to confirm their identification and date. Irrigation in that area was mainly spring based, so if the identification is correct the date must remain very uncertain. At Tajirhi there are what appear to be three wide channels to the south-west of the main settlement. These need confirming on the ground, but there is plentiful evidence for Garamantian-style *qsur* and shaft/drum tomb cemeteries in the immediate environs of the oasis.

---

[78] Sterry *et al.* 2012; Sterry and Mattingly 2013.   [79] Mattingly *et al.* 2015, 20, 22.

In sum, the total number of foggaras known for Fazzan now exceeds 800, with the vast majority evidently of Garamantian date and very little indication that they continued in use in this region far into the Medieval period.

Ghadamis, Nafzaoua and Jarid

The main source of irrigation at Ghadamis is an artesian spring; however, there are 21 foggaras in two groups to the north (at Qasr Ghlul) and to the west (at Tunin) indicating an attempt at some point in time to augment the cultivable area there beyond the restricted zone that could be fed from the main spring and from a number of *shaduf* wells within the core oasis.[80] A brief visit was made to these sites during fieldwork at Ghadamis in 2011, but no dating material was recovered from the foggaras (though Qasr Ghlul appears to have been established in late antiquity).[81] There is a very strong correlation between individual foggaras and groups of gardens which allows us to calculate that the irrigated areas range between 0.13 and 1.19 ha. None of the foggaras appears still to be working, but three channels flow into a cistern on the edge of Tunin that is still in existence implying that they were in use until quite recently. In two cases foggaras have been redirected to a lower set of gardens, presumably in response to a dropping water table.

Located to the east of Ghadamis, Darj appears to have a natural artesian spring, but the strip of cultivation just to the north (Terguddah) was originally fed by at least 20 foggara channels. None is very long, but they range from very small to large shafts, perhaps suggesting that they tap water reservoirs at different depths. A further 12 foggaras of similar type have been identified at the tiny oasis of Chawan, 90 km to the north.

Moving into southern Tunisia, small, short foggaras are known in the Nafzaoua, although they have been mostly destroyed by modern development. A small number are still visible 4 km to the north of Telmine (the likely location of the regional capital Turris Tamalleni in the Roman period) on the slope of the Jabal Tebaga and these appear to have irrigated an area that is now abandoned. Foggaras here were still functioning in 1947,[82] and a survey in 1962 recorded 57 channels stretching along the escarpment as far as Zaouia, but these have since all been replaced by deeply dug artesian wells.[83] Of those that still survive, some have been dug

---

[80] Goblot 1979, 117 mentions their existence on the basis of information provided by his son, who had seen them. They are not mentioned by Aucapitaine 1857, despite Goblot's implication that they were. On the irrigation at Ghadamis, see Mattingly and Sterry 2010.

[81] Mattingly *et al.* 2018, 220–21.   [82] Moreau 1947.   [83] Suter 1962.

out as open channels and are used in conjunction with a number of dams for floodwater farming. At least one foggara is also known from Douz, although it has not been possible to locate this on satellite imagery and it may have been destroyed in the last few years.

Little is known of foggaras in the Jarid oasis group to the west, but at least two examples can be identified south of Daqas. Special mention should be made of an isolated single foggara that is 32 km north of Tozeur, near the Wadi Zrizer. Not previously recorded, the foggara runs for 1.2 km into an area of gardens of *c.*1 ha (although the current arrangement is a later layout). A possible *opus Africanum* farm of Roman date is located 110 m to the east of the foggara. There are very few settlements (either ancient or modern) in this region and this foggara may well be a pioneering and ultimately not very successful experiment of foggara technology in a new environment.

Foggaras within the Roman Province: Gafsa and the Aurès Mountains

Another large group of foggaras is found 17 km to the east of Gafsa under the villages of Lortes and El Guettar. A total of 31 channels were reportedly active in 1910, some of which appear to have been of substantial size and ran for between 600 m and 1 km with shafts up to 35 m deep at the mother wells; only 21 are now visible, the others having been destroyed by the expansion of the modern settlements.[84]

One of the most celebrated foggara systems is to be found at Badès (ancient Badias). Aerial photographs by Baradez identified a foggara system that feeds into a probably Roman field system.[85] Although large parts of this have been destroyed, channels and fields are still visible to the north of Badès. At Lamasba (Bellezma), north of the Aurès, the Aqua Claudiana irrigation aqueduct, for which we have a detailed irrigation schedule of the third century AD, connects to underground tunnels with shafts every 10 m that tap a hillside aquifer.[86] Other foggaras are known in the Aurès Mountains (at Souma el Kiata, Henchir Oxhmida, Menaa, Vegesala, Ain Ferhat, Ain Chabor, Ain Kharoubi) and both Birebent and Fentress suggest that these are all of Roman date (broadly second to fourth century AD).[87]

---

[84] Bursaux 1910, 369; Gruet 1954, 4–5. Megdiche and Moussa 2014 present data on 29 channels recorded from 1940s aerial photographs. They record shaft spacing as 15–20 m and a depth of 21–25 m.

[85] Baradez 1949, 169, photos A, B and C.

[86] Birebent 1962, 385–89; Fentress 1979, 168–70. Irrigation schedule: *ILAlg* 1.2139; for the remains of the aqueduct, a tunnel with access shafts every 10 m, see Ballu and Groslambert 1997, 311.

[87] Birebent 1962; Fentress 1979; cf. Wilson 2009.

Many of these systems have refinements – the enclosure of the water channel in a stone conduit or terracotta pipeline at the base of the tunnel, the gallery above being backfilled to prevent collapse and thus eliminate the need for regular maintenance – that suggest that they are Roman developments of foggara technology that had percolated north from the Sahara.[88] They all lie in areas that receive between 400 and 200 mm of precipitation annually and most consist of only a single channel. Except at Badès, agriculture in these areas would have been possible without irrigation, but the foggara-type irrigation aqueducts north of the Aurès may have allowed more intensive forms of agriculture reliant on a continuous and predictable water supply.

At Sidi Nasrallah, near Kairouan, in central Tunisia, a long-abandoned foggara was put back into service in 1901, and its association with Roman ruins and the masonry steining of its shafts suggest a Roman date.[89] Apart from the fact that this is the most northerly recorded foggara in Tunisia, it is perhaps also significant for its alternative name, Henchir al-Khattara, which may refer to the word for foggara used in Morocco.[90]

Further individual foggaras have been reported from Jerba, the Ekjus valley, El Jem, between Gafsa and Tebessa, and a still-working foggara at Oum Jdour, Kasserine, but these remain unverified and no further details are currently available.[91]

Central and Western Algeria

Wargla comprises a cluster of oases in the Algerian Sahara *c.*160 km south-west of Tuggurt. The oasis was an early centre of Ibadite resistance in the tenth century AD and numerous 'Berber ruins' are reported, but undated. The abandoned town of Sedrata (*c.*30 ha) and its gardens are partially buried below the dunes immediately to the south of Wargla. Beyond them there are ruins of a number of buildings of unknown date on top of the isolated hilltop site of Gara Krima. The palm groves (500,000 palms in the early twentieth century) are sustained by the subterranean waters of the

---

[88] Wilson 2005, 232–33; 2006; 2009.   [89] Gresse 1901; Wilson 2006; 2009.   [90] Hbaieb 2013.

[91] See the work of the project: *Foggara. Inventory, analysis and valorisation of traditional water techniques of European and Saharan drainage tunnels* (Project ID: ICA3-CT-2002-10029). The example at Carthage reported by this project is in fact not a foggara, but a foggara-type aqueduct of Roman date coming from the plain of La Soukra, that seems to have had water-lifting devices for irrigation mounted over some of its shafts: see Renault 1912, 471–75; Fornacciari 1928; Wilson 2003, 121–22. It is not clear that it was dug in foggara fashion, as a tunnel between pairs of vertical shafts, rather than in a cut-and-cover ditch (the inside of the gallery is lined with masonry).

Wadi Mya and artesian springs. The remains of a small number of foggaras are also to be found on the west side of the oasis. From Wargla a route runs south across hostile terrain towards the Ahaggar and Tamanrasset (1,500 km) and west to the Mzab.[92]

A route leads from Ghardaia down the east edge of the Great Western Erg to al-Golea *c.*270 km to the south. Beyond al-Golea, the route continues south to In Salah (400 km) and then Tamanrasset and the Ahaggar (650 km). Foggaras are known at al-Golea, in the Wargla, at In Salah, and in dense concentrations in the Tidikelt and Tuwat oases to the west.[93] A number of finds of Roman artefacts are reported from the general area of the Mzab, Tuggurt and Wargla oases by Salama, including coins and Roman pottery.[94] The case for pre-Islamic origins is suggestive, if unproven at present.

Between the Gourara, Tuwat and Tidikelt oases there are 1,470 foggaras which Capot-Rey has estimated to comprise a combined total of 1,520 km of channels with the largest up to 13 km long.[95] By any measure they are the largest group of foggaras in the Sahara. Dating is largely absent as elsewhere in the Algerian Sahara, but the more northerly group, the Gourara, has more ruined fortified settlements or *ksour* and may be the location of the oldest foggaras. Foggaras across these three oasis zones have been the subject of intensive study, but not from an archaeological point of view.[96] Local traditions recorded in the sixteenth to eighteenth centuries ascribed Gaetulian and Jewish (pre-Islamic) origins to at least some of the *ksour*.[97] Goblot suggested that the foggaras of this region were constructed by successive waves of immigrants who brought the technology with them: first, Jews or Judaised Zenata Berbers in the ninth century, then Barmacid refugees from Persia in the eleventh century and finally Almoravids from Morocco in the later middle ages.[98] This is all speculation, however, and

---

[92] Heywood 1926, 257–58.   [93] Capot-Rey 1953, 320, Carte VII; 1958.

[94] Remini and Achour 2013a; Remini *et al.* 2014.

[95] Capot-Rey 1953, 324–26 (this is almost certainly an underestimate); Capot-Rey and Damade 1962.

[96] Voinot 1909; Cornet 1952; Lô 1953/1954; Capot-Rey 1953; Chaintron 1957/1958; Bisson 1957; 1989; Echallier 1972; Kobori 1989, 13–22.

[97] Martin 1908, 25–55. One mosque at Tamentit was reported in the late eighteenth century as bearing an inscription mentioning its origins as a pre-existing *kasr* built in the sixth century AD (p. 45). On the other hand the seventeenth-century chronicler al-Haj Ahmad ben Yousef at-Tinilani associated the commencement of foggara irrigation with the first Arab migration into the area in the later tenth century: 'Ils y organisèrent des irrigations au moyen de canaux souterrains, tels que n'en avaient jamais établi de semblables les populations qui les avaient précédés; ces canaux furent dénommés foggaras' (Martin 1908, 61–62). See Wilson 2009 for a full discussion of rival traditions of the origins of these foggaras.

[98] Goblot 1979, 167–69.

the first author has argued instead that similarities in terminology (*foggara*, pl. *feggaguir*, rather than *khettarat*) between the groups in these oases and those in Fazzan, and probably also in the social status of those who dug them (*haratin* slaves rather than specialist groups in Algeria; and the likelihood of the Garamantes using slave labour for foggara construction in Fazzan), may point instead to diffusion of the technology from the foggaras of the Libyan Sahara.[99] Moreover, at Tamentit in the Tuwat oasis there are two groups of foggaras on different alignments, one set with Arabic names, whose water is divided simultaneously among different users by a grille or *kesria* leading into different channels, and the other with Berber names, whose entire flow is channelled to different users in rotation each for a set period of time.[100] The different nomenclature and distribution arrangements point to two different cultural backgrounds, and coupled with the different alignments this suggests two main chronological phases of construction and operation. Only four of the Berber-group foggaras were still functioning in the mid-twentieth century, but they are on the same alignment as a multitude of abandoned foggaras. The Berber group is presumably therefore earlier than the Arabic-named group, and they may indeed be pre-Islamic.[101]

To the west of Laghouat, towards the west end of the Saharan Atlas, there are further oases that lie *c.*250 km south of the Roman frontier forts of Mauretania Caesariensis. These are Moghrar (two foggaras), Tahtani, Foukani, Maryam, Boussemghoune (one foggara?), Beni Ounif (five foggaras), Ain Sefra (two foggaras), Figig and Bechar (22 foggaras), Kenadsa (40 foggaras), Lahmar (one?) and Wakda (one?), known for the remains of fortified villages of presumed Medieval date.[102]

The foggaras at Figig have been studied in detail. They are not true foggaras in that they do not tap a groundwater supply; instead the galleries each connect to a different artesian well.[103] There were 30 or 39 channels in total ranging from 50 to 1,000 m in length, but these have been almost entirely destroyed.[104] Flow rates varied hugely from <0.1 to 88 l/sec and together they irrigated an area of *c.*700 ha. The distribution networks of three of the foggaras through basins and irrigation channels (*seguia*) have also been mapped and provide a useful comparison to ancient systems.

---

[99] Wilson 2005, 232–33; 2006, 213–14; 2009, 30–32.   [100] Capot-Rey and Damade 1962.
[101] Wilson 2009.   [102] Heywood 1926, 94–100; Remini *et al.* 2010.   [103] Popp 1990, 82.
[104] Fitzwilliam Hall n.d. – his discussion is the most comprehensive review of foggara distribution in Morocco.

At Kenadsa there are 40 underground channels running 150 m from a cliff to the north into the oasis gardens.[105] Although referred to by some as foggaras and tapping a combination of artesian wells and groundwater, they do not have any vertical access/ventilation shafts along their tunnels and so cannot be considered true foggaras. They were in regular use until the latter part of the twentieth century, but only ten still survive, with flow rates down to as little as 1–2 l/s.

Between Figig and Adrar at the north of the Tuwat oases are a number of small oases that lie on the banks of the Wadi Saoura, many of which are foggara-fed.

Tabalbala is a small oasis some 240 km to the east of the southern tip of the Draa and 300 km to the west of the Tuwat. The most remarkable aspect of the archaeology of this oasis relates to the *c*.200 foggara channels that flowed from the sand sea towards the escarpment. Either these required regular replacement or the oasis once sustained a substantially larger population than it does today (around 5,000).[106]

Morocco

In Morocco Fitzwilliam Hall has inventoried at least 1,600 foggaras.[107] At Marrakech there are more than 50 foggaras totalling several hundred kilometres with the longest over 8 km in length. The system is dated to the reign of the Almoravid ruler Ali (1107–1143) by the contemporary writer al-Idrisi who lived in the city.[108] It has sometimes been argued that these are the oldest foggaras in Morocco, although this is in part due to an assumption that they were an Arab introduction to North Africa from Spain.[109]

In the Tafilalat, around the city of Sijilmasa, there are 80 foggaras forming a network of *c*.300 km of channels that have been mapped from a combination of satellite imagery, fieldwork and interviews (see Fig. 3.3 for an example).[110] These irrigated an area of 3,000 ha. Although Sijilmasa was described by 14 Medieval authors no mention was made of the foggaras which are themselves closely associated with later *qsur* that lie to the north of the city. Lightfoot and Miller therefore argue for a post-fourteenth-century date for this group.[111] This argument is not, however, at all decisive, since the artificial derivation of the seasonal floodwaters of

---

[105] Remini *et al.* 2014.   [106] Champault 1969.   [107] Fitwilliam Hall n.d.
[108] Al-Idrisi, in Dozy and De Goeje, 1866, 78; Goblot 1979.
[109] E.g. Goblot 1979, 152–55, followed by Lambton 1989, 5.
[110] Castellani 1999, 231–38; Lightfoot 1996; Margat 1961.   [111] Lightfoot and Miller 1996.

the Wadis Rheris and Ziz (the largest artificial scheme in the region, dated by Lightfoot to the eleventh century) is also not mentioned in these sources; one cannot assume that the foggaras would necessarily be mentioned either.[112] The canalisation of wadi floodwaters constituted the mainstay of the Tafilalat oasis but it is clear that foggaras were also common, with as many as 570 (*c*.3,000 km) in more than 155 locations recorded in 1967, although less than 20 per cent are still in use today.[113] They continue to be utilised to service a band of small oases along the entire corridor between the High Atlas and Anti-Atlas with 80 around the palmeries at Skoura, 28 at Boudenib, and at least four at Beni Taijit.[114]

Foggaras are also widespread across much of the rest of southern Morocco. In the Souss valley there is a well-preserved group at Oulad Berhil with 25 channels extending over 50–75 km.[115] At Tata there are at least 40 foggaras.[116] The Trans-Saharan trading town of Tamdult (which was abandoned in the fourteenth century) is not irrigated by foggaras, even though they are to be found in neighbouring Tinzounine (about five foggaras) and Akka (about five foggaras). This could imply that, as with the Tafilalat, foggaras were a late Medieval introduction to southern Morocco. Further notable examples are found throughout the Anti-Atlas: to the west of Guelmim (*c*.20 foggaras), Taghjijt (*c*.5 foggaras), Tissint (*c*.5 foggaras), Foum Zguid (*c*.10 foggaras), on the upland plateau of Tazenakht (*c*.50 foggaras), the villages south of Taliouine (*c*.25 foggaras) and Tazzarine (*c*.5 foggaras).[117] In the Draa irrigation comes primarily from diverting water from the river into open canals, but there are *c*.10 examples of foggaras. At least one of these near Tamegroute was in use within living memory and all seem likely to be Medieval or more recent in date.

Ahaggar, Mauritania and Western Sahara

The Ahaggar group of foggaras is the most southerly known in the Sahara. The foggaras are dug exclusively along the bottom of wadis and collect rainwater from the alluvium rather than tapping a supply of groundwater.[118] They are therefore prone to collapse and tend to be short-lived; they are highly

---

[112] This position may seem a little contradictory to the argument advanced below in relation to the absence of reference in Arab sources mentioning foggaras in Fazzan as suggesting early abandonment. However, there is a further factor to consider for the Sijilmasa area, in that there the primary water resource was the near perennial stream of the Wadi Ziz and its tributaries. Foggaras around Sijilmasa will always have been of minor significance in the overall irrigation regime, though at some point in time serving to augment the irrigated area.

[113] Ouhssain 2004.   [114] Mahdane *et al.* 2011.   [115] Popp 1986, 35.
[116] Barathon *et al.* 2005.   [117] For Guelmim see Hart 1973.   [118] Capot-Rey 1953.

dependent on precipitation for their recharge, and some only run seasonally.[119] They range in length from a few hundred metres to 5 km and, as in the Tuwat and Tidikelt oases, they were mainly dug by Harratin communities. Gast considers them to be as recent as the nineteenth century, with initial foggaras dug by farmers from the Tidikelt, but Remini and Achour suggest a fourteenth-century date.[120] In any case the largest number appear to date to the mid-twentieth century when 184 were in use.[121] However, this was seemingly short-lived and the systems were much in decline by the start of the twenty-first century with most channels no longer visible.

Goblot records foggaras at Bir Moghrein (Mauritania) and Guetta-Zemmur (Western Sahara) that were discovered by the French in 1935.[122] At least one other foggara has been claimed in the Oued Seguelil near the Trans-Saharan centres of Wadan and Chinguetti. However, no known research has been conducted into any of these systems and satellite reconnaissance has failed to locate any likely remains. The presence of linear geological features around Bir Moghrein must raise the possibility that they were mistakenly identified. Certainly, there is no evidence to suggest that they were a major contributor to oasis irrigation in this region.

The Spread of Irrigation Technologies: Diffusion versus Transfer

Three of the key irrigation technologies considered above – the foggara, the *shaduf* and *dalw* wells – seem to have spread westward from the Near East or the Arabian Peninsula via Egypt along routes to Fazzan and thence further west still. The *shaduf* seems to have reached Fazzan from Egypt in the first half of the first millennium BC, although its history elsewhere remains unclear.

The emerging picture suggests a progressive westward spread of the foggara through the Northern Sahara from the oases of the Western Desert of Egypt, through al-Jufra and Fazzan, northwards through Ghadames and Derj to the Nafzaoua and southern Tunisia and the Aurès, and westward to the main oasis centres of the Tuwat/Tidikelt/Gourara, beyond which the technology radiated to points further west, south-west and north-west, ultimately (perhaps after the twelfth century AD) reaching the Ahaggar in the south and Marrakech in the north (Fig. 3.5). In contrast to earlier models – which saw the introduction of foggaras to various parts of the Sahara as the result either of imperial expansion on the part of Rome

---

[119] Sanlaville 1957.   [120] Gast 1995; Remini and Achour 2013b.   [121] Sanlaville 1957.
[122] Du Puigaudeau and Senones 1947; Goblot 1979, 165.

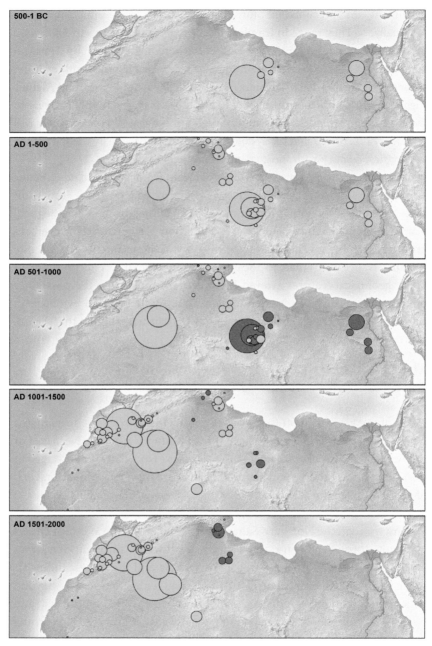

Figure 3.5 Hypothetical distribution of active (blue) and failing/abandoned (grey) foggaras by phase across the Trans-Saharan region (M. Sterry for Trans-SAHARA Project).

or as brought in by various groups of refugees from supposedly *qanat*-using parts of the world (for example improbably, Jews from Cyrenaica, or Barmakid Persians), or Islamic settlers[123] – the chronological data now at our disposal, in large part as a result of fieldwork by the Fazzan and Desert Migrations Projects, suggest that the technology spread along Saharan trade routes. It both enabled the development of oases that could become nodes on a trade network and spread throughout the network that resulted. The dissemination of foggara technology throughout the Sahara in antiquity is an integral and inseparable aspect of the history of Saharan, and early Trans-Saharan, trade.[124]

The general outline of the diffusion of this technology is clear, but the chronology remains very hazy. Our fixed points are: the presence of foggaras at Ain Manawir in Egypt in the fifth century BC (and the subsequent Ptolemaic and Roman development of foggaras at various places in the Kharga, Dakhla and Farafra oases); the AMS date on the mudbrick lining of a foggara at al-Hatiya, calibrated to 391–206 calBC, together with the intensive use of foggara irrigation throughout the Garamantian Fazzan, more generally between the latter centuries BC and around the middle of the first millennium AD, or a little after. By the Roman period (first to fourth centuries AD) we can see that the technology had reached the Aurès Mountains and southern Tunisia; and during the first half of the twelfth century the first *khattara*/foggaras were dug at Marrakech in Morocco. By the eleventh and twelfth centuries irrigation in Fazzan seems to have relied on wells equipped with *shadufs* or the *dalw*, and not on foggaras.

We can hazard some guesses to interpolate between these fixed points; guesses which while currently unproven at least appear plausible, even likely, and can provide a hypothesis for future testing. It appears that foggara irrigation technology was introduced from Egypt to Fazzan in the second half of the first millennium BC, along Trans-Saharan routes, and that it intensified the development of a Garamantian agricultural society in Fazzan, which controlled Trans-Saharan trade.[125] The foggaras of Fazzan appear to have been used perhaps until the early middle ages, but probably not beyond this; regional settlement appears to have already contracted by the seventh or eighth centuries AD, and as we have seen, Arab Medieval geographers refer to irrigation by shadufs and *dalw* wells in Fazzan in the eleventh and twelfth centuries, but not to foggaras. Given the association with large settlements that have yielded Roman-era pottery, it seems probable that the foggaras at

---

[123] Goblot 1979.

[124] Wilson and Mattingly 2003, 275–77; Mattingly and Wilson 2004; Wilson 2005; 2006; 2009; 2012.

[125] Wilson and Mattingly 2003; Mattingly and Wilson 2004; Wilson 2006; 2012; Mattingly 2006; 2011.

Hun and Waddan in the al-Jufra oasis are broadly contemporary with the Garamantian floruit of foggaras in Fazzan, that is sometime between the latter centuries BC and the latter first millennium AD. From Fazzan and the al-Jufra, foggaras spread north to the fringes of the Garamantian world, to southern Tunisia and the southern Aurès in the Roman period. Berber legends from the Aurès firmly identify the foggara as a Saharan or Berber technology for water provision, in contradistinction to Roman technologies of spring development and aqueduct construction.[126] It would seem very likely that, as Ghadamis, Derj and Sinawin lie on the route from Fazzan to southern Tunisia, the foggaras there may go back to Garamantian times.

At some point, and very probably *before* intensive foggara usage had ceased in Fazzan, the development of oasis zones in the western parts of the Central Sahara (especially the Tuwat and Gourara in Algeria) facilitated the subsequent development of new north–south trade routes through what is now the Algerian Sahara. These oases are today the zones of most highly developed foggara use anywhere outside Iran; local tradition puts foggara use here as early as the eleventh century AD, and as we have seen there are grounds for thinking it may go back even earlier. There are strong similarities, in construction and nomenclature, between the foggaras of Fazzan and those of the Algerian Sahara, and it is most likely that the foggaras of the Tuwat and Gourara were introduced from Fazzan, and therefore before the Garamantian foggaras had fallen out of use.[127] From these oases the foggara subsequently spread to the Tidikelt, Tafilalat and Figig, enabling the development of these oases as trading centres. The history of the foggara in the Sahara is part of the history of Trans-Saharan trade; and the foggara has for centuries defined much of the character of irrigated agriculture in Saharan oases, leading to characteristic field systems and even the migration of fields and villages across the landscape as a foggara is deepened to maintain flow in a declining aquifer and its outlet point consequently emerges further downhill.

Factors in the Spread of Irrigation Technologies

The mapping and dating of this technological diffusion does not in itself provide an explanatory framework. As outlined in Chapter 1 of this volume, the irrigation technologies discussed were part of a range of agricultural innovations that also included crops, animals, implements and management practices. However, the first agricultural revolution in the Sahara, based on the adoption of a developed agricultural package of crops, most likely relied on surficial or spring-fed irrigation. Foggaras in

[126] Wilson 2009, 36–39.   [127] Wilson 2006; 2009.

particular appear to have spread later, marking a secondary phase of intensification of oasis cultivation. This section will examine the way in which the spread and adoption of the innovation was entangled with technologies, environments and economic, social and cultural factors.

Only in certain parts of the Sahara do we find the right combination of water sources, geologies and topographies to support foggara irrigation. Understanding of this terrain and how to manipulate it requires some expertise, and specialists (if only for directing work) should be considered a prerequisite, especially in new zones. The tunnelling process was labour intensive and costly in materials, as in addition to being fed the workforce needed supplying with metal tools for digging shafts and tunnelling through rock and mudbricks for lining shafts dug through sand. This high level of capital investment severely limited the speed at which foggara irrigation could be developed in an oasis without some form of external stimulus and favoured building foggaras next to pre-existing systems rather than in entirely new locations where expertise, labour and materials might have been lacking. As the foggaras were transformative of the water sources that they tapped, they required the cooperation (or pacification) of all who would be affected (both permanent and transitory land users).

An important question to answer is what foggaras offered that the initial irrigation strategies in the Saharan oases did not. The start-up costs of constructing a foggara irrigation scheme were high. There had to be significant and tangible gains expected of such an extraordinary invest-ment in labour and other resources. Crucially, foggaras offered a possible means to augment the supply of free-flowing water in an oasis. As with the construction of man-made artesian wells, the attraction was in having the equivalent of a new spring source, allowing a considerable extension of the irrigated area. Springs, foggaras and artesian wells that did not involve mechanical labour to lift water into irrigation channels were not simply more efficient, they enabled a community to extend the oasis and thus to support a growing population. They also helped extend the growing season through the hot summer months, a process also helped by the adoption of new crop species suited to rapid summer maturation, like sorghum and pearl millet or water-hungry cotton. Foggaras were not a guaranteed success – they were prone to internal collapse and required high levels of maintenance on top of the ruinous initial construction costs. If a foggara became seriously blocked at the wrong moment, crops could be killed before flow was restored. Depending on the nature of the water source they tapped, they might decline in flow after some years of opera-tion, requiring deepening or augmentation of the mother well. The fact that so many oasis communities have constructed foggaras suggests that they not only tap into groundwater but also into communal optimism and a desire or need for oasis expansion.

The foggara irrigation may seem to have an intrinsic benefit in a desert environment (an increase in the cultivable area and overall reduction in day-to-day labour needed for water lifting resulting in increased output), but it is only likely to have been attractive where there was a perceived overall benefit.[128] One possible reason for needing to increase agricultural output may be a growing population, either sedentary due to growth and migration into oases or transitory due to increasing numbers of people and animals moving through the Sahara such as pastoralists and trade caravans. In a connected Sahara, food surpluses were also a ready trade good. Social and cultural factors may have been as important in determining the spread and adoption of irrigation technologies.[129] The nature of pre-existing land ownership and water management would have influenced the appeal and success of a new system that required considerable levels of cooperation between multiple farms. For example, in the early to mid-twentieth century, foggaras were in use in regions where most land was held by a small number of (often absentee) landlords, as at Tamanrasset, but they were absent from regions dominated by large numbers of smallholders, as in the Murzuq basin.[130]

There can also be no straightforward answer as to who drove the spread and adoption of irrigation technologies in the Sahara. The celebrated example of the Marrakech foggaras certainly appears to be state-backed and to this we can perhaps add the systems linked to the Garamantian urban centres of Jarma and Qasr ash-Sharraba and certainly those of Badès. However, recent descriptions of foggara construction emphasise the role of the local community in planning and funding the construction of individual systems in line with their personal resources and needs. Distinguishing between these different types of venture is difficult, but we can note that in those oases where foggaras are less connected to one another they tend to be smaller in size and located in marginal locations in relation to the main oasis core, suggesting that these were more independent ventures. The largest concentrations of foggaras, in Tuwat and the Wadi al-Ajal, include some of the longest and most complex systems in the Sahara (suggesting a greater level of centralised control in their construction), but their link to separate small fortified villages implies that they were also related to individual communities. At Ain Manawir in Egypt, the ostraca recording sales of water shares

[128] Van der Veen and Westley 2010, 517.   [129] Van der Veen and Westley 2010, 516–17.
[130] Eldblom 1968.

in the fifth and fourth centuries BC point to the foggaras having been created as an investment, with the returns expected through sales of water. Certainly, as Kirchner has demonstrated, peasants are perfectly capable of constructing complex irrigation systems, including foggaras, without state involvement.[131] At the same time, it must be stressed that the spread of foggaras across the Sahara was not a simple triumph of progress. Indeed, for a variety of reasons (social, economic and hydrological), foggara technology was only appropriate to certain places at certain times. The foggara was always one of a range of tools available on the 'technological shelf' for Saharan cultivators, and less technologically complex solutions continued to be deployed alongside the foggara in many regions and in some locations were never supplanted by the foggara.[132]

Stress and Collapse

If we can suggest some broad chronology for the spread of foggara irrigation, end dates for its use in regions such as Fazzan are harder to come by. The widespread abandonment of Garamantian sites in the Wadi al-Ajal and in southern Fazzan in the sixth to tenth centuries provide a very strong clue. The evidence of al-Bakri and al-Idrisi suggests that by the eleventh and twelfth centuries foggara irrigation had been replaced first by *shadufs* and then by *dalw* wells. Elsewhere we have even less idea; the foggaras of Umm al-Abid had been abandoned long before Clapperton passed through in 1822, such that the local inhabitants did not understand what they were, and those of the al-Jufra oasis group, and some at least of those close to Ghadamis, had also been abandoned long before living memory. Very possibly their abandonment, like those of Fazzan, also dates to the second half of the first millennium AD.

While we cannot date their abandonment with precision, we can say something about the process, and probably the cause, which seems to be that the water table that the foggaras tapped fell continuously. A survey to the west of the Taqallit peninsula in the Wadi al-Ajal identified three main phases of foggara development. First, several foggaras were constructed, starting some distance north of the foot of the escarpment. Second, as more foggaras were added, those of the first phase were extended backwards almost to the escarpment base, with tributary branches added to them to maximise the collection area within the aquifer. In a third phase, the

[131] Kirchner 2009, 152.

[132] For explanations of the 'technological shelf' approach to the adoption and deployment of technology, see Greene 1994; Mattingly 1996.

downstream sections of many foggaras fell out of use and their upstream
sections were diverted by means of cross-linking tributaries to the foggaras
that remained in use, so that a reduced number of functioning foggaras was
tapping the aquifer across a broad front of the escarpment (Fig. 3.6). The
same process can be seen further east, at Tuwash (Fig. 3.7).

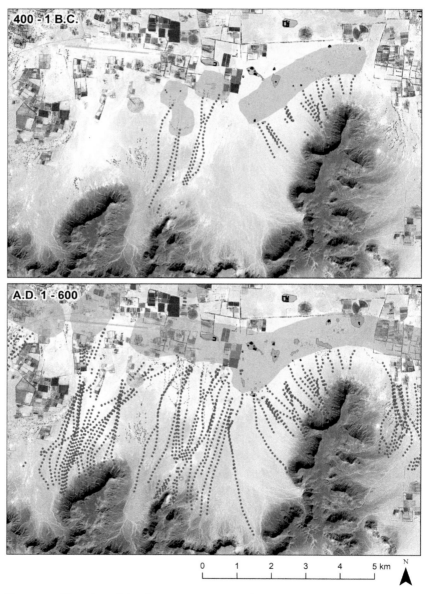

Figure 3.6 Hypothetical development sequence in the Taqallit landscape (WorldView-2
image, 14 January 2013, copyright DigitalGlobe).

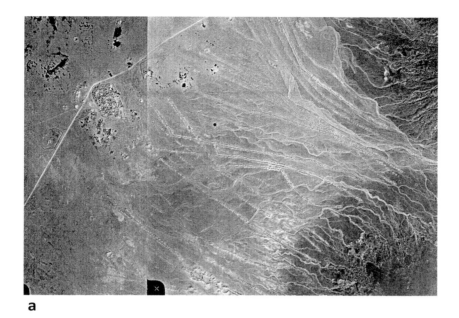

Figure 3.7 Foggaras at Tuwash in the Wadi al-Ajal: (a) air-photograph and (b) plan of tributary branches in the upstream (southern) part of some foggaras, and foggara capture via cross-links in the downstream sections.

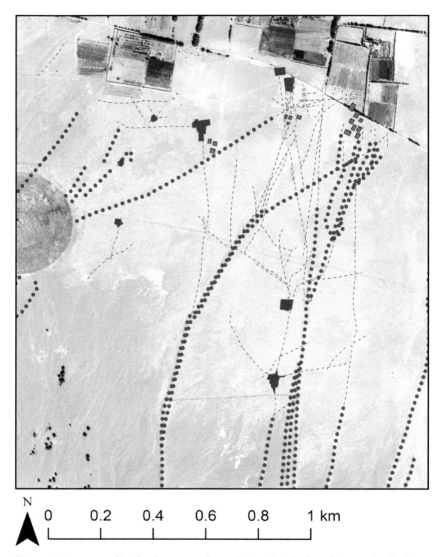

N

0   0.2   0.4   0.6   0.8   1 km

Figure 3.8 Foggara distribution network at ad-Disa (Wadi al-Ajal, Fazzan). Thick-dotted: subterranean foggara channels; thin-dashed: surface channels; blue blocks: reservoirs. (WorldView-2 image, 14 January 2013, copyright DigitalGlobe).

Just to the east of Taqallit, in the area known as ad-Disa, is an area where the outflow zone and distribution arrangements of a number of foggaras has not yet been destroyed by modern agriculture. Here, channels and reservoirs can be traced cut through the duricrust surface of a prehistoric palaeolake (Fig. 3.8). We can see a successive northward (downslope) migration of distribution reservoirs as foggara channels were deepened, necessitating recutting the reservoirs and distribution channels further north where the ground surface was lower. For example, at the lower right centre of Figure 3.8 we can see a subterranean foggara line (blue dotted line) emerging to feed a reservoir (blue) from which three distribution channels depart to the north-west, north and north-east. Further along the central one of these is another square reservoir, which essentially replaces the first one; this too has several distribution channels leading off it. One of these in turn leads to a third reservoir further north, which is also fed by distribution channels from other foggaras. A later stage still seems to be represented by a subterranean foggara (dotted blue line) which crosses this surface distribution channel, running at a greater depth from south-west to north-east. The settlements found by the survey (red) are grouped around the northern reservoirs and outlet points.

These alterations to the foggara network show a progressive and continual response to the problem of a falling water table, which required foggaras to be constantly deepened. The eventual abandonment of the foggaras, and of many of the sites associated with them, must have occurred when the water table dropped below a level at which the foggaras could still tap it and deliver water to the surface. Coupled with a declining water table, problems of labour and maintenance gradually led to the abandonment of most foggaras, and a shift to smaller-scale agriculture supported by wells, either *shaduf* or, at some point after the Arab invasions of North Africa, the *dalw* type. At a few sites in the Wadi al-Ajal, such as EDS10, occupation continued into the early Medieval period, sustained by *shaduf* wells, but these irrigated a smaller area. In the area to the east of Murzuq, where the variation in relief is very feeble, a slight drop in the water table would have put the foggaras there out of use, and indeed the few foggaras here do not seem to have been used for long (their spoil rings are very faint, perhaps reflecting only a short period of maintenance).[133] Instead, this area relied chiefly on *shaduf* wells, and these too would have gone out of use if the water table dropped more than a few metres.

With the decline of the foggaras as a result of the falling water table, agricultural production and the population that could be sustained evidently collapsed substantially, bringing an end to the Garamantian floruit of population, urban development and irrigated agriculture at some point within the second half of the first millennium AD. The exact timing of this process,

[133] Sterry *et al.* 2011.

though, remains unclear. The decline of Garamantian power will have had a further effect on Saharan and Trans-Saharan trade, although other factors, including fourth-century disruption to the cities of the Tripolitanian coast, by earthquakes and by the raids of the Austuriani, also played a part. Indeed, some of these other factors may be interrelated with the decline of foggara irrigation in the Sahara, and cause and effect are sometimes difficult to disentangle.

A similar process of foggara deepening and eventual exhaustion appears to have happened in the al-Jufra oasis group: at Waddan, the foggaras also show the same characteristics of tributary branches and the downstream migration of successive reservoirs that we have seen in Fazzan and which indicate efforts to combat a falling water table. Here too this presumably led ultimately to the abandonment of these foggaras, and settlement reliance on springs and wells. Subsequently the settlement and agricultural pattern appears to have become far more nucleated around the urban sites with little or no hinterland settlements on the edge of large field systems laid out on areas of *sabkha*. It is tempting to see the foggaras as broadly con-temporary with similar developments in the Garamantian Fazzan and marking a maximal expansion of agriculture and population here. The loss of foggara irrigation did not mark catastrophic collapse, but a return to a core oasis zone.

Conclusion

Much of the core Garamantian territory has foggaras: the Wadi al-Ajal, southern Fazzan, and even the Wadi ash-Shati despite the abundance there of artesian springs. The intensive use of this technology in the Garamantian region went hand in hand with a combination of a Mediterranean and Sub-Saharan crop package,[134] and supported a settled, agricultural society living in a mixture of urban and scattered rural settlements, with a symbiotic interac-tion with more mobile pastoral groups of animal herders, and particularly cameleers.[135] Foggaras have also been identified from satellite imagery in areas where they were previously unknown or little known, notably in the al-Jufra oases and at Ghadamis and other oases on the northern fringes of Garamantian territory. Much work remains to be done on the chronology both of construction and of abandonment of foggaras in most regions of the

[134] Duckworth *et al.*, Chapter 1, this volume.   [135] Scheele 2017.

Sahara. It would be audacious to claim that the distribution of early foggaras in the Libyan Sahara is coterminous with the area of Garamantian control, or that foggaras outside the core Garamantian heartlands are an indicator of Garamantian influence. But the presence both of clusters of foggaras and of early urban centres in Hun and Waddan invite reflections on the degree and nature of contact between the population of these oases and the Garamantes, while the rarity of foggaras in the Wadi Tanzzuft is one more factor among several that underscores the differences in material culture and settlement morphology between this region and the core Garamantian territory of Fazzan. The overall picture suggests a striking degree of agricultural intensification in the Sahara in antiquity, and this is linked with the development of Saharan and Trans-Saharan trade.[136] It is a clear demonstration of the idea that oases are not self-sufficient, and that oasis agriculture is also inherently dependent on long-distance trade connections.[137]

Key desiderata for future research include dating the introduction, use and abandonment of the foggaras of the oases of the Northern Sahara, and also dating the shift in foggara usage to the Algerian Sahara – especially to the Gourara and Tuwat – and its onward diffusion westward to Morocco and Mauretania. While the most intensive periods of foggara usage here were clearly Medieval and later, the traditional view that the technology was introduced to the Algerian Sahara only in the Islamic era needs to be kept under review. Finally, if foggaras enabled the intensification of agriculture and population growth not only in Fazzan, but also in some of the more northerly oases of the Libyan Sahara, the implications of their eventual failure for understanding migrations and the various waves of incursions by Saharan peoples into Roman, Vandal and Byzantine territory in late antiquity are potentially considerable, and deserve further exploration.[138]

References

Agut-Labordère, D. 2018. The agricultural landscape of Ayn Manawir (Kharga oasis, Egypt) through the Persian period ostraca (Vth–IVth century BC). In Purdue *et al.* 2018, 359–77.

Aucapitaine, H. 1857. R'adamès, une ville du Sahara. *Revue Contemporaine* 31: 199–204.

---

[136] Mattingly *et al.* 2017; Wilson 2012.   [137] Liverani 2000; Scheele 2010; Wilson 2012.
[138] Fentress and Wilson 2016.

Ballu, A. and Groslambert, A. 1997. *L'Archéologie Algérienne de 1895 à 1915: Les Rapports d'Albert Ballu Publiés au Journal Officiel de la République Française de 1896 à 1916.* Lyon: Centre d'Etudes Romaines et Gallo-romaines.

Baradez, J. 1949. *Vue aérienne de l'organisation romaine dans le sud Algérien: Fossatum Africae.* Paris: Arts et Métiers Graphiques.

Barathon, J.-J., El Abbassi, H. and Lechevalier, C. 2005. Les oasis de la région de Tata (Maroc): Abandon de la vie oasienne traditionnelle et adaptation à la vie urbaine. *Annales de Géographie* 114.644: 449–61.

Barker, G.W., Gilbertson, D., Jones, B. and Mattingly, D. 1996. *Farming the Desert: The UNESCO Libyan Valleys Archaeological Survey, Vol. 1 Synthesis.* Paris: UNESCO.

Bárta, M. and Brůna, V. 2013. The re-emergence of the El-Hayz Oasis. In M. Dospěl and L. Suková (eds), *Bahriya Oasis: Recent Research into the Past of an Egyptian Oasis*, Prague: Faculty of Arts, Charles University, 19–34.

Beaumont, P., Bonine, M. and McLachlan, K. (eds) 1989. *Qanat, Kariz and Khattara: Traditional Water Systems in the Middle East and North Africa.* London: Middle East Centre, School of Oriental and African Studies, University of London; Wisbech: Middle East and North African Studies Press.

Berbrugger, A. 1862. *Les puits artésiens des oasis méridionales de l'Algérie* (2nd edition). Alger: Bastide.

Birebent, J. 1962. *Aquae Romanae: Recherches d'hydraulique romaine dans l'est algérien.* Alger: Service des Antiquités.

Bisson, J. 1957. *Le Gourara: Etude de géographie humaine.* Mémoires de l'Institut de recherches sahariennes 3. Alger: Institut de Recherches Sahariennes.

Bisson, J. 1989. The origin and evolution of foggara oases in the Algerian Sahara. In Beaumont *et al.* 1989, 178–209.

Bousquet, B. 1996. *Tell-Douch et sa région. Géographie d'une limite de milieu à une frontière d'empire.* Cairo: Institut Français d'Archéologie Orientale.

Briant, P. 2001. *Irrigation et drainage dans l'antiquité. Qanâts et canalisations souterraines en Iran, en Egypte et en Grèce: Séminaire du Collège de France, mars 2000.* Paris: Thotm.

Bruce-Lockhart, J. and Wright, J. (eds) 2000. *Difficult and Dangerous Roads: Hugh Clapperton's Travels in Sahara and Fezzan 1822–1825.* London: Sickle Moon.

Buongarzone, R. and De Angeli, S. 2011. L'Oasi di Farafra: Sistemi idrici a qanat e insediamenti di età romana e bizantina. Risultati preliminari della seconda missione dell'Università degli Studi della Tuscia. *Ricerche Italiane e Scavi in Egitto* 5: 53–69.

Bursaux. 1910. L'oasis de Guettar: Ses ressources; sa décadence; moyens d'y remédier. *Revue Tunisienne* 83.1: 364–73.

Capot-Rey, R. 1953. *Le Sahara Français* (L'Afrique Blanche Francaise II). Paris: Presses Universitaires de France.

Capot-Rey, R. 1958. L'eau et le sol à el Goléa. *Travaux de l'Institut de Recherches Sahariennes* 17: 83–125.

Capot-Rey, R. and Damade, W. 1962. Irrigation et structure agraire à Tamentit (Touat). *Travaux de l'Institut de Recherches Sahariennes* 21: 99–119.

Caputo, G. 1937. Archeologia. In Reale Società Geographica Italiana 1937, 301–30.

Castellani, V. 1999. *Civiltà dell'acqua. Archeologia del territorio da Roma arcaica alle antiche civiltà mediterrannee*. Rome: Editorial Service System E.S.S.

Chaintron, J.F. 1957/1958. Aoulef: Problèmes économiques et sociaux d'une oasis à foggaras. *Travaux de l'Institut de Recherches Sahariennes* 16: 101–29; 17: 127–56.

Champault, D. 1969. *Une oasis du Sahara nord-occidental: Tabelbala*. Paris: Éditions du Centre National de la Recherche Scientifique.

Charbonneau, J. (ed.) 1955. *Le Sahara Français*. Vichy: Wallon.

Chauveau, M. 1996. Les archives d'un temple des oasis au temps des Perses. *Bulletin de la Société française d'Égyptologie* 137: 32–47.

Chauveau, M. 2001. Les qanats dans les ostraca de Manâwir. In Briant 2001, 137–42.

Colin, G.S. 1932. La noria marocaine et les machines hydrauliques dans le monde arabe. *Hespéris* 14: 22–61.

Cornet, A. 1952. Essai sur l'hydrogéologie du Grand Erg occidental et des régions limitrophes (les foggaras). *Travaux de l'Institut de Recherches Sahariennes* 8: 71–122.

Cressey, G.-B. 1958. Qanats, karez and foggaras. *Geographical Review* 48: 27–44.

Daniels, C.M. 1973. The Garamantes of Fezzan: An interim report of research, 1965–1973. *Libyan Studies* 4: 35–40.

De Angeli, S. 2013. Qanat landscapes in the oases of the Western Desert of Egypt: The case of the Bahriya and Farafra oases. In Dospěl and Suková 2013, 271–85.

Desanges, J. 1980. *(Pline l'ancien) Histoire naturelle Livre V.1–46 (L'Afrique du nord)*. Paris: Les Belles Lettres.

Despois, J. 1946. *Mission scientifique du Fezzan (1944–1945) III: Géographie humaine*. Algiers: Imbert.

Despois, J.J. 1960. Bir, iii, the Maghrib. In H.A.R. Gibb, J.H. Kramers, E. Lévi-Provençal, J. Schacht, B. Lewis and C. Pellat (eds), *Encyclopaedia of Islam, Volume 1*, Leiden: Brill, 1231–32.

De Villiers, M. and Hirtle, S. 2002. *Sahara: A Natural History*. New York: Walker and Co.

Dospěl, M. and Suková, L. 2013. *Bahriya Oasis: Recent Research into the Past of an Egyptian Oasis*. Prague: Charles University.

Dozy, R. and De Goeje, M.J. 1866. *Description de l'Afrique et de l'Espagne par Edrîsî*. Leiden: Brill.

Drake, N., Wilson, A., Pelling, R., White, K., Mattingly, D. and Black, S. 2004. Water table decline, springline desiccation and the early development of irrigated agriculture in the Wadi al-Ajal, Libyan Fazzan. *Libyan Studies* 35: 95–112.

Du Puigaudeau, O. and Senones, M. 1947. Le cimetière de Bir 'Umm Garn. *Journal de la Société des Africanistes* 17: 51–56.

Durand, J.H. and Guyot, J. 1955. L'irrigation des cultures dans l'oued Righ. *Travaux de l'Institut de Recherches Sahariennes* 13: 75–130.

Echallier, J.-C. 1972. *Villages désertés et structures agraires anciennes du Touat et du Gourara*. Paris: RMG.

Eldblom, L. 1968. *Structure foncière: Organisation et structure sociale. Une étude comparative sur la vie socio-économique dans les trois oasis libyennes de Ghat, Mourzouk et particulièrement Ghadamès*. Lund: Uniksol.

English, P.W. 1968. The origin and spread of qanats in the Old World. *Proceedings of the American Philosophical Society* 112: 170–81.

Estorges, P. 1964. L'irrigation dans l'oasis de Laghouat. *Travaux de l'Institut de Recherches Sahariennes* 23: 111–37.

Fakhry, A. 1942. Bahria and Farafra Oases: Third Preliminary Report. In A. Fakhry and E. Drioton (eds), *Recent Explorations in the Oases of the Western Desert*, Cairo: Press of the French Institute of Oriental Archaeology, 71–113.

Fentress, E.W.B. 1979. *Numidia and the Roman Army: Social, Military and Economic Aspects of the Frontier Zone*. Oxford: BAR.

Fentress, E.W.B. and Wilson, A.I. 2016. The Saharan Berber diaspora and the southern frontiers of Vandal and Byzantine North Africa. In J. Conant and S. Stevens (eds), *North Africa under Byzantium and Early Islam, ca. 500–ca. 800*, Washington, DC: Dumbarton Oaks Research Library and Collection, 41–63.

Fitzwilliam Hall n.d., *The Living Khettāras of Southern Morocco: A Traditional Water Harvesting Technology on the Brink*. https://www.academia.edu/5069877, accessed 9 May 2016.

Fornacciari, C. 1928. Note sur le drain romain de la Soukra: Communication à la séance de la Commission de l'Afrique du Nord, 10 décembre 1929. *Bullétin archéologique du comité des travaux historiques et scientifiques* 1928: 413–15.

Gast, M. 1995. Des graines nourricières qu'on ne broie pas: les confusions de l'agriculture néolithique saharienne. In G. Camps and R. Chénorkian (eds), *L'homme méditerranéen*, Aix-en-Provence: Publications de l'Université de Provenance, 249–57.

Gaucher, G. 1948. Irrigation et mise en valeur du Tafilalet. *Travaux de l'Institut de Recherches Sahariennes* 5: 95–120.

Gautier, E.-F. 1935. *Sahara: The Great Desert* (translated from the French by D.F. Mayhew). New York: Columbia University Press.

Goblot, H. 1979. *Les qanats: Une technique d'acquisition de l'eau*. Industrie et artisanat 9. Paris and New York: Mouton.

Gonon, T. 2018. La gestion de l'eau dans le désert oriental égyptien durant les temps historiques, de l'époque perse à nos jours: Le site de 'Ayn Manâwîr et la prospection du bassin sud de l'oasis de Kharga. In Purdue *et al.* 2018, 269–90.

Greene, K. 1994. Technology and innovation in context: The Roman background to Medieval and later developments. *Journal of Roman Archaeology* 7: 22–33.

Gresse, A. 1901. Restauration des travaux hydrauliques anciens de Sidi-Nasseur-Allah. In P. Gauckler (ed.), *Enquête administrative sur les installations hydrauliques romaines en Tunisie*, Tunis: Imprimerie rapide, 311–17.

Gruet, M. 1954. Le gisement moutérien d'El Guettar. *Karthago. Revue d'Archéologie Africaine* 5: 3–79.

Hart, D.M. 1973. The Ait Ba 'Amran of Ifni: An ethnographic survey. *Revue des Mondes Musulmans et de la Méditerranée* 15.1: 61–74.

Hbaieb, M.A. 2013. Notes préliminaires à propos d'un système de captage et de partage d'eau dans les environs de Kairouan: La foggara de Sidi Ali b. Nasrallah. In N. Boukhchim, J. Ben Nasr and A. El Bahi (eds), *Kairouan et sa Région: Nouvelles recherches d'archéologie et de patrimoine. Actes du 3ème colloque international du Département d'Archéologie (Kairouan 1–4 avril 2009)*, Kairouan: Faculté des Lettres et Sciences Humaines, Université de Kairouan, 301–15.

Heywood, C. 1926. *Algeria and Tunisia*. Paris and London: Librairie Hachette.

Jamil, N. 1999. Calph and Qutb: Poetry as a source for interpreting the transformation of the Byzantine cross on steps on Ummayad coinage. In J. Johns (ed.), *Bayt al-Maqdis* (Oxford Studies in Islamic Art 9), Oxford: Oxford University Press, 11–57.

Kirchner, H. 2009. Original design, tribal management and modifications in Medieval hydraulic systems in the Balearic Islands (Spain). *World Archaeology* 41.1: 151–68.

Klitzsch, E. and Baird, D.W. 1969. Stratigraphy and palaeohydrology of the Germa (Jarma) area southwest Libya. In W.H. Kanes (ed.), *Geology, Archaeology and Prehistory of the Southwestern Fezzan, Libya* (Petroleum Exploration Society of Libya, eleventh annual field conference 1969), Tripoli: Petroleum Exploration Society of Libya, 67–80.

Kobori, I. 1989. Comparative studies on the formation of qanat water system – Pt. I. *The Bulletin of the Institute of Social Sciences, Meiji University* 12.1: 1–40.

Lambton, A.K.S. 1989. The origin, diffusion and functioning of the qanat. In Beaumont 1989, 5–12.

Laureano, P. 1991. *Sahara: Jardin méconnu*. Paris: Larousse.

Lethielleux, J. 1948. *Le Fezzan: Ses jardins, ses palmiers. Notes d'ethnographie et d'histoire*. Tunis: Institut des Belles Lettres Arabes.

Levtzion, N. and Hopkins, J.F.P. (eds) 2001. *Corpus of Early Arabic Sources for West African History*. Cambridge: Cambridge University Press.

Lightfoot, D.R. 1996. Moroccan khettara: Traditional irrigation and progressive desiccation. *Geoforum* 27.2: 261–73.

Lightfoot, D.R. and Miller, J.A. 1996. Sijilmassa: The rise and fall of a walled oasis in Medieval Morocco. *Annals of the Association of American Geographers* 86.1: 78–101.

Liverani, M. 2000. The Libyan caravan road in Herodotus IV.181–184. *Journal of the Economic and Social History of the Orient* 43.4: 496–520.

Lô, Capitaine 1953/1954. Les foggaras du Tidikelt. *Travaux de l'Institut de Recherches Sahariennes* 10: 139–79; 11: 49–77.

Mahdane, M., Lanau, S., Ruf, Th. and Valony, M.-J. 2011. La gestion des galeries drainantes (khettaras) dans l'oasis de Skoura, Maroc. In T. Dahou, M. Elloumi, F. Molle, M. Gassab and B. Romagny (eds), *Pouvoirs, sociétés et nature au Sud de la Méditerranée*, Paris: Karthala, 209–31.

Malouta, M. and Wilson, A.I. 2013. Mechanical irrigation: Water-lifting devices in the archaeological evidence and in the Egyptian papyri. In A. Bowman and A. Wilson (eds), *The Roman Agricultural Economy: Organization, Investment, and Production* (Oxford Studies on the Roman Economy), Oxford: Oxford University Press, 273–305.

Margat, J. 1961. *Carte Hydrogéologique au 1/50000 de la Plaine du Tafilalt*. Rabat: Notes et Mémoires du Service Géologique, Service Géologique du Maroc.

Martel, A. 1965. *Les confins Saharo-Tripolitains de la Tunisie (1881–1911)*. 2 vols. Paris: Presses Universitaires de France.

Martin, A.G.P. 1908. *Les oasis sahariennes (Gourara – Touat – Tidikelt)*. Alger: Imprimerie Algérienne.

Mattingly, D.J. 1996. Olive presses in Roman Africa: Technical evolution or stagnation? *L'Africa romana* 11: 577–95.

Mattingly, D.J. (ed.) 2003. *The Archaeology of Fazzan. Volume 1, Synthesis*. London: Society for Libyan Studies, Department of Antiquities.

Mattingly, D.J. 2006. The Garamantes: The first Libyan state. In Mattingly *et al.* 2006: 189–204.

Mattingly, D.J. (ed.) 2007. *The Archaeology of Fazzan. Volume 2, Site Gazetteer, Pottery and other Survey Finds*. London: Society for Libyan Studies, Department of Antiquities.

Mattingly, D.J. (ed.) 2010. *The Archaeology of Fazzan. Volume 3, Excavations carried out by C.M. Daniels*. London: Society for Libyan Studies, Department of Antiquities.

Mattingly, D.J. 2011. The Garamantes of Fazzan: An early Libyan state with Trans-Saharan connections. In A. Dowler and E.R. Galvin (eds), *Money, Trade and Trade Routes in Pre-Islamic North Africa* (British Museum Research Publications 176), London: British Museum, 49–60.

Mattingly, D.J. (ed.) 2013. *The Archaeology of Fazzan. Volume 4, Survey and Excavations at Old Jarma (Ancient Garama) carried out by C.M. Daniels (1962–69) and the Fazzan Project (1997–2001)*. London: Society for Libyan Studies, Department of Antiquities.

Mattingly, D.J. and Sterry, M.S. 2010. *Ghadames Archaeological Survey. Phase 1 Desk-top Report*. Unpublished consultancy report produced for Libyan Department of Antiquities, Ghadames Development Authority and BP.

Mattingly, D.J. and Wilson, A.I. 2004. Farming the Sahara: The Garamantian contribution in southern Libya. In M. Liverani (ed.), *Arid Lands at the Time of the Roman Empire*, Firenze: All'Insegna del Giglio, 39–52.

Mattingly, D.J., McLaren, S., Savage, E., al-Fasatwi, Y. and Gadgood, K. (eds) 2006. *The Libyan Desert: Natural Resources and Cultural Heritage*. London: Society for Libyan Studies.

Mattingly, D., Sterry, M. and Edwards, D. 2015. The origins and development of Zuwila, Libyan Sahara: An archaeological and historical overview of an ancient oasis town and caravan centre. *Azania* 50.1: 27–75.

Mattingly, D.J., Leitch, V., Duckworth, C.N., Cuenod, A., Sterry, M. and Cole, F. (eds) 2017. *Trade in the Ancient Sahara and Beyond*. Trans-Saharan Archaeology, Volume 1. Series editor D.J. Mattingly. Cambridge: Cambridge University Press and the Society for Libyan Studies.

Mattingly, D.J., Sterry, M., al-Haddad, M. and Bokbot, Y. 2018. Beyond the Garamantes: The early development of Saharan oases. In Purdue *et al.* 2018a, 205–28.

Megdiche, F. and Moussa, M. 2014. The qanat as crucial antique water acquisition system common to arid zones' communities: Two case studies, foggaras in Tunisia and afalaj in Oman. *Research Journal of Social Science and Management* 3.12. www .theinternationaljournal.org/ojs/index.php?journal=tij&page=article&op=view& path%5B%5D=2864.

Merlo, S., Hakenbeck, S. and Balbo, A.L. 2013. Desert Migrations Project XVIII: The archaeology of the northern Fazzan. A preliminary report. *Libyan Studies* 44: 141–61.

Mirti, T.H., Wallender, W.W., Chancellor, W.J. and Grismer, M.E. 1999. Performance characteristics of the shaduf: A manual water-lifting device. *Applied Engineering in Agriculture* 15.3: 225–31.

Moreau, P. 1947. Des lacs de sel au chaos de sable: Le pays des Nefzaouas. *IBLA. Revue de l'Institut des Belles Lettres Arabes* 10.37: 19–47.

Nachtigal, G. 1974. *Sahara and Sudan: Tripoli and Fezzan, Tibesti or Tu* (translation and notes by A.G.B. Fisher and H.J. Fisher). London: Hurst.

Nesson, C. 1965. Structures agraire et evolution sociale dans les oasis de l'Oued Righ. *Travaux de l'Institut de Recherches Sahariennes* 24: 85–127.

Oleson, J.P. 1984. *Greek and Roman Mechanical Water-Lifting Devices: The History of a Technology*. Toronto: University of Toronto Press.

Oleson, J.P. 2000. Water-lifting. In Ö. Wikander (ed.), *Handbook of Ancient Water Technology* (Technology and Change in History 2), Leiden: Brill, 207–302.

Ouhssain, M. 2004. Système d'irrigation traditionnelle par khettaras dans le sud est Marocain fonctionnement et role dans la sauvegarde de la vie dans les oasis. *Homme Terre et Eaux* 129: 8–10.

Pantalacci, L. and Denoix, S. 2008. Travaux de l'Institut français d'archéologie orientale en 2007–2008. *Bulletin de l'Institut Français d'Archéologie Orientale* 108: 371–521.

Popp, H. 1986. L'agriculture irriguée dans la vallée du Souss. Formes et conflits d'utilisation de l'eau. *Méditerranée* 59: 33–47.

Popp, H. 1990. Oasenwirtschaft in den Maghrebländern: Zur Revision des Forschungsstandes in der Bundesrepublik (Oasis Economy in the Maghrib Countries). *Erdkunde* 44.2: 81–92.

Purdue, L., Charbonnier, J. and Khalidi, L. (eds) 2018. *Des refuges aux oasis: Vivre en milieu aride de la Préhistoire à aujourd'hui. XXXVIIIe rencontres internationales d'archéologie et d'histoire d'Antibes*, Antibes: Éditions APDCA.

Rayne, L., Sheldrick, N. and Nikolaus, J. 2017. Endangered archaeology in Libya: Recording damage and destruction. *Libyan Studies* 48: 23–49.

Reale Società Geographica Italiana (ed.) 1937. *Il Sahara Italiano: Fezzan e oasi di Gat*. Rome: Società italiana arti grafiche.

Remini, B. and Achour, B. 2013a. The foggaras of In Salah (Algeria): The forgotten heritage. *Larhyss Journal* 15: 85–95.

Remini, B. and Achour, B. 2013b. Les foggaras de l'Ahaggar: disparition d'un patrimoine hydraulique. *Larhyss Journal* 14: 149–59.

Remini, B., Achour, B. and Kechad, R. 2010. Les types de foggaras en Algérie. *Revue Sciences de l'eau (Canada-France)* 25.4: 293–306.

Remini, B., Rezoug, C. and Achour, B. 2014. The foggara of Kenadsa (Algeria). *Larhyss Journal* 18: 93–105.

Renault, J. 1912. Les bassins du trik Dar-Saniat à Carthage. *Revue Tunisienne* 19.95: 471–98.

Riser, J. 1996. Dra. In G. Camps (ed.), *Encyclopédie Berbère 17: Douiret-Eropaei*, Aix-en-Provence: Edisud, 2537–41.

Sanlaville, P. 1957. Les centres de cultures de l'Ahaggar. *Revue de Géographie de Lyon* 32.4: 333–41.

Savornin, J. 1947. Le plus grand appareil hydraulique du Sahara (nappe artésian dite de l'Albia). *Travaux de l'Institut de Recherches Sahariennes* 4: 25–66.

Savornin, J. 1950. Le Bas Sahara (l'appareil artésian le plus simple du Sahara). *Travaux de l'Institut de Recherches Sahariennes* 6: 45–62.

Scarin, E. 1934. *Le oasi del Fezzan*. 2 vols. Bologna: Zanichelli.

Scarin, E. 1937. Descrizione delle oasi e gruppi di oasi. In Reale Società Geographica Italiana 1937: 603–44.

Scarin, E. 1938. *La Giofra e Zella (le oasi del 29 parallelo della Libia occidentale)*. Firenze: Sansoni.

Schacht, I. 2003. A preliminary survey of the ancient qanat systems of the northern Kharga Oasis. *Mitteilungen des Deutschen Archäologischen Instituts Abteilung Kairo* 59: 411–23.

Scheele, J. 2010. Traders, saints and irrigation: reflections on Saharan connectivity. *Journal of African History* 51.3: 281–300.

Scheele, J. 2017. The need for nomads. Camel-herding, raiding and Saharan trade and settlement. In Mattingly *et al.* 2017, 55–79.

Sterry, M. and Mattingly, D.J. (eds) 2020. *Urbanisation and State Formation in the Ancient Sahara and Beyond*, Trans-Saharan Archaeology, Volume 3, series editor D.J. Mattingly, Cambridge: Cambridge University Press and the Society for Libyan Studies.

Sterry, M. and Mattingly, D.J. 2013. Desert Migrations Project XVII: Further AMS dates for historic settlements from Fazzan, South-West Libya. *Libyan Studies* 44: 127–40.

Sterry, M., Mattingly, D., Ahmed, M., Savage, T., White, K. and Wilson, A.I. 2011. DMP XIII: Reconnaissance survey of archaeological sites in the Murzuq area. *Libyan Studies* 42: 103–16.

Sterry, M., Mattingly, D.J. and Higham, T. 2012. Desert Migrations Project XVI: Radiocarbon dates from the Murzuq region, Southern Libya. *Libyan Studies* 43: 137–47.

Sterry, M., Mattingly, D.J. and Wilson, A.I. Forthcoming. Foggaras and the Garamantes: Hydraulic landscapes in the Central Sahara. In S. Rost (ed.), *Irrigation in Early States: New Directions*. Chicago: The Oriental Institute of the University of Chicago.

Suter, K. 1962. Über Queltöpfe, Quellhügel und Wasserstollen des Nefzaoua (Südtunesien). *Vierteljahrsschrift der Naturforschenden Gesellschaft in Zürich* 107: 49–64.

Thiry, J. 1995. *Le Sahara Libyen dans l'Afrique du Nord Médiévale*. Orientalia Lovaniensia Analecta 72. Leuven: Peeters, Departement Oosterse Studies.

Trousset, P. 1986. Les oasis présahariennes dans l'antiquité: Partage de l'eau et division du temps. *Antiquités Africaines* 22: 161–91.

Van der Veen, M. and Westley, B. 2010. Palaeoeconomic studies. In Mattingly 2010, 488–522.

Voinot, L. 1909. *Le Tidikelt: Etude sur la géographie, l'histoire, les moeurs du pays*. Oran: Editions Jacques Gandini.

Walpole, G.F. 1932. *An Ancient Subterranean Aqueduct West of Matruh. Survey of Egypt* 42. London: Ministry of Finance.

Ward, P. 1968. *Touring Libya. The Southern Provinces*. London: Faber.

Wilson, A.I. 2002. Machines, power and the ancient economy. *Journal of Roman Studies* 92: 1–32.

Wilson, A.I. 2003. Classical water technology in the Early Islamic world. In C. Bruun and A. Saastamoinen (eds), *Technology, Ideology, Water: From Frontinus to the Renaissance and Beyond*, Roma: Institutum Romanum Finlandiae, 115–41.

Wilson, A.I. 2005. Foggara irrigation, early state formation and Saharan trade: The Garamantes of Fazzan. *Schriftenreihe der Frontinus-Gesellschaft* 26: 223–34.

Wilson, A.I. 2006. The spread of foggara-based irrigation in the ancient Sahara. In Mattingly *et al.* 2006, 205–16.

Wilson, A.I. 2009. Foggaras in ancient North Africa: Or how to marry a Berber Princess. In V. Bridoux (ed.), *Contrôle et distribution de l'eau dans le Maghreb antique et médiéval*, Rome: École française de Rome, 19–39.

Wilson, A.I. 2012. Saharan trade: Short-, medium- and long-distance trade networks in the Roman period. *Azania: Archaeological Research in Africa* 47.4: 409–49.

Wilson, A.I. and Mattingly, D.J. 2003. Irrigation technologies: Foggaras, wells and field systems. In Mattingly 2003, 234–78.

Wuttmann, M. 2001. Les qanats de ʾAyn-Manâwîr. In Briant 2001, 109–35.

Wuttmann, M., Barakat, H., Bousquet, B., Chauveau, M., Gonon, T., Marchand, S., Robin, M. and Schweitzer, A. 1998. ʿAyn Manawir (oasis de Kharga): Deuxième rapport préliminaire. *Bulletin de l'Institut Français d'Archéologie Orientale* 98: 367–462.

Wuttmann, M., Gonon, T. and Thiers, C. 2000. The qanats of ʿAyn-Manâwîr (Kharga Oasis, Egypt). *Journal of Achaemenid Studies and Researches* 1. https://halshs.archives-ouvertes.fr/halshs-02051616/file/The_Qanats_of_Ayn_Manawir_Kharga_Oasis_E.pdf.

4 | Crafts in Roman North Africa

Technical Transfer and Permanence through
Grain Mills and Fullonicae

TOUATIA AMRAOUI

Introduction

Since the second half of the twentieth century, various general and specific studies have been devoted to describing and analysing Roman workshops, products and tools found in North Africa. Some of these were uncovered in recent stratigraphic excavations, but the majority were discovered during the nineteenth century or the first half of the twentieth century. Even if ancient craft facilities were difficult to identify unequivocally by our predecessors because they knew little about them, the size and characteristic features of these discoveries were sufficiently original and specific to be mentioned in excavation reports.

However, the available documentation on different production activities is very unequal; there are many differences depending on the type of craft, the region, the chronological context and so forth. First of all, we can observe that some crafts are much better represented in studies than others. We have many attestations of 'olive oil' presses[1] found in cities but especially in the countryside during surveys in Tunisia and Algeria.[2] Pottery production is mentioned in many studies because of the ubiquitous nature of this material and its importance in dating and understanding economic relationships, but these are mainly concerned with Tunisian production.[3] Following the study of Ponsich and Tarradell on the Moroccan and Spanish coasts in the 1960s, research on the fish salting and purple industries has advanced in Tunisia and Libya, and more recently in Algeria.[4] General and specific studies have

---

[1] Recent studies, mostly the works of J.-P. Brun, have shown that an important number of the presses found in North Africa were in fact used to produce wine (see Brun 2003).

[2] Leveau 1984; Mattingly and Hitchner 1993; Sehili 2009.

[3] Ben Moussa 2007; Bonifay 2004; Salomonson 1968.

[4] For Tunisia: Fentress *et al.* 2009; Slim *et al.* 2004; for Libya: Tébar Megias and Wilson 2008; for Algeria: Amraoui 2014 and Amraoui Forthcoming.

also focused on other types of crafts such as textile and glass production.[5]
Nonetheless, the archaeological information available is rarely sufficient to
understand fully the functioning of the workshops and their evolution, or to
establish typo-chronologies of the products.

The archaeologist is faced with a double imbalance. First, workshops
and technology in North Africa are often known very superficially.
Concerning pottery production, for instance, one can observe that not
a single workshop has been studied in its entirety: the different discoveries
or studies always focused on kilns or tools, but rarely on other parts of the
workshop. Second, in Africa the lack of overall research into crafts usually
leads authors of economic syntheses to focus upon the finished products,
such as the mosaics or the vessels.

As a specialist in the study of ancient crafts, my main goal is to understand
and restore craft praxis from North African archaeological discoveries, and
more specifically from urban Algerian sites (Fig. 4.1). I have gathered data
concerning discoveries of tools and workshops of various kind of activities.[6]
All in all, I have identified 135 workshops in Algeria. Given the relative lack
of field data, the documentation I have assembled for workshop remains,
including plans, drawings and photographs, forms a new basis on which to
study more precisely the characteristics of the workshops, their spatial
organisation and the typology of the tools employed in each craft process.
Conducted with the aim of dating and understanding the functioning of the
productive process, this new analysis was based mainly on discoveries and
work carried out in other regions of the Roman world, in which the research
is much more developed. Because of their remarkable state of conservation,
most of the best studied ancient workshops are located in Italy, at Pompeii,
Herculaneum and Ostia.[7] At times, however, ethnographic studies developed for other historical periods that describe traditional practices have also
been very useful for the understanding of ancient remains.[8]

The results of this research are numerous: they lead to reflections on
historiography, technical functioning, production, scales of production
and economic systems. For the purposes of the present volume, I focus
on two aspects of technical characteristics, the value of which has become
increasingly apparent as my study has progressed. These are the adoption
and the diffusion of Roman technology in African provinces, and the
permanence of local African *savoir faire*.

---

[5] For textiles: Johannesen 1954; Wilson 2001; Wilson 2002. For glass: Foy 2003.
[6] Amraoui 2017.   [7] Borgard 2002; Botte 2009; Flohr 2013; Monteix 2010.
[8] See below, section on the cage of the *fullo*.

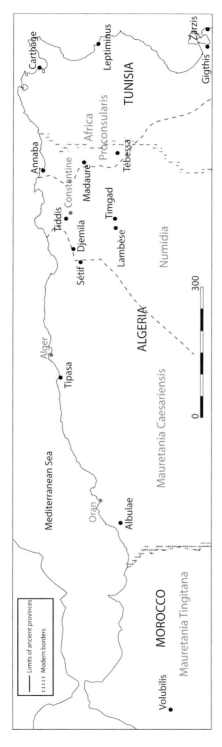

Figure 4.1 Map of the main sites discussed (ancient borders relate to the third century) (T. Amraoui).

A hugely important diversity in production activities, down to the individual stages of production, has been identified in Algeria and neighbouring countries: presenting the whole story would be impossible in a short contribution. Instead, this chapter is a good opportunity to concentrate on those crafts that are less frequently discussed in publications. The baking and textile industries presented are perfect examples of the combination of Roman techniques with African *savoir faire*. Indeed, through the description of their technological aspects, I shall discuss their origins as well as their influences and adaptations.

Examples of Food Production Technology: Ancient Bakeries and Grain Mills

The processing of wheat into flour and the baking of bread have been little discussed for Roman Africa, with the exception of M. Leduc's recent study of the bakeries of Volubilis,[9] and a few isolated studies for other areas of the Maghreb.[10] It is important to recall that three steps are necessary in the readying of bread for consumption. These are: grain milling, preparation of the dough and baking. Based on the archaeological remains of the Vesuvian cities, it is possible to distinguish these activities by the location of the specific equipment and facilities. Thus, in plan, the basic Roman bakery or *pistrinum* should contain one or more grain mills and mechanical dough mixers, and an oven, with specific workstations arranged in different parts of the workshop.[11]

During my investigation, I found that only a few bakeries have been clearly identified in Algeria. This state of affairs can partly be explained by the fact that the tools were not identified by our predecessors and therefore are rarely mentioned in the publications, but it is also due to stone equipment found during old excavations often having being subsequently moved and displayed in lapidary deposits or archaeological gardens (Fig. 4.2). At several sites, I observed numerous grain mills and mechanical mixers that were totally decontextualised; unfortunately, as their provenance is unknown it is

---

[9] For example: Leduc 2008.

[10] Lake El Biben area and Gighti (Drine 2001); *Leptiminus* (Stone *et al.* 2011, 485–92); or the hinterland of Dougga and Annaba surveyed by M. De Vos (De Vos 2000).

[11] As we can see for example in Herculanum in the Insula Orientalis II^a (Monteix 2010, 409, fig. 226) or Ostia (Bakker 1999, 18, fig. 8a). In Antiquity, baking workshops are often *pistrina*, but there is also some evidence of places where the grain milling step was not present in bakeries where only dough preparation and baking took place. In this chapter I focus on the facilities of the *pistrinum*.

Figure 4.2 A lapidary deposit in Timgad where different kinds of stone objects, mostly grain mills, were moved and stored after their discovery (T. Amraoui).

impossible to determine if they originally belonged to workshops or domestic contexts.

Currently, only three or four urban bakeries (*pistrina*) have been identified, mostly in Djemila, ancient Cuicul.[12] Generally, they occupied one to three rooms; their commercial status is marked by an opening onto the street. As an example, the workshop of the so-called 'Maison orientale' in the eastern *intra muros* area was located in three rooms, 7 to 9 in the southern part of the house (Fig. 4.3). The remains are much damaged today, but the report published by Allais indicates that equipment found in room 7 consisted of a grain mill, a mechanical mixer, a terracotta jar that could have been used to store grain and perhaps an oven, which was discovered already destroyed.[13] The presence of a mechanical mixer as well as a large opening towards the street through rooms 8 and 9 could lead us to assume that these were the remains of a commercial bakery, rather than domestic equipment.

---

[12] In North Africa, bakeries are not well known; some have been found in Morocco, in Volubilis (Leduc 2008); for Tunisia, one published example was discovered at Gightis (Drine 2001).

[13] Allais 1954, 352. She also mentions water supply facilities in room 8.

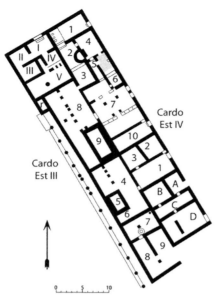

Figure 4.3 The 'Maison orientale', Djemila. The *pistrinum* occupied rooms 7 to 9 in the southern part of the house (T. Amraoui after Allais 1954).

Obviously, it is difficult to discuss local technical characteristics from the sparse evidence of bakeries without focusing on the stone equipment, specifically grain mills. Contrary to other remains, there are enough examples of these: more than 60 complete mills found in Algeria, plus those published for Tunisia, Morocco and Libya.

Appearance and Evolution of the Classical Roman Grain Mill: The 'Pompeian Type'

The Classical Roman grain mill, usually called the 'Pompeian' grain mill, was the main form used in the Mediterranean provinces of the Empire. It is composed of a fixed conical millstone, the *meta*, and a mobile one with an hourglass shape called the *catillus*, which fits on to the first (see Figs 4.4a and 4.6a).

Generally, the main studies of grain mills – which especially concern discoveries in Italy at Ostia, Pompeii and Herculaneum – focus on the *molae asinariae*. As their name indicates, it is assumed that they were all activated by equidae.[14] However, in reality two sizes were developed by the Romans:

---

[14] It is also attested through ancient texts and archaeology (Monteix 2010, 139–41); in the *pistrinum* IX 12, 6 of Herculanum, the bones of seven equidae were found.

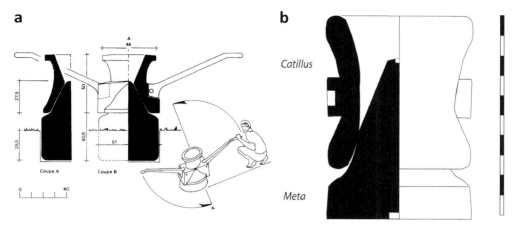

Figure 4.4 (a) Byrsa Punic grain mill type (Amouretti 1986, pl. 24a); (b) African Roman grain mill Type 1 (T. Amraoui).

the large model or 'meules à sang' (animal mills) adapted to equidae – and probably turned by human labour too[15] – and a smaller one, similar to the dimensions of pre-Roman types operated only by people.

Indeed, the Pompeian grain mill type resulted from an evolution of a 'pre-Pompeian type' that seems to have appeared around the third century BC following various discoveries. These models featured a *catillus* and a *meta* measuring 0.50 and 0.65 m respectively (Fig. 4.4a). According to Amouretti, this semi-alternative mill was manipulated by human power.[16] She argued that the Carthaginian world played a significant role in the stages of experimentation and improvement of the rotary mill. Indeed, following the discovery of a fragment of *catillus* type C1 in Lattara (France), dated to the first century BC and belonging to a 'meule à bras' (hand mill), Py has also pointed out that this kind of grain mill was elaborated little by little in the Punic world (Motyé, Morgantina, Byrsa/Carthage). In this light, the Pompeian-type grain mill was a technical evolution of the Byrsa or Morgantina type which was adopted in Republican Italy around the beginning of the second century BC. It was then perfected by the Romans, particularly with the invention of the *anille*, a piece of metal that permitted adjustment of the height and the pressure of the *meta* on the *catillus*.[17] These technical changes enabled a complete rotation, contrary to the Punic model which was only semi-rotary.

In North Africa, the majority of the identified grain mills or *molae* seems to belong to the Classical form known as the Pompeian grain mill; in this

---

[15] Amouretti 1986, 146; Monteix 2010, 140 (*contra* Moritz 1958, 97–102). See below.
[16] Amouretti 1986, 245.   [17] Py 1992, 213.

study they are referred to as 'Type 1'[18] (Fig. 4.4b). However, even though this typology has been qualified as Pompeian in some studies,[19] it appears that grain mills found in Algeria and Tunisia differ from Italian examples in three main respects: shape, raw material choice and dimensions.

Shape of African Roman Grain Mills

While the *metae* of African grain mills are very similar in shape, a more precise study of the typology of the African Roman grain mills allows us to distinguish two different profiles for the *catilli:* Types 1a and 1b. The majority of the *catilli* belong to Type 1a; they present the shape of an hourglass which is quite well defined inside and out, although there can be some variations in the general review of the outside 'ears' depending certainly on the dexterity of the stone-mason rather than on chronological differences. Type 1b, well represented by two examples found in Albulae (western Algeria), is much less Classical than Type 1a (Fig. 4.5). The hourglass shape of the *catilli* is barely marked, especially on the outside, and their 'ears' are hardly projecting; thus, this upper part of the grain mill looks like a cylindrical barrel. This particular morphology raises the question of the location where these objects were manufactured: were they imported or made locally?

Raw Materials: The Choice of the Stone

In the Gulf of Naples, as in Gaul (e.g. at Lyon),[20] and also at certain African sites such as Leptiminus[21] and Cyrene,[22] grain mills were mostly made of basalt. Yet in Algeria, my field observations demonstrate that there were only a few made of volcanic stone. The main parts of *catilli* and *metae* were made from regionally available stones, generally the same that were used to build local cities.[23] At Tebessa (Fig. 4.6b) and Madaure, the few examples

---

[18] Some sites also present small-format manual mills that can be referred to as 'Type 2'. However, because of their size and their technical specifications they can only be considered as domestic tools. Moreover, as we have only a small number of examples and little information about their context of discovery, they will not be further discussed here.

[19] Akerraz and Lenoir 2002, 198; De Vos 2000; Leduc 2008, 482.

[20] From examples exhibited at the *Musée gallo-romain de Fourvière* of Lyon.

[21] Stone *et al.* 2011, 485–87, table 19.1.   [22] Riley 1980.

[23] For now, it is impossible to determine precisely which local quarry was used because there is no new research in this domain and no petrographic analysis.

Type 1a

Timgad

Tiddis

Type 1b

Albulae
(Demaeght et Doumergue 1932, fig. 9)

Timgad

Figure 4.5 Grain mill Types 1a and 1b, and some variations in local stones (T. Amraoui).

present in the museum gardens or visible on the sites seem to be cut in the local sandstone. At Tiddis, with the exception of one *meta* of sandstone, the three others visible at the site were made from the grey limestone peculiar to the region. At Djemila, one *meta* found in a little bakery located on the *cardo maximus* was made of puddingstone; it is not yet possible to determine whether it is a local stone. In any case, for the examples found at

Tiddis, Madaure, Tebessa and also Annaba,[24] we can hardly doubt the local nature of their production.

In a large sample group from Timgad, only two of the 44 *catilli* and three of the 43 *metae* were cut in a volcanic stone, and in any case this was different to the Italian basalts. De Vos, who has also observed the presence of some grain mills made of basalt during her surveys around Annaba and Dougga, supposed that they were imported. Without petrographic analyses, however, we are not able to precisely determine their provenance. In the *Catalogue raisonné des objets archéologiques du musée de la ville d'Oran*, the authors indicate the presence of two complete grain mills of Type 1b produced with 'the basalt of the country'; they were found at Albulae, present-day Aïn Temouchent (north of Tlemcen) (Fig. 4.5). Geological studies confirm the presence of basalt in the hinterland of this city, but also in other areas as close as Nemours (present-day Ghazaouet). They also indicate the existence of this rock elsewhere on the Algerian coast, at Dellys in Grande Kabylie.[25] However, the presence of basalt quarries in diverse regions of Mauretania Caesariensis does not prove that they all served to produce the grain mills found in Algeria, because there was also an active Mediterranean sea-borne trade in mills.[26] Volcanic stone milling equipment found in harbour cities such as Annaba, Cyrene and Leptiminus indicate the existence of trade and economic links with other provinces, mainly Italy as confirmed by petrographic analysis.[27] But these objects could also travel within Africa and reach more inland regions: recent research has identified at Djemila a grain mill produced with the basalt of Orvieto (Italy).[28]

To sum up, a great part of the grain mills discovered at North African sites clearly belong to local production. This probably reflects ease of supply and the lower cost of local materials. The general use of stones that were not volcanic in origin, along with the good condition of the local grain mills, could indicate that they resisted sufficiently the wear caused by the friction of the *catillus* on the *meta*, and that the flour quality was not too bad: in other words, they 'did the job'. But, where available, volcanic stones were certainly employed. At Volubilis, the grain mills seem to have been exclusively made in basalt which was probably of local provenance.[29] This conclusion regarding local mill production is not specific to North Africa:

---

[24] A photograph in Delestre 2005 shows a Type 1 grain mill made in limestone similar to the blocks used to build local walls.

[25] Peron 1883, 8, 178.

[26] Stone wrote that analyses on some grain mills made of volcanic stones found in North Africa showed different geographical origins; stones came in particular from Sardinia, Sicily and the western part of Libya (Stone *et al.* 2011, 486).

[27] Riley 1980; Stone *et al.* 2011.   [28] Antonelli and Lazzarini 2010, 2084.   [29] Leduc 2008, 482.

a   b

Figure 4.6 (a) *Mola asinaria* in a *pistrinum* at Pompeii (D. Mattingly); (b) grain mill Type 1 (Tebessa). (T. Amraoui).

recent research in Gaul indicates a regional production of grain mills there too, with sandstones coming from quarries typically located within a 40 to 130 km radius around consumption sites.[30]

The examples of volcanic stone equipment are still few in number, and it is necessary to carry out new fieldwork in North Africa and also more petrographic analysis in order to distinguish local from imported products, to better define their geographical distribution and to understand the commercial links between the different regions of the western Mediterranean Sea.

Dimensions

The third major difference between the Pompeian mill type and the African Type 1 concerns their dimensions. As seen above, grain mills found in Campanian cities and in Ostia could be very large;[31] their main part measuring over 1.50 m high (Fig. 4.6a) and sometimes more when the *meta* rested on a masonry base. Those *molae asinariae* – or donkey mills – were most likely activated by equidae (donkeys or horses).[32]

In Algeria and Tunisia, grain mills are smaller. They generally had a height between 0.80 and 1.20 m, and the majority of complete examples do not exceed 1 m in height (Figs 4.4b and 4.6b). What can we conclude

---

[30] Jaccottey and Longepierre 2011, 103.   [31] See Bakker 1999.
[32] Amouretti 1986, 144; Bakker 1999, 5, fig. 1; Monteix 2010, 137–42.

about the use of African Type 1? Were they activated by donkey? With an average height of 0.70 cm, it appears improbable that they were turned by a 1–1.20 m high adult donkey.

The *mola* of Tebessa proves that this kind of mill must have been human-operated (Fig. 4.6b) because even if some grain mills were elevated by setting them on a masonry base, their height would have been insufficient to connect them to a donkey. Moreover, in the bakeries found the rooms with mills do not have any trace of pavement. This problem is not peculiar to Africa as there are also small grain mills in Italy and Gaul. Whereas Moritz argued that this kind of small mill functioned with donkeys,[33] for Amouretti they could only be operated by people.[34] Monteix specifies that the possibility of using human power must be considered for some small grain mills copying the form of *molae asinariae* and found in a limited number of cases in Pompeii. Moreover, I think this option must also be considered for some of the largest examples discovered in Pompeii, because in some bakeries mills and walls are very close together and the floor unpaved. In those cases the work was almost certainly supplied by human labour.[35]

To date, I have not found evidence of *molae asinariae* (donkey mills) in Algeria: they were not as widely used here as they had been on the northern shores of the West Mediterranean. The typology of local examples tends to confirm that the most common and widespread model is the 'moulin à bras' (hand mill).[36] In Roman Africa, the use of human labour could have followed an established local habit, but it might also reflect different production needs to those of Italian cities.

Characteristics of Grain Mills and Transfer of Technology in Africa

The study of the grain-milling technology in Africa prompts several tentative conclusions. First of all, there was obviously some standardisation of the production of these tools, and we can surmise some continuity in the use of the small grain mill from the pre-Roman to the Roman period. Despite this traditional aspect, however, the examples discovered also demonstrate that the Type 1 mill moved in tandem with Roman technical evolutions as it presents both the '*anille*' and the *catillus* shape of the Italian grain mills. Contextualised discoveries show that this small model was used both in domestic and commercial contexts and that the few identified

---

[33] Moritz 1958, 97–102.   [34] Amouretti 1986, 144.   [35] Monteix 2010, 140–42, fig. 67.
[36] Except maybe for the rare copies presenting a height of 1.2 m, but their size remains modest.

bakeries were small production units. At the moment, in Africa, there is no evidence of large units of production such as the big *pistrina* found in Italy. Consequently, production needs seem to have been different in Africa, where modest units with small grain mills may have been sufficient in middle-sized cities. This urban production was likely aimed at responding to the demand of inhabitants who did not possess a domestic grain mill and other facilities to make bread at home. Further research needs to be done in larger African cities such as Carthage, Cherchel or Lambese in order to determine if there were big grain mills and *pistrina* to answer to the needs of a more numerous population, or if a different kind of supply, such as hydraulic grain mills, existed.[37]

Concerning its geographical repartition, the Type 1 mill was present throughout the North African territory from Annaba to Tebessa and from Mauretania Tingitana to Byzacena. In Volubilis, only a few examples were found, as in the local bakeries the more widespread model was the '*meule annulaire*' predominant not only at this site – at last 39 models were discovered – but also in Morocco, and present too in southern Spain.[38] In this particular case we can more easily argue that the evidence reveals some traditional or local pre-Roman habit.[39] This kind of grain mill was not used in the territory from western Algeria to Libya. What about eastern African provinces and the pre-Saharan or Saharan regions? At the moment it is difficult to answer this question properly because the available data are still limited. Some grain mills were discovered in coastal regions of Libya, especially in Cyrene or Tocra,[40] but this particular part of North Africa, along with the others, needs further research. For Algeria, the Roman grain mill is present in pre-desert areas north of the Roman frontier (*limes*). In the Hodna, I have observed several Roman grain mills at sites such as Zabi where the architecture was mostly mudbrick, but where presses and grain mills were cut in local or imported stones and belong to the Roman models found in northern Algeria. In other Saharan regions the influence of Roman technology seems weaker. At Saniat Jibril, excavations prove that between the first and the fourth century two kinds of mills where used: mostly the traditional saddle querns or grinders – or '*meules va-et-vient*' – with the appearance by the second century AD of rotary querns. At the

---

[37] Many archaeological attestations have already been listed in Wilson 1995.

[38] According to Akerraz and Lenoir 2002, 198: four *metae* and only two *catilli* were found in Volubilis whereas Leduc 2008, 482, N. 19 listed three *catilli* and no *meta*.

[39] On the pre-Roman development of the ring/'annulaire' form in both Morocco and Spain, see Alonso Martinez 2002.

[40] Riley 1980. A special thanks to Andrew Wilson and Ahmad Buzaian for giving me references concerning discoveries in Libya.

moment it seems that the Roman grain mill type was not present south of the *limes*. Even in recent times, in the Saharan regions we can observe that those same simple techniques of saddle querns and rotary querns were still the only ones attested for traditional grain milling[41] whereas in the northern regions only the rotary quern was still used traditionally among Berber populations like the Chaouias or the Kabyles.[42]

Textile Treatment and Typology of the African *Fullonicae*

Textile production and trade was evidently an important element of the ancient economy in North Africa, although the evidence remains elusive.[43] Textile production is composed of different steps that can be more or less studied through archaeological remains. Unfortunately, during early excavations the tools used in two important activities of the textile process – spinning and weaving – were lost for the greater part. In the Maghrib, museums do not present a lot of spindle whorls or loomweights in their collections, and, where present, mostly there is no indication of provenance or of chronological contexts. Nonetheless, from the few discoveries made in North Africa some general characteristics can be defined.

Concerning spinning, although the spindle whorls found in North Africa were sometimes made from bone, wood or even stone, the most widespread models were ceramic. Most of these were not purpose made in raw clay, however, but were cut from pottery sherds. This kind of reuse is attested in Algeria at Cuicul for example,[44] in Tunisia at Carthage,[45] in Libya at Benghazi[46] and in the oasis of Saniat Jibril.[47] It is difficult to date the introduction of this Mediterranean technique of spinning that may be anterior to the Roman conquest. It was widely adopted in North Africa, however, in coastal regions as well as in oases and according to ethnological studies it is still used nowadays in those same areas.

For weaving, the data are even poorer as this activity can be only attested with loomweights made of terracotta – or more rarely of stone – since the other components of the loom were made of wood.[48] They are very rare in Algeria's museums as well as in the other countries of the Maghreb, but an interesting discovery of some 54 loomweights at the oasis site of Saniat Jibril in Garamantian Fazzan attests to textile production in this region.

---

[41] See for example Gast 2010.   [42] See for example Gaudry 1928, 148–49.
[43] Bender Jørgensen 2017; Guédon 2017.   [44] Amraoui 2017.   [45] Hurst *et al.* 1984, 251.
[46] Tébar Megias and Wilson 2008, 50, 53, fig. 6.   [47] Mattingly 2010, 197, fig. 3.85.
[48] On traditional looms, see Bender Jørgensen 2017, 240–43.

Generally, in a Mediterranean context, the rarity of loomweights in the northern areas of Roman Africa could be partly explained by the appearance at the beginning of the empire of the vertical loom with two horizontal bars, which did not require weights.[49] With the example of Saniat Jibril, it appears that once adopted the same technique of weaving was used from a period yet to be defined, until at least the fourth century AD.

The Archaeology of the *Fullonicae* in Africa

To address the general problematic about both Roman technical transfer and local habits, I focus here on a very specific step of the process: the fulling. This is principally because of the large sample of well-conserved fulling workshops (*fullonicae*) found in Algeria. The role of the fullers (*fullones*) was twofold: they were in charge of giving the final treatment to materials that had just been woven, but they were also commissioned to wash old textiles to enhance their aspect with different kinds of 'detergents'. Each step of the work required proper facilities and tools: fulling stall with tubs, rinsing basins, a space to hang the clothes, a press, etc.[50] Thanks to the *fullonicae* discovered in Pompeii and Ostia, we know that the principal facilities that facilitate their identification are the fulling tubs, which are characteristic of the fuller's work.

In Algeria, at the present time, fulling is the most represented urban craft, mainly due to the good conservation of the remains. To date, I have identified with certainty 12 *fullonicae* in Timgad and 10 in Tiddis, located in southern and central Numidia respectively (Fig. 4.1). This is quite exceptional by comparison with the other African provinces: in Morocco or Libya there is as yet no evidence of *fullonicae*, and in Tunisia only a few small facilities have been identified at Thuburbo Majus.[51] Thanks to the documentation that I have gathered on old excavations and direct observation of extant elements, it is possible to summarise the typological characteristics of these *fullonicae* and to compare them with the 'classic' type of Italian examples. Yet it remains difficult to date the workshops: the chronological range is between the end of the third century and the fifth century AD.

The historiography of their discovery reveals some biases concerning their identification and interpretation.[52] The *fullonicae* found in Timgad were actually interpreted as dye-works by Ballu and Christofle,[53] but the

---

[49] See for example Forbes 1964, 202.   [50] Monteix 2010, 193–98.
[51] Ben Abed-Ben Khader 1987, 129–31, 133–34 and Plans 10 and 11; Wilson 2004, 157.
[52] Amraoui 2017, 241–42.   [53] Christofle 1935, 74.

characteristics of their facilities are far removed from those used to dye clothes. There were no heated vats for instance. Contrary to a common confusion, the *fullones* had no part in dyeing: they were charged simply with treating new textiles or washing old clothes; the dye process was handled by the *infector* and the *offector*.[54] The fulling tubs found at Tiddis were also misinterpreted by Berthier, who identified them as '*cuves de potiers*' (that is, as tubs used in the preparation of clay as part of pottery production), as some *fullonicae* were located near to kilns.[55] Yet, as demonstrated below, these discoveries correspond clearly to the equipment for fulling as we know it from ancient iconography or archaeological remains elsewhere.

The Typology of Fulling Facilities

The *fullonicae* generally featured 2–10 fulling tubs made of terracotta and inserted into the ground.[56] The 49 examples of tubs have a circular or oval shape, a diameter of between 0.70 and 0.97 m, and a depth of 0.50–0.70 m; most of them are bigger than the examples from Ostia (Fig. 4.7). Some examples from Tiddis are highly original because the inner side of the tub has mineral inclusions that look like grains of basalt. This abrasive surface probably served to wash the textile with more efficiency; for now, these are the only examples presenting such a technical characteristic in the Mediterranean region.

The surface around the tubs was paved with *opus testaceum*, *opus tesselatum* or *opus spicatum* – as at Tiddis – or simply covered with broken tile mortar, as at Timgad. They were surrounded by low walls that were either monolithic blocks of stone (Timgad) or built of small pieces of limestone (Tiddis). Contrary to Italian examples, in Algeria, and also in Tunisia at Thuburbo Majus,[57] the tubs are surrounded by walls on four sides, rather than simply three sides: these are not fulling 'stalls', but fulling 'compartments', generally disposed along the walls of the workshops (Fig. 4.7). This arrangement has not been described or observed in previous studies: neither in excavation reports, nor in later syntheses. It is present in all *fullonicae* of Timgad and Tiddis with the exception of some workshops in which the compartments are not preserved. Of the preserved partitions, the highest remaining ones measure 0.30–0.40 m.

---

[54] For further information, see Borgard 2002 from the example of Pompeii.

[55] Berthier 2000, 116–20.   [56] Some late and rare examples are in stone.

[57] Ben Abed-Ben Khader 1987.

Figure 4.7 *Fullonica* A1 (Tiddis), fulling compartments with tubs surrounded by *opus testaceum*. The tubs present mineral inclusions on the inner part (T. Amraoui).

This particular typology must have impacted upon working methods. Following the example of the Italian discoveries, it was supposed that all workers acted according to the same movements. To enact the essential *saltus fullonius*, the *fullo* was assumed to have worked while leaning on the two lateral low walls of the stall in order to reach enough force and pressure to wash the clothes with his or her feet (Fig. 4.8a–b). In this case, the low side walls had to be close enough to the tub to serve as support. In Numidia, however, the compartments are often rectangular and are larger than Italian stalls: I realised in the field that it would have been impossible for the workers to reach the two low side walls. However, it appears that the tub was always placed close to at least one of the partitions (Fig. 4.9). As a consequence, I suggest that the workers leant on only one side – which was rarely the one facing the main room (Figure 4.8c). I also realised that the height of one of the low walls was always adapted in order to be easily stepped over, to allow the worker to reach the tub.[58]

---

[58] For Thuburbo Majus, it is impossible to specify if they were similar because the partitions are destroyed, we cannot know their height, but they seem finer.

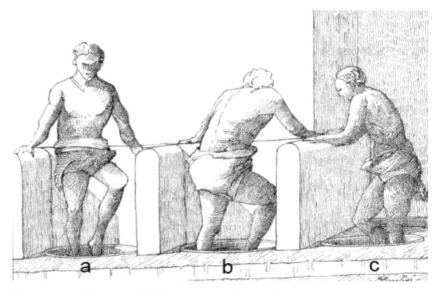

Figure 4.8 *Fullones* at work (after Pietrogrande 1976, fig. 26). Models (a) and (b) illustrate the double side support of the Pompeian or Ostian type. Model (c) represents a support of a single side, typical and systematic to Tiddis and to Timgad.

Figure 4.9 *Fullonica* of Insula 30 (Timgad), the well surrounded with low walls in the middle, and around it the other compartments containing tubs. Notice that the floor of the workshop – visible on the left – is paved with limestone (T. Amraoui).

Water Supply of the *Fullonicae*

Water was the main resource used in a *fullonica*; the proper functioning of workshops depended on its supply.[59] Each the two case study sites reveals evidence for its own particular supply system. At Timgad, the majority of the *fullonicae* had their own well; they were generally circular in shape, built in sandstone rubble and surrounded by a rectangular edge. They were usually placed in the centre of the room: it is assumed that they were a primary element of construction and that the workshop's layout and facilities were designed around that basic equipment.

Moreover, most of the wells in Timgad's *fullonicae* were surrounded by monolithic blocks like the tub compartments while those of domestic spaces were not (Figs 4.9 and 4.11). The most probable explanation for this is that clean well water had to be preserved from infiltration and splashes coming from the compartments as the detergents used could pollute them. Also, due to their height we can presume that the partitions helped to keep the workers safe from the well. These hypotheses are confirmed by the existence of some workshops in which the tubs were more distant from the wells, as in these cases there were no protecting walls. Only 3 of the 12 *fullonicae* identified did not have a well; they were probably supplied by cisterns.

At Tiddis, the situation was quite different from Timgad as there were no wells at the site due to its elevated topography. The only water-supplying system available in Tiddis seems to have been cisterns. Most of them appear to be part of domestic spaces but there are also some rare examples settled in secondary streets. The excavations led by Berthier revealed the presence of a large 'château d'eau' (20 × 13 m) composed of three cisterns and located on the top of the mountain. According to Berthier, this construction was supplied with water by the rains that streamed from the summit, with pipes allowing secondary distribution from this reservoir to some parts of the settlement.

We have only two workshops in Tiddis where water supply is identifiable – in these, a pipe coming from an adjoining cistern was in direct connection with the fulling compartments. Otherwise, at Tiddis as at Timgad, we must conclude that the water was supplied manually by artisans using buckets. Also, there is no convincing evidence for evacuation of compartments: it had to be done manually and the waste water thrown on the floor of the workshop and evacuated towards the street, or else dirty water could have been emptied directly into the street (Figs 4.9–4.11).

[59] Amraoui 2018.

Figure 4.10 Terracotta pipe used to supply water within a compartment with tub in a *fullonica* at Tiddis (T. Amraoui).

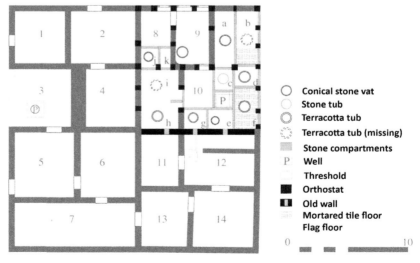

Figure 4.11 Plan of Insula 30 (Timgad), the *fullonica* is located in the north-east corner (T. Amraoui).

Rinsing without Basins?

After the fulling process, the clothes had to be rinsed. At Pompeii and Ostia this step was practised in one large and deep basin or in three long basins generally disposed in the middle of the room. As the tubs were placed laterally, against the walls, the workers could reach the rinsing facilities easily. This appears to be a logical spatial organisation. The basins were supplied with water by pipes connected to the urban hydraulic network.[60]

In Algeria, the typology is different. With the exception of some very rare and particular cases, the tubs generally occupy the lateral parts of the room, freeing up space in the centre. This central space remains relatively small and contains no evidence of basins. In the *fullonica* of Insula 30 at Timgad, there is only one small compartment, *k*, without a tub: it is impossible that the workers fulling in the ten other compartments all rinsed the clothes in this one. Consequently, we have to consider how were the textiles rinsed. The only probable answer is that the compartments with a tub were also used for rinsing. There are many supporting arguments for this conclusion. Contrary to the Italian examples where the stalls closely surrounded the tubs, many of the African compartments included a much greater space than was required by the size of the tub. Sometimes the space defined by the low walls was so large that it might be thought more profitable to install one or even two additional tubs. Thus, the presence of the fourth partition may also find an explanation: it was used to isolate completely a space used both for fulling and for rinsing. With their double function, the compartments presenting a tub could thus be identified as 'basins with tub'. This use is confirmed by the water pipes found in Tiddis that brought water directly into the compartments. Flohr reports the absence of basins in eight of the Italian *fullonicae* and supposes that it is because they were not preserved. Yet, for Timgad's workshops the general preservation of the remains and the presence of stone pavements proves that there were no basins (Figs 4.9 and 4.11).

Moreover, at both sites, inside the compartments the paved surface is sloped in order to facilitate the flow of water into the tub. This would have been particularity useful during the fulling process, keeping the liquids within the tubs, but also when the spaces were cleaned: the workers had only to recover the dirty waters collected in that main container.

Compared to the Italian discoveries, African *fullonicae* present generally the same typical facilities, the most important feature of which is the

---

[60] See for example Flohr 2013.

terracotta tub bounded by low walls. However, their system of compartmentalisation makes them clearly different from Italian examples. In Numidia, it seems to have been related with the necessity of installing multiple facilities in a restricted space, but also in conserving limited water supplies.

The absence of a continuous, abundant water supply forced craftsmen to develop other arrangements, because large basins would have required a regular water supply to fill and clean them. However, the wells and the small cisterns described were evidently sufficient for this purpose when washing and rinsing took place in the same small tubs.

As we have no information about pre-Roman workshops or about the treatment of textiles before the Roman presence, it is impossible to suggest a traditional cultural habit. On the other hand, these facilities demonstrate the permanence of water issues in areas which were not provided with a developed hydraulic network that facilitated a supply of continuous running water. Even if we can consider the absence of basins as an adaptation to local water supply issues, it does not appear to have been an obstacle to the proper functioning or the prosperity of the workshops.

An Example of the Ethnoarchaeological Contribution to the Study of Techniques: The Cage of the *Fullo*

The observations on the craft activities that I presented above can be enriched by a very important aspect of the study of ancient technology: ethnoarchaeology. This approach generally contributes to the development of new lines of thought in order to help the understanding of ancient processes. Here, I present an example that shows the importance of considering possible continuity in techniques from antiquity to more recent periods. It concerns textile activity; more precisely, one particular step relating to the whitening of wool.

Paintings found in the workshops at Pompeii show *fullones* at work; two of them represent a cage, one in the *fullonica* of L. Veranius Hypsaeus, the other in the *fullonica* VI 14, 21–22. In the first, we can see a worker holding a cage and a small bucket (Fig. 4.12a).[61] It has been argued that these tools were used to produce fumigations of sulphur. During my research on textile production in ancient Africa, I examined different ethnographic studies carried out in the Maghreb during the colonisation period, between

---

[61] Special thanks to M. Flohr for permission to publish here his photograph.

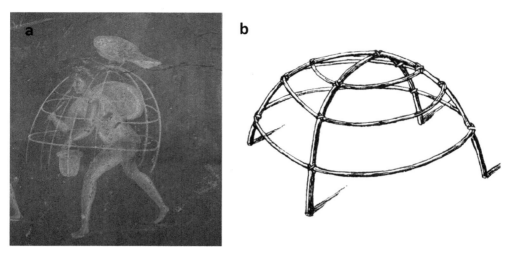

Figure 4.12 (a) Cage represented on a painting of the *fullonica* of L. Veranus Hypsaeus at Pompeii (Flohr 2013, fig. 140); (b) Mseḥna in wood used at Tlemcen at the beginning of the twentieth century (Bel and Ricard 1913, 26, fig. 11).

the end of the nineteenth and the early twentieth century. Some of them described in detail the different traditional steps of the work. At Tlemcen (western Algeria), they reveal that women were using a very similar cage to the one of Pompeii. They moistened the wool and then arranged it on the *mseḥna*, a cage made in wicker (Fig. 4.12b) that seems a bit smaller than the one in the Pompeii painting. The woman placed a terracotta brazier below the cage, and sulphur powder was thrown on the embers; the wool was then rinsed in cold water. This process was aimed at whitening the wool, but contrary to the Pompeian example where it was reserved for finished clothes, at Tlemcen it was carried out prior to spinning. Some studies concerning other areas of the Mediterranean basin in antiquity or for more recent times demonstrate that raw wool could be treated before weaving.[62] This action was reserved for white wool or garments and could not be used on coloured textiles.

Thanks to an ethnoarchaeological comparison, it has been possible to show that this process was also used in modern North Africa. As well as helping to better understand the technique used in antiquity, it demonstrates its permanence in the Mediterranean area until at least the twentieth century.

---

[62] For example, Forbes 1964, 21, 81.

Conclusion

The sample of craft activities presented in this chapter reveals that the African provinces adopted Roman techniques with their integration to the empire, just as did Gaul and Spain. This situation is related to the adoption of the Roman way of life in cities that were inspired by the *urbs* through monumental architecture and institutions, and whose inhabitants, new citizens of the empire, lived '*à la romaine*'. Yet these standardised tools seem to have been adapted to local techniques or preferences. We observe that some of their characteristics could result from cultural continuity with already established pre-Roman traditions, but their typology also reveals the importance of space and the supply of natural resources.

This study, however, has some limitations. The main problem remains the difficulty of identifying the inheritance from pre-Roman periods. It also highlights the difficulties of defining what is and what is not native. In addition, it is impossible to specify whether the adoption of Roman techniques was gradual or fast. Did it begin after the fall of Carthage or before? In fact, we cannot yet define the role of Carthage in their diffusion and whether that city had a role in technical transfer before the integration of the western territories, or whether it had started through independent economic trade between the two Mediterranean coasts. Or, on the contrary, did it take place after their final annexation to Rome? At the moment, most of the discoveries of workshops belong to late antiquity, as the excavations reflect especially the last stages of activity: we still know very little about their first appearance.

Concerning the local African particularities, compared with what we often consider to be the 'classic' Italian model, we need to step back a little. In his *Naturalis Historia*, Pliny mentioned the specificities of transformation or consumption in the various regions of the 'world' that he describes: they were often dependent on diverse local habits. Thus, we must admit that it is entirely normal to find variants to the 'classic' model, and that these could have been arbitrarily identified at times. In other words, considering the fact that African remains are mainly late, Italian discoveries could appear as reflecting a particular – early – period in a specific region of Italy, and we can only observe that we do not yet have enough information about previous or later workshops to fully comprehend the complexity of technological transfers.

While my research has helped to develop our understanding of technological diffusion in North Africa, one must recognise that the history of ancient techniques remains complex. In the future, although it will be important to keep collecting numerous and varied data concerning different local craft activities, it will also be essential to focus on their chronology and their geographical distribution. To be able to renew, or even in certain cases to initiate the reflection on the penetration of Mediterranean techniques in southern regions, we need new field research. Data concerning previous periods in Roman African provinces have to be studied, but so must remains located beyond the *limes*. For the Saharan areas, most of the investigations are limited to the prehistoric ages except for recent research, especially that led by David J. Mattingly and his team in the Saharan oases. From the discoveries of Saniat Jibril, for example, it appears that Saharan regions were aware of 'Mediterranean' techniques and used them, but that they were not concerned by the latest Roman technical changes, in contrast to more northern African regions. Why? One part of the investigation would be to define the chronology of their adoption and then try to explain how and why they were maintained. These limitations in the transfer of techniques cannot be explained only by geography, but are also the result of socio-economic and political factors that need to be studied in more detail in the future.

References

Akerraz, A. and Lenoir, M. 2002. Instruments de broyage en Maurétanie tingitane à l'époque Romaine, le cas de Volubilis. In Procopiou and Treuil 2002, 198–207.

Allais, Y. 1954. Les fouilles de 1950–1952 dans le quartier Est de Djemila. *Libyca* 2.2: 343–61.

Alonso Martinez, N. 2002. Le moulin rotatif manuel au nord-est de la péninsule ibérique: Une innovation technique dans le contexte domestique de la mouture de céréales. In Procopiou and Treuil 2002, 111–27.

Amouretti, M.-C. 1986. *Le pain et l'huile dans la Grèce antique: De l'araire au moulin*. Paris: Belles Lettres.

Amraoui, T. 2014. La production urbaine de salaisons en Algérie romaine: L'exemple de Tipasa (Maurétanie césarienne). In E. Botte and V. Leitch (eds), *Fish and Ships: Production and Commerce of Salsmenta during Antiquity*, Aix-en-Provence: Centre Camille Jullian, 91–101.

Amraoui, T. 2017. *L'artisanat dans les cités antiques de l'Algérie (Ier siècle avant notre ère –VIIe siècle après notre ère)*. Roman Archaeology series, 26. Oxford: Archaeopress.

Amraoui, T. 2018. Alimentation et gestion de l'eau dans les ateliers antiques de Numidie: Le cas des fullonicae. In V. Brouquier-Reddé and F. Hurlet (eds), *L'eau dans les Villes de l'Afrique du Nord et leur Territoire, Actes du Colloque ANR EauMaghreb, 6–8 décembre 2012, Bordeaux*, Bordeaux: Editions Ausonius, 195–204.

Amraoui, T. Forthcoming. Les ateliers antiques de transformation du poisson en Algérie: Typologie, localisation et répartition géographique. In *Actes du XIe Colloque international de la SEMPAM, 'Histoire et Archéologie de l'Afrique du Nord', Hommes et animaux au Maghreb, de la Préhistoire au Moyen-Âge: exploration d'une relation complexe, 8–11 octobre 2014, Marseille-Aix-en-Provence*.

Antonelli, F. and Lazzarini, L. 2010. Mediterranean trade of the most widespread Roman volcanic millstones from Italy and petrochemical markers of their raw materials. *Journal of Archaeological Science* 37.9: 2081–92.

Bakker, J.T. 1999. *The Mills-Bakeries of Ostia: Description and Interpretation.* Amsterdam: J.C. Gieben.

Bel, A. and Ricard, P. 1913. *Le travail de la laine à Tlemcen: Les industries indigènes de l'Algérie.* Alger: A. Jourdan.

Ben Abed-Ben Khader, A. 1987. Thuburbo Majus, Les Mosaïques dans la région ouest. *Corpus des Mosaïques de Tunisie* 2.3. Tunis: Institut national d'archéologie et d'arts.

Ben Moussa, M. 2007. *La production de sigillées africaines: Recherches d'histoire et d'archéologie en Tunisie septentrionale et centrale.* Barcelona: Universitat de Barcelona.

Bender Jørgensen, L. 2017. Textiles and textile trade in the first millennium AD: Evidence from Egypt. In Mattingly *et al.* 2017, 231–58.

Berthier, A. 2000. *Tiddis, cité antique de Numidie.* Paris: De Boccard.

Bonifay, M. 2004. *Études sur la céramique romaine tardive d'Afrique.* BAR International Series 1301. Oxford: Archaeopress.

Borgard, P. 2002. À propos des teintureries de Pompéi: l'exemple de l'officina infectoria. In J.-C. Béal and J.-C. Goyon (eds), *Les artisans dans la ville antique.* Lyon: Université Lumière-Lyon 2, 55–67.

Botte, E. 2009. *Salaisons et sauces de poissons en Italie du sud et en Sicile durant l'antiquité.* Naples: Centre Jean Bérard.

Brun, J.-P. 2003. Les pressoirs à vin d'Afrique et de Maurétanie à l'époque romaine. *Africa (ns Séances Scientifiques)* 1: 7–30.

Christofle, M. 1935. *Rapport sur les travaux de fouilles et consolidations effectués en 1930–1931–1932 par le Service des monuments historiques de l'Algérie.* Alger: J. Carbonel.

Delestre, X. 2005. *Hippone.* Aix-en-Provence: Édisud.

De Vos, M. 2000. *Rus Africum: Terra, acqua, olio nell'Africa settentrionale: scavo e ricognizione nei dintorni di Dougga (Alto Tell tunisino).* Trento: Università degli studi di Trento.

Drine, A. 2001. Meules à grain et pétrins autour du lac El Bibèn et à Gighti. In J.-P. Brun and P. Jockey (eds), *Technai: Techniques et sociétés en Méditerranée:*

Hommage à Marie-Claire Amouretti. Paris: Maison méditerranéenne des sciences de l'homme, 251–60.

Fentress, E., Drine, A. and Holod, R. (eds) 2009. *An Island through Time: Jerba Studies. Vol 1, the Punic and Roman Periods*. JRA Supplementary series 71. Portsmouth: Journal of Roman Archaeology.

Flohr, M. 2013. *The World of the Fullo: Work, Economy, and Society in Roman Italy*. Oxford: Oxford University Press.

Forbes, R.J. 1964. *Studies in Ancient Technology, Volume* 4 (2nd edition). Leiden: Brill.

Foy, D. 2003. Le verre antique en Tunisie: L'apport des fouilles récentes tuniso-françaises. *Journal of Glass Studies* 45: 59–89.

Gast, M. 2010. Meules et molettes (Sahara). *Encyclopédie Berbère* 31: 4954–59.

Gaudry, M. 1928. *La femme Chaouia de l'Aurès: Etude de sociologie Berbère*. Paris: Librairie orientaliste Paul Geuthner.

Guédon, S. 2017. Circulation and trade of textiles in the southern borders of Roman Africa. In Mattingly *et al.* 2017, 259–84.

Hurst, H.R., Fulford, M. and Peacock, D.P.S. 1984. *Excavations at Carthage: The British Mission. Vol. I.2, the Avenue du Président Habib Bourguiba, Salambo: The Pottery and Other Ceramic Objects from the Site*. Sheffield: British Academy and University of Sheffield Department of Prehistory and Archaeology.

Jaccottey, L. and Longepierre, S. 2011. Les moulins de type Pompéi en France. In O. Buchsenschutz, L. Jaccotey, F. Jodry and J.-L. Blanchard (eds), *Évolution typologique et technique des meules du néolithique à l'an mille: Actes des IIIe rencontres archéologiques de l'achéosite Gaulois. Aquitania* (Supplément 23), Bordeaux: Aquitania, 95–107.

Johannesen, R. 1954. The textile industry in Roman North Africa. *The Classical Journal* 49.4: 157–60.

Leduc, M. 2008. Les *pistrina* volubilitains, témoins majeurs du dynamisme économique municipal. In *L'Africa Romana: Le Richezze dell'Africa: Risorse, Produzioni, Scambi: Atti del XVII Convegno di Studio, Sevilla, 14–17 dicembre 2006*. Roma: Carocci, 475–506.

Leveau, P. 1984. *Caesarea de Maurétanie, une ville romaine et ses campagnes*. Rome: École française de Rome.

Mattingly, D.J. (ed.) 2010. *The Archaeology of Fazzan. Volume 3, Excavations Carried out by C.M. Daniels*. London: Society for Libyan Studies, Department of Antiquities.

Mattingly, D.J. and Hitchner, R.B. 1993. Technical specifications for some North African olive presses of Roman date. In M.-C. Amouretti and J.-P. Brun (eds), *La Production du Vin et de l'Huile en Méditerranée*, Athènes: Ecole Française d'Athènes, 439–62.

Mattingly, D.J., Leitch, V., Duckworth, C.N., Cuenod, A., Sterry, M. and Cole, F. (eds) 2017. *Trade in the Ancient Sahara and Beyond*. Trans-Saharan Archaeology, Volume 1. Series editor D.J. Mattingly. Cambridge: Cambridge University Press and the Society for Libyan Studies.

Monteix, N. 2010. *Les lieux de métier: Boutiques et ateliers d'Herculanum.* BEFAR, 344. Rome: École française de Rome.

Moritz, L.A. 1958. *Grain-Mills and Flour in Classical Antiquity.* Oxford: Clarendon Press.

Peron, A. 1883. *Essai d'une description géologique de l'Algérie pour servir de guide aux géologues dans l'Afrique française.* Paris: G. Masson.

Pietrogrande, A.L. 1976. *Scavi di Ostia, volume ottavo, Le Fulloniche.* Rome: Libreria dello Stato.

Procopiou, H. and Treuil, R. (eds) 2002. *Moudre et broyer, l'interprétation fonctionnelle de l'outillage de mouture et de broyage dans la préhistoire et l'antiquité, II, archéologie et histoire du paléolithique au moyen âge.* Paris: Éditions du CTHS.

Py, M. 1992. Meules d'époque protohistorique et romaine provenant de Lattes. *Lattara* 5: 183–232.

Riley, J.A. 1980. Imported grain mills at Cyrene. *Libyan Studies* 12: 55–59.

Salomonson, J.W. 1968. Etudes sur la céramique romaine d'Afrique. *Babesch* 43: 80–154.

Sehili, S. 2009. *Huileries antiques de Jebel Semmama – région de Kasserine.* Tunis: Centre de Publication Universitaire.

Slim, H., Trousset, P., Paskoff, R. and Oeslati, A. 2004. *Le littoral de la Tunisie: Etude géoarchéologique et historique.* Paris: CNRS.

Stone D.L., Mattingly, D.J. and Ben Lazreg, N. 2011. *Leptiminus (Lamta) Report no. 3: The Field Survey.* JRA, Suppl. 87. Portsmouth: Journal of Roman Archaeology.

Tébar Megias, E. and Wilson, A. 2008. Classical and Hellenistic textile production at Euesperides (Benghazi, Libya): Preliminary results. In C. Alfaro Giner and L. Karali (eds), *Vestidos, textiles y tintes: Estudios sobre la producción de bienes de consumo en la Antigüedad,* Actas del II symposium internacional sobre textiles y tintes del Mediterraneo en el mundo antiguo (Atenas, 24 al 26 de noviembre, 2005), Valencia: Universitat de València, 49–59.

Wilson, A. 1995. Water-mills in North Africa and the development of the horizontal water-wheel. *Journal of Roman Archaeology* 8: 499–510.

Wilson, A. 2001. Timgad and textile production. In D.J. Mattingly and J. Salmon (eds), *Economies Beyond Agriculture in the Classical World,* London: Routledge, 271–96.

Wilson, A. 2002. Urban production in the Roman world, the view from North Africa. *Papers of the British School at Rome* 70: 231–74.

Wilson, A. 2004. Archaeological evidence for textile production and dyeing in Roman North Africa. In C. Alfaro, J.P. Wild and B. Costa (eds), *Purpureae vestes: Actas del I Symposium internacional sobre textiles y tintes del Mediterráneo en época romana (Ibiza, 8–10 novembre 2002),* Valencia: Universitat de València, 155–64.

5 | Movement and Management of Animals in the North and West of Africa from 1000 BC to AD 1000

B. TYR FOTHERGILL, VEERLE LINSEELE AND SILVIA
VALENZUELA LAMAS

Introduction

There are several possible paths of introduction for domestic species brought into North and West Africa. For the early phases (sixth to first millennium BC), the dominant idea is that translocation of most domestic animals and many domestic plants originated from the Levant, with most species entering Africa first through modern Egypt.[1] These species are then thought to have been moved in a general east to west direction, travelling along routes which then branch southward: either the Central Saharan route through Fazzan to the Lake Chad or eastern Niger Bend regions, or south from Morocco to Senegal through Mauritania (or across to the western Niger Bend). The earliest agricultural economies presumably reached large parts of coastal northern Africa by sea,[2] although as far as animal bones are concerned there is very little actual archaeological evidence for these early stages. Later on, domestic animal species (possibly the chicken) may also have been introduced through a Mediterranean route, perhaps transported by Phoenician trade networks and then moved southward, oasis by oasis. In addition, from the first millennium AD domesticated animal species were also spread in an east–west direction along the Sahel zone, starting from the Horn of Africa and reaching Sub-Saharan West Africa in this way.[3] It is possible that the route itself impacted the dissemination of some species (for example, sites in Burkina Faso have chickens but not camels present in early levels; Senegalese sites have camels or equids but not chickens), although the archaeological evidence could be purely coincidental.

These early introductory narratives sometimes also consider 'packages' or combinations of species moving together into the Sahara, such as

---

[1] Gautier 2002.   [2] Barich 2014; Zeder 2008.   [3] Linseele 2007.

cattle, caprines and possibly dogs, which arrived first in Egypt from the Levant and then spread gradually, reaching the western and eventually southern regions of the African continent.[4] In Sub-Saharan West Africa, archaeological data for periods preceding the arrival of the first animal domesticates (in the second half of the third millennium BC) are limited. Animals were moving in the company of people, but there is little material evidence for technology transfer and interaction with local communities, at least in the earliest stages. It is probable that multiple, repeated translocations of the same domestic species occurred across North and West Africa. Some of these were probably unsuccessful in the sense that they did not lead to the establishment of local, breeding populations of the animals concerned. This option is not often considered and is difficult to detect archaeologically. However, osteometric data in Sub-Saharan Africa highlights the existence of different types of the same species, which may represent separate introduction events.[5]

Although the archaeological evidence seems to generally support these paths of introduction, the narratives are often inherently colonial in nature and there are some issues of interpretation. First, there is a bias towards the excavation of large urban sites along the North African coastlines, with Greek, Phoenician and Punic colonies frequently the target of research. Second, domestication is an 'ongoing co-evolutionary process rather than an event or invention'.[6] The fact that a domestic species originated outside of Africa (and is then charted at sites across the landscape in order of its earliest appearance in a region) does not accurately reflect the continued adaptation of the species and the impact of local management strategies over time. For example, the genetic history of domestic cattle in Africa is immensely complex, but a review of the evidence concludes that the Y-chromosome haplotype diversity in African cattle breeds is directly indicative of deliberate, long-term efforts by pastoralists to enhance their herds.[7] Furthermore, some of this diversity is likely to be the result of genetic contributions from wild male African aurochsen.[8]

Previous synthetic research on North African faunal material is limited.[9] Anthony King's review of mammal bones from sites across the Roman world was the first to present a regional view of the evidence from sites in North Africa.[10] This was a groundbreaking and vital piece of work, but North Africa was not his primary focus and interpretations were limited by

---

[4] See relevant chapters in Blench and MacDonald 2000.   [5] Linseele 2007.
[6] Gifford-Gonzalez and Hanotte 2011, 1–4.   [7] Stock and Gifford-Gonzalez 2013.
[8] Stock and Gifford-Gonzalez 2013, 67.
[9] For broad surveys, see Grant 2006; MacKinnon 2017.   [10] King 1999.

period and species. Leone and Mattingly focused solely on North Africa and contextualised the role of domestic species within the rural landscapes and agricultural practices of the late antique, Vandal and Arab periods (roughly the third to eighth centuries AD),[11] but the role of faunal data in this piece was relatively minor. More synthetic papers exist on Sub-Saharan West Africa,[12] and a large amount of West African faunal data have been synthesised by one of us.[13] This chapter is unique in its geographical approach (see Fig. 5.1), presenting faunal data for domestic animals across the Sahara as well as adjacent regions both north and south of it, with the aim of studying relations and connections between these areas. We will discuss species translocation and then proceed to the biological requirements, husbandry, movement, roles and archaeological evidence of key species.

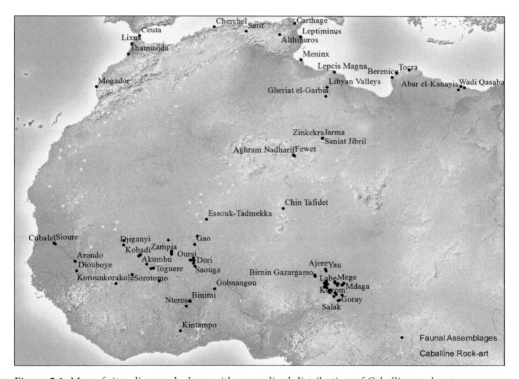

Figure 5.1 Map of sites discussed, along with generalised distribution of Caballine rock art.

---

[11] Leone and Mattingly 2004. That paper built on Mattingly and Hitchner 1995, 196–98.
[12] For example, MacDonald and MacDonald 2000; Van Neer 2002.   [13] Linseele 2007.

Translocation of Species

The introduction of domestic species to new areas requires human-driven relocation of animals to unfamiliar environments. A veritable host of terminological nomenclature exists to describe this idea, ranging from characterising it as an activity, to a process or product, and the usage of terms varies substantially across and even within disciplines. For this chapter we have chosen to use the broadest general definition of translocation as a change of location; substitution of the conservation biology term 'introduction' is not appropriate as it does not capture the process of movement and transportation, and is by definition focused on the establishment of a species in a specific habitat.[14] Although the term 'translocation' is defined as 'the deliberate and mediated movement of organisms, from any source, captive or wild, from one area to free release in another' by International Union for Conservation standards,[15] animals are not often released as a matter of course through the process with which we are concerned, and the framework of conservation is not fully suitable for studying the past movements of domestic species. Additionally, although the processes and risks of translocation are fully applicable to domestic species, much of the literature on animal translocation is limited to wild species; this is probably due in part to research priorities which are driven by concern for the survival of endangered species and at-risk habitats. The movement of domestic species is thus subsumed by the movement of humans, despite issues of clear relevance in common (such as stress, disease and environmental requirements). In two archaeologically framed papers in which the concept of translocation is explicitly considered,[16] the authors discuss the human-aided movement of domesticates and commensal species, and then either focus on species viewed as exotic rarities or go on to state that they are concerned only with 'non-domesticated' animals.[17] Other contributions take the arrival of species in a new area as the main investigative focus and do not fully consider the process (and the requisite animal management skills and technology) of moving these creatures across large distances.[18] The sheer economic cost, technological challenge and potential risks presented by the translocation of domestic species in the ancient world at any scale is surely worth further consideration – to say nothing of the ways in which past human lifeways and activities would have been altered by the arrival of novel species.

---

[14] Fischer and Lindenmayer 2000, 3.   [15] Seddon *et al.* 2012, 6.
[16] Albarella 2007; Grayson 2001.   [17] Albarella 2007, 136; Grayson 2001, 17.
[18] For example, the introduction of various domestic species to Britain, O'Connor and Sykes 2010.

Domestic species have widely varying life and health requirements, and their needs (both behavioural and biological) would have substantially affected the methods used to transport them. Animals with higher water requirements would, by necessity, have to stop more frequently and perhaps travel across less direct routes with more available water. Specialised knowledge and skills would have played no small part in moving animals across past landscapes and quite possibly also in managing them upon arrival in unfamiliar environments.[19]

With regard to the translocation of species across North and West Africa, transportation mechanisms of various sorts could have been utilised. In terms of cross-country movement, some animals can be herded or led by tether, possibly with the assistance of dogs (this is likely to have been the case for camels, cattle, caprines and equids) and others (chickens) could have been packed onto the backs of transport animals or into carts or other vehicles. It is possible that horses in particular accompanied the chariot into North Africa.[20] Pigs are a bit more problematic with regard to land-based movement; they require frequent watering, their foraging habits make them unsuitable for herding over long distances[21] and they would lose valuable weight during transit. Land-based translocation of pigs may thus have required specialised skills and a substantial amount of time and effort to achieve, particularly in the Sahara. Maritime transport is a plausible alternative for moving pigs and could certainly have played a role in the movement of other domestic species along the coast of North and West Africa. In the case of West Africa, arrivals of domesticates by sea probably continued as late as the sixteenth century AD.[22]

There are notable ecological and biological considerations which must be taken into account when investigating the range of impacts which might have occurred as a result of domestic species translocation. The success of a translocated species in any environment is innately tied to disease vulnerability and exposure. It is possible that camel populations were not established in certain parts of North Africa (and most of West Africa) due to their vulnerability to fly-borne ailments of humid climes, including trypanosomiasis.[23] Camels can also face health difficulties if they are not provided with enough salt or access to halophytic plants, as salt deficiencies can lead to necrosis of the skin and cramps.[24] Some West African breeds of cattle, sheep and goats are trypanotolerant (resistant to trypanosomiasis),

---

[19] For example, the hire of elephant handlers from India by the Ottoman Empire in Egypt (AD 1770–1830) and other areas, Mikhail 2013.
[20] Camps and Chaker 1993.   [21] Zeder 1991.   [22] Linseele 2007.   [23] Köhler-Rollefson 1991.
[24] Köhler-Rollefson 1991.

possibly a locally developed adaptation. Trypanotolerance appears to be associated with dwarfism and can therefore be reasonably inferred, based on archaeozoological evidence.[25]

There are other disease factors to consider within the translocation framework. It is possible that the animals being moved brought along pathogens and parasites which had the potential to affect the local people, wildlife and livestock already present.[26] One archaeological example of this is the human-aided movement of osteopetrosis (caused by avian leucosis viruses) in chickens.[27] Alternatively, newly translocated species may encounter new pathogens and parasites upon introduction and their population could suffer as a result.[28] A good Saharan example of this is *Trypanosoma evansii* (commonly referred to as surra, a form of trypanosomiasis) which is endemic to the Sub-Saharan tsetse fly, but which was introduced into the horsefly population of North Africa via the blood of infected camels (or other livestock).[29] The health of the newly translocated animal would have been at risk for other reasons: although domesticate species are ostensibly well cared for by their human keepers, the combination of atypical movement and a new environment causes significant amounts of stress and can potentially increase mortality rates.[30]

People moved animals in the past for many reasons; Albarella suggests that 'people moving to new lands ... bring with them elements of the world that they are about to leave', and specifically refers to live animals.[31] It is probable that species were transported for other reasons, including economic gains or increased power and status on the part of the person moving or receiving the animal. It is also likely, especially with regard to the nature of animal movement across the Sahara,[32] that species in the process of translocation passed through many sets of hands (or were moved on the backs of several different camels) throughout their journey.

Translocated species, by definition, are introduced to areas outside their previous realms of experience. People meeting an animal that they have never encountered before are unlikely to have the same perception of that species as the person who raised or transported it to that location. In fact, unless substantial transfer of knowledge has preceded the arrival of a new species, the translocated animal may be viewed and managed in a totally different way (for example, the same chicken stock used for egg production in some parts of the Roman Empire might have been desirable for sacrifice or other purposes in different parts). Even if a domestic animal successfully

[25] Linseele 2007; MacDonald and MacDonald 2000.   [26] Cunningham 1996.
[27] Fothergill 2017; Gál 2008.   [28] Cunningham 1996.   [29] Desquesnes *et al.* 2013.
[30] Seddon *et al.* 2012.   [31] Albarella 2007, 133.   [32] Mattingly *et al.* Forthcoming.

accompanied people migrating to a new area, other factors such as climate could well have affected the methods used to establish and manage it. New strategies might have been developed in response to differences between the area from which the animal was originally taken and the region to which it was translocated (for example, seasonal movement during only the winter or spring, or species-specific housing).

Key Domestic Species

A diverse range of fauna was transported across North and West Africa by various methods and at different times. Here we focus on key domesticate taxa: chickens (we also discuss guinea fowl and francolins), dogs, equids, pigs, camels (dromedaries), caprines (sheep and goats) and cattle (unhumped and humped). We review the biological needs and requirements of each taxon or group, probable methods of transportation and movement, the earliest archaeological evidence for their arrival or adoption and factors that would have affected approaches to their management and husbandry. When possible, we also contextualise taxa with regard to both environments and the peoples who kept them.

Chickens and Guinea Fowl

In comparison with a mammal of similar size, chickens require little water (43 ml per kg, depending upon the size of the individual and the climate). For the purpose of comparison, a rabbit (as a similarly sized mammal) requires 90 ml per kg.[33] If allowed to forage freely and presented with a rich environment (and/or kitchen scraps), chickens can support themselves almost entirely. Water intake is vital for egg-laying hens and if prevented from drinking, laying hens can take days to resume normal activity;[34] provision of water would therefore have been key to egg-laying success in the past. Susceptibility to dehydration and predation would have been substantial practical risks of chicken translocation. However, in terms of movement alone, chickens are quite portable. Due to behavioural differences, it is unlikely that chickens could be safely herded across large distances like other galliformes.[35] As their tendency to flight would require some form of restraint, it is probable that another method of transport would have been used.

---

[33] Anonymous 1984.   [34] Winchell 2001.   [35] Fothergill 2014.

There are some issues with the identification of chicken from archae-ological assemblages. First, small taxa, especially avians, are underrepre-sented (in comparison to mammals) in assemblages which are not sieved through fine mesh.[36] Additionally, avian bones have thinner walls and are more easily destroyed than those of mammals. Although bird elements are morphologically distinct from mammal elements, avian identification can present substantial difficulty to the non-specialist, and bird bones some-times go completely unidentified. Importantly, an enormous challenge is presented by the process of distinguishing domestic chicken elements (*Gallus gallus*) from those of other galliform birds, more specifically guinea fowl (family Numididae) and members of the francolin genera (*Peliperdix, Dendroperdix, Scleroptila* and *Pternistis*), especially in Sub-Saharan Africa.[37] It is unclear from many older reports if the only bird elements recovered from a site were clearly identified as chicken to the exclusion of other galliform birds in the same size range.

There is no literary record of francolin translocation, but guinea fowl were likely to have been traded northward into Europe as a rare exotic domesticate, as they are described in recognisable detail as an African bird by Roman authors from the first century BC, including Varro.[38] The guinea fowl is referred to in other sources from Italy and Greece,[39] but the geographic origin of the guinea fowl which was moved into Europe is not currently known. As there is little evidence of a guinea fowl population becoming established in Europe in the Roman period, it would seem that either the husbandry methods used to keep the birds did not travel with them, or they were initially unsuccessful in a new environment. It is worth noting here that the domestication status of *Numida meleagris* has been debated, at least for areas within its natural range. Based upon environ-mental interactions and behaviour, Blench concludes that it is 'only partly domesticated',[40] while MacDonald refers to it as a 'certain African domes-ticate' in the same volume.[41] While they admit that the guinea fowl is quite behaviourally difficult, Gifford-Gonzalez and Hanotte describe it as a domesticate species.[42] At any rate, since the birds were translocated into Europe by the first century BC,[43] a close relationship of some kind with people is clear. Consideration for domestication as a co-evolutionary process rather than a singular event after which immense physiological and behavioural changes are clearly evident might be a productive

---

[36] O'Connor 2008, 34.   [37] MacDonald 1992.   [38] Varro, *De Re Rustica*, 3.9.17.
[39] Hughes 2003.   [40] Blench 2000a, 315.   [41] MacDonald 2000, 10.
[42] Gifford-Gonzalez and Hanotte 2011, 16–17.   [43] Mongin and Plouzeau 1984.

framework for future research and debates on the status and role of the guinea fowl.

The earliest chicken bones in North Africa were excavated from the Phoenician colony of Mogador on the Atlantic coast of Morocco and were dated to the seventh century BC.[44] Although it is possible that later construction at the site could have disturbed some contexts, this date is consistent with the movement of chickens along the Mediterranean coastline. The first depictions of chickens in North Africa are 25 small bronze figurines which were recovered from Cyrene at the sanctuary of Demeter and Persephone; these were dated to the sixth century BC on a stylistic basis,[45] and chicken bones were identified in later components of the same site.[46] Although no chickens were identified at Carthage before the fifth to fourth centuries BC,[47] there is some (as yet unpublished) evidence for chickens at Carthage from the sixth century BC.[48] Another coastal site, Sidi Khrebish, had chicken bones present from the second century BC.[49] Prior to the end of the first millennium BC, chicken elements were only present at sites along the coast, which probably reflects a bias towards excavating Greek, Phoenician and Punic colonies and a lack of interest in indigenous settlements. However, it is notable that no chickens were identified at the inland site of Althiburos prior to the arrival of the Romans.[50]

By the first millennium AD, the majority of assemblages across North Africa have chickens present, regardless of location. Sites such as Fewet and Zinkekra in the Central Sahara have no chicken elements present in assemblages from the first millennium BC.[51] Yet, perhaps as a result of increased Garamantian trade, chickens turn up in contexts from the second century AD onward at Jarma, capital of the Garamantes.[52] This general trend may indicate rather swift adoption of the species across North Africa.

In West Africa, chickens have been identified at Arondo (AD 428–635) in the Faleme Valley of the Upper Senegal region.[53] In Burkina Faso, Kirikongo has elements which are likely to be chicken dating from the first to fifth centuries AD, and definitively identified elements dated to calAD 560–660.[54] A 1.8 m diameter feature overlaid with large sherds and with shallow post-holes was tentatively classed as a chicken coop at the site of Houlouf

---

[44] Becker 2012.   [45] Warden *et al.* 1990.   [46] Crabtree and Monge 1987.
[47] Phase B of the German excavations, Nobis 1999.   [48] Linseele, personal communication.
[49] Barker 1979.   [50] Valenzuela Lamas 2016.
[51] Alhaique 2013, Fothergill 2012, van der Veen and Westley 2010; the last notes that a chicken-sized bird was present.
[52] Holmes and Grant 2013.   [53] Watson 1999.
[54] Dueppen 2011; Beta 236234 charcoal, range not given.

south of Lake Chad (calAD 660–775),[55] although no avian remains from the site were speciated. In the subsequent centuries, the chicken appears to have been adopted at a large proportion of communities throughout arid West Africa.[56] This is unsurprising, given that chickens can be raised in small spaces and in marginal environments as long as they are managed with care and kept safe from predators. Chickens produce multiple, highly useful products in addition to their flesh, including eggs, dung and feathers; they have also been valued for their roles in divination and entertainment. With regard to the spread of chickens to Sub-Saharan West Africa, a Trans-Saharan route as well as an east to west route across the Sahel has been suggested, and it is possible that multiple introductions happened.[57] Linguists have also argued for an earlier presence of chicken in West Africa than the animal bone evidence can currently support.[58]

Dogs

Dogs were present in North Africa and the Sahara by the sixth millennium BC.[59] It is assumed that they spread together with domestic cattle and caprines as herding animals. The presence of cut and burn marks on dog bones from the Late Bronze Age and Iron Age levels of Althiburos (Tunisia) suggests that they were occasionally eaten.[60] However, in Saharan rock art, dogs are mainly depicted in hunting scenes.[61] Dogs reached Sub-Saharan West Africa at about the same times as cattle and caprines.[62] For the first half of the second millennium AD, there is evidence that dogs were eaten and this has been connected to similar practices among Berbers in northern Africa.[63] Recent research suggests that movement of dogs south of the Sahara may have been challenged by the presence of canine-specific pathogens in addition to those which affect a range of species.[64] Apart from the risks presented by disease in southern regions, the dispersal of dogs throughout North and West Africa was probably less problematic than moving species such as pigs.

Equids: Horses

The horse was and continues to be a prominent and meaningful figure to the peoples of the Sahara,[65] and may have been specifically associated with

---

[55] Holl 2002, 150; laboratory details not available.   [56] Linseele 2007.
[57] Linseele 2007; Mwacharo *et al.* 2013.   [58] Blench 1995.   [59] Mitchell 2015.
[60] Valenzuela Lamas 2016.   [61] Cesarino 1997.   [62] Linseele 2007.   [63] Linseele 2003.
[64] Mitchell 2015.   [65] Daumas 1968.

early oasis communities.[66] This connection is evident in figurines and rock art; there are numerous depictions of horsemen and chariots in the Wadi al-Ajal and near Ghat.[67] Muzzolini estimates that these depictions are dated from 700 BC to AD 500.[68] Paintings and engravings of horses are also present from Saharan Mauritania near Dhar Tichitt all the way north to Morocco and east to Chad.[69] Horses have historically been viewed as prestige animals in many cultures and the Sahara was no exception;[70] they may have been favoured for riding and display due to this association. High-ranking Garamantes of Fazzan were described as using chariots drawn by four horses in the fifth century BC,[71] and Strabo stated that horse breeding was an activity avidly pursued by Saharan peoples.[72] This might indicate the incipient development of Saharan horse breeds by the end of the first millennium BC, and suggests the existence of specialised oasis husbandry methods.

Estimates for the water requirements of horses vary wildly, but range from 30 to 90 litres a day, depending upon the ambient temperature, what the horse is eating and whether or not it is lactating. Horses can pack approximately a third of their weight; a North African horse of relatively small stature could probably carry about 90 kg,[73] and in the nineteenth century an average horse could be purchased for 10 or 20 slaves – an excellent horse might be worth 100 camels.[74]

Despite the fact that local conditions pose challenges to routine horse maintenance and care, horses in present-day West Africa are kept as a marker of prestige and mode of transport by wealthy individuals.[75] Humidity-related diseases in western Africa (such as trypanosomiasis) have a serious effect on horse mortality. Law has described how the overall health of horses progressively decreases from north to south.[76] Horses are also vulnerable to heat exposure, which can limit their use to cooler hours of the day.[77] Some pony breeds, however, have become trypanotolerant and generally better adapted to the West African climate and conditions.[78] There were firm links between horse ownership, socio-political power and high status in pre-colonial Islamic societies of West Africa.[79] Furthermore, due to the association of horses with raids and warfare, the symbolic worth of horses increased over time. Because of the endemic diseases of West

[66] Mattingly *et al.* Forthcoming.   [67] Barnett and Mattingly 2003; Muzzolini 1996.
[68] Muzzolini 1996.   [69] Challis *et al.* 2007; see distribution of caballine rock art in Figure 5.1.
[70] Strabo, *Geography*, 17.3.19.   [71] Herodotus 4.183.   [72] Strabo, *Geography*, 17.3.19.
[73] Vigneron 1968.   [74] Lydon 2009, 132–33.
[75] Connah 1981, 43; Geis-Tronich 1991, 438–52.   [76] Law 1980, 76–82.
[77] Geis-Tronich 1991, 438–52.   [78] Blench 1993.   [79] Law 1980, 176–96; Law 1995.

Africa that limited successful horse breeding, horses continued to be imported from the north; these transactions contributed to the formation of large-scale, long-distance trade in the pre-colonial era.[80] The combination of husbandry, environmental requirements and disease vulnerability probably proved challenging for those moving horses in the past.

Identification of horse material from archaeological contexts and differentiation of their elements from those of donkeys, mules and hinnies can present considerable difficulty, depending upon the degree of fragmentation present in the assemblage and other issues. It seems most likely that the horse arrived in Egypt at some point in the early second millennium BC,[81] which coincides neatly with the dates of diffusion for chariot technology.[82] Rock art depictions of chariots and horses are present across the Sahara,[83] and a distal equid femur fragment (considered too large to be a domestic donkey) was recovered near a human ribcage in an antenna tomb (00/195bis) in Wadi Tanzzuft (dated to *c*.1000 BC).[84] Based on size alone, this fragment could potentially have originated from either a horse or a wild ass.[85]

The earliest definitively identified horse bones in North Africa are associated with Althiburos and date to the eighth century BC.[86] Maghribian coastal cities also have early horse remains: the Phoenician/ Punic site of Mogador in Morocco and Carthage in Tunisia.[87] Considering the fact that domesticated horse material has been identified at sites from the fourth and third millennia BC in the Levant, and Egypt has horse bones from the second millennium BC, it seems possible that the earliest horse in the Maghrib may have been introduced prior to the arrival of the Phoenicians in the ninth century BC.[88]

The earliest identifiable horse material in West Africa comes from the site of Akumbu (AD 600–1000).[89] Skeletal evidence from the first millennium AD also includes five burials, which were excavated from Aissa Dugjé in northern Cameroon.[90] Two scholars have independently suggested that a small horse (perhaps the progenitor of the present-day local pony types) was extant in West Africa from the first millennium BC to the first millennium AD.[91] This possibility is supported by linguistic evidence and perhaps also the trypanotolerance and other environmentally specific

---

[80] Law 1980, 54–58; Law 1995.   [81] Chaix 2000.   [82] Camps and Chaker 1993.
[83] Camps and Gast 1982.   [84] Alhaique 2002, 183.
[85] See Marshall 2007 for a discussion of early domestic donkey size.
[86] Valenzuela Lamas 2016.   [87] Becker *et al.* 2012; Nobis 1999.
[88] Mattingly *et al.* Forthcoming.   [89] MacDonald and MacDonald 2000, 140.
[90] MacEachern *et al.* 2001.   [91] Blench 2000b; Law 1980, 3; 1995.

adaptations of the local modern ponies.[92] Additionally, Medieval Arabic source material describes the presence of very small horses in multiple regions of West Africa;[93] this suggests that such animals were introduced prior to Arab contact. Finally, equestrian equipment which technologically predates the set of paraphernalia used by Arab peoples (for example, a bridle with bit, a saddle with stirrups) is known from some regions of West Africa.[94]

Equids: Donkeys, Mules and Hinnies

Donkeys are well adapted to hot and arid climes,[95] and Libyan donkeys were considered to be second only to the camel in terms of their hardiness and desert adaptation.[96] In terms of water consumption, donkeys can survive for one or two days with very little water,[97] but a working donkey requires about ten litres a day. Donkeys can carry about 65 kg,[98] and were no doubt a great benefit to the past communities who adopted them. Apart from their vital role as a general pack animal and in operating wells and mills, Marshall has noted their importance in bringing water to other types of livestock in arid environments across North and East Africa during the modern era.[99] Mules and hinnies (the offspring of a female donkey and a stallion or a male donkey and a mare respectively) present an ideal compromise between the characteristics of each species: more resilient than a horse, and capable of carrying approximately 70–90 kg. However, the infertility of mules and hinnies presents a considerable drawback. Considering the hardiness of donkeys, mules and hinnies, human-aided movement of these animals may have been comparatively less difficult than moving species with more stringent environmental or husbandry needs (for example, pigs and horses).

Equus africanus, the wild ass, is native to North Africa and found at Holocene sites across the Maghrib and Sahara.[100] The conventional narrative suggests that wild donkeys were domesticated in Egypt by around 4000 BC, but given the occasional rock art portrayals across the Sahara and abundant populations of *Equus africanus*, it may well be that Saharan donkeys were independently domesticated,[101] although further research is necessary to investigate this possibility. Debates regarding donkey

---

[92] Blench 1993; Law 1980, 5–7.   [93] Levtzion and Hopkins 1981, 81, 185, 263.
[94] Law 1980, 93–96; Law 1995.   [95] Camps *et al.* 1988.   [96] Bates 1970, 29.
[97] Bovill 1968; Sidebotham 2011, 25.   [98] Barker *et al.* 2007, 344–45.
[99] Marshall 2007, 375.   [100] Blench 2000b; Marshall 2007, 376–78.
[101] Mattingly *et al.* Forthcoming.

domestication continue, but ancient DNA research supports the idea of the donkey as an African domesticate; some results have hinted at a strong affiliation between domestic donkeys and the Nubian and Somali clades of wild donkeys.[102]

An equid mandible and teeth were excavated from a Middle Pastoral corbeille (4044–3960 calBC) in the northern part of the Messak Settafet.[103] All other faunal remains from this site were identified as domestic cattle or caprine; this may be an indicator that the specimen represents a domestic donkey,[104] and the date of the find is consistent with pre-dynastic and early dynastic donkey finds in Egypt.[105] The existence of a desert caravan route for donkeys (the Abu Ballas trail) during the late Old Kingdom period/First Intermediate period (second half of the third millennium BC) and between Oxyrhynchos and Bahariya in the Ptolemaic period (second century AD), both in the Egyptian Western Desert, shows that it was possible to use the animals for desert transport to some extent.[106]

Outside of the Nilotic region, the first securely dated *Equus asinus* originates from a context dated to 2197–1435 calBC at the site of Wadi Hariq in western Sudan.[107] By this point, it is possible that domestic donkeys were present in the Sahara and the Maghrib, but a lack of excavated sites from that period hampers any such interpretations.[108] Many rock art depictions of people riding equids are found throughout the Garamantian heartlands in the Libyan Sahara. Equid remains were recovered from first millennium BC contexts at Zinkekra, an Early Garamantian hill fort in the Sahara.[109] These are small in size, indistinct in morphology and are thought to probably be donkey. However, another site in the same region, Fewet, has no equid bones present (though the sample concerned is rather small).[110]

The earliest identified equid (tentatively identified as *Equus* cf. *asinus*) in Sub-Saharan West Africa was excavated at Siouré in the Middle Senegal Valley, and is dated to AD 1–250.[111] A single donkey element dating to the first millennium BC is reportedly present at Walaldé (also in the Middle Senegal Valley).[112] As few details of the faunal assemblage have been published, this designation should probably be regarded with some caution.

---

[102] Kimura *et al.* 2013; see Gifford-Gonzalez and Hanotte 2011 for a review of the evidence.
[103] di Lernia *et al.* 2013; 07/39 C1 UGAMS-3757 charred bone 5190 ± 30.
[104] Mattingly *et al.* Forthcoming.   [105] Marshall 2007.   [106] Förster 2007; Thissen 2013.
[107] Jesse *et al.* 2004; radiocarbon details not available.   [108] Mattingly *et al.* Forthcoming.
[109] Fothergill 2012; van der Veen and Westley 2010.   [110] Alhaique 2013.
[111] MacDonald and MacDonald 2000, 140.   [112] Deme and McIntosh 2006.

Some of the earliest settlement assemblages from Maghribian sites such as Althiburos, Carthage and Mogador have equids present,[113] and although it is often impossible to differentiate between the skeletal remains of horses, mules and hinnies or donkeys, the first and last species were certainly present and widespread by the mid-first millennium BC. Mules or hinnies have not been definitively identified in assemblages from the areas considered here, but the difficulty presented by their identification makes this unsurprising. In Sub-Saharan Africa, donkeys and horses become ubiquitous in the later first millennium AD.[114] Hopefully future excavations and analyses will help to clarify the appearance and movement of equids across these regions.

Pigs

Pigs present a particular challenge in terms of movement, and special skills were probably required to transport them. Apart from the logistical problems of moving pigs, there are other issues of serious concern. As a species, pigs are ill-suited to hot environments. They sunburn easily, do not have sweat glands and lack an effective mechanism to keep cool in high temperatures; ample shade and water is required in order to avoid high death rates from heat stress.[115] Of all the species discussed here, pigs would probably have benefitted the most from being moved at the coolest parts of the year. Adult pigs may have been impossible to move long distances across the high-temperature areas of the Sahara Desert. Pigs farrow in the autumn, and with a gestation period of roughly 115 days followed by a four-to-eight-week weaning period, piglets may have been light enough (modern piglet weights range from 7 to 21.3 kg depending upon the age at which they are weaned)[116] for transport by pack animals in the spring months. Of all the species discussed here, pigs may have been the most difficult to transport and manage due to the probable necessity of packing them onto another animal, their rapid maturation and their environmental requirements.

Pigs were present in Egypt from the fifth millennium BC and have been identified in Fazzan in the Phase 8 levels at Jarma (150 BC–AD 50) and every subsequent phase up to the Early Modern period.[117] A single suid cranial fragment came from a Period 2 layer at Zinkekra (ZIN002.11), and

---

[113] Becker *et al.* 2012; Nobis 1999; Valenzuela Lamas 2016.
[114] MacDonald and MacDonald 2000.   [115] Misztal *et al.* 2010; Zeder 1998.   [116] Carr 1998.
[117] Holmes 2013; Linseele *et al.* 2014.

although this has not been directly dated it is considered a part of the Early Garamantian Phase (1000–500 BC).[118]

Most evidence points towards a European introduction of the domestic pig in West Africa, although bone finds at one Early Iron Age site in South Africa suggests that the animal may already have been propagated over the African continent by around AD 600.[119] Pigs are generally not kept by nomadic pastoralists, and therefore they probably did not spread across the Sahara from North Africa together with the domestic cattle and caprines. Linguists have argued for a pre-European introduction and proposed that domestic pigs may have been taken from north-eastern Africa down the Nile, spreading further overland to west-central Africa along a corridor from Darfur to Lake Chad and reaching central Nigeria in Medieval times.[120] However, there are no archaeological bone remains to support this hypothesis.

Camels

Due to their tolerance for heat and ability to withstand water shortages, camels have a reputation for being ideally suited to the environmental extremes of North Africa and are typically kept in areas which have less than 250 mm of annual rainfall.[121] Camels are able to conserve moisture very effectively, can sustain a fluid loss of roughly 30 per cent of their body weight and are able to rehydrate safely and quickly. In high temperatures, camels can go without water for three to five days, and for up to six or seven days in cool conditions. In addition, they are able to mediate the effects of extreme temperatures and regulate their body temperatures more efficiently than other animals. They also possess other adaptive advantages, including bushy eyelashes which prevent windblown sand and dust from entering their eyes, and feet with cutaneous pads, which allow them to move with relative ease over difficult terrain. Camels can carry up to 150–200 kg and are potentially sources of milk and meat if necessary. They are popularly thought of as the desert pack animal par excellence, and frequently contrasted with horses in terms of their slower land speed,[122] but a direct comparison between these two species is not viable. Beyond the social and symbolic differences in how people perceived camels and horses, they have adapted to very different environments and are not suitable for

---

[118] Van der Veen and Westley 2010.   [119] Plug and Badenhorst 2001, 113.
[120] Blench 2000c.
[121] Camps *et al.* 1996; Gigliarelli 1932, 189–96; Lydon 2009, 208–14; Shaw 1979.
[122] From nineteenth-century accounts, 25–30 km a day, Lydon 2009, 209–10.

the same types of terrain. Speed is also not the only factor worth considering: calculations involving water weight and horse carrying capacity reveal that horses require more water than they can physically carry during heavy activity,[123] which is less of an issue for camels. Conversely, rocky terrain is very difficult for camels and can cause lameness; camels are also vulnerable to the fly-borne diseases which are so prevalent throughout the northern Maghrib and parts of West Africa.[124] The variation in vegetation and environment across the Sahara and the rest of the Maghrib has led to camels becoming highly adapted to specific regions. As it is likely that camel deaths would be unsustainably high if one type of camel was taken directly across the Sahara, the nineteenth-century caravan practice was to change camel teams entirely at different points along the route.[125] If this tradition originated in earlier practices, it may suggest that distinct breeds of camels were developed for regional trade purposes, and then linked up together across wider stretches of landscape.

The earliest identified camel skeletal material in North Africa outside of Egypt has been excavated from Carthage in Tunisia and is dated to the fifth to third centuries BC.[126] Camel has also been identified at Utica from a first millennium BC context.[127] About a quarter of coastal sites in the Maghrib from the second century BC to the seventh century AD had camel present, but the species is typically only represented by a handful of bones. Since the climate of the northern Tunisian and Moroccan sites in particular is unsuitable for camels, the animals at these sites were probably used in transport. The camel arrived in the Sahara by the first millennium AD. The first camel bones from a Saharan context date to no later than the second century AD and were recovered from the sites of Aghram Nadharif and Jarma, the Garamantian capital.[128] Later remains from Saniat Jibril date from the first to the fourth century AD.[129] The proportion of camels appears to have increased over time at these sites, which might hint at their rapid adoption. However, the sample sizes are very small and reconstructing changes in the structure of the camel population with any confidence is not possible. It is possible that camels were being raised outside of oasis settlements as no unfused (juvenile) bones were noted at Jarma.[130] This is consistent with the management requirements and foraging

---

[123] Mattingly *et al.* Forthcoming.
[124] Johnson 1969, 8; Lydon 2009; Mitchell 2005, 145–46; Shaw 1979.   [125] Scheele 2010.
[126] Nobis 1999, 602.   [127] Elizabeth Fentress, personal communication.
[128] Alhaique 2006; Holmes 2013; Holmes and Grant 2013.
[129] Van der Veen and Westley 2010.   [130] Holmes and Grant 2013.

tendencies of camels, which could have been quite destructive within an oasis settlement.

The earliest dated, definitively identified camel remains in Sub-Saharan Africa were excavated in Senegal from the site of Cubalel/Siouré (AD 250–400);[131] this may indicate the use of camels in Trans-Saharan trade by the early first millennium AD. However, possible camel remains were reported from Walaldé along the Middle Senegal (from W2; c.800–300 BC).[132] If the dating and speciation were confirmed, it would dramatically change the current narrative about the introduction of the camel to West Africa. Linguistic evidence supports a northern route of introduction for the species into West Africa.[133] Nevertheless, an east–west introduction through the savannah corridor is argued for by some.[134] Dromedaries cannot thrive south of the Sahel zone because of their vulnerability to endemic diseases in the region,[135] but it is possible that certain regional varieties used in trade were marginally more successful. At least the species enjoyed a form of iconographic success in the southern Lake Chad region of the Sahel, as is indicated by the presence of a camel figurine at the site of Houlouf (c.AD 1400–1600).[136]

Caprines (Sheep and Goats)

Caprines were spread overland from the Levant to Africa, passing first through Egypt. The earliest evidence for domesticated sheep/goats dates to the late seventh millennium BC, and several sites across the Egyptian deserts are known for fifth-millennium BC caprine material, although bone evidence is usually very limited.[137] By the mid-fifth millennium BC, caprines were probably introduced into the Sahara.[138] Coastal northern Africa may, as part of the Mediterranean zone, have seen the arrival of the earliest domesticated animals and agricultural economies through several waves of seafaring.[139] Caprines reached Sub-Saharan West Africa in the late third millennium BC (Late Stone Age).[140] Size analyses suggest that new types of sheep/goat appeared in West Africa after the Late Stone Age (mid-first millennium BC–early first millennium AD; Iron Age). This may have involved new introductions that were associated with the documented renewal of population movement, but could also represent locally developed breeds.

---

[131] MacDonald and MacDonald 2000.   [132] Deme and McIntosh 2006.   [133] Blench 1995.
[134] Bulliet 1990.   [135] Wilson 1984, 17.   [136] Holl 2002, 180.   [137] Linseele et al. 2014.
[138] Gifford-Gonzalez and Hanotte 2011.   [139] Zeder 2011.   [140] Linseele 2007.

   In the arid environments of Africa, sheep and goats are probably the most easily kept of the larger domesticated food animals. Sheep are grazers, and may compete with cattle for the same type of pasture, while goats are browsers and can subsist on a more varied diet.[141] In general, caprines (and especially sheep) need to drink more often than cattle, but their intake is smaller and they can therefore be sustained by more limited sources that would not support cattle.[142] This factor, combined with their comparatively rapid terrestrial movement speed, probably made caprines (especially goats) less challenging to translocate than other species.

Cattle

The oldest uncontroversial African cattle remains were found in the Egyptian Western Desert and date to the fifth millennium BC. Cattle thus appeared about simultaneously with the domesticated caprines and were quickly spread to the Sahara,[143] reaching West Africa in the third millennium BC as well. As we suggested for the caprines, it is also possible that new cattle types were introduced during the subsequent Iron Age. The available evidence points to the introduction of humped cattle (zebu) from Asia by way of the Arabian Sea, entering the Horn during the first millennium AD and spreading rapidly over Africa from there.[144] Osteologically, zebu cattle are difficult to differentiate from unhumped cattle, and crossbred types (Sanga) also existed.

   Cattle are ecologically demanding animals which need more drinking water and better pasture than sheep or goats,[145] but their characteristics and requirements vary according to their type. Pastoral nomads keep mainly humped cattle, although pure types do not occur in Africa. African cattle all have taurine (humpless) origins, but with zebu introgression, decreasing in a north–south and east–west direction.[146] Zebu need less food and water and are better suited to long-distance migration than humpless cattle. Moreover, their milk production is less affected by food shortages, and they are less sensitive to ticks, gastrointestinal parasites and rinderpest (cattle plague; genus *Morbillivirus*).[147] Taurines are mainly kept in transhumant systems or by sedentary farmers, and are more resistant to trypanosomiasis.[148] Sanga cattle, usually humpless but sometimes with a small, muscular hump, are sometimes considered as a third type of African

---

[141] Dahl and Hjort 1976, 253.   [142] Dahl and Hjort 1976, 249.
[143] Alhaique 2006; 2013; Holmes 2013; van der Veen and Westley 2010.
[144] Gifford-Gonzalez and Hanotte 2011; Hanotte *et al.* 2002.   [145] Dahl and Hjort 1976.
[146] Hanotte *et al.* 2002.   [147] FAO 2001; Marshall 1989.   [148] FAO 2001.

cattle.[149] Some authors consider the Sanga to be the descendants of locally domesticated African aurochs, while others argue that they are the result of cross-breeding taurine and zebu cattle. They are less resistant to rinderpest and produce less milk than zebu, but they are trypanotolerant.[150] At the end of the nineteenth century AD, a rinderpest epidemic eradicated taurine and Sanga cattle from most of the African continent.[151] Cattle often have a high symbolic value, especially in pastoral nomadic cultures, an importance to which their numerous appearances in Saharan rock art also testify. However, it appears that in economic terms or with regard to the numbers of bones in archaeological assemblages, caprines are usually more important. In any case, it is likely that mixed herds, consisting of both cattle and caprines, were kept in order to moderate and reduce risks, maintain good pasture, make maximum use of available resources and to better spread yields throughout the year.

Data and Discussion

The geographic distribution of sites with published faunal assemblages, many of which have been referenced in the text and some of which have been incorporated into the graphs, is shown in Figure 5.1. This map illustrates the staggering spatial scope of our chapter and reflects the traditional research bias towards colonial sites on the Mediterranean coast and other favoured regions.

Figures 5.2–5.7 (created using the assemblage data in Table 5.1) show aspects of the faunal data collated from the phased assemblages from different regions across North Africa, West Africa and the Sahara. In these graphs, the proportion of each species (y-axis) is plotted over time (x-axis). The lines across each graph (trendlines) are rolling averages of the proportion of each species (points) against the total number of cattle, caprine and pig elements (as these three species were consistently reported across all regions). The rolling average (also called a moving mean) trendlines show the mean average proportion of the indicated species over a 250-year period. Each point on the graphs represents the temporal midpoint of a single phased assemblage to illustrate the complexity and variation in the faunal data.[152]

---

[149] Grigson 1991.   [150] Porter 1991, 193.   [151] Payne 1964.

[152] This approach is similar to modelling political polling data. Although a version sensitive to the size, quality and dating of an assemblage could be constructed, this model is presented here for clarity and replicability.

Table 5.1 *Faunal data, organised by region and time period*

Municipality or region	Site or project	Date span or period	Reference
Algeria	Cherchel	200 BC–AD 1400	Clark 1993
Algeria	Sétif	AD 400–1200	King 1991
Cyrenaica	Berenice, Area CC, H2, SK1-SK4	200 BC–700 AD	Barker 1979
Cyrenaica	Tocra	Late Roman	Buzaian 2000
Fazzan	Zinkekra	900 BC–AD 100	Van der Veen and Westley 2010; Fothergill 2012
Fazzan	Jarma	300 BC–AD 1850	Holmes and Grant 2013
Fazzan	Aghram Nadharif	AD 1–400	Alhaique 2006
Fazzan	Saniat Jibril	AD 1–400	Van der Veen and Westley 2010
Fazzan	Fewet	200 BC–AD 100	Alhaique 2013
Lake Chad (southern)	Daima	550 BC–AD 1150	Connah 1981
Lake Chad (southern)	Deguesse	1900 BC–AD 1800	Holl 2002
Lake Chad (southern)	Krenak	1900 BC–AD 1400	Holl 2002
Lake Chad (southern)	Hamei	AD 500–1800	Holl 2002
Lake Chad (southern)	Mishiskwa	AD 500–1800	Holl 2002
Lake Chad (southern)	Madaf	AD 500–1800	Holl 2002
Lake Chad (southern)	Blé	AD 250–1400	Holl 2002
Lake Chad (southern)	Krenak-Sao	AD 500–1000	Holl 2002
Lake Chad (southern)	Holouf	AD 1–1800	Holl 2002
Marmarica	Wadi Umm el-Ashdan	100 BC–AD 500	Pöllath and Rieger 2013
Marmarica	Abar el-Kanayis	AD 1–600	Pöllath and Rieger 2013
Marmarica	Gheriat el-Garbia	AD 300–450	Pöllath and Rieger 2013
Morocco	Lixus	Punic to Islamic	Iborra Eres 2001
Morocco	Mogador	700–500 BC	Becker 2012; Becker *et al.* 2012.
Morocco	Thamusida	200 BC–AD 400	De Grossi Mazzorin and De Venuto 2006
Morocco	Al-Basra	AD 600–1050	Loyet 2004

Table 5.1 (*cont.*)

Municipality or region	Site or project	Date span or period	Reference
Morocco	Ceuta	600–700 BC	Camarós and Estévez 2010
Niger Bend	Gadei	AD 600–1600	Stangroome 2000
Niger Bend	Kobadi	2000 BC–AD 1	Raimbault *et al.* 1987
Niger Bend	Mouyssam II (KNT 2)	AD 1–1000	Guérin and Faure 1991
Niger Bend	Akumbu	AD 400–1400	MacDonald and Van Neer 1993
Niger Bend	Kolima-Sud	1700–500 BC	MacDonald 1994
Niger Bend	Dia-Shoma	800 BC–AD 1700	MacDonald and MacDonald 2000
Niger Bend	Jenné-jeno	250 BC–AD 1400	MacDonald 1995
Niger Bend	Tongo Maaré Diabel	AD 1–1000	MacDonald *et al.* 1994
Niger Bend	Gao Saney	AD 900–1200	MacDonald and MacDonald 1996
Niger Bend	Gao Ancien	AD 500–1600	MacDonald and MacDonald 1996
Tripolitania	Libyan Valleys	AD 1–700	Van der Veen *et al.* 1996
Tripolitania	Lepcis Magna	AD 300–1000	Sidell 1997
Tunisia	Althiburos	900 BC–AD 600	Valenzuela Lamas 2016
Tunisia	Carthage (Karthago)	Punic to late Roman	Nobis 1999
Tunisia	Carthage Circus	AD 500–600	Rielly 1988
Tunisia	Carthage Cisterns 1977.1, 1977.2, 1977.3	AD 500–700	Reese 1981
Tunisia	Carthage Kobbat Bent el Rey	Late Roman	Von den Driesch and Baumgartner 1997
Tunisia	Carthage House of the Greek Charioteers	Roman, Vandal, Byzantine	Reese 1977
Tunisia	Carthage Ecclesiastical Complex	Late Roman to Islamic	Reese 1977
Tunisia	Carthage Avenue Habib Bourgiba	Vandal to Byzantine	Schwartz 1984
Tunisia	Carthage Bir Messaouda	760 BC–AD 1800	Slopsma *et al.* 2009

Table 5.1 (*cont.*)

Municipality or region	Site or project	Date span or period	Reference
Tunisia	Meninx	AD 200–500	Drine *et al.* 2009
Tunisia	Leptiminus	AD 200–700	Burke 2001
Burkina Faso	BF 94/133	2200–1000 BC	Linseele 2007; 2013
Burkina Faso	BF 94/96	2200–1000 BC	Linseele 2007; 2013
Burkina Faso	BF 97/5	2200–1000 BC, AD 1–500	Linseele 2007; 2013
Burkina Faso	BF 94/45	2200–1000 BC, AD 1–500	Linseele 2007; 2013
Burkina Faso	BF 97/13	AD 1–1400	Linseele 2007; 2013
Burkina Faso	BF 97/30	AD 1000–1400	Linseele 2007; 2013
Burkina Faso	BF 96/22	AD 500–1000	Linseele 2007; 2013
Burkina Faso	BF 97/31	AD 1000–1400	Linseele 2007; 2013
Burkina Faso	BF 94/120	AD 1000–1400	Linseele 2007; 2013
Burkina Faso	BF 95/7	AD 1000–1400	Linseele 2007; 2013
Lake Chad (south-east Nigeria)	NA 90/5 C	1500–1200 BC	Linseele 2007; 2013
Lake Chad (south-east Nigeria)	NA 90/5A	1200–800 BC	Linseele 2007; 2013
Lake Chad (south-east Nigeria)	NA 90/5BI	1500–800 BC	Linseele 2007; 2013
Lake Chad (south-east Nigeria)	NA 90/5BII	1000–800 BC	Linseele 2007; 2013
Lake Chad (south-east Nigeria)	NA 91/1A	1800–1400 BC	Linseele 2007; 2013
Lake Chad (south-east Nigeria)	NA 93/42	1800–1400 BC	Linseele 2007; 2013
Lake Chad (south-east Nigeria)	NA 97/18	1800–1400 BC	Linseele 2007; 2013
Lake Chad (south-east Nigeria)	NA 97/24	1800–1400 BC	Linseele 2007; 2013

Table 5.1 (*cont.*)

Municipality or region	Site or project	Date span or period	Reference
Lake Chad (south-east Nigeria)	NA 93/36	1500–1200 BC	Linseele 2007; 2013
Lake Chad (south-east Nigeria)	NA 99/65	1500–800 BC	Linseele 2007; 2013
Lake Chad (south-east Nigeria)	NA 93/10	1000–800 BC	Linseele 2007; 2013
Lake Chad (south-east Nigeria)	NA 97/37	600–400 BC	Linseele 2007; 2013
Lake Chad (south-east Nigeria)	NA 97/33	1500–1000 BC	Linseele 2007; 2013
Lake Chad (south-east Nigeria)	NA 96/45	1500–1000 BC	Linseele 2007; 2013
Lake Chad (south-east Nigeria)	NA 95/1	1500–1000 BC	Linseele 2007; 2013
Lake Chad (south-east Nigeria)	NA 97/26	AD 1–700	Linseele 2007; 2013
Lake Chad (south-east Nigeria)	NA 99/75	AD 1–700	Linseele 2007; 2013
Lake Chad (south-east Nigeria)	NA 97/13	AD 1–700	Linseele 2007; 2013
Lake Chad (south-east Nigeria)	NA 92/2 C	AD 1800–1900	Linseele 2007; 2013
Lake Chad (south-east Nigeria)	NA 93/46	1300 BC–AD 600	Linseele 2007; 2013
Lake Chad (south-east Nigeria)	NA 94/7	550 BC–AD 1983	Linseele 2007; 2013
Lake Chad (south-east Nigeria)	NA 93/45	AD 600–2000	Linseele 2007; 2013

Note: Some 'site' entries use codes which can be linked to the appropriate reference (for example, BF 94/133, NA 93/45), and others include multiple subsites (for example, Libyan Valleys, Berenice, the Carthage cisterns). The 'date span or period' column includes the temporal range of all reported assemblages for each site, and gaps in the overall chronology may therefore be present. NB Since data compiled in 2015, further faunal assemblages have been published: Morocco (Rirha, Volubilis); Tunisia (Bir Ennahal, Utica, Zama, Zita); Egypt (Amheida); Mali (Tadmakka, Tongo Maare Diabal); and Senegal (Middle Senegal Valley).

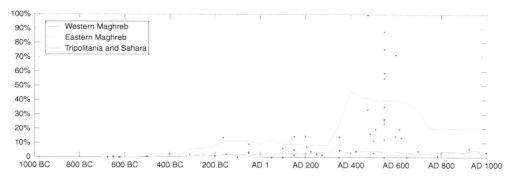

Figure 5.2 Chickens as a proportion of cattle, caprines and pigs in assemblages. Points represent individual assemblage percentages.

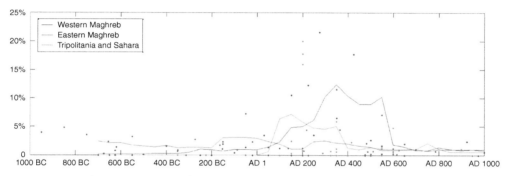

Figure 5.3 Equids as a proportion of cattle, caprines and pigs in assemblages. Points represent individual assemblage percentages.

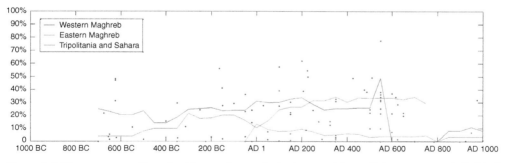

Figure 5.4 Pigs as a proportion of cattle, caprines and pigs in assemblages. Points represent individual assemblage percentages.

Figures 5.2–5.5 use three regions due to the low overall numbers of chickens, equids and camels as well as the near absence of pigs in Niger River and Lake Chad assemblages. However, we were able to develop more nuanced graphs for caprines and cattle. Figures 5.6 and 5.7 present the

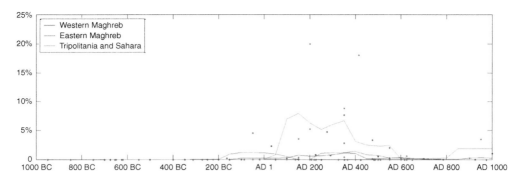

Figure 5.5 Camels as a proportion of cattle, caprines and pigs in assemblages. Points represent individual assemblage percentages.

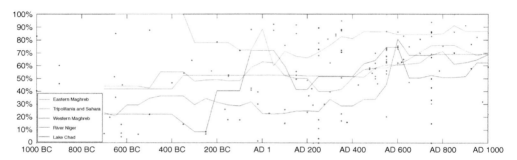

Figure 5.6 Caprines as a proportion of cattle, caprines and pigs in assemblages. Points represent individual assemblage percentages.

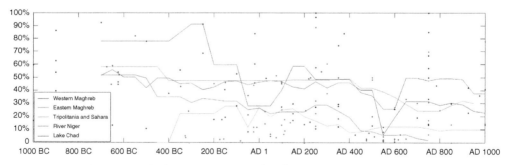

Figure 5.7 Cattle as a proportion of cattle, caprines and pigs in assemblages. Points represent individual assemblage percentages.

greater study area as divided into five geographic regions: Cyrenaica and Tunisia, Tripolitania and the Sahara, Mauretania (sites in the western Maghrib), the Niger River (predominantly sites in Mali and Burkina

Faso) and Lake Chad (sites mainly south of Lake Chad, including northern Nigeria and Cameroon).

As previously noted, there are some inherent biases in the data, including a preponderance of late Roman and Byzantine material in Cyrenaica/Tunisia with a clearly observable spatial and functional distribution of only a few inland and rural sites (see Figure 5.1; 27 assemblages originated from Carthage alone). This particular bias affects Tripolitania/Sahara and Mauretania as well to some extent. The Niger River and Lake Chad assemblages are somewhat more widely dispersed, but spatial biases are evident in all regions. No graph is included for dogs because although the species was an important component of pastoral animal husbandry and was eaten by some Saharan peoples, they often occur as associated bone groups (ABGs), especially in the periods which dominate this dataset. This can skew the relative proportions of other species which tend not to be encountered as ABGs; the material from the Carthage Circus excavations (which included 14 equid ABGs) has not been included in the equid graph for the same reason.[153] Despite these exclusions and issues, a number of patterns are clear and merit discussion.

There are unsurprisingly strong differences between regions with regard to relative species proportions, and even when considering only the temporal data, the data are not evenly distributed across space and time due to excavation biases and other factors. However, the relative frequency of caprines increases over time in all regions, rather in keeping with King's paper.[154] Conversely, the relative frequency of cattle decreases over time, especially after the first century BC, although this is by no means an evenly distributed development. It is possible that these two trends (a general increase in caprines and concomitant decrease in cattle) may be linked to changes in landscape and climate that encouraged raising more drought-tolerant livestock in some regions. Pigs are another matter altogether; they initially turn up in comparatively high percentages in Cyrenaica/Tunisia, and their relative frequency wavers over time. Domestic pigs are present at Jarma in the Sahara and at Tripolitanian sites but are missing from Niger River and Lake Chad assemblages (it is possible that some specimens tentatively identified as warthog or another suid may be *Sus scrofa* f. domestica), but were clearly of importance from at least the Medieval period.[155] In North Africa, pigs are an important part of urban assemblages from the mid-first millennium AD, but are only infrequently identified after AD 600 (though the number of analysed assemblages is low), which broadly coincides with the adoption of Islam across the region.[156] One

---

[153] Rielly 1988.   [154] King 1999.   [155] Blench 2000c.   [156] MacKinnon 2017.

possibility for the introduction of pigs and their husbandry to parts of northern Africa is their inclusion in a 'package' of agricultural skills and techniques specific to oasis environments which was disseminated across the Sahara and perhaps into other areas. The point at which pigs enter a prolonged period of increased frequency in Cyrenaican/Tunisian and Tripolitanian/Saharan assemblages (AD 400–450) is also the point at which the chicken is most frequent, perhaps a reflection of urban animal husbandry regimes at large coastal sites, in which both the chicken and the pig would have flourished. However, skeletal evidence for pigs predates the occurrence of chicken remains at all sites.

Chickens are vanishingly rare at some West African sites, which is likely to be accounted for by the use of a single identification category for all avians (or only presence/absence data) in some reports.[157] Equids and camels both appear more frequently in assemblages dating to the early first millennium AD, particularly in North Africa and the Sahara; this might be a reflection of the use of some of these animals in pre-Islamic Trans-Saharan trade. Archaeological visibility of these species may also have been impacted by diachronic changes in culinary practices and disposal of carcasses outside of habitation areas.[158] It is worth noting here that in reviewing the collated data, certain sites appear to group more closely with husbandry practices prevalent in other regions: Aghram Nadharif, located squarely in the Sahara, has a high proportion of cattle; Gao has a very high proportion of caprines and camel remains are present, which may be a reflection of its prominent role in Trans-Saharan trade.

Concluding Remarks

Many aspects of the processes involved in moving animal species in the past remain conjectural, although tantalising possibilities exist for 'packages' of species and skills, mechanisms for transporting certain animals and the applicability of translocation as a way of approaching some of these matters. Some evidence for the development of animal breeds which are more suitable for specific environments or regions (through trypano-tolerance or highly localised adaptations) presents an enticing avenue for further research.

[157] Holl 2002; Bedaux *et al.* 1978.   [158] Linseele 2007, 83.

Various biases in knowledge frustrate attempts at large-scale interpretation and have already been mentioned, but substantial gaps remain. We know little regarding the movement and introduction of domesticate species between the Late Stone Age (when the earliest domesticates arrived) and the introductions made by Arab peoples or during the Islamic period; perhaps horses and new types of cattle and caprines made it through the Sahara to West Africa in this period. Some specific themes have emerged through this study, chief of which is the number of practical obstacles that affect the movement of different species. There are significant environmental differences between the Sahara and Sub-Saharan Africa which would have impacted the movement, establishment and management of domestic animal species across and between the regions; chief among these is disease. Dogs, horses, camels and some cattle are vulnerable to trypanosomiasis and other fly-borne diseases of humid regions. Other health-related concerns abound: camels will become unwell if they do not have access to enough salt in the form of halophyte plants. Pigs are easily sunburned and have an extremely low tolerance for heat. All species have water requirements in order to survive and be productive, and fulfilling these needs in the Sahara and parts of West Africa would have been a continuous challenge.

We are in general agreement with Liverani regarding the species composition and nature of caravans across the Sahara,[159] but are not entirely comfortable regarding the idea that the southern regions of North and West Africa had little impact with regard to innovation overall. While it is clear that most domestic species were introduced mainly from the north and east, and that pre-existing husbandry and transport skills would have been necessary to accomplish translocation, local methods and inventions (for example, the construction of huts to prevent biting insects from accessing horses as found at Houlouf,[160] the development of trypanotolerant breeds of dwarf sheep and goats) were critical to the management and success of said species. Unfortunately, it is difficult to detect the extent to which more archaeologically ephemeral innovations spread out of the Sahelian belt and West Africa.

Various narratives and conjectures for north to south movement of animals in North and West Africa exist, but the translocation of animals from the south to the north is another story. Although we do not know the geographic origin of the guinea fowl that were

---

[159] Liverani, Chapter 2, this volume.   [160] Holl 2002, 156.

translocated to Europe and described by Roman authors, it is possible that these originated in West Africa and may even have been moved northward across the Sahara. The south to north trade in hippopotamus and elephant ivory is particularly of note and probably worth investigating. One archaeological example is a cache of hippopotamus ivory that was excavated from a context dating to the eleventh century AD in Gao (Mali), a 'terminus for Trans-Saharan trade'.[161] Giraffe elements were identified in second-century AD and fifth- to ninth-century levels at Jarma.[162] These elements may represent the skin of a giraffe which included lower leg and foot bones rather than a complete live animal; in-depth investigation of the movement of animal parts and products thus has the potential to enhance our understanding of regional connections.

Other lines of investigation might prove to be particularly valuable. The introduction of foggara technology to the Wadi al-Ajal in the late first millennium BC is roughly in line with the first appearance of pigs and plant species associated with oasis agriculture.[163] This lends some support to the idea that if there was an oasis agriculture 'package', pigs may have been part of it, complemented it or were well suited to such circumstances. Ostrich eggshell was a valuable and widely traded item which is present across the Sahara and North Africa at sites such as Jarma and Althiburos.[164] Ostriches have been extinct from much of this area since at least the beginning of the twentieth century, but ancient ostrich ranges included Egypt, parts of the Sahara, the North African pre-desert and southern Tunisia;[165] the origins of the eggshell at these sites is therefore uncertain.

The husbandry requirements, behaviour and archaeological and textual evidence for the movement of the key species we have discussed in this chapter highlight the complexity and importance of these processes and the value of animal management knowledge to past peoples of the Sahara and surrounding regions. We hope to have illuminated some Trans-Saharan and West African connections through the framework of animal translocation and created a platform upon which future research on the roles of animals and their management can be built.

---

[161] Insoll 1995, 327.   [162] Holmes and Grant 2013.
[163] See Wilson *et al.*, Chapter 3, this volume.
[164] Holmes and Grant 2013; Valenzuela Lamas 2016.
[165] Kacem *et al.* 1994; Manlius 2001; Wilson 2012.

References

Albarella, U. 2007. Companions of our travel: The archaeological evidence of animals in exile. In S. Hartmann (ed.), *Fauna and Flora in the Middle Ages: Studies of the Medieval Environment and Its Impact on the Human Mind*, Frankfurt am Main: Verlag Peter Lang, 133–54.

Alhaique, F. 2002. Archaeozoology of funerary structures. In S. di Lernia and G. Manzi (eds), *Sand, Stones, and Bones: The Archaeology of Death in the Wadi Tanezzuft Valley (5000–2000 BP)*, Firenze: All'Insegna del Giglio, 181–96.

Alhaique, F. 2006. The faunal remains. In M. Liverani (ed.), *Aghram Nadarif: A Garamantian Citadel in the Wadi Tannezzuft*, Firenze: All'Insegna del Giglio, 349–60.

Alhaique, F. 2013. The faunal remains. In L. Mori (ed.), *Life and Death of a Rural Village in Garamantian Times: Archaeological Investigations in the Oasis of Fewet (Libyan Sahara)*, ZAZ 6. Firenze: All'Insegna di Giglio, 191–98.

Anonymous 1984. *Guide to the Care and Use of Experimental Animals*. Ottawa: Canadian Council on Animal Care, Volumes 1 and 2.

Barich, B.E. 2014. Northwest Libya from the Early to Late Holocene: New data on environment and subsistence from the Jebel Gharbi. *Quaternary International* 320: 15–27.

Barker, G. 1979. Economic life at Berenice: The animal and fish bones, marine molluscs and plant remains. In J. Lloyd (ed.), *Excavations at Sidi Khrebish Benghazi (Berenice), Volume 2*. Supplements to Libya Antiqua 5. Tripoli: Department of Antiquities, 1–49.

Barker, G., Gilbertson, D. and Mattingly, D.J. 2007. *Archaeology and Desertification: The Wadi Faynan Landscape Survey, Southern Jordan*. Oxford: Oxbow, CBRL.

Barnett, T.F. and Mattingly, D.J. 2003. The engraved heritage: rock-art and inscriptions. In D.J. Mattingly (ed.), *The Archaeology of Fazzan. Volume 1, Synthesis*, London: Society for Libyan Studies, Department of Antiquities, 279–326.

Bates, O. 1970. *The Eastern Libyans* (new impression). Abingdon: Frank Cass and Company, Limited.

Becker, C. 2012. Hühner auf einem langen Seeweg gen Westen – frühe Nachweise von *Gallus domesticus* aus der phönizisch-punischen Niederlassung von Mogador, Marokko. *Festschrift für Helmut Kroll. Offa* 69.70: 225–38.

Becker, C., von den Driesch, A. and Küchelmann, C. 2012. Mogador, eine Handelsstation am westlichen Rand der phönizischen und römischen Welt – die Tierreste. In G. Grupe, G. McGlynn and J. Peters (eds), *Current Discoveries from Outside and Within*, München: Documenta Archaeobiologiae Jahrbuch der Staatssammlung für Anthropologie und Paläoanatomie 10, 11–159.

Bedaux, R.M.A., Constandse-Westermann, T.S., Hacquebord, L., Lange, A.G. and Van der Waals, J.D. 1978. Recherches archéologiques dans le Delta intérieur du Niger (Mali). *Palaeohistoria Bussum* 20: 91–220.

Blench, R.M. 1993. Ethnographic and linguistic evidence for the prehistory of African ruminant livestock, horses and ponies. In T. Shaw, P. Sinclair, B. Andah and A. Okpoko (eds), *The Archaeology of Africa: Food, Metals and Towns*, London and New York: Routledge, 71–103.

Blench, R.M. 1995. A history of domestic animals in northeastern Nigeria. *Cahiers des Sciences Humaines* 31: 181–238.

Blench, R.M. 2000a. African minor livestock species. In Blench and MacDonald 2000, 314–38.

Blench, R.M. 2000b. A history of donkeys, wild asses and mules in Africa. In Blench and MacDonald 2000, 339–54.

Blench, R.M. 2000c. A history of pigs in Africa. In Blench and MacDonald 2000, 355–67.

Blench, R.M. and MacDonald, K. (eds) 2000. *The Origins and Development of African Livestock: Archaeology, Genetics, Linguistics and Ethnography*. London: Routledge.

Bovill, E.W. 1968. *The Golden Trade of the Moors* (2nd edition). Oxford: Oxford University Press.

Bulliet, R.W. 1990. *The Camel and the Wheel*. New York: Columbia University Press.

Burke, A. 2001. Patterns of animal exploitation at Leptiminus: Faunal remains from the East Baths and from the Roman cemetery Site 10. In L.M. Stirling, D.J. Mattingly and N. Ben Lazreg (eds), *Leptiminus (Lamta) Report No. 2 The East Baths, Cemeteries, Kilns, Venus Mosaic, Site Museum and Other Studies*. Portsmouth, RI: Journal of Roman Archaeology Supplement 41, 442–56.

Buzaian, A.M. 2000. Excavations at Tocra (1985–1992). *Libyan Studies* 31: 59–102.

Camarós, E. and Estévez, J. 2010. Los restos arqueozoológicos de mamíferos: Gestión y explotación del recurso animal en los niveles del siglo 7 aC de Plaza de la Catedral (Ceuta). In F. Villada, J. Ramon and J. Suárez (eds), *El asentamiento protohistórico de Ceuta: Indígenas y fenicios en la orilla norteafricana del Estrecho de Gibraltar*, Ceuta: Archivo General, 383–406.

Camps, G. and Gast, M. 1982. *Les chars préhistoriques du Sahara: Archéologie et techniques d'attelage. Actes du colloque de Sénanque, 21–22 mars 1981*. Aix-en-Provence: Université de Provence.

Camps, G. and Chaker, S. 1993. Cheval. In *Encyclopédie berbère 12 (Capsa – Cheval)*, Aix-en-Provence: Edisud, 1907–11.

Camps, G., Musso, J.-C. and Chaker, S. 1988. Âne. In *Encyclopédie berbère 5 (Anacutas – Anti-Atlas)*, Aix-en-Provence: Edisud, 647–57.

Camps, G., Peyron, M. and Chaker, S. 1996. Dromadaire. In *Encyclopédie berbère 17 (Douiret – Eropaei)*, Aix-en-Provence: Edisud, 2541–54.

Carr, J. 1998. *Garth Pig Stockmanship Standards*. Sheffield: 5 M Enterprises for the Garth Veterinary Group.

Cesarino, F. 1997. I cani del Sahara. *Sahara* 9: 93–113.

Chaix, L. 2000. A Hyksos horse from Tell Heboua (Sinai, Egypt). In M. Mashkour, A.M. Choyke, H. Buitenhuis and F. Poplin (eds), *Archaeozoology of the Near East: Proceedings of the Fourth International Symposium on the Archaeozoology of Southwestern Asia and Adjacent Areas*, Groningen: ARC, 177–86.

Challis, W., Campbell, A., Coulson, D. and Keenan, J. 2007. Funerary monuments and horse paintings: A preliminary report on the archaeology of a site in the Tagant region of South East Mauritania near Dhar Tichitt. *The Journal of North African Studies* 10.3–4: 459–70.

Clark, G. 1993. The faunal remains. In N. Benseddik and T. Potter, *Fouilles du Forum de Cherchel 1977–1981, Bulletin d'archéologie algérienne*, supplément 6, Algiers: Agence Nationale d'Archéologie, 159–95.

Connah, G. 1981. *Three Thousand Years in Africa: Man and His Environment in the Lake Chad Region of Nigeria*. Cambridge: Cambridge University Press.

Crabtree, P.J. and Monge, J.M. 1987. The faunal remains from the sanctuary of Demeter and Persephone at Cyrene, Libya. *Masca Journal* 4.3: 139–43.

Cunningham, A.A. 1996. Disease risks of wildlife translocations. *Conservation Biology* 10.2: 349–53.

Dahl, G. and Hjort, A. 1976. *Having Herds: Pastoral Herd Growth and Household Economy*. Stockholm: Liber Tryck.

Daumas, E. 1968. *The Horses of the Sahara* (translated by S.M. Ohlendorf). Austin: University of Texas Press.

De Grossi Mazzorin, J. and De Venuto, G. 2006. Ricerche archeozoologiche a Thamusida (Marocco): Allevamento, alimentazione e ambiente di un insedia-mento mauro e di una citta romana. In A. Tagliacozzo, I. Fiore, S. Marconi and U. Tecchiati (eds), *Atti del 5 Convegno Nazionale di Archeozoologia (10–12 Novembre, Roverto, 2006)*, Roverto: Osiride, 389–93.

Deme, A. and McIntosh, S.K. 2006. Excavations at Walaldé: New light on the settlement of the Middle Senegal Valley by iron-using people. *Journal of African Archaeology* 4.2: 317–47.

Desquesnes, M., Holzmuller, P., Lai, D.-H., Dargantes, A., Lun, Z.-R. and Jittaplapong, S. 2013. Trypanosoma evansi and surra: A review and perspectives on origin, history, distribution, taxonomy, morphology, hosts, and pathogenic effects. *BioMed Research International* 194176: doi:10.1155/2013/194176.

di Lernia, S., Tafuri, M., Gallinaro, M., Alhaique, F., Balasse, M., Cavorsi L. and Fullagar P.D. 2013. Inside the African cattle complex: Animal burials in the Holocene Central Sahara. *PloS one* 8.2: e56879.

Drine, A., Ferchiou, N., Bagnall, R.S., Várhelyi, Z., Fabis, M. and King, A. 2009. Faunal remains. In E. Fentress, A. Drine and R. Holod (eds), *An Island through Time: Jerba Studies, Vol. 1, the Punic and Roman Periods*, Portsmouth, RI: Journal of Roman Archaeology Supplementary Series 71: 328–47.

Dueppen, S. 2011. Evidence for chickens at Iron Age Kirikongo (c.AD 100–1450), Burkina Faso. *Antiquity* 85: 142–57.

FAO 2001. *Pastoralism in the New Millennium.* Rome: FAO Animal Production and Health Paper 150.

Fischer, J. and Lindenmayer, D.B. 2000. An assessment of the published results of animal relocations. *Biological Conservation* 96.1: 1–11.

Förster, F. 2007. With donkeys, jars and water bags into the Libyan Desert: The Abu Ballas trail in the late Old Kingdom/First Intermediate period. *British Museum Studies in Ancient Egypt and Sudan* 7: 1–39.

Fothergill, B.T. 2012. A short report on faunal remains from sites at Zinkekra. Unpublished report, University of Leicester.

Fothergill, B.T. 2014. The husbandry, perception and 'improvement' of the turkey in Britain, 1500–1900. *Post-Medieval Archaeology* 48.1: 207–28.

Fothergill, B.T. 2017. Human-aided movement of viral disease and the archaeology of avian osteopetrosis. *International Journal of Osteoarchaeology* 27.5: 853–66.

Gál, E. 2008. Bone evidence of pathological lesions in domestic hen (Gallus domesticus Linnaeus, 1758). *Veterinarija ir zootechnika* 41.63: 42–48.

Gautier, A. 2002. The evidence for the earliest livestock in North Africa: Or adventures with large bovids, ovicaprids, dogs and pigs. In F.A. Hassan (ed.), *Droughts, Food and Culture: Ecological Change and Food Security in Africa's Later Prehistory*, Dordrecht and London: Kluwer Academic and Plenum Publishers, 195–207.

Geis-Tronich, G. 1991. *Materielle Kultur der Gulmanceba in Burkina Faso.* Köln: Rüdiger Köppe Verlag.

Gifford-Gonzalez, D. and Hanotte, O. 2011. Domesticating animals in Africa: Implications of genetic and archaeological findings. *Journal of World Prehistory* 24.1: 1–23.

Gigliarelli, U. 1932. *Il Fezzan.* Tripoli: Governo della Tripolitania.

Grant, A. 2006. Animal bones from the Sahara: Diet, economy and social practice. In D.J. Mattingly, S. McLaren, E. Savage, Y. al-Fasatwi and K. Gadgood (eds), *The Libyan Desert: Natural Resources and Cultural Heritage*, London: Society for Libyan Studies, 179–85.

Grayson, D.K. 2001. The archaeological record of human impacts on animal populations. *Journal of World Prehistory* 15.1: 1–68.

Grigson, C. 1991. An African origin for African cattle? Some archaeological evidence. *The African Archaeological Review* 9: 119–44.

Guérin, C. and Faure, M. 1991. La faune: Les mammiferes holocenes du site KNT 2 (région de Tombouctou, Mali). In M. Raimbault and K. Sanogo (eds), *Recherches archéologiques au Mali*, Paris: Editions Karthala, 372–77.

Hanotte, O., Bradley, D.G., Ochieng, J.W., Verjee, Y., Hill, E.W. and Rege, J.E.O. 2002. African pastoralism: Genetic imprints of origins and migrations. *Science* 296: 336–39.

Holl, A. 2002. *The Land of Houlouf: Genesis of a Chadic Polity 1900 BC–AD 1800.* Memoirs of the Museum of Anthropology, University of Michigan, Number 35. Ann Arbor: University of Michigan Museum of Anthropology.

Holmes, M. 2013. Faunal data appendices. In Mattingly 2013: 853–64.

Holmes, M. and Grant, A. 2013. The animal bone assemblage. In Mattingly 2013: 495–501.

Hughes, J.D. 2003. Europe as consumer of exotic biodiversity: Greek and Roman times. *Landscape Research* 28.1: 21–31.

Iborra Eres, P. 2001. Estudio Faunístico. In C. Aranegui Gascó (ed.), *Lixus Colonia, Fenicia y Ciudad Púnico Mauritana. Anotaciones sobre su ocupación medieval*, Saguntum Extra 4, Valencia: University of Valencia, 200–04.

Insoll, T. 1995. A cache of hippopotamus ivory at Gao, Mali and a hypothesis of its use. *Antiquity* 69: 327–36.

Jesse, F., Kröpelin, S., Lange, M., Pöllath, N. and Berke, H. 2004. On the periphery of Kerma – the Handessi Horizon in Wadi Hariq, Northwestern Sudan. *Journal of African Archaeology* 2: 123–64.

Johnson, D.L. 1969. *The Nature of Nomadism*. Chicago: Department of Geography, University of Chicago.

Kacem, S.B.H., Muller, H.-P. and Weisner, H. 1994. *Gestion de la faune sauvage et des parcs nationaux en Tunisie: Reintroduction, gestion, et amenagement*. Tunis: Direction Générale des Forêts and Deutsche Gesellschaft für Technische Zusammenarbeit.

Kimura, B., Marshall, F., Beja-Pereira, A. and Mulligan, C. 2013. Donkey domestication. *African Archaeological Review* 30.1: 83–95.

King, A.C. 1991. *Animal bones*. In A. Mohamedi, A. Benmansour, A.A. Amamra and E. Fentress (eds), *Fouilles De Sétif (1977–1984), 5ème Supplément au Bulletin d'Archéologie Algerienne*, Algeria: Agence nationale d'archéologie et de protection des sites et monuments historiques, 247–59.

King, A.C. 1999. Diet in the Roman world: A regional inter-site comparison of the mammal bones. *Journal of Roman Archaeology* 12: 168–202.

Köhler-Rollefson, I.U. 1991. *Camelus dromedarius*. Mammalian Species No. 375. Oxford: Oxford University Press for the American Society of Mammalogists.

Law, R. 1980. *The Horse in West African History: The Role of the Horse in the Societies of Pre-Colonial West Africa*. London: Oxford University Press, for the International Africa Institute.

Law, R. 1995. The horse in pre-colonial West-Africa. In G. Pezzoli (ed.), *Cavalieri dell'Africa*, Milano: Centro studi archaeologia Africana, 175–84.

Leone, A. and Mattingly, D.J. 2004. Vandal, Byzantine, and Arab rural landscapes in North Africa. In N. Christie (ed.), *Landscapes of Change: Rural Evolutions in Late Antiquity and the Early Middle Ages*, Aldershot: Ashgate, 135–62.

Levtzion, N. and Hopkins, J. 1981. *Corpus of Early Arabic Sources for West African History*. Cambridge: Cambridge University Press.

Linseele, V. 2003. Cultural identity and the consumption of dogs in western Africa. In S.J. O'Day, W. Van Neer and A. Ervynck (eds), *Behaviour Behind Bones: The Zooarchaeology of Ritual, Religion, Status and Identity*, Oxford: Oxbow Books, 318–26.

Linseele, V. 2007. *Archaeofaunal Remains from the Past 4000 Years in Sahelian West Africa: Domestic Livestock, Subsistence Strategies and Environmental Changes.* Oxford: Archaeopress.

Linseele, V. 2013. From the first stock keepers to specialised pastoralists in the West African savannah. In M. Bollig, M. Schnegg and H.-P. Wotzka (eds), *Pastoralism in Africa: Past, Present and Future*, Oxford: Berghahn Books, 145–70.

Linseele, V., Van Neer, W., Thys, S., Phillipps, R., Cappers, R., Wendrich, W. and Holdaway, S. 2014. New archaeozoological data from the Fayum 'Neolithic' with a critical assessment of the evidence for early stock keeping in Egypt. *PLoS ONE* 9.10: e108517.

Loyet, M. 2004. Food, fuel, and raw material: Faunal remains from al-Basra. In N.L. Benco (ed.), *Anatomy of a Medieval Islamic Town: Al-Basra*, Morocco: BAR International Series 1234, 21–30.

Lydon, G. 2009. *On Trans-Saharan Trails: Islamic Law, Trade Networks and Cross-cultural Exchange in Nineteenth-century Western Africa.* Cambridge: Cambridge University Press.

MacDonald, K.C. 1992. The domestic chicken (Gallus gallus) in Sub-Saharan Africa: A background to its introduction and its osteological differentiation from indigenous fowls (Numidinae and Francolinus sp.). *Journal of Archaeological Science* 19: 303–18.

MacDonald, K.C. 1994. Socio-economic diversity and the origin of cultural complexity along the Middle Niger (2000 BC to AD 300). Doctoral thesis, University of Cambridge.

MacDonald, K.C. 1995. Analysis of the faunal remains. In S.K. McIntosh (ed.), *Excavations at Jenne-jeno, Hambarketolo, and Kaniana (Inland Niger Delta, Mali), the 1981 Season*, Oakland: University of California Press, 271–318.

MacDonald, K.C. 2000. The origins of African livestock: Indigenous or imported? In Blench and MacDonald 2000, 2–17.

MacDonald, K.C. and MacDonald, R.H. 2000. The origins and development of domesticated animals in arid West Africa. In Blench and MacDonald 2000, 127–62.

MacDonald, R.H. and MacDonald, K.C. 1996. A preliminary report on the faunal remains recovered from Gao Ancien and Gao-Saney. In T. Insoll, *Islam, Archaeology and History: Gao Region (Mali)*, Oxford: Tempus, 124–26.

MacDonald, K.C. and Van Neer, W. 1993. Appendix 1: An Initial Report on the Fauna of Akumbuu (Mali). In T. Togola, *Archaeological Investigations of Iron Age Sites in the Mema Region, Mali (West Africa)*. Doctoral Thesis, Rice University.

MacDonald, K.C., Togola, T., MacDonald, R.H. and Capezza, C. 1994. Douentza, Mali. *Past: Newsletter of the Prehistoric Society* 17: 12–14.

MacEachern, S., Bourges, C. and Reeves, M. 2001. Early horse remains from Northern Cameroon. *Antiquity* 75: 62–67.

MacKinnon, M. 2017. Animals, acculturation, and colonization in ancient and Islamic North Africa. In U. Albarella (ed.), *The Oxford Handbook of Zooarchaeology*, Oxford: Oxford University Press, 466–78.

Manlius, N. 2001. The ostrich in Egypt: Past and present. *Journal of Biogeography* 28: 945–53.

Marshall, F. 1989. Rethinking the role of Bos indicus in Sub-Saharan Africa. *Current Anthropology* 30: 235–39.

Marshall, F. 2007. African pastoral perspectives on domestication of the donkey: A first synthesis. In T.P. Denham and L. Vrydaghs (eds), *Rethinking Agriculture: Archaeological and Ethnoarchaeological Perspectives*, London: UCL Press, 537–94.

Mattingly, D.J. (ed.) 2013. *The Archaeology of Fazzan. Volume 4, Survey and Excavations at Old Jarma (Ancient Garama) Carried Out by C.M. Daniels (1962–1969) and the Fazzan Project (1997–2001)*. London: Society for Libyan Studies, Department of Antiquities.

Mattingly, D.J. and Hitchner, R.B. 1995. Roman Africa: An archaeological review. *Journal of Roman Studies* 85: 165–213.

Mattingly, D., Fothergill, B.T. and Sterry, M. Forthcoming. Animal traffic in the Sahara. In V. Blanc-Bijon (ed.), *Hommes et animaux au Maghreb, de la Préhistoire au Moyen Age. Explorations d'une relation complexe. XIe Colloque international Histoire et Archéologie de l'Afrique du Nord (Marseille – Aix-en-Provence, 8–11 octobre 2014)*, Aix-en-Provence: Presses universitaires de Provence.

Mikhail, A. 2013. *The Animal in Ottoman Egypt*. Oxford: Oxford University Press.

Misztal, I., Aguilar, I., Tsuruta, S., Sanchez, J.P. and Zumbach, B. 2010. Studies on heat stress in dairy cattle and pigs. In G. Erhardt (ed.), *Proceedings of the 9th World Congress on Genetics Applied to Livestock Production, ID625*, Leipzig: German Society of Animal Science, 1–5.

Mitchell, P.J. 2005. *African Connections: Archaeological Perspectives on Africa and the Wider World*. Walnut Creek: Altamira Press.

Mitchell, P.J. 2015. Did disease constrain the spread of domestic dogs (*Canis familiaris*) into Sub-Saharan Africa? *Azania: Archaeological Research in Africa* 50.1: 1–44.

Mongin, P. and Plouzeau, M. 1984. Guinea fowl. In I.L. Mason (ed.), *Evolution of Domesticated Animals*, London: Longman, 322–25.

Muzzolini, A. 1996. Les équidés dans les figurations rupestres sahariennes. *Anthropologie (Brno)* 24.1–2: 185–202.

Mwacharo, J.M., Bjørnstad, G., Han, J.L. and Hanotte, O. 2013. The history of African village chickens: An archaeological and molecular perspective. *African Archaeological Review* 30: 97–114.

Nobis, G. 1999. Die Tierreste von Karthago. In F. Rakob (ed.), *Karthago Volume 3, Die Deutschen Ausgrabungen in Karthago*, Mainz: Philipp von Zabern, 574–631.

O'Connor, T. 2008. *The Archaeology of Animal Bones*. College Station: Texas A&M University Press.

O'Connor, T. and Sykes, N.J. 2010. *Extinctions and Invasions: A Social History of British Fauna*. Oxford: Windgather Press.

Payne, W.J.A. 1964. The origin of domestic cattle in Africa Empire. *Journal of Experimental Agriculture* 32: 97–113.

Plug, I. and Badenhorst, S. 2001. *Distribution of Macromammals in Southern Africa over the Past 30000 Years as Reflected in Animal Remains from Archaeological Sites*. Pretoria: Transvaal Museum.

Pöllath, N. and Rieger, A. 2013. Insights in diet and economy of the Eastern Marmarica: Faunal remains from Greco-Roman sites in North-western Egypt (Abar el-Kanayis, Wadi Umm el-Ashdan and Wadi Qasaba). In *Mitteilungen des Deutschen Archäologischen Instituts Abteilung Kairo, Band 67*, Berlin and Boston: Walter de Gruyter GmbH, 163–80.

Porter, V. 1991. *Cattle: A Handbook to the Breeds of the World*. London: Christopher Helm and A&C Black.

Raimbault, M., Guérin, C. and Faure, M. 1987. Les vertébrés du gisement néolithique de Kobadi (Mali). *Archaeozoologia* 1: 219–38.

Reese, D.S. 1977. Animal bone report. In J.H. Humphrey (ed.), *Excavations at Carthage 1976 Conducted by the University of Michigan, Volume 3*, Ann Arbor: The University of Michigan Press, 131–62.

Reese, D.S. 1981. Faunal remains from three cisterns (1977.1, 1977.2, and 1977.3). In J.H. Humphrey (ed.), *Excavations at Carthage 1977 Conducted by the University of Michigan, Volume 6*, Ann Arbor: The University of Michigan Press, 191–219.

Rielly, K. 1988. A collection of equid skeletons from the cemetery. In J.H. Humphrey (ed.), *The Circus and a Byzantine Cemetery at Carthage, Volume 1*, Ann Arbor: The University of Michigan Press, 297–323.

Scheele, J. 2010. Traders, saints and irrigation: Reflections on Saharan connectivity. *Journal of African History* 51: 281–300.

Schwartz, J.H. 1984. The (primarily) mammalian fauna. In H.R. Hurst (ed.), *Excavations at Carthage: The British Mission. Volume 1, part 1, The Avenue du Président Habib Bourguiba, Salammbo: The Site and Finds Other than Pottery*, Sheffield: The British Academy and the University of Sheffield, 229–56.

Seddon, P.J., Strauss, W.M. and Innes, J. 2012. Animal translocations: What are they and why do we do them? In J.G Ewen, D.P. Armstrong, K.A. Parker and P.J. Seddon (eds), *Reintroduction Biology: Integrating Science and Management*, Oxford: Wiley-Blackwell, 1–32.

Shaw, B.D. 1979. The camel in ancient North Africa and the Sahara: History, biology and human economy. *Bulletin de l'IFAN B* 41.4: 663–721.

Sidebotham, S. 2011. *Berenike and the Ancient Maritime Spice Route*. Berkeley: University of California.

Sidell, J. 1997. Appendix 3: The Animal Bone. In Walda *et al.* 1997, 68–70.

Slopsma, J., van Wijngaarden-Bakker, L. and Maliepaard, R. 2009. Animal remains from the Bir Messaouda excavations 2000/2001 and other Carthaginian settlement contexts. *Carthage Studies* 3: 21–63.

Stangroome, C. 2000. The faunal remains from Gadei (excluding fish). In T. Insoll (ed.), *Urbanism, Archaeology and Trade: Further Observations on the Gao Region (Mali): The 1996 Field Season Results*, Oxford: BAR International Series 829, 261–73.

Stock, F. and Gifford-Gonzalez, D. 2013. Genetics and African cattle domestication. *African Archaeological Review* 30.1: 51–72.

Thissen, H.-J. 2013. Donkeys and water: Demotic ostraca in Cologne as evidence for desert travel between Oxyrhynchos and the Bahariya Oasis in the 2nd century BC. In F. Förster and H. Riemer (eds), *Desert Road Archaeology in Ancient Egypt and Beyond*, Köln: Heinrich Barth Institut, 391–97.

Valenzuela Lamas, S. 2016. Alimentation et élevage à *Althiburos* à partir des restes fauniques. In N. Kallala and J. Sanmartí (eds), *Althiburos, Volume 2*, Tarragona: Monographies ICAC, 421–48.

Van der Veen, M. and Westley, B. 2010. Palaeoeconomic studies. In D.J. Mattingly (ed.), *The Archaeology of Fazzan. Volume 3, Excavations of C.M. Daniels*, London: Society for Libyan Studies, Department of Antiquities, 488–522.

Van der Veen, M., Grant, A. and Barker, G. 1996. Romano-Libyan agriculture: Crops and animals. In G. Barker (ed.), *Farming the Desert: The UNESCO Libyan Valleys Archaeological Survey. Volume 1, Synthesis*, Paris and London: UNESCO and Society for Libyan Studies, 227–63.

Van Neer, W. 2002. Food security in Western and Central Africa during the late Holocene: The role of domestic stock keeping, hunting and fishing. In F.A. Hassan (ed.), *Droughts, Food and Culture: Ecological Change and Food Security in Africa's Later Prehistory*, New York, Boston, Dordrecht, London and Moscow: Kluwer Academic and Plenum Publishers, 251–74.

Vigneron, P. 1968. *Le cheval dans l'antiquité gréco-romaine, Volumes 1 and 2*. Nancy: Faculté des Lettres de Nancy, Annales de l'Est 35.

Von den Driesch, A. and Baumgartner, I. 1997. Die Spätantiken Tierreste Aus Der Kobbat Bent El Rey in Karthago. *Archaeozoologia* 9: 155–72.

Walda, H.M., Ashton, S.-A., Reynolds, P., Sidell, J., Welsby Sjöstrom, I. and Wilkinson K. 1997. The 1996 Excavations at Lepcis Magna. *Libyan Studies* 28: 43–70.

Warden, P.G., Oliver, A., Crabtree, P.J. and Monge, J. 1990. *The Extramural Sanctuary of Demeter and Persephone at Cyrene, Libya Final Reports 4: The Small Finds; Glass; Faunal and Human Skeletal Remains*. Philadelphia: University Museum of Pennsylvania.

Watson, D. 1999. Appendix E1: The Faleme Valley faunal assemblages. In I. Thiaw, *Archaeological Investigations of Long-term Culture Change in the Lower Falemme (Upper Senegal Region) AD 500–1900*. Doctoral thesis, Rice University, 371–84.

Wilson, A. 2012. Saharan trade in the Roman period: Short-, medium- and long-distance trade networks. *Azania: Archaeological Research in Africa* 47.4: 409–49.

Wilson, R.T. 1984. *The Camel*. London: Longman Group Limited.

Winchell, W. 2001. *Water Requirements for Poultry*. Canada Plan Service, Report 5603.

Zeder, M.A. 1991. *Feeding Cities: Specialised Animal Economies in the Ancient Near East*. Washington, DC: Smithsonian Institution Press.

Zeder, M.A. 1998. Pigs and emergent complexity in the ancient Near East. In S.M. Nelson (ed.), *Ancestors for the Pigs: Pigs in Prehistory*, MASCA Research Papers in Science and Archaeology 15. Philadelphia: University of Pennsylvania Museum of Archaeology and Anthropology, 109–22.

Zeder, M.A. 2008. Domestication and early agriculture in the Mediterranean Basin: Origins, diffusion, and impact. *Proceedings of the National Academy of Science* 105: 11597–604.

Zeder, M.A. 2011. The origins of agriculture in the Near East. *Current Anthropology* 52: 221–35.

6 | The Early History of Weaving in West Africa

A Review of the Evidence

SONJA MAGNAVITA

Introduction

Exploring the onset of weaving technology in prehistoric West Africa is comparable to fishing in the dark. At a certain point in time, full light falls on to an already developed weaving tradition, focused mainly on the production of cotton textile for various purposes. This coincides with an eventful period in the early second millennium AD, with the rise and decline of powerful empires, drastic changes in religious beliefs and practices, the impact of increased urbanism and an intensification of long-distance trading networks. Far from being merely one out of many technologies, textile production in early second-millennium AD West Africa was intimately related to these movements: local demand for textiles increased under the influence of Islam, especially in urban centres, and long-distance trade stimulated both demand and supply. In the first centuries of the second millennium AD, evidence for textiles comes from several sources: directly in the form of archaeological textiles and written testimonies, and indirectly in the form of tools or materials related to textile production. Taken together these pieces of evidence clearly indicate that from the early second millennium AD onwards woven textiles were both produced and traded within West Africa, as well as to and from elsewhere. Much more obscure, however, are the origins of this technology and the means of its diffusion. If we want to explore the *status quo ante* the established weaving tradition of early second-millennium AD West Africa, a look at its direct precursors in the preceding centuries is essential. However, this is the point where the situation becomes most delicate, because both direct and indirect evidence amount to questionable fragments only. Within this chapter I first review the developed weaving tradition of the early second millennium AD and then progress back in time for an evaluation of

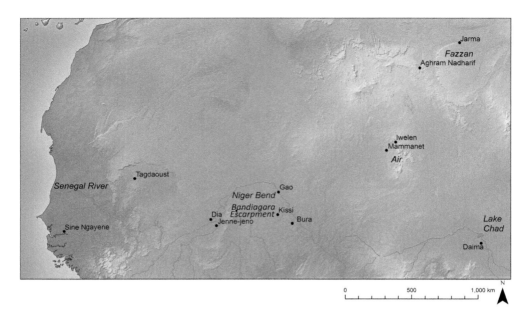

Figure 6.1 Map of the main locations discussed (M. Sterry for Trans-SAHARA Project).

its precursors (see Fig. 6.1 for a map showing the main locations referred to).

Textiles in Early Second Millennium AD West Africa

Direct Archaeological Evidence

Bandiagara Escarpment, Mali (Eleventh Century AD and Later)

The vast majority of direct archaeological evidence for early second-millennium AD West African textiles comes from a single archaeological landscape: the caves in the Bandiagara escarpment, Mali. Textiles were found in caves that were used for funerary purposes during roughly the eleventh to eighteenth centuries AD by sedentary farming and iron-producing communities living nearby, that is pre-Dogon (or Tellem) in the earlier part of this period, and Dogon from the sixteenth century onwards.[1] The textiles were worn by the dead at the moment when they were deposited in the caves, but due to disturbances most of the textiles were no longer in a clear context associated with a specific skeleton when

---

[1] Bedaux and Bolland 1980, 10; Mayor *et al.* 2014.

they were recovered. Textiles from two funerary caves were assigned an absolute date between the eleventh to twelfth centuries AD (Cave C) and the fifteenth to sixteenth centuries AD (Cave F) by means of conventional radiocarbon dating of human bones,[2] while other caves were dated relatively only. However, as has been remarked by Mayor,[3] the age ranges are considerably wider when these radiocarbon dates are newly calibrated (see Table 6.1). The earliest dates, the eleventh to twelfth centuries AD, should thus be treated with caution.

From the textiles taken for analysis and belonging to the earliest contexts it became apparent that only two raw materials had been used: cotton in most, and – much less frequently – wool.[4] Regardless of the raw material, all studied single threads were spun clockwise, while two or more single Z-spun threads were plied together in the counter-direction, thus forming an S-ply yarn. Simple Z-spun yarn was used for wefts. Warp yarns were often set in pairs of single Z-spun yarn (cotton textiles only), or two Z-spun strands were S-plied (woollens only). This knowledge of West African material needs to be related to broader discussions of textile terminology and preserved textiles in the Sahara and Egypt.[5]

The Bandiagara textiles were made into a range of products, such as clothing (mainly shirts and tunics) and accessories (coifs, shawls, bands and others), as well as blankets.[6] The general weaving technique identified is the plain weave technique, seemingly in different systems for different products: clothes were made in a balanced plain weave. The blankets are exclusively in weft-faced plain weave, which is in principle the same weaving technique but the amount of weft threads is considerably higher than of warp threads, with the result that the warps are covered entirely by the weft threads. A few woven bands are in a warp-faced plain weave pattern, which is the counterpart of the weft-faced pattern, due to a higher number of warp over weft threads. Equally, the choice of raw material seems to have been linked to both the technique and the type of garment: cotton textiles occur in all three techniques and in all types of garments, while wool has been used for blankets only and was woven exclusively in weft-faced plain weave.[7] Both cotton and wool (threads or whole garments) were either dyed or undyed; those that were dyed

---

[2] Bedaux and Bolland 1980, table 1.   [3] Mayor 2011, 170–71.
[4] Bedaux and Bolland 1980, 13.
[5] Trans-Saharan aspects of ancient textile production featured in Volume 1 of this series, Mattingly *et al.* 2017. For illustrations of yarns, details on textile types and categorisation, and discussion of Egyptian textiles, see Bender Jørgensen 2017; for textiles in the Sahara, see Mattingly and Cole 2017.
[6] Bolland 1991.   [7] Bolland 1991, 71.

Table 6.1 *Chronology of archaeological textiles in West Africa*

	Lab #	Uncalibrated radiocarbon age BP	Calibrated age range (1-sigma) calAD	Calibrated age range (2-sigma) calAD	Median probability	Material	Context	Reference
Iwelen, Niger	PA-764	1220 ± 60	711–745, 764–885	669–901 (920–961)	802 calAD	Textile (wool tunic)	Tunic from woman burial no. 68	Paris 1996, 210–11
	PA-768	1165 ± 60	774–900 (921–950)	(694–746) 763–991	859 calAD	Leather	Leather shroud from woman burial no. 68	Paris 1996, 210–11
Mammanet, Niger	PA-?	1270 ± 65	664–777 (792–803, 844–857)	648–893 (933–936)	749 calAD	Textile (cotton shroud)	Shroud from child burial MMNT 1.1	Paris et al. 1986
	PA-86	1280 ± 60	660–776	652–882	739 calAD	Textile (tunic)	Tunic from child burial MMNT 1.1	Paris et al. 1986
	PA-100	1025 ± 60	(902–920), 962–1046 (1093–1120, 1140–1147)	891–1156	1009 calAD	Textile	Textile from child burial MMNT 1.7	Paris et al. 1986
Igbo-Ukwu, Nigeria	BM-2142 R	940 ± 370	(691–749), 761–1320 (1350–1391)	336–1681 (1739–1751, 1762–1802, 1937–1950)	1046 calAD	Wood	Wooden stool from burial chamber	Shaw 1995, 43
Igbo Richard, Nigeria	I-2008	1000 ± 120	773–1028	675–1161	921 calAD			Shaw 1975, Table. 1, 504
Sine Ngayene, Senegal	Dak-201	867 ± 117	1043–1103, 1118–1256	(901–920, 954–957), 961–1311 (1359–1387)	1148 calAD	Charcoal from stone circle No. 25	Textile pseudomorph on spearhead found in stone circle No. 32	Thilmans et al. 1980, 153
Bandiagara, Cave C, Mali	GX-0470	895 ± 95	1040–1110, 1115–1215	981–1281	1130 calAD	Human bone	Deposit inside cave	Bedaux 1972
	GX-0752	855 ± 55	1056–1076, 1154–1254	1040–1108, 1116–1266	1177 calAD	Human bone	Deposit inside cave	Bedaux 1972
	GX-0469	780 ± 95	(1058–1065, 1068–1072), 1154–1298 (1372–1378)	1033–1321 (1348–1392)	1224 calAD	Human bone	Deposit inside cave	Bedaux 1972

Note: For calibration, the Intcal13 calibration curve was used (Reimer et al. 2013).

exhibited colours of red, green, yellow and blue, the last being more frequent than other colours. With a few exceptions, the cotton textiles were made of relatively narrow strips measuring between 18 and 25 cm in width, sewn together selvedge to selvedge to create larger garments. These fabrics in fact provide the earliest direct evidence for narrow-strip cotton weaving in Sub-Saharan Africa, which was likely carried out by means of a horizontal treadle loom. However, in contrast to this, all wool garments represent relatively broad webs, implying minimum loom widths between at least 23 and 64 cm, but possibly even more.[8] For the broadest woollen fabrics, it has been suggested that such textiles were likely made on a single-heddle vertical loom and were reaching West Africa probably as imports from across the Sahara.[9] The similarity to Berber wool textiles is mentioned at least for one blanket: the authors refer to similarities with Nubian fabrics in design and colour pattern.[10]

Sine Ngayène, Senegal (c.Eleventh Century AD or Later)

At the megalithic site of Sine Ngayène in Senegal, excavation at stone circle No. 32 revealed burials and burial goods, among them several iron spearheads.[11] On the blade of one of the spearheads, a textile pseudomorph has been detected. Pseudomorphs are the mineralised form of the textile, a result of mineral salts exchanging with the organic material. In the case of the Sine Ngayène discovery, the corrosion products deriving from the iron spearhead produced the pseudomorph over the part where the fabric once touched the metal. The extent of such a pseudomorph is limited to the size of the mineralisation salt donor – in this case the spearhead. The information value of such small fragments is clearly rather limited. Neither the raw material nor the exact weaving technique could be identified for the Sine Ngayène fabric; Boser-Sarivaxévanis commented on this fragment that it might have been made either in plain weave technique ('*armure toile*'), or by a semi-weaving technique that resulted in a similar pattern.[12] Equally problematic is the determination of the age of this piece of textile; charcoal found in the course of excavations in a neighbouring stone circle (No. 25) was conventionally radiocarbon dated in the 1970s.[13] When newly calibrated, the age of the charcoal falls into the range of the tenth to fourteenth centuries AD (Table 6.1). More recent excavations in the double monolith

---

[8] Bolland 1991, tables 1 to 4.   [9] Bedaux and Bolland 1980, 15.
[10] Bedaux and Bolland 1980, 15.
[11] Thilmans *et al.* 1980, 37; cf. also Thilmans and Ravisé 1980.   [12] Thilmans *et al.* 1980, 38.
[13] Thilmans *et al.* 1980, 153.

circle No. 27, positioned slightly closer to No. 32, delivered an even wider age range between the end of the eighth and fourteenth centuries AD for that monument.[14]

Spindle Whorls and Loomweights

Many excavated sites in West Africa have delivered spindle whorls made out of baked clay (to name but a few, Tagdaoust, Niani, Dia, Jenné-jeno, Gao and Daima).[15] None of these stem, to my knowledge, from a context that clearly predates the eighth century AD. Spindle whorls are not per se an indication of local weaving; the find of a spindle whorl only indicates that fibres were spun, and spun fibres are a prerequisite for weaving with yarn. Weaving with unspun fibres is, however, not uncommon in West Africa – raffia, for example, can be woven with unspun threads. Moreover, the lack of spindle whorls in a certain region at a certain point in time does not necessarily indicate that spinning and weaving with spun yarn were not practised; spindle whorls are not essential for the spinning process, indeed even fine yarn can be spun without any whorl. Since spindle whorls might also have been made out of more perishable material (such as wood, bone or ivory), it is possible that such objects were used but simply are not preserved in the archaeological record. Moreover, some small-sized spindle whorls might have been misidentified as beads. Spindle whorls are thus neither evidence for weaving, nor is their absence proof that weaving was not practised. What can we thus infer from the find of a spindle whorl? If it is complete, the weight of the object can give an indication of the technically feasible fineness of the yarn produced. In general, two rules apply for the weight of spindle whorls: (1) the heavier the whorl, the thicker the resultant yarn; (2) the shorter-stapled the fibres, the lighter the required whorl. Heavy whorls are thus not useful when short fibres should be processed into thin yarn. However, it is not reasonable to infer the fibre raw material just from the weight or size of a spindle whorl; light, small-sized spindle whorls cannot be directly equated with cotton spinning, although this has often been asserted.[16]

Most of the spindle whorls found in West African archaeological sites from the early second millennium AD onwards are small-sized terracotta whorls, with a bi-conical, conical or more or less spherical shape. The weight of such objects is rarely documented in African archaeological

[14] Holl *et al.* 2007, 135, Table 1.
[15] Ordered according to the sites mentioned: Robert-Chaleix 1983; Filipowiak 1979; Schmidt and Bedaux 2006; McIntosh 1995; Insoll 1996; Connah 1981.
[16] Johnson 1977, 169; Bedaux 1993, 456; Berthier 1997, 95.

publications, making it hard to estimate for what type of yarn they were possibly used. Interestingly, at none of the textile-bearing sites mentioned above were spindle whorls found (nor any other textile tool), and vice versa: the sites with spindle whorls have not yielded textile fragments. At Daima near Lake Chad some ceramic sherds were modified for secondary use possibly as spindle whorls,[17] and a fragment of a charred, *c.*3 mm thick cord was found in the same layer.[18] This, of course, does not indicate that weaving was practised too.

Loomweights have not been found in Sub-Saharan West Africa, to my knowledge. This could be a problem of identification – it might be challenging to differentiate, for example, between a loom weight and a fishing net sinker, probably depending much on the interpretation of the context and environment. But it is equally possible that looms requiring weights, that is the warp-weighted vertical loom, were not in use in West Africa. The southernmost evidence for the use of a warp-weighted loom has been found in southern Libya, at the south-western periphery of the Garamantian kingdom. At the early first millennium AD site of Aghram Nadharif, items convincingly interpreted as loomweights were found in close connection to one another.[19] This indication of the use of a warp-weighted loom in the Central Sahara is not a mere coincidence; similar indications have equally been found in the Garamantian heartlands of the Wadi al-Ajal near Jarma.[20] The use of the warp-weighted loom seems to have persisted there at least up to Late Garamantian times.[21]

Textual Evidence

Several early Arabic text sources inform us that at least in some areas of Sub-Saharan Africa, textiles were in use in the early second millennium AD. The general impression is, however, that textiles were not at that time widely available, affordable for everyone or used as cloth by all peoples from the Sahel. In text passages from various authors, socio-economic differences are clearly stated in the ways people dressed themselves:

Among them are peoples who clothe themselves in skins, going otherwise naked; others who cover themselves with grass, and those who fix horns of animal bones on their heads. (Text attributed to al-Masudi, writing in the late tenth century AD)[22]

---

[17] Phase Daima III, *c.*eighth–twelfth centuries AD; Connah 1981, 165.
[18] Connah 1981, 189–90.   [19] Mori 2006b.   [20] Mattingly *et al.* 2010, 194–97.
[21] Mattingly *et al.* 2010, 194.   [22] Al-Masudi, § 87 in Levtzion and Hopkins 1981, 35.

The clothes of the people there [between Tadmakka and Kawkaw] are like those of the other Sudan, consisting of a robe (*milhafa*) and a garment of skins or some other material, according to each man's individual means. (al-Bakri, *c.* 1068)[23]

The clothing of the common people of Kawkaw consists of skins with which they cover their nudity. Their merchants wear chemises (*qadawir*) and mantles (*aksiya*), and woollen band s rolled around their heads (*karazi*). Their ornaments are of gold. The nobles and eminent persons among them wear waist-wrappers (*uzur*). (al-Idrisi, *c.* 1154)[24]

The common people [of Sila and Takrur] wear chemises (*qadawir*) of wool and woollen bands (*kurziyya*) wound round their heads. The notables dress themselves in garments of cotton and mantles (*mi'zar*). (al-Idrisi, *c.* 1154)[25]

The last passage by al-Idrisi in particular, which discusses the different ways people of the Takrur region once dressed themselves, has led to the conclusion that wool weaving in West Africa might be older than cotton weaving.[26] While al-Idrisi's statement clearly aims at reporting differences in social status, it possibly suggests that the use of cotton as raw material for clothes was a later and possibly foreign achievement, and that cotton clothes were rare and therefore a valuable good not accessible for everyone. It is, however, unclear whether the term for wool in this reference really referred to the raw material or rather to a particular product, such as a coarse type of garment.[27] Despite this, it is worth noting that the vast majority of the woollen Bandiagara textiles (mostly blankets) date to the earliest contexts, while cotton clearly replaced wool in the later centuries.

The earliest known textual evidence for West African cotton cultivation and weaving (possibly narrow-strip weaving) is found in al-Bakri's text of the second half of the eleventh century AD.[28] It indicates that at least in areas with good water supply – in this case the Middle Senegal River – people were weaving cotton and even supplied larger towns with woven products. There are many more text sources with such precious pieces of information, and it becomes apparent that the meagre archaeological evidence by no means reflects the actual facts.

[23] Al-Bakri, § 183 in Levtzion and Hopkins 1981, 87.
[24] Al-Idrisi, § N28/11 in Levtzion and Hopkins 1981, 113.
[25] Al-Idrisi, § N18/3 in Levtzion and Hopkins 1981, 107.
[26] Mauny 1961, 344; Boser-Sarivaxévanis 1972, 206.   [27] Johnson 1977, 172.
[28] Al-Bakri, §173 in Levtzion and Hopkins 1981, 78.

Textiles in West Africa before the Eleventh Century AD

Direct Archaeological Evidence

Prior to the eleventh century, archaeological evidence for textiles in West Africa is rare, and even if we encompass the Southern Sahara, the corpus remains very small, although the conditions for textile preservation are certainly better within the desert than in the more humid regions to the south.

Igbo-Ukwu, Nigeria

At the site of Igbo-Ukwu in southern Nigeria, textile fragments made of vegetal fibres were discovered in association with metal artefacts.[29] The site has been dated to approximately the ninth to eleventh centuries AD (Table 6.1). It is only due to the metal corrosion products that textile fragments directly in contact were prevented from total decay. The nature of the vegetal fibres has not been identified with certainty.[30] All the webs had been made in plain weave technique. The fibres were spun in S-direction; for stronger yarn, two S-strands were plied together to make a Z-yarn, which was used for both wefts and warps.[31] None of the fragments have been identified as belonging to a piece of clothing; they were probably all used for wrapping or covering copper alloy objects.

Aïr Mountains, Niger

More substantial finds of textiles were discovered in the Southern Sahara, at the archaeological sites of Mammanet and Iwelen in northern Niger.[32] In graves dating to between the seventh and eleventh centuries AD, tunics, shrouds and a veil were partially preserved and some of them directly dated. At Mammanet (Grave MMNT 1.1), located at the north-western edge of the Aïr Mountains, a two- or three-year-old child had been buried according to Muslim rites. The child was wearing an indigo-dyed cotton tunic and was covered with a white cotton shroud. The textiles in this grave were directly radiocarbon dated to the seventh to ninth centuries AD (see Table 6.1).[33] In another grave at Mammanet (MMNT 1.7), an approximately seven-year-old child had been buried according to the same rites, and similar cotton textiles were found. They were directly dated to the

---

[29] Shaw 1970, 240–44.   [30] Shaw 1970, 243.   [31] Shaw 1970, 240.   [32] Paris 1996.
[33] Paris *et al.* 1986, 514.

ninth to twelfth centuries AD (see Table 6.1).[34] I could not find further information on the weaves.

In the northern centre of the Aïr Massif, the necropolis of Iwelen was investigated and one of the graves (WLN 1.68) contained the skeleton of a woman, buried within a leather shroud.[35] She was wearing bronze anklets and bracelets made of horn, and a well-preserved long tunic. The tunic is made of wool dyed in red, green and blue colours (Fig. 6.2). The head of the woman was covered by a veil of white cotton, embroidered with a Berber design in indigo-blue wool. The investigators assume that both garments were imported from North Africa, probably from southern Tunisia.

Figure. 6.2 The wool tunic from Iwelen, grave 68, after restoration, on display at the IRSH Niamey, Niger (photo: S. Magnavita, taken Spring 2007).

[34] Paris 1996, 231.   [35] Paris 1996, 209–11.

Several radiocarbon samples were taken from this grave, including the tunic and leather shroud. These were dated to the seventh to tenth centuries AD (see Table 6.1).[36] I could not find further information on the weaves and spinning of either garment, but have seen the original wool tunic on display in the *Institut de Recherches en Sciences Humaines* (IRSH) in Niamey in 2007 (Fig. 6.2). The main weave pattern of the tunic is weft-faced plain weave. While a closer look at the fibres' spinning direction was not possible, it was nevertheless visible that the warp yarn is stronger than the weft and was apparently Z-plied, but not set in pairs. The tunic has not been made up from narrow-woven bands, but instead displays a very broad web; it is thus likely that a broad vertical loom was used.

Bura Asinda-sikka, Niger

The necropolis of Bura Asinda-sikka in south-western Niger has become famous mostly because of the terracotta figures erected over the graves.[37] The figures were mounted on the round bases of upturned ceramic pots. While these pots were probably standing visibly on the ground, the human remains were buried at a regular depth in the earth directly below. The terracotta figures display elaborate hairstyle, dress, jewellery and weapons. This personal garb is in part reflected by the type of burial goods accompanying the dead in the graves below the figures, such as beads of different kinds, as well as rings and bracelets of iron and copper alloys. Textiles that were in close contact with these metals and their corrosion products were preserved in small fragments. Due to their very restricted size, it is not discernible whether these textiles were part of clothes, blankets or funerary shrouds.

The investigation of these textiles is not yet complete, but it can be preliminarily stated that all fragments seem to be of cotton, woven in plain weave technique. For some, a balanced plain weave pattern is clearly discernible (Fig. 6.3). One fragment has Z-spun warp threads occurring in pairs (Fig. 6.4), matching well with the cotton textiles of the Bandiagara escarpment. Although it does not seem to be the rule, several yarns in other fragments seem to be spun in S-direction, but this remains to be examined more closely.

The age of these textiles is not certain; generally, an age range between the third and eleventh century is assigned to the whole necropolis.[38] An attempt has been made recently to increase the precision of this broad range by

---

[36] Paris 1996, 210.   [37] Gado 1993.   [38] Gado 1993.

Figure 6.3 Cotton fabric in balanced plain weave on a copper alloy bracelet from Bura Asinda-sikka, Niger (photo: S. Magnavita).

Figure 6.4 Plain weave cotton fabric with visible warps, set in pairs. Copper alloy bracelet from Bura Asinda-sikka, Niger (photo: S. Magnavita).

directly AMS dating organic remains attached to the metallic burial goods. In a first test, the dating was accomplished, but rejected by me due to an implausibly high age of the sampled organic remains attached to an iron arrow, falling into the mid-third millennium BC. Another sample, consisting of cotton fibres attached to a bronze bracelet, failed because of insufficient carbon content – the cotton fibres were obviously highly mineralised. While these could easily be the oldest West African cotton textiles, we shall have to wait until more precise dates are gained before drawing further conclusions.

Kissi, Burkina Faso

The oldest West African textiles yet found come from excavations at the burial sites of Kissi, in north-east Burkina Faso. Similarly to the sites of Bura, Igbo-Ukwu and Sine Ngayène, textile fragments (but also other organic remains such as wood, vegetal fibres, leather and fur) were preserved due to the corrosion of metal objects in graves (Fig. 6.5). AMS dating was run on these organic remains, mostly of wood, leather or vegetal fibres.[39] Most of the better preserved textiles come from the cemetery Kissi 3, in graves dating between the fifth and seventh centuries AD, where metal objects were extraordinarily numerous. The oldest woven fibres, however, were found in cemetery Kissi 14 C, Grave 2 – most likely a woman's grave, dating to around the first to fourth centuries AD. The buried person was wearing a heavy apron made up of stone and iron beads; a few woven fibres were preserved adhering to iron beads, suggesting that a piece of woven fabric was part of the apron. A blanket or shroud wrapped around the dead would more likely have led to a considerably higher amount of textile fragments on top of these iron beads.

The textile fragments are all of the same material: fine animal hair or wool.[40] The fragments are not large enough to reconstruct the garments they were part of, but it was possible to study their manufacture.

Most of the yarns are relatively thin, both weft and warp yarns measuring generally between 0.4 and 0.7 mm in diameter. For weft yarn, fibres were spun in Z-direction, and the resulting yarn was not plied together with other strands. In contrast to this, the warp yarn was S-plied from two strands, meaning the last twist was counter-clockwise. It is not totally clear in which direction the single strands for warp yarns were twisted before they were plied together – they give the impression of being S-spun and then plied in the *same* direction. Commonly one assumes that the single threads in an S-plied yarn are spun in the counter-direction, because spinning and plying in the same direction can be awkward. However, the Egyptian weaving tradition made almost exclusive use of S-spun, S-plied yarn; this possibility should therefore not be ruled out per se for the Kissi textiles. On the other hand, the tension in the warps is higher than in the wefts and although it looks as if they were spun in the same S-direction as they were plied, according to a handspinning specialist this visual effect might also happen if the yarn was 'overtwisted'.[41]

All identifiable webs were woven in a weft-faced plain weave pattern (see for example Fig. 6.5). The Kissi textiles do not give clues about the type of loom used, as even the largest fragments, some of which are up to 18 cm long, have their greatest length in warp direction only. In the more loom-diagnostic weft direction, the broadest fragment has a minimum width of 6 cm. In view of their fragmentary condition, it is unclear to which kind of items the Kissi textiles belonged. However, for several textile fragments, adhesion to the upper side of the metal object was observed, while some of

[39] See Magnavita 2008 and 2015 for details.   [40] Magnavita 2008, 246.
[41] I. Gelhaar, personal communication.

Figure 6.5 Fragment of a musical instrument from Kissi, Burkina Faso, cemetery Kissi 3, Grave 11, with fine animal hair or wool fabric in weft-faced plain weave (photo: S. Magnavita).

these have no textile, but leather adhering to the opposite side of the object, that is, the side facing the body of the dead. This seems to indicate the use of leather or skin clothes below woven textiles.[42]

No spindle whorls have been found at Kissi, and nor have any other textile tools or weaver's equipment. The raw material of the fibres is also not in favour of local weaving, since there is no evidence for the presence of wool-bearing animals in the region in the early and mid-first millennium AD, such as wool sheep or dromedary.[43] While dromedary bones dating to the third to fourth centuries AD have been identified in Senegal,[44] the eastern Niger Bend still lacks such finds at that time. On the other hand, wool-bearing sheep remains are difficult to identify among the large corpus of ovicaprine bones found in Iron Age sites throughout West Africa. Today, wool sheep seem to be mainly confined to areas close to the Niger River: the Macina sheep in the Inland Niger Delta region of Mali, and the Goundoun sheep (a subtype of the former) at the eastern Niger Bend, mainly between Gao and Niamey (Fig. 6.6).[45] Nowadays they are mainly, if not exclusively, bred and exploited by Fulani shepherds. The date of their arrival in West Africa is unknown, but some think this might have happened in the context of Arab-Islamic trading activities.[46]

Nearest Textile-Bearing Sites Outside of West Africa

Although it is not in the scope of this chapter to review all African textile evidence, it makes sense to take a brief look at least at the next closest find spots of pre-eleventh-century archaeological textiles outside of West Africa (Fig. 6.1). Proximity in this case is relative, since the nearest comparable finds were made in Fazzan in Libya, at a distance of about

---

[42] Magnavita 2008; 2015.   [43] Magnavita 2008; see also Fothergill *et al.*, Chapter 5, this volume.
[44] MacDonald and MacDonald 2000, 141.   [45] Wilson 1991, 125–27.   [46] Linseele 2007, 70.

Figure 6.6 Wool sheep near Tillabéri, Niger (photo: S. Magnavita).

700 km north-east of Iwelen and over 1,600 km from Kissi, for example. Textiles were also present in the *c.*fourth to fifth centuries tomb at Abalessa in southern Algeria, merely 1,000 km from Kissi and less than 500 km from Iwelen; however, these apparently did not survive the excavation and therefore cannot serve us here for comparison.[47] There are also some important textiles from the early Medieval occupation of the site of Ghirza in the Libyan pre-desert to the north of Fazzan and these seem to have been part of an assemblage linked to Saharan trade.[48]

In the Watwat cemeteries near Jarma, wool textiles were found in several graves dating to approximately the second century AD.[49] Their typical weaving pattern is weft-faced plain weave and the spinning direction is mostly Z, although some are reported to be S-spun; there are multicoloured fragments and some have thick, coloured cords at their selvedges.[50] Weave, colours and selvedges bear similarities to the Iwelen tunic (Fig. 6.7; compare with Fig. 6.2), although this item is considerably younger (see above).

Textile fragments were also found in the Wadi Tanzzuft near Ghat in south-western Libya, dating to the second to third centuries AD.[51] In the 'Royal Tumulus' of In Aghelachem, fragments of textiles possibly made of dromedary hair and woven in weft-faced plain weave technique have been reported.[52] At Aghram Nadharif, a first to second century site in the Ghat area, where loomweights indicating the use of a warp-weighted vertical loom have been found (see above),[53] a piece

---

[47] Camps 1974, 504.   [48] Wild 1984; Franca Cole, personal communication.
[49] Mattingly *et al.* 2008.
[50] Mattingly *et al.* 2008, 253–55; cf. also Edwards *et al.* 2010, 360, 363, for another Garamantian find from the Royal cemetery near Jarma.
[51] Maspero *et al.* 2002.   [52] Maspero *et al.* 2002, 162–63.   [53] Mori 2006b, 319–21.

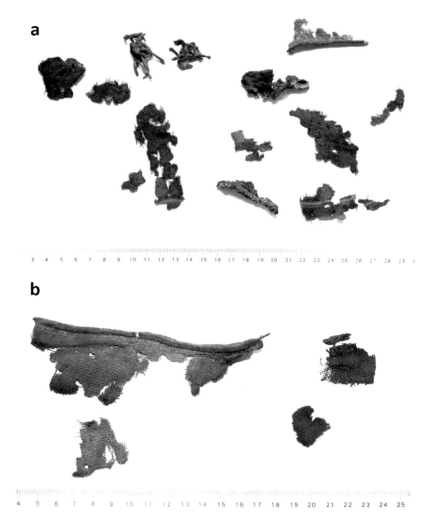

Figure 6.7 Textile fragments approximately dated to the second century AD from Garamantian graves at the Watwat cemetery UAT008: (a) T86; (b) T87 (Toby Savage for Fazzan Project, Mattingly *et al.* 2008: figs 19 and 20).

of textile was found in the coarse mortar of a mudbrick wall.[54] Weave and material have not been reported.

Older textiles were found at Zinkekra, where two fragments were discovered within a rectangular mudbrick building radiocarbon dated to the

---

[54] Mori 2006a, 119.

first millennium BC (790–416 calBC).[55] Both fragments are made of wool and woven in a plain weave pattern. Although the author does not explicitly state it, both the illustrations and the fact that the amount of weft threads is about four times higher than of warp threads indicates that this is a weft-faced plain weave.[56] In both fragments, the threads are Z-spun. Some of the warp threads at the edge of one of the fragments are set in pairs, but the main web has single warp and weft threads.[57]

Indirect Archaeological Evidence

Other than primary evidence in the form of preserved textiles and tools, more indirect evidence can throw some light on the early history of West African weaving. A large corpus of artistic representations of humans wearing cloth exists, especially in rock art and sculpture. One problem that concerns all textile studies by means of artistic representations is that the nature of the displayed cloth cannot be identified – at least not with certainty. For example, the numerous representations on Nok terracotta figures that seem to imply a sort of garment might equally represent leather, felted (bark cloth) or plaited fabrics. Although many different types of garments are discernible, such as waist-wrappers, aprons, coifs and hats, none of the original Nok figures shows an unambiguous depiction of a woven cloth.

Further indirect evidence comes from impressions on pottery. Decorating pottery with various tools made of strings and cords can be seen as characteristic for many regions in Sub-Saharan West Africa throughout the last 3,000 years,[58] but this usually has nothing in common with woven fabrics. Mat impressions on pottery, on the other hand, are frequent in many regions throughout the Sahel and sometimes considerable details on the construction of the mat and the fibres used can be gathered from well-preserved impressions on sherds.[59] While going into details on the relationship between matting and weaving would be beyond the scope of this chapter, one type of mat typical for the interior of the Niger Bend should nevertheless be mentioned for its apparently close relation to woven fabrics. At the Niger Bend between Dogon Country and south-western Niger, Iron Age pottery frequently bears impressions deriving from a kind of mat that was made up of twined elements in a semi-

---

[55] Wild in Hoffmann *et al.* 2010, 487. Detail of date in Mattingly *et al.* 2007, 295: OxA-3075: 2490 ± 70 BC recalibrated here using IntCal13.

[56] Hoffmann *et al.* 2010, 486, fig. 8.32.   [57] Wild in Hoffmann *et al.* 2010, 487–88.

[58] See, for example Haour *et al.* 2010 and references therein.

[59] See, for example, Wiesmüller 2001.

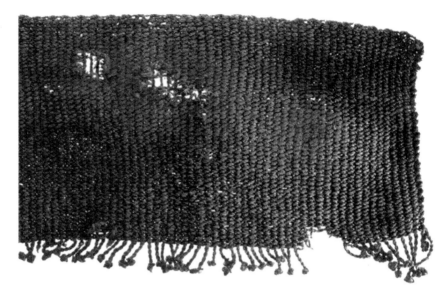

Figure 6.8 The typical twine-mat used for potting in Dogon land (photo courtesy A. Mayor).

weaving technique, resembling a sort of weft-faced plain weave. Inspection of modern samples of such mats still in use in Dogon Country show that these are made of vegetal fibres twisted in S-direction, two or more strands of which are then plied to form a Z-cord, used for both thread systems (Fig. 6.8). What might be relevant for this review of early weaving in West Africa is not only its regional occurrence near the Niger Bend, but also its age: ceramic studies show that this type of twine-mat and a slightly different but related type were already present in parts of this region about 2,000 years ago or even more.[60] Semi-weaving techniques employing spun fibres were thus known in West Africa well before the proven establishment of a loom-weaving tradition, and it is probable that the knowledge of such a technique much facilitated the adoption and spread of weaving techniques in later times.

Textual Evidence

Compared to the textual sources from the eleventh century onwards, those that were written in the preceding centuries do not inform us much about the use of textiles in Saharan or Sub-Saharan Africa. Ibn al-Faqih, writing at the beginning of the tenth century AD, provides one of the earliest Arab

[60] Mayor 2011, 193–94.

documents about clothing practice in West Africa: 'Their [the people of Ghana] clothes are [made of] panther skins, panthers being abundant there' (Ibn al-Faqih, *c.*AD 903).[61] Other authors allude to Sub-Saharan peoples as being naked (such as Ibn Khurradadhbih, writing around AD 846 and often repeated by later writers: 'and the naked Sudan as far as the opposite sea').[62] Nakedness is also mentioned by Pliny the Elder as well as Pomponius Mela in their accounts of African tribes, where they describe the North African Gamphasantes as being naked.[63] Herodotus, describing the discontinued effort of a circumnavigation of Africa by Sataspes, mentions that 'at the farthest point to which he had reached, the coast was occupied by a dwarfish race, who wore a dress made from the palm-tree'.[64] Since none of the Classical authors' descriptions can be clearly ascribed to a specific region in West Africa, the scant textual fragments concerning clothing remain nebulous at best.

Conclusion

Taking the eleventh/twelfth centuries as a *terminus ante quem* for the regional spread of woven fabrics and weaving techniques over parts of West Africa, the following key points emerge and can be used for comparisons with earlier times:

- The use of cotton was dominant, but wool and bast fibres were used too.
- Spinning was usually clockwise (Z-direction, sometimes S-ply).
- Light whorls were common.
- Weaving of narrow bands was common, which were then sewn together into larger garments.
- Plain weave was most common (especially balanced and weft-faced).
- Dye was used, indigo was common.

When this is compared to the evidence from the late first millennium AD (textiles from Igbo-Ukwu and the Aïr Mountains, and possibly Bura), we see that the older textiles do not contradict most of the key points raised above. For the eighth to eleventh centuries AD, therefore, we can confirm the following:

[61] Ibn Al-Faqih, §87.11 in Levtzion and Hopkins 1981, 28.
[62] Ibn Khurradadhbih, §89.7 in Levtzion and Hopkins 1981, 17.
[63] Pliny the Elder, *Naturalis Historia* 5.8 (*c.*AD 50); Mela, *Cosmographia* 1.8 (*c.*AD 43).
[64] Herodotus, *Histories* 4.43 (fifth century BC).

- Use of cotton, wool and possibly bast.
- Plain weave (weft-faced and balanced).
- Broad webs (?).
- Different spinning directions (?).
- Dye was used, including indigo.

The spinning direction of the Igbo-Ukwu bast fabrics is said to have been counter-clockwise (S) and at least the warp yarns in the Iwelen wool tunic seem to be Z-plied. In contrast to the prevailing horizontal narrow-strip weaving of later times, these textiles were not made of narrow strips but rather on broader, possibly vertical looms. For none of these find spots can local textile production be truly ascertained; the Iwelen tunic is even supposed to stem from north of the Sahara (see above).

If we continue then to the (as yet) oldest preserved textile remains found in West Africa, that is, the largely mid-first millennium finds from Kissi, we can raise these points:

- Use of wool only;
- Spinning was clockwise (Z) for wefts and counter-clockwise (S) for warps.
- Plain weave (weft-faced only).

It remains undetermined whether the Kissi textiles were made of broad or narrow webs. That there is no cotton present at Kissi might indicate that wool weaving predates cotton weaving in West Africa. But since it is not clear if these wool textiles were woven in the region or rather imported from far away, we can only state that the *use* of woollen fabrics seems to predate that of cotton fabrics in West Africa. At least in the case of Kissi, leather garments were possibly in use too and wool fabrics were perhaps more exceptional. However, this argument is problematic because the evidence is biased: the Kissi textiles were preserved only due to the corrosion of metals. Those graves with the highest amount of iron and copper alloy objects were therefore those with high numbers of preserved textile fragments. Since the type and amount of metal objects might indicate differences in social or socio-economic status of the buried person, the conclusion that textiles were more frequent in high-status graves is circular reasoning. What is more, many of the textile fragments have only become visible during the cleaning and conservation work on the metal objects, and this has been done preferentially on material from the more richly adorned graves.[65] However, if we take into account the historical sources cited above, which are about half a millennium younger than the Kissi textiles, it may be concluded that textiles were a rather uncommon, and therefore a relatively expensive commodity in first-millennium AD West Africa, especially if they were not locally manufactured.

Due to the highly fragmentary evidence, the origins of West African weaving are thus difficult to trace. It is possible that the technology of weaving on a loom was transferred from one region to the other, and mobile groups such as nomads and pastoralists were perhaps the first carriers of both the technology and the animal raw material. When this happened is difficult to assess; at least we know that during the first half of the first millennium AD, wool fabrics were consumed in Sub-Saharan West Africa, and their weaving pattern and material does not speak against a Saharan origin. It remains unknown, however, whether by this time the technology was transferred too, or just the products. What is known is that woven woollens reached West Africa at a time when mat and basket weaving had already been widely practised for a long time, as was the production of clothing in leather, fur and possibly vegetal material. At the same time, semi-weaving techniques, as seen by twine-mat impressions on pottery, had already been known in West Africa for at least a couple of centuries, possibly even more. Weaving technology certainly started to take off in West Africa around the end of the first millennium AD with the arrival of Islam and the traders linked to this movement. The demand for cloth increased and cotton became especially popular, not only due to Islamic clothing customs but certainly also for economic reasons, given cotton's easier cultivation and higher yield in tropical Africa in contrast to the exploitation of wool-bearing animals. The spread of cotton and the use of the horizontal treadle loom had a visible and lasting impact on local West African crafts; the increased demand for such products went hand in hand with a higher production efficiency and better raw material availability. In some regions, cotton strips even served as a sort of currency from the first half of the second millennium AD until modern times.[66] Cotton then largely replaced wool textiles, although some traditions remained alive up to modern times, such as the production of woollen blankets near the Niger Bend.

---

[65] Magnavita 2008.   [66] Johnson 1977; Kriger 2006.

References

Bedaux, R.M.A. 1972. Tellem, reconnaissance archéologique d'une culture de l'Ouest africain au Moyen Age: Recherches architectoniques. *Journal de la Société des Africanistes* 42.2: 103–85.

Bedaux, R.M.A. 1993. Les plus anciens tissus de l'Afrique de l'Ouest. In J. Devisse (ed.), *Vallées du Niger*, Paris: Editions de la Réunion des Musées nationales, 456–63.

Bedaux, R.M.A. and Bolland, R. 1980. Tellem, reconnaissance archéologique d'une culture de l'Ouest africain au Moyen-Age: Les textiles. *Journal des Africanistes* 50.1: 9–23.

Bender Jørgensen, L. 2017. Textiles and textile trade in the first millennium AD: Evidence from Egypt. In Mattingly *et al.* 2017, 231–58.

Berthier, S. 1997. *Recherches archéologiques sur la capitale de l'empire de Ghana: Etude d'un secteur d'habitat à Koumbi Saleh, Mauritanie: Campagnes II–III–IV–V, (1975–1976) – (1980–1981)*. BAR International Series 680. Oxford: Archaeopress.

Bolland, R. 1991. *Tellem Textiles: Archaeological Finds from Burial Caves in Mali's Bandiagara Cliff*. Leiden: Tropenmuseum and Royal Tropical Institute.

Boser-Sarivaxévanis, R. 1972. *Les tissus de l'Afrique Occidentale*. Basel: Basler Beiträge zur Ethnologie.

Camps, G. 1974. L'âge du tombeau de Tin Hinan, ancêtre des Touareg du Hoggar. *Zephyrus* 25: 497–516.

Connah, G. 1981. *Three Thousand Years in Africa: Man and His Environment in the Lake Chad Region of Nigeria*. Cambridge: Cambridge University Press.

Edwards, D.N., Mattingly, D.J., Daniels, C.M. and Hawthorne, J. 2010. Excavations of other Garamantian cemeteries and burials. In Mattingly 2010, 343–74.

Filipowiak, W. 1979. *Etudes archéologiques sur la capitale médiévale du Mali*. Szczecin: Muzeum Narodowe.

Gado, B. 1993. Un 'village des morts' à Bura en République du Niger: Un site méthodiquement fouillé fournit d'irremplaçables informations. In J. Devisse (ed.), *Vallées du Niger*, Paris: Editions de la Réunion des Musées Nationaux, 365–74.

Haour, A., Manning, K., Arazi, N., Gosselain, O., Guèye, N.S., Keita, D., Livingstone Smith, A., MacDonald, K., Mayor, A., McIntosh, S. and Vernet, R. 2010. *African Pottery Roulettes Past and Present: Techniques, Identification and Distribution*. Oxford: Oxbow Books.

Hoffmann, B., Mattingly, D.J., Tagart, C., Cole, F. and Wild, J.P. 2010. Non-Ceramic finds from CMD's excavations and the work of M.S. Ayoub. In Mattingly 2010, 411–88.

Holl, A., Bocoum, H., Dueppen, S. and Gallagher, D. 2007. Switching mortuary codes and ritual programs: The double-monolith-circle from Sine-Ngayène, Senegal. *Journal of African Archaeology* 5.1: 127–48.

Insoll, T. 1996. *Islam, Archaeology and History: Gao Region (Mali) ca.* AD *900–1250.* Oxford: Tempus Reparatum, BAR International Series 647.

Johnson, M. 1977. Cloth strips and history. *West African Journal of Archaeology* 7: 169–78.

Kriger, C.E. 2006. *Cloth in West African History.* Lanham: Altamira Press.

Levtzion, N. and Hopkins, J.F. (eds) 1981. *Corpus of Early Arabic Sources for West African History.* Cambridge: Cambridge University Press.

Linseele, V. 2007. *Archaeofaunal Remains from the Past 4000 Years in Sahelian West Africa: Domestic Livestock, Subsistence Strategies and Environmental Changes.* BAR International Series 1658, Cambridge Monographs in African Archaeology 70. Oxford: Archaeopress.

Liverani, M. (ed.) 2006. *Aghram Nadharif: The Barkat Oasis (Sha'abiya of Ghat, Libyan Sahara) in Garamantian Times.* The Archaeology of Libyan Sahara Volume 2. Firenze: All'Insegna del Giglio.

MacDonald, K.C. and MacDonald, R.H. 2000. The origins and development of domesticated animals in arid West Africa. In R.M. Blench and K.C. MacDonald (eds), *The Origins and Development of African Livestock: Archaeology, Genetics, Linguistics and Ethnography*, London: Routledge, 127–63.

Magnavita, S. 2008. The oldest textiles from sub-Saharan West Africa: Woolen facts from Kissi, Burkina Faso. *Journal of African Archaeology* 6.2: 243–57.

Magnavita, S. 2015. *1500 Jahre am Mare de Kissi: Eine Fallstudie zur Besiedlungsgeschichte des Sahel von Burkina Faso.* Frankfurt am Main: Africa Magna Verlag.

Maspero, A., Bruni, S., Cattaneo, C. and Lovisolo, A. 2002. Textiles and leather: Raw materials and manufacture. In S. di Lernia and G. Manzi (eds), *Sand, Stones and Bones: The Archaeology of Death in the Wadi Tanezzuft Valley (5000–2000 BP)*, The Archaeology of Libyan Sahara I, Arid Zone Archaeology Monographs 3, Firenze: All'Insegna del Giglio, 157–68.

Mattingly, D.J. (ed.) 2010. *The Archaeology of Fazzan. Volume 3, Excavations of C. M. Daniels.* London: Society for Libyan Studies, Department of Antiquities.

Mattingly, D.J. and Cole, F. 2017. Visible and invisible commodities of trade: The significance of organic materials in Saharan trade. In Mattingly *et al.* 2017, 211–30.

Mattingly, D.J., Thomas, D.C., Meadows, J., Pelling, R., Dore, J.N. and Edwards, D. 2007. AMS and radiometric radiocarbon dates from the CMD work and FP. In D. J. Mattingly (ed.), *The Archaeology of Fazzan. Volume 2, Site Gazetteer, Pottery and Other Survey Finds*, London: Society for Libyan Studies, Department of Antiquities.

Mattingly, D., Dore, J., Lahr, M., Ahmed, M., Cole, F., Crisp, J. and Moussa, F. 2008. DMP II: 2008 fieldwork on burials and identity in the Wadi al-Ajal. *Libyan Studies* 39: 223–62.

Mattingly, D.J., Hawthorne, J. and Daniels, C.M. 2010. Excavations at the Classic Garamantian settlement of Saniat Jibril (GER002). In Mattingly 2010, 123–204.

Mattingly, D.J., Leitch, V., Duckworth, C.N., Cuénod, A., Sterry, M. and Cole, F. 2017. *Trade in the Ancient Sahara and Beyond.* Trans-Saharan Archaeology, Volume 1. Series editor D.J. Mattingly. Cambridge: Cambridge University Press.

Mauny, R. 1961. *Tableau géographique de l'Ouest africain au Moyen-âge: D'après les sources écrites, la tradition et l'archéologie.* Dakar: IFAN.

Mayor, A. 2011. *Traditions céramiques dans la boucle du Niger: Ethnoarchéologie et histoire du peuplement au temps des empires précoloniaux.* Journal of African Archaeology Monograph Series 7. Frankfurt am Main: Africa Magna Verlag.

Mayor, A., Huysecom, E., Ozainne, S. and Magnavita, S. 2014. Early social complexity in the Dogon Country (Mali) as evidenced by a new chronology of funerary practices. *Journal of Anthropological Archaeology* 34: 17–41.

McIntosh, S.K. 1995. *Excavations at Jenné-Jeno, Hambarketolo, and Kaniana (Inland Niger Delta, Mali), the 1981 Season.* Berkeley: University of California Press.

Mori, L. 2006a. The excavation of residential unit AN9-13. In Liverani 2006, 121–33.

Mori, L. 2006b. The loom weights. In M. Liverani (ed.), *Aghram Nadharif: The Barkat Oasis (Sha'abiya of Ghat, Libyan Sahara) in Garamantian Times*, The Archaeology of Libyan Sahara, Volume 2, Firenze: All'Insegna del Giglio, 319–21.

Paris, F. 1996. *Les sépultures du Sahara nigérien du Néolithique à l'islamisation, 1: Coutumes funéraires, chronologie, civilisations.* Paris: Orstom.

Paris, F., Roset, J.-P. and Saliège, J.-F. 1986. Une sépulture musulmane ancienne dans l'Air séptentrional (Niger). *Comptes Rendus de l'Académie des Sciences, Série 3: Sciences de la Vie* 303.12 : 513–18.

Reimer, P.J., Bard, E., Bayliss, A. *et al.* 2013. INTCAL and MARINE13 radiocarbon age calibration curves 0–50,000 years Cal BP. *Radiocarbon* 55 (4): 1869–87.

Robert-Chaleix, D. 1983. Fusaioles décorées du site de Tegdaoust. In J. Devisse, O. Babacar and T.M. Bah (eds), *Tegdaoust III: Recherches Sur Aoudaghost (Campagnes 1960–1965, Enquêtes générales)*, Paris: Éditions Recherche sur les Civilisations (ADPF), 447–514.

Schmidt, A. and Bedaux, R. 2006. Fusaioles. In R. Bedaux, J. Polet, K. Sanogo and A. Schmidt (eds), *Recherches archéologiques à Dia dans le Delta intérieur du Niger (Mali): Bilan des saisons de fouilles 1998–2003*, Mededelingen van het Rijksmuseum voor Volkenkunde 33, Leiden: CNWS Publications, 282–87.

Shaw, T. 1970. *Igbo-Ukwu, 2 volumes.* London: Faber and Faber.

Shaw, T. 1975. Those Igbo-Ukwu radiocarbon dates: Facts, fictions and probabilities. *The Journal of African History* 16.4: 503–17.

Shaw, T. 1995. Those Igbo-Ukwu dates again. *Nyame Akuma* 44: 43.

Thilmans, G. and Ravisé, A. 1980. *Protohistoire du Sénégal: Recherches archéologiques*, Volume 2. Dakar: IFAN.

Thilmans, G., Ravisé, A., Descamps, C. and Khayat, B. 1980. *Protohistoire du Sénégal: Les sites mégalithiques*, Volume 1. Dakar: IFAN.

Wiesmüller, B. 2001. *Die Entwicklung der Keramik von 3000 BP bis zur Gegenwart in den Tonebenen südlich des Tschadsees.* PhD thesis, Goethe-University Frankfurt am Main.

Wild, J.P. 1984. Textiles from Building 32. In O. Brogan and D. Smith (eds), *Ghirza: A Libyan Settlement in the Roman Period*, Tripoli: Department of Antiquities, 291–308.

Wilson, R.T. 1991. *Small Ruminant Production and the Small Ruminant Genetic Resource in Tropical Africa.* FAO Animal Production and Health Paper 88. Rome: FAO.

PART III

Metallurgy

7 | Metalworking in Pre-Islamic North Africa

A View from the Garamantian Oases

AURÉLIE CUÉNOD

Metalworking in the Trans-Saharan Area

In this section of the volume, we turn our attention to technologies related to the production of metal objects, and reflect on whether it is possible or not to discuss the 'mobile' nature of metallurgical technologies. To this end I seek to identify elements of the *chaîne opératoire* that might have been transmitted in time or in space between different people within the Trans-Saharan region, and to discuss possible mechanisms involved in this transmission. As a prerequisite, it is therefore necessary to be able to reconstruct the *chaîne opératoire*. Although metallurgical activities leave some traces behind, such as slag (the by-product of smelting and smithing), remains of furnaces or technical ceramics such as crucibles or *tuyères* (used to force air into the furnace), sometimes unprocessed ore or the finished objects themselves, all in various states of preservation, a detailed understanding of the processes and human choices leading to the production of metal does not always easily follow. As made evident in Robion-Brunner's chapter (Chapter 9), many different processes can lead to the production of iron, and Africa is particularly renowned for the diversity of its iron-smelting practices,[1] but this diversity is more easily grasped from elements that can be missing from the archaeological record (furnace superstructure, ore and fuel choice, and the technical practices and organisation of the people carrying out the production). While some of these can be reconstructed by specialist analysis of the production remains, it has been noted that many different processes can lead to similar results, since the principles of thermodynamics governing their production are often similar, regardless of the processes used.[2]

---

[1] Killick 2015.   [2] Miller and Killick 2004; Rehren *et al.* 2007.

Once elements of the *chaîne opératoire* are understood, we can attempt to identify patterns that are repeated, with likely adaptations, in different regions or at different times. However, depending on the degree of adaptation encountered these may not be easily recognised. As inventiveness has been demonstrated to be an important characteristic of African metallurgy, with many variants of the bloomery process having been developed to adapt to a multitude of different environments and ores, identifying related technologies can prove difficult.[3] This difficulty is compounded by the patchiness of the data available so far: for the period with which this volume is concerned (1000 BC–AD 1500), detailed studies of metalworking remains are few and far between, very far in fact. As discussed below, physical distance between sites is not necessarily the best indicator of connectivity but can nonetheless be an illustration of the vastness of the landscape in question: sites with known metallurgical remains in the Trans-Saharan region are often separated by more than 1,000 km as the crow flies: *c.*1,700 km from Fazzan to the Nile Valley, *c.*1,100 km to the Aïr Massif, *c.*1,200 km to Carthage. On the southern fringe of the desert, known metalworking sites are not quite so distant, in part due to a number of research programmes in the last few decades in the Senegal River valley, the Dhar Néma, the Inland Niger Delta, the eastern Niger Bend and the area near Lake Chad, but this remains only a handful of sites in a very vast region. How then can we reconstruct the transmission of technological aspects of metalworking, when at the same time there can exist significant diversity in a limited area?[4] If metalworking remains are taken in isolation, this might seem like a futile game of connect the dots between various 'lamppost areas' where our understanding of metalworking is fairly high, but which misses out vast swathes of so far unexplored 'dark' areas. When taken in conjunction, however, with what we know about other technologies, settlement patterns, potential migrations and so forth, and when we try to address the reasons why particular technologies might have been adopted or not in various areas (be that due to environmental constraints, societal organisation or cultural and religious beliefs) this exercise becomes more fruitful. Moreover, as discussed in the general introduction to this volume, the vast distances between known archaeological sites are not only the product of a lack of archaeological research (and of the difficulties of carrying out more in the present political climate) but also result from the nature of the area: a largely hyper-arid and sparsely

---

[3] Killick 2015; for examples of many different processes see also Cline 1937.
[4] See for example Robion-Brunner, Chapter 9, this volume.

populated landscape, but one in which mobility was paramount to survival,[5] and which we know was being crossed by trade routes and was interconnected from early periods.[6] In this context it might therefore not be so absurd to think that ideas, knowledge, styles or practices related to metalworking technologies might have crossed vast expanses of land along with the people and goods involved in trade, and that we might be able to observe some elements of these transfers even with the large geographical gaps in the current state of knowledge.

Once connections have been recognised between different areas, the next logical step is to try to establish a chronological framework for the transfer of knowledge. This can only be done with the aid of secure dating, and discussions on early African metallurgy have struggled with the problem for many decades now. The difficulty of obtaining secure dating evidence in areas within the Trans-Saharan region has already been highlighted.[7] Issues include the 'old wood' problem causing the radiocarbon dates on charcoal samples found in furnaces to be potentially much earlier than the furnace itself; the deflation caused by wind that can occur at desertic sites, meaning that finding datable samples securely associated with metalworking is difficult; and the flattening of the radiocarbon calibration curve between *c.*730 and 400 calBC, meaning that we have a very poor resolution for metalworking evidence in this time period, which unfortunately corresponds to many of the earlier examples of African metalworking.[8] Questions on dating and antecedence become more virulently debated the further back we go in time,[9] and have been the primary focus of the longstanding debate on the origins of metalworking in Africa. This debate has been reviewed at length elsewhere,[10] but deserves a mention here as it revolves around the ideas of invention, adaptation and dispersal of technologies, which are at the heart of this volume.

Since the 1950s,[11] there has been a split between the proponents of a diffusion of metallurgical knowledge from North Africa and Egypt (influenced by the civilisations of the Mediterranean and the Near East) into Sub-Saharan Africa and proponents of an independent invention on the African continent. On one side of the debate, scholars have highlighted the technical complexity of iron smelting and expressed doubts as to

[5] Scheele 2017.   [6] Mattingly *et al.* 2017.   [7] See particularly Killick 2004 ; 2015, 310–11.
[8] See IntCal13 curve: Reimer *et al.* 2013.   [9] MacEachern 2010, 39–40.
[10] Alpern 2005; Holl 2009; Killick 2009.
[11] The paper most frequently cited as the starting points of this debate was published in 1952 by Mauny, who explored possible diffusion routes of iron technology through East and West Africa from a presumed single invention by the Hittites in the second millennium BC, with a rebuttal in the same year by Lhote. Mauny 1952; Lhote 1952.

whether it could have been invented in a place that mostly lacks a copper industry predating the iron metallurgy.[12] They have therefore taken the view that dates for Sub-Saharan ironworking earlier than those known from Carthage, Egypt or Sudan, that is to say generally before the flattening of the radiocarbon calibration curve in the mid-first millennium BC, are so exceptional that they need to be accompanied by substantial and reliable corroborating evidence.[13] Reports of early metalworking or metal objects from the Aïr by Grébénart, the Termit Massif by Quéchon and co-authors and at the nearby site of Egaro by Paris *et al.*, to cite only the Saharan examples,[14] have thus been received with scepticism if not rejected (and in the case of the Aïr, corrected in a paper co-authored by Grébénart himself), citing that the chronological, stratigraphic or archaeometallurgical evidence was not beyond doubt, due notably to the methodological difficulties encountered with dating described above.[15] On the other side of the debate, this has been seen as a systematic rejection of all of the potential proofs for an independent invention in Africa, at best betraying a bias regarding the ingenuity of African peoples, at worst a deliberate support for old colonialist ideas of the technological and intellectual inferiority of Africa.[16] While there are calls to move the debate towards the way the technologies were embedded in society and how they impacted said societies,[17] there is no doubt that this question still causes a lot of discussion. As an illustration, important new evidence of iron forging from Cameroon and the Central African Republic presented as going back to the late third/early second millennium BC published by Zangato in 2007 was met with a wide range of reactions, which were collected by Pringle for a paper in the journal *Science*.[18] These ranged from strong support for the early dates based on a very good clustering of radiocarbon dates for the metalworking structures, to doubts concerning the possible disturbance of contexts and the state of preservation of the objects, which seemed in too good a condition given their age and the nature of the soil. A further publication of the results in 2010 in the *Journal of African Archaeology* was accompanied by comments from four scholars,[19] and was followed in 2012 by another response by Clist.[20] Some of the comments published in 2010

---

[12] Childs and Killick 1993, 321; Craddock 2010, 33–34; Phillipson 2005, 215–16.

[13] Clist 2012; McIntosh 2005, 77–78.   [14] Grébénart 1983; Paris *et al.* 1992; Quéchon 2001.

[15] Killick *et al.* 1988; McIntosh 1994, 173; Killick 2004.

[16] Concerning the Termit dates see Quéchon 2001, 253; see also Alpern 2005, 89–93 and references therein.

[17] Chirikure 2010; Herbert 2001, 42.   [18] Zangato 2007; Pringle 2009.

[19] Zangato and Holl 2010; with Chirikure 2010; Craddock 2010; Eggert 2010; MacEachern 2010.

[20] Clist 2012.

promoted a positive approach, genuinely considering all new evidence and accepting that each individual's research will necessarily be influenced by past ideas and models and be carried out within a political context. They encouraged colleagues working in Africa to keep publishing such discoveries with detailed stratigraphies, pottery sequences and as wide an array of dating methods as funding will allow.[21]

Unfortunately, such a detailed approach cannot always be taken. The present chapter, for example, which studies the metallurgical activities of the Garamantes, suffers from the current lack of access to Libya. An effort is made in the three chapters of this section to explore questions that, although not directly related to the debate of the appearance of ironworking in Africa, should in time expand our understanding of the way the technology could have developed in the Saharan and Sahelian landscapes (Fig. 7.1). For example, issues such as the adaptation of techniques to local conditions and the availability or need to import raw materials are addressed, as are the relationships between metalworking and other

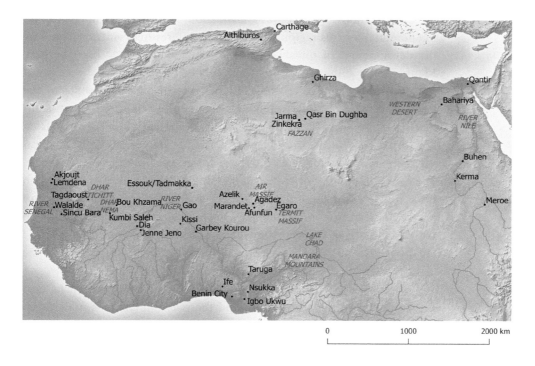

Figure 7.1 Locations of the main sites and regions discussed.

[21] Chirikure 2010; MacEachern 2010.

aspects of the material culture. In this first chapter I focus on the results of the Trans-SAHARA Project's analytical work on metalworking and trade in Fazzan in the Garamantian period and its relevance within the wider region. In Chapter 8, Humphris concentrates on the recent advances of work aimed at clarifying ironworking at the Kushite site of Meroe in Sudan and explores the potential and difficulties of applying network analysis to iron technology in the Nile area. Robion-Brunner (Chapter 9) summarises work from four recent projects at sites in Mali, Benin, Togo and Burkina Faso in West Africa, spanning periods from the seventh to the twentieth centuries AD, investigating, in particular, the significance of diversity in iron smelting.

Metals Finds in Fazzan

Prior to the work of the Charles Daniels in the 1960s and 1970s in and around Jarma, during which metal objects and a few pieces of slag were discovered, almost nothing was known about metalworking in Fazzan, yet the potential for this region to bring some interesting evidence regarding the development of metalworking in Africa had already been noticed. Mauny, for example, from the very onset of the debate on the origin of metalworking, highlighted the potential role of Saharan people in the transfer of metalworking technologies across the Sahara. In a map summarising his work, Fazzan appears as a node in the diffusion of iron from the Libyan coast to the Lake Chad area and the Aïr Massif.[22] Although his views are now outdated and echo the political climate at the time he wrote, one cannot help but notice the influential position of the Garamantes on trade routes in the Central Sahara and wonder what role they could have played in the transfer of technologies, including metalworking, not only in the periods corresponding to the early adoption of metalworking in the area, but also in subsequent periods; in particular at the height of the Garamantian kingdom in the first half of the first millennium AD.

The following sections present the current evidence for metal and metalworking remains in Fazzan, and the scientific analysis undertaken on this material by the Trans-SAHARA Project to better understand the activities of the Garamantian metalworkers and their wider significance in the history of metalworking in North Africa.

---

[22] Mauny 1952.

Context and Typology of the Metal Finds

Ayoub's problematic excavations at the Garamantian capital of Jarma between 1962 and 1965 produced a number of unremarkable fragments of copper alloys and iron, but also some impressive fragments of bronze statuary as well as pieces of gold and silver jewellery and vessels. Unfortunately the context of these finds was very poorly recorded and it is likely that less exceptional finds may not have been recorded at all.[23] Although it was made clear from this early work that the Garamantes used a variety of metals, traces of metalworking activities were only reported a few years later, following Daniels' excavations in the 1960s and 1970s, and later became a recurring feature in the survey work of the Fazzan Project from 1997 to 2002, and in the Desert Migrations Project from 2007 to 2011. During these projects, a total of over 380 fragments of copper objects, 90 of iron, 11 of silver, 6 of gold, 5 of bi-metallic (copper/iron) artefacts and at least 14 kilograms of slag were recovered. It must be noted that these numbers represent material recovered from the excavation and survey of only a handful of cemeteries and settlements out of possibly hundreds of Garamantian sites in the Wadi al-Ajal.

Metal does not at first sight appear to have been an important feature of Garamantian burials. For example, of the 134 tombs excavated by the Desert Migrations Project, only 14 presented metal objects.[24] The objects recovered in the tombs were mostly small items of personal ornament: silver or copper alloy finger rings or earrings, and copper or iron 'rivet plates'. These small plates, with rivets at either end, are remarkably frequently found in Fazzan and might have been used to embellish textile, leather or wood items that have now disappeared, or – as suggested by Vanacker for similar plates found at the Mauritanian site of Tagdaoust – to reinforce damaged wooden objects.[25] Unfortunately, many of the tombs had been robbed and as metal objects are likely to have been particularly prized by the robbers, it is very difficult to assess the frequency with which the Garamantes might have been depositing metal objects in tombs and whether or not larger metal artefacts would have occasionally been part of the grave goods.

The impression that copper was used primarily for small ornaments, however, carries through to the objects recovered at settlement sites. With the exception of the statuary fragments recovered by Ayoub, the copper finds at Jarma, the Garamantian capital, consist mostly of pins or rods,

---

[23] Mattingly 2013, 67–71, for a detailed account of Ayoub's work.
[24] Mattingly *et al.* 2019, 88–100, for a summary of the finds from Garamantian burials.
[25] Vanacker 1983, 93.

rings, bracelets and rivet plates.[26] At the site of Saniat Jibril in the vicinity of Jarma, the density of the copper fragments is much higher and is linked to metalworking activities as described in more detail below. The types of objects recovered, however, remains much the same, with the addition of many indistinct fragments. The use of copper contrasts with that of iron: many of the iron objects are highly corroded and cannot be easily identified, but it seems that aside from a few rivet plates and bangle fragments found in tombs, iron was mostly reserved for nails, tools or weapons. A small number of copper and iron objects of similar types to the ones found in the Wadi al-Ajal were also recovered from Garamantian levels in the Fewet area of the Wadi Tanzzuft.[27]

As mentioned above, slag was found on many Garamantian sites. The slag recovered by the Fazzan Project and a small number of Daniels' slag finds are published in a detailed report by Schrüfer-Kolb.[28] In this section, we present the evidence for metalworking on some of the better documented sites of the Wadi al-Ajal, but metallurgical slag was recognised at many more sites in the area (a total of 11 sites during the Fazzan Project and about 20 more during the Desert Migration Project)[29] and was also present at Aghram Nadharif and Tan Ataram in the Wadi Tanzzuft dating from the last centuries of the first millennium BC and the first half of the first millennium AD. The samples from Aghram Nadharif were analysed and thought to most likely represent the small-scale forging of iron.[30] Heavy duty stone tools, probably used for the sharpening and finishing of metal artefacts, were also found at the site.[31]

Chronology of the Metal Finds

Most of the metal objects excavated from datable contexts in the Wadi al-Ajal are from the Classic and Late Garamantian Periods (AD 1–300 and AD 300–700). Iron and copper are however both present, although in very small numbers from earlier phases: four iron objects can be relatively securely dated from Proto-Urban Garamantian levels of the last few centuries BC at Tinda and Jarma, and one copper object from Jarma comes from a level dated to the end of the Proto-Urban Garamantian period or the beginning of the Classic Garamantian period. Very few contexts from periods before the Classic Garamantian period have been excavated so far, and these low numbers may reflect a lack of excavation rather than be a reliable indicator of when metals started being used in Fazzan.

---

[26] Cole 2013b, 810–13.   [27] Mori 2013b, 77; Mori *et al.* 2013, 65.
[28] Schrüfer-Kolb 2007, 448–62.   [29] Schrüfer-Kolb 2007, 448.
[30] Gida and Vidale 2006, 323–26; Mori 2013b, 77.   [31] Lemorini and Cristiani 2006, 303.

Analysis of the Metalwork and Metalworking Debris

Methodological Difficulties

It must be stated at the outset that due to the political situation in Libya at the time of this work the sampling of objects to be analysed had to be made on a subset of artefacts that had been brought to Europe after earlier excavations (especially those by Daniels). A further limitation was that sampling had to focus on those items that had enough uncorroded material left for analysis. One always wishes to analyse artefacts from secure, well-dated contexts, but in these circumstances it was simply not always possible. The conclusions and suggestions of this chapter have to be understood with this caveat in mind, in the hope that a more detailed programme of analysis will one day follow.

Chemical Analysis of the Copper

Some 42 copper-base objects from Fazzan were analysed to shed light on the type of alloys being used in Fazzan and the possible provenance of the metal. Of these, 16 were subjected to surface X-ray fluorescence (XRF) analysis as part of a preliminary study (for which the data have already been published elsewhere).[32] A further 26 samples were subjected to electron probe microanalysis (EPMA). The methodology and data are given in Appendix 7.1 (Tables 7.1–7.4). Most of the other objects were entirely remineralised and were therefore not subjected to chemical analysis. The results of the analysis have already been discussed in the first volume of this series.[33] They suggest that much of the copper found in Fazzan was probably imported from the Mediterranean area, alongside Roman ceramics and glass also found on Garamantian sites. Indeed, many objects were found to be made of brass, an alloy of copper and zinc whose production on a significant scale started with the Romans and is not known to have taken place in Sub-Saharan Africa before the modern colonial period.[34] Many of the samples also included antimony, a minor element which is also frequent in Roman objects.[35] It is possible that the Garamantes could have used copper from African sources, but on present evidence it seems less likely, as the chemical signature of the Fazzan objects, with arsenic and nickel rarely present in significant amounts, does not correspond to those of analysed objects from regions with known

---

[32] Duckworth *et al.* 2015.   [33] Leitch *et al.* 2017. See also Duckworth *et al.* 2015.
[34] Craddock 1978; 1985.   [35] Craddock 1978.

deposits, such as the area of Afunfun in Niger, or even further afield in the Akjoujt region of Mauritania.[36]

The chemical composition of the copper artefacts, many of which contained two or three of the alloying elements tin, lead and zinc, also suggests that much of the metal used by the Garamantes was recycled. These alloys can indeed be interpreted as the result of the mixing of bronze, brass and leaded-copper during recycling/remelting activities. Since the practice of recycling metal was common in the Roman world,[37] the presence of such a mixed composition in Fazzan does not in itself indicate that recycling was practised there, but the remains of metalworking described below strongly suggest that it was.

Lead Isotope Analysis

In an attempt to clarify the provenance of the Fazzan copper objects and investigate trade in the wider region, 23 samples were subjected to lead isotope analysis (LIA).[38] In this technique the relative amounts of four isotopes of lead present in archaeological objects (^{204}Pb, ^{206}Pb, ^{207}Pb and ^{208}Pb) are measured and compared to known ratios of ore sources. The proportion of these isotopes in a given ore deposit depends on the age of the deposit and its composition at the time of formation, and can therefore be seen as a signature for the deposit. The proportion of the different isotopes has been shown not to be altered during the smelting of the ore or the further processing of the metal, which enables us to trace the provenance of metal objects using LIA.[39] The results of the LIA of the Fazzan material are presented in Appendix 7.1 and in Figures 7.2 to 7.6.

The data cluster in two areas, and there are two outliers. One of the outliers (TSM 185, a pin from Zinkekra made of low tin bronze) has extremely low ratios of ^{208}Pb/^{206}Pb and ^{207}Pb/^{206}Pb and very high ^{206}Pb/^{204}Pb which do not seem to correspond to any known ore sources or archaeological objects and cannot at present be satisfactorily explained. It will therefore not be discussed any further or shown on the graphs below. The biggest group is composed of 19 objects: the majority of these objects come from the workshop site of Saniat Jibril, but some are from Jarma and a piece of oxidised copper was found in slag from Qasr Bin Dughba. A second group with higher ratios of ^{208}Pb/^{206}Pb and ^{207}Pb/^{206}Pb and lower ratios of ^{206}Pb/^{204}Pb is formed by two objects, one from

---

[36] Bourhis 1983; Lambert 1983.   [37] Craddock 1978, 12–13; Pollard *et al.* 2015.
[38] The analysis was carried out by J.A. Evans and V. Pashley at the British Geological Survey using MC-ICP-MS. The analysis of the second batch of 13 samples was made possible by a grant awarded by the Society for Libyan Studies for which I am grateful.
[39] Gale and Stos-Gale 1996.

Zinkekra and one from Jarma. A single object – a small coil from Zinkekra – has lower ratios of $^{208}Pb/^{206}Pb$ and $^{207}Pb/^{206}Pb$ and higher ratios of $^{206}Pb/^{204}Pb$ than the main group. Unfortunately, none of these last three objects come from securely dated contexts, but the fact that they plot separately to all of the Saniat Jibril objects may indicate changes of metal source with time, the peak of activity at Zinkekra being earlier in date than Saniat Jibril. It could potentially also represent the use of different metal for different purposes, for example metal imported for direct use at Jarma and Zinkekra, as opposed to metal destined to be reworked at Saniat Jibril; or a change in isotopic signature may have been induced by the work carried out at Saniat Jibril, such as the mixing of metal from different sources.

Going further in the interpretation of the results and the discussion of possible sources, it is important to reiterate that the metal from Fazzan represents a wide variety of alloys. This seriously complicates the question of the provenance of the objects as all of the alloying elements, as well as the copper itself, will contribute to the observed isotopic signature. In leaded alloys in particular, the signature of the added lead will prevail, drowning out the signature of the copper or of other alloying elements. The situation with brasses is delicate, as the zinc and the copper can contribute to a similar extent to the final lead composition. Indeed, lead and zinc generally occur together in ore deposits and are difficult to separate, resulting in lead being added with the zinc.[40] The lead isotope ratios of brasses will therefore fall on a mixing line between the ratios of the ores used for the copper and for the zinc. Following these considerations, it becomes apparent that the different types of alloys found in Fazzan must be considered separately if we hope to shed light on their provenance. We have therefore divided the results between objects with no lead or zinc, regardless of the amount of tin (as tin did not seem responsible for any pattern), objects with over 1 per cent lead regardless of tin or zinc contents and objects with over 1 per cent zinc and no lead. Theoretically, in the first group the signature of the copper should prevail; in the second that of the lead; and the third should fall on a mixing line between that of the copper and that of the zinc. The results shown on Figure 7.2 are not clear cut and with so little data could be incidental: we can only very tentatively suggest that the leaded alloys roughly cluster together with $^{207}Pb/^{206}Pb$ values between 0.8447 and 0.8489, representing a lead source, while the four analysed objects with the higher $^{207}Pb/^{206}Pb$ of the main cluster are all brasses, perhaps indicative of the influence of a zinc source.

---

[40] Craddock and Meeks in Weisgerber 2007.

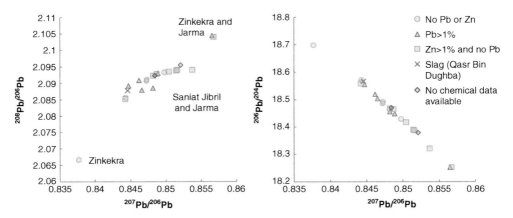

Figure 7.2 Lead isotope ratios for copper-base objects from Fazzan. The error bars are smaller than the size of the markers.

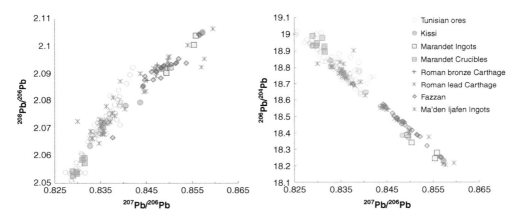

Figure 7.3 Lead isotope ratios for copper-base objects from Fazzan compared to those of Tunisian lead ores, Kissi objects, Marandet objects and crucibles, and Roman lead and bronze from Carthage.

The comparison of the LIA from Fazzan with other available data on archaeological objects from North and West African sites has shown interesting similarities (Fig. 7.3). Two brass anklets from fifth- to seventh-century AD contexts from the site of Kissi in Burkina Faso and two brass ingots from the sixth- to ninth-century AD site of Marandet in Niger fall close to our main group, although with slightly lower $^{206}Pb/^{204}Pb$ values, while a set of chain links from the second to ninth centuries AD from Kissi and two further Marandet ingots plot near our group of two objects from Jarma and Zinkekra. Roman lead and bronze objects from Carthage also fall in close proximity to these two groups. These similarities may suggest the use of a similar pool of metal at these sites, and thus metal trade between them. Chronology is of course an important factor to consider, and the majority of the objects from Fazzan are thought to date from the first to fourth centuries AD, so at least some of the Kissi objects and certainly the Marandet ingots are later in date. The fact that similarities exist despite this time difference may indicate the continued used of metal from the same sources, or the curation or recycling of the same pool of metal for a prolonged period of time. The slight differences in the $^{206}Pb/^{204}Pb$ values for the Kissi anklets and two of the Marandet ingots could of course represent a different source altogether, but they could also be an indication that metal was transformed at these sites, for example through the addition of local metal. This has already been suggested by Fenn for the Kissi material,[41] and is a practice that was described by travellers in the Early Modern period for the trade centre of Kano in particular, where old copper and zinc imported from Tripoli were added to copper extracted from a mine in Wadai.[42] Unfortunately, there is at present relatively little reference lead isotope data for metal deposits in Africa, making it difficult to verify this theory.

As mentioned above, the chemical composition of the objects seems to indicate that a significant proportion of the metal found in Fazzan would have come from the Roman Mediterranean. The Fazzan LIA data were therefore compared to areas that are known to have been mined in the area of influence of the Romans between the first and fourth centuries AD. Tunisian ores do not seem to have contributed to the composition of much or any of the metal found in Fazzan (Fig. 7.3), contrary to some of the objects from Carthage, Kissi and Marandet which were very likely extracted from a Tunisian source.[43] The coil from Zinkekra does fall near the range of isotope ratios of these deposits, but is slightly peripheral to them and may indicate mixing, or a different source altogether. This lack of metal from Tunisian sources is intriguing considering that pottery was clearly imported from there.[44] It must however be noted that we only have at our disposal here data on lead ores in Tunisia, and do not currently know

---

[41] Fenn *et al.* 2009, 130.   [42] Barth 1858 [1890], 33–39.

[43] Tunisian lead ores, Skaggs *et al.* 2012; Kissi objects, Fenn *et al.* 2009; Marandet objects and crucibles, Willett and Sayre 2006; Roman lead and bronze from Carthage, unpublished reports by Gibbins 1991 and Farquhar and Vitali 2009, for which the data were published in Fenn *et al.* 2009; Skaggs *et al.* 2012.

[44] Leitch *et al.* 2017.

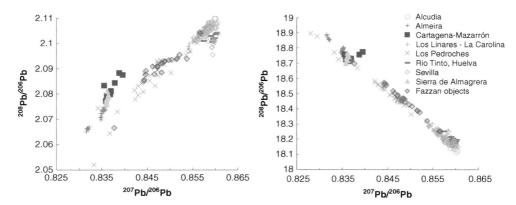

Figure 7.4 Lead isotope ratios for copper-base objects from Fazzan compared to those of Spanish ores.

if the much less widespread copper deposits of the country, some of which show traces of ancient exploitation,[45] share the same isotopic signature.

We consider the Iberian Peninsula next as it was a major metal producer in the Roman period. Lead and copper ores, among other minerals, were mined in various districts that were most active between the first century BC and the second century AD. Figure 7.4 shows the lead isotope ratios for various Spanish ore deposits and the Fazzan objects.[46] There is some overlap between the ore sources of the Los Pedroches area in the Sierra Morena and the main group of Fazzan material. Both lead and copper ores were mined in this region, which could explain the lack of a clear difference in the Fazzan material between leaded and unleaded items, as the lead and copper that constitutes them could both have come from this region and therefore have the same signature. Ores from the Los Pedroches area have only been sampled fairly recently,[47] and have since been suggested as the source of copper coins of Augustus and Tiberius,[48] and Roman copper ingots found in a shipwreck in the Mediterranean.[49] It is conceivable that some of this metal would also have been transported to North Africa. The Zinkekra and Jarma objects with the higher $^{208}Pb/^{206}Pb$ ratios, along with the Kissi chain links, correspond to ores of the Los Pedroches, Linares-La Carolina and the Alcudia lead- and copper-mining districts, all in the Sierra Morena region. The shipment of Iberian metal to

[45] Tekki 2009.
[46] On the comparative data for Spanish ores, see Dayton and Dayton 1986; Klein *et al.* 2009; Santos Zalduegui *et al.* 2004; Stos-Gale *et al.* 1995.
[47] Santos Zalduegui *et al.* 2004; cf. Klein *et al.* 2009.   [48] Klein *et al.* 2004; 2009.
[49] Rico *et al.* 2005.

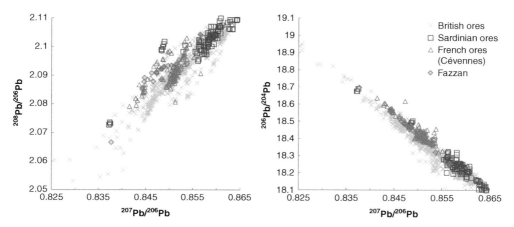

Figure 7.5 Lead isotope ratios for copper-base objects from Fazzan compared to those of ores from Britain, France (Cévennes) and Sardinia.

North Africa is unfortunately not well documented. To our knowledge the only physical evidence for this is a first-century BC shipwreck containing lead ingots from the Cartagena district found in the harbour of Cherchell in present-day Algeria.[50] If Spain was indeed the original source for copper found in Fazzan, it remains unclear whether the Fazzan copper would have been traded directly from Iberia to African ports, then to Fazzan, or if it is more generally representative of the copper in circulation in the Roman world, traded as finished objects or scrap to Fazzan.

Some of the objects from the main group also have similar ratios to ore from southern France, where mostly lead but also copper ores were mined in the Roman period on a seemingly much smaller scale than in Spain (Fig. 7.5).[51] Sardinia and Britain, where lead production took place following the decline of the Spanish mines, also show peripheral matches to our data, and cannot be ruled out as participating in the composition of the Fazzan objects, especially as one of several mixed metals (Fig. 7.5).[52]

The provenance of the zinc ore used in the Fazzan brasses is problematic since relatively little is known of the location of the zinc ore (smithsonite) deposits mined in Roman times. Mining has now been attested in Germany near Aachen and Stolberg,[53] while brass cementation crucibles have been found in Xanten also in western Germany[54] and Colchester and

---

[50] Domergue and Rico 2014.   [51] Domergue *et al.* 2006.

[52] On British ores, see Rohl 1996; on French ores, see Baron *et al.* 2006; Bode *et al.* 2009; Le Guen *et al.* 1991; on Sardinian ores, see Boni and Koeppel 1985; Ludwig *et al.* 1989; Stos-Gale *et al.* 1995; Swainbank *et al.* 1982.

[53] Gechter 1993.   [54] Rehren 1999.

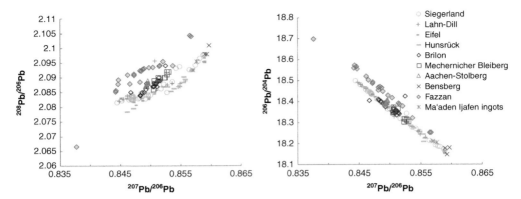

Figure 7.6 Lead isotope ratios for copper-based objects from Fazzan compared to those of ores from Germany.

Canterbury in England,[55] and suggested in Lyon, Autun and Alesia in France.[56] The brasses from Fazzan with ^{207}Pb/^{206}Pb between 0.8504 and 0.8537 could perhaps be seen as a falling on a mixing line between the main group of leaded and unleaded copper and bronze, and a source of zinc unclear at present, but the ores from the Aachen-Stolberg area do not seem to be good candidates for this (Fig. 7.6).[57]

In summary, the Sierra Morena and potentially Britain, France and Sardinia seem plausible candidates as the original sources of the copper and lead found in the copper alloys from Fazzan, while the origin of the zinc remains unclear. We have also highlighted similarities between the lead isotope signature for objects from Fazzan, Niger and the Niger Bend area, which, along with the presence of other northern imports at all of these sites, suggests that they were involved in a regional network of trade beginning in the first millennium AD. To go further, a detailed sampling of ores from Niger would be crucial as it could help clarify the potential mixing of Saharan metal with metal imported from further afield.

Evidence of Copperworking

The clearest evidence for the transformation of copper in Fazzan comes from the sites of Jarma and Saniat Jibril. In the Classic Garamantian levels

[55] Bayley 1998.
[56] Chardron-Picault and Picon 1998; Desbat *et al.* 2000; Picon *et al.* 1995. Craddock and Eckstein have however since expressed doubts regarding the use of these vessels to produce brass (Craddock and Eckstein 2003, 225).
[57] On German ore sources, Bode *et al.* 2009; Durali-Müller *et al.* 2007.

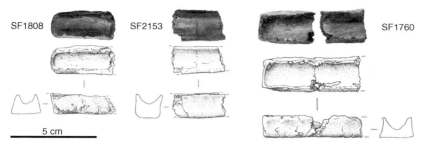

Figure 7.7 Ingot moulds found in Jarma (SF1760, SF1808 and SF2153).

of Jarma, the Garamantian capital, the Fazzan Project found three fragments of copper ingot moulds.[58] They were hand moulded from clay in
a rectangle shape with a semicircular channel (channel width: 10 to 13 mm,
depth: 4 to 8 mm), and fired by contact with the molten metal (Fig. 7.7).[59]
One of the fragments showed traces of copper on its upper lip. This mould
design is unlike the models known to us from other sites in the Sahara or
West Africa and are also earlier in date. Examples found at Marandet (sixth
to ninth centuries AD) were made of fired earth with multiple narrow
channels.[60] Others were found at Tagdaoust in Mauritania. These were
'bricks' of fired clay measuring at least 10.5 × 11 × 4 cm, with several
channels of trapeze or rectangular sections with rounded angles,[61] and date
approximately from the tenth to the twelfth centuries AD.

   At the Classic Garamantian settlement site of Saniat Jibril, located 300 m
east of Jarma and occupied between the second to first centuries BC and
the fifth century AD, the Fazzan Project recorded a particularly high
concentration of copper fragments and slag representative of metallurgical
activities. Many fragments of stones, glass and shells used in the production of beads were also found, giving the overall impression that Saniat
Jibril included of a range of workshops specialised in the production of
jewellery. Detailed descriptions of the excavated and surveyed features, and
catalogues listing the slag and metal small finds from the site, can be found
in the *Archaeology of Fazzan* series.[62] Many ashy patches covered the area
surveyed by the Fazzan Project. One of these was excavated in 2001 and
was found to be a hearth differing from the traditional domestic hearth of
Garamantian date. It had a roughly hemispherical bowl *c.*75 cm in diameter and 40 cm deep, and presented features that could be interpreted as

---

[58] Cole 2013a, 462.   [59] Figure 7.7 is taken from Mattingly 2013, 811.
[60] Fenn 2006, 39; Magnavita *et al.* 2007.   [61] Vanacker 1983.
[62] Mattingly 2010, 123–204; Schrufer-Kolb 2007, 448–62.

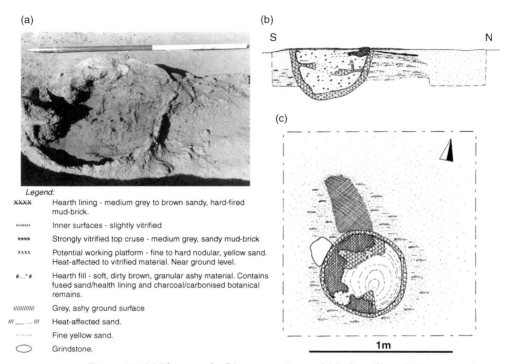

Legend:

××××	Hearth lining - medium grey to brown sandy, hard-fired mud-brick.
××××××	Inner surfaces - slightly vitrified
★★★★	Strongly vitrified top cruse - medium grey, sandy mud-brick
××××	Potential working platform - fine to hard nodular, yellow sand. Heat-affected to vitrified material. Near ground level.
#...°#	Hearth fill - soft, dirty brown, granular ashy material. Contains fused sand/health lining and charcoal/carbonised botanical remains.
/////////	Grey, ashy ground surface
/// ___ ... ///	Heat-affected sand.
....	Fine yellow sand.
◯	Grindstone.

Figure 7.8 (a) Photograph, (b) cross-section and (c) plan of hearth 20 excavated at Saniat Jibril by the Fazzan Project in 2001.

remains from a blow-hole and a collapsed superstructure (Fig. 7.8).[63] Schrüfer-Kolb considered that there was little doubt that it would have been used for fairly high-temperature processes, probably to work both copper and iron, but that it may also have been used for other activities.[64] Other remains included a number of smithing hearth bottoms, spheroidal hammerscales, fragments of iron slag with some adhering copper oxidation products and two possible crucible fragments, from which she concluded that both ironworking (forging and possible bloom consolidation) and copper alloy working took place at the site, sometimes in close proximity.

Intriguingly, there was a greater concentration of silver coins in Saniat Jibril than in other Garamantian sites including the capital Jarma.[65] As the Garamantes do not seem to have had a coin-based economy, it was suggested that the coins might have been collected to be recycled at the site, although there is at present no firm evidence for this.[66]

---

[63] Figure 7.8 is from Schrüfer-Kolb 2007, 450.   [64] Schrüfer-Kolb 2007, 451.
[65] These are Roman coins from the second to fourth centuries AD.   [66] Sauer 2007, 463.

TSM 601c   TSM 602c   5 cm

Figure 7.9 Fragments of slag TSM 601c and TSM 602 from Qasr Bin Dughba.

Evidence for copperworking was also found at the site of Qasr Bin Dughba, a large enclosed settlement site of the eastern Wadi al-Ajal, briefly surveyed by both Daniels and the Fazzan Project. Radiocarbon dates suggest occupation between the late fourth and early sixth centuries AD,[67] but the full chronology and extent of the settlement are unclear. Traces of metalworking were found in the form of a roughly plano-convex piece of slag with large lumps of corroded metallic copper (TSM 601c found at GBD 001; Fig. 7.9) and fragments of crust-like greenish pieces of slag that are very porous and light (for example, TSM 601a and 602; Fig. 7.9), which according to Daniels' notes were common at site GBD 003. A lump of oxidised copper from the former was included in the set of objects chosen for LIA presented above. The ratios measured fall within the main group of Fazzan objects, and if Qasr Bin Dughba is indeed of later date than Jarma, Zinkekra and Saniat Jibril, could represent a continuity in the source of copper used in the region. Microscopy also revealed the presence of copper sulphide inclusions in this lump. The crust-like pieces were mostly composed of a glassy matrix with various calcium-rich pyroxene crystals and inclusions of iron sulphides. I hesitate to discuss these poorly contextualised finds in too much detail, but they do indicate that metal was worked at the site. When access to Libya becomes possible again, it would be very interesting to revisit the site to try to reach a better appreciation of the type of activities carried out there.

In order to appreciate the craft of the Garamantian coppersmiths, I also turned to the objects themselves. Not all objects found in Fazzan are necessarily representative of the metalworking carried out there, as some were probably directly imported and were never

[67] Mattingly *et al.* 2007, 229–31.

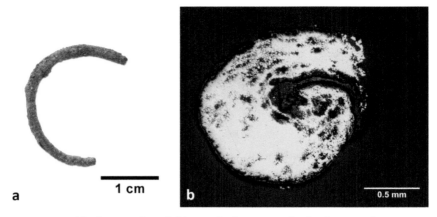

a   1 cm   b   0.5 mm

Figure 7.10 (a) Photograph and (b) unetched micrograph of a thin ring from Saniat Jibril (TSM 160). The micrograph shows evidence for coiling or wire-drawing.

subsequently altered. Nevertheless, the evidence at Saniat Jibril makes it clear that ornaments were produced on site. The morphology of the objects as well as their microstructure (twin grains and slip bands) shows that they were mostly produced using cold-working and annealing. Many of the artefacts are indeed made of sheet metal, rods or wires of variable thickness, which were then cut, pierced, bent, coiled or segmented to make various types of artefacts, such as tubes, coiled pins or pendants (see Fig. 7.15 in Appendix 7.1). Some of the wires were probably produced by coiling a strip of metal as revealed by the spiralling microstructure observed on the cross-section of a ring (Fig. 7.10). Repoussé, to produce simple dotted decorations, and riveting, in particular for the production of the 'rivet plates', seem to also have been part of the repertoire of the Garamantes.

As seen above, there is evidence of ingots being cast in open clay moulds, and we can also suggest the use of sand moulds which would not have survived to this day, but we have very few examples of objects that might have been made using more complex casting techniques such as lost-wax or bivalve mould casting, and it is unclear whether these techniques would have been used in Fazzan.

Evidence of Ironworking

At Jarma, the Fazzan Project found evidence for iron-smithing slag compatible with what one might expect from relatively small-scale metalworking in smithies or household environments. The Classic and Late Garamantian levels stood out as having a higher concentration of metalworking remains, suggesting a more intense activity in this period. As mentioned above, at the site of Saniat Jibril ironworking was carried out in a quasi-urban setting as one of several manufacturing activities. The fragments of slag from Saniat Jibril are either undiagnostic or appear to be iron-smithing slag, including some plano-convex hearth bottoms. Detailed descriptions of the metal finds and metalworking debris recovered at Jarma and Saniat Jibril can be found in previous publications.[68]

The promontory of Zinkekra, 4 km south-west of modern Jarma, is the 'type site' for Early and Proto-Urban Garamantian settlements. Daniels' extensive survey and excavation work there produced the earliest metalworking evidence known in Fazzan to date: slag and pieces of iron-rich minerals identified by one of Daniels' contacts as limonite. The majority of these remains most likely dates to between the late first millennium BC and the first century AD, but a few samples could date from as early as the first half of the first millennium BC.[69] Although many hearths were found at various sites on the Zinkekra escarpment, in particular at ZIN002.11, where a great number are concentrated in a small area, most of these appear to have been of a domestic nature and it is unclear whether any of those were associated with metalworking.

A fragment of undiagnostic slag (SF61) came from layer 87 in a deeply stratified section on the north side of Zinkekra (ZIN002.218), which was dated by radiocarbon dating of a date stone to 791–540 calBC.[70] From layer 86, immediately above, came a second piece of slag, of the 'run slag' type discussed below (SF55). This layer was dated, also from a date stone, to 792–542 calBC.[71] Another potentially early fragment (TSM 620) comes from a context that has been identified as belonging to the second period of occupation of Zinkekra in the Early Garamantian Period (*c.*1000–500 BC).[72] This fragment was black to brown, dense, about 2.5 cm thick and had rusty patches. Metallographic analysis has shown it to be slightly porous, with some

---

[68] Schrüfer-Kolb 2007, 448–62; Cole 2013a, 461–63; 2013b, 808–13.

[69] Mattingly 2010, 19–84.   [70] OxA-29242: 2510 ± 30 BP.   [71] OxA-X-2632-19: 2515 ± 27 BP.

[72] Hawthorne *et al.* 2010, 78–82. The slag fragment TSM 620 was found in Context 10 at ZIN002.011 identified as belonging to Period 2, a period characterised by oval, stone-built buildings. This period has been dated on the basis of two radiocarbon dates taken at ZIN002.013 and of associated material culture to the Early Garamantian Period. The dates from Period 2 levels at ZIN002.013 were both from charcoal samples analysed in 1972 by Teledyne Isotopes Ltd and were as follow: I-6321: 920–410 calBC (2595±90 BP), I-6322: 920–390 calBC (2560±110 BP).

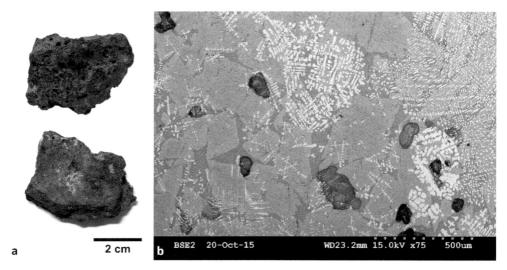

Figure 7.11 (a) Side and top view of TSM 620; (b) micrograph showing dendrites of wüstite (light grey), blocky fayalite (middle grey) and glass (darker grey).

cracks, and to be composed of dendritic wüstite of variable fineness and blocky fayalite in a glassy matrix (Fig. 7.11). This piece results from either iron smelting or smithing. Distinguishing between the two based on micro-structure and chemical analysis is notoriously difficult,[73] and its morphology is fairly non-diagnostic, but the presence of ore fragments in the same area of Zinkekra could indicate smelting. The well-developed crystals of fayalite indicate a relatively slow cooling rate, probably inside the base of the furnace.

These early examples of slag should of course be treated with caution as they are isolated pieces, but the stratified nature of the deposits and the consistent Early Garamantian dates are strongly suggestive that metallurgy was well established by the middle of the first millennium BC.

Of the other fragments of slag found at Zinkekra and available in Leicester, many are of a type sometimes referred to as 'slag prills' or 'run slag'. They are relatively small pieces, most of them complete with no obvious top or bottom, smooth shiny surfaces and a shape clearly resulting from the flowing of once-fluid material (Fig. 7.12). One of the pieces presented embedded charcoal fragments.

Metallographic analysis of two of these fragments (TSM 619 and TSM 628) showed them to be slightly porous and composed of elongated crystals of fayalite in a glassy matrix. In TSM 628 the size of the fayalite crystals varied from area to area, probably representing different deposition events. Wüstite

---

[73] Miller and Killick 2004, 31.

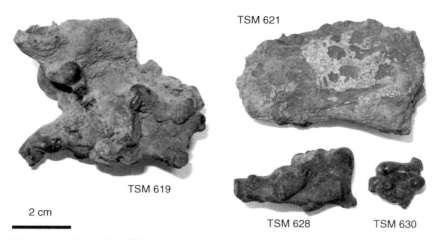

Figure 7.12 Examples of fragments of 'run slag' (TSM 619, 628 and 630) and iron bearing rock (TSM 621) from Zinkekra.

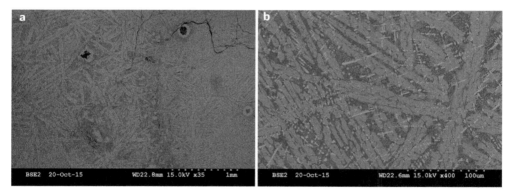

Figure 7.13 (a) and (b) Micrographs of slag sample TSM 628 at two different magnifications showing elongated fayalite crystals (middle grey) in a glassy matrix (darker grey) and fine dendrites of wüstite (light grey). Pores and cracks appear black.

was also present in this sample in the form of very fine dendrites (Fig. 7.13) and grains of sand were found in TSM 619. This type of slag can be interpreted as drips falling out of the hot zone of the furnace during smelting, or possibly expelled from a bloom during its consolidation. Slag of a similar morphology was found at sites of the Nok culture in Nigeria dating from the mid-first millennium BC.[74] These seemingly resulted from the iron-smelting operations in non-slag-tapping furnaces. Other (very remote) examples were found at the Iron Age sites of Shooter's Hill and Trevelgue Head in Britain and, in the absence of tap slag or large furnace bottoms, were interpreted as the result

[74] Junius 2016.

of the smelting of a small quantity of the rich iron ore found at the site. This is thought to have produced only a small volume of slag, for which no tapping or vertical separation in a pit would be required.[75] A similar process is conceivable in Fazzan making use of the reddish iron ore found at the site during Daniels' excavations.

Iron deposits are known in Fazzan in the Wadi ash-Shati about 100 km north of the Wadi al-Ajal across the Ubari Sand Sea. These are extremely large, but of low grade according to modern standards.[76] Although some pre-Islamic settlements have been recognised there, no true archaeological work has yet been carried out, meaning that we can only speculate as to the existence of smelting sites in that area, or the transport of ores across the sand sea. There are no deposits of such a scale in the Wadi al-Ajal, but small iron oxide deposits and locally enriched sandstones have been found, notably at al-Ghrayf immediately north of Zinkekra which could potentially have been used in metallurgical activities.[77] The smelting of iron in Fazzan from the mid-first millennium BC is on present evidence a possibility, although strong archaeological evidence in the form of furnaces clearly linked to metalworking, tuyères or slag clearly ascribable to smelting is so far lacking.

Ironworking of course does not only require metallic ore, but also a great quantity of fuel which can be problematic in arid environments. Wood charcoal, in particular from date palm, was used in Fazzan,[78] but other possible sources of fuel to be considered are date stones and dung. There is a large amount of dung at Zinkekra from the sheep, goat and cattle kept at the site. A 'small brick-like cube of dung which presented every appearance of being a piece of unused fuel' found at site ZIN002.011 during Daniels' excavations indicates that dung was most probably used as a fuel there,[79] and the use of dung fuel is also attested at Jarma.[80] Burned date stones are also frequently found in Fazzan and thought to have been used for fuel. Piles of burned date stones radiocarbon dated to the second half of the first millennium BC were, for example, found at ZIN700.[81] Strabo mentions the use of date stones by Mesopotamian bronze-workers,[82] and it seems possible that they could also have been used for metalworking in Fazzan, although most likely for activities other than smelting, for which charcoal is preferable to biomass fuels.[83] The relationship between dung, date stones and the metallurgical features would certainly be an interesting avenue of investigation when fieldwork in Libya becomes possible again.

---

[75] Dungworth and Mepham 2012.   [76] Schrüfer-Kolb 2007, 453.
[77] Schrüfer-Kolb 2007, 453.   [78] Pelling 2013, 490; Schrufer-Kolb 2007, 453.
[79] Daniels 1968, 142.   [80] See review in Pelling 2013, 490.   [81] Mattingly *et al.* 2007.
[82] Strabo, *Geography* 16.1.14.   [83] Rehder 2000, 63–65.

Evidence for the further processing of metals at Zinkekra is limited: this comprises a few fragments of undiagnostic metallurgical slag, a plano-convex slag cake (found at ZIN002.219) indicative of smithing activities and a grooved stone (found at ZIN001.060), interpreted as having been used for the sharpening of a metal blade.[84] Fragments of copper alloys are rare, and fragments of iron from Zinkekra are non-existent in the list of small finds compiled from Daniels' archives and the Fazzan Project's work as well as from the material available in Leicester, all in all giving the impression of relatively small-scale metallurgical activities.

The Emerging Picture for Metalworking in Fazzan

The evidence described above can clearly only provide an incomplete picture of the relationship the Garamantes had with metal and metalworking, given that hundreds of sites in the Wadi al-Ajal have yet to be studied in detail. What seems to be emerging so far is the image of an industry mainly of transformation, where finished objects were produced from stock or recycled metal. This took the form of the production of small objects of copper, notably jewellery making, and the forging of more substantial iron tools. It took place in both household settings, as at Jarma, and potentially many other sites across the Wadi where iron slag was found, and in more specialised workshops, like at Saniat Jibril. While in the Classic Garamantian period the bulk of the metal, or of the copper alloys at least, was likely imported from the Mediterranean area, there is some evidence that iron might also have been produced locally from the smelting of ores, probably on a small scale. It may be significant that this evidence seems to predate the period of most intense trade with the Roman world during which the smelting of ores may have been a less attractive investment than trade. In the following section, we look at the place of Garamantian metalworking in the Trans-Saharan context and its potential relationship with other industries.

Garamantian Metal in a Trans-Saharan Network

Copper Metallurgy

As discussed above, chemical analysis and LIA of metal from Fazzan, Marandet and Kissi show similarities suggesting a shared source of metal, and trade between these regions from the first millennium AD. It

---

[84] Hawthorne *et al.* 2010, 34 and fig. 1.24.

is difficult to ascertain whether metalworking practices were also transmitted across this network, and if so, how early these interactions could have started. Techniques for the working of sheets and wires of copper could conceivably have been shared between Fazzan and Niger. Indeed, during the first millennium BC, native copper, copper oxides and copper carbonates were smelted in the region of Agadez in Niger (Grébénart's Copper II sites).[85] As in Garamantian Fazzan, the volume of metal handled was apparently low and the objects were mostly small in dimensions, and hammered rather than cast.[86] The Nigerian assemblage, however, seems to include more utilitarian objects alongside the ornaments, such as small arrowheads, spatulas and chisels. The ingots are also different: sub-rectangular, and cast in sand moulds unlike the clay moulds found in Fazzan. Interestingly, however, the pottery associated with the Copper II furnaces corresponds to a Saharan Neolithic tradition. This, along with the absence of permanent settlement structures at the sites, has led Grébénart to suggest that the work was carried out by itinerant metalworkers turned towards the desert regions in the north. Evidence for copper working in the first millennium BC is so far lacking in Fazzan, however, so we have no indication of whether these itinerant metalworkers could have exchanged knowledge or raw materials with the people of Fazzan.

Starting in the mid-first millennium AD we find examples of secondary working of copper at many other sites across the Sahara and the Sahel (Garbey Kourou, Jenné-jeno), and the evidence increases by the end of the millennium (Tadmakka, Marandet, Gao Saney, Sincu Bara).[87] The evidence takes the form of small crucibles and fragments of copper, as well as traces of the production or transformation of ingots. The secondary working of copper has, for example, been described in some detail at Tagdaoust (eighth to eleventh centuries AD) where it seems to have operated in a similar setting to Saniat Jibril: copper was worked in a specialised area alongside stones, ostrich eggshell and small quantities of iron.[88] There are of course a number of stylistic and technological differences across this vast region. For example, geometric incised decorations and wire decorations applied to the body of objects, seemingly unknown in Fazzan, are seen at various West African sites. The use of lost-wax casting, for which there is currently no evidence at any period in Fazzan, is attested around the ninth

---

[85] Grébénart 1983; Killick *et al.* 1988.   [86] Grébénart 1983.

[87] Garbey Kourou: Magnavita 2017; Jenné-jeno: McIntosh 1995, 264–90; Tadmakka: Nixon 2009; Marandet: Magnavita *et al.* 2007; Magnavita 2017; Gao Saney: Cissé 2010, 228–41; Sincu Bara: Garenne-Marot *et al.* 1994.

[88] Vanacker 1983.

century at Tagdaoust,[89] between the tenth and the thirteenth centuries at Sincu Bara[90] and between the eleventh and thirteenth centuries at Toguere Doupwil,[91] although the exact details of its appearance and spread are unclear.

Despite these differences, the Saharan and Sahelian sites present some common elements. The working of wire, rods and sheets into small ornaments is frequent, and perforated or riveted plates are found at several sites, while statuary, vessels or weapons are to our knowledge absent in sites of this period. This marks them apart from the earlier traditions of Punic and Roman North Africa to the north, which included larger cast objects such as figurines and statues, mirrors and vessels,[92] from the first-millennium BC copper production in the Akjoujt region of Mauritania, where it was made into axes and arrowheads,[93] and farther south from the traditions of southern Nigeria that were Igbo-Ukwu, Ife and later Benin, with their iconic cast heads and plaques.[94] This can perhaps be explained by limitations in the volume of metal available to work, since in many cases it had to be imported through middle- or long-distance trade due to the absence of copper deposits nearby, or limitations in fuel resources in these arid regions. While the volume of metal worked may have been related to environmental constraints, the type (most finds are ornaments) may have to do with the fact that ironworking was already well established in these regions, and that, as seems to have been the case in Fazzan, iron was preferred for the production of tools and weapons. The differences in object types observed in the Akjoujt region, where copper weapons and tools were found, could be attributed to the local availability of the copper ore, as well as the fact that the production of copper predated that of iron. Indeed, while the copper deposits of the region were exploited from the first millennium BC, the iron deposits apparently remained unexploited.[95]

We can hope that future research will help to determine whether the similarities in copper metallurgy observed at Saharan and the Sahelian sites are associated with a diffusion of technologies across a Trans-Saharan network which was developing in the first millennium AD, or are related to similar responses to comparable environmental constraints. Either way, it seems that its development was accelerated by the import of metal from

---

[89] Vanacker 1983.   [90] Garenne-Marot *et al.* 1994.   [91] Bedaux *et al.* 1978.

[92] See notably Boube-Piccot 1995 and Tekki 2009.

[93] See notably the Boudhida assemblage Vernet 1993, 343–52.

[94] Herbert 1984 and references therein; Shaw 1970.

[95] Lambert 1983. McIntosh 2020 warns that the dating of these surface finds to the first millennium BC is based on typology and needs to be verified with finds from closed and dated contexts.

the north, with the advent of Islamic rule and in the centuries immediately before it, and coincides with the emergence of increasingly complex societies, in particular in the Middle Senegal Valley and the Middle Niger. This trade is attested by the appearance of imported material, including brass, in the assemblages of these sites at around the same time as people started to transform copper.[96] Indeed, if the metal arrived as ingots or in forms deemed unsuitable for the local markets, it would then have necessitated the development of cutting, melting, casting and hammering techniques so that it could be redistributed locally.

Iron Metallurgy

Iron seems to have first been worked, if not smelted, in Fazzan at some point between *c.*800 and 500 BC, with the volume of evidence for it increasing towards the end of the millennium. Putting the controversial early dates of the Termit Massif aside,[97] it seems that in many sites in the Trans-Saharan region and West Africa ironworking was present around this early to mid-first-millennium BC mark, unfortunately coinciding with the flattening in the radiocarbon calibration curve. This is true for sites in the northern peripheries of the Mandara Mountains in Nigeria and Cameroon,[98] for Nok culture sites[99] and sites in the Nsukka area in Nigeria,[100] for Grébénart's Iron I in Niger,[101] but also in the Mauritanian area of the Dhar Nema,[102] the Inland Niger Delta at Dia[103] and the Senegal River valley at Walalde.[104] Metallurgy has been the subject of surprisingly little attention in the Nile Valley with the exception of the site of Meroe in Sudan (see Chapter 8), where the earliest dates currently point to around the seventh to sixth centuries BC, although earlier dates may still emerge upon dating the lower layers of the slag heaps. A review of archaeological evidence in Egypt has shown that although iron objects appeared from the second millennium BC, it was not until the seventh to fifth centuries that tools were regularly made of iron.[105] Similar dates are available for the Maghrib: iron was worked in Carthage from the eighth century BC,[106] and metal was worked both on a small scale in households and in large

---

[96] See Volume 1 in this series (Mattingly *et al.* 2017) and also Cissé 2010; Fenn *et al.* 2009; Magnavita 2017; McIntosh 1995, 264.

[97] Grébénart 1983; Quéchon 2001. And see critical assessment in Killick 2004, 100–7.

[98] MacEachern 1996.   [99] Junius 2016.   [100] Okafor 2002.

[101] Grébénart 1983; Killick *et al.* 1988.   [102] MacDonald *et al.* 2009.   [103] Schmidt 2005.

[104] Deme and McIntosh 2006, 336–37.   [105] Wuttmann 2001.

[106] Niemeyer 1990; Rakob 1990; see also Alpern 2005, 51 and note 37 on the debate on whether this is smithing or smelting slag.

industrial centres such as Bir Massouda between the seventh and fifth centuries BC, and Byrsa Hill between the fifth and the third centuries BC.[107] Slag was also found at the inland Tunisian site of Althiburos in layers from the eighth century BC to the late Numidian period,[108] hinting at the possibility that metalworking was widely practised in the so far greatly understudied pre-Roman periods of North Africa.

The technological characteristics of these early incidences of iron-working are of little more help than the dates in reconstructing potential transmission patterns, given the remarkably small number of sites where remains of metalworking furnaces have so far been identified. Most of these seem to be forced draught low-shaft furnaces, but there are significant differences in their geometry, from very small diameters in Walaldé (*c.*25–30 cm)[109] to about *c.*110 cm for the recently excavated Nok culture furnaces,[110] and up to *c.*126 cm in the Nsukka region.[111] Construction methods were also variable, with the use of coarse stones bound by clay for the furnace walls in Bou Khzama, while clay or sand-rich material alone seems to have been preferred elsewhere. Slag appears not to have been tapped at Walaldé and Bou Khzama, whereas in Opi it was tapped into pits via connecting channels,[112] and at Meroe there was a combination of tapping and internal slag formation.[113] The environmental conditions in the forested regions of Nigeria and the arid area of the Dhar Nema, for example, clearly imposed very different constraints on the metalworkers. Fuel, in particular, was probably scarce at the latter site, which has been suggested as the reason no charcoal was found inside the excavated furnace.[114] The availability of ores of different grades and the social setting of the production would have been other factors influencing the technological choices of the metalworkers.[115] But there is simply too little evidence at present to determine whether or not these shared a common origin. If they did, they seem to have been relatively rapidly adapted to make the most of the local conditions.

Given the lack of precision in the dating of early iron production and the relatively few technological characteristics to go on, it is difficult to know whether the appearance of metalworking in Fazzan

---

[107] Kaufman 2014, 161–63.   [108] Sanmarti *et al.* 2012.

[109] Note that the dimensions of the Walade furnaces appear to only have been assessed through the geometry of the slag since no *in situ* furnaces were observed (Deme and McIntosh 2006).

[110] Junius 2016.   [111] Okafor 2002.   [112] Okafor 2002.

[113] Humphris, Chapter 8, this volume.   [114] MacDonald *et al.* 2009, 41.

[115] Robion-Brunner, Chapter 9, this volume.

Figure 7.14 Iron pick-axe found in Jarma, Fazzan (TSM016).

was the result of external influences, and if so where from; or if Fazzan itself would have played a role in the transmission of some aspects of ironworking technologies. One angle of investigation that was discussed among contributors to this volume is the relationship between the production of iron and the digging of the irrigation systems known as the foggaras. These consist of an underground channel and a series of vertical shafts, which when dug through rock would have required strong tools, for which iron would have been well suited.[116] A possible example of such a tool is the iron pick-axe found in Jarma of uncertain date (TSM016 GER001.3 69, see Fig. 7.14). A well-established ability to maintain, if not produce, iron in the vicinity of the foggaras would then have been worth investing in. Chapters 2 and 3 detailed the east to west spread of the foggara technology across North Africa. It most likely originated from the Near Eastern *qanat* and first appeared on the African continent in the Western Desert of Egypt in the mid-first millennium BC. Whether this wave of innovation also brought along changes in ironworking technologies, or whether iron was truly a prerequisite for the spread of the foggara, is for the moment a matter of speculation, especially given the absence, to our knowledge, of evidence for metalworking in the oases of the Western Desert.[117] A few points are worth consideration, however: the appearance of the foggara in Fazzan dates from around the fourth to third centuries BC. This is later than the

---

[116] Wilson *et al.*, Chapter 3, this volume.

[117] It may be interesting to note that the Bahariya Oasis is an important modern source of iron ore (haematite, limonite and goethite), and might be an area worthy of attention (Ogden 2000, 166).

first possible indications of metalworking, but corresponds to the time when slag appears more frequently in the archaeological record. This follows the pattern observed in the Near East where the *qanat* appears at the transition between the Bronze Age and the Iron Age, that is, in the first half of the first millennium BC; not when iron first appeared, but when it became commonplace, and replaced bronze for the production of tools and weapons.[118] This suggests a possible relationship between the two technologies, although not necessarily a direct one. The building of the foggaras may indeed have increased the demand for iron, but many other factors should be considered, as the period of their appearances corresponds to a variety of other changes. In Fazzan it comes with the second phase of agricultural innovations that included the adoption of Sub-Saharan crops, and was marked by an intensification of cultivation.[119] These changes were accompanied by a shift in settlement pattern and a population increase. The increased food production would have fed the growing population, but also may have created a food surplus for trade. We can envisage that this developing trade might have brought in new ideas and raw materials. Could this have included iron in the form of a finished or semi-finished product, or ironworking knowledge? An increased agricultural output would also have increased the demand for tools, not only for the digging of foggaras, but also for a variety of other agricultural activities.

The evidence for metalworking available to date unfortunately does not allow us to investigate in detail who worked the metal. There seems to have been an element of household and workshop production, probably from the sedentary part of the population in the Classic Garamantian period, but could we envisage, perhaps for earlier periods, the involvement of itinerant metalworkers? Deme and McIntosh indeed remarked that iron smelting appeared at Walalde, Jenné-jeno and Bou Khzama 'with pastoral or agropastoral peoples who transhume and have wide-reaching networks for movement and exchange'.[120] We think also of the endogamous social group of the potters and blacksmiths found in the Sahel and well documented by

---

[118] For the appearance of the *qanat*, see Liverani, Chapter 2 and Wilson *et al.*, Chapter 3, this volume and references therein; for the development of iron metallurgy in the Near East see notably Pigott 1999.

[119] See further discussion in Duckworth *et al.*, Chapter 1, and Wilson *et al.*, Chapter 3, this volume.

[120] Deme and McIntosh 2006, 344.

anthropological research, where the men practice ironworking and the women make pottery. Livingstone Smith suggests, as a very tentative hypothesis but one worth exploring, the involvement of this group in the spread of the use of both rouletted pottery decoration and iron metallurgy.[121] He highlights the simultaneous appearance of iron objects and roulette decoration at a number of sites in the Lake Chad area, Nigeria and Niger. He also remarks that the matrimonial strategies of these groups led them to be highly mobile and facilitated the crossing of social or ethnic boundaries.[122]

Twisted cord roulette is common in Fazzan in the Classic and Late Garamantian periods, but the earliest example was found at Zinkekra and dates from the early first millennium BC.[123] As summarised in Chapter 13, a whole spectrum of possible explanations for shared pottery decorations between Sub-Saharan and Central Saharan sites can be envisaged, from completely independent inventions to a loose notion of shared style, or the movement of pots, individuals or groups. In this context it would be unwise to make any assumption as to the potential links between pottery styles and the appearance of ironworking in Fazzan, although as research continues on both pottery (decoration, but also tempering and shaping) and metalworking, it may be an avenue of research that enables us to think of the people behind these technologies and their spread in this vast area, rather than being limited to drawing parallels between sets of very distant sites.

Conclusion

The recent analysis of metalworking remains from Fazzan has helped to clarify the range of metallurgical activities carried out by the Garamantes. The emerging picture is necessarily incomplete due to the relatively low number of sites excavated in Fazzan and the lack of access to excavated material stored in Libya. It is, however, starting to show not only the trade of metal between the Mediterranean area and Fazzan, especially during the first half of the first millennium AD, but also trade and possible shared technological choices between Fazzan and sites on the southern edge of the desert. The constraints of limited fuel and restricted access to copper, which in many cases had to be traded in, would have played a role in the development of the techniques used to work with it: the work of sheet

---

[121] Livingstone Smith 2007.
[122] Livingstone Smith 2007, 207. See also MacEachern 1998, 127.
[123] Pot HM315 at ZIN002.023W. Figure 1.55 in Hawthorne *et al.* 2010.

metal, wires and rods, and the casting of small ingots. But we have also shown that the development of ferrous and non-ferrous metalworking in Fazzan could have been entangled with that of other technologies, in particular foggara irrigation and agriculture which would likely have created more demand for iron, but also enabled the production of food surpluses and manufacturing capacity facilitating trade. It is at present difficult to appreciate who the metalworkers were. In the context of household or workshop production in settlements such as Jarma or Saniat Jibril, we can envisage that they formed part of the sedentary population, but their relationship with the oasis farmers is unclear. We can also only speculate as to the involvement of the pastoral people of the Central Sahara. Their involvement in trade is likely, and it is tempting to suggest that they could have participated in the spread of iron and copper metallurgy, but there is no firm evidence for that in Fazzan so far.[124]

Appendix 7.1 Analysed Objects

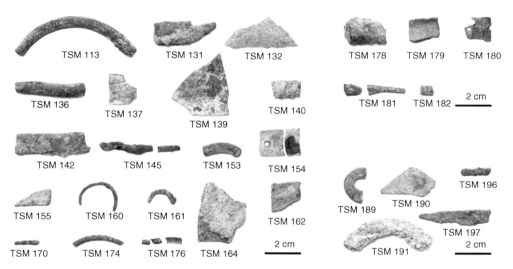

Figure 7.15 Fazzan objects from Saniat Jibril (left), Zinkekra (top right) and Jarma (bottom right) subjected to chemical or lead isotope analysis

[124] The lead isotope analysis was supported by a grant from the Society for Libyan Studies to which we are grateful. We also thank J.A. Evans and V. Pashley from the British Geological Survey who carried out the lead isotope analysis and John Spratt of the Natural History Museum in London for his assistance with the electron microprobe analysis.

Table 7.1 *Objects subjected to chemical and lead isotope analysis*

Sample no.	Description	Date	Site	Context	LIA	EPMA	Small find no.	Publication
TSM 113	Bangle/ring segment		Saniat Jibril	GER 002 unstratified	x	x	CMD SF56?	AF3 p.477
TSM 131	Blade	Probably 1st–4th cent. AD	Saniat Jibril	GER 002 4 11 top soil		x	CMD SF3	AF3 p.479
TSM 132	Thin folded sheet	4th cent. AD	Saniat Jibril	GER 002 4 26	x	x	CMD SF13	AF3 p.479
TSM 136	Rod	4th cent. AD	Saniat Jibril	GER 002 4 30	x		CMD SF34	AF3 p.479
TSM 137	Sheet fragment	Mid-2nd–late 3rd cent. AD	Saniat Jibril	GER 002 4 37	x	x	CMD SF14	AF3 p.479
TSM 139	Thick sheet fragment (mirror?)	50/80–mid-2nd cent. AD	Saniat Jibril	GER 002 4 101	x	x		AF3 p.479
TSM 140	Rod fragment	Mid-2nd–late 3rd cent. AD	Saniat Jibril	GER 002 6 9	x	x	CMD SF19	AF3 p.479
TSM 142	Strip fragment	Probably 1st–4th cent. AD	Saniat Jibril	GER 002 7 S	x	x	CMD SF62	AF3 p.479
TSM 145	Rod	Mid-2nd–late 3rd cent. AD	Saniat Jibril	GER 002 7 1	x	x	CMD SF43	AF3 p.479
TSM 153	Rod/bracelet fragment?	Probably 1st–4th cent. AD	Saniat Jibril	GER 002 7 44	x	x	CMD SF37	AF3 p.479
TSM 154	Perforated sheet fragment	Probably 1st–4th cent. AD	Saniat Jibril	GER 002 7 55	x	x	CMD SF47	AF3 p.479
TSM 155	Thick sheet fragment (mirror?)	Probably 1st–4th cent. AD	Saniat Jibril	GER 002 7 55	x	x	CMD SF53	AF3 p.479
TSM 160	Ring fragment	Probably 1st–4th cent. AD	Saniat Jibril	GER 002 8 S		x	CMD SF66	AF3 p.479
TSM 161	Ring fragment	Probably 1st–4th cent. AD	Saniat Jibril	GER 002 8 S	x	x	CMD SF67	AF3 p.480
TSM 162	Sheet fragment	Probably 1st–4th cent. AD	Saniat Jibril	GER 002 8 S	x	x	CMD SF68	AF3 p.480
TSM 164	Thick sheet fragment (mirror?)	Probably 1st–4th cent. AD	Saniat Jibril	GER 002 8 1	x	x		AF3 p.480
TSM 170	Rod fragment	Probably 1st–4th cent. AD	Saniat Jibril	GER 002 8 3	x	x		AF3 p.480
TSM 174	Segmented bracelet fragment	Probably 1st–4th cent. AD	Saniat Jibril	GER 002 G		x		AF3 p.477
TSM 176	Rod fragment	Probably 1st–4th cent. AD	Saniat Jibril	GER 002 G		x		AF3 p.477
TSM 178	Lump	Late 1st millennium BC?	Zinkekra	ZIN 002 slope		x		AF3 p.480
TSM 179	Sheet fragment	Late 1st millennium BC?	Zinkekra	ZIN 002 slope		x		AF3 p.480
TSM 180	Perforated and folded strip	Late 1st millennium BC?	Zinkekra	ZIN 002 slope	x	x		AF3 p.480
TSM 181	Tapered cone	Late 1st millennium BC?	Zinkekra	ZIN 002 slope		x		AF3 p.480
TSM 182	Coiled wire (bead?)	300 BC–1st cent. BC/1st cent. AD?	Zinkekra	ZIN 002 11 S	x			AF3 p.480

TSM 185	Coiled wire (pin?)	1st cent. AD?	Zinkekra	ZIN 002 125 E	x	x	CMD SF1364	AF3 p.480
TSM 189	Bead?		Jarma	GER 001 G/1		x		
TSM 190	Thick sheet fragment (mirror?)		Jarma	GER 001 G/1	x	x		
TSM 191	Bracelet fragment		Jarma	GER 001 G/1	x	x		
TSM 196	Rod fragment	c.AD 180–400	Jarma	GER 001 G1 748	x		FP 2001 SF1358	
TSM 197	Blade?	c.AD 180–400	Jarma	GER 001 G1 764	x		FP 2001 SF1440	
TSM 601c	Copper oxide inclusion in slag	Late 4th–early 6th cent. AD?	Qasr Bin Dughba	GBD 001	x			

Note: In the 'small find no.' column CMD numbers are from Charles Daniel's excavations and FP2001 from the Fazzan Project 2001 excavations. In the 'publication' column AF3 refers to *The Archaeology of Fazzan, Volume 3* (Mattingly 2010).

Microprobe Analysis

Small samples were taken from 79 artefacts from Fazzan and the Libyan pre-desert site of Ghirza using a jeweller's saw. Many of these were completely remineralised and only objects with significant amounts of metal remaining were selected for analysis. The samples were then mounted in epoxy resin, ground and polished down to 1 μm following normal procedures. They were analysed at the Natural History Museum in London using a Cameca SX100 Electron Microprobe using wavelength dispersive spectrometers. The operating conditions were 20 keV and 20 nA. Sixteen elements were sought for, including copper and elements commonly alloyed with it (Sn, Pb, Zn), as well as elements often associated with copper deposits and frequently found in ancient copper (Si, S, Mn, Fe, Co, Ni, As, Ag, Sb, Bi, Au, Cl). Pure metal and geological standards were used to calibrate the instrument and calculate overlap corrections factors. The average detection limits are given in Table 7.2.

The spot size of the electron beam was too small to directly obtain a bulk composition that accurately accounted for the amount of lead present in the samples. Indeed, lead is not soluble in copper at room temperature and when an alloy of copper and lead is cast and cooled, the lead segregates in globular particles. The amount of lead was instead determined using backscattered electron images of the regions analysed. Imaging software was used to determine the surface percentage represented by the lead inclusions, from which the volume percentage and weight percentage were then calculated. Measurements taken on the inclusions themselves showed that these sometimes contained a few per cent of chlorine, traces of bismuth and in one case silver. The composition of the matrix was obtained by averaging measurements taken in several points (the number of points is given in Table 7.3). The two sets of results were combined to obtain the overall composition of the sample.

This method was used on three certified copper alloys from MBH Analytical Ltd. The results are given in Table 7.2 along with the standard deviations from the multiple measurements in the main phases of these alloys, giving an idea of both the accuracy and precision of the method. The lead percentage was found to show some discrepancies with the certified lead contents, but is close enough to confidently discuss the absence or presence of lead as an alloying element. Uncertainties in the measurement of other elements is reflected in the number of significant numbers given in Table 7.3.

Table 7.2 *Composition of brass, leaded bronze and bronze standards analysed using EPMA*

		no. of points	Si	S	Mn	Fe	Co	Ni	Cu	Zn	As	Ag	Sb	Pb	Bi	Au	Sn	Total
31X B22	Weight % measured	8	0.14	bdl	bdl	0.12	0.10	0.13	80.49	16.73	0.20	bdl	0.18	0.51	0.21	bdl	0.23	99.04
	Standard deviation		*0.02*			*0.05*	*0.04*	*0.02*	*1.87*	*1.06*	*0.13*		*0.13*				*0.14*	
	Given composition		0.05	0.03		0.16	0.14	0.15	82.47	15.92	0.17		0.16	0.15	0.17		0.16	
	Absolute error		*–0.10*			*0.04*	*0.04*	*0.02*	*1.98*	*–0.81*	*–0.04*		*–0.02*	*–0.36*	*–0.04*		*–0.07*	
32X LB17	Weight % measured	11	0.11	bdl	0.19	0.25	bdl	0.43	75.73	0.64	1.24	0.68	4.28	7.45	bdl	bdl	6.45	97.44
	Standard deviation		*0.02*		*0.03*	*0.12*		*0.02*	*0.26*	*0.03*	*0.12*	*0.05*	*0.17*				*0.22*	
	Given composition				0.30	0.49	0.01	0.47	74.83	0.63	1.51	0.91	4.10	9.83	0.22		5.97	
	Absolute error				*0.11*	*0.23*	*0.04*	*0.04*	*–0.90*	*–0.01*	*0.27*	*0.23*	*–0.18*	*2.38*			*–0.48*	
32X SN7	Weight % measured	12	0.07	bdl	bdl	0.04	0.39	0.17	80.92	2.21	0.69	0.21	0.21	2.27	0.07	bdl	10.22	97.47
	Standard deviation		*0.01*			*0.02*	*0.07*	*0.01*	*1.39*	*0.16*	*0.23*	*0.04*	*0.04*				*1.38*	
	Given composition				0.00	0.06	0.44	0.18	80.30	1.96	1.07	0.31	0.26	2.60	0.05	0.00	12.60	
	Absolute error					*0.02*	*0.06*	*0.01*	*–0.62*	*–0.25*	*0.38*	*0.09*	*0.06*	*0.33*	*–0.01*		*2.38*	
	Average detection limits (ppm)		164	330	267	244	300	312	758	502	355	447	368	721	628	762	454	

Note: The lead and bismuth contents were assessed using the method described in the text. The certified compositions of the standards also contained small amounts of aluminium, phosphorus, chromium and cadmium which were not sought for in our analysis and are not included here. bdl = below detection limit.

Table 7.3 *Composition of the Fazzan objects given in weight percentages*

Sample	No. of points	Si	S	Fe	Ni	Cu	Zn	As	Ag	Sb	Pb	Bi	Au	Cl	Sn	Total
TSM 113	10	bdl	0.10	0.06	0.03	82	0.07	bdl	bdl	0.09	9	0.05	bdl	0.8	6.5	98.8
TSM 131	2	0.06	0.05	0.39	bdl	84	9.7	0.26	0.14	1.1	bdl	bdl	bdl	bdl	4.0	100.0
TSM 132	3	0.05	0.8	0.21	bdl	82	13	bdl	bdl	0.19	bdl	bdl	bdl	0.07	1.8	98.1
TSM 137	10	bdl	bdl	0.22	bdl	86	11	bdl	0.07	0.21	bdl	bdl	bdl	0.03	2.0	99.5
TSM 139	*22*	*0.28*	*0.10*	*bdl*	*bdl*	*45*	*bdl*	*bdl*	*0.04*	*0.11*	*11*	*bdl*	*bdl*	*1.6*	*25*	*82.4*
TSM 140	*6*	*0.03*	*0.04*	*0.26*	*bdl*	*82*	*bdl*	*bdl*	*bdl*	*bdl*	*<1%*	*bdl*	*bdl*	*0.37*	*0.12*	*83.0*
TSM 142	2	0.02	0.16	0.19	0.03	58	0.06	bdl	bdl	0.12	35	bdl	bdl	0.05	6.7	100.1
TSM 145	10	bdl	0.10	0.6	bdl	88	4.9	0.07	bdl	0.21	<1%	bdl	bdl	bdl	5.6	99.9
TSM 153	5	bdl	bdl	0.6	0.04	81	12	0.08	0.06	0.24	bdl	bdl	bdl	0.04	5.2	99.5
TSM 154	11	bdl	0.09	0.05	0.04	97	1.9	0.04	0.08	0.17	<1%	bdl	0.09	bdl	0.8	101.0
TSM 155	*7*	*0.29*	*0.09*	*0.08*	*bdl*	*51*	*0.07*	*0.07*	*bdl*	*0.08*	*6*	*bdl*	*bdl*	*1*	*26*	*84.5*
TSM 160	19	bdl	0.13	0.12	bdl	85	12	0.06	bdl	0.21	1	bdl	bdl	bdl	0.27	99.2
TSM 161	10	0.10	0.13	0.32	bdl	85	13	0.05	bdl	0.11	<1%	bdl	bdl	bdl	0.17	99.0
TSM 162	9	0.02	0.05	0.20	bdl	63	10	bdl	bdl	0.06	21	bdl	bdl	0.02	5.0	99.9
TSM 164	*19*	*bdl*	*0.24*	*bdl*	*bdl*	*44*	*bdl*	*0.06*	*bdl*	*0.12*	*4*	*bdl*	*bdl*	*0.41*	*37*	*85.9*
TSM 170	5	bdl	0.04	0.34	0.06	80	18	bdl	bdl	bdl	<1%	0.00	bdl	0.02	0.17	98.8
TSM 174	13	0.06	bdl	0.7	bdl	75	14	0.07	0.09	3.3	5	0.02	bdl	0.01	bdl	98.5
TSM 176	9	0.08	bdl	0.10	bdl	92	0.05	bdl	bdl	0.08	bdl	bdl	bdl	bdl	6.4	98.3
TSM 178	5	bdl	bdl	0.21	0.14	70	24	0.23	0.06	0.04	3	0.02	bdl	0.22	0.18	99.1
TSM 179	6	0.05	bdl	0.13	0.09	93	bdl	0.05	bdl	0.04	3	bdl	bdl	0.13	2.7	99.1
TSM 180	8	0.06	bdl	0.08	bdl	82	13	bdl	0.07	0.10	<1%	0.01	bdl	0.02	2.0	98.0
TSM 181	5	bdl	0.05	0.04	0.06	92	bdl	bdl	bdl	0.07	2	0.01	bdl	bdl	5.6	99.8
TSM 185	6	0.09	0.38	0.19	0.08	91	bdl	bdl	bdl	bdl	bdl	bdl	bdl	0.13	6.5	98.0
TSM 189	6	0.02	bdl	0.6	0.02	77	15	bdl	bdl	0.07	4	0.02	bdl	0.43	1.5	99.2
TSM 190	12	0.02	0.15	0.31	bdl	65	0.5	bdl	0.04	0.09	11	bdl	bdl	bdl	22	99.4
TSM 191	10	0.04	bdl	bdl	bdl	78	bdl	0.7	0.13	bdl	21	0.12	bdl	0.03	bdl	99.3
TSM 211	13	bdl	bdl	bdl	bdl	100	bdl	bdl	bdl	bdl	bdl	bdl	bdl	bdl	bdl	99.9
TSM 217	8	bdl	0.03	0.13	0.05	89	bdl	0.16	bdl	0.06	<1%	0.01	bdl	0.03	7.8	98.5

Note: Given the limitations of the equipment, values for all element but lead that were >10 per cent are rounded to the nearest whole number, values between 0.5 and 10 per cent to the first decimal place, and values <0.5 per cent to two decimal places. For lead, values >1 per cent are all rounded to the nearest whole number, and values under 1 per cent are marked <1%. bdl = below detection limit. Cells left blank indicate the element was not sought for. Objects for which low totals were obtained are given in italics.

Three of the samples (TSM 139, 155 and 164) presented complex microstructures with multiple phases, some of which were very rich in tin. Unfortunately, they were severely corroded, with some phases more affected than others, and poor totals were obtained. These are flat and relatively thick fragments of metal, and given their high tin contents we can tentatively suggest that they were mirrors, with tin added to achieve a reflective surface. For these samples, the numbers given represent an overall average on points taken in the different phases of the objects. They give a rough estimate of the samples' compositions, but the reader must be aware of their limitations. TSM 190 is also a piece of thick sheet metal with a very high tin content (22 per cent) and may also belong to the same category of objects (mirrors?), but as it wasn't corroded and satisfactory totals were obtained, its composition could be evaluated using the method described above.

The results are given in Table 7.3. Mn and Co were also sought for, but were always under the detection limit, so are not included in the table.

Lead Isotope Analysis

The analysis was carried out by J.A. Evans and V. Pashley at the British Geological Survey. Lead was extracted from the samples using ion exchange chromatography. The lead fraction was brought into solution using HNO_3 and spiked with a thallium solution to allow for the correction of instrument-induced mass bias. It was then analysed using a Thermo Fisher Neptune Plus multiple collector inductively coupled plasma mass spectrometer (MC-ICP-MS). Each individual ratio presented in Table 7.4 represents the average of 25 acquisitions. A reference solution of lead (NBS 981) was also repeatedly analysed. The data on the copper samples were then normalised according to the deviation between the known and measured values of the reference solution. The errors presented in Table 7.4 are propagated relative to the reproducibility of the reference solution.

Table 7.4 *Lead isotope ratios of Fazzan objects*

Sample number	Lab code	$^{206}Pb/^{204}Pb$	Error (2σ)	$^{207}Pb/^{206}Pb$	Error (2σ)	$^{208}Pb/^{206}Pb$	Error (2σ)
TSM 113	'P713:1'	18.5549	1.78E-03	0.8447	5.32E-05	2.089292	1.59E-04
TSM 132	'P744_11'	18.3908	3.31E-03	0.85143	8.51E-05	2.0939	3.56E-04
TSM 136	'P744_12'	18.5028	3.70E-03	0.84656	8.47E-05	2.0879	3.55E-04
TSM 137	'P744_13'	18.3872	3.31E-03	0.85158	8.52E-05	2.0941	3.56E-04
TSM 139	'P744_14'	18.4291	3.32E-03	0.84975	8.50E-05	2.0934	3.56E-04
TSM 140	'P744_15'	18.5726	3.34E-03	0.84427	8.44E-05	2.0857	3.55E-04
TSM 142	'P713:2'	18.5193	1.89E-03	0.8462	5.42E-05	2.090883	1.63E-04
TSM 145	'P713:3'	18.4174	1.75E-03	0.8504	5.53E-05	2.093554	1.59E-04
TSM 153	'P744_16'	18.559	3.34E-03	0.84419	8.44E-05	2.0852	3.54E-04
TSM 154	'P713:4'	18.4674	1.74E-03	0.8482	5.51E-05	2.092341	1.63E-04
TSM 155	'P744_17'	18.4859	3.33E-03	0.84723	8.47E-05	2.0908	3.55E-04
TSM 161	'P713:5'	18.3212	1.81E-03	0.8537	5.46E-05	2.094032	1.65E-04
TSM 162	'P713:6'	18.4548	1.73E-03	0.8482	5.34E-05	2.088545	1.61E-04
TSM 164	'P744_18'	18.4917	3.33E-03	0.84725	8.47E-05	2.0912	3.56E-04
TSM 170	P713:7	18.4652	1.75E-03	0.8487	1.27E-05	2.092882	1.07E-04
TSM 180	'P713:8'	18.2531	1.68E-03	0.8567	5.40E-05	2.10402	1.58E-04
TSM 182	'P744_19'	18.6985	3.37E-03	0.83767	8.38E-05	2.0667	3.51E-04
TSM 185	'P744_20'	21.4453	3.86E-03	0.73544	7.35E-05	1.8007	3.06E-04
TSM 190	'P744_21'	18.4485	3.32E-03	0.8489	8.49E-05	2.0931	3.56E-04
TSM 191	'P713:9'	18.2527	1.81E-03	0.8565	5.48E-05	2.104378	1.64E-04
TSM 196	'P744_22'	18.379	3.49E-03	0.85209	8.52E-05	2.0955	3.56E-04
TSM 197	'P744_23'	18.4707	3.14E-03	0.84843	8.48E-05	2.0923	3.56E-04
TSM 601c	'P713:10'	18.566	1.80E-03	0.8446	5.32E-05	2.087817	1.59E-04

References

Alpern, S.B. 2005. Did they or didn't they invent it? Iron in Sub-Saharan Africa. *History in Africa* 32: 41–94.

Baron, S., Carignan, J., Laurent, S. and Ploquin, A. 2006. Medieval lead making on Mont-Lozère Massif (Cévennes-France): Tracing ore sources using Pb isotopes. *Applied Geochemistry* 21: 241–52.

Barth, H. 1858 [1890]. *Travels and Discoveries in North and Central Africa.* London: Ward, Lock and Co.

Bayley, J. 1998. The production of brass in antiquity with particular reference to Roman Britain. In P.T. Craddock (ed.), *2000 Years of Zinc and Brass*, London: British Museum, 7–26.

Bedaux, R.M., Constandse-Westermann, T.S., Hacquebord, L., Lange, A.G. and Van der Waals, J.D. 1978. Recherches archéologiques dans le Delta Intérieur du Niger (Mali). *Palaeohistoria Bussum* 20: 91–220.

Bode, M., Hauptmann, A. and Mezger, K. 2009. Tracing Roman lead sources using lead isotope analyses in conjunction with archaeological and epigraphic evidence – a case study from Augustan/Tiberian Germania. *Archaeological and Anthropological Sciences* 1: 177–94.

Boni, M. and Koeppel, V. 1985. Ore-lead isotope pattern from the Iglesiente-Sulcis Area (SW Sardinia) and the problem of remobilization of metals. *Mineralium Deposita* 20.3: 185–93.

Boube-Piccot, C. 1995. Bronzes antiques: Productions et importations au Maroc. In P. Trousset (ed.), *L'Afrique du Nord Antique et Médiévale: Productions et Exportations Africaines. Actualités archéologiques*, Paris: Editions du CTHS, 65–78.

Bourhis, J.-R. 1983. Résultats des analyses d'objets en cuivre, bronze, laiton et des résidus de métallurgie antique d'Afrique. In Echard 1983, 127–52.

Chardron-Picault, P. and Picon, M. 1998. La fabrication du laiton à Autun, durant la période romaine: Premières recherches. *Mémoires de la Société Eduenne* 56.2: 171–81.

Childs, S.T. and Killick, D. 1993. Indigenous African metallurgy: Nature and culture. *Annual Review of Anthropology* 22: 317–37.

Chirikure, S. 2010. On evidence, ideas and fantasy: The origins of iron in Sub-Saharan Africa. Thoughts on É. Zangato and A.F.C. Holl's 'On the Iron Front'. *Journal of African Archaeology* 8.1: 25–28.

Cissé, M. 2010. *Archaeological Investigations of Early Trade and Urbanism at Gao Saney (Mali)*. Unpublished PhD thesis, Rice University, Houston.

Cline, W.B. 1937. *Mining and Metallurgy in Negro Africa*. Menasha: Gorge Banta Publishing Company.

Clist, B. 2012. Vers une réduction des préjugés et la fonte des antagonismes: Un bilan de l'expansion de la métallurgie du fer en Afrique sub-saharienne. *Journal of African Archaeology* 10.1: 71–84.

Cole, F. 2013a. Small finds reports and catalogue of small finds. In Mattingly 2013, 455–72.

Cole, F. 2013b. Catalogue of small finds. In Mattingly 2013, 793–840.

Craddock, P.T. 1978. The composition of the copper alloys used by the Greek, Etruscan and Roman civilizations: 3. The origins and early use of brass. *Journal of Archaeological Science* 5.1: 1–16.

Craddock, P.T. 1985. Medieval copper alloy production and West African bronze analyses – Part I. *Archaeometry* 27: 17–41.

Craddock, P.T. 2010. New paradigms for old iron: Thoughts on É. Zangato A.F.C. Holl's 'On the Iron Front'. *Journal of African Archaeology* 8.1: 29–36.

Craddock, P.T. and Eckstein, K. 2003. Production of brass in antiquity by direct reduction. In P.T. Craddock and J. Lang (eds), *Mining and Metal Production through the Ages*, London: The British Museum Press, 216–30.

Daniels, C.M. 1968. Garamantian excavations: Zinchecra 1965–67. *Libya Antiqua* 5: 113–94.

Dayton, J.E. and Dayton, A. 1986. Use and limitations of lead isotopes in archae-
ology. In J.S. Olin and M.J. Blackman (eds), *Proceedings of the 24th International
Archaeometry Symposium, Smithsonian, Washington, DC, May 14–18, 1984*,
Washington, DC: Smithsonian Institution Press, 13–42.

Deme, A. and McIntosh, S.K. 2006. Excavations at Walaldé: New light on the
settlement of the Middle Senegal Valley by iron-using peoples. *Journal of African
Archaeology* 4.2: 317–47.

Desbat, A., Meille, E. and Picon, M. 2000. La préparation du laiton par cémentation, à
l'époque romaine. In P. Pétrequin, P. Fluzin, J. Thiriot and P. Benoit (eds), *Arts du
Feu et Productions Artisanales: Actes des XXe Rencontres Internationales
d'Archéologie et d'Histoire d'Antibes, 21–23 oct. 1999*, Antibes: Éditions APDCA,
183–88.

Descoeudres, J.-P., Huysecom, E., Serneels, V. and Zimmermann, J.-L. (eds) 2001.
*The Origins of Iron Metallurgy: Proceedings of the First International Colloquium
on the Archaeology of Africa and the Mediterranean Basin. Mediterranean
Archaeology* 14. Sydney: University of Sydney.

Domergue, C. and Rico, C. 2014. Les itinéraires du commerce du cuivre et du
plomb hispaniques à l'époque romaine dans le monde méditerranéen. In *La
Corse et le Monde Méditerranéen, des Origines au Moyen Ag : Echanges et Circuits
Commerciaux. Actes du colloque de Bastia, 21–22 novembre 2013. Bulletin de la
Société des sciences historiques et naturelles de la Corse* 746–47: 135–68, Bastia:
Société des Sciences Historiques et Naturelles de la Corse.

Domergue, C., Serneels, V., Cauuet, B., Pailler, J.-M. and Orzechowski, S. 2006.
Mines et métallurgies en Gaule à la fin de l'âge du Fer et à l'époque romaine. In
D. Paunier (ed.), *Celtes et Gaulois, l'Archéologie face à l'Histoire, 5: la
Romanisation et la Question de l'Héritage Celtique*, Glux-en-Glenne: Bibracte,
Centre archéologique européen, 131–62.

Duckworth, C.N., Cuénod, A. and Mattingly, D.J. 2015. Non-destructive µXRF
analysis of glass and metal objects from sites in the Libyan Pre-Desert and
Fazzan. *Libyan Studies* 46: 15–34.

Dungworth, D. and Mepham, L. 2012. Prehistoric iron smelting in London:
Evidence from Shooters Hill. *Historical Metallurgy* 46: 1–8.

Durali-Müller, S., Brey, G.P., Wigg-Wolf, D. and Lahaye, Y. 2007. Roman lead
mining in Germany: Its origin and development through time deduced
from lead isotope provenance studies. *Journal of Archaeological Science*
34: 1555–67.

Echard, N. (ed.) 1983. *Métallurgies Africaines: Nouvelles contributions. Mémoires
de la Société des Africanistes* 9. Paris: Société des Africanistes.

Eggert, M. 2010. Too old? Remarks on new evidence of ironworking in
north-central Africa. *Journal of African Archaeology* 8.1: 37–38.

Farquhar, R.M. and Vitali, V. 2009. *Lead Isotope Analyses of Punic and Roman
Artifacts. Unpublished report*. Toronto: Geophysics Laboratory, University of
Toronto.

Fenn, T. 2006. Copper metallurgy and Trans-Saharan commerce: Report on summer 2006 field research in the western Agadez region, central Niger. *Nyame Akuma* 66: 25–34.

Fenn, T.R., Killick, D.J., Chesley, J., Magnavita, S. and Ruiz, J. 2009. Contacts between West Africa and Roman North Africa: Archaeometallurgical results from Kissi, northeastern Burkina Faso. In S. Magnavita *et al.* (eds), *Crossroads Carrrefour/Sahel: Cultural and Technological Developments in the First Millennium* BC/AD *West Africa*, Frankfurt: Africa Magna Verlag, 119–46.

Gale, N.H. and Stos-Gale, Z.A. 1996. Lead isotope methodology: The possible fractionation of lead isotope compositions during metallurgical processes. In S. Demirci, A.M. Ozer and G.D. Summers (eds), *Archaeometry 94: The Proceedings of the 29th International Symposium on Archaeometry*, Ankara: Tubitak, 287–99.

Garenne-Marot, L., Wayman, M.L. and Pigott, V.C. 1994. Early copper and brass in Senegal. In T. Childs (ed.), *Society, Culture and Technology in Africa*, MASCA Research Papers in Science and Archaeology, Supplement to Volume 11, Philadelphia: University of Pennsylvania Museum, 45–62.

Gechter, M. 1993. Römischer Bergbau in der Germania Inferior: Eine Bestandaufnahme. In H. Steuer and U. Zimmermann (eds), *Montanarchäologie in Europa*, Sigmaringen: Jan Thorbecke, 161–66.

Gibbins, H. 1991. *Lead Isotope Analyses of Artifacts from Carthage and Roccagloriosa. Unpublished report.* Edmonton: Department of Chemical and Materials Engineering, University of Alberta.

Gida, G. and Vidale, M. 2006. Analytical observations on some iron finds. In Liverani 2006, 323–26.

Grébénart, D. 1983. Les métallurgies du cuivre et du fer autour d'Agadez (Niger), des origines au début de la période médiévale. In Echard 1983, 109–25.

Hawthorne, J., Mattingly, D.J. and Daniels, C.M., with contributions by Barnett, T., Dore, J.N. and Leone, A. 2010. Zinkekra: an Early Garamantian escarpment settlement and associated sites (ZIN001–003). In Mattingly 2010, 19–84.

Herbert, E.W. 1984. *Red Gold of Africa: Copper in Precolonial History and Culture.* Madison: University of Wisconsin Press.

Herbert, E.W. 2001. African metallurgy: The historian's dilemma. In Descoeudres *et al.* 2001, 41–48.

Holl, A.F. 2009. Early West African metallurgies: New data and old orthodoxy. *Journal of World Prehistory* 22.4: 415–38.

Junius, H. 2016. Nok early iron production in Central Nigeria: New finds and features. *Journal of African Archaeology* 14.3: 291–311.

Kaufman, B. 2014. *Empire without a Voice: Phoenician Iron Metallurgy and Imperial Strategy at Carthage.* Unpublished PhD thesis. Los Angeles: University of California.

Killick, D. 2004. Review essay: What do we know about African iron working? *Journal of African Archaeology* 2.1: 97–112.

Killick, D. 2009. Cairo to Cape: The spread of metallurgy through eastern and southern Africa. *Journal of World Prehistory* 22.4: 399–414.

Killick, D. 2015. Invention and innovation in African iron-smelting. *Cambridge Archaeology Journal* 25.1: 307–19.

Killick, D., Van der Merwe, N.J., Gordon, R.B. and Grébénart, D. 1988. Reassessment of the evidence for early metallurgy in Niger, West Africa. *Journal of Archaeological Science* 15: 367–94.

Klein, S., Lahaye, Y., Brey, G.P. and von Kaenel, H.-M. 2004. The early Roman imperial aes coinage II: Tracing the copper sources by analysis of lead and copper isotopes – copper coins of Augustus and Tiberius. *Archaeometry* 46.3: 469–80.

Klein, S., Domergue, C., Lahaye, Y., Brey, G.P. and von Kaenel, H.-M. 2009. The lead and copper isotopic composition of copper ores from the Sierra Morena (Spain). *Journal of Iberian Geology* 35.1: 59–68.

Lambert, N. 1983. Nouvelle contribution à l'étude du Chalcolithique de Mauritanie. In Echard 1983, 63–87.

La Niece, S., Hook, D.R. and Craddock, P.T. (eds) 2007. *Metals and Mines: Studies in Archaeometallurgy*. London: Archetype Publications in association with the British Museum, 148–58.

Le Guen, M., Orgeval, J.-J. and Lancelot, J. 1991. Lead isotope behaviour in a polyphased Pb-Zn ore deposit: Les Malines (Cévennes, France). *Mineralium Deposita* 26: 180–88.

Leitch, V., Duckworth, C., Cuénod, A., Mattingly, D.J., Sterry, M. and Cole, F. 2017. Early Saharan trade: The inorganic evidence. In Mattingly *et al.* 2017, 287–340.

Lemorini, C. and Cristiani, E. 2006. Functional analysis of abraded heavy duty tools. In Liverani 2006, 295–308.

Lhote, H. 1952. La connaissance du fer en Afrique occidentale. *Encyclopédie Mensuelle d'Outre-Mer* 1.25: 269–72.

Liverani, M. (ed.) 2006. *Aghram Nadharif: The Barkat Oasis (Sha'abiya of Ghat, Libyan Sahara) in Garamantian Times*. Arid Zone Archaeology Monographs 5. Florence: All'Insegna del Giglio.

Livingstone Smith, A. 2007. Histoire du décor à la roulette en Afrique subsaharienne. *Journal of African Archaeology* 5.2: 189–216.

Ludwig, K.R., Vollmer, R., Turi, B., Simmons, K.R. and Perna, G. 1989. Isotopic constraints on the genesis of base-metal ores in southern and central Sardinia. *European Journal of Mineralogy* 1.5: 657–66.

MacDonald, K.C., Vernet, R., Martinón-Torres, M. and Fuller, D.Q. 2009. Dhar Néma: From early agriculture to metallurgy in southeastern Mauritania. *Azania: Archaeological Research in Africa* 44.1: 3–48.

MacEachern, S. 1996. Iron Age beginnings north of the Mandara Mountains, Cameroon and Nigeria. In G. Pwiti and R. Soper (eds), *Aspects of African Archaeology: Papers from the 10th Congress of the Pan African Association for Prehistory and Related Studies*, Harare: University of Zimbabwe Publications, 489–95.

MacEachern, S. 1998. Scale, style, and cultural variation: Technological traditions in the Northern Mandara mountains. In M.T. Stark (ed.), *The Archaeology of Social Boundaries*, Washington and London: Smithsonian Institution Press, 107–31.

MacEachern, S. 2010. Thoughts on É. Zangato and A.F.C. Holl's 'On the Iron Front'. *Journal of African Archaeology* 8.1: 39–41.

Magnavita, S. 2017. Track and trace: Archaeometric approaches to the study of early Trans-Saharan trade. In Mattingly *et al.* 2017, 393–413.

Magnavita, S., Maga, A., Magnavita, C. and Idé, O.A. 2007. New studies on Marandet (central Niger) and its trade connections: An interim report. *Zeitschrift für Archäologie Außereuropäischer Kulturen* 2: 147–65.

Mattingly, D.J. (ed.) 2007. *The Archaeology of Fazzan. Volume 2, Site Gazetteer, Pottery and Other Survey Finds*. London: Society for Libyan Studies, Department of Antiquities.

Mattingly, D.J. (ed.) 2010. *The Archaeology of Fazzan. Volume 3, Excavations carried out by C.M. Daniels*. London: Society for Libyan Studies, Department of Antiquities.

Mattingly, D.J. (ed.) 2013. *The Archaeology of Fazzan. Volume 4, Survey and Excavations at Old Jarma (Ancient Garama) carried out by C.M. Daniels (1962–69) and the Fazzan Project (1997–2001)*. London: Society for Libyan Studies, Department of Antiquities.

Mattingly, D.J., Lahr, M., Armitage, S., Barton, H., Dore, J., Drake, N., Foley, R., Merlo, S., Salem, M., Stock, J. and White, K. 2007. Desert migrations: People, environment and culture in the Libyan Sahara. *Libyan Studies* 38: 115–56.

Mattingly, D.J., Leitch, V., Duckworth, C.N., Cuenod, A., Sterry, M. and Cole, F. (eds) 2017. *Trade in the Ancient Sahara and Beyond*. Trans-Saharan Archaeology, Volume 1. Series editor D.J. Mattingly. Cambridge: Cambridge University Press.

Mattingly, D.J., Gatto, M., Ray, N. and Sterry, M. 2019. Dying to be Garamantian: Burial and migration in Fazzan. In M. Carmelo Gatto, D.J. Mattingly, N. Ray and M. Sterry (eds), *Burials, Migration and Identity in the Ancient Sahara and Beyond*. Trans-Saharan Archaeology, Volume 2. Series editor D.J. Mattingly. Cambridge: Cambridge University Press and the Society for Libyan Studies, 51–107.

Mauny, R. 1952. Essai sur l'histoire des métaux en Afrique occidentale. *Bulletin de l'IFAN* 14.2: 545–95.

McIntosh, S.K. 1994. Changing perceptions of West Africa's past: Archaeological research since 1988. *Journal of Archaeological Research* 2.2: 165–98.

McIntosh, S.K. 1995. *Excavations at Jenné-Jeno, Hambarketolo, and Kaniana (Inland Niger Delta, Mali), the 1981 Season*. Berkeley: University of California Press.

McIntosh, S.K. 2005. Archaeology and the reconstruction of the African past. In J. E. Philips (ed.), *Writing African History*, Rochester, NY: University of Rochester Press, 51–85.

McIntosh, S.K. 2020. Long-distance exchange and urban trajectories in the first millennium AD: Case studies from the Middle Niger and Middle Senegal River valleys. In M. Sterry and D.J. Mattingly (eds), *Urbanisation and State Formation in the Ancient Sahara and Beyond*, Trans-Saharan Archaeology, Volume 3, series editor D.J. Mattingly, Cambridge: Cambridge University Press, 521–63.

Miller, D. and Killick, D. 2004. Slag identification at southern African archaeological sites. *Journal of African Archaeology* 2.1: 23–47.

Mori, L. (ed.) 2013a. *Life and Death of a Rural Village in Garamantian Times: Archaeological Investigations in the Fewet oasis (Libyan Sahara)*. Arid Zone Archaeology Monographs 6. Firenze: All'Insegna del Giglio.

Mori, L. 2013b. The survey in the Tan Ataram area. In Mori 2013a, 71–78.

Mori, L., Gatto, M.C. and Ottomano, C. 2013. Excavations and soundings at Tan Afella. In Mori 2013a, 30–70.

Niemeyer, H.G. 1990. A la recherche de la Carthage archaïque: Premiers résultats des fouilles de l'Université de Hambourg en 1986 et 1987. In *Carthage et son Territoire dans l'Antiquité, Actes du IVe colloque international sur l'histoire et l'archéologie de l'Afrique du Nord réuni dans le cadre du 113e Congrès national des Sociétés savants, Strasbourg, 5–9 avril 1988*. Paris: CTHS, 45–52.

Nixon, S. 2009. Excavating Essouk-Tadmakka (Mali): New archaeological investigations of Early Islamic Trans-Saharan trade. *Azania: Archaeological Research in Africa* 44.2: 217–55.

Ogden, J. 2000. Metals. In P. Nicholson and I. Shaw (eds), *Ancient Egyptian Materials and Technology*, Cambridge: Cambridge University Press, 146–76.

Okafor, E.E. 2002. La réduction du fer dans les Bas-Fourneaux – Une industrie vieille de 2500 ans au Nigeria. In H. Bocoum (ed.), *Aux origines de la métallurgie du fer en Afrique*, Paris: Editions UNESCO, 35–48.

Paris, F., Person, A., Quéchon, G. and Saliège, J.-F. 1992. Les débuts de la métallurgie au Niger septentrional. *Journal des Africanistes* 62.2: 55–68.

Pelling, R. 2013. The archaeobotanical remains. In Mattingly 2013, 473–94.

Phillipson, D.W. 2005. *African Archaeology*. Cambridge: Cambridge University Press.

Picon, M., Le Nezet-Celestin, M. and Desbat, A. 1995. Un type particulier de grands récipients en terre réfractaire utilisés pour la fabrication du laiton par cémentation. In L. Rivet (ed.), *Actes du Congrès de Rouen*, Marseille: Société Française d'Etude de la Céramique Antique en Gaule.

Pigott, V.C. (ed.) 1999. *The Archaeometallurgy of the Asian Old World*. University Museum Monograph 16/MASCA Research Papers in Science and Archaeology 16. Philadelphia: University of Pennsylvania.

Pollard, A.M., Bray, P., Gosden, C., Wilson, A. and Hamerow, H. 2015. Characterising copper based metals in Britain in the first millennium AD: A preliminary quantification of metal flow and recycling. *Antiquity* 89.345: 697–713.

Pringle, H. 2009. Seeking Africa's first iron men. *Science* 323.5911: 200–2.

Quéchon, G. 2001. Les datations de la métallurgie du fer à Termit (Niger): Leur fiabilité, leur signification. In Descoeudres *et al.* 2001, 247–53.

Rakob, F. 1990. La Carthage archaïque. In *Carthage et son territoire dans l'Antiquité, Actes du IVe colloque international sur l'histoire et l'archéologie de l'Afrique du Nord réuni dans le cadre du 113e Congrès national des Sociétés savants, Strasbourg, 5–9 avril 1988.* Paris: CTHS, 31–43.

Rehder, J. 2000. *Mastery and Uses of Fire in Antiquity.* Montreal: McGill-Queen's University Press.

Rehren, Th. 1999. Small size, large scale Roman brass production in Germania Inferior. *Journal of Archaeological Science* 26.8: 1083–87.

Rehren, Th., Charlton, M., Chirikure, S., Humphris, J., Ige, A. and Veldhuijzen, H. A. 2007. Decisions set in slag: The human factor in African iron smelting. In La Niece *et al.* 2007, 211–18.

Reimer, P.J., Bard, E., Bayliss, A., Beck, J.W., Blackwell, P.G., Bronk Ramsey, C., Grootes, P.M., Guilderson, T.P., Haflidason, H., Hajdas, I., Hattž, C., Heaton, T.J., Hoffmann, D.L., Hogg, A.G., Hughen, K.A., Kaiser, K.F., Kromer, B., Manning, S. W., Niu, M., Reimer, R.W., Richards, D.A., Scott, E.M., Southon, J.R., Staff, R.A., Turney, C.S.M. and Van der Plicht, J. 2013. IntCal13 and Marine13 Radiocarbon Age Calibration Curves 0–50,000 Years cal BP. *Radiocarbon* 55.4: 1869–87.

Rico, C., Domergue, C., Rauzier, M., Klein, S., Lahaye, Y., Brey, G. and von Kaenel, H.-M. 2005. La provenance des lingots de cuivre romains de Maguelone (Hérault, France). Étude archéologique et archéométrique. *Revue Archéologique de Narbonnaise* 38.1: 459–72.

Rohl, B.M. 1996. Lead isotope data from the Isotrace Laboratory, Oxford: Archaeometry data base 2, galena from Britain and Ireland. *Archaeometry* 38.1: 165–80.

Sanmarti, J., Kallala, N., Carme Belarte, M., Ramon, J., Telmini, B.M., Jornet, R. and Miniaoui, S. 2012. Filling gaps in the protohistory of the eastern Maghreb: The Althiburos Archaeological Project (El Kef, Tunisia). *Journal of African Archaeology* 10.1: 21–44.

Santos Zalduegui, J.F., Garcia de Madinabeitia, S., Gil Ibarguchi, J.I. and Palero, F. 2004. A lead isotope database: The Los Pedroches – Alcudia area (Spain): Implications for archaeometallurgical connections across southwestern and southeastern Iberia. *Archaeometry* 46.4: 625–34.

Sauer, E. 2007. Fazzan Project survey small finds reports: The coins. In Mattingly 2007, 463–64.

Scheele, J. 2017. The need for nomads: Camel-herding, raiding, and Saharan trade and settlement. In Mattingly *et al.* 2017, 55–79.

Schmidt, A. 2005. 7.2 Métaux. In R. Bedaux, J. Polet, K. Sanogo and A. Schmidt (eds), *Recherches Archéologiques à Dia dans le Delta intérieur du Niger (Mali): Bilan des Saisons de Fouilles 1998–2003*, Leiden: CNWS Publications, 257–62.

Schrüfer-Kolb, I. 2007. Metallurgical and non-metallurgical industrial activities. In Mattingly 2007, 448–62.

Shaw, T. 1970. *Igbo-Ukwu: An Account of Archaeological Discoveries in Eastern Nigeria*. London: Faber and Faber.

Skaggs, S., Norman, N., Garrison, E., Coleman, D. and Bouhlel, S. 2012. Local mining or lead importation in the Roman province of Africa Proconsularis? Lead isotope analysis of curse tablets from Roman Carthage, Tunisia. *Journal of Archaeological Science* 39: 970–83.

Stos-Gale, Z., Gale, N.H., Houghton, J. and Speakman, R. 1995. Lead isotope data from the Isotrace Laboratory, Oxford: Archaeometry data base 1, ores from the western Mediterranean. *Archaeometry* 37.2: 407–15.

Swainbank, I.G., Shepherd, T.J., Caboi, R. and Massoli-Novelli, R. 1982. Lead isotopic composition of some galena ores from Sardinia. *Periodico di Mineralogia* 51: 275–86.

Tekki, A. 2009. *Recherches sur la métallurgie punique, notamment les objets en alliages à base de cuivre à Carthage*. Unpublished PhD dissertation, Université de Provence.

Vanacker, C. 1983. Cuivre et métallurgie du cuivre à Tegdaoust (Mauritanie Orientale). Découvertes et problèmes. In Echard 1983, 89–107.

Vernet, R. 1993. *Préhistoire de la Mauritanie*. Nouakchott: Sépia.

Weisgerber, G., with contributions by Craddock, P.T. and Meeks N.D., Baumer, U. and Koller, J. 2007. Roman brass and lead ingots from the western Mediterranean. In La Niece *et al.* 2007, 148–58.

Willett, F. and Sayre, E.V. 2006. Lead isotopes in West African copper alloys. *Journal of African Archaeology* 4.1: 55–90.

Wuttmann, M. 2001. La métallurgie du fer dans l'Egypte ancienne: Les données de l'archéologie. In Descoeudres *et al.* 2001, 205–07.

Zangato, É. 2007. *Les Ateliers d'Oboui: Premières communautés métallurgistes dans le Nord-Ouest du Centrafrique*. Paris: Editions Recherches sur les Civilisations.

Zangato, É. and Holl, A.F.C. 2010. On the iron front: New evidence from north-central Africa. *Journal of African Archaeology* 8.1: 7–23.

8 | Is the Archaeometallurgical Record a Valuable Tool when Considering Meroe within a Trans-Saharan Landscape?

JANE HUMPHRIS

Introduction

From around the middle of the eighth century BC, the Kingdom of Kush ruled a vast territory stretching from south of modern-day Khartoum to beyond the Nile Delta in the north, through the imposition of kingship sanctioned by complex religious and political systems.[1] From its capital of Napata at the fourth cataract on the Nile, the most important Kushite religious site, this 'Double Kingdom' period lasted until the middle of the seventh century BC.[2] Kushite withdrawal from Egypt was followed by over 300 years of continuous rule from Napata, until *c.*280 BC when Meroe, on the east bank of the Nile between the fifth and sixth cataracts, became the primary royal seat of the kingdom.[3] Long before this time, Meroe was an important economic centre.[4] As the main royal capital for the next *c.*600 years, Meroe was famed as a cosmopolitan trade hub[5] and a melting pot of external influences as well as a hive of local technological production, testified by the rich material culture and architectural expressions uncovered during excavations at the site.[6]

Since it was first 'discovered' in the late 1700s by the Scottish explorer James Bruce, Meroe has attracted the fascination of the academic world as the capital of one of Africa's great ancient kingdoms. Stories of Africa's 'Black Pharaohs', pyramids, palaces and temples, as well as a recent

---

[1] Bianchi 2004, 147–213; Edwards 2004, 112; Pope 2014; Török 1997a, 131–407; 2015; Welsby 1996, 12–71.

[2] Pope 2014.

[3] On the role of Meroe and Nubian urbanism more generally, see Edwards 2020.

[4] Humphris and Scheibner 2017.

[5] Edwards 1999a; Haaland and Haaland 2007, 378 and references therein.

[6] Bagh 2015, 21–82; Garstang *et al.* 1911; Shinnie and Anderson 2004; Török 1997a, 527–31, 1997b; Wolf *et al.* 2009.

UNESCO World Heritage listing, ensures a continuing interest in the ruins of the ancient city, and in the role of Meroe within the ancient world. Local and external expressions evident in the manufacture and design of Meroitic material culture are used to identify key insights into the past interconnectedness of the wider region, as well as local traditions and innovations. It is this Meroitic materiality that creates the potential for considering Meroe within a Trans-Saharan landscape and beyond.

Building on the excavations of the twentieth century, notably those led by Peter Shinnie,[7] UCL Qatar launched a new archaeological research project at Meroe in 2012 to investigate iron production and other pyro-technologies associated with the Kingdom of Kush. At the time of writing, 11 field seasons of extensive geophysical surveys and archaeological excavations incorporating a systematic sample collection and laboratory analysis programme have revealed much about the role and impact of iron production within the development of Kush.[8] In addition to contributing to the archaeometallurgical understanding of ancient Sudan, the research aims to use the medium of technology, and especially of iron production, to reveal the relationships that existed between Meroe and contemporary ancient societies.

This chapter first considers the theoretical framework by which Meroe can be positioned within its wider geographical context, by exploring the manner in which different types of connections across space and time can be studied. Our current state of knowledge concerning the position of Kush within an apparently extensive trade network will be summarised to high-light the body of data from which connections to other regions could be identified (Fig. 8.1). The technology of iron production is then used to explore potential links from Meroe across the Sahara and beyond by considering the available data. Future research foci to expand our under-standing of Meroe within its immediate and more distant landscapes through material culture and technology are evaluated, as well as what this may reveal about the positioning of Meroe within the wider world.

Identifying Local Networks in the Archaeological Record

Network analysis can be used by archaeologists to contribute to some of the most fundamental questions concerning how people, objects and ideas

---

[7] Shinnie and Anderson 2004; Shinnie and Bradley 1980; Shinnie and Kense 1982; Tylecote 1970; 1982.

[8] Humphris 2014; Humphris and Carey 2016; Humphris and Rehren 2014; Rehren 2001.

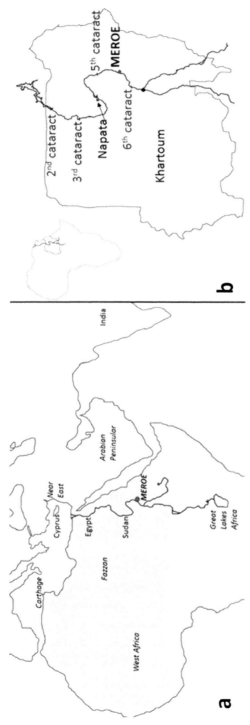

Figure 8.1 (a) Map illustrating the regions mentioned in the text; (b) the location of Kushite sites.

moved and were transmitted across space and time.[9] While this approach
has been used successfully to improve the interpretations of particular case
studies, for example considering the Mesoamerican obsidian trade,[10] many
archaeological studies have not yet attempted to make use of the tools
available within this framework to explore interconnections across cultures, spaces and time.[11]

A network science approach considers that *nodes* (for example people or
groups) are situated within various networks, and the connections, or
edges, between the *nodes*, as well as the positioning of the nodes within
the network of *edges* (relationships), creates or enables the future of the
nodes.[12] This concept provides a structure for archaeologists to reveal past
relationships and their cause and effect. Situating archaeological data
within such a framework when considering connections, or relationships,
between ancient sites or societies within a defined geographical context
allows for a detailed consideration of the nodes and edges (that is, the sites
or people and their relationships with others), and therefore the opportunities created within such an environment: 'The central point of network
science for archaeology is that it *places relationships at the heart of our
analytical techniques*'.[13] In order to make use of such a theoretical tool
through the identification of relationships, the actors, as well as the nodes
and edges, need to be recognised. Archaeologists studying technological
processes do so by grounding their research within the concept of the
chaîne opératoire, which facilitates extrapolation of technological choices
made by the actors themselves. A sound reconstruction of the *chaîne
opératoire* at a particular point in time, preferably across multiple contemporary technological practices, reveals ancient technologies as inter-
linked webs of transformative actions performed by actors embedded
within multifaceted socio-cultural, political, economic and environmental
contexts.[14] Therefore, a well-contextualised technological investigation
theoretically provides a solid reference for implementing a network
analysis approach.

While network analysis using ancient technology is quite clearly an ideal
approach, success requires substantial data, including the chronological and
technological details from all sites under investigation. To apply a networks
analysis approach to consider Meroe in a Trans-Saharan landscape,
contemporary nodes and edges would be defined, and technological practice
at each site reconstructed temporally and spatially. A very brief

---

[9] Brughmans 2013, 624.   [10] Golitko *et al.* 2012; Golitko and Feinman 2015.
[11] Brughmans 2013, 654; Collar *et al.* 2015, 2–3.   [12] Collar *et al.* 2015, 2.
[13] Collar *et al.* 2015, 6.   [14] Gosselain 2000; Ingold 1990; Lemonier 1990; Pfaffenberger 1992.

consideration of the possibility of such an approach in the case under consideration immediately leads to the assumption that network analysis is currently impossible. Major challenges in terms of Meroe's own archaeo-metallurgical reconstruction relate to the long time period under considera-tion (iron was produced at Meroe for over 1,000 years)[15] and the limited amount of data currently available concerning the vast majority of the iron production remains present at the site, despite the 11 field seasons of excavation. However, perhaps more fundamental to Meroe, and to the broader question of the use of iron production as the medium through which to consider ancient connections across regions, is the currently problematic radiocarbon calibration curve during the key period in time (800–400 BC) relating to the apparent appearance of iron in the archae-ological record of the wider region. Any radiocarbon dates falling within this period are impossible to refine and involve significant error margins.[16] Even where radiocarbon sequences are modelled, for example using OxCal's Bayesian analysis functions,[17] the fact remains that the chronologies pro-duced are uncertain. Considering that an evaluation of connections between sites or regions through the medium of technology ultimately relies on a sound understanding of the *appearance* of the technology in question, before then moving towards a comparison of technological practice, it would seem we are far from achieving the aim of this chapter. Rather, the answer to the question posed in the title of this chapter would be: perhaps – following decades of well-funded, extensive archaeometallurgical research at Meroe and all iron production sites in the broader region. Nevertheless, a review of currently available data and the impression this provides regard-ing the place of Meroe in the wider ancient world is valuable, and reveals important insights into the history of iron production and of Meroe itself.

The well-developed terminology used during network analysis provides a comprehensive view for considering connected landscapes. Nodes are commonly sites, but can also be more discrete units such as production areas within one site, for example individual workshops. At Meroe, two furnace workshop spaces were identified on the north settlement mound of the city by Shinnie, and one was identified on the south settlement mound by the UCL Qatar team in 2014.[18] More recently, two additional iron production workshops have been discovered in the easternmost cluster of iron production debris (Fig. 8.2).[19] Hence we know of five discrete furnace

---

[15] Humphris and Scheibner 2017.   [16] Walanus 2009.
[17] Bronk Ramsey 2009; Humphris and Scheibner 2017.
[18] Humphris and Carey 2016; Shinnie 1985; Shinnie and Kense 1982; Tylecote 1970; 1982.
[19] Map of city after Shinnie and Anderson 2004.

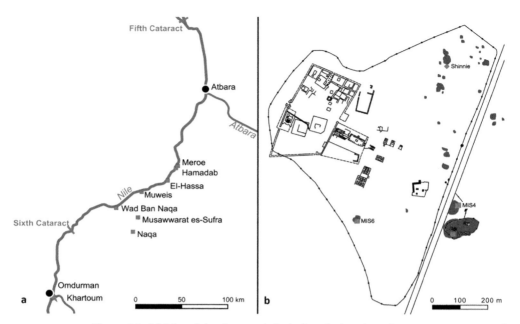

Figure 8.2 (a) Meroe's local network, including the location of some Meroitic sites and those where iron production remains are known; (b) the site of Meroe with the slag heaps (blue) and furnace workshop locations marked (red squares with slag heap designations).

workshops at the site. Across the site, significant areas are dominated by the remains of iron production waste in the form of slag heaps. These heaps, even when furnace workshops are lacking, can be considered as the dumping ground from workshops located nearby (assuming the metallurgical debris was not carried far). Based on the results of radiocarbon dating at only six out of the more than 30 slag heaps visible at the surface, combined with radiocarbon dates produced from earlier excavations and our evolving model of the development of the site over time, the workshops and slag heaps can be placed within a (partially hypothetical) chronological framework that allows approximately contemporary iron-producing locations to be identified and considered. In this way we can begin to reveal the local technological network and the spatio-temporal significance of this.

Currently the available data indicate that the remains of Napatan and early Meroitic iron production are found to the east of the Amun Temple, while Late Meroitic and post-Meroitic remains are found to the north-east and south-east of the temple.[20] This view of a chronological change in iron

---

[20] Carey et al. 2019; Humphris and Scheibner 2017.

production locations at Meroe may change as research progresses. However, the development of the site as a royal capital, and the subsequent incorporation of the eastern area of the site, traditionally dominated by large-scale iron production activity, into the city's evolving urban and religious organisation, is significant. This eastern area of the site is that closest to the royal cemeteries. It forms the easternmost aspect of the monumentality of the capital, which visitors approaching from the east would pass through. In place of furnaces and craftspeople involved in the dirty activities associated with iron production, from around the first century BC visitors to the site, or those returning from the cemeteries, would have passed impressive newly constructed temples, elevated in the landscape by their positioning on top of the old slag heaps. From here they moved to the grand processional way leading to the Amun Temple, behind which was the Royal Enclosure. Meanwhile, the iron production activity had been relocated to the north and south of the processional way. Whether or not early iron production layers will also be found to the north-east and south-east of the Amun Temple, there was a distinctive shift in iron production, away from the eastern area of the site in later times. The cause and effect of this can therefore begin to be considered and placed within our broader understanding of the history of the site, especially because, due to the long periods of time involved in the creation of the larger slag heaps, and despite a poorly refined radiocarbon sequence, overlaps in production can be identified.

Expanding on the notion of nodes, the Meroitic environs can be considered: Meroe was not the only Kushite iron production location. Iron slag in small quantities has been found at the site of Musawwarat es-Sufra, *c.*80 km to the south-south-west, and in larger quantities at the riverine site of El Hassa, *c.*20 km to the south-west of Meroe. Relatively extensive remains of iron production are also known at the Meroitic site of Muweis near the modern-day city of Shendi, *c.*45 km to the south-west of Meroe (Fig. 8.2).[21] However, a lack of radiocarbon dating or published information concerning the technological style of production associated with these remains makes it currently impossible to incorporate them into a broader Meroitic network-landscape. At the site of Hamadab, a few kilometres to the south of Meroe, archaeometallurgical research revealed iron production dating to the late post-Meroitic time.[22] This means that it cannot simply be assumed that iron production at a Meroitic site dates to a classic Meroitic period. The Hamadab remains are fortunately

---

[21] Baud 2008.   [22] Wolf and Nowotnick 2005; Wolf *et al.* 2015.

contemporary to later iron production remains at Meroe, providing the future opportunity for a fascinating comparison between a capital and non-capital site, as the kingdom moved through its period of decline.

Therefore it is clear that the technological network of the site and the immediate region is poorly populated and only partially understood within a chronological framework. The identification of such local nodes and edges (in this case iron production locations), however, will prove fundamental in developing our understanding of the movement and spread of iron technology throughout the Meroitic region. Furthermore, the extensive archaeological research conducted at many Meroitic sites provides an impressive framework within which to apply networks science to consider ancient technology in this region of the ancient world.

Constructing an understanding of the more far-reaching networks within which Meroe existed is even more challenging. Partly due to the extreme environmental conditions and landscapes, and sparsity of modern settlements and water, but mostly due to decades of civil unrest, archaeological data are particularly lacking in the wider geographical region. To the west lies Kordofan and Darfur, to the south, South Sudan and Northern Uganda, all of which have been (and partly continue to be) ravaged by years or even decades of civil war and genocide, making archaeological research impossible. Archaeological evidence for Kushite populations and contacts even more immediately on the west bank of the Nile is lacking (although little archaeological exploration of areas in that direction has so far been carried out).[23] Thus, large gaps exist in our archaeological understandings of broader areas through which goods and people would have had to move to connect Meroe to the broader Saharan world.

Despite these difficulties, a significant amount of archaeological work has been carried out on the subject of iron production in the wider region, including for the first time archaeometallurgical research in northern Ethiopia associated with the contemporary Kingdom of Aksum,[24] and this research can be drawn upon to begin to understand Meroe's positioning in the wider continental context and beyond, as will be described below. As mentioned above, as a first step primarily requires a consideration of the initial appearance of technology, the early periods under consideration will be explored. Despite the apparent 'black hole' that exist in the regions immediately surrounding Meroe (except along the Nile to the north), there is still much data that can be drawn on to begin to consider how we may view Meroe's place in Trans-Saharan Africa and beyond.

---

[23] Welsby 1996, 61; Wolf 2019.   [24] Humphris 2017.

The Kingdom of Kush and Early Connections
with the Wider World

In order to consider the position of Meroe within a wider landscape, longer-term relationships need to be assessed. The movement of goods, people and ideas in ancient Sudan certainly had a great antiquity and can be traced back to at least the Bronze Age, as evidenced at the site of Kerma in northern Sudan near the third cataract. Kerma became the centre of Bronze Age Sudan, and even during this early time significant quantities of Egyptian artefacts and Egyptian cultural traits such as burial practices are found there. There are also similarities in material culture found between populations living in Lower Nubia and around Kerma.[25]

By the early third millennium BC, imported bronze and copper artefacts from the north appeared in the region, eventually perhaps leading to the diminishing occurrence of stone tools.[26] By the Early Kerma period (*c*.2500 BC), people were working bronze at Kerma,[27] indicating that the technology of bronzeworking travelled to the region relatively late (perhaps a few hundred years) after the objects themselves appear in the archaeological record. Egyptian pottery vessels found at various sites suggest that Egyptian food goods were also being imported to the south during these early times. In return, Egyptians were receiving ivory, gold, ebony and animal skins, all transported north along the River Nile as well as via caravan routes to the west of the Nile.[28] Egyptian influences and power struggles continued to dominate the region for the next thousand years, as seen for example in the material culture of the forts built to protect Egyptian gold-mining endeavours.[29] Meanwhile, Egypt's contacts with the wider world are well documented, for example along the Red Sea to the land of Punt to trade for exotic items.[30] Influences from these broader contacts certainly reached Meroe. However, while Egyptian influences can be seen during the early history of the site, for example in the construction of an early Amun temple, the more far-reaching influences are perhaps less evident compared to the time after Meroe became the capital – as could be expected.

Gold was one of the most sought-after Nubian commodities that would have been traded to the north to satisfy the Egyptian love of exotic goods. According to Shinnie, trade networks from farther south than Kerma, down to the Blue and White Nile and beyond, and to the west perhaps via the network of wadis crossing parts of the desert, also existed during these early

---

[25] Edwards 2004, 75–78.   [26] Killick 2009, 403.   [27] Edwards 2004, 86.
[28] Shinnie 1991, 49–50.   [29] Edwards 2004, 90–94.   [30] Killick 2009, 404.

times.[31] Others would dispute the claim of trade goods or of many people ever travelling much to and from the south, citing the major swamps of the Sudd and the gorge of the Ethiopian plateau, as barriers to such (large-scale) movement.[32] Eventually with the introduction of the camel, more land routes could have been exploited to import and export goods. However, as Shinnie wrote over 20 years ago, 'To reconstruct the routes by which these were obtained is extremely hazardous in the face of lack of evidence'.[33] We are still far from obtaining a better understanding of these southern trade routes.

From around 1500 BC, weakening Egyptian power led Kerma to expand north into Upper Egypt, increasing the flow of diverse goods and wealth. This period is particularly marked by the development in style and quantity of local ceramic production, with metal vessels apparently providing influence for the shiny surfaces, colouring and unusual forms of some of the pottery vessel types produced.[34] Kerma's power diminished with the rise of the Egyptian 18th Dynasty which extended its influence as far south at least as the forth cataract. Following a related period of increase in Egyptian culture in Nubia, the Kingdom of Kush then expanded from its capital at Napata as the 25th Dynasty, as outlined above. This enduring relationship along the Nile, facilitated by the opportunity of river transport and availability of good land to support populations through which these relationships could be maintained, is perhaps one of the most significant networks of the ancient world. This connection with the north continued during Meroitic Kush, evidenced not only by the copious amounts of Egyptian or Egyptian influenced materials found at Meroitic sites, but also in the Hellenistic and Roman influences which also appeared.

Meroe Royal City

Archaeological work at the Royal City of Meroe has provided an insight into various aspects of royal and elite life. Complete with elaborate water features,[35] impressive temples, shrines and palatial residential buildings, the upper echelons of society lived opulent lives surrounded by impressive, beautifully decorated architecture, imported material culture and locally made goods.[36] Material examples are to be found in collections housed in the National Museum of Sudan as well as in institutions around the world (Fig. 8.3). Objects of glass, faience, ivory, copper, iron, brass, ceramic and

[31] Shinnie 1991, 51.   [32] Welsby 1996, 58.   [33] Shinnie 1991, 50.   [34] Edwards 2004, 96.
[35] Wolf *et al.* 2009.
[36] Garstang *et al.* 1911; Grzymski 2005; Shinnie 1967; Török 1997a, 527–31.

Figure 8.3 Examples of Meroitic material culture inspired or imported from abroad: (a) the reclining man excavated at the so-called Royal Baths at Meroe, famous for its Hellenistic-inspired decoration; (b) the Egyptian Bes god, depicted on a column excavated at the Amun Temple at Meroe (both photographed at the Glyptotek, Copenhagen); (c) a copper alloy figurine recently excavated from within a Garstang spoil heap at Meroe's Apedemak Temple, possibly originating from the Mediterranean world, or even from the east; (d) and (e) cowrie shells, including evidence of shell working, most likely from the east coast of Africa.

gold create a truly impressive material repertoire.[37] The so-called Royal Baths provide a particularly nice example of external influences interdigitating with local technological and artistic traditions, with the friezes surrounding the main water pool depicting Grecian-style musicians, African elephants, Kushite lions, Egyptian lotus flowers and a complex water management system.[38]

---

[37] Bagh 2015. [38] Wolf *et al.* 2009.

Relatively little is known about the lives of 'normal' people at Meroe, due to traditional research bias and a general lack of archaeological investigation across much of the site. It is suggested here that technology, embedded with social meaning and the choices and influences under which the artisans (actors) themselves worked, provides the perfect opportunity to access this facet of society. A great diversity of technologies was practised at Meroe by (presumably) the non-elites. Meroitic ceramics, both imported and locally produced, have been studied at particular sites,[39] with Török noting, 'Decorated pottery is the finest achievement of Meroitic art'.[40] Interestingly, a very small proportion of ceramics found at Meroe was imported, rather the local artisans produced the vast majority of the ceramics used throughout the history of the site. Earlier excavations found evidence of faience production and the working of cowrie shells (as seen in Fig. 8.3). There has been limited, extensive material science-based investigations of the technological remains at Meroe, and concurrently limited attempts so far to place these technologies within a broader geographical framework. This is despite the common assertion that Meroe was a cosmopolitan hub linking east, west, south and north. Shinnie, referring to Meroe and its connections to the wider world, commented that 'Trade with Egypt was the dominant commercial activity and information is only readily available for that – details of what trade there was with south, west and east is scarcely recoverable although some hypotheses can be suggested but must wait further investigation before certainty is gained.'[41] Can iron production be used as a medium through which such connections can be viewed?

Iron Production at Meroe as a Means for Identifying External Links and Contacts

As mentioned above, multiple, geographically distinct, chronologically grounded technological reconstructions are required to use technology as a means through which to consider connections. Such data are not yet available. However, certain information regarding Meroe's ferrous technology, in addition to that relating to the earliest radiocarbon dates, which will be considered below, are worth highlighting. Recent research at the site has confirmed that the technology of iron production most likely dates back to as early as the Napatan period, and lasted for over 1,000 years.[42] The famous, largest slag heap at Meroe, sectioned by the construction of the Cape to Cairo

---

[39] Adams 1964; Edwards 1998; 1999b; Grzymski 2003.   [40] Török 1997a, 529.
[41] Shinnie 1991, 49.   [42] Humphris and Scheibner 2017.

a   b

Figure 8.4 Meroe's largest slag heap, known as MIS4 (Meroe Iron Slag 4) within this research, sectioned by the railway.

railway by the British in the nineteenth century, has produced the earliest dates so far (Fig. 8.4).[43] Understanding how far back in time people were producing iron at Meroe allows for a consideration of not only early connections across space, through which this technological knowledge may have been transfused, but also provides data that contribute towards the ongoing debates surrounding the issue of the appearance of iron production in Africa.[44]

Information gained from the furnace workshops that have been excavated so far at the site, dating from (probably) the Napatan and early Meroitic times, and the later and post-Meroitic times, can be combined with data generated from the currently limited reconstructions of the technological approaches used by the ancient smelters to highlight certain key characteristics of Meroitic iron production.[45] The furnaces have an internal base diameter of up to *c.*90 cm,[46] were partly slag tapping although a significant amount of slag solidified inside the furnace and were supplied by air that was forced from ceramic pot bellows situated around the back of the furnaces through tuyères.[47] Tuyère production seems more standardised in early periods and less so in later times.[48] The furnaces were constructed with a sand-rich lining which seems to have been consistently produced in the same manner. The furnaces were relined between smelts and the old vitrified lining was dumped with other metallurgical waste. A predominantly goethite, oolithic ore was mined from thin, shallow lenses found on the surface of plateau lands *c.*9 km from the city (Fig. 8.5).[49] Occasional slag finds within this mining landscape indicate that the smelters sometimes tested the ore before transporting it the significant distance back to their furnaces in the city. The ore was prepared

[43] Humphris and Scheibner 2017.   [44] Alpern 2005; Holl 2009; Killick 2009.
[45] Mapunda 1997, 112.   [46] Shinnie and Kense 1982, 23.   [47] Shinnie and Kense 1982.
[48] Ting and Humphris 2017.   [49] Humphris *et al.* 2018b.

Figure 8.5 An area within the Meroitic mining landscape under excavation.

(roasted and crushed to specific sizes) close to the smelting furnaces, evidenced by the bands of ore-processing debris visible in the slag heaps (mainly small grains of reddish brown material) (Fig. 8.6).[50] The smelters continuously and almost exclusively used the highly calorific and structurally stable *Acacia*-type *nilotica* tree for their wood charcoal.[51] The smelters worked in defined workshop areas with either two furnaces or perhaps one furnace and a secondary refining installation at opposite ends of the working space, within which was situated (at least in later times) a useful pit.

The scientific reconstruction of the smelting processes at Meroe is hampered by the sheer quantity of material being systematically collected during extensive excavations. However, the limited details provided above can be considered in relation to what is known from elsewhere to explore the topic of interconnections.

[50] Tylecote 1977, 163–64.   [51] Humphris and Eichhorn 2019.

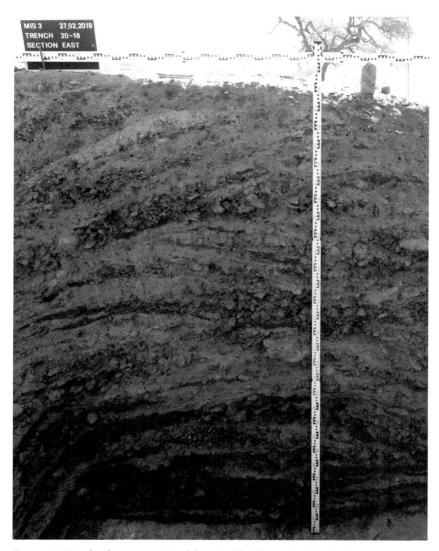

Figure 8.6 Bands of ore-processing debris (reddish brown) within the deposits of a slag heap at Meroe.

Early Iron Production in the Wider Region

Early dates for iron production in various regions of Africa are being produced and synthesised. These can be combined with a study of stylistic traits and practices, and used to consider early connections across the continent and beyond.[52] However, the above-mentioned major problems

---

[52] Alpern 2005; Clist 1987; de Maret and Thiry 1996; Holl 2009; Killick 2004; 2009; Van Grunderbeek 1992; Wotzka 2006; Yahalom-Mack and Eliyahu-Behar 2015.

regarding the radiocarbon calibration curve and resulting chronologies should be continually borne in mind.

Looking South

Although a generally limited amount of archaeological research has been carried out in the Great Lakes region of Africa,[53] in relation to ancient metallurgy more has been conducted in Rwanda, Burundi and north-western Tanzania that has generated a sound picture of the Early Iron Age iron production traditions of this region. Early Iron Age iron furnaces have been radiocarbon dated to the first millennium BC.[54] These furnaces were designed to allow slag to drain into a pit that was often packed with vegetation prior to the smelt (as seen by the plant impressions within the slag fragments). Built of sometimes decorated clay bricks or slabs that were often slotted together, the furnaces were supplied by air through multiple tuyères.[55] The well-defined Early Iron Age Urewe ceramics of this period,[56] along with a spike in social activity indicated through a study of radiocarbon dates,[57] and the quite stylised and intricate furnace designs which seem to parallel the Urewe ceramic design in attention to aesthetic detail, have all been used to suggest a level of social organisation and coordination of technologies across this region, even at this early time. However, it is clear that based on stylistic approaches to iron smelting there is little indication of a link between the Meroitic smelting technologies and those happening at the same or similar times to the south in the Great Lakes region. In fact, as pointed out by Killick, if copper metallurgy was not transmitted from the Nile Valley to the regions of the Great Lakes in spite of the apparent affinity shown to copper in Sub-Saharan Africa, why should we assume it is likely that iron production traditions travelled down this southward route?[58]

Looking North and North-West

The extensive, longstanding and embedded connections between Egypt and Nubia have been well documented and are briefly described above.

---

[53] Killick 2009, 400–1.
[54] Killick 2004, 100–1; 2009; Schmidt and Childs 1996, 205–6; Van Grunderbeek *et al.* 2001, 276.
[55] Hiernaux and Maquet 1960; Nenquin 1971, 183–87; Schmidt and Childs 1985; 1996; Van Grunderbeek 1988; Van Grunderbeek *et al.* 1983; Van Noten 1983.
[56] Ashley 2005; 2010; Clist 1987; Giblin 2013; MacLean 1995; Reid 1995; Van Grunderbeek 1988; 1992.
[57] Wotzka 2006, 285.   [58] Killick 2009, 404; see also Herbert 1984.

Worked meteoric iron beads have been dated to around 3200 BC,[59] but dedicated archaeometallurgical studies of Egyptian materials are rare,[60] and this situation is not helped by the prohibition of the exportation of archaeological samples for analysis outside Egypt.[61] Currently, iron production in Egypt seems not to have predated the sixth century BC.[62] The evolution of iron production in Egypt may have been hindered by a very productive bronze-producing economy, as well as a lack of a sustainable source of good wood for fuel and a general lack of high-quality iron ores. However, at a few sites such as the Greek-settled delta site of Naukratis, dated to the sixth century BC, as well as Defenna, and in the eastern desert from the fourth century BC, iron production was occurring.[63] Based on the data currently available and in light of the calibration issue, this Egyptian iron production does not appear to have been any earlier than the iron production evident at Meroe, but could have a contemporary appearance. Whether or not there was a technological link between the two production regions will remain unknown until archaeometallurgical data are available from Egypt.

In the Central Sahara (Fazzan, southern Libya), a number of small fragments of iron slag have been excavated in layers dating to the first half of the first millennium BC,[64] placing this area also possibly contemporary to the early iron production at Meroe. The few samples available from these Garamantian sites seem to have been produced from a smelting process, which combined with the possible ore samples and smithing cakes could suggest that smelting as well as smithing was being carried out at this early time in Fazzan, at least on a small scale. Unfortunately, the current situation in Libya now prevents further work being conducted into this intriguing and promising avenue of archaeometallurgical investigation. Interestingly, the time period over which metal production debris is found in Fazzan, totalling over a millennium, is also similar to Meroe where we have over 1,000 years of iron production. It will be very interesting to compare the diachronic nature of metallurgy between these two significant, contemporary political powers. However, it should be noted that while the dates may be similar, the technological approach to smelting in Fazzan appears to have been quite different to that of Meroe, based on the few samples analysed so far. The general absence of tapped slag, and the generally very small scale indicative of more local, home-based metal

---

[59] Rehren *et al.* 2013.   [60] Killick 2009, 402.
[61] Rehren and Rosenow, Chapter 12, this volume.
[62] Killick 2004, 99; Shinnie and Kense 1982.   [63] Chirikure 2015, 71.
[64] Cuénod, Chapter 7, this volume.

production, as well as the design of the furnace, point to quite different origins and developments of iron production to that seen at Meroe. As Cuénod mentions, a lack of large quantities of fuel may well have been a defining factor in the development of the scale and style of metalworking in Fazzan, and this difference compared to the rich, fertile Nile Valley may well be a key feature in leading to the different technological approaches between the two regions.

Iron production investigated recently at Carthage also seems different to that seen at Meroe.[65] The style of iron production found at Carthage is noted as being non-slag tapping, and in particular as making use of double tuyères (rectangular tuyères with two parallel air holes). Such distinctive features have not been found at Meroe. At Carthage the industry, including workshops, was situated surrounding the city walls,[66] which is similar to the situation at Meroe but could be circumstantial, as those in power within both states sought to control such valuable economic facets of society as production locations.

Further to the north in the Central and Western Mediterranean and in Greece, iron production debris has been dated to the early to mid-first millennium BC.[67] In Cyprus iron appears earlier, in the late second millennium BC, with the production of bi-metallic knives. Some scholars have postulated Cyprus as an origin for the spread of iron metallurgy, although based on object types this is seen as unlikely, despite the early appearance of iron objects in this location.[68]

Looking East

Evidence for early iron production across the Horn of Africa, including Ethiopia, Djibouti, Eritrea and Somalia, is particularly scarce.[69] Recent research has produced radiocarbon dates for iron production in the first few centuries AD and further archaeometallurgical research in Tigrai may well produce earlier dates.[70] Contacts between Meroe and Aksum, and as far east as present-day Yemen and the western cost of Saudi Arabia, have been suggested as dating back to at least the end of the second millennium BC.[71] Certainly in the Ethiopian highlands during the first millennium BC pre-Aksumite period, links to the Arabian world are evident in features such as the monarchical system adopted and the

[65] Kaufman 2014; Tekki 2009.   [66] Aubert 2001, 219.   [67] Renzi *et al.* 2013.
[68] Yahalom-Mack and Eliyahu-Behar 2015.   [69] Mapunda 1997, 114.   [70] Humphris 2017.
[71] Mapunda 1997, 116–17; Munro-Hay 1993, 609–11.

architecture preferred by those in power, while imported pottery from the Nile Valley and non-ceramic imports from Arabia are also found.[72]

Information concerning iron production in the Arabian Peninsula is almost completely lacking.[73] Iron production was apparently being carried out in Yemen although no dates are provided.[74] In south-eastern Arabia, excavations at Muweilah in Sharjah, United Arab Emirates indicate that iron objects were used in the area during the Iron Age II period, dating from 800 BC onwards.[75] Magee suggests that iron objects dating to this early period found in the south-east of Arabia probably came from western Iran.[76] In general and according to the available evidence, iron was not produced in this region until later times, although trade and contact with the east was certainly occurring.

Meanwhile, in the Near East literary evidence suggests that the Hittites were adept at producing iron.[77] Evidence for iron smelting appears at a few sites dated to the early first millennium BC and earlier, while the use of iron for utilitarian purposes appears to drastically increase at this time.[78] The evidence from the site of Tell Hammeh in Jordan indicates that at the very beginning of the first millennium BC smelters were making use of sacrificial tuyères and tapped their slag from the furnaces which were constructed within a compact rubble platform. A particular feature of tuyères excavated at Tell Hammeh and Beth Shemesh, a smithing site in modern-day Israel dating from the early first millennium BC, approximately 75 km from Tell Hammeh, are their square sections.[79] Tuyères with square sections were also excavated at the large slagheap at Meroe mentioned above. However, round tuyères also exist within the same contexts, which are in any case dated to a period of a few hundred years later that the Near Eastern examples, and so a direct connection perhaps should not be postulated. It should be noted that these Near Eastern sites show no signs of invention, just as is the case at Meroe. Therefore, the earlier iron production locations where smelters experimented to perfect their crafts continue to elude the archaeologists working in this region.

A final point of interest is the use of furnaces that could both tap slag and were designed so that slag would form inside the furnace pit, found in the Near East during the early first millennium BC.[80] At Meroe the furnaces seem to have been designed in the same manner. Could this, alongside the

---

[72] Munro-Hay 1993, 612. [73] Martina Renzi, personal communication.
[74] Weisgerber 2006, 1. [75] Magee 1998, 113. [76] Magee 1998, 115.
[77] Yahalom-Mack and Eliyahu-Behar 2015. [78] Veldhuijzen 2013. [79] Veldhuijzen 2013.
[80] Yahalom-Mack and Eliyahu-Behar 2015.

square tuyères, be an adaptation of technological knowledge brought to Meroe from this region?

Looking West

Looking to West Africa, a once popular theory among diffusionists suggested that while the swamps of South Sudan may have created a barrier against diffusion of iron technology and other cultural traits spreading from Meroe to the south, the eventual transmission of knowledge to Sub-Saharan Africa must have moved from Meroe to the west, and then to the south and east.[81] However, much earlier substantiated dates are available from across the western region as compared to the dates we currently have at Meroe for iron production. Holl provides a succinct summary of the numerous early dates for iron production across West Africa (spanning the first millennium BC and earlier).[82] When considering early iron technologies, for example in Nigeria, it also seems the approach to smelting is slightly different to that seen at Meroe, with smelters either tapping their slag from the furnaces *or* allowing the slag to form in a pit, whereas at Meroe it seems the furnaces were designed to facilitate both the tapping of the slag and the formation of slag inside the furnace.[83]

In addition, contacts between the Darfur region and the Nile Valley can only be identified from the mid-first millennium AD according to the pottery record,[84] which seems to indicate that contacts between the Nile Valley and locations farther to the west occurred much later, long after iron production technologies appear in Chad.[85] Jemkur notes that if iron technology were to have spread from Meroe to West Africa, it (or rather the people carrying the knowledge) would presumably have travelled through the corridor formed by the Mandara Mountains and Lake Chad. The site of Daima in Nigeria close to the border with Cameroon would lie in the path of this route, which may have led from the Nile Valley through southern Darfur. However, iron smelting at this location is much later (up to 800 years later), than the iron-producing Nok culture site of Taruga much farther to the south-west in Nigeria, leading Jemkur to state, 'neither iron objects nor iron technology diffused from Meroe to the Nok'.[86] Clist provides a critical summary of radiocarbon dates for iron production sites in Central Africa and demonstrates clearly the presence of iron production traditions in operation long before those currently dated at Meroe.[87]

---

[81] Mapunda 1997, 119.   [82] Holl 2009.   [83] Humphris and Carey 2016; Okafor 2004, 53.
[84] Pole 1985.   [85] Mapunda 1997, 119.   [86] Jemkur 2004, 36.   [87] Clist 2013.

Further Considerations

Decades ago, the first archaeometallurgist to work at Meroe, Ronnie Tylecote, suggested that in general the stylistic approach to iron production at Meroe could be most closely paralleled to the Norican pre-Roman and Roman style of production.[88] Reasons for this, aside from his particular familiarity and interest in this smelting, are numerous. The perceived similarity of the furnaces and metallurgical debris over time, and the sheer scale of production remains present in large stratified heaps, reminded Tylecote of Roman production.[89] The number of tuyères and the partial slag-tapping technology, as well as the apparently Egyptian nature of the attachment of the bellows to the tuyères mentioned above, also contributed to this supposition: 'It seems that this is yet another example of Roman-inspired diffusion using Egypt as the intermediary.'[90] However, Tylecote also mentions the diversity apparent in Roman iron-smelting furnaces,[91] and there are a number of features which seem quite unique in the combination at Meroe, for example the fact that the furnaces were designed to tap and hold a large quantity of slag; that two furnaces were situated at opposite ends of a sunken workshop (at least in later times); and that they used six tuyères which is more than the majority of examples of furnaces studied in the Roman world. The central pit, evident at least in the later workshops in the middle of the workshop floor, seems uniquely Meroitic. Recent experimental work suggests this was used not only for slag and bloom removal, but also to offer a very advantageous view into the furnace during the smelting operations.[92]

Another consideration is the potential ritual or symbolic expressions associated with iron production at Meroe, notably with the positioning of a temple, ascribed by Garstang as the Apedemak Temple,[93] on top of a mound of iron production debris. If we assume Garstang's interpretation was correct, it is interesting that this temple, dedicated to the god of warfare and fertility, can be found deliberately positioned on a mound of iron production debris. Ritual and symbolic associations of iron production with fertility, kingship and power (either beneficial or negative to society) in Sub-Saharan Africa, both archaeologically and ethnographically, are well attested, although examples displaying no such links are also common.[94] It is well known that Meroe was involved in warfare to protect

[88] Cech 2014; Tylecote 1982, 41.
[89] See Cleere 1976 for comments on Roman-British slagheaps.   [90] Tylecote 1982, 41.
[91] Tylecote 1986, 155–62.   [92] Humphris *et al.* 2018a.   [93] Garstang *et al.* 1911; Haaland 1985.
[94] For example see Childs and Killick 1993; De Maret 1985; Reid and MacLean 1995; Schmidt 1996.

Figure 8.7 Excavations underway at Meroe's so-called Apedemak Temple, constructed on top of a large slag heap. Approximate extent of the architectural features, *c.*55 m.

its borders, and the size of the city and its environs implies that a significant population had to be fed and protected by the state. Thus iron production for tools and weapons could well have been a particularly important technology for the Meroitic elite, and the function of the iron products and the nature of the god Apedemak may have been symbolically linked, which could be the reason for the positioning of this temple on top of a mound of iron production debris.[95] However, no other obvious signs of ritual association within Meroitic iron smelting have yet been found, or at least noticed, by modern archaeologists. Despite ongoing, extensive excavations at the Apedemak Temple and its slag heap platform (Fig. 8.7) and the so-called Ox Temple which is also situated on a slag heap, it remains to be seen whether or not further evidence for ritual, symbolism or religion will be revealed.

As a final consideration, the role of potential influences from even farther to the east should be mentioned. Randi Haaland, writing in 2013, notes a number of potential connections between the Meroitic state and India. For example, when discussing some of the temple decorations, she notes, 'Elements such as the lotus flower, snake, yoga-like posture, finger positions, three-headed representations, four armed gods and the high relief are all design features that display similarities to those found in

---

[95] Haaland and Haaland 2007; Haaland 2013a; 2013b.

comparable Indian contexts.'[96] Shinnie also noted possible connections to India when discussing the same depictions.[97] The earliest iron production in eastern India potentially dates to the late second millennium BC, while solidly dated iron production evidence apparently came from 800 to 700 BC (antedating the period of the calibration issue).[98] While Bocoum discounted links between Meroe and the rest of Africa when considering early iron production ('the dates obtained in West Africa, Central Africa ... and East Africa today form a body of evidence sufficiently consistent for all authors to agree that the Meroitic hypothesis – that is, of borrowing from Meroe – has definitely collapsed'),[99] early Indian Ocean ancient trade networks are known. It may be just as appropriate or even more appropriate to look to the east for connections visible in the technological practices of the craftspeople of Meroe.

Conclusions

Until we understand the earliest, and even the beginnings of iron production at Meroe, placing this site within a concept of 'mobile technologies' will be very difficult, not least because we still have no idea of the stylistic approach to the earliest iron technology at Meroe, or when this occurred. The biggest challenge to understanding the inception of iron production in all of the regions discussed above has to be the production of sound chronologies. As Killick has noted a number of times, early dates of around the early to mid-first millennium BC lie within the problematic time period for using the radiocarbon calibration curve, which does not allow for the generation of a tight chronological framework. The answer to this problem is the use of additional dating methods such as luminescence or archaeomagnetic dating in combination with radiocarbon methods. However, these approaches are also not unproblematic and have not been widely adopted. As a result, and in combination with budgetary and logistical limitations on fieldwork, our understanding of the earliest dated iron production locations are still hindered.[100] Whether it is financial constraints or methodological challenges which are responsible for prohibiting the widespread adoption of luminescence or archaeomagnetic dating at early metallurgical sites in Africa and beyond, such approaches should be particularly encouraged in future.

---

[96] Haaland 2013a, 152–53. [97] Shinnie 1967, 22.
[98] Craddock 1995, 265; Tripathi 2001, 65–85. [99] Bocoum 2004, 10.
[100] Killick 2009, 406–7; see also Clist 2013, 26–27.

The value of archaeological science in creating in-depth understandings of the material culture and, importantly, of the production technologies present in societies throughout time and across the world, is clear.[101] Using these data within archaeological theoretical frameworks to consider the interconnectedness of past societies holds great potential. The challenge is to make use of both the scientific approaches and the theoretical frameworks available, including network science, to generate a comprehensive picture of diachronic, local, regional and transregionally linked societies.

Despite the new dating of iron slagheaps at Meroe clearly demonstrating that iron production was being carried out there at similar time periods to the early iron smelting in the north, south and east, the technological differences currently seem to suggest that Meroe stood alone in the development of its iron technologies, at least in terms of large-scale technology from potentially around the seventh to sixth centuries BC. Our challenge is to reveal what, if anything, preceded the technological approach to iron production at Meroe before the relatively standardised approach to the operating parameters of iron production which left apparently quite similar archaeometallurgical remains over a period of 1,000 years. Future research questions include: was there an evolution of technology at this site (or even an invention of iron metallurgy), or did iron production arrive as a fully formed industry, perfectly suited for major exploitation at Meroe where ores, clays, water, labour and fuel were in abundance? It should be noted that the new archaeometallurgical excavations at Meroe have so far focused on slag *heaps* as opposed to subsurface remains. From the excavations of Garstang in the early twentieth century,[102] and Shinnie in the 1960s and 1970s,[103] we know that many metres of archaeology should still be preserved subsurface at certain locations, and we also know that furnace workshops can overlay each other and that slag exists below ground at Meroe. This means that there is great potential to reveal earlier-dated iron production at the site. The team will continue to develop and implement innovative methods to investigate Meroe's iron production history, and continue with the major excavations and programme of laboratory analysis already underway. In addition, the combination of gradiometry and resistivity surveys are continuing to reveal the locations of potential furnace workshops, of which we need to find and excavate many more to understand the nature of iron production at the site and how this may have changed over time. Experimental archaeology is also contributing to our

[101] Martinón-Torres and Killick 2014.   [102] Garstang *et al.* 1911.
[103] Shinnie and Anderson 2004.

understanding of Meroitic smelting as we try to reconstruct not just when, but how the people at Meroe produced iron.[104] The task is great and funding not unlimited, but it is hoped that over the coming years more data will be generated that will help us appreciate the iron producers of Meroe and the role and impact they had on the rise, power and fall of Kush, and appreciate the position of Meroe within the Trans-Saharan region, and in general its continental contexts.[105]

References

Adams, W.Y. 1964. An introductory classification of Meroitic pottery. *Kush* 12: 126–73.

Alpern, S.B. 2005. Did they or didn't they invent it? Iron in Sub-Saharan Africa. *History in Africa* 32: 41–94.

Ashley, C.Z. 2005. *Ceramic Variability and Change: A Perspective from Great Lakes Africa.* Unpublished PhD thesis, University College London.

Ashley, C.Z. 2010. Towards a socialised archaeology of ceramics in Great Lakes Africa. *African Archaeological Review* 27: 135–63.

Aubert, M.E. 2001. *The Phoenicians and the West: Politics, Colonies, and Trade.* Cambridge: Cambridge University Press.

Bagh, T. 2015. *Finds from the Excavations of J. Garstang in Meroe and F. Ll. Griffith in Kawa in the Ny Carlsberg Glyptotek.* Copenhagen: Ny Carlsbery Glyptotek.

Baud, M. 2008. The Meroitic royal city of Muweis: First steps into an urban settlement in riverine Upper Nubia. *Sudan & Nubia* 12: 52–63.

Bianchi, R.S. 2004. *Daily Life of the Nubians.* Westport, CT and London: Greenwood Press.

Bocoum, H. (ed.) 2004. *The Origins of Iron Metallurgy in Africa: New Light on Its Antiquity: West and Central Africa.* Paris: UNESCO.

Bronk Ramsey, C. 2009. Bayesian analysis of radiocarbon dates. *Radiocarbon,* 51.1: 337–60.

Brughmans, T. 2013. Thinking through networks: A review of formal network methods in archaeology. *Journal of Archaeological Method and Theory* 20: 623–62.

---

[104] Charlton and Humphris 2019; Humphris *et al.* 2018a.

[105] Years of discussions with David Killick regarding the origins of iron technology in Africa, and the limitations of radiocarbon dating, have been invaluable in shaping the work presented here. Additionally, the contribution of UCL Qatar Sudan Project team members Thomas Scheibner and Saskia Buchner, and our associated, constant deliberations, continue to contribute significantly to our growing understanding of the archaeology of Meroe.

Carey, C., Stremke, F. and Humphris, J. 2019. Investigating the ironworking remains in the Royal City of Meroe: New insights on the Nile Corridor and the Kingdom of Kush. *Antiquity* 93 (368): 432–49.

Cech, B. 2014. The production of ferrum Noricum at Hüttenberg, Austria: The results of archaeological excavations carried out from 2003 to 2010 at the site Semlach/Eisner. In B. Cech and Th. Rehren (eds), *Early Iron in Europe*, Montagnac: Éditions Monique Mergoil, 11–20.

Charlton, M.F. and Humphris, J. 2019. Exploring iron making practices at Meroe, Sudan: A comparative analysis of archaeological and experimental data. *Journal of Archaeological and Anthropological Sciences* 11.3: 895–912.

Childs, S.T. and Killick, D. 1993. Indigenous African metallurgy: Nature and culture. *Annual Anthropological Review* 22, 317–37.

Chirikure, S. 2015. Domesticating nature. In S. Chirikure (ed.), *Metals in Past Societies: A Global Perspective on Indigenous African Metallurgy*, Cham: Springer, 61–98.

Cleere, H.F. 1976. Some operating parameters for Roman iron-works. *Bulletin of the Institute of Archaeology of the University of London* 13: 233–46.

Clist, B. 1987. A critical reappraisal of the chronological framework of Early Urewe Iron Age industry. *Muntu* 6: 35–62.

Clist, B. 2013. Our iron smelting 14C dates from Central Africa: From a plain appointment to a full blown relationship. In Humphris and Rehren 2013, 22–28.

Collar, A., Coward, F., Brughmans, T. and Mills, B.J. 2015. Networks in archaeology: Phenomena, abstraction, representation. *Journal of Archaeological Method and Theory* 22.1: 1–33.

Craddock, P.T. 1995. *Early Metal Mining and Production*. Edinburgh: Edinburgh University Press.

De Maret, P. 1985. The smith's myth and the origin of leadership in Central Africa. In Haaland and Shinnie 1985, 73–87.

De Maret, P. and Thiry, G. 1996. How old is the Iron Age in Central Africa? In P. R. Schmidt (ed.), *The Culture and Technology of African Iron Production*, Gainesville: University Press of Florida, 29–39.

Edwards, D.N. 1998. Report on the Musawwarat pottery, 1997. *MittSAG* 8: 62–67.

Edwards, D.N. 1999a. Meroe in the savannah: Meroe as a Sudanic Kingdom. *Meroitica* 15: 312–20.

Edwards, D.N. 1999b. Meroitic ceramic chronology: Exploring the Meroe west cemeteries. *Azania* 34: 25–44.

Edwards, D.N. 2004. *The Nubian Past: An Archaeology of Sudan*. London and New York: Routledge.

Edwards, D.N. 2020. Early states and urban forms in the Middle Nile. In M. Sterry and D.J. Mattingly (eds), *Urbanisation and State Formation in the Ancient Sahara and Beyond*, Trans-Saharan Archaeology, Volume 3, series editor D. J. Mattingly, Cambridge: Cambridge University Press, 359–95.

Garstang, J., Sayce, A.H. and Griffith, F.L.L. 1911. *Meroë, the City of the Ethiopians: Being an Account of the First Season's Excavations on the Site, 1909–1910.* Oxford: The Clarendon Press.

Giblin, J.D. 2013. A reconsideration of Rwandan archaeological ceramics and their political significance in a post-genocide era. *African Archaeological Review* 30.4: 501–29.

Golitko, M. and Feinman, G.M. 2015. Procurement and distribution of Pre-Hispanic Mesoamerican obsidian 900 BC–AD 1520: A social network analysis. *Journal of Archaeological Method and Theory* 22.1: 206–47.

Golitko, M., Meierhoff, J., Feinman, G.M. and Williams, P.R. 2012. Complexities of collapse: The evidence of Maya obsidian as revealed by social network graphical analysis. *Antiquity* 86: 507–23.

Gosselain, O.P. 2000. Materialising identities: An African perspective. *Journal of Archaeological Method and Theory* 7.3:˙187–217.

Grzymski, K.A. 2003. *The Meroe Expedition: The Meroe Reports 1.* Mississauga: Benben Publications.

Grzymski, K.A. 2005. Meroe, the capital of Kush: Old problems and new discoveries. *Sudan & Nubia* 9: 47–58.

Haaland, G. and Haaland, R. 2007. God of war, worldly ruler, and craft specialists in the Meroitic Kingdom of Sudan. *Journal of Social Anthropology* 7.3: 372–92.

Haaland, R. 1985. Iron production, its socio-cultural context and ecological implications. In Haaland and Shinnie 1985, 50–72.

Haaland, R. 2013a. Meroitic iron working in a global Indian Ocean context. In Humphris and Rehren 2013, 146–55.

Haaland, R. 2013b. The Meroitic Empire: Trade and cultural influences in an Indian Ocean context. *African Archaeological Review* 31.4: 649–73.

Haaland, R. and Shinnie, P. (eds) 1985. *African Iron Working: Ancient and Traditional.* Oslo: Norwegian University Press.

Herbert, E.W. 1984. *Red Gold of Africa: Copper in Precolonial History and Culture.* Wisconsin: University of Wisconsin Press.

Hiernaux, J. and Maquet, E. 1960. *Cultures préhistoriques de l'âge des métaux aux Ruanda-Urundi et au Kivu (Congo Belge), deuxième partie.* Brussels: Académie Royale des Sciences d'Outre-Mer.

Holl, A.F.C. 2009. Early West African metallurgies: New data and old orthodoxy. *Journal of World Prehistory* 22: 415–38.

Humphris, J. 2014. Post-Meroitic iron production: Initial results and interpretations. *Sudan & Nubia* 18: 121–29.

Humphris, J. 2017. A letter from Ethiopia. *The Crucible: Historical Metallurgy Society Newsletter.*

Humphris, J. and Carey, C. 2016. New methods for unlocking the secrets of slagheaps: Integrating geoprospection, excavation and quantitative methods at Meroe, Sudan. *Journal of Archaeological Science* 70: 132–44.

Humphris, J. and Eichhorn, B. 2019. Fuel selection during long-term ancient iron production in Sudan. *Azania* 54.1: 33–54.

Humphris, J. and Rehren, Th. (eds) 2013. *The World of Iron*. London: Archetype Publications.

Humphris, J. and Rehren, Th. 2014. Iron production and the Kingdom of Kush: An introduction to UCL Qatar's research in Sudan. In A. Lohwasser and P. Wolf (eds), *Ein Forscherleben zwischen den Welten: Zum 80. Geburtstag von Steffen Wenig*, Berlin: Sonderheft MittSAG, 177–90.

Humphris, J. and Scheibner, T. 2017. A new radiocarbon chronology for ancient iron production in the Meroe region of Sudan. *African Archaeology Review* 34: 377–413.

Humphris, J., Charlton, M.F., Keen, J., Sauder, L. and AlShishani, F. 2018a. Iron smelting in Sudan: Experimental archaeology at the Royal City of Meroe. *Journal of Field Archaeology* 43.5: 399–416.

Humphris, J., Bussert, R., AlShishani, F. and Scheibner, T. 2018b. The ancient iron mines of Meroe. *Azania* 53.3: 291–311.

Ingold, T. 1990. Society, nature and the concept of technology. *Archaeological Review from Cambridge* 9.1: 5–17.

Jemkur, J.F. 2004. The beginnings of iron metallurgy in West Africa. In H. Bocoum (ed.), *The Origins of Iron Metallurgy in Africa: New Light on Its Antiquity, West and Central Africa*, Paris: UNESCO Publishing, 33–42.

Kaufman, B. 2014. *Empire Without a Voice: Phoenician Iron Metallurgy and Imperial Strategy at Carthage*. Unpublished PhD thesis. Los Angeles: University of California.

Killick, D. 2004. What do we know about African iron working? *Journal of African Archaeology* 2.1: 97–112.

Killick, D. 2009. Cairo to Cape: The spread of metallurgy through eastern and southern Africa. *Journal of World Prehistory* 22.4: 399–414.

Lemonier, P. 1990. Topsy turvy techniques: Remarks on the social representation of techniques. *Archaeological Review from Cambridge* 9.1: 27–37.

MacLean, R. 1995. Late Stone Age and Early Iron Age settlement in the Interlacustrine region: A district case study. *Azania* 29–30: 296–302.

Magee, P. 1998. New evidence of the initial appearance of iron in southeastern Arabia. *Arabian Archaeology* 9: 112–17.

Mapunda, B.B.B. 1997. Patching up evidence for ironworking in the Horn. *African Archaeological Review* 14.2: 107–24.

Martinón-Torres, M. and Killick, D. 2014. Archaeological theories and archaeological sciences. In A. Gardner, M. Lake and U. Sommer (eds), *The Oxford Handbook of Archaeological Theories*, Oxford: Oxford Handbooks Online. doi:10.1093/oxfordhb/9780199567942.013.004.

Munro-Hay, S. 1993. State development and urbanism in northern Ethiopia. In T. Shaw, P. Sinclair, B. Andah and A. Okpoko (eds), *The Archaeology of Africa: Food, Metals and Towns*, London: Routledge, 609–21.

Nenquin, J. 1971. The Congo, Rwanda, and Burundi. In P.L. Shinnie (ed.), *The African Iron Age*, Oxford: Oxford University Press, 183–214.

Okafor, E.E. 2004. Twenty-five centuries of bloomery iron smelting in Nigeria. In H. Bocoum (ed.), *The Origins of Iron Metallurgy in Africa, New Light on its Antiquity: West and Central Africa*, Paris: UNESCO Publishing, 43–54.

Pfaffenberger, B. 1992. Social anthropology of technology. *Annual Review of Anthropology* 21: 491–516.

Pole, L.M. 1985. Furnace design and the smelting operation: Survey of written reports of iron smelting in west Africa. In Haaland and Shinnie 1985, 142–63.

Pope, J. 2014. *The Double Kingdom under Taharqo: Studies in the History of Kush and Egypt, c.690–664 BC.* Leiden: Brill.

Rehren, Th. 2001. Meroe, Iron and Africa. *MittSAG* 12: 102–9.

Rehren, Th., Belgya, T., Jambon, A., Káli, G., Kasztovszky, Z., Kis, Z., Kovács, I., Maróti, B., Martinón-Torres, M. 2013. 5,000 years old Egyptian iron beads made from hammered meteoritic iron. *Journal of Archaeological Science* 40: 4785–92.

Reid, D.A.M. 1995. Early settlement and social organisation in the Interlacustrine region. *Azania* 29–30:303–13.

Reid, D.A.M. and MacLean, R. 1995. Symbolism and the social context of iron production in Karagwe. *World Archaeology* 27: 144–61.

Renzi, M., Rovira, S., Carme Rovira-Hortalà, M. and Ruiz, I.M. 2013. Questioning research on early iron in the Mediterranean. In Humphris and Rehren 2013, 178–87.

Schmidt, P.R. 1996. Reconfiguring the Barongo: Reproductive symbolism and reproduction among a work association of iron smelters. In P.R. Schmidt (ed.), *The Culture and Technology of African Iron Production*, Gainesville: University Press of Florida, 74–127.

Schmidt, P.R. and Childs, S.T. 1985. Innovation and industry during the Early Iron Age in East Africa: KM2 and KM3 sites in northwest Tanzania. *African Archaeological Review* 3: 53–94.

Schmidt, P.R. and Childs, S.T. 1996. Actualistic models for interpretation of two Early Iron Age industrial sites in northwestern Tanzania. In P.R. Schmidt (ed.), *The Culture and Technology of African Iron Production*, Gainesville: University of Florida Press, 186–233.

Shinnie, P.L. 1967. *Meroe: A Civilization of the Sudan.* New York: Praeger.

Shinnie, P.L. 1985. Iron working at Meroe. In R. Haaland and P.L. Shinnie (eds), *African Iron Working: Ancient and Traditional*, Oxford: Oxford University Press, 28–35.

Shinnie, P.L. 1991. Trade routes of the ancient Sudan: 3,000 BC–AD 350. In W. V. Davies (ed.), *Egypt and Africa, Nubia from Prehistory to Islam*, London: British Museum Press, 48–53.

Shinnie, P.L. and Anderson, J.R. (eds) 2004. *The Capital of Kush 2: Meroe Excavations 1973–1984.* Wiesbaden: Harrassowitz Verlag.

Shinnie, P.L. and Bradley, R.J. 1980. *The Capital of Kush 1, Meroe excavations 1965–1972. Meroitica* 4. Berlin: Akademie Verlag.

Shinnie, P.L. and Kense, F.J. 1982. Meroitic iron working. *Meroitica* 6: 17–28.

Tekki, A. 2009. Recherches sur la métallurgie punique, notamment les objets en alliages à base de cuivre à Carthage. Unpublished PhD thesis, Université de Provence.

Ting, C. and Humphris, J. 2017. The technology and craft organisation of Kushite technical ceramic production at Meroe and Hamadab, Sudan. *Journal of Archaeological Science: Reports* 16: 34–43.

Török, L. 1997a. *The Kingdom of Kush: Handbook of the Napatan-Meroitic Civilization*. Leiden, New York and Köln: Brill.

Török, L. 1997b. *Meroe City: An Ancient African Capital: John Garstang's Excavations in the Sudan*. London: Egypt Exploration Society.

Török, L. 2015. *The Periods of Kushite History from the Tenth Century* BC *to the* AD *Fourth Century*. Budapest: Ízisz Foundation.

Tripathi, V. 2001. *The Age of Iron in South Asia: Legacy and Tradition*. New Delhi: Aryan Books.

Tylecote, R.F. 1970. Iron working at Meroe, Sudan. *Bulletin of the Historical Metallurgy Group* 2: 23–50.

Tylecote, R.F. 1977. Iron working at Meroe, Sudan. *Wissenschaftliche Arbeiten Bgld* 59: 157–71.

Tylecote, R.F. 1982. Metal working at Meroe, Sudan. *Meroitica* 6: 29–42.

Tylecote, R.F. 1986. *The Prehistory of Metallurgy in the British Isles*. London: The Institute of Metals.

Van Grunderbeek, M.-C. 1988. Essai d'étude typologique de céramique urewe dans la région des collines au Burundi et Rwanda. *Azania* 23: 11–55.

Van Grunderbeek, M.-C. 1992. Essai de délimitation chronologique de l'Age du Fer Ancien au Burundi, au Rwanda et dans la région des Grand Lacs. *Azania* 27: 53–80.

Van Grunderbeek, M.-C., Roche, E. and Doutrelepont, H. 1983. *Le Premier Age du Fer au Rwanda et au Burundi, Archéologie et Environment*. Brussels: Institut National de Recherche Scientifique.

Van Grunderbeek, M.-C., Roche, E. and Doutrelepont, H. 2001. Un type de fourneau de fonte de fer associé à la culture Urewe (Age de Fer Ancien) au Rwanda et au Burundi. *Mediterranean Archaeology* 14: 271–97.

Van Noten, F. 1983. *Histoire Archéologique du Rwanda*. Brussels: Musee Royal de l'Afrique Centrale – Tervuren.

Veldhuijzen, H.A. 2013. Early iron in the Near East. In Humphris and Rehren 2013, 203–13.

Walanus, A. 2009. Systematic bias of radiocarbon method. *Radiocarbon*, 51.2: 433–36.

Weisgerber, G. 2006. The mineral wealth of ancient Arabia and its use I: Copper mining and smelting at Feinan and Timna – comparison and evaluation of techniques, production, and strategies. *Arabian Archaeology* 17: 1–30.

Welsby, D.A. 1996. *The Kingdom of Kush: The Napatan and Meroitic Empires.* Princeton: Markus Wiener Publishers.

Wolf, P. 2019. Settlement in the Meroitic Kingdom. In D. Raue (ed.), *Handbook of Ancient Nubia*, Berlin: De Gruyter, 715–83.

Wolf, P. and Nowotnick, U. 2005. Hamadab: A Meroitic urban settlement. Excavations 2001–2003. *Archéologie du Nil Moyen* 10: 1–8.

Wolf, S., Hof, C. and Onasch, H.-U. 2009. Investigations in the so-called Royal Baths at Meroë in 2000, 2004 and 2005: A preliminary report. *Kush* 19: 106–16.

Wolf, P., Nowotnick, U. and Hof, C. 2015. Hamadab: Insights into development and lifestyle of a Meroitic urban settlement. In M.H. Zach (ed.), *Proceedings of the 11th International Conference for Meroitic Studies, Vienna, 1–4 September 2008*, Vienna: Verein der Förderer der Sudanforschung, 123–39.

Wotzka, H.-P. 2006. Records of activity: Radiocarbon and the structure of Iron Age settlement in Central Africa. In H.-P. Wotza (ed.), *Grundlegungen: Beiträge zur europäischen und afrikanischen Archäologie für Manfred K. H. Eggert*. Tübingen: Francke, 271–89.

Yahalom-Mack, N. and Eliyahu-Behar, A. 2015. The transition from bronze to iron in Canaan: Chronology, technology, and context. *Radiocarbon* 57.2: 285–305.

9 | What Is the Meaning of the Extreme Variability of Ancient Ironworking in West Africa?

A Comparison between Four Case Studies

CAROLINE ROBION-BRUNNER

Introduction

One of the distinctive features of West African ironworking is its extreme variability. West African metallurgists developed many different ways to produce the same material: iron. Compared to the Europeans, they multiplied the technical and cultural choices to an unparalleled degree.[1] In West Africa, the bloomery process is the only one to have been used, but dozens of variants of it were developed.

This diversity has long enabled researchers to draw comparisons between the techniques used,[2] to reconstruct changes in techniques over time[3] and to examine associated settlement patterns.[4] Several analytical systems have tried to characterise the variants and to understand their presence: why, in West Africa, do we find evidence of so many methods to make iron?

Four recent research projects offer the possibility of re-examining the diversity of iron smelting at a regional scale (Fig. 9.1). For my PhD (incorporating ten field seasons between 2002 and 2010),[5] more than 100 bloomery and mining sites were inventoried, mapped and studied for the first time in Dogon Country, Mali.[6] This study highlights an outstanding archaeological heritage of iron metallurgy and led to the selection of relevant criteria for the differentiation of seven ironworking traditions. This analytical method was then tested in 2013 and 2014 in Dendi Country (Benin) to understand the development and importance of iron production there.[7] Here again, there

---

[1] Pleiner 2000.   [2] Cline 1937.   [3] Killick 1991; 2015.   [4] David and Robertson 1996.

[5] This PhD was carried out in the framework of the project entitled Human Populations and Paleoclimatic Evolution in West Africa directed by Eric Huysecom (Huysecom 2002).

[6] Robion-Brunner 2010; Robion-Brunner et al. 2013.

[7] These two missions were carried out in the framework of the Crossroads of Empires project led by Anne Haour (Haour et al. 2011). Robion-Brunner 2018; Robion-Brunner et al. 2015.

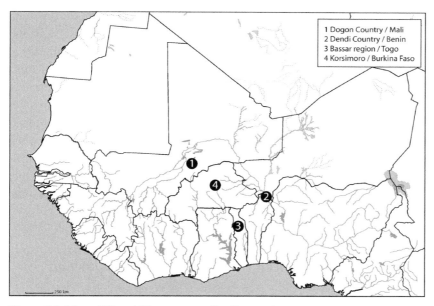

Figure 9.1 Map of West African case studies discussed.

are several different iron traditions in a specific area. Known as one of the most important African ironworking centres,[8] it is clear why de Barros suggested the Bassar Region (Togo) to me as a case study to address the issues of the societal and environmental impact of ancient iron production.[9] In 2013, the 'SIDERENT' project was awarded funding by the French research agency (ANR). The innovative character of this project consists in mobilising researchers from five different disciplines (ethnology, archaeology, archaeometry, metallography and environmental sciences) and in addressing the social, ritual and symbolic dimensions of ironworking, the nature of the exploited resources and the technologies utilised, as well as the economic and political contexts within which iron production developed. Since 2011, Serneels has led research in Burkina Faso and Côte d'Ivoire.[10] In Burkina Faso, he found an immense iron production site, Korsimoro, where five chronologically consecutive technical traditions were identified. My use of the same methodological approach allows me to incorporate his data as a fourth comparative case study.

---

[8] De Barros 1985; 1986; 1988.

[9] Since 2014, the team of the SIDERENT, Iron Smelting and Environment in Togo project led by Caroline Robion-Brunner has conducted three field seasons (Robion-Brunner *et al.* 2014).

[10] This research has been the subject of the project entitled the Origine et développement de la métallurgie du fer au Burkina Faso et en Côte d'Ivoire led by Vincent Serneels (Serneels *et al.* 2012; 2013; 2014; 2015).

In this contribution, I use these case studies to assess each of the possible factors that caused diversity in West African iron smelting. I begin by looking into the material constraints and the ways in which metallurgists adapted to these. Next, I examine the link between the diversity of iron traditions and the identity of the metallurgists. Similarities between traditions may reflect the transmission of knowledge and the mechanisms by which technologies are learned. The scale of production also has an impact on the bloomery process. I explore how certain iron traditions may support intensive production. I conclude with thoughts on possible distinctions between culture, economic context and population dynamics to explain the extreme variability in West African ironworking, and I reflect on possible future research to better understand this question.

Diversity in West African Iron Smelting: A Phenomenon Still under Debate

Since the pioneering work of W. Cline,[11] many researchers have attempted to explain the considerable diversity in West African iron smelting. To this end, different typological systems have been developed. The first is based on furnace morphology and considers the shape and size of the super-structure, the number of openings, the construction materials, etc.[12] The second is based on technological criteria in order to identify iron-smelting practices: presence or absence of a superstructure, natural or forced draught, tapped slag or slag-pit furnace.[13] The third classifies metallurgical workshops based on social, political and economic organisa-tion, taking into consideration the social identity of the metallurgists.[14] These typological systems have demonstrated the diversity of technologi-cal, cultural and economic choices, but they do not explain it or clarify the underlying meaning of this phenomenon.

In 1991, Childs considered 'why a great diversity of iron smelting furnaces exists in Sub-Saharan Africa'.[15] She discussed the factors involved in stylistic variation and concluded: 'the great diversity of iron smelting furnaces in Bantu-speaking Africa is related to the many localised, cultural influences on the smelting process'.[16] Through this technological activity,

---

[11] Cline 1937.   [12] Celis 1991; Martinelli 1993; McNaughton 1993; Sutton 1985.
[13] Chirikure *et al.* 2009; Kense 1985; Killick 1991; Miller and Van der Merwe 1994; Pole 1985; Tylecote 1987.
[14] Childs and Killick 1993; Langlois 2006; de Maret 1980; 1985; Martinelli 2004.
[15] Childs 1991, 332.   [16] Childs 1991, 353.

African societies 'express their views of the structure of nature and society'.[17] Beyond the material requirements, ironworking is also charged with meaning. The bloomery process is difficult to execute because specific chemical and physical conditions must be met if metallic iron is to be made. It is no little matter for humans to develop the requisite skills to modify the properties of a natural resource (ore) in order to change it into a useful material (metal), reducing iron oxide to metallic iron. Studying the methods of iron smelting can reveal belief systems, rituals which mark the technical acts, technical alternatives and cultural preferences developed by the metallurgists.[18]

These questions about technological choice are often overshadowed by the debate on the origins of ironworking in Africa. After over 60 years it is still current and finds a prominent place in the Africanist archaeological community.[19] Even if the majority of scientists agree upon the independence of the invention of African iron metallurgy, they continue to debate the early dates. Behind these discussions we have the political history of the relationship between Europe and Africa, and the difficulty of simply examining the raw data. With this debate on the oldest dates we lose sight of the technical aspects of the first smelting processes and the evidence of their spread across Africa. Like Gallay,[20] Killick encourages Africanist archaeologists to move beyond the issue of 'diffusion or invention'.[21] For him, the confusion between invention and innovation leads to an erroneous idea of the historical evolution of African ironworking and crystallises the debate on the capacity or lack thereof of Africans for technological invention. The huge variation in West African iron-smelting practices is not called into question: 'African ironworkers invented many novel iron-smelting processes. Some of these have not yet been noted anywhere else in the world.'[22] But for inventions to become innovations, several conditions are required: dense populations; large towns and cities; and literacy. Both historical and archaeological studies show a low population density in Sub-Saharan Africa before the seventeenth century and a pattern of settlements with large empty spaces between them. These factors seem to have favoured not the development of innovations, but rather the presence of many variants of the bloomery process in Africa.

---

[17] Childs and Killick 1993, 333.
[18] Childs 1991; Gordon and Killick 1993; Herbert 1993; Schmidt 1996b.
[19] See notably *Journal of African Archaeology* 8.1 (2010); Alpern 2005; Bocoum 2004; Clist 2012; Holl 2009; Killick 2004; Mauny 1952; Trigger 1969.
[20] Gallay 2001.   [21] Killick 2015.   [22] Killick 2015, 314.

Drawing connections between technological and social phenomena is hardly novel. The study of technological systems is as much the affair of the archaeologist as the ethnologist.[23] Given the fact that there are different ways to smelt iron ore, to try to explain these variants is to explore not only their material but also their socio-cultural context. This highlights relevant links between a technical phenomenon and a social reality. In contrast to studies that emphasise the distribution of technical parameters on the scale of the African continent,[24] a new systematic regional survey of West African iron districts allows us to revise our thinking[25] by contributing to the appreciation of diversity in a single area, change or continuity over time, and the causes of longevity or change in iron production traditions.

Adaptation to Local Conditions: The Choice of Raw Materials for Smelting

Africa is a vast continent with variable local conditions. The diversity of raw material leads to local adaptations of the bloomery process. The smelting of ore to produce metal demands specialised skills in order to maintain a balance between the different variables for the smelt to be successful. In nature, iron may be found in five different compounds: as oxide, hydroxide, carbide, sulphide and silicate. The oxides (hematite and goethite) present in lateritic formations are the most common in Africa, but there are many different types of iron ore. Variability in available ore can influence the smelting technology used, and thus the diversity seen in the slag produced. For example, the melting point depends on the nature of the ore. Killick argues that 'African ironworkers adapted bloomery furnaces to an extraordinary range of iron ores, some of which cannot be used by modern blast furnaces'.[26] He took the example of magnetite-ilmenite ores used both in northern South Africa[27] and in the Pare Mountains of northern Tanzania,[28] noting that, 'High-titanium iron ores can be smelted in bloomery furnaces because these operate at lower temperatures and have less-reducing furnace atmospheres than blast furnaces.'[29]

---

[23] Balfet 1975; Chamoux 1978; Lemonnier 2010; Leroi-Gourhan 1971; Mauss 1947.
[24] Chirikure *et al.* 2009; Kense 1985; Killick 1991.
[25] Fabre 2009; Guillon 2013; Robion-Brunner 2010; 2018; Robion-Brunner *et al.* 2015; Serneels *et al.* 2012; 2013; 2014; 2015.
[26] Killick 2015, 314.   [27] Killick and Miller 2014.   [28] Louise Iles, pers. comm., 2013.
[29] Killick 2015, 314.

In some places several different types of iron ore are available in a single area and archaeometric analyses have shown that metallurgists either consciously or unconsciously chose a particular type to produce their iron. In the southern and northern Republic of Benin, slag and ore were collected from six archaeological contexts (Fig. 9.2).[30] Our first analysis of the global chemical compositions of the sampled slag reflects differences in the choice of raw materials from place to place (Table 9.1).[31] Indeed, at Kompa Moussekoubou and Gorouberi a lateritic ore was employed, whereas at Tin Tin Kanza, Mommassaga and Gbanago an oolitic ore was used. Evidence for the mining of the oolitic ore exists,[32] notably at Pekinga, but the mining of a lateritic ore still remains to be proved. The geological map shows the presence of soils that could contain some nodules of iron and manganese oxides or of a lateritic crust (from yellow to brown on the map, Fig. 9.3) that could have been exploited and could explain the specific compositions measured in the slag of Kompa and Gorouberi. The oolitic ore is well known to be present in the Terminal Continental layer in Dendi Country (purple on the map, Fig. 9.3).[33]

On the basis of the geological data, some preliminary hypotheses concerning the ore can be proposed but will need to be supported by the collection and analysis of more samples both in the mining areas and at the smelting sites. Further archaeological investigations and archaeometric analyses are necessary to understand how culture, economics and technical pressure played their parts in raw material choice, in the smelting process and in the treatment of the metal produced in Dendi Country. It is interesting to see that the ironworkers of Kompa Moussekoubou did not choose to exploit the iron ore that was geographically the closest. Behind the constraint of raw materials, there could also have been the issue of political control over resources. The landholder may have forced metallurgists to use their ore or to obtain ore, perhaps of a lesser quality, elsewhere. It is important to take into account the relationship between the different agents involved in iron production. The identity of the metallurgists is plural: different statuses (landholders,

---

[30] Robion-Brunner *et al.* 2015.

[31] Marie-Pierre Coustures (Toulouse University) was responsible for archaeometric analyses on the metallurgical samples. Chemical compositions of the minerals were determined by electron microprobe analysis and global compositions measured by ICP-AES (induced coupled plasma atomic emission spectrometry) and ICP-MS (induced coupled plasma mass dispersive spectrometry).

[32] The oolitic ore present in the north of Dendi Country was sampled at Pekinga (Fig. 9.1) and analysed. The thin section analysis shows it is mainly composed of goethite (2% of P_2O_5 in the ancient oolites) with interstitial quartz, sillimanite and rutile cemented by goethite. The high P_2O_5 content also appears in the global composition (Table 9.1).

[33] Viennot 1978.

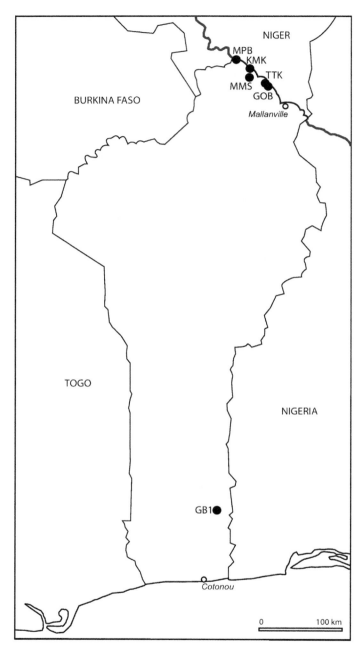

Figure 9.2 Map of Benin, showing the location of samples of ore and slag analysed in the laboratory (MPB = Pekinga; KMK = Kompa Moussekoubou; GOB = Gorouberi; MMS = Momassaga; TTK = Tin Tin Kanza; GB1 = Gbanago).

Table 9.1 Global major element compositions of selected ore and slag samples from Dendi Country measured by ICP-AES at ALS Minerals, Seville, Spain

Sample	Label	Oxide (weight %)														
		SiO_2	Al_2O_3	Fe_2O_3	CaO	MgO	Na_2O	K_2O	Cr_2O_3	TiO_2	MnO	P_2O_5	SrO	BaO	LOI	Total
Oolitic ore from Pekinga	MPB-13-1	4.83	3.87	77.9	0.15	0.08	0.02	0.03	0.02	0.06	0.18	1.96	<0.01	0.01	12.4	101.51
Oxidised slag from Kompa Moussekoubou	KMK-13-1	11.9	5.97	84.7	0.21	0.33	0.03	0.07	0.01	0.51	1.8	0.44	<0.01	0.06	−5.97	99.96
'Footed bowl with no base' slag from Kompa Moussekoubou	KMK-13-1B	29.3	8.38	59.5	1.6	0.87	0.04	0.42	0.01	0.72	1.85	0.46	0.02	0.07	−4.86	98.38
Tapped slag from Gorouberi	GOB-13-SII-1	28.2	8.3	56.5	3.84	0.89	0.05	0.68	0.15	0.45	4.34	0.5	0.04	0.4	−5.26	99.08
Smelting slag from Gorouberi	GOB-13-SII-2	33.7	8.12	52	3.56	0.86	0.09	0.98	0.05	0.45	2.61	0.49	0.04	0.18	−4.32	98.81
Tapped slag from Mommassaga	MMS-13-1	28	5.73	71.2	0.19	0.08	0.03	0.07	0.01	0.19	0.07	1.34	0.01	0.01	−5.91	101.02
Smelting slag from Gbanago	GB1-13-2	25.2	10.25	60.1	4.11	0.5	0.05	0.7	0.02	0.63	0.49	1.7	0.06	0.04	−4.77	99.08
Tapped slag from Tin Tin Kanza	TTK-13-2-1	25.4	6.06	71.9	0.36	0.14	0.04	0.18	0.02	0.35	0.92	1.36	<0.01	0.07	−6.39	100.41

Note: LOI = limit of identification.

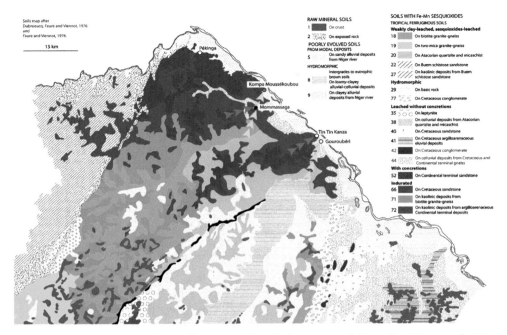

Figure 9.3 The smelting sites of Dendi Country overlain on the soils map after Faure *et al.* 1976 for the Kandi sheet and after Faure and Viennot 1976 for the Karimama sheet. Potential oolitic ore deposits are shown in shades of purple and potential lateritic ore deposits in shades of ochre. The possible supply routes are represented by arrows.

possessors of magic and technological knowledge, labour force) operate at each of the principal stages of the bloomery process (extraction, smelting, smithing), and differ depending on the level of production. In Dogon Country in Mali, the available ethnological data yield valuable information concerning the later periods of traditional iron production (from the eighteenth century to the beginning of the twentieth century AD) and allows a determination of the identity of ironworkers. In this area,

the holder of the land from which the iron ore was extracted belongs to the social category of the cultivators. Indeed, the mines are always situated within the respective village's territories, which are under the responsibility of the land masters (descendants of the village founders). The technically more complex blacksmithing activities are a domain exclusively executed and controlled by the blacksmiths and gives them their status of endogamous craftspersons separate from the cultivators.[34]

The local heterogeneity in technological practice and the archaeological evidence could be the result of the control of resources.

---

[34] Robion-Brunner *et al.* 2013, 263.

Wood, or wood transformed into charcoal, was the most important fuel for African iron smelting. The wood species that can be used are numerous, although naturally the metallurgists prefer those with a high calorific value. In Africa the vegetation is variable, being affected by climate and human activities. We can therefore observe different choices in fuel use reflecting local conditions. For example, in Dogon Country ironworkers used several wood species to smelt iron. 'This corresponds well with Kiethega (2009, 249ff.) who similarly lists a large number of species traditionally used for iron production in Burkina Faso [. . .] The spectra are nevertheless dominated in number by some taxa, namely *Prosopis Africana* and *Terminalia species*, *Vittellaria paradoxa* and *Pterocarpus lucens* followed by members of the *Combretaceae* family.'[35] This non-selectivity of wood species contrasts with the situation observed at the Meroitic sites in Sudan.[36] There, the results of charcoal analysis show a high selectivity in fuel: only one species – the *Acacia nilotica* – was exploited. This is not the only taxon in the area; the composition of the anthracological samples is completely different on domestic sites and more diversified.[37] These choices, linking both strategies of exploitation and adaptation to local conditions, may also be reflected in the bloomery process. Natural draught furnaces require a lot of fuel; their geographical distribution 'corresponds exactly to the areas of infertile, dry, deciduous savannah woodlands in Africa, in which trees were plentiful'.[38] Therefore, it makes sense that Dogon ironworkers used a varied spectrum of wood to produce their iron. They needed a huge quantity of charcoal to operate their natural draught furnaces and could not be too selective if they did not want to damage the environment. For the Meroe sites, excavations have yielded six pots that had been used as bowls for bellows surrounding the furnace dated to around AD 200.[39] This is the earliest and best known archaeological bellows from Africa. The forced draught needs less charcoal than the natural draught process: the Meroe ironworkers may have had a selective strategy for a long time.

'Show Me Your Slag, I'll Tell You Who You Are!'

Similarly to many stylistic analyses of ceramics, differences in iron technologies can reflect social identity.[40] The style or the manner in which

---

[35] Eichhorn 2012, 144–45.
[36] On Meroitic ironworking, see Humphris, Chapter 8, this volume.
[37] Barbara Eichhorn, personal communication, 2014.   [38] Killick 2015, 313–14.
[39] Shinnie 1985. Also see Humphris, Chapter 8, this volume.   [40] Celis 1991; Sutton 1985.

something is done can be conceived as the assertion of an identity, and identity cannot be conceived without opposition and a sense of otherness.[41] It signals the customs of a specific group of people. Moreover, craftsmen recognise themselves by the way in which they make things. Analyses of the material data allows us to distinguish between the different traditions and identities of the metallurgists, and to propose scenarios which can help to explain settlement history.

The diversity of West African ironworking is of much interest in terms of ways of 'making' and 'thinking' about the actions applied to the material. In addition to ways of 'thinking', there are also technical, social and cultural factors. It is thus logical to consider which driving forces cross-cut this variability. For Childs, 'iron smelting furnaces exhibit style [. . .] I define technological style as the formal integration of the behaviours performed during the manufacture and use of material culture which, in its entirety, expresses social information'.[42] The term 'style' allows inclusion of all the factors involved in the observed diversity and contributes to a better understanding of it. Furnaces, slag and the spatial organisation of iron workshops materialise the beliefs, skills, economic context, identity and history of the metallurgists. It should be noted that ironworkers are aware that there are many different techniques to produce iron, and that it is possible to distinguish them. Like potters and their pots, ironworkers recognise their slag.

In Dogon Country (Mali), seven smelting traditions have been identified (Figs 9.1 and 9.4).[43] A series of 14 AMS dates and oral tradition show that this activity started at least in the beginning of the second millennium AD and gradually ceased in the early twentieth century, having been taken over by imported European iron. Six of the seven traditions produced iron at the same time between the sixteenth and the eighteenth centuries. While all metallurgical traditions of this region use a low-temperature, natural draught bloomery iron-smelting process, the individual technologies show more or less substantial differences in furnace morphologies, the slag separation process and the type and nature of the waste products. A slag-tapping process characterises the Fiko, Ouin, Ama, Wol and Tinntam traditions; a substantial part of the slag from these sites was tapped and shows more or less specific morphologies. The Aridinyi smelters used slag-pit furnaces, and the slag formed large furnace slag blocks in the pit. The Ennde furnaces did not have tap holes, and the slag flowed into the lower part of the furnace where it cooled down with characteristic,

[41] Gallay 2000.   [42] Childs 1991, 332.   [43] Robion-Brunner 2010; Robion-Brunner *et al.* 2013.

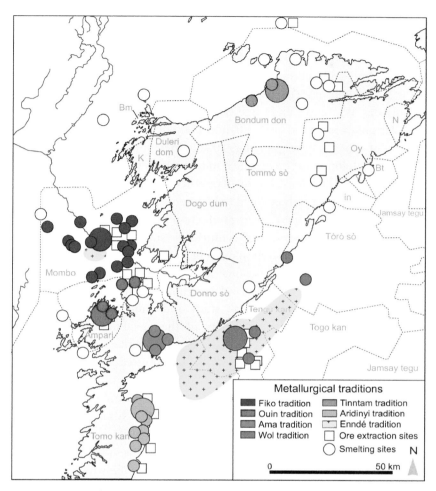

Figure 9.4 Map of Dogon Country, showing the extraction and bloomery sites and the seven metallurgical traditions.

intricate vertical flow structures. From a morphological point of view, the furnaces of the different traditions demonstrate a high degree of architectural diversity. In a geographically limited area, the Dogon metallurgists showed creativity in the construction of bloomery structures. All of the bloomery furnaces have a pit, mostly of circular section, and a door to remove slag and raw iron. However, the number of openings, the presence or absence of steps or peephole, and the nature of the construction materials differ. In the end, each tradition has its own characteristic bloomery structures. Of course, this does not exclude a degree of variability within a single tradition, in particular for those that persisted over long periods. From an economic point of view, the spatial organisation and volume of slag heaps indicate high diversity in the intensity and level of production. Enormous craters of waste, with 15 sites each containing a slag volume of more than 10,000 m³, characterises the Fiko tradition. Sites in the Tinntam and Aridinyi traditions generally have slag volumes of between 1,000 and 10,000 m³. The spatial organisation and waste volume for the Ouin, Ama, Wol and Ennde traditions reflect smaller-scale metallurgies, with slag volumes on the order of 10 to 1,000 m³. A global estimate of the tonnage of slag is in the region of 400,000 tonnes – or 40,000 tonnes of iron objects over 1,400 years[44] – of which more than 75 per cent belongs to the Fiko traditions. The intensification of production at Fiko, destined for a vast external market, was carbon dated to between AD 1000 and 1600.

This diversity of primary iron production in a geographically limited area, and extending over several centuries, is surprising. It suggests that technological differentiation should not be considered from a purely functional perspective because functional factors do not satisfactorily explain the causes underlying the observed variability. Cultural and economic factors are essential if we want to study and understand metallurgical production as a whole. The diversity of the metallurgical remains is certainly also related to the complex historical context of this region, where the identity of the metallurgists is expressed through material culture. Ethnohistorical data reveal that the smith caste on the Bandiagara Plateau developed out of the local population substrate, but also shows that other people were incorporated into this caste from later-arriving populations, mostly from the Inland Niger Delta, but also from the north-west and north-east of the Gondo Plain. These individuals did not originally all belong to the social category of smiths. Following a voluntary or restrained social transformation, local cultivators, of Dogon or external origin, and slaves became iron specialists in order to meet economic needs. The information collected shows a level of production that goes well beyond local needs, or even those of the whole of Dogon Country. Increasing external demand, which could tentatively be related to the emergence of the West African empires, may have driven the intensification of production. This economic and historical context allowed the

---

[44] Through the quantification of slag (Robion-Brunner 2010) and the material mass balance established at the Fiko site (Perret and Serneels 2006), we can propose an estimation of iron production: each tonne of slag corresponds to the production of between 300 and 600 kg of iron, so 400,000 tonnes of slag = 120,000 tonnes of bloom; after refining of the bloom and smithing of the iron objects, 100 to 200 kg of iron objects can be expected to have been produced from the 300 to 600 kg of bloom, so 120,000 tonnes of bloom = 40,000 tonnes of iron objects. 40,000 tonnes of iron objects produced over 1400 years corresponds to 26 tonnes of iron objects per year (without taking into account fluctuations in production).

encounter between diverse populations with different metallurgical traditions. These populations shared a territory and had to maintain their methods of producing iron as a cultural signature. However, the presence of a certain similarity between the metallurgical traditions perhaps shows the existence of technological transmission. In Dogon Country, there was no population replacement but rather cohabitation in the same space of several human groups of different geographical and social origins.[45]

The preservation of variants within the same region could reflect the mechanisms by which technologies are learned. Depending on the technology (ironworking, ceramics, weaving, etc.), the mechanisms of apprenticeship would either facilitate or obstruct the conditions of adoption of exogenous technical skills and the agency to adapt techniques and technological approaches. The beliefs underlying the techniques may restrain and model each step of the *chaîne opératoire*. In contrast to ceramics[46] and forging,[47] the apprenticeship of iron smelting has not been the focus of ethnological studies. Researchers have, however, described 'real' or re-enacted smelting sessions that they attended. They discuss technical and quantified details, beliefs and rituals claimed to be necessary for the success of the operations, and finally the social and economic context.[48] The status of the participants is given. There is a head smelter or an elder's council, as well as young people or apprentices. These ethnographic descriptions show the major importance of rituals. They mark each step and allow them to be remembered. Under the leadership of a master, the metallurgists seem to take part collectively in the smelting. Even if the learning can be individual,[49] the smelting is really collective; it is impossible to smelt alone. The apprentices must follow and remember the rituals, but they do not seem to learn technical knowledge. Each member of a smelting session detects the physical and chemical changes of the material being processed inside the furnace through different senses: sight, hearing, smell and touch.[50] If the smelting does not work, the methods of the master and the group are not called into question. Instead, a taboo has been transgressed. The success of a smelt is guaranteed by the respect of taboos, ancestors, traditions, genies and so forth: 'dans le domaine de la métallurgie traditionnelle du fer en Afrique, les croyances sont indissociables des techniques et forment ensemble une pratique complexe dont le résultat immédiat est la production de richesse sociale au service de la

---

[45] Robion-Brunner 2012.   [46] Bril and Roux 2002; Gallay 2010; Gosselain 1995.
[47] Kante 1993; Martinelli 1996.
[48] Bellamy 1904; Echard 1986; Huysecom and Agustoni 1996; Van der Merwe and Avery 1987.
[49] Jane Humphris, personal communication, 2015.   [50] Andrieux 2012.

collectivité'.[51] It is therefore difficult to innovate in a technical activity with a deep-rooted symbolic system. Beyond expertise, the head smelter transmits a way of viewing the world and the skills to modify it. These skills are both technological and magical in scope.

Large or Small, it is not the Same!

The scale at which ironworking was practised makes a difference in the way the metallurgists managed their space and their production in terms of quantity and quality. Consequently, the artefacts resulting from different levels of production cannot be the same. Varying production output modifies the raw material supply networks, the organisation of the site and the structure of production. 'Furnace size was also influenced by local economic and social phenomenon, such as market demands, long distance trade networks, the use of bride price, and the available labour pool. These were usually unconscious relationship set in tradition within a wide cultural context.'[52]

At Korsimoro (Burkina Faso), five smelting traditions have been identified in the same place,[53] and the 18 radiocarbon dates obtained show that these traditions follow one another in time, with each corresponding to a different period of production (Fig. 9.5).[54] The KRS 1 tradition (seventh to tenth century AD) was characterised by average-sized furnaces (diameters of 0.8 m) with natural draught and single utilisation. The furnaces were grouped in lines of 5–12 units. In the KRS 2 tradition (eleventh to thirteenth century AD), the furnaces were larger (diameters of 1 m), with natural draught and multiple utilisations. The slag was caught at the back of the furnace, in which spent tuyères had been placed. Waste materials formed a large but not very thick spread. The KRS 3 tradition (fourteenth to sixteenth century AD) saw the appearance of furnaces with outside slag spilling (natural draught/multiple utilisation/reconstruction in the same place). Each furnace was surrounded by a circular accumulation of slag. The furnaces of the KRS 4 tradition (seventeenth century AD) were very small (diameters of 0.2 m), with a single utilisation and forced draught. They were placed in lines or in groups. The KRS 5 tradition (eighteenth/ nineteenth centuries AD?) seems to belong to the last period of production. The slag heaps were small (0.1 to 1 m high) with large furnaces (diameters

---

[51] Huysecom 2001, 82.   [52] Childs 1991, 345.
[53] The site extends almost continuously over 10 km.   [54] Serneels *et al.* 2012; 2014.

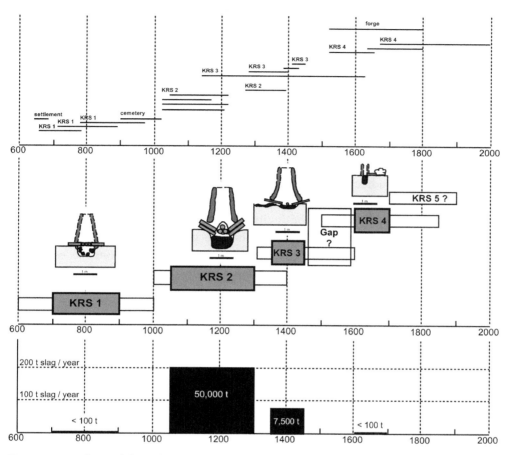

Figure 9.5 Synthesis of chronological data and stages of production at the Korsimoro site (after Serneels *et al.* 2014, fig. 49 p.102).

of 1.5 m) installed among them, without specific organisation. No opening in the furnaces has been recorded, but the local informants mention the simultaneous use of four bellows. A global estimate of the tonnage of slag is in the region of 200,000 tonnes, of which more than 80 per cent belongs to the second and third traditions. This large volume testifies to intensive production between AD 1000 and 1500, destined for a vast external market as suggested above.[55] In the current state of knowledge, the reasons for these technical changes are poorly understood: they seem rather radical.

---

[55] Building on the calculation elaborated at the Fiko site (see footnote 44 and Perret and Serneels 2006): 200,000 tonnes of slag = 60,000 tonnes of bloom = 20,000 tonnes of iron objects; 80 per cent were produced between AD 1000 and 1500, that is 16,000 tonnes of iron objects produced over 500 years, corresponding to 32 tonnes of iron objects per year.

Indeed, Serneels did not detect any gradual evolution from one technique to another. It is very difficult to discuss continuity or discontinuity in iron production. If the technical changes correspond to population movements, we could envisage periods of abandonment between two phases of activity. In fact, only the iron workshops of KRS 2 were reoccupied by those of KRS 3 during the next period, which could support some continuity of activity. The transitions between KRS 1/KRS 2, KRS 3/KRS 4 and KRS 4/KRS 5 are also unclear. Finally, the available radiocarbon dates are too few to discern the evolution of iron production at this site: to clarify such change, additional radiocarbon dates are needed as well as work on other types of sites and artefacts (settlements, burial sites, ceramics, etc.).

When discussing continuity between two traditions, development and innovation can play a significant role. Certain techniques may support modifications, improvements and adaptations in response to economic and social contexts. Childs observes that 'large-scale production was accomplished in furnaces of all sizes'. However:

> The Njanja group of the MaShona, for example, mobilised a large labour force to operate many small furnaces simultaneously. . . . Other groups used fewer, but larger furnaces with a slag outlet so that a bigger bloom could accumulate in the space left by the tapped slag.[56]

On the other hand, certain technical systems are more effective for large-scale production. The possibility of reusing the same furnace several times limits the time needed for construction. This is related to the smelting process (slag running into the bottom of the furnace or out of the furnace) and the ability to clean the pit of the furnace for future use. We therefore suggest that multiple reuse of a furnace is an enabling factor for large-scale production.

Other technological elements could be influenced or encouraged by local economic needs. For example, the large natural draught iron-smelting furnace is considered by both Martinelli and Killick as a technological innovation.[57] In choosing natural draught, iron smelters opted for efficiency and labour saving, thereby using fewer workers than would have been necessary with mechanical blowers. For Martinelli, this choice is the result of social transformations and a reflection of the associated technological, cultural and political issues: 'The technical system of the Yatenga blacksmiths is characterised by the desire to produce surpluses for exportation to other areas in the Mossi (Moose) region and to

---

[56] Childs 1991, 345.   [57] Killick 2015; Martinelli 2004.

Figure 9.6 Natural draught iron-smelting furnace at the Tatré site (Bassar Region, Togo) (photo: C. Robion-Brunner).

neighbouring countries as far as the border with Ghana.'[58] The choice of natural draught and the creation of a caste of blacksmiths frees up people to treat the raw iron, make iron objects and develop long-distance trade and exchange. For Killick, the widespread use of this kind of furnace was favoured by local environmental conditions:

These [large natural draught iron-smelting furnaces] were particularly common in the West African Sudanic woodland zone from Senegal to Nigeria and in the *miombo* woodlands of Tanzania, Zambia, Malawi and Mozambique (Cline 1937; Killick 1991). [. . .] Both of these zones of savannah woodlands soils have very infertile soils, so swidden (slash-and-burn) agriculture was dominant. [. . .] I suggest that the labour requirements for swidden agriculture conflicted with those for iron smelting, and that this conflict favoured the spread of the natural draught furnace.[59]

Whether the result of economic or environmental pressure, several major West African centres of iron production (Dogon Country, Mali; Bassar Region, Togo; and Korsimoro, Burkina Faso) used natural draught furnaces (Fig. 9.6).

[58] Martinelli 2004, 187.   [59] Killick 2015, 316.

Preliminary Reflections on the Meaning of Diversity

West African iron production is diverse and multiple. The data currently available to us come from over a century and a half of research. It is thus extremely difficult to determine the factors underlying the observed diversity, develop generalisations and propose explanations. Nevertheless, a number of recent research programmes have contributed significantly to data renewal.

Africa has extremely diverse physical and environmental conditions. Metallurgists need to adapt their iron production process to local resources, which play a significant role in the variability in iron waste and the processes used. To estimate their role, more analyses of the global chemical compositions of the ore and the slag are needed, along with archaeobotanical investigations. In spite of raw material constraints, metallurgists made a fundamental choice to exploit them. The issue of political control over resources could also be a factor in local heterogeneity in technological practices and the archaeological evidence.

Systematic regional studies show that style is a factor in different approaches to iron smelting. The use of diverse means to manufacture the same product suggests the presence of populations belonging to several cultures. As smelting is a social act, smelting techniques reflect social identity. But the presence of several smelting styles in a single area, such as Dogon Country (Mali) and the Korsimoro site (Burkina Faso), can be proof of population movement, technical transmission or increased production. Based upon archaeological artefacts alone, do we have the elements necessary to differentiate between these possibilities? With regional studies, we can acquire much information from different periods and examine whether metallurgical diversity is linked with a single factor (raw material constraints, settlement history, technological transmission, technological evolution, economic level of production, etc.) or with several. In the case of Dogon metallurgy, the presence of different traditions reflects the successive arrival of different population groups. Their long-term cohabitation reflects the desire or need for cultural differentiation, emphasised by methods of knowledge transmission. The force of the beliefs underlying the techniques and their ability to maintain the confidential character of this power – the power to change the nature of the material – by secrecy and fear is also a major component. The five metallurgical traditions at Korsimoro belong to different periods. The presence in the last periods of two traditions producing a poor quality iron and in small quantity shows that we are not dealing with a linear evolution of technology. I suggest, instead, that these technological changes were probably linked with significant changes in population settlement.

The final factor affecting technological diversity is the level of production. The same technological traditions are not used for small- and large-scale production. For small-scale production, a furnace, typically a slag-pit furnace, was generally used only a single time. For large-scale production several elements are always present: multiple uses of a furnace; strategies to evacuate the slag during the smelt (slag tapping) or after the smelt (using tuyères, or a block of clay placed in the furnace before the smelt); furnaces in a battery system; organisation of the waste, etc. In Dogon and Korsimoro iron production we saw both the impact of population displacement and the wider effects of the economy. But we do not as yet have material evidence that African iron smelters had adapted or changed their technique to intensive production, although it seems that certain techniques are more suitable for increased output. Further archaeological investigations and comparisons with European cases are necessary to better understand and validate this interpretation. To compare the African iron-smelting sites and African sites with European sites, we need to develop a common approach and improve the bridge between French and English terminology, particularly for the descriptions of slag.[60]

References

Alpern, S.B. 2005. Did they or didn't they invent it? Iron in Sub-Saharan Africa. *History in Africa* 32: 41–94.

Andrieux, P. 2012. La réduction métallurgique: Des sens aux savoirs transmis. In Robion-Brunner and Martinelli 2012, 227–43.

Balfet, H. 1975. Technologie. In R. Cresswell (ed.), *Eléments d'ethnologie. 2, Six approches*, Paris: A. Colin, 44–79.

Bellamy, C.V. 1904. A West African smelting house. *Journal of the Iron and Steel Institute* 66: 99–126.

Bocoum, H. (ed.) 2004. *The Origins of Iron Metallurgy in Africa: New Light on Its Antiquity: West and Central Africa*. Paris: UNESCO.

---

[60] I am grateful to Aurélie Cuénod for inviting me to the Mobile Technologies conference and suggesting that I present the results of my recent archaeological and ethnohistorical research on West African metallurgy, and to Marie-Pierre Coustures, Alain Gallay, Vincent Serneels, Pierre de Maret and David Killick for many discussions about diversity, techniques, African iron smelting, etc. I must also express my gratitude to François-Xavier Fauvelle for his valuable comments and Becky Miller for her helpful corrections of the English text.

Bril, B. and Roux, V. (eds) 2002. *Le geste technique: Réflexions méthodologiques et anthropologiques*. Ramonville Saint-Agne: Editions Erès (= *Revue d'Anthropologie des connaissances, Technologies/Idéologies/Pratiques* 14.2).

Celis, G. 1991. *Les fonderies africaines du fer, un grand métier disparu*. Frankfurt: Museum für Völkerkunde.

Chamoux, M.-N. 1978. La transmission des savoir-faire: Un objet pour l'ethnologie des techniques? *Techniques et Culture* 3: 46–83.

Childs, S.T. 1991. Style, technology and iron smelting furnaces in Bantu-speaking Africa. *Journal of Anthropological Archaeology* 10: 332–59.

Childs, S.T. and Killick, D. 1993. Indigenous African metallurgy: Nature and culture. *Annual Review of Anthropology* 22: 317–37.

Chirikure, S., Burret, R. and Heimann, R.B. 2009. Beyond furnaces and slags: A review study of bellows and their role in indigenous African metallurgical process. *Azania* 44.2: 195–215.

Cline, W. 1937. *Mining and Metallurgy in Negro Africa*. General Series in Anthropology 5. Menasha: George Banta Publishing.

Clist, B. 2012. Vers une réduction des préjugés et la fonte des antagonismes: Un bilan de l'expansion de la métallurgie du fer en Afrique Sub-Saharienne. *Journal of African Archaeology* 10.1: 71–84.

David, N. and Robertson, I.G. 1996. Competition and change in two traditional African iron industries. In Schmidt 1996a, 128–44.

De Barros, P. 1985. *The Bassar: Large-scale Iron Producers of the West African Savanna*. Unpublished PhD thesis, University of California, Los Angeles.

De Barros, P. 1986. Bassar: A quantified, chronologically controlled, regional approach to a traditional iron production centre in West Africa. *Africa: Journal of the international African Institute* 56.2: 148–74.

De Barros, P. 1988. Societal repercussions of the rise of large-scale traditional iron production: A West African example. *The African Archaeological Review* 6: 91–113.

De Maret, P. 1980. Ceux qui jouent avec le feu: La place du forgeron en Afrique Centrale. *Africa: Journal of the International African Institute* 50.3: 263–79.

De Maret, P. 1985. The smith's myth and the origin of leadership in Central Africa. In Haaland and Shinnie 1985, 73–87.

Descoeudres, J.-P., Huysecom, E., Serneels, V. and Zimmermann, J.-L. (eds) 2001. *Aux origines de la métallurgie du fer. Table ronde internationale d'archéologie: L'Afrique et le bassin méditerranéen (1; 4–7 juin 1999; Genève). Mediterranean Archaeology* 14. Sydney: University of Sydney.

Echard, N. 1986. Histoire du peuplement et histoire des techniques: L'exemple de la métallurgie hausa du fer au Niger. *Journal des Africanistes* 56.1: 21–34.

Eichhorn, B. 2012. Woody resource exploitation for iron metallurgy of the Fiko tradition: Implications for the environmental history of Dogon Country, Mali. In Robion-Brunner and Martinelli 2012, 141–52.

Fabre, J.-M. 2009. La métallurgie du fer au Sahel burkinabé à la fin du 1er millénaire AD. In S. Magnavita, L. Koté, P. Breunig and O.A. Idé (eds), *Crossroads, Cultural and Technological Developments in First Millennium* BC/AD *West Africa*, Frankfurt: Africa Magna, 167–78.

Faure, P. and Viennot, M. 1976. *Carte Pédologique de Reconnaissance à 1: 200,000. Porga-Karimama. République Populaire du Bénin.* Bondy: Office de la recherche scientifique et technique outre-mer.

Faure, P., Viennot, M. and Dubroecq, D. 1976. *Carte Pédologique de Reconnaissance à 1: 200,000. Kandi. République Populaire du Bénin.* Bondy: Office de la recherche scientifique et technique outre-mer.

Gallay, A. 2000. Cultures, styles, ethnies: Quel choix pour l'archéologue? In R. De Marinis and S. Biaggio (eds), *I Leponti: Tra mito e realtà, 1. Cat. di mostra (maggio–dicembre 2000; Locarno, Castello Visconteo – Casorella)*, Locarno: Gruppo Archeologia Ticino, 71–78.

Gallay, A. 2001. Diffusion ou invention: Un faux débat pour l'archéologue? In Descoeudres *et al.* 2001, 73–82.

Gallay, A. 2010. Les mécanismes de diffusion de la céramique traditionnelle dans la boucle du Niger (Mali): Une évaluation des réseaux de distribution. In C. Manen, F. Convertini, D. Binder and I. Sénépart (eds), *Premières sociétés paysannes de Méditerranée occidentale: Structure des productions céramiques. Séance de la Société préhistorique française*, Paris: Société Préhistorique Française, 265–81.

Gordon, R.B. and Killick, D.J. 1993. Adaptation of technology to culture and environment: Bloomery iron smelting in America and Africa. *Technology and Culture* 34.2: 243–70.

Gosselain, O.P. 1995. *Identités techniques, le travail de la poterie au Cameroun méridional.* Unpublished PhD thesis, Université Libre de Bruxelles.

Guillon, R. 2013. *Relation société-milieu en domaine sahélien au sud-ouest du Niger au cours des quatre derniers millénaires: Approche géoarchéologique.* Unpublished PhD thesis, Université de Dijon.

Haaland, R. and Shinnie, P. (eds) 1985. *African Iron Working: Ancient and Traditional.* Oslo: Norwegian University Press.

Haour, A., Banni Guene, O., Gosselain, O., Livingstone Smith, A. and N'Dah, D. 2011. Survey along the Niger River Valley at the Benin-Niger border, winter 2011. *Nyame Akuma* 76: 23–32.

Herbert, E.W. 1993. *Iron, Gender and Power: Rituals of Transformation in African Societies.* Bloomington: Indiana University Press.

Holl, A.F.C. 2009. Early West African metallurgies: New data and old orthodoxy. *Journal of World Prehistory* 22: 415–38.

Huysecom, E. 2001. Technique et croyance des forgerons africains: Eléments pour une approche ethnoarchéologique. In Descoeudres *et al.* 2001, 73–82.

Huysecom, E. 2002. Palaeoenvironment and human population in West Africa: An international research project in Mali. *Antiquity* 292: 335–36.

Huysecom, E. and Agustoni, B. 1996. *Inagina, l'ultime maison du fer*. Genève: Télévision Suisse Romande.

Kante, N. 1993. *Forgerons d'Afrique noire: Transmission des savoirs traditionnels en pays malinké*. Paris: Editions de l'Harmattan.

Kense, F.J. 1985. The initial diffusion of iron to Africa. In Haaland and Shinnie 1985, 11–27.

Killick, D.J. 1991. The relevance of recent African iron-smelting practice to reconstructions of prehistoric smelting technology. *MASCA Research Papers in Science and Archaeology* 8.1: 47–54.

Killick, D.J. 2004. Review essay: What do we know about African iron working? *Journal of African Archaeology* 2.1: 97–112.

Killick, D.J. 2015. Invention and innovation in African iron-smelting technologies. *Cambridge Archaeological Journal* 25.1: 307–19.

Killick, D.J. and Miller, D.M. 2014. Smelting of magnetite and magnetite-ilmenite ores in the northern Lowveld, South Africa, ca.1000 CE to ca.1880 CE. *Journal of Archaeological Science* 43: 230–55.

Langlois, O. 2006. De l'organisation bipartite du travail du fer dans les monts Mandara septentrionaux. *Techniques et Culture* 46–47: 175–209.

Lemonnier, P. 2010. L'étude des systèmes techniques. *Techniques et Culture* 54–55.1: 49–67.

Leroi-Gourhan, A. 1971. *Evolution et techniques: L'homme et la matière*. Paris: Albin Michel.

Martinelli, B. 1993. Fonderies ouest-africaines: Classement comparatif et tendances. *Techniques et Culture* 21: 195–221.

Martinelli, B. 1996. Sous le regard de l'apprenti: Paliers de savoir et d'insertion chez les forgerons Moose du Yatenga (Burkina Faso). *Techniques et Culture* 58: 9–47.

Martinelli, B. 2004. On the threshold of intensive metallurgy: The choice of slow combustion in the Niger River Bend (Burkina Faso and Mali). In Bocoum 2004, 165–88.

Mauny, R. 1952. Essai sur l'histoire de métaux en Afrique occidentale. *Bulletin de l'Institut Français de l'Afrique Noire* 14.2: 545–95.

Mauss, M. 1947. *Manuel d'ethnographie*. Paris: Payot.

McNaughton, P.R. 1993. *The Mande Blacksmith: Knowledge, Power and Art in West Africa*. Bloomington and Indianapolis: Indiana University Press.

Miller, D.E. and Van der Merwe, N.J. 1994. Early metal working in Sub-Saharan Africa: A review of recent research. *Journal of African History* 35.1: 1–36.

Perret, S. and Serneels, V. 2006. Technological characterization and quantification of a large scale iron smelting site in Fiko, Mali. In J.-F. Moreau, R. Auger, J. Chabot and A. Herzog (eds), *Proceedings/Actes ISA2006, 36th International Symposium on Archaeometry, Quebec Canada, 2–6.05.2006*, Québec: CELAT (*Cahiers d'archéologie du CELAT* 25.7), 453–63.

Pleiner, R. 2000. *Iron in Archaeology: The European Bloomery Smelters*. Praha: Archeologicky ustav AVCR.

Pole, L.-M. 1985. Furnace design and the smelting operation: A survey of written reports of iron smelting in West Africa. In Haaland and Shinnie 1985, 142–63.

Robion-Brunner, C. 2010. *Peuplements des forgerons et traditions sidérurgiques: Vers une histoire de la production du fer sur le plateau de Bandiagara (pays dogon, Mali) durant les empires précoloniaux.* Frankfurt: Africa Magna Verlag.

Robion-Brunner, C. 2012. The role of ethnohistoric data in reconstructing ancient siderurgy in Dogon Country (Mali). *P@lethnology* 4: 209–34.

Robion-Brunner, C. 2018. Ironworking. In A. Haour (ed.), *Two Thousand Years in Dendi, Nothern Benin*, Leiden: Brill, 174–92.

Robion-Brunner, C. and Martinelli, B. (eds). 2012. *Métallurgie du fer et sociétés africaines: Bilans et nouveaux paradigmes dans la recherche anthropologique et archéologique.* Oxford: BAR International Series 2395.

Robion-Brunner, C., Serneels, V. and Perret, S. 2013. Variability in iron smelting practices: Confrontation of technical, cultural and economic criteria to explain the metallurgical diversity in the Dogon area (Mali). In J. Humphris and T. Rehren (eds), *The World of Iron*, London: Archetype Publications, 257–65.

Robion-Brunner, C., Aboki, T., de Barros, P., Coustures, M.-P., Ilaboti, D., Dugast, S., Eichhorn, B., Le Drezen, Y., Mahou-Hekinian, V., Robert, V., Soulignac, R. and Tidjougouna, L. 2014. *The Project 'SIDERENT'*. Poster of the 14th Congress of the Pan African Archaeological Association for Prehistory and Related Studies, University of Johannesburg.

Robion-Brunner, C., Haour, A., Coustures, M.-P., Champion, L. and Béziat, D. 2015. Iron production in northern Benin: Excavations at Kompa Moussékoubou. *Journal of African Archaeology* 13.1: 39–57.

Schmidt, P.R. (ed.) 1996a. *The Culture and Technology of African Iron Production.* Gainesville: Press of Florida.

Schmidt, P.R. 1996b. Cultural representations of African iron production. In Schmidt 1996a, 1–28.

Serneels, V., Kiénon-Kaboré, H.T., Koté, L., Kouassi, S.K., Ramseyer, D. and Simporé, L. 2012. Origine et développement de la métallurgie du fer au Burkina Faso et en Côte d'Ivoire. Premiers résultats sur le site sidérurgique de Korsimoro (Sanmatenga, Burkina Faso). *Jahresbericht 2011 der Schweizerisch-Liechtensteinische Stiftung für Archäologische Forschungen im Ausland (SLSA):* 23–54.

Serneels, V., Kiénon-Kaboré, H.T., Koté, L., Kouassi, S.K., Mauvilly, M., Ramseyer, D. and Simporé, L. 2013. Origine et développement de la métallurgie du fer au Burkina Faso et en Côte d'Ivoire. Premiers résultats sur le site sidérurgique de Siola (Kaniasso, Danguélé, Côte d'Ivoire). *Jahresbericht 2012 der Schweizerisch-Liechtensteinische Stiftung für Archäologische Forschungen im Ausland (SLSA):* 113–43.

Serneels, V., Donadini, F., Kiénon-Kaboré, H.T., Koté, L., Kouassi, S.K., Ramseyer, D. and Simporé, L. 2014. Origine et développement de la métallurgie du fer au Burkina Faso et en Côte d'Ivoire: Avancement des recherches en 2013 et quantification des vestiges de Korsimoro (Burkina Faso). *Jahresbericht 2013 der Schweizerisch-Liechtensteinische Stiftung für Archäologische Forschungen im Ausland (SLSA):* 65–112.

Serneels, V., Jobin, P., Kiénon-Kaboré, H.T., Koté, L., Kouassi, S.K., Ramseyer, D., Thiombiano-Ilbi-oudo, E. and Simporé, L. 2015. Origine et développement de la métallurgie du fer au Burkina Faso et en Côte d'Ivoire: Seconde campagne dans la region de Kaniasso (Folon, Côte d'Ivoire) et autres recherches. *Jahresbericht 2014 der Schweizerisch-Liechtensteinische Stiftung für Archäologische Forschungen im Ausland (SLSA):* 23–60.

Shinnie, P.L. 1985. Iron working at Meroe. In Haaland and Shinnie 1985, 28–35.

Sutton, J.E.G. 1985. Temporal and spatial variability in African iron furnaces. In Haaland and Shinnie 1985, 164–91.

Trigger, B.G. 1969. The myth of Meroe and the African Iron Age. *International Journal of African Historical Studies* 2: 23–50.

Tylecote, R.F. 1987. *The Early History of Metallurgy in Europe.* London: Longman.

Van der Merwe, N.J. and Avery, D.H. 1987. Science and magic in African technology: Traditional iron smelting in Malawi. *Africa* 57.2: 143–72.

Viennot, M. 1978. *Notice explicative no,66 (9) de la carte pédologique de reconnaissance de la République Populaire du Bénin, Feuille de Kandi-Karimama.* Paris: Orstom.

PART IV

Glass Technology

10 | Shattering Illusions

Using Analytical Evidence to Establish Clearer Pictures
of Glass Production and Trade within Africa

CHLOË N. DUCKWORTH

Introduction

There are two main aims of this chapter. The first part will provide further general introduction to some specific issues of glass production and glassworking technology that are relevant to the three chapters in this section of the book. In recent years there have been significant advances in the chemical and isotopic analyses of glass, allowing researchers to reconstruct the raw ingredients, and even potentially the provenance, of glass used to make objects such as beads and vessels. Much of this research has focused on the contiguous zones of the Eastern Mediterranean and Western/Southern Asia. Several distinct 'groups' of glass have been defined by their major and minor elemental composition. Furthermore, trace element and isotope data have allowed tentative reconstructions of the different raw material sources utilised, providing a route to provenance.

A growing number of researchers have recognised the value of compositional data for the analysis of glasses, particularly beads, as a proxy for reconstructing African trade routes and interconnectivity from the late first millennium BC to the period of Islamic trade in the second millennium AD. To date, this work could best be described as 'pioneering', as the tiny number of objects analysed stands in sharp contrast to the vastness of the geographical area from which glass vessel fragments and beads have been recovered. Comparisons with the well-established compositional groups from the East Mediterranean and West Asia are essential, but should be undertaken with caution, given the overwhelming bias to analysis of samples from these areas, and the low representation of other areas including the Iberian Peninsula and North and West Africa.

The second part of this chapter presents the results of my analysis of glass from the Garamantian heartlands in the Libyan Central Sahara, including several fragments of imported Roman vessel glass. Results are contextualised in relation to those of other published studies, to develop a broader picture against which new analyses can be interpreted. I aim to demonstrate the crucial importance of moving beyond a simple association between composition and provenance. Less archaeologically 'visible' practices such as recycling, which may take place periodically, in small and archaeologically ephemeral installations, often leave subtle traces in the glass chemistry. The potential of data from trace element analyses in investigating these effects is explored. In addition, the possibilities of local African glass production, recycling and reworking are discussed.

Glass is an excellent means by which to track technological change. It is relatively inert, and often survives well in the archaeological record. Depending on the period and place in question, it may also be a fairly common archaeological find, increasing its potential for sampling and chemical analysis. Glass cannot yet be scientifically analysed for the purpose of dating, but chemical analysis of even tiny surviving fragments reveals a wealth of information about the raw ingredients, recipes and production processes used to make them. Because these things change depending on the location of glass production and the knowledge of the glassmakers, the analysis of multiple samples of glass provides chronometric and geographical resolution on technology transfer and change over time and space.

For the Sahara, however, and for North Africa more broadly, only very few analyses of glass have been conducted to date. This chapter seeks to illustrate the immense value of analysing glass found in North African contexts, by presenting the results of a large-scale programme of analysis of materials from the Trans-SAHARA Project, and previous archaeological investigations in Fazzan. The materials range from Roman glasses imported from the Mediterranean, to Islamic glass bangles that littered Saharan trade routes until as late as the nineteenth and early twentieth centuries.[1] In contrast with traditional approaches that have focused primarily on assigning the geological origin of the raw ingredients used to make glasses, this chapter will give more weight to questions such as modification of materials through heat treatment and recycling, and to the whole biography of the glass that ended up being recovered from archaeological contexts in the Sahara. For the reader who seeks a deeper understanding of the scientific background to glass analysis, and the

---

[1] An interesting point in studies of glass from the Trans-Saharan zone is that to date most attention has been devoted to the distribution and compositional analysis of beads, with less attention to the potential transport and provenance of bangles and vessel glass.

history of glass analysis in a North African context, the next section will be of use. Readers who are already familiar with these matters, or who wish only to know about the case study in question, may skip to 'Material Analysed from South-West Libya'.

The Scientific Analysis of Archaeological Glass: Major, Minor and Trace Elements

Although archaeological glasses are characterised by their chemistry, glass itself is best defined as a state of matter. More specifically, glass (along with plastics and gels) is an amorphous solid, lacking the long-range order which characterises crystalline solids such as pure metals and minerals, but with the short-range order of the molecules in a liquid such as water (H_2O). In simple terms, this state can be achieved by cooling a material more rapidly than it is able to arrange itself into a crystallise form. Most historical glasses are thus based on silica (silicon dioxide; SiO_2), which is particularly viscous and thus suited to glass formation. The short-range order they possess is in the form of the silica tetrahedron, SiO_4.

Despite its suitability for glassmaking, pure silica ($>c.93$ per cent SiO_2) melts at a temperature of 1,600°C and cannot be worked below 1,500°C,[2] for which reason historical man-made glasses also required a so-called 'flux', or network modifier, which disrupts the continuity of the network of the silica (the network former). The most suitable fluxes are the alkali metal oxides soda (Na_2O) and potash (K_2O). Most archaeological glasses thus consist of the short-range order of silica tetrahedra, each with an Si^{4+} ion directionally bonded to four O^{2-} ions. Each O^{2-} ion can either be shared between two tetrahedra (forming a 'bridging' oxygen ion), or can bond with a network modifier such as Na^+ (forming a 'non-bridging' oxygen ion). Also found in most glasses are so-called 'network stabilisers', most importantly lime (CaO), which prevents alkali-silica glasses from dissolving in water.

From their earliest consistent production in the mid-second millennium BC, the majority of man-made glasses were formed by the fusion of silica and an alkali metal (typically sodium or potassium). In addition to an alkali, most silica-based glasses (or at least most of those which have survived in the archaeological record) included lime, which acts as a stabiliser. Differences between the sources of these three ingredients (silica,

---

[2] Pollard and Heron 1996, 151.

alkali and lime) and between the recipes and production processes employed gave rise to compositional variations in the glasses. Changes over time and place can thus be reflected in the chemistry of the glasses.

The use of chemical markers to distinguish between the ingredients found in ancient glasses now has a long history. Sayre and Smith were among the first to distinguish between glasses made in different periods and places, based on the quantity of certain key oxides within them.[3] They identified five categories of ancient Western glass: second millennium BC, antimony-rich, Roman, Early Islamic and Islamic lead.[4] A key discriminator between different glass compositions was found to be the quantity of magnesia (MgO) and potash (K_2O) in a glass. Glasses with high magnesia and potash (known as HMG) were made using the ashes of halophytic plants, which grow in saline environments and take up salts including soda but also potash, magnesia and lime during their growth. Glasses with low magnesia and potash (LMG) were made with a relatively pure, mineral alkali source such as natron. According to Sayre and Smith,[5] HMG second millennium BC glasses average *c.*3.6 per cent MgO and 1.1 per cent K_2O. A further group that has since been distinguished is low-magnesia, high-potash (LMHK, or 'mixed alkali') glass, typical of the earliest European (particularly north Italian) glass production of the late second and early first millennia BC.[6]

In the earliest glass production of the mid-second millennium BC in Mesopotamia and Egypt, halophytic plant ashes were combined with a pure silica source, probably crushed quartz pebbles. Around the eighth century BC, glasses produced in Western Asia and the Mediterranean began to be made with a mineral alkali, the most prominent source of which was Wadi Natrun in the Western Desert of Egypt. The mineral was combined not with quartz, but with silica sands, which brought with them various impurities, some of which were more beneficial than others, including – for beach sands – lime introduced along with seashells (though deliberate addition of lime may also have occurred). Other sand-sourced impurities include iron and aluminium, and a host of trace elements (usually defined as elements present at fewer than 100 parts per million, ppm).

To date, mineral alkali glasses have been characterised by these sand-borne impurities, as well as of various colourants or decolourants added to the glasses (see below), as it is difficult to distinguish between the mineral

---

[3] Sayre and Smith 1961.   [4] Sayre and Smith 1961, 1825.   [5] Sayre and Smith 1967, 281–93.
[6] Henderson 1988.

sources themselves due to their purity. Recent work by Devulder *et al.* investigated the possibility of discriminating between sources of mineral alkali using boron (B) isotopes: they have shown that the B isotopic composition of 33 Graeco-Roman glasses analysed was most compatible with the δ^{11}B values of Wadi Natrun, Egypt.[7] The lower δ^{11}B value glasses are also compatible, however, with samples of the mineral alkali sources at al-Barnuj and in Fazzan, but not those from Lake Pikrolimni in Greece. It is thus likely that most Roman glasses were made using mineral alkali from Wadi Natrun, but it does not automatically follow that this was the only source.

At some point in the eighth and ninth centuries AD there was a shift in the Mediterranean back to the use of halophytic plant ashes, now combined with silica of varying levels of purity. The shift may in part have stemmed from a disruption to trade routes which led to a lack of mineral alkali in glassmaking regions. It is thought that plant ashes had continued to be used in areas to the east of the Euphrates throughout the period when mineral alkali glasses were being made in the west. In northern Europe, glassmakers began to rely instead on the ashes of trees such as beech, which provide the required alkali primarily in the form of potash rather than soda.

Glasses made yet farther afield may also be of relevance to African glass composition. The glass type most commonly encountered in South and Southeast Asia is mineral-soda-alumina glass (m-Na-Al), characterised by relatively high alumina concentrations (>4 per cent Al_2O_3) and thought to result from the combination of impure, granitic sand with mineral soda.[8] The occurrence of this general glass type dates from the fourth century BC to the sixteenth century AD.[9] Two subtypes have been identified. The first comprises glass samples mostly from South India, Sri Lanka and Southeast Asia, which date from the fifth century BC to the tenth century AD. This glass is rare in Africa. It can be easily characterised by its uranium concentration (*c.*20 ppm U) and relatively high barium (<*c.*2,500 ppm Ba), so that it has been dubbed 'low uranium – high barium' (lU-hBa) glass.[10] It is thought to have been produced at South Indian and Sri Lankan sites, and dates to between the fourth century BC and the fifth century AD. The second subtype of m-Na-Al glass is that linked to the so-called 'trade wind beads', which travelled west from southern Asia. It differs from the first type, with higher uranium (average 100 ppm U) and lower barium than the

---

[7] Devulder *et al.* 2014.   [8] Dussubieux *et al.* 2009.   [9] Dussubieux *et al.* 2008.
[10] Dussubieux *et al.* 2008; 2009, 158–59.

first subtype, and has thus been named 'high-uranium – low-barium' (hU-lBa) glass.[11] This type is also later, dating to between the ninth and nineteenth centuries AD.

Other, rarer categories of glass can also be identified and are generally more specific to certain regions and/or periods. Two such groups are discussed in more detail below. These are: (1) high-lead glasses, which can be subdivided between lead-silica, lead-soda-silica and lead-potash-silica types, and which are mainly associated with the late first and early second millennia AD Islamic and Christian worlds with a possible emphasis on the Maghrib; and (2) high-alumina, high-lime glasses, which were manufactured in and around Ile-Ife, southern Nigeria, from the later first millennium AD.

As noted above, impurities in the raw ingredients of glassmaking can provide useful compositional 'markers', but if present in high enough quantities they had noticeable effects on the properties of the resultant glasses. Iron, a frequent impurity in glasses made from sand, imparts a strong, often undesirable colour to the glass, which can range from brown to green depending on the redox conditions of the furnace. To counter this, various metals and minerals were added as colourants or decolourants in addition to the primary ingredients of glass production. The purpose of the decolourants was to create something as close as possible to the transparent, colourless glass we take for granted today. An alternative mechanism by which glass could be decoloured was through purification of the raw ingredients, although this processing could also have the effect of removing 'desirable' impurities such as calcium, and weakening the resultant glass. Glass colourants and decolourants are discussed in more detail below, as and when they are relevant to the results of the analyses presented.

Glass in Africa

Here I make a broad division between research into glass composition in North Africa, and Sub-Saharan (but north of the equator) Africa. To date there has been little research on glass found within the Sahara itself, and one of the aims of this chapter is to start to explore what Trans-Saharan influences may have been at play in the production and manipulation of glass.[12] Several other contributions in this series will be of interest to the

---

[11] Dussubieux *et al.* 2008; 2009.

[12] The PhD by Truffa Giachet 2019 includes a significant body of new analyses of glass beads from West Africa, and will be a key point of future reference, but appeared too late for full consideration to be taken here.

reader in this regard: Chapter 11 by Peter Robertshaw (with a focus on beads that is particularly complementary to my arguments below) and Chapter 12 co-authored by Thilo Rehren and Daniela Rosenow (presenting a comparative diachronic view of Egyptian glass production), both presented in this volume; and the chapters by Laure Dussubieux and Sonja Magnavita in a previous volume.[13] Nonetheless, it will be helpful to elucidate some of the key details of our chemical understanding of glass in Africa below, to better situate the results presented.

North Africa

The Mediterranean coast of Africa can be contextualised within the broader sweep of Mediterranean technology transfer and trade, although it is important to consider how far such influences penetrated inland, and the extent to which North Africa contributed to, as well as being influenced by, technological change in the Mediterranean. The main compositional groupings of glass encountered in the Mediterranean are outlined above. Egyptian glass is discussed in detail elsewhere in this volume.[14]

Studies which have focused on the chemical analysis of North African assemblages include the LA-ICP-MS analysis of 30 glass beads of diverse shape and colour from Medieval al-Basra, Morocco,[15] among which six major glass types were identified (lead-silica; lead-soda-silica; lead-silica with high phosphorous and lime; soda-lime-silica with low alumina; soda-lime-silica with high alumina; and potash-lime), suggesting a complex picture of long-distance trade, recycling and modification of glass. Some of this glass may have travelled south, at least as far as Essouk-Tadmakka in Mali, as noted by Robertshaw *et al.*[16] Analytical studies of Roman Africa are more numerous,[17] although they still do not approach the scale of analysis conducted on glass from Egypt, Italy or the East Mediterranean.

One category of glass which may be of relevance to North African archaeology is high-lead glass. Lead has been employed as a colourant and opacifier in glasses since the earliest glassmaking of the Late Bronze Age in Egypt and Mesopotamia, but it can also be added to glasses in larger quantities. Before the Early Modern period, three main types of high-lead glasses have been identified outside of China and East Asia. All are broadly contemporary, and occurred in the late first and early second millennia AD. These are: lead-silica (also known as Islamic high lead); lead-soda-

---

[13] Dussubieux 2017; Magnavita 2017.   [14] Rehren and Rosenow, Chapter 12, this volume.
[15] Robertshaw *et al.* 2010.   [16] Robertshaw *et al.* 2010, 376.
[17] See for example Gliozzo *et al.* 2013.

silica; and lead-potash-silica (also known as Central European lead glass). Lead-silica glasses, although rare, were one of the categories established early on by Sayre and Smith and typically contain over 60–70 per cent PbO by weight.[18] Lead-soda-silica glasses, with anything from *c.*5 to 60 per cent PbO, seem to be even rarer than lead-silica glasses, although this may be in part due to geographical biases in glass analysis. Indeed, recent attempts to address this bias by analysing glass from Medieval Iberia (Spain and Portugal) have identified a prevalence of lead-soda-silica among assemblages of tenth- and eleventh-century glasses from Madinat al-Zahra and nearby Cordoba.[19] Lead-soda-silica glasses have been identified elsewhere in Spain, albeit in a smaller proportion,[20] and were among the ninth- to eleventh-century glasses from al-Basra, Morocco, as noted above.[21] They were also identified in one bead from Jenné-jeno;[22] eight from Gao Saney (see below); and several glasses from ninth- to fourteenth-century Essouk-Tadmakka, Mali.[23] This group may thus be significant for North and West African archaeology, and may have been manufactured (perhaps from recycled materials) in the Maghrib, either in North-West Africa, or in the Iberian Peninsula. Lead-potash-silica glasses are encountered in Medieval Europe, and are thought to be the result of adding lead to raw or recycled potash glasses made to regional recipes using tree ash.[24] It is possible that lead-soda-silica glasses were made in the same way,[25] or in at least some cases through the mixing of high-lead and soda-lime-silica glasses during recycling.[26]

Few comparative datasets exist for the Central Sahara. Seven glass and five faience beads were collected in the oasis of Fewet, south-west of Ghat, and analysed by energy-dispersive X-ray microanalysis.[27] Four of the glass beads were identified as mineral alkali glass and two as soda ash glass; another bead, blue-grey in colour, could not be classified into either group as it had low potassium oxide (0.45 per cent K_2O) but high magnesia (4 per cent MgO). For the mineral alkali beads, Verità argues that the variable content of aluminium oxide (1.2–2.7 per cent Al_2O_3) and calcium oxide (3.5–8.4 per cent CaO) indicates the use of siliceous-calcareous sands of different origins in their production.[28] The plant ash beads are interpreted as being fairly recent in date, at least one of them being thought to date to the eighteenth to nineteenth century.

---

[18] Sayre and Smith 1961.   [19] Duckworth *et al.* 2015a.
[20] De Juan Ares and Schibille 2017, 11.   [21] Robertshaw *et al.* 2010.   [22] Brill 1995.
[23] P. Robertshaw, J. Lankton, L. Dussubieux and S. Nixon, personal communication.
[24] Mecking 2013.   [25] Duckworth *et al.* 2015a.   [26] Robertshaw *et al.* 2010.   [27] Verità 2013.
[28] Verità 2013, 171.

Sub-Saharan Africa

Overland trade across Sub-Saharan Africa renders the Indian Ocean trade connection with East Africa of relevance in understanding the composition of African glasses (Indian Ocean trade was also linked with that in the Mediterranean via the Red Sea and the Nile). For glass found in Sub-Saharan Africa, the most significant of the Asian glass compositions mentioned above is the high-uranium, low-barium (hU-lBa) form of the mineral-soda-alumina (m-Na-Al) glass, associated with the so-called trade wind beads, which are thought to have been shipped across the Indian Ocean.[29] It is important to recognise, however, that there remain many gaps in our knowledge of glass composition, and that new data may alter the assignment of some of these glasses to distant provenances.

The earliest glass bead from a West African site analysed to date was a cobalt-blue fragment of a large cylindrical bead, dated to between *c.*250 BC and AD 50 and found at Jenné-jeno, Mali.[30] This bead was subject to atomic absorption and atomic emission spectroscopy, along with five other beads and two 'glass fragments' from the site, by Robert H. Brill and Sidney Goldstein of the Corning Museum of Glass. It was found to have a composition unexpectedly rich in potash (13 per cent K_2O). Brill interprets this as indicating an Indian or East Asian origin for the bead, given the early date assigned to it.[31] Another bead from Jenné-jeno is hypothesised by Brill to have been made in India on the basis of its high alumina and low lime content.[32] The analysed sample of beads also yielded plant ash and mineral alkali glasses, including one glass which seems to have been made to a typical Roman mineral alkali recipe and contains 0.52 per cent Sb_2O_5, the main glass decolourant used in the Mediterranean world until the second century AD (discussed in more detail below). Overall, the small number of analysed glasses from Jenné-jeno form a rather mixed compositional bag, although this is perhaps unsurprising given their wide date range (250 BC to AD 1400).

On the other hand, as summarised by Magnavita, most beads analysed from West African Sub-Saharan sites have been found to have been made to a recipe using halophytic plant ashes as the alkali source.[33] This is taken to be consistent with dates in the Islamic period, or – for those glasses deemed to be pre-Islamic – interpreted as indicating a production location

[29] Lankton and Dussubieux 2006.

[30] Truffa Giachet 2019 includes a new analysis of a Phoenician eye bead found at another Malian site Nin-Bèrè 3, with a Mediterranean mineral flux composition, in a context dated to the seventh–fifth centuries BC.

[31] Brill 1995, 252.   [32] Brill 1995, 255.   [33] Magnavita 2017.

to the east of the Euphrates, as the use of plant ashes in glassmaking is thought to have continued there unabated throughout the later first millennium BC and early first millennium AD. It includes two beads from Marandet, dated to the sixth to ninth centuries AD; two from Dourou Boro, Mali; and the majority of beads analysed from Igbo-Ukwu. Robertshaw *et al.* report the results of analysis of 37 glass beads from the cemetery of Kissi 13, Burkina Faso.[34] Four beads from Kissi were fluxed with a mineral alkali, and one bead was made of the high-alumina, high-lime glass characteristic of West African manufacture (see discussion of Ile-Ife below). The majority (32 beads), however, were found to be plant ash soda-lime-silica glasses. The authors note that several of these glasses have a ratio of lime to alumina in the region of 1.5:1 to 3:1, similar to glasses from Nishapur and to Sasanian glasses, which they ascribe to the use of sand rather than quartz pebbles in the production of the glasses, but which they further argue implies a provenance east of the Euphrates.[35]

Analysis of the glass recovered from excavations at Gao Saney (dating to the eighth century AD and later) was conducted by Laure Dussubieux at the Field Museum in Chicago, and is briefly reported in Cissé *et al.*[36] Of 47 beads analysed, 44 were found to have been made with a plant ash alkali and two with a mineral alkali. The remaining bead was a very high-lead glass. Among the 44 plant ash beads from Gao Saney, eight were found to have a high level of added lead (>10 per cent), along with elevated tin, which might indicate trade connections or technological links with the north given the findings of high-lead glasses in Morocco and Spain discussed above (though elevated tin is not a consistent feature of these). The Gao Saney beads are relatively low in alumina (with the exception of two, all have <3 per cent Al_2O_3). In addition, a number of fragments of glass vessels were also found at Gao Saney and Gao Ancien, some of which are undergoing chemical analysis.[37] Although the results of these analyses are yet to be published, the glass vessel fragments are typologically consistent with importation from Egypt and the Maghrib, and possibly also from al-Andalus.

Problems with the Provenance Model for West African Beads

The interpretation given in Cissé *et al.*,[38] that the plant ash beads from Gao Saney were made 'east of the Euphrates', appears to rest on the assumption

---

[34] Robertshaw *et al.* 2009a.   [35] Robertshaw *et al.* 2009a, 101–3.   [36] Cissé *et al.* 2013.
[37] Cissé 2017; Insoll 1996, 66.   [38] Cissé *et al.* 2013, 29.

that these beads predate the eighth century AD, since it is well established that plant ash glasses were widely dispersed west of the Euphrates from that time on. I suggest that other finds of plant ash beads in early contexts, such as those discussed above, should also be treated with caution. Although it is by no means impossible that the glasses from Kissi originated in Asia, the assumption of provenance based primarily on a positive match between lime and alumina ratios may in future be falsified, not least because there remain many gaps in our knowledge of the glass chemistry of different regions. Plant ash glasses with similar lime to alumina ratios have also been recently identified in the Iberian Peninsula,[39] one of the areas which to date has been virtually uncharted in the chemical analysis of glass. Admittedly, these glasses are rather variable in their alumina content and not all of them could be cited as a match for the Kissi glasses, but their existence highlights that we need to refine our understanding of Sub-Saharan glass composition in the light of new evidence from hitherto underrepresented areas, particularly Saharan and North Africa and the Iberian Peninsula.

In summary, although there is some evidence that glass beads from east of the Euphrates were finding their way to West Africa, possibly by rather circuitous routes and 'down-the-line' trade via the Indian Ocean and East or Mediterranean Africa, it must be remembered that a number of factors contribute to chemical composition, including the use of similar raw ingredients from diverse sources, and that the major and minor composition of a sample of glass cannot be taken as a direct indication of its provenance. Given the relatively small amount of analytical data for African glasses, we cannot be certain that the production of plant ash glasses was only taking place east of the Euphrates until the eighth century AD. The earliest glass production of the second millennium BC, including that in Egypt, was based on a plant ash recipe, as outlined above, and it is thus feasible that small-scale plant ash production continued, or was reinvented in some areas, despite the overwhelming predominance of glasses made with mineral alkalis in the Mediterranean region.

As mentioned by Fothergill *et al.* in Chapter 5 of this volume, camels need to consume halophytic plants to access vital salts, so an association with these plants could have been a feature across much of the Sahara and Sahel. Furthermore, and as noted by Robertshaw, beads are small and mobile, which lends them a propensity for intrusiveness into older archaeological contexts.[40]

---

[39] Duckworth *et al.* 2015a.   [40] Robertshaw, Chapter 11, this volume.

West African Production

The clearest evidence for early glass*making* in Sub-Saharan Africa comes from Ile-Ife, in southern Nigeria. Abundant archaeological evidence, including glassworking waste and glass-lined crucibles, attests to glass production activities in this region from at least the eleventh century. This may have been an indigenous development; perhaps filling a niche opened by the long West African tradition of importing glass beads,[41] or responding to local demands and traditions of making and using beads of other materials including cowrie shells. Analysis of vitreous waste and finished objects by Lankton *et al.* demonstrates that the productive activities included primary glassmaking, and that the resultant glasses can be recognised by their unique chemical composition, which is high in lime and alumina (>10 per cent CaO and Al_2O_3): a glass type consequently dubbed 'HLHA'.[42] In addition, compositional evidence suggests that other glasses were imported to Ile-Ife, and that a proportion of these imported glasses was recycled along with the locally produced material, resulting in some glasses with compositions intermediate between the two. High-lime, high-alumina glass dated to the eighth to twelfth centuries has also been identified among those analysed from Igbo-Ukwu, 300 km south-east of Ile-Ife.[43] Three samples of HLHA glasses were also reported from Gao and dated to the eleventh to fourteenth centuries, and two samples from Kissi, dated to the eleventh century at the latest, in addition to a few scattered examples from farther afield.[44]

More recent evidence may also help to shed light on social-historical aspects of glass production practices and the importance of considering the effects of different production practices on the compositional characteristics of the finished glasses. At Nupe, in west-central Nigeria, primary glassmaking was conducted since at least the mid-nineteenth century, from which time it was in the hands of a guild known as the '*masagá*', immigrants to the region of eastern origin, previously suggested to be Egyptian but perhaps more likely from the Kanem-Bornu region, which – as noted by Robertshaw *et al.* – fits well with the observation that the mineral soda used to make glass was imported from around Lake Chad.[45] The glasses were made by combining this mineral soda with local sands, along with a handful of slag from the blacksmith's forge, which was added to the glass-making furnace near the mid-point of the production process resulting in

---

[41] Freestone 2006.   [42] Lankton *et al.* 2006.   [43] Lankton *et al.* 2006, 125–27.
[44] See Lankton *et al.* 2006, 127.   [45] Robertshaw *et al.* 2009b, 83–84.

the characteristically deep black glass known as *bíkini*.[46] In addition, the *masagá* recycled imported European bottle-glass and beads of a range of colours. Eventually, the ready availability of these seems to have had negative consequences for the manufacture of *bíkini* glass. A key compositional feature of the Nupe glasses is their heterogeneity, a likely result of accidental contamination from tools and relatively uncontrolled recycling and mixing: it is noted by Robertshaw *et al.* that 'the glass recovered from the bottom of the furnace was referred to as *bíkini* glass by the *masagá*, but … observations suggested that there could have been variable amounts of recycled glass mixed in with it'.[47]

Material Analysed from South-West Libya

Vessels

The glasses analysed were mainly from excavations in Fazzan, south-west Libya. Over 3,500 fragments of glass have been recovered from excavations and surveys directed by various individuals who worked in the area at different times: the Italian-led excavations of the 1930s;[48] Mohammed Ayoub, 1961–1969; Charles Daniels, 1958–1977;[49] and David Mattingly, with the Fazzan Project, 1997–2001,[50] and Desert Migrations Project, 2007–2011. Most of these glasses remain in Libya, but a small number, from excavations by Charles Daniels, were held in the Trans-SAHARA Project archives at the University of Leicester, and it was these which were sampled and analysed: 83 fragments of vessel glass, 30 fragments of glass bangles, 18 beads, 7 samples of vitreous production waste, 1 'drip' or possible hairpin, 1 'raw' glass chunk and 1 glass stirrer. In addition, 13 vessel and mirror glass fragments from Ghirza in the Libyan pre-desert, and 2 vessel glass fragments from Sabratha on Libya's coast, were also sampled and analysed for comparison.

Bangles

The bangles recovered from Fazzan and analysed in this study are dated on stylistic grounds to between the thirteenth and nineteenth centuries, but

---

[46] Robertshaw *et al.* 2009b, 84.   [47] Robertshaw *et al.* 2009b, 85.

[48] Pace *et al.* 1951, figs 85, 88, 95, 101–4, 106, colour plate III; cf. also Mattingly 2010, 360–61, figs 6.23–6.24.

[49] See Mattingly 2010.   [50] Mattingly 2007; Mattingly 2013.

the tradition of bangle making is much older. Drawn glass canes that could be heated and manipulated to form were in use from the earliest period of vessel making in the latter half of the second millennium BC, and such canes were later used in other ways; including closing them around a mould to form glass bangles, leaving a characteristic seam on the finished object, where the two ends of the cane had come together. The earliest unequivocal evidence for the use of this technology comes from La Tène burials of the later first millennium BC.[51] There is some tentative evidence for the manufacture of glass bangles in India at around the same time.[52]

Also from La Tène contexts is possible evidence for the use of the 'seamless' technique of bangle construction, in which bangles were made by expanding a gob of glass on a rapidly rotating cone-shaped object, or between two sticks.[53] Glass bangles became popular in the Roman world from approximately the third century AD, when darkly coloured, seamed bangles are known.[54] A Byzantine style of glass bangle developed, and was widely imitated (for example, in the Balkans). This style of bangle continued to be made under Islamic rule, but from the seventh century it was made alongside polychrome bangles, which slowly increased in popularity. The greatest expansion of glass bangle production occurred between the thirteenth and fifteenth centuries.[55] Its output is commonly referred to as 'Mamluk', because most of the work to date on bangle typology has taken place in areas that were ruled by the Mamluk dynasty at that time. Most of these later polychrome and monochrome bangles were manufactured using the 'seamless' technique, and this is still employed today in traditional workshops.

As noted, 30 samples of polychrome glass bangle fragments were sampled and analysed (Figure 10.1). All were recovered from the surface collection surveys conducted by Charles Daniels in Fazzan.

The samples analysed form a significant proportion of the total number of bangle fragments recovered from Fazzan, of which there are 67 recorded from the excavations of Charles Daniels and David Mattingly. Glass bangles are rather difficult to date, as few stratified examples are known. The majority of the Fazzan bangles have been suggested to date to between the thirteenth and fifteenth centuries AD, by comparison with the typology produced by Maud Spaer for Palestinian bangles.[56] Their strongest parallels, however, are the less well-dated Saharan bangles illustrated by

[51] Vellani 1996; Nicolas 2012.   [52] See Kanungo and Brill 2009.   [53] Rolland *et al.* 2012.

[54] Spaer 1988, 52; Antonaras and Anagnostopoulou-Chatzipolichoroni 2002.

[55] See Meyer 1992; Shindo 1996, 269; Spaer 1992, 56.   [56] Spaer 1988; 1992.

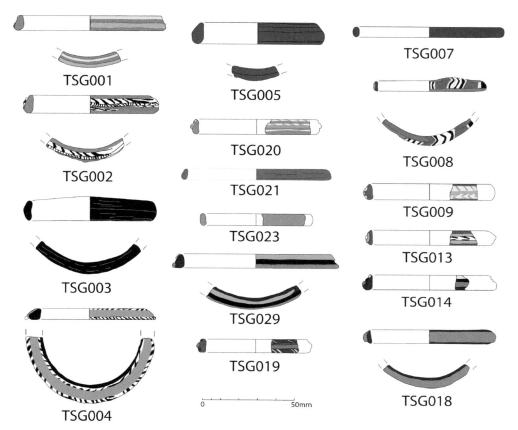

Figure 10.1 Colour illustrations of selected sampled and analysed glass bangles from Fazzan (drawings by Mike Hawkes, University of Leicester).

Théodore Monod from Djado and Azelik (Tadekka) in Niger,[57] which may imply regional production in a widespread technological tradition of bangle making, rather than long-distance trade. Nonetheless, the bangles were clearly traded over long distances. In a Saharan context, glass bangle fragments often turn up in large quantities in oasis sites, the stopping points in Saharan and Trans-Saharan trade. Monod himself collected over five kilograms of bangle fragments at Awjila, a major stopping point on the route from Fustat in Egypt to Zuwila in Fazzan.[58]

Other work on bangles worthy of note includes that of Boulogne,[59] Boulogne and Henderson,[60] Carboni,[61] Meyer,[62] Monod,[63] Shindo[64] and

[57] Monod 1975.   [58] Monod 1975, 707.   [59] Boulogne 2007a; 2007b.
[60] Boulogne and Henderson 2009.   [61] Carboni 1994.   [62] Meyer 1992.
[63] Monod 1978; 1982.   [64] Shindo 1996; 2001.

Spaer.[65] Bangles are also mentioned, sometimes with an accompanying discussion, in various excavation reports. Ten Islamic glass bangles were more recently recovered by the Fazzan Project in Jarma, in contexts dated to various periods from the mid-thirteenth century to the eighteenth to twentieth centuries, and may provide a (very) broad chronological framework for the rest, although they were not available for sampling and analysis. As late as 1821, the accounts of Captain George Lyon included glass bangles among the commodities being traded from Fazzan to West Africa. Indeed, 'according to a number of elderly women in Jarma very similar bangles are still worn by some families, making the [chronological, regional] differentiation of different groups difficult'.[66]

Assessing the meaning or the symbolic and exchange value of bangles is difficult without deeper contextual evidence than we currently possess, although historical accounts allow us access to the later centuries under consideration. European observers seem to have been surprised by the apparent weight of the bangles and other jewellery worn by Saharan women. In her diary, Mrs Tully, sister-in-law to the British consul in Tripoli, who lived there from 1783 to 1795, remarked that the Bedouin living in an oasis outside Tripoli did not 'remove their arm or leg bracelets, nor the earrings, with which they may be said to be weighed down'.[67] This note seems to refer primarily to metal bracelets, particularly of gold and silver. Among the notes compiled by a French surgeon in Tripoli, where he was imprisoned between 1668 and 1676, are descriptions of the dress and abundant jewellery worn by local women, including a note that 'on their arms and legs they wear thick anklets and bracelets which probably weigh a pound'.[68] Antonio Mordini, an Italian scholar of the early twentieth century, noted that the wealthier among the Tuareg in Ghadames wore silver bangles and other jewellery, while poorer women wore leather and glass beads.[69] No mention is made of glass bangles, but it seems that bangles of many different materials could be worn together, as shown in an early twentieth-century image of women from Fazzan presented by Alberini.[70] Certainly, these accounts emphasise that bangles were typically worn by women, as shown in Figure 10.2. The polychromy of glass bangles may have served an apotropaic function, which also fits with their use by women (and possibly also children): the evil eye (*ain*) was believed to be particularly dangerous for younger women, because of their beauty.[71]

---

[65] Spaer 1988; 1992.   [66] Mattingly 2013, 416.   [67] Alberini 1998, 27.   [68] Alberini 1998, 26.
[69] Mordini 1937.   [70] Alberini 1998, 23.   [71] Mordini 1937.

Figure 10.2 Women wearing bangles: (a) Tebu woman wearing multiple bangles of different colours, *c.*1820 (from Lyon 1821); (b) Zuwaya woman wearing jewellery, including what appears to be a metal bangle (from a report on the travels of Rosita Forbes in *The Illustrated London News*, 4 June 1921, 757).

The bangles are clearly much later in date than the other materials discussed here, but they are an important class of artefact, and – as can be seen in the discussion below – their analysis casts a much-needed light on questions such as the life cycle of glass, and the detection of practices such as recycling, which are typically less visible in the archaeological record.

Beads

The prevalence of beads at many African sites, and their potential as proxies for the reconstruction of the routes of trade and contact, makes

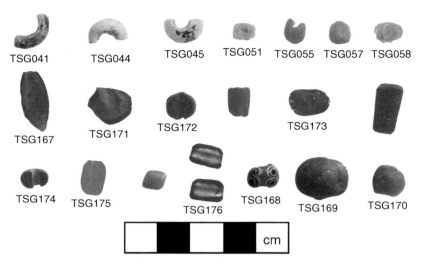

Figure 10.3 Selected bead fragments from Fazzan, subjected to sampling and chemical analysis. The unlabelled beads were not sampled for analysis.

their analysis a priority. Sadly, relatively few beads were available for analysis from the Trans-SAHARA Project archives: of over 824 recorded glass beads or fragments from the excavations of Charles Daniels and David Mattingly in Fazzan, only 18 were available and suitable for sampling and analysis (Fig. 10.3). Several of these were surface finds and thus lacking in precise archaeological context.

One Islamic bead from Ghirza was analysed by micro-XRF at the School of Archaeology and Ancient History, University of Leicester, but the semi-quantitative results were highly distorted by surface corrosion, matrix effects and the limitations of XRF for analysing light elements, and are thus difficult to interpret. They are reported in a previous paper.[72] As noted in that paper, the beads from Zuwila (the quantitative results for four of which are reported here) are especially interesting because they are malformed, and appear to be the product of relatively low-temperature, perhaps unskilled workmanship: they are streaky in appearance and several of them have closed thread-holes or other flaws which render them impossible to string. A series of similar beads seems to have been found in or around Jarma: according to Hoffmann,[73] there are 16 unprovenanced, blue-green opaque cylinder beads in Jarma Museum, all of which either have a partial perforation or no perforation at all.

[72] Duckworth *et al.* 2015b.   [73] Hoffmann 2013b, 720.

It is worth mentioning that some of the beads which were not available for analysis are of well-recognised types and thus provide useful information on changes in long-distance trade routes to Fazzan over time. As noted by Cole, many glass and faience beads at Jarma were probably imported via Egypt or Carthage from farther afield, with material from the Classic Garamantian period including Indo-Pacific beads, thought to have come from Sri Lanka; a layered glass eye-bead (SF1054), segmented bead (SF2196) and two wound beads (SF220, SF2201), all closely paralleled at Carthage; and two beads which may have come from Alexandria (SF2072 and SF953).[74] Some of the later glass beads from Jarma fall into recognised categories of Indian and European trade beads, such as SF923, a Venetian feather bead.

Glass Mirrors

Among the material available for analysis within the context of the Trans-SAHARA Project were several fragments of glass mirrors, and one complete mirror, with some of the backing still intact. The mirror glass was recovered, along with other items including probable wooden mirror boxes, from Building 32 at Ghirza in the Libyan pre-desert (Fig. 10.4). The original construction of the building is dated to between the fourth and sixth centuries, but it was thereafter abandoned and not reoccupied

a   **b**

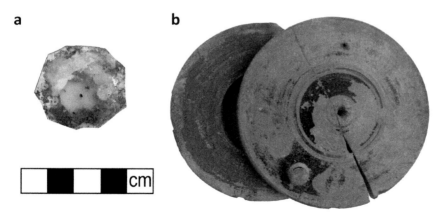

Figure 10.4 Finds from Building 32 at Ghirza: (a) complete, slightly convex glass mirror; (b) painted cedarwood mirror box.

---

[74] Cole 2013, 460–61.

until the tenth century. The second phase of use of the building, which disturbed the earlier contexts, spanned the later tenth and early eleventh centuries. At this time it seems the building was in use as either a shop or a warehouse.[75]

The appearance of the mirrors is consistent with traditional production methods described by Kock and Sode, in which a large bubble of glass is blown, filled with molten lead or tin to provide a thin coating on the interior, cooled and cut.[76] The complete mirror was analysed by non-destructive micro-XRF and the backing material used was found to be lead, with some contamination from an iron-based accretion which may have related to the original housing of the mirror, or have resulted from some other contamination during burial.[77] One of the other mirror fragments was sampled for quantitative analysis, and the results are discussed below.

Materials Indicative of Local Glass Working

A further category is that of vitreous production waste. This category can be subdivided into: partially worked or malformed beads, some of which were analysed and are reported here; a chunk of raw glass in Jarma Museum, of unknown provenance, and another chunk from Saniat Jibril which was analysed; a piece of glass, which has previously been interpreted as a 'drip' or 'spill', from Zinkekra; some fragments of glass 'slag', found at Zinkekra, as well as pellets and pieces cut from a glass rod, all unstratified; and 19 stratified fragments of unformed vitreous waste or glass drops, several adhering to ceramics, and all found at Jarma.

Jarma Production Waste

Nine examples of what seem to be fragments of glass production waste were recovered from Jarma during the 1997–2001 Fazzan Project excavations, and are reported by Hoffmann.[78] These come from Phase 2 (AD 1250–1650, 1 fragment), Phase 5 (AD 400–850, 2 fragments), Phase 6 (AD 180–400, 4 fragments), Phase 6/7 (AD 100–200, 1 fragment) and Phase 7 (AD 50–150, 1 fragment). It is notable that the dates are for the most part consistent with the typological dates suggested for the peak imports of glass wares in the Classic Garamantian era. It is also possible, indeed likely, given the similarities between many of the fragments, that the material from the

[75] Brogan and Smith 1984, 81.   [76] Kock and Sode 2002.   [77] Duckworth *et al.* 2015b.
[78] Hoffmann 2013b, 721.

more recent phases was residual, and that the activities which resulted in this vitreous waste material all took place in the Classic Garamantian periods.

These remains, although unavailable for analysis, are the only ones to provide unequivocal evidence for the high-temperature working of glass in Fazzan in the first millennium AD. The adherence of vitreous production waste to locally produced ceramics demonstrates beyond reasonable doubt that some kind of activity was taking place at a temperature high enough to fuse a vitreous, silica-based substance onto a pottery sherd. The evidence does not seem to fit the model we might expect from accidental melting (for example, due to a building fire), which usually results in complete but deformed objects. It was taking place at temperatures hot enough to make the glass 'splash' onto the sherd.

The most notable 'splashed' examples are illustrated in Figure 10.5a and b. Both were found at Jarma in levels of Phase 6 date, AD 180–400, and are briefly described by Hoffmann, who examined them. Of Figure 10.5b she said: 'Body sherd of handmade local pottery (fabric 1). Globular vessel? On inside splash of dark blue glass and knocked off trail? Also white splashes of unknown substance. Dims 77 × 61, Th 7 [mm]'.[79] Although I was unable to re-examine theses sherds, some interesting deductions can be made. The 'trail' is not clearly visible on the photograph, but its presence as described by Hoffmann suggests that some tool may have been used to draw out the glass, in possible (but admittedly rather tentative) evidence for working. The white patches in the photograph, described by Hoffmann as an 'unknown substance', could be a glass frit, a calcareous material or even mineral soda (natron), which was locally available in Fazzan.

This evidence does not, of course, demonstrate that people in Fazzan were able to melt glass in crucibles, or necessarily to form glass beads. What it does provide is an important clue regarding the way they engaged with the material. They may have imported Roman glass vessels and traded in glass beads, but they were also aware that glass could be manipulated at high temperature. At the very least they were experimenting with such manipulation, but they may have been doing much more.

Analysed Production Waste

Analysis of the samples of vitreous waste that were available in Leicester was thus undertaken with the intention of identifying whether any of this

---

[79] Hoffmann 2013b, 721.

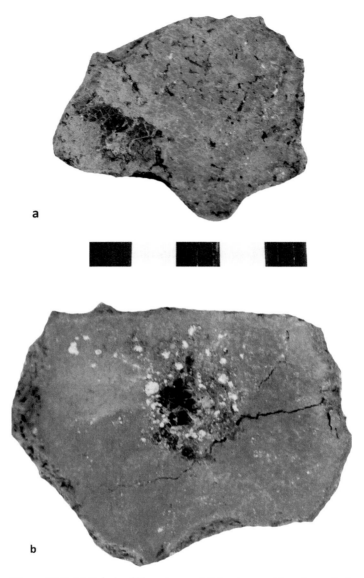

Figure 10.5 (a) Splash of blue glass and (b) unknown blue glass splash and white substance on two sherds of local, handmade pottery. Excavated in Jarma, late second to fourth century AD.

material could have been recycled Roman glass; whether there were any indications of primary production using local ingredients; and whether the vitreous waste showed any chemical signs of being related to beads found in any of the areas connected by the Sahara.

Figure 10.6 (a) An example of the semi-fused, heterogeneous vitreous production waste from Ayoub's 'Building 1' in Jarma; (b) the glass chunk from Saniat Jibril; (c) the glass 'drip' from Zinkekra.

Ten fragments of semi-fused and heterogeneous glassy production waste from the excavations of Charles Daniels were analysed, an example of which is shown in Figure 10.6a. They are in various shades of dark, cloudy green, adhering to (and sometimes incorporating) a buff-coloured, fine-grained ceramic material. They came from Building 1, Ayoub's 'Building A' in Jarma, from a pit feature filled with ash and 'mortar lumps' (GER001.001 10), cut into by a hearth feature (GER001.001 7).[80] A thicker glassy fragment, adhering to a flattish lump of the same ceramic material (TSG150), came from the context directly below (GER001.001 16) and was associated with some Flavian Cypriot Sigillata (Hayes 1b). It is reasonably likely that all ten available fragments were the result of the same production activity, given the similarity in colour and in the buff-coloured ceramic to which they adhere. Of the ten fragments of vitreous waste analysed, only those with up to 74.12 per cent SiO_2 have been included in the results presented below. The other samples have much higher SiO_2 and lower Na_2O: if these fragments were the remains of deliberate glass production and not some other process they must have been semi-fused or failed attempts.

Raw Glass Chunk

The chunk of glass analysed was found in the manufacturing site of Saniat Jibril (Figure 10.6b). Glass chunks – many of which were much larger than

---

[80] Mattingly 2013, 73–86.

this – were transported from primary production centres across the Mediterranean to secondary production centres where they could be remelted and worked into objects at temperature (for example, by glass-blowing). The presence of this chunk in Saniat Jibril alongside the remains of a range of production activities, many of them associated with bead making, implies that the Garamantes were working glass in some form. It does not, however, necessarily imply the hot-working of glass, as it would also be possible to grind beads from a glass chunk using 'cold-working' techniques, such as those employed in shaping carnelian (a slightly harder material than soda-lime-silica glass).

A second chunk of glass, of unknown provenance, is in Jarma Museum.[81] It is a different colour to this one – a dark, 'yellow brown' according to Hoffmann's assessment – suggesting that chunks of glass may have been taken to Jarma with more frequency than previously acknowledged. A much larger chunk is on display in the Hotel Zumit, Tripoli, shown in Figure 10.7. It has never been sampled and analysed, but it may well be an example of raw Roman glass. As noted by David Hill, large lumps of glass such as this one, once taken to shore, would not have travelled far before being further broken down, due to their bulk and weight.[82] Given the hotel's coastal location, it is possible that the lump was cargo in a shipwreck, although its unweathered appearance may suggest otherwise.

Glass 'Drip'

The bulbous end of the 'drip' (Figure 10.6c) is similar to some fragments of glass still in Jarma, notably six possible hairpins, identified by Birgitta Hoffmann.[83] Three of these are of similar size but only survive to a very short length, so it is not possible to tell whether they are truly comparable with this object. The other hairpins are thinner, and in two of them the drawn part leading out from the bulbous end survives, and is slender and straight.[84] In our analysed fragment, the drawn part is slightly curved, and rather thick by comparison. On the other hand, it does not show any signs of tapering to a point as one might expect of a 'drip' or 'spill' from glassworking activities. It is thus unclear whether this is a fragment of a broken object, a drip from glassworking activities or simply a malformed hairpin, stirrer or similar type.

---

[81] Hoffmann 2013b, 720.
[82] Special thanks are due to Caroline Lawrence, who very kindly provided me with her photograph of the raw glass lump in Hotel Zumit, Tripoli, and to David Hill for bringing it to my attention in the first place.
[83] Hoffmann 2013b, 717–18.   [84] Hoffmann 2013b, 718, fig. 24.4.

Figure 10.7 The 'raw' glass lump in Hotel Zumit, Tripoli. It is approximately the size of a football, as shown in the image on the right (Images courtesy of Caroline Lawrence of Roman Mysteries Ltd).

Analytical Methodology

The glasses were first analysed using electron probe microanalysis (EPMA) in collaboration with Victoria Smith at the Research Laboratory for Archaeology and the History of Art, University of Oxford. Quantitative analysis was performed using a JEOL-8600 wavelength dispersive electron microprobe with 15 kV accelerating voltage, 7 nA current and 10 μm diameter beam (the relatively small beam diameter used may have been behind low readings for some of the more corroded glasses that are omitted from this study). Peak counting times were 20 s for Ca and K; 30 s for Si, Al and Mg; 40 s for Fe; 50 s for Cl, Mn and Pb; 60 s for Sn and Sb; and 80 s for P and Cu. The microprobe was calibrated using a suite of mineral standards, and quantified using the PAP absorption correction method. The accuracy of the electron microprobe analyses was assessed using Corning reference glasses and the values are reported elsewhere.[85] Each result presented in this chapter is the mean of three spot analyses.

Following microprobe analysis, the glasses were further subjected to laser ablation inductively coupled plasma mass spectrometry (LA-ICP-MS), conducted in collaboration with Simon Chenery at the Centre for

---

[85] Duckworth *et al.* 2016b.

Environmental Geochemistry, British Geological Survey, Keyworth. The instrument consists of a NewWave FX 193 nm excimer laser with integral microscope and ablation cell coupled to an Agilent 7500c series ICP-MS using a He gas flow. The instrument was calibrated using SRM610 glass (NIST, USA), and quality was assessed using SRM612 and Corning glass. Initial comparisons with the EPMA data have shown good agreement for most elements between the two techniques, although as might be expected there is some discrepancy between the results for those elements which are heterogeneously dispersed in the glass (for example, lead or tin).

Analytical Results

Results are presented in Tables 10.1, 10.2 and 10.3 in Appendix 10.1, reporting the physical characteristics and archaeological context of the glass, and the EPMA and LA-ICP-MS results, respectively. The analysis and interpretation of the glass bangles is reported elsewhere.[86]

The trace element results for the full dataset were only available shortly after my contract with the Trans-SAHARA Project expired, and I have not yet been able to do justice to the complexity of these. I have decided nonetheless to publish the full set of data here, so that other researchers may access it in the meantime.

Roman Vessel Glass

One of the aims of analysis was to identify compositional groups within the Roman vessel glass which was found in Sabratha, Ghirza and the sites in Fazzan. Of 83 fragments of vessel glass analysed, four were removed as outliers, either due to corrosion effects (TSG112, TSG123 and TSG124) or – in one case – because the fragment was deemed to be modern (TSG077).

As shown in Figure 10.8, almost all fragments of vessel glasses were found to be compositionally consistent with those produced in the Hellenistic and Roman tradition; that is, glasses made with a mineral alkali that has low magnesia (MgO) and potash (K_2O).

The vessel glasses were subdivided into established Roman compositional groups using the reference group parameters set by Gliozzo *et al.*,[87] which were based on the collated results of previously published sets of data, as shown in Figure 10.9. Figure 10.10 illustrates these groups divided by broad date categories. Broadly speaking, the diachronic compositional

---

[86] Duckworth *et al.* 2016a.   [87] Gliozzo *et al.* 2013.

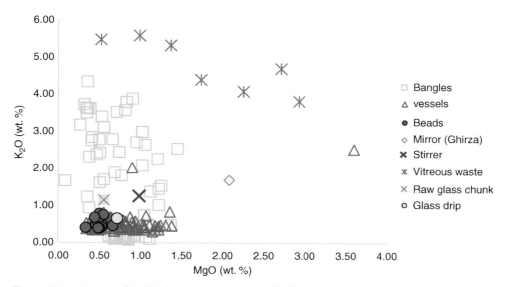

Figure 10.8 Magnesia (MgO) plotted against potash (K₂O) for all samples. Based on
EPMA results. Glasses made with a mineral source of alkali have low MgO and K₂O
(typically under 1.5 per cent of each), and are clustered in the bottom left of the plot.

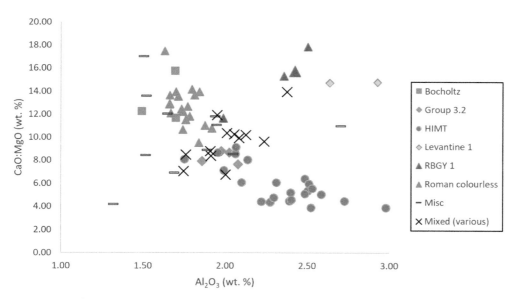

Figure 10.9 Alumina (Al₂O₃) plotted against the ratio of CaO:MgO. Based on EPMA
results. Groups based on Gliozzo *et al.* (2013). The distinction between the high iron,
manganese, titanium glass (HIMT) and Roman colourless glasses can be clearly seen.
The miscellaneous (uncategorised) glasses are shown as blue dashes, and the glasses
thought to be a mix between two or more compositional groups are shown as black 'X's.

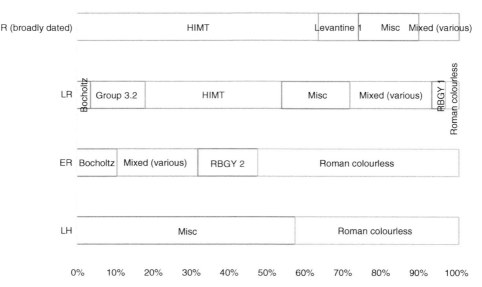

Figure 10.10 The vessel glass groups plotted by broad date brackets. Dates are based on typology and/or archaeological context (groups based on Gliozzo *et al.* 2013). R (broadly dated) = Roman (broadly dated) (n=19); LR = Late Roman (n=28); ER = Early Roman (n=19); LH = Late Hellenistic (n=7).

changes within the Fazzan assemblage follow those encountered in glasses from within the Roman world: these results are discussed further below. Several of the vessel glasses have been interpreted as being of mixed composition, falling between two or more of the well-defined compositional groups. These are indicated simply as 'mixed (various)' in the plots. Glasses that do not fit clearly into any groups, and do not show clear indications of mixed composition, are labelled 'misc'.

As can be seen in Figure 10.9, the mixed composition glasses tend to fall between the established compositional groups. This implies either mixing of differently composed glasses or recycling (melting together used and broken objects, with or without additional newly made, 'raw' glass). One way to establish a strong likelihood that glasses are the result of recycling is to look at the presence of 'decolourants' (manganese and antimony) that served to counter the colouring effects of impurities such as iron in the raw ingredients for glassmaking. There would be little reason for mixing the two different decolourants together deliberately, so it can be reasonably assumed that elevated manganese *and* antimony is indicative of recycling practice, in which glasses of various compositions were remelted together.

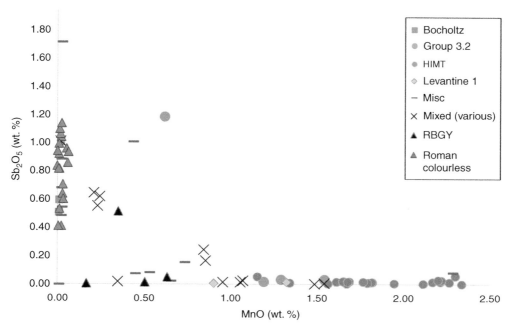

Figure 10.11 Manganese oxide (MnO) plotted against antimony oxide (Sb_2O_5) for the Roman vessel glasses, divided by compositional group.

In a plot of manganese (MnO) against antimony (Sb_2O_5) for the Roman vessel glasses (Figure 10.11), it is immediately apparent that some of the samples fit this model, containing both elevated antimony and manganese (these are visible in the plot as any samples *not* clinging to either the 'X' or 'Y' axis). Several of the glasses that were deemed to be of mixed composition fall into this group, while a few others seem to have been mixed from two or more compositional groups that were alike in using manganese as a decolourant. Several of the 'miscellaneous' glasses also plot here, and it is possible that these were the result of mixing several different compositional types.

Beads and Vitreous Waste

The beads and vitreous waste, like the vessel glasses, are compositionally consistent with production using a mineral alkali. The aqua/greenish colour of the Zuwila beads results from their Fe_2O_3 and CuO contents, which are higher than those of most of the vessel glasses.

Given that we know manufacturing activities occurred at Saniat Jibril, the question arises as to whether we can see any evidence for the recycling

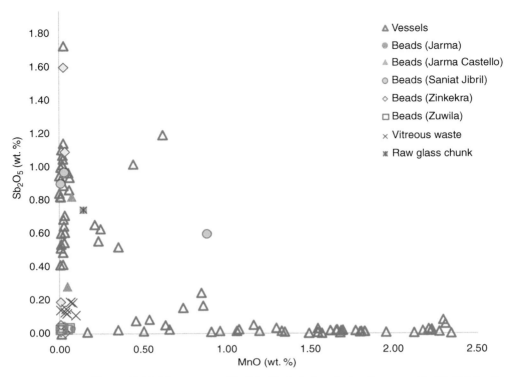

Figure 10.12 Manganese oxide (MnO) plotted against antimony oxide (Sb$_2$O$_5$) for the Roman vessel glasses, the various beads, the glass chunk and the vitreous waste. Samples with >2 per cent Sb$_2$O$_5$ were omitted, as the antimony was intentionally added in these cases as a colourant-opacifier.

or reuse of imported Roman vessel glass. While the beads from Zuwila are compositionally distinct from the Roman vessel glasses, there is some indication that beads from Saniat Jibril and Zinkekra may have been either manufactured in the Roman world or made in Fazzan from imported, and remelted or recycled, Roman glass. As shown in Figure 10.12, two glass fragments found in Saniat Jibril – the green portion of a bead (TSG172_grntint) and the glass chunk (TSG151) – have slightly elevated manganese *and* antimony, indicative of manufacture due to recycling (see above). That this may have taken place within Fazzan is tantalisingly hinted at by the mixed composition of the chunk of glass from Saniat Jibril, although it must also be acknowledged that this chunk of glass could have been mixed elsewhere and imported into Fazzan. Regardless of this, the combined evidence for hot-working of glass in Fazzan, particularly the splashes of glass on local pottery sherds, and the fact that several fragments of glass vessel cullet (scrap, broken vessel glass) were encountered in Saniat Jibril, lend weight to the hypothesis that glass beads were manufactured there. In light of this, the presence of both beads and unworked glass that have compositions consistent with recycled Roman vessel glass should be considered as possible evidence for glass bead making within Fazzan.

Several beads were found to have been coloured and opacified by lead-antimonate: TSG044, an opaque yellow ring bead; the opaque yellow decoration of polychrome bead TSG175; and lead-tin opacifiers in TSG051, an opaque green bead. Because antimony, lead and tin are rather heterogeneously distributed within opaque glass, and therefore may differ depending on which area of a sample was analysed, the reader is advised to consult both the EPMA and the LA-ICP-MS results in Tables 10.2 and 10.3. Lead-antimonates have been used as opacifiers since the sixteenth century BC; lead-tin opacifier (lead stannate) was first used in Europe from the second to first centuries BC, and again throughout the later Roman and Byzantine Empires from the fourth century AD onwards.[88]

All four unstratified beads from Zuwila contained elevated lead: the EPMA results show 0.93–4.91 per cent PbO, which is consistent with XRF findings for similar beads from Zuwila that could not be subjected to destructive sampling, as reported in an earlier article.[89] By contrast, all but three vessel glasses (TSG079, TSG119 and TSG128, with <0.45 per cent PbO) contained low lead (<0.16 per cent PbO), although the levels of lead in the beads are consistent with those found in several of the bangles and the mirror from Ghirza.

The vitreous waste from Fazzan is rather heterogeneous in composition, and it does not provide a clear compositional match for any of the other glasses analysed. As seen in Figure 10.8, the amount of magnesia measured varied widely, from 0.53 to 2.92 per cent MgO. The potassium oxide content, on the other hand, was consistently rather high, at 3.8–5.56 per cent K_2O, which could be indicative of the use of plant ashes as an alkali in the higher-magnesia glasses (TSG146–150) but which is more difficult to interpret in the low-magnesia glasses (TSG144 and TSG145), as discussed below. The amount of calcium also varies widely between the vitreous waste samples analysed to date, whereas the alumina is rather high (5.2–9.05 per cent Al_2O_3). The glasses also contain a significant iron impurity (0.91–3.63 per cent Fe_2O_3).

It is worth at least considering the possibility that the vitreous waste in Fazzan was the result of local primary production. Fazzan itself was a

---

[88] Tite *et al.* 2008.   [89] Duckworth *et al.* 2015b.

potential source of mineral alkali suitable for glass production, as discussed by Devulder *et al.*,[90] and analyses of samples of this material from Lake Trona, to the north of the Wadi al-Ajal, have revealed a wide variation in potassium oxide.[91] Local sands have been reported to be fairly mature, quartzitic sands, with a modest grain coating of amorphous iron oxides and silicates,[92] which might explain the iron and alumina content of the glasses. It could also help to explain the low calcium content, which we would expect of a glass made from mineral alkali and inland sand. Perhaps the best we can say is that, on the present state of the evidence, local glassmaking remains a possibility. In any case, it should be borne in mind that vitreous waste will not always be compositionally representative of the finished products being made at a site: the very presence of vitreous production remains in the archaeological record more often than not testifies to their failure and consequent discard.

Saharan Glass Bangles and the Question of Recycling

The following is a summary of the interpretation of the chemical results obtained by analysis of the glass bangles.[93] Fragments of 30 bangles were analysed, but because most of these are polychrome this amounted to 66 samples.

All analysed bangle fragments fall into the compositional range of silica glasses made with a soda flux, with 14.68–22.61 per cent soda (Na_2O^*) and 64.94–74.92 per cent silica (SiO_2^*) (asterisks indicate that the results shown were normalised to 100 per cent following removal of oxides associated primarily with colouring). Lime content varies greatly from one bangle to another (1.07–10.47 per cent CaO^*). In addition, the samples exhibit a broad range of lead contents (from trace to 34.1 per cent PbO, with 41 samples containing >1 per cent PbO).

The iron content of the bangles from Fazzan is relatively low, with only three samples having >1 per cent Fe_2O_3. Alumina contents range from 0.85–2.21 per cent Al_2O_3, and the highest alumina was found in the same three samples with >1 per cent Fe_2O_3. These quantities of iron, and its correlation with alumina, imply that the bangles were made using an intentionally purified or relatively mature sand source. There is a broad correlation between elements associated with the silica source (iron, aluminium, titanium) and those associated with the source of lime

---

[90] Devulder *et al.* 2014.   [91] Duckworth *et al.* 2016b; Fabri 2013.
[92] Kevin White, personal communication.
[93] For the full analytical interpretation and tables of results, see Duckworth *et al.* 2016a.

(magnesium, calcium), so it is likely that the lime was introduced along with the silica.[94]

Strontium (Sr), which as noted above is an important indicator for the source of lime in glasses, was far from consistent in these samples, ranging from 24.73 to 397 ppm (unsurprisingly, in the bangle with the highest lime content). Freestone *et al.* note that coastal sands tend to have heavy mineral assemblages low in zircon (*c.*60 ppm), although examples from Carthage may have both high zirconium (*c.*160 ppm) and high strontium, perhaps indicative of the use of a non-Levantine sand source coupled with marine shell as a source of calcium.[95] The bangles exhibit a very different calcium to strontium ratio from that of the Roman vessel glass, due to the fact that lime in Roman vessel glasses was derived from seashells in coastal sands (see above). Exceptions are TSG005, 021, 025 and 030, all of which are monochrome, and the two colours of TSG022. Limestone, having undergone diagenesis, has a higher Ca:Sr ratio than seashells, and it could have entered the glass through an inland sand source. As shown in Figure 10.13, most of the Roman vessel glasses can be seen to cluster around the high-strontium, low-zirconium brackets established by Freestone *et al.*[96] The low strontium of the bangles is combined with variable zirconium. The low strontium in both waste glasses and bangles *could* be indicative of Saharan production using non-coastal sands, but the evidence is far from conclusive at present, and it should be noted that the waste glasses have exceptionally low lime.

The relatively low concentration of other impurities not directly associated with colouration, particularly magnesia (0.08–1.45 per cent MgO), suggests that the soda was derived from a soda-rich mineral, rather than from the halophytic plant ashes with their characteristic impurities, notably lime, magnesia and potash (see above). The potash content of several bangle fragments, however, is relatively high – up to 4.8 per cent K_2O^*. Similar results were found by Boulogne and Henderson, for Mamluk- to Ottoman-period Jordanian bangles.[97] A high K_2O:MgO ratio was also a feature of several of the fragments of vitreous waste recovered from first millennium AD contexts at Jarma (see Fig. 10.8).

Boron (B) is a common element in evaporite sequences, so it can be a useful marker of the source of soda in glasses. The analytical results indicated that B is present in elevated but relatively consistent traces throughout the sample set (55–146 ppm B), which could imply the use of

---

[94] See Duckworth *et al.* 2016a, 148.   [95] Freestone *et al.* 2000.   [96] Freestone *et al.* 2000.
[97] Boulogne and Henderson 2009.

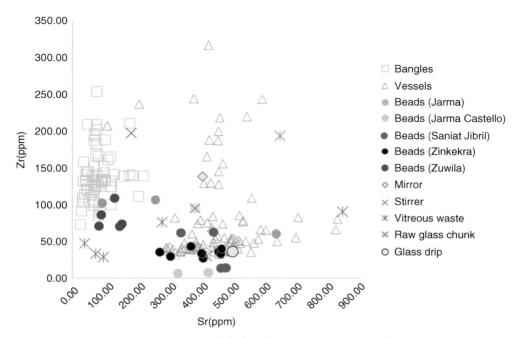

Figure 10.13 Strontium (Sr) plotted against zirconium (Zr) for the analysed dataset.

the same soda source for all the bangles. The boron levels of the bangles are within the lower range of those encountered in Roman glass (the Roman vessel glasses from Fazzan have 13–279 ppm B). The unstratified beads from Zuwila once again share similarities with the bangles in this regard, having consistently low boron between 53.1 and 61.2 ppm; the beads from Saniat Jibril and Jarma are – as might be expected – variable, but within the Roman range (49.5–279.3 ppm B).

Various colourants, both deliberately added and present as contaminants, were used in the bangles. These include 'natural' colourants (mainly iron) present as impurities in the raw ingredients; manganese, which was primarily responsible for dark glasses of black appearance; lead or tin, which produced opaque white glasses; and lead combined with either tin or antimony, which produced opaque glasses in shades of yellow, orange and (when associated, for example, with copper) green.

Most of the bangles exhibited heterogeneous features both macroscopically and under optical and electron microscopy. These included streaks and patches of different colours, or variation in the hue or translucence of the glass, and numerous air bubbles. These features are indicative of low-temperature mixing of one or more glasses, or of low-temperature addition of colourants to a glass batch.

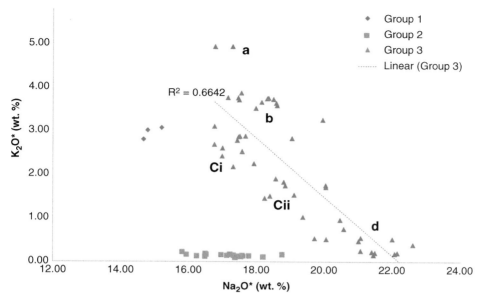

Figure 10.14 Soda (Na_2O) plotted against potash (K_2O), using normalised EPMA results (excluding colourants). The letters a–d refer to Group 3 subgroups.

The bangles can be divided broadly between three compositional groups, as shown in a plot of the two main alkalis (soda and potash) in Figure 10.14.[98] Except for TSG013, all of the colours in each bangle fall within the same groups, confirming the robustness of the groupings. Furthermore, the different colours within a single bangle are chemically similar for elements not directly associated with their colouration, and there are certain stylistic similarities within the groups.[99]

Much of the patterning in the data, however, is indicative of gradual changes between samples, rather than clearly demarcated compositional groups, with the exception of compositional Group 1 which consists of just three colours of glass from a single bangle (TSG001). Groups 2 and 3 are distinguished by their different quantities and ratios of alkali oxides ($Na_2O^* + K_2O^*$): <19 per cent alkali in Group 2 and >19 per cent alkali in Group 3. The Group 3 samples fall along an apparent mixing line between soda (Na_2O) and potash (K_2O), which are negatively correlated for this group. By contrast, the samples in Group 2 are unanimously low in potash (<0.22 per cent K_2O). Other attempts to divide the glasses into

---

[98] These groups are discussed in more detail in Duckworth *et al.* 2016a, 151–53, where an explanation of the sub-groups (a, b, ci, cii and d) can also be found.

[99] See Duckworth *et al.* 2016a, 152.

clearly demarcated groups were unsuccessful. For the rare earth elements (REEs), the Group 2 and 3 bangles shared a negative europium (Eu) anomaly in relation to crustal abundance, but were extremely heterogeneous for the heavier REEs and could vary significantly even within a single bangle. It is likely that the REEs had been affected by several factors, including the mixing of different glasses, mixed raw materials and the addition of colourants.

Discussion, Synthesis and Contextualisation

Trade Routes

If we are to reconstruct the direction from which glass entered Fazzan in the Garamantian period, we might consider the proportion of the identified glass groups at different sites in Libya. This is most clearly apparent for the later Roman glasses, over a third of which are of the HIMT composition, thought to have been made in Egypt. In attempting to trace trade routes, we can make a broad division between late Roman vessel glass from Sabratha on the coast (two samples, both HIMT), Ghirza in the Libyan pre-desert (12 samples, 5 HIMT, 3 Group 3.2, 4 of mixed composition) and the various sites in Fazzan (14 samples, 4 HIMT, one Group 3.2 and several of varying compositions, including some mixed). Of 24 samples of glass that could only be dated broadly as 'Roman' by their typology or archaeological context, 12 are HIMT, which dates them by comparison to the later Roman period.

These results are relatively few and thus difficult to interpret. As a new glass industry opened up in Egypt, we might expect that some of this material reached Fazzan, but it is not clear whether it did so via direct trade routes across the desert or via the coast, reaching Fazzan after travelling (by direct or indirect routes) through places such as Sabratha and Ghirza. The evidence to date is not incompatible with either scenario. In her typological assessment, Birgitta Hoffmann noted that the later glass assemblage shows more Egyptian influence, whereas the glass vessels from the first two centuries AD have more affinity with the western Roman Empire (although her assertion that the consignments of glass from the first and second centuries AD arrived directly from Italy may be less easy to support).[100] In any case, from a compositional perspective this is still a rather small sample upon which to base any interpretation: more data are needed on Roman and other glasses in North Africa.

---

[100] Hoffmann 2013a, 417–18.

Recycling and Modification

Recycling of glass requires less fuel, as it can be achieved at more modest temperatures than those required for its primary fusion. Thus, glass recycling could be achieved at lower cost and with less advanced pyrotechnological know-how than glassmaking, regardless of the knowledge of recipes and raw ingredients themselves. In many cases it may have been simply more efficient to recycle imported glass than to manufacture it locally from raw materials.

Reuse of a material may take several forms. Because glass can be made in one location, transported to another and remelted, we must be careful to distinguish between remelting of glass to work it into shape and recycling using fragments of broken glass objects (known as cullet). Powder-glass beads are made by placing ground glass into clay moulds, firing and then (sometimes) regrinding the edges.[101] This technique would have allowed recycling of imported glass, possibly from many different sources, with less need for compositional predictability than that demanded by hot-working. It should be emphasised that any heating of glass, whether it involves mixing of glasses from different sources or not, affects the chemical composition and appearance of the glass, for example, via the loss of some elements by volatilisation, contamination by fuels and tools, and the reduction or oxidation of the glass in the furnace atmosphere. Recycling can also affect the composition by the mixing of glasses with different chemical characteristics.

I suggest that the compositional patterning noticed in the thirteenth- to nineteenth-century bangles from Fazzan is the result of recycling practice. The dataset is characterised by compositional gradations (notably CaO, PbO and K_2O), indicating that although they are part of a single broad compositional group (soda glass with low impurities and added colourants), they have been subject to numerous manipulations, possibly involving both recombination (that is, recycling) and the addition of raw ingredients to preformed glasses in later stages of production.[102] It is further suggested that the bangles are recycling end products: glasses that, due to repeated mixing, were typically strongly coloured (masking any ill effects of mixing) and worked into simple forms. The addition of lead to many of the bangles would also have helped to lower the working temperature. As the bangle glasses were now highly coloured, and compositionally

---

[101] Sprague 1985, 97.   [102] Duckworth *et al.* 2016a, 153.

rather heterogeneous, they could not be recycled further, and when they broke were unceremoniously dumped, sometimes in large quantities.

In the context of African glass bead production, a third category of reuse should be distinguished: that of modification – but not full remelting – of existing beads. Davison *et al.* note stretch marks and surface opacity as possible markers of heat alteration of imported dichroic beads in West Africa from the eighteenth century or later,[103] and other reports of bead modification are known.[104] One-quarter of the 800 beads recovered from the 2001–2002 and 2009 excavations at Gao Saney were 'melted, malformed or unfinished and may represent glass-manufacturing debris': the glass beads are thought to have been cut from drawn canes and heated on a flat surface to smooth the ends.[105] Within the sample set analysed here, a drawn glass cane is included in the group of malformed glass beads from Zuwila, Fazzan, which was analysed by XRF. Modification of existing beads or drawn glass canes could thus provide one explanation for the malformed appearance of the glass beads from Zuwila, although their streaky appearance suggests that, even if their distorted shapes were the result of heat modification, these beads are also the result of recycling. Similar examples crop up in a range of contexts. For example, specimen 5528 from Jenné-jeno, a plant ash glass coloured by cobalt and bronze and dated AD 300–800, appears to have been modified at relatively low temperature, 'by someone not very experienced in the handling of hot glass'.[106]

Cold-working of existing beads is also a possibility, and lapidary techniques are often encountered as a means of modifying glass objects in other regions of the world. There is abundant evidence of the working of stone beads in and around Jarma. Carnelian was worked into beads at Jarma and its satellite settlement of Saniat Jibril and it may have been heat-treated as well as cold-worked, as evidenced by the range of shades of carnelian chippings found in Jarma. Bead grinders were used to rough out the shapes of ostrich eggshell and carnelian beads and over 100 fragments of bead grinders have been identified from Classic Garamantian levels at Saniat Jibril.[107]

One problem with studying glass recycling from a chemical perspective is that it is arguably more likely to effect composition when practised on a relatively small, haphazard scale, due to the greater chance of contaminants entering the glass, or mixing between different compositions,[108] but that it

[103] Davison *et al.* 1971.   [104] For example, Bowdich 1819.   [105] Cissé *et al.* 2013, 27.
[106] Brill 1995, 255.   [107] Cole 2013, 456–61.
[108] See for example Robertshaw *et al.* 2009b and the discussion of this paper above.

is analytically most traceable when dealing with large datasets. This is in part because recycling is only chemically detectable where we are able to identify 'end-members' (the original glasses of different composition which are mixed to produce a compositionally intermediate glass).

This being the case, the clearest chemical evidence we have for recycling among the Libyan glasses, with the exception of the bangles, comes from the Roman vessel glass (see above, and Figures 10.8–10.12), which can be contextualised within widely accepted compositional categories of Mediterranean glasses and which is consistent with both chemical and literary evidence for this practice from at least the later first century AD.[109]

Production Locations

Glass production, especially when practised on a small scale, can leave surprisingly few traces in the archaeological record. In fact, as noted above, the transmutability of glass means that the remains found at workshop sites are equally, if not more likely, to relate to failed glasses that for whatever reason could not be remelted and used.

An ongoing assumption of compositional analysis is that there is something like a 'standard' composition for a particular workshop at a given time. This assumption works rather well when dealing with the mass production of glass for vessel blowing, because mass production operated on a large scale, and because the glassblower needed to have a clear understanding of the properties of the glass (s)he is working with (this is one reason that glass cullet for recycling may have been quite well sorted, at least in the Roman Mediterranean). It is also the case that much glass may have been produced according to a 'partial batch melting model', in which the glass formed will have a composition determined by the eutectic, meaning that diverse production processes could have led to compositionally very similar outcomes.[110] When we are talking about the small-scale production of glass for bead or bangle making, however, we might allow for a somewhat higher degree of compositional variability. The use of unrefined raw materials from more than one location, lower furnace temperatures and the recycling of pre-made glasses of varying compositions, could

---

[109] See Silvestri 2008, 1489.   [110] Rehren 2000.

all lead to compositional heterogeneity between glasses from the same workshop and even within a single object.

The vitreous waste from Fazzan has a highly heterogeneous composition and is difficult to interpret, although a planned programme of isotope analysis may provide more clues as to whether it is the result of the fusion of locally sourced raw ingredients. The high soda content (10.15–14.26 per cent Na_2O) of the vitreous waste supports the interpretation that it was a man-made glass rather than a by-product of some other activity, and it is also true that all such fragments were found in Jarma and Saniat Jibril, sites which have also provided evidence for other productive activities including metalworking and carnelian working.[111] Bead furnaces themselves, generally small and temporary, would not necessarily leave an archaeological trace. It should also be noted that glass could have been melted and adapted for other purposes: recent work at Essouk-Tadmakka, for example, has uncovered evidence for the use of a glass flux – probably made from crushed glass beads – in gold-refining activities.[112]

If glass production (whether primary or secondary) was taking place in Fazzan during the Classic Garamantian and Islamic periods, it is reasonable to consider what fuel would have been available to reach the required temperatures. Primary soda-lime-silica glass production requires temperatures in the region of 1,100°C, broadly similar to those required for copper smelting, and experimental work has demonstrated that the attainment of such temperatures could consume a significant amount of fuel. Following replication and experimental firing of a Late Bronze Age furnace from Amarna, Egypt, Nicholson and Jackson report that 380 kg of dry wood fuel (consisting of palm rib, pine and eucalyptus) was required to fire a furnace with an internal diameter of 1.5 m and containing two differently sized crucibles of glass, for 8 hours and 50 minutes, up to a maximum temperature of 1,150°C, which was reached after 6 hours and 20 minutes.[113] A temperature of 1,100°C, probably sufficient to cause fusion of the glass, was maintained for a full four hours. Aside from the fuel, the furnace charge consisted of just 860 cm^3 of ground glass-forming raw materials split between the two crucibles, although Nicholson and Jackson felt that the yield could be significantly improved by 'topping up' the crucibles during firing.[114]

---

[111] Cole 2013, 459.   [112] Rehren and Nixon 2014.   [113] Nicholson and Jackson 2007, 94–97.
[114] Nicholson and Jackson 2007, 98.

It is possible, indeed likely, that glass production activities in Fazzan used smaller structures than that described above, which would presumably consume less fuel. Nonetheless, the amount of fuel required to produce even a small amount of glass could be considerable and a potential obstacle to pyrotechnological activities in a desert environment. One possibility is that animal dung was used. Experiments by Kenoyer demonstrated the efficacy of dried dung cakes as fuel in small-scale semi-industrial activities: it was found that herbivorous dung could attain temperatures of 1,095°C in one hour and 20 minutes.[115] Pelling notes that evidence for fodder and forage was present in the archaeobotanical record from Jarma, which implies either the stabling and penning of animals within the site, or the deliberate collection of dung, including possible indicators for camel dung in phases 6 and 7 (AD 50–400) and the presence of sheep and goat droppings mixed with chaff and animal penning waste in a context (358) associated with a bread oven.[116] Another possible fuel source for Fazzan is date palm wood and fronds, and the date stones themselves: of 1,434 date stones identified in the archaeobotanical record for Jarma, 1,382 were charred and just 52 desiccated,[117] although, as noted by Nesbitt, date stones could also have been fed to animals and burned as a constituent in dung.[118] If glass recycling, but not glassmaking, was taking place in Fazzan, then the required temperatures would be lower, certainly below 1,000 °C and thus far more attainable in a small bead furnace or similar structure.

If the vitreous waste from Jarma or the chunk of glass from Saniat Jibril are indicative of either recycling or primary glass production (and it is difficult to see why else a chunk of glass might have been present in Fazzan, if not for some productive activity), we might ask what objects were being produced from the recycled glasses. We can, I think, rule out vessel glasses: the vessel glasses known to us are wholly consistent with Mediterranean and Egyptian forms, and there is no indication of a local manufacture of glass vessels. The glass bangles are from later dates than the contexts in which the vitreous waste and raw glass was found, and although the former may have been locally produced in recent centuries, this cannot provide an explanation for the latter.

---

[115] Kenoyer, cited in Lancelotti and Madella 2012. [116] Pelling 2013, 488–90.
[117] Pelling 2013, 490. [118] Nesbitt 1993.

This leaves us with beads. Most beads from Fazzan were not available for quantitative analysis, either because they remain in Jarma Museum or because they are preserved as complete objects and we did not wish to destructively sample them. The few beads analysed to date have shown a fair degree of compositional heterogeneity, as have the vitreous waste materials. Compositional heterogeneity could be the result of different workshops, different provenances or simply a lack of predictability in glass production (as we might expect from small-scale recycling or a non-industrial glass industry using local raw ingredients). Despite our current lack of direct evidence, it is well worth considering whether recycled or locally produced glasses from Fazzan were finding their way south and west along trade routes extending to the Lake Chad or the Niger Bend areas. The odd intriguing find, such as the glass bead of typical Roman vessel composition from Jenné-jeno,[119] may support such an idea, but only further excavation and analysis will tell whether this is a question we might ever hope to answer.

Conclusions

When did the earliest Trans-Saharan glass trade emerge? In the introduction to this chapter I considered various pre-Islamic contexts in which glass beads and, occasionally, vessel glass have been discovered. Although most evidence currently dates to the Islamic period, the fact that glass beads were so widely traded in the later first millennium AD suggests that glass may already have been a common reference point across several different groups spread over a wide geographical area. Indeed, the material properties of glass, particularly its propensity for hot-working, are often visible in its finished forms (for example, wound beads; trailed or eye beads; blown vessels). It is therefore no surprise that the hot-working properties of glasses were recognised and manipulated in several instances, regardless of whether this technology was transferred from person to person or 'invented' on multiple separate occasions. Others seem to have been equally happy with modifying glass beads when cold, in the same way as they might modify beads of stone.

---

[119] Brill 1995.

Perhaps the key point is that glass was, and is, open to manipulation. We are dealing with a vast area and time span, but it should not surprise us that glasses found in one location may have undergone several processes of alteration prior to their deposition. Glasses could have been subject to many episodes of reformation throughout their cultural biographies, even perhaps being transformed from vessel to bead, or from one type of bead to another.

I also postulate the addition of further raw ingredients to a glass melt. There are many reasons this might occur: additional ingredients could be added as colourants; to compensate for the loss of volatiles during reheating; accidentally, due to contamination; or for a variety of other reasons. When we trace the chemical signature of a glass bead, we may be examining the remnants of any number of episodes in its history. We can only ever hope to glimpse a small proportion of the events surrounding any material object, of course, but by careful consideration of the chemical and archaeological evidence, including indications of provenance and recycling as provided by trace element and isotope analysis, we can start to put these events back into the archaeological record. There is no straight line from production to deposition, but perhaps in the end it is the path between the two that is most interesting.[120]

Appendix 10.1 Data for the Glass Samples Analysed
Tables 10.1–10.3 follow overleaf.

[120] Thanks are due to Simon Chenery and Victoria Smith, for their expertise in the acquisition of chemical data, to Andrew Wilson for commenting upon and presenting the first draught of this text and for all his brilliant insights, and to every participant in the conference, all of whom enriched it with their discussion, especially Tom Fenn, Touatia Amroui, Martin Sterry and Aurélie Cuénod. As well as writing excellent children's literature, Caroline Lawrence has a keen eye for Roman glass remains, and I thank her warmly for letting me use her image for Figure 10.7. I am forever indebted to David J. Mattingly for giving me the opportunity to work on this material as part of his Trans-SAHARA Project.

Table 10.1 *Physical characteristics and archaeological context details of glass samples from Libya selected for analysis*

VESSELS

	Group	Colour	Site	Description	Typology	Context
TSG069	Roman Colourless	Colourless	Zinkekra	Wheel-polished rim of conical vessel, two abraded lines below rim	Late Hellenistic	1st to 2nd century AD
TSG070	Bocholtz	Colourless	Zinkekra	High footring, traces of wheel-polishing on exterior	Early Roman	1st to 2nd century AD
TSG071	Misc	Colourless	Zinkekra	Rim fragments, traces of wheel-polishing, conical body(?)	Early Roman	1st to 2nd century AD
TSG072	Misc	Colourless	Zinkekra	High footring, traces of wheel-polishing on exterior	Early Roman	Undated tomb
TSG073	Roman Colourless	Colourless	Zinkekra	Fire-rounded rim of deep, conical bowl	Early Roman	Undated tomb
TSG074	Roman Colourless	Colourless	Zinkekra	Outsplayed, cracked off rim, ground smooth, globular vessel body, two wheel-cut lines below rim and two more on body	Early Roman	Undated tomb
TSG075	Roman Colourless	Colourless	Zinkekra	Body fragment of beaker, cup or bottle with two bands of three wheel-cut lines each	Roman	Undated tomb
TSG076	Roman Colourless	Colourless	Zinkekra	Rim and body fragment, slightly outsplayed rim, ground smooth, tall conical body, wheel-cut groove below rim and oval facets below	Early Roman	Undated tomb
TSG078	RBGY 1	Colourless	Saniat Jibril	Slightly outsplayed, fire-rounded rim fragment	Late Roman	2nd to 5th century AD
TSG079	Mixed (Roman Colourless, RBGY 1)	Colourless	Saniat Jibril	Applied base of goblet or lamp	Roman	Mid-2nd to 3rd century AD
TSG080	Roman Colourless	Colourless	Saniat Jibril	Applied decorative element from beaker – probably conch shell	Roman, 4th century AD	Mid-2nd to 4th century AD

ID	Type	Colour	Site	Description	Period	Date
TSG081	Roman Colourless	Colourless	Saniat Jibril	Folded footring, almost complete	Roman	Mid-1st to mid-2nd century AD
TSG082	Mixed (RBGY 2, Levantine 1)	Blue-green	Saniat Jibril	Rim fragment of moulded, ribbed bowl	Early Roman	Mid-1st to mid-2nd century AD
TSG083	RBGY 2	Blue-green	Saniat Jibril	Rim fragment of moulded, ribbed bowl	Early Roman	Mid-1st to mid-2nd century AD
TSG084	RBGY 2	Blue-green	Saniat Jibril	Body fragment of moulded, ribbed bowl	Early Roman	Mid-1st to mid-2nd century AD
TSG085	Misc	Colourless	Saniat Jibril	Rim (outsplayed, cracked off and ground smooth) of beaker with wheel-cut lines below rim and on body	Early Roman	Mid-1st to 4th century AD
TSG086	Levantine 1	Blue-green	Saniat Jibril	Fragment of tubular base ring	Roman	Mid-2nd to 3rd century AD
TSG087	HIMT	Colourless	Saniat Jibril	Body fragment of blown glass vessel	Roman	Mid-1st to 4th century AD
TSG089	Misc	Colourless	Saniat Jibril	Body fragment of cast glass vessel	Hellenistic or Roman	Mid-1st to 4th century AD
TSG090	HIMT	Light green	Saniat Jibril	Body fragment of glass vessel		Mid-1st to 4th century AD
TSG091	Bocholtz	Colourless	Saniat Jibril	Body fragment of glass vessel with applied, trailing elements	Roman	4th century AD
TSG092	Roman Colourless	Colourless	Tinda	Rim fragment of straight-rimmed, wheel-polished, conical glass vessel, wheel-cut groove below rim on interior	Late Hellenistic	From a disturbed burial, t.a.q. AD 500
TSG093	Roman Colourless	Colourless	Tinda	Rim fragment of straight-rimmed, wheel-polished, conical glass vessel, wheel-cut groove below rim on interior	Late Hellenistic	From a disturbed burial, t.a.q. AD 500
TSG094	Roman Colourless	Colourless	Tinda	Rim fragment of straight-rimmed, wheel-polished, conical glass vessel, wheel-cut groove below rim on interior	Late Hellenistic	From a disturbed burial, t.a.q. AD 500
TSG095	HIMT	Olive green	Royal Cemetery	Body fragment of straight-sided, cylindrical bottle with abraded body decoration (horizontal and diagonal lines)	Late Roman	Unknown

Table 10.1 (*cont.*)

	Group	Colour	Site	Description	Typology	Context
TSG096	HIMT	Olive green	Royal Cemetery	Body fragment with abraded decoration (horizontal and diagonal lines)	Roman	Unknown
TSG097	HIMT	Colourless	Royal Cemetery	Body fragment with single band of wheel-cut lines	Roman	Unknown
TSG098	HIMT	Colourless	Royal Cemetery	Body fragment with two bands of wheel-cut lines	Roman	Unknown
TSG099	HIMT	Olive green	Royal Cemetery	Body fragment	Roman	Unknown
TSG100	Levantine 1	Blue-green	Al Fjayj Cemetery	Rim fragment of flask or jug, slightly everted, fire-rounded rim and globular body	Roman	Unknown
TSG101	HIMT	Colourless	Qasr Bin Dughba	Body fragments of straight-sided, cylindrical vessel, abraded decoration (horizontal and vertical lines with round facets)	Late Roman	Unknown
TSG102	Misc	Colourless	Qasr Bin Dughba	Body fragments of straight-sided, cylindrical vessel, abraded decoration (horizontal and vertical lines with round facets)	Late Roman	Unknown
TSG103	Group 3.2	Colourless	Qasr Bin Dughba	Body fragments of straight-sided, cylindrical vessel, abraded decoration (horizontal and vertical lines with round facets)	Late Roman	Unknown
TSG104	Mixed (HIMT, Roman Colourless)	Colourless	Qasr Bin Dughba	Body fragment with abraded, curved decoration	Late Roman	Unknown
TSG105	Misc	Colourless	Qasr Bin Dughba	Body fragment with slightly curved abraded line on exterior	Late Roman	Unknown
TSG106	Mixed (HIMT, Roman Colourless)	Colourless	Qasr Bin Dughba	Undecorated body fragment	Late Roman	Unknown
TSG107	Misc	Colourless	Qasr Bin Dughba	Undecorated body fragment	Late Roman	Unknown
TSG108	HIMT	Colourless	Nesciya Cemetery	Body fragment with applied blue blob and thin, wheel-cut line	Late Roman	Unknown

TSG	Glass group	Colour	Site	Description	Period	Date
TSG109	HIMT	Colourless	Zuwila	Body fragment with narrow, abraded decoration (horizontal line and thick, oblong shape)	Late Roman	Unknown
TSG110	Roman Colourless	Colourless	Saniat bin Huwaydi	Base and body of thin-walled, flat-based vessel with slightly flaring walls		1st to mid-2nd century AD
TSG111	Roman Colourless	Colourless	Saniat bin Huwaydi	Body fragments of heavily corroded glass beaker		1st to mid-2nd century AD
TSG114	Roman Colourless	Colourless	Saniat bin Huwaydi	Deep bowl base with applied base ring, corroded	Roman	Mid-1st to 2nd century AD
TSG115	Roman Colourless	Colourless	Saniat bin Huwaydi	Body fragments of heavily corroded glass vessel		Mid-1st to 2nd century AD
TSG117	Mixed (HIMT, Roman Colourless)	Colourless	Saniat bin Huwaydi	Rim fragments of heavily corroded glass vessel		Mid-1st to 2nd century AD
TSG118	Mixed (HIMT, Roman Colourless)	Colourless	Saniat bin Huwaydi	Conical bowl with tubular rim, convex base with tubular base ring and pointed kick, heavily corroded	Roman	Mid-1st to 2nd century AD
TSG119	Bocholtz	Colourless	Saniat bin Huwaydi	Glass bottle, heavily corroded		Mid-1st to 2nd century AD
TSG120	Mixed (HIMT, Roman Colourless)	Light green	Saniat bin Huwaydi	Conical tubular rimmed bowl	Roman	Mid-1st to 2nd century AD
TSG121	HIMT	Colourless	Saniat bin Huwaydi	Thin glass bottle, heavily corroded	Roman	Mid-1st to 2nd century AD
TSG122	Roman Colourless	Colourless	Saniat bin Huwaydi	Body of heavily corroded glass vessel		Mid-1st to 2nd century AD
TSG125	Group 3.2	Olive green	Ghirza	Fragment of base ring of shallow bowl	Late Roman	Mid-4th to 6th century AD
TSG128	Group 3.2	Light blue	Ghirza	Body fragment of glass vessel		4th to mid-5th century AD
TSG129	Mixed (HIMT, Roman Colourless)	Colourless	Ghirza	Body fragment of glass vessel		4th to mid-5th century AD
TSG130	HIMT	Olive green	Ghirza	Body fragment of glass vessel		4th to mid-5th century AD
TSG131	HIMT	Olive green	Ghirza	Cracked off, everted rim from lamp	Late Roman	4th to mid-5th century AD
TSG132	HIMT	Colourless	Ghirza	Fire-rounded rim of glass vessel	Roman	4th to mid-5th century AD
TSG133	Mixed (HIMT, Roman Colourless / RBGY 2)	Colourless	Ghirza	Body fragment of glass vessel with thin, applied horizontal trails in opaque white		4th to mid-5th century AD

Table 10.1 (*cont.*)

	Group	Colour	Site	Description	Typology	Context
TSG134	Group 3.2	Colourless	Ghirza	Body fragment of glass vessel		4th to mid-5th century AD
TSG135	Mixed (HIMT, RBGY 2)	Light green	Ghirza	Rim fragment of cup or deep bowl, fire-rounded rim, slightly tapering sides		4th to mid-5th century AD
TSG136	Mixed (HIMT, Levantine 1)	Light yellow	Ghirza	Fire-rounded rim fragment of stemmed cup	Late Roman	4th to mid-5th century AD
TSG137	HIMT	Light green	Ghirza	Pushed-in tubular base and part of stem of stemmed cup or lamp	Late Roman	4th to mid-5th century AD
TSG138	HIMT	Green	Ghirza	Pushed-in tubular base and part of stem of stemmed cup or lamp	Late Roman	4th to mid-5th century AD
TSG139	HIMT	Light green	Sabratha	Drawn stem from stemmed cup or lamp	Late Roman to early Medieval	
TSG140	Misc	Light green	Sabratha	Body fragment from stemmed cup or lamp	Late Roman to early Medieval	
TSG153	RBGY 2	Colourless	Zinkekra	Vessel fragment with two abraded lines	Late Roman	2nd century BC to 2nd century AD
TSG154	Misc	Turquoise	Zinkekra	Vessel fragment of thick-walled vessel with incised decoration	Late Roman	Unknown
TSG155	Mixed (HIMT, Roman Colourless)	Colourless	Unknown (Fazzan)	Fragment of honeycomb beaker or cup	Roman	Unknown
TSG156	HIMT	Colourless	Zinkekra	Rim fragment of glass vessel	Roman	1st to 4th century AD
TSG157	Misc	Colourless	Zinkekra	Vessel fragment with abraded lines	Roman	Unknown
TSG158	HIMT	Colourless	Saniat Jibril	Fragment of cracked off rim	Roman	Mid-1st to mid-2nd century AD
TSG159	HIMT	Colourless	Saniat Jibril	Body fragment of glass vessel	Roman	1st to 4th century AD
TSG160	Roman Colourless	Colourless	Saniat Jibril	Body fragment of glass vessel	Roman	Mid-2nd to 3rd century AD
TSG161	Misc	Colourless	Zuwila	Rim fragment	Roman	Unstratified
TSG162	HIMT	Colourless	Unknown (Fazzan)	Colourless vessel with applied, blue-green ring base	Roman	Unknown

ID	Glass group	Colour	Site	Description	Period	Date
TSG163	Roman Colourless	Colourless	Unknown (Fazzan)	Rim fragment of large, oval plate	Roman	Unknown
TSG164	HIMT	Colourless	Unknown (Fazzan)	Base fragment of large vessel	Roman	Unknown
TSG165	Misc	Blue-green	Zuwila 2 Cemetery	Fragment of glass vessel	Roman	Unknown
TSG177	HIMT	Light green	Unknown (Fazzan)	Fragment of light green vessel with horizontal rows of dark blue blobs	Roman	Unknown
TSG178	Roman Colourless	Colourless	Watwat	Body fragment of colourless vessel with painted (enamel?) decoration red, yellow and green	Roman	Unstratified
TSG180	Roman Colourless	Colourless	Saniat Jibril	Body fragment of vessel with engraved, curved line	Roman	Mid-1st to 3rd century
BEADS						
TSG166		Blue-green	Zuwila 2 Cemetery	Bead fragment, from set of deformed beads with closed thread-holes		Unknown
TSG167		Cobalt-blue	Zinkekra	Oblate bead fragment		3rd century BC to 1st century AD
TSG168_turq	Consistent with Roman Colourless	Turquoise	Zinkekra	Eye-bead fragment (turquoise, with white opaque and blue 'eyes')		Unstratified
TSG168_blue		Blue	Zinkekra	Eye-bead fragment (turquoise, with white opaque and blue 'eyes')		Unstratified
TSG168_white		White opaque	Zinkekra	Eye-bead fragment (turquoise, with white opaque and blue 'eyes')		Unstratified
TSG169	Consistent with Roman Colourless	Blue-green	Zinkekra	Globular bead fragment		Unstratified
TSG170	Consistent with mixed Levantine 1, Roman Colourless	Turquoise opaque	Zinkekra	Globular bead fragment		Unstratified
TSG171	Consistent with mixed RBGY 2, Roman Colourless	Turquoise	Zinkekra	Globular bead fragment		3rd century BC to early 1st century AD
TSG172_blueopq		Turquoise opaque	Saniat Jibril	Globular bead fragment, with translucent green core and outer opaque turquoise		Unstratified

Table 10.1 (*cont.*)

	Group	Colour	Site	Description	Typology	Context
TSG172 _grntint		Very light green	Saniat Jibril	Globular bead fragment, with translucent green core and outer opaque turquoise		Unstratified
TSG173		Cobalt-blue	Zinkekra	Globular bead fragment		1st millennium BC
TSG174	Consistent with Levantine 1	Turquoise opaque	Zinkekra	Globular bead fragment		1st millennium BC
TSG175_cless	High potash and lead	Colourless	Saniat Jibril	Red translucent bead fragment with white and yellow opaque trails		1st millennium BC
TSG175 _pinkstreak	High potash and lead	Pink	Saniat Jibril	Red translucent bead fragment with white and yellow opaque trails		1st millennium BC
TSG175 _yell	High potash and lead	Yellow	Saniat Jibril	Red translucent bead fragment with white and yellow opaque trails		Unknown
TSG176_red	High potash and lead	Red	Germa Castello	Complete (broken in half) bead, white opaque core with translucent red overlay	Post-Roman	Unstratified
TSG176_white	High potash and lead	White opaque	Germa Castello	Complete (broken in half) bead, white opaque core with translucent red overlay		Unstratified
TSG041	Lead-soda-silica	Yellow opaque	Jarma	Ring bead or pendant fragment		T.p.q. 400 BC
TSG044		Yellow opaque	Jarma	Ring bead fragment		Topsoil
TSG045		Green	Jarma	Ring bead fragment		Topsoil
TSG051		Light green opaque	Zuwila	Bead fragment		Unstratified
TSG055		Blue-green	Zuwila	Bead fragment		Unstratified
TSG057		Green	Zuwila	Bead fragment		Unstratified
TSG058		Blue-green	Zuwila	Bead fragment		Unstratified
MIRROR						
TSG068	Plant ash glass	Colourless	Ghirza	Lead-backed, convex glass mirror fragment		Mid-10th to mid-11th century AD

	Composition	Colour	Site	Description		Date
STIRRER						
TSG179		Turquoise	Jarma	End of stirrer or 'glass pin', straight shaft topped by flat, circular head	Early Roman	Unstratified
VITREOUS WASTE						
TSG144	High alumina and iron	Green opaque	Jarma	Lump of friable frit or ceramic-type material with surface glaze on one side		Mid-1st to mid-4th century AD
TSG145	High alumina and iron	Green opaque	Jarma	Lump of semi-fused glassy material with surface glaze		Mid-1st to mid-4th century AD
TSG146	High alumina and iron	Green opaque	Jarma	Lump of friable frit or ceramic-type material with surface glaze on surface		Mid-1st to mid-4th century AD
TSG147	High alumina and iron	Green opaque	Jarma	Frit with traces of buff-coloured ceramic adhering to one side		Mid-1st to mid-4th century AD
TSG148	High alumina and iron	Green opaque	Jarma	Lump of friable frit or ceramic-type material with surface glaze on surface		Mid-1st to mid-4th century AD
TSG149	High alumina and iron	Green opaque	Jarma	Lump of friable frit or ceramic-type material with surface glaze on surface		Mid-1st to mid-4th century AD
TSG150		Green opaque	Jarma	Buff-coloured ceramic with thick glaze layer adhering to the top		Late 1st century AD
RAW GLASS CHUNK						
TSG151	Elevated potash, antimony – recycled?	Green	Saniat Jibril	Chunk of 'raw' glass		Unstratified
GLASS 'DRIP'						
TSG152	Consistent with mixed Levantine 1, RBGY 2	Green	Zinkekra	Glass 'drip' or end of cane		2nd century BC to 2nd century AD

Table 10.2 *Glass compositional analysis: EPMA results (weight %)*

	Na$_2$O	MgO	Al$_2$O$_3$	SiO$_2$	P$_2$O$_5$	Cl	K$_2$O	CaO	TiO$_2$	MnO	Fe$_2$O$_3$	CuO	SnO$_2$	Sb$_2$O$_5$	PbO
TSG069	19.15	0.43	1.66	69.64	0.01	1.55	0.42	5.53	0.05	0.03	0.36	0.00	0.00	0.6	0.0
TSG070	21.25	0.46	1.49	67.03	0.02	1.58	0.47	5.61	0.05	0.02	0.35	0.00	0.01	1.0	0.0
TSG071	20.88	0.68	1.69	65.11	0.05	1.42	0.53	4.67	0.14	0.44	0.67	0.00	0.02	1.0	0.4
TSG072	19.55	0.56	1.65	66.35	0.02	1.49	0.52	6.78	0.06	0.02	0.40	0.00	0.01	0.9	0.1
TSG073	19.69	0.52	1.66	67.70	0.03	1.50	0.50	6.73	0.06	0.01	0.43	0.00	0.01	0.9	0.1
TSG074	19.35	0.41	1.70	70.53	0.04	1.58	0.38	5.79	0.05	0.02	0.36	0.00	0.01	0.4	0.1
TSG075	18.78	0.42	1.71	70.96	0.02	1.63	0.43	5.70	0.06	0.01	0.40	0.00	0.00	0.4	0.0
TSG076	19.67	0.47	1.67	69.29	0.01	1.73	0.36	5.74	0.07	0.00	0.35	0.00	0.00	0.8	0.0
TSG078	17.66	0.56	1.99	69.62	0.09	1.37	0.82	6.52	0.07	0.35	0.52	0.00	0.02	0.5	0.0
TSG079	17.91	0.58	1.95	68.69	0.04	1.34	0.68	6.97	0.08	0.02	0.51	0.00	0.00	1.0	0.0
TSG080	18.92	0.62	1.74	68.98	0.05	1.55	0.39	6.62	0.07	0.03	0.45	0.01	0.01	0.6	0.0
TSG081	18.08	0.35	1.63	70.39	0.02	1.56	0.54	6.10	0.06	0.05	0.34	0.00	0.02	1.0	0.0
TSG082	15.48	0.64	2.37	69.87	0.14	1.36	0.60	8.97	0.05	0.35	0.34	0.00	0.03	0.0	0.0
TSG083	15.94	0.52	2.36	70.48	0.19	1.33	0.73	7.91	0.06	0.63	0.34	0.00	0.05	0.1	0.0
TSG084	16.50	0.47	2.43	71.09	0.13	1.52	0.54	7.38	0.05	0.50	0.31	0.00	0.00	0.0	0.0
TSG085	18.44	0.61	1.95	68.15	0.04	1.50	0.61	6.78	0.09	0.03	0.43	0.00	0.00	1.7	0.0
TSG086	14.71	0.55	2.92	69.80	0.09	1.32	0.55	8.14	0.06	1.33	0.34	0.00	0.00	0.0	0.0
TSG087	20.11	0.96	2.49	64.70	0.06	1.50	0.37	6.12	0.36	2.22	1.12	0.01	0.01	0.0	0.1
TSG089	18.95	0.50	1.52	69.36	0.02	1.58	0.38	6.75	0.06	0.03	0.34	0.00	0.01	0.7	0.0
TSG090	18.80	1.19	2.40	67.13	0.06	1.62	0.45	5.25	0.31	2.30	0.97	0.01	0.02	0.1	0.0
TSG091	17.95	0.38	1.70	71.30	0.03	1.52	0.43	5.95	0.06	0.01	0.32	0.00	0.01	0.6	0.0
TSG092	19.10	0.45	1.76	70.35	0.03	1.68	0.36	5.21	0.06	0.02	0.37	0.00	0.03	1.0	0.0
TSG093	20.68	0.46	1.78	68.28	0.03	1.81	0.41	5.40	0.06	0.01	0.39	0.00	0.02	0.8	0.0
TSG094	19.19	0.42	1.74	70.32	0.03	1.69	0.36	5.14	0.06	0.02	0.33	0.00	0.02	1.1	0.0
TSG095	18.35	1.22	2.59	65.89	0.07	1.18	0.43	6.08	0.50	2.34	1.37	0.00	0.00	0.0	0.0
TSG096	20.00	1.05	2.53	66.71	0.05	1.70	0.35	4.04	0.47	2.27	1.46	0.01	0.01	0.0	0.1
TSG097	18.67	0.69	2.07	68.32	0.05	1.41	0.31	5.84	0.25	1.80	0.86	0.00	0.00	0.0	0.0
TSG098	19.72	0.94	2.11	66.45	0.06	1.59	0.38	5.70	0.25	1.95	1.00	0.00	0.01	0.0	0.0
TSG099	18.66	1.05	2.41	67.77	0.04	1.39	0.39	5.42	0.39	2.17	1.27	0.00	0.01	0.0	0.0

TSG100	15.47	0.56	2.64	69.61	0.12	1.44	0.66	8.32	0.08	0.90	0.41	0.00	0.04	0.0	0.0
TSG101	19.67	0.93	2.00	68.14	0.03	1.69	0.36	6.57	0.10	1.34	0.59	0.01	0.00	0.0	0.0
TSG102	18.06	0.36	1.51	69.83	0.03	1.48	0.45	6.17	0.07	0.66	0.44	0.00	0.01	0.0	0.0
TSG103	18.38	0.88	1.86	69.99	0.00	1.55	0.37	6.93	0.09	1.19	0.37	0.00	0.02	0.0	0.0
TSG104	20.09	0.78	1.75	66.82	0.06	1.62	0.44	5.52	0.09	1.07	0.36	0.01	0.02	0.0	0.0
TSG105	19.75	0.73	1.52	66.12	0.02	1.39	0.44	6.10	0.07	0.74	0.34	0.03	0.01	0.2	0.0
TSG106	20.39	0.78	1.76	69.99	0.06	1.63	0.48	6.63	0.08	0.86	0.46	0.03	0.01	0.2	0.0
TSG107	21.55	0.76	1.89	66.09	0.06	1.93	0.37	6.70	0.08	0.45	0.95	0.00	0.00	0.1	0.1
TSG108	21.89	1.18	2.51	63.48	0.06	1.87	0.36	6.23	0.28	1.67	1.11	0.00	0.01	0.0	0.0
TSG109	21.71	1.22	2.49	62.91	0.06	1.83	0.35	6.20	0.29	1.69	1.07	0.00	0.00	0.0	0.0
TSG110	19.81	0.35	1.66	70.06	0.01	1.86	0.39	4.77	0.05	0.01	0.36	0.00	0.02	0.8	0.0
TSG111	19.45	0.57	1.92	68.41	0.05	1.62	0.50	6.11	0.09	0.06	0.52	0.00	0.02	0.9	0.0
TSG114	19.08	0.50	1.74	69.02	0.02	1.57	0.43	6.23	0.07	0.01	0.45	0.00	0.00	1.0	0.1
TSG115	17.97	0.38	1.80	71.22	0.03	1.58	0.52	5.42	0.06	0.03	0.28	0.00	0.01	0.7	0.2
TSG117	18.95	0.66	2.08	68.30	0.11	1.42	0.68	6.53	0.10	0.23	0.53	0.00	0.01	0.6	0.0
TSG118	19.07	0.65	2.13	68.75	0.11	1.45	0.69	6.60	0.10	0.25	0.53	0.00	0.03	0.6	0.0
TSG119	21.49	0.50	1.70	67.25	0.02	2.11	0.35	5.80	0.06	0.01	0.33	0.00	0.00	0.5	0.4
TSG120	18.98	0.64	2.06	68.43	0.09	1.43	0.69	6.54	0.10	0.21	0.54	0.00	0.02	0.6	0.1
TSG121	18.42	0.97	2.28	70.44	0.05	1.60	0.44	4.22	0.17	1.82	0.57	0.00	0.00	0.0	0.1
TSG122	20.08	0.42	1.77	69.31	0.03	1.76	0.42	5.38	0.06	0.01	0.36	0.00	0.02	1.1	0.0
TSG125	20.83	0.82	1.98	65.47	0.07	1.08	0.57	7.23	0.11	1.29	0.56	0.00	0.01	0.0	0.0
TSG128	18.02	0.87	2.08	65.47	0.14	1.26	0.70	6.67	0.12	0.62	0.86	0.42	0.03	1.2	0.3
TSG129	20.70	0.61	2.01	67.46	0.05	1.26	0.43	6.32	0.08	1.06	0.43	0.00	0.01	0.0	0.0
TSG130	20.71	1.38	2.98	62.60	0.06	1.33	0.46	5.35	0.61	2.22	2.23	0.01	0.01	0.0	0.0
TSG131	18.42	1.05	2.52	64.37	0.15	1.35	0.43	6.23	0.44	1.66	3.61	0.01	0.00	0.0	0.0
TSG132	20.34	1.11	1.75	63.10	0.08	1.25	0.47	8.91	0.11	1.82	0.53	0.00	0.02	0.0	0.0
TSG133	18.88	0.82	1.91	67.54	0.08	1.14	0.55	7.24	0.14	0.96	0.61	0.00	0.03	0.0	0.0
TSG134	18.74	0.83	2.03	66.58	0.09	1.14	0.51	7.17	0.17	1.54	0.69	0.01	0.02	0.0	0.0
TSG135	19.50	1.07	2.00	66.14	0.21	1.22	0.73	7.26	0.13	0.85	0.86	0.09	0.02	0.2	0.1
TSG136	20.04	0.91	2.24	63.81	0.07	1.01	0.45	8.78	0.16	1.49	0.75	0.00	0.02	0.0	0.0
TSG137	19.80	0.90	2.14	66.48	0.06	1.15	0.56	7.20	0.12	1.57	0.64	0.00	0.00	0.0	0.0
TSG138	19.66	0.79	2.07	65.82	0.07	1.22	0.60	7.14	0.15	1.16	0.83	0.04	0.01	0.1	0.2
TSG139	17.93	1.36	2.32	64.69	0.17	0.99	0.84	8.18	0.14	2.20	0.66	0.01	0.00	0.0	0.0

Table 10.2 (cont.)

	Na$_2$O	MgO	Al$_2$O$_3$	SiO$_2$	P$_2$O$_5$	Cl	K$_2$O	CaO	TiO$_2$	MnO	Fe$_2$O$_3$	CuO	SnO$_2$	Sb$_2$O$_5$	PbO
TSG140	19.02	0.94	2.05	66.36	0.07	1.29	0.57	8.02	0.10	0.02	0.63	0.00	0.01	0.5	0.0
TSG153	16.12	0.45	2.50	71.19	0.14	1.46	0.48	8.10	0.05	0.17	0.36	0.04	0.00	0.0	0.0
TSG154	16.11	0.56	1.94	63.59	0.07	1.15	0.74	6.61	0.08	0.03	0.64	4.45	0.32	0.5	3.5
TSG155	18.59	0.79	1.91	68.40	0.02	1.69	0.41	6.62	0.09	1.54	0.38	0.01	0.01	0.0	0.0
TSG156	18.83	0.77	1.96	68.44	0.07	1.66	0.40	6.59	0.09	1.62	0.36	0.00	0.00	0.0	0.0
TSG157	11.09	3.59	0.44	71.47	0.35	0.94	2.52	8.58	0.11	0.54	0.20	0.00	0.01	0.1	0.0
TSG158	19.62	1.31	2.54	62.94	0.11	1.45	0.48	7.22	0.39	1.79	2.26	0.04	0.01	0.0	0.0
TSG159	18.52	1.25	2.73	66.46	0.04	1.42	0.47	5.54	0.05	2.12	1.45	0.01	0.01	0.0	0.0
TSG160	17.28	0.46	1.81	71.21	0.03	1.32	0.56	6.34	0.07	0.06	0.41	0.01	0.02	0.9	0.0
TSG161	17.89	0.90	1.32	69.74	0.14	1.60	2.01	3.72	0.17	2.29	0.24	0.00	0.00	0.1	0.0
TSG162	20.87	1.04	2.41	66.10	0.06	1.67	0.49	4.73	0.15	1.65	1.05	0.20	0.01	0.0	0.0
TSG163	19.42	0.53	1.88	69.89	0.02	1.54	0.44	5.90	0.07	0.00	0.39	0.00	0.00	0.9	0.0
TSG164	18.90	0.91	2.30	69.56	0.04	1.66	0.42	4.25	0.15	1.68	0.61	0.01	0.00	0.0	0.0
TSG165	14.50	0.92	2.71	69.08	0.09	1.30	0.36	10.15	0.34	0.01	1.24	0.02	0.01	0.0	0.0
TSG177	20.29	1.15	2.23	67.35	0.05	1.81	0.30	5.01	0.26	1.77	0.89	0.02	0.02	0.0	0.0
TSG178	19.34	0.41	1.84	69.45	0.02	1.64	0.49	5.70	0.06	0.03	0.37	0.00	0.04	1.1	0.3
TSG180	19.38	0.58	1.84	70.24	0.05	1.65	0.42	5.56	0.07	0.01	0.30	0.02	0.06	0.5	0.0
TSG166	18.79	0.46	2.13	67.83	0.11	1.83	0.48	2.40	0.15	0.06	0.67	1.31	0.31	0.0	3.9
TSG167	17.80	0.33	1.71	71.68	0.03	1.70	0.42	6.32	0.05	0.03	0.79	0.12	0.00	0.0	0.0
TSG168_turq	13.56	0.50	2.20	69.87	0.06	1.00	0.53	8.37	0.06	0.04	0.46	1.12	0.03	1.1	0.7
TSG168_blue	12.45	0.51	2.29	69.61	0.05	0.85	0.79	8.90	0.00	0.03	2.10	0.50	0.03	1.6	0.1
TSG168_white	12.01	0.55	2.10	66.93	0.04	0.63	0.68	7.93		0.03	0.56	0.02	0.03	8.8	0.0
TSG169	18.39	0.54	1.77	70.55	0.05	1.05	0.49	5.24	0.05	0.01	0.37	1.47	0.01	0.0	0.0
TSG170	15.36	0.46	1.76	64.41	0.03	1.11	0.50	7.87	0.06	0.04	0.40	3.30	0.02	3.7	0.7
TSG171	17.73	0.55	2.17	66.74	0.07	1.47	0.76	7.24	0.07	0.01	0.41	1.88	0.02	0.1	0.0
TSG172_blueopq	19.12	0.64	1.91	63.15	0.03	1.53	0.56	4.33	0.15	0.07	0.62	4.75	0.25	3.5	0.1
TSG172_grntint	19.47	1.88	1.89	63.09	0.41	1.46	0.84	7.43	0.12	0.88	0.97	0.40	0.00	0.6	0.0

TSG173	20.39	0.49	2.26	65.18	0.06	1.47	0.55	7.81	0.04	0.01	0.91	0.14	0.01	0.2	0.0
TSG174	13.79	0.45	2.42	65.21	0.03	1.41	0.68	7.69	0.07	0.01	0.60	3.56	0.10	3.1	0.0
TSG175_cless	6.77	0.73	0.59	51.32	0.32	0.95	12.67	4.97	0.03	0.03	0.32	0.03	0.01	1.0	14.8
TSG175 _pinkstreak	6.54	0.66	0.53	50.73	0.34	1.00	12.81	4.92	0.03	0.01	0.32	0.02	0.00	0.9	15.4
TSG175_yell	6.69	0.91	0.51	46.70	0.36	0.59	6.01	5.16	0.04	0.10	0.38	0.05	0.30	2.7	25.5
TSG176_red	7.10	0.73	0.28	48.78	0.43	0.99	13.01	4.22	0.02	0.08	0.23	0.01	0.01	0.8	18.4
TSG176 _white	5.40	0.35	0.29	44.36	0.29	1.06	9.58	2.92	0.02	0.05	0.18	0.05	0.05	0.3	25.2
TSG041	12.73	0.87	2.50	72.59	0.10	0.97	1.03	8.54	0.08	0.08	0.72	0.11	0.01	0.0	0.0
TSG044	6.39	0.13	1.17	47.39	0.03	0.33	0.35	4.30	0.11	0.02	2.72	0.03	0.00	3.0	32.5
TSG045	15.25	0.57	1.49	68.06	0.11	1.10	0.74	8.99	0.11	0.03	0.97	2.87	0.05	0.1	0.1
TSG051	20.62	0.53	2.06	62.58	0.09	1.69	0.43	4.37	0.19	0.02	0.93	0.94	0.42	0.0	4.9
TSG055	20.89	0.50	2.35	66.89	0.09	1.55	0.39	3.78	0.19	0.01	1.11	0.72	0.08	0.0	1.2
TSG057	19.41	0.67	2.65	66.68	0.10	1.64	0.46	2.78	0.26	0.05	1.04	1.43	0.28	0.0	2.5
TSG058	20.73	0.49	2.34	66.98	0.07	1.54	0.39	3.76	0.20	0.00	1.08	0.91	0.08	0.0	0.9
TSG068	12.40	2.08	1.43	66.11	0.46	1.04	1.69	8.56	0.12	2.98	0.64	0.04	0.01	0.0	1.9
TSG179	17.44	0.98	1.56	73.07	0.10	0.36	1.25	2.84	0.18	0.08	2.70	0.01	0.00	0.1	0.0
TSG144	12.86	0.53	5.20	73.51	0.04	0.38	5.46	1.70	0.27	0.08	0.91	0.00	0.00	0.2	0.0
TSG145	10.15	0.99	5.18	74.12	0.07	0.27	5.56	2.14	0.37	0.07	1.82	0.02	0.01	0.2	0.1
TSG146	14.26	2.92	6.59	63.30	0.26	0.07	3.80	5.65	0.51	0.10	2.67	0.00	0.01	0.1	0.0
TSG147	12.12	2.25	9.05	65.29	0.13	0.08	4.07	3.90	0.25	0.04	3.63	0.00	0.00	0.1	0.0
TSG148	10.43	1.37	8.63	68.82	0.14	0.03	5.30	1.15	0.24	0.01	3.87	0.00	0.00	0.1	0.0
TSG149	12.35	2.71	5.94	65.70	0.18	0.06	4.68	4.59	0.45	0.03	2.81	0.00	0.04	0.1	0.0
TSG150	10.30	1.74	5.32	69.60	0.13	0.29	4.37	6.37	0.28	0.04	1.94	0.00	0.00	0.1	0.0
TSG151	15.60	0.56	2.13	69.37	0.10	1.32	1.15	8.19	0.10	0.14	0.64	0.00	0.03	0.7	0.0
TSG152	17.39	0.72	2.29	68.58	0.10	1.32	0.66	9.18	0.06	0.04	0.37	0.02	0.01	0.0	0.0

Table 10.3 Glass compositional analysis: LA-ICP-MS results. The table is in two parts (a) and (b), with two lines of data for each sample analysed (units are ppm).

Part (a)	Li	B	Mg	Al	P	Ti	V	Cr	Mn	Fe	Co	Ni	Cu	Zn	As	Rb	Sr	Y	Zr	Nb	Mo	Sn
TSG069	3	193	1,957	9,348	179	327	6	7	140	2,152	1	2	4	11	20	5	350	5	39	1	0	4
TSG070	3	175	1,905	8,253	179	308	5	8	94	1,952	1	2	8	12	34	4	338	5	37	1	0	5
TSG071	5	158	2,758	9,290	225	865	16	16	2,663	4,387	4	7	9	37	60	4	320	6	82	3	1	71
TSG072	3	135	2,252	9,153	187	376	7	9	115	2,364	1	2	8	14	17	5	477	5	42	1	0	16
TSG073	3	139	2,289	9,140	199	384	7	9	120	2,513	1	3	9	16	19	5	501	5	43	1	0	16
TSG074	3	158	1,851	9,213	155	328	6	8	73	1,920	1	2	7	13	7	4	340	4	36	1	0	4
TSG075	3	177	1,888	9,203	139	367	6	8	85	2,154	1	3	9	15	9	5	391	5	43	1	0	8
TSG076	3	175	2006	9,592	177	399	5	9	97	2,023	1	3	4	14	7	5	350	6	47	2	0	7
TSG078	7	181	2,609	11,453	339	431	15	11	2,728	3,207	4	6	33	25	22	10	439	6	49	2	1	11
TSG079	5	196	2,706	10,850	227	509	9	10	130	3,447	2	4	22	26	30	8	638	6	50	2	0	7
TSG080	4	140	2,946	10,257	239	447	8	10	232	3,073	2	4	65	22	67	6	495	7	50	2	0	18
TSG081	3	234	1,755	9,200	154	349	5	8	102	2,002	1	2	7	16	22	6	402	6	39	1	0	6
TSG082	3	147	3,297	13,140	507	325	11	11	2,623	2,486	6	10	22	18	2	8	557	8	36	1	1	6
TSG083	4	106	2,670	13,227	647	351	13	10	4,727	2,789	18	11	34	22	2	8	492	7	37	1	2	13
TSG084	3	138	2,326	13,247	459	313	13	9	3,940	2,137	6	10	11	15	2	7	458	7	32	1	2	7
TSG085	5	144	2,740	10,857	173	525	9	10	163	3,027	6	3	9	21	15	6	502	5	54	2	0	8
TSG086	3	102	2,817	16,633	373	383	18	13	10,633	3,547	8	11	10	14	21	8	494	7	36	1	2	6
TSG087	4	211	4,527	13,657	299	2,173	38	46	15,963	8,987	9	16	41	27	4	6	455	10	200	4	5	6
TSG089	3	198	2,268	8,260	178	356	6	8	91	2,004	1	3	11	18	28	5	471	6	38	1	0	6
TSG090	4	165	5,693	13,153	292	1,836	38	37	16,240	7,633	10	14	53	25	2	5	419	9	166	4	5	6
TSG091	3	220	1,802	9,557	193	381	6	9	89	1,990	1	2	4	13	20	5	340	6	41	1	0	6
TSG092	3	228	1,974	9,670	183	353	6	8	78	1,977	1	2	6	15	16	5	293	5	42	1	0	6
TSG093	3	149	1,974	9,719	186	353	6	8	101	2,145	1	3	7	12	44	4	295	5	41	1	0	5
TSG094	3	237	1,969	9,577	198	374	6	9	84	2,043	1	3	5	16	16	5	305	5	43	1	0	6
TSG095	5	179	5,873	13,737	223	3,013	57	70	19,467	10,967	10	14	28	28	3	4	592	10	243	6	6	6
TSG096	4	172	4,643	13,640	242	2,813	49	62	18,300	10,933	14	13	43	30	4	5	378	10	245	6	9	6
TSG097	4	96	3,147	11,773	236	1,491	33	35	13,967	6,817	8	15	32	22	4	5	456	8	128	3	4	5
TSG098	4	218	4,190	12,157	285	1,497	39	33	15,147	7,947	7	18	35	25	4	5	430	9	130	3	4	5
TSG099	4	212	5,003	13,647	270	2,311	44	50	16,563	9,920	11	17	39	27	3	5	453	10	187	5	5	5
TSG100	3	104	2,837	15,283	518	457	22	17	7,133	3,023	6	9	12	14	2	9	517	7	40	2	3	5
TSG101	5	218	4,079	11,348	256	618	24	14	9,653	4,390	5	8	51	14	3	5	474	7	55	2	3	5

TSG102	3	46	1,523	8,313	201	423	15	11	4,853	3,023	3	4	19	12	3	6	408	6	46	1	1	5
TSG103	4	182	3,830	10,583	189	549	22	12	9,610	3,353	4	7	29	12	2	6	520	6	51	2	3	6
TSG104	4	203	3,775	10,267	207	547	17	12	9,403	3,720	7	8	52	17	3	5	511	6	51	2	5	8
TSG105	4	132	3,117	8,720	223	444	14	10	5,840	3,167	6	7	204	18	11	5	524	6	47	2	2	19
TSG106	4	143	3,373	9,183	236	482	15	11	6,270	3,383	6	7	224	19	12	6	567	6	48	2	2	21
TSG107	4	205	3,463	10,437	247	499	24	11	3,360	6,467	2	9	25	21	12	5	541	7	50	2	1	5
TSG108	4	200	5,680	14,137	212	1,698	30	34	10,830	7,240	7	13	29	22	4	5	468	9	156	4	5	7
TSG109	4	199	5,603	14,340	205	1,757	31	36	11,200	7,283	7	12	28	20	4	5	456	9	145	4	4	7
TSG110	2	148	1,702	9,187	168	310	5	7	85	2,077	1	2	3	11	6	5	299	5	38	1	0	6
TSG111	4	173	2,701	11,357	255	563	9	12	550	3,118	2	4	11	18	26	5	452	6	58	2	0	13
TSG114	4	205	2,451	10,287	148	439	7	11	123	2,600	1	2	9	13	238	4	388	5	48	1	0	47
TSG115	3	202	1,901	10,327	206	342	5	9	87	1,969	1	2	10	19	25	5	314	5	39	1	0	32
TSG117	5	153	2,962	12,400	444	604	13	11	1,631	3,476	3	6	36	21	14	7	400	6	79	2	1	22
TSG118	5	163	2,856	11,723	409	590	12	11	1,386	3,437	3	6	36	22	16	6	434	6	69	2	1	20
TSG119	3	229	2,282	9,787	156	377	6	9	91	2,190	1	3	6	9	14	4	382	6	45	1	0	54
TSG120	5	165	3,053	12,270	370	621	13	11	1,493	3,463	3	6	35	23	15	7	420	6	76	2	1	24
TSG121	4	156	4,727	13,537	225	1,033	34	21	13,440	5,437	8	12	17	16	3	5	437	7	84	3	5	8
TSG122	3	191	2,053	10,276	165	343	6	8	109	2,092	1	2	7	15	35	5	378	5	41	1	0	8
TSG125	5	158	3,625	10,893	329	687	33	13	8,603	4,317	8	10	39	20	3	7	603	7	65	2	2	15
TSG128	6	190	4,303	12,117	475	709	19	15	4,150	5,593	80	11	3,360	59	41	9	374	5	61	2	2	180
TSG129	4	163	2,897	11,313	173	482	21	11	7,543	3,813	5	9	17	11	3	7	444	6	54	2	1	7
TSG130	5	227	6,297	16,543	291	3,646	65	85	16,640	16,293	14	19	78	34	10	6	423	12	317	7	3	7
TSG131	4	122	5,050	14,227	620	2,667	97	63	11,750	24,717	10	37	80	46	23	6	459	15	219	5	3	7
TSG132	5	168	5,203	9,982	287	674	35	14	13,393	5,237	7	11	38	17	4	6	821	8	66	2	3	9
TSG133	5	135	3,985	11,477	315	828	22	18	7,077	4,613	4	7	26	13	3	7	534	7	79	2	1	9
TSG134	5	153	4,283	12,223	324	1,007	28	21	10,917	5,513	5	9	43	16	5	6	559	7	110	3	2	14
TSG135	6	177	5,343	11,537	706	776	24	16	5,893	6,377	9	10	745	33	11	8	531	7	77	2	2	77
TSG136	5	152	4,600	12,670	273	956	31	23	10,567	6,247	7	12	26	21	3	6	704	8	83	3	3	7
TSG137	6	150	4,177	11,810	271	719	31	14	11,157	5,283	6	10	35	15	3	7	587	7	66	2	3	7
TSG138	7	155	3,783	11,193	299	913	28	21	8,067	5,910	10	10	287	21	5	8	521	7	86	2	2	55
TSG139	7	182	7,060	13,250	691	864	32	18	16,267	6,130	7	18	43	27	4	8	827	8	81	3	2	12
TSG140	5	167	4,480	11,703	268	606	11	12	192	4,397	2	5	25	22	40	7	698	7	55	2	0	10
TSG153	3	92	2,390	13,902	542	322	8	10	1,310	2,334	5	5	8	12	1	8	442	7	36	1	1	3
TSG154	5	137	2,930	10,843	267	494	8	10	197	4,436	71	23	35,330	989	79	7	580	6	53	2	0	2,167
TSG155	4	158	3,857	10,630	183	563	27	11	12,693	3,840	8	9	21	16	3	6	495	6	54	2	4	3
TSG156	4	159	3,897	10,543	188	565	27	10	12,043	3,823	8	9	21	16	3	6	497	6	52	2	4	3

Table 10.3 (cont.)

Part (a)	Li	B	Mg	Al	P	Ti	V	Cr	Mn	Fe	Co	Ni	Cu	Zn	As	Rb	Sr	Y	Zr	Nb	Mo	Sn
TSG157	7	101	19,877	2,686	1,241	645	14	6	3,769	1,673	3	5	8	30	1	10	427	4	188	2	2	2
TSG158	6	177	6,247	14,310	460	2,320	67	48	14,001	16,729	19	23	106	39	13	6	544	12	220	5	2	22
TSG159	3	85	2,238	12,987	500	298	7	9	1,296	2,154	5	5	7	12	1	6	408	7	33	1	0	2
TSG160	4	112	2,353	9,823	131	407	7	9	130	2,469	1	3	4	16	5	5	390	5	43	1	0	2
TSG161	7	93	4,173	7,233	567	1,006	16	17	17,293	3,443	6	9	43	175	4	5	108	5	207	3	1	3
TSG162	5	166	4,821	12,683	299	925	34	19	14,033	9,146	10	17	3,535	283	18	5	469	7	74	3	5	56
TSG163	4	191	2,495	10,232	169	391	7	8	156	2,588	1	3	16	19	117	5	365	5	41	1	0	5
TSG164	4	144	4,352	12,442	185	911	30	28	13,112	5,198	7	11	16	14	3	5	390	6	74	2	4	3
TSG165	5	132	4,617	15,084	449	2029	25	31	183	8,409	4	9	3	19	1	5	209	8	237	5	0	2
TSG177	4	222	5,543	11,983	164	1,530	28	29	13,503	7,167	10	13	28	20	4	5	409	7	130	3	3	2
TSG178	3	150	1,969	9,717	131	362	6	7	179	2,330	1	2	13	17	10	5	438	5	43	1	0	34
TSG180	3	186	2,738	9,938	134	394	7	8	90	2,175	1	2	5	12	16	6	369	5	39	1	0	2
TSG166	3	59	2,212	11,960	507	917	12	18	269	4,859	3	12	9,943	52	21	5	148	5	71	2	0	2,213
TSG167	4	120	1,843	8,867	183	291	5	6	68	5,567	566	5	945	104	4	6	306	5	30	1	0	2
TSG168_turq	7	63	2,872	11,903	276	358	7	8	107	7,373	957	9	1991	120	16	11	456	7	36	1	1	4
TSG168_blue	7	74	2,957	12,167	283	360	7	8	113	13,973	2,240	13	3,902	216	14	12	463	7	33	1	1	5
TSG169	3	106	2,528	9,566	225	301	8	6	61	2,052	20	4	11,277	16	12	6	273	5	36	1	0	3
TSG170	5	61	2,471	9,596	205	352	9	8	85	2,817	6	11	26,153	17	47	9	370	6	44	1	0	153
TSG171	4	113	2,845	12,307	236	411	9	9	144	2,750	8	8	15,000	10	22	12	464	7	40	1	1	18
TSG172_blueopq	5	182	5,059	10,751	865	743	16	15	2,444	7,573	4	10	7,991	50	31	6	439	5	63	2	2	355
TSG172_grntint	6	197	3,110	10,913	330	871	12	27	611	4,616	4	16	35,873	138	97	8	339	6	61	3	0	1,661
TSG173	3	107	2,186	12,254	209	263	5	6	97	5,656	557	6	968	170	6	9	408	7	27	1	0	3
TSG174	6	46	2,403	13,634	214	434	7	9	129	3,907	9	14	27,827	26	41	10	403	7	34	1	0	497
TSG175_cless	11	57	4,339	3,400	1,266	203	6	6	95	2,153	1	4	40	34	18,737	21	477	1	14	1	0	49
TSG175_pinkstreak	12	59	4,343	3,312	1,295	205	6	6	95	2,124	1	5	40	32	20,147	21	479	1	14	1	0	50
TSG175_yell	10	67	5,803	3,528	1,498	229	6	6	813	2,988	4	17	332	169	7,410	16	463	5	14	1	0	3,863
TSG176_red	12	65	4,394	2003	1,541	110	4	3	324	1,193	2	5	71	32	19,700	32	423	7	7	0	1	17
TSG176_white	10	50	3,485	1,859	1,275	97	3	7	210	1,067	3	7	118	26	52,830	21	329	1	6	0	0	183
TSG041	5	279	4,475	14,063	454	475	11	9	571	4,623	369	15	916	78	11	14	636	8	60	1	7	33
TSG044	5	49	999	7,005	251	652	11	10	67	17,020	5	6	206	24	40	7	93	5	102	2	0	4
TSG045	9	150	2,897	8,583	474	679	12	12	126	5,997	76	17	22,943	43	50	9	259	5	107	2	0	348
TSG051	4	53	2,286	11,173	453	1,109	15	18	212	5,623	4	14	7,493	449	33	4	155	5	74	2	0	4,290
TSG055	3	63	2,190	11,743	348	1,147	17	23	122	6,110	4	15	5,733	261	17	5	84	5	71	2	0	383

TSG057	3	60	2,962	382	1,553	21	36	172	6,700	5	19	11,400	774	46	6	132	6	109	3	0	1947
TSG058	3	61	2,173	375	1,220	17	22	120	6,470	4	18	7,300	332	22	5	92	7	87	3	0	617
TSG068	40	86	10,593	1,589	699	28	12	21,633	5,717	17	21	287	73	8	11	406	7	139	3	10	159
TSG179	19	69	4,837	455	1,078	15	8	720	18,063	53	13	6	52	7	12	184	9	197	5	13	3
TSG144	21	13	4,713	287	1,597	30	24	411	13,277	4	11	8	437	0	29	73	7	33	15	1	4
TSG145	112	14	6,840	403	2,220	40	35	402	14,533	5	16	127	1,133	0	72	280	14	76	9	1	8
TSG146	54	72	17,900	993	3,070	51	25	463	19,867	7	18	23	289	1	24	646	22	193	13	1	5
TSG147	21	16	5,974	298	1,496	36	30	186	13,548	5	14	6	140	0	15	38	10	47	7	0	2
TSG148	5	15	9,117	489	1,453	43	26	293	18,683	7	18	3	37	1	106	418	7	30	6	0	1
TSG149	26	47	12,755	511	2,713	49	31	359	21,727	7	17	11	225	1	36	843	14	91	11	1	5
TSG150	7	15	5,733	339	1,657	31	25	533	16,533	5	10	3	234	0	30	99	10	29	7	1	3
TSG151	13	185	2,994	337	614	12	11	913	4,738	3	6	33	29	19	21	383	6	95	2	0	22
TSG152	4	92	3,681	437	357	9	12	306	2,678	1	4	5	9	2	9	500	8	36	1	1	3

Part (b)	Sb	Cs	Ba	La	Ce	Pr	Nd	Sm	Eu	Gd	Tb	Dy	Ho	Er	Tm	Yb	Lu	Hf	Pb	Th	U
TSG069	3,793	0	133	5	8	1	4	1	0	1	0	1	0	1	0	0	0	1	9	1	1
TSG070	6,053	0	130	5	8	1	4	1	0	1	0	1	0	1	0	0	0	1	13	1	1
TSG071	5,940	0	124	6	11	1	5	1	0	1	0	1	0	1	0	0	0	2	4,160	1	1
TSG072	5,083	0	130	5	9	1	4	1	0	1	0	1	0	0	0	1	1	1	493	1	1
TSG073	5,237	0	131	5	9	1	5	1	0	1	0	1	0	0	0	0	0	1	496	1	1
TSG074	1950	0	113	4	7	1	4	1	0	1	0	1	0	0	0	0	0	1	71	1	1
TSG075	2,153	0	137	5	9	1	4	1	0	1	0	1	0	0	0	0	0	1	96	1	1
TSG076	5,617	0	155	6	9	1	5	1	0	1	0	1	0	1	0	0	0	1	22	1	1
TSG078	3,377	0	240	6	10	1	5	1	0	1	0	1	0	1	0	1	0	1	98	1	1
TSG079	6,874	0	163	7	11	1	6	1	0	1	0	1	0	1	0	1	0	1	47	1	1
TSG080	4,138	0	159	6	11	1	6	1	0	1	0	1	0	1	0	1	0	1	119	1	1
TSG081	3,668	0	145	6	9	1	5	1	0	1	0	1	0	1	0	1	0	1	14	1	1
TSG082	−1	0	243	6	11	1	6	1	0	2	0	1	0	1	0	1	0	1	7	1	1
TSG083	93	0	255	6	11	1	6	1	0	1	0	1	0	1	0	1	0	1	51	1	1
TSG084	19	0	241	6	10	1	6	1	0	1	0	1	0	1	0	1	0	1	16	1	1
TSG085	10,300	0	144	5	10	1	5	1	0	1	0	1	0	1	0	0	0	1	146	1	1
TSG086	8	0	385	6	11	2	6	1	0	1	0	1	0	1	0	0	0	1	6	1	1
TSG087	1	0	385	9	16	2	9	2	0	2	0	2	0	1	0	1	0	4	13	2	2
TSG089	4,227	0	123	5	9	1	5	1	0	1	0	1	0	1	0	0	0	1	26	1	1
TSG090	0	0	410	8	15	2	7	2	0	0	0	1	0	1	0	1	0	4	6	2	1
TSG091	3,700	0	134	5	9	1	5	1	0	1	0	1	0	1	0	0	0	1	13	1	1
TSG092	6,097	0	133	5	8	1	4	1	0	1	0	1	0	0	0	0	0	1	20	1	1
TSG093	4,697	0	131	5	8	1	4	1	0	1	0	1	0	0	0	0	0	1	9	1	1
TSG094	6,127	0	140	5	8	1	4	1	0	1	0	1	0	0	0	0	0	1	21	1	1
TSG095	3	0	2,423	9	16	2	9	2	1	2	0	2	0	1	0	1	0	5	17	2	2
TSG096	1	0	893	10	17	2	9	2	0	2	0	2	0	1	0	1	0	6	8	2	1
TSG097	0	0	269	9	14	2	8	2	0	2	0	1	0	1	0	1	0	3	16	1	1
TSG098	0	0	252	9	13	2	8	1	0	2	0	2	0	1	0	1	0	3	10	1	1
TSG099	0	0	249	10	16	2	10	2	1	2	0	2	0	1	0	1	0	5	8	2	2
TSG100	0	0	423	7	12	2	6	1	0	1	0	1	0	1	0	1	0	1	5	1	1
TSG101	2	0	216	6	11	2	6	1	0	1	0	1	0	1	0	1	0	1	7	1	1

ID																							
TSG102	0	0	394	5	9	1	5	1	0	1	0	1	0	1	0	1	0	0	1	1	5	1	1
TSG103	22	0	232	6	10	1	5	1	0	1	0	1	0	1	0	1	1	0	1	1	8	1	1
TSG104	18	0	304	6	10	1	6	1	0	1	0	1	0	1	0	1	1	0	1	1	47	1	1
TSG105	773	0	246	5	9	1	5	1	0	1	0	1	0	1	0	1	0	0	1	1	106	1	1
TSG106	825	0	278	6	11	1	6	1	0	1	0	1	0	1	0	1	1	0	1	1	115	1	1
TSG107	736	0	143	7	11	2	7	1	0	1	0	1	0	1	0	1	1	0	1	1	295	1	1
TSG108	1	0	366	9	14	2	8	2	0	2	0	2	0	1	0	2	1	0	4	1	9	2	1
TSG109	1	0	346	9	13	2	8	2	0	1	0	1	0	1	0	1	1	0	3	1	7	1	1
TSG110	5,203	0	144	5	8	1	4	1	0	1	0	1	0	1	0	1	0	0	1	1	6	1	1
TSG111	5,517	0	148	5	10	1	5	1	0	1	0	1	0	1	0	1	0	0	1	1	126	1	1
TSG114	6,323	0	143	5	9	1	5	1	0	1	0	1	0	1	0	1	0	0	1	1	910	1	1
TSG115	4,257	0	145	5	8	1	5	1	0	1	0	1	0	1	0	1	0	0	1	1	993	1	1
TSG117	3,678	0	190	6	11	1	6	2	0	1	0	1	0	1	0	1	1	0	2	1	238	1	1
TSG118	4,060	0	178	6	11	1	6	2	0	1	0	1	0	1	0	1	1	0	2	1	244	1	1
TSG119	3,098	0	131	5	9	1	5	1	0	1	0	1	0	1	0	1	0	0	1	1	2,757	1	1
TSG120	4,063	0	189	6	11	1	6	1	0	1	0	1	0	1	0	1	1	0	2	1	229	1	1
TSG121	7	0	317	7	13	2	7	1	0	2	0	1	0	1	0	1	1	0	2	1	12	1	1
TSG122	7,420	0	149	5	9	1	5	2	0	1	0	2	0	0	0	1	0	0	1	1	51	1	1
TSG125	9	0	288	6	10	1	6	1	0	1	0	1	0	1	0	1	1	0	2	1	63	1	1
TSG128	5,913	0	247	6	11	2	6	1	0	1	0	1	0	1	0	1	1	0	2	1	2,233	1	1
TSG129	9	0	488	6	11	1	6	1	1	1	0	1	0	1	0	1	0	0	1	1	9	1	1
TSG130	1	0	803	12	21	3	12	2	1	2	1	2	1	1	0	2	0	0	7	1	9	2	2
TSG131	1	0	238	15	19	4	15	3	1	3	1	3	1	1	0	3	0	0	5	1	27	2	2
TSG132	17	0	446	8	13	2	7	2	0	1	0	1	0	2	1	1	0	0	2	1	38	1	1
TSG133	50	0	248	7	13	2	7	2	0	1	0	1	0	1	0	1	0	0	2	1	34	1	1
TSG134	255	0	280	7	12	2	7	3	0	1	0	1	0	1	0	1	0	0	3	1	94	1	1
TSG135	1,583	0	328	7	12	2	6	2	0	1	0	1	0	1	0	1	0	0	2	1	867	1	1
TSG136	0	0	466	8	13	2	8	2	0	1	0	1	0	1	0	1	0	0	2	1	42	2	2
TSG137	6	0	337	7	12	2	6	2	0	1	0	1	0	1	0	1	0	0	2	1	11	1	1
TSG138	249	0	397	6	12	2	6	1	0	1	0	1	0	1	0	1	0	0	2	1	1,463	1	1
TSG139	72	0	289	7	13	2	6	1	0	1	0	1	0	1	0	1	0	0	2	1	56	1	1
TSG140	3,242	0	152	7	13	2	7	1	0	1	0	1	0	1	0	1	0	0	1	1	81	1	1

(*cont.*)

Part (b)	Sb	Cs	Ba	La	Ce	Pr	Nd	Sm	Eu	Gd	Tb	Dy	Ho	Er	Tm	Yb	Lu	Hf	Pb	Th	U
TSG153	1	0	215	6	11	1	6	1	0	1	0	1	0	1	0	1	0	1	7	1	1
TSG154	3,402	0	141	6	11	1	6	1	0	1	0	1	0	1	0	0	0	1	33,407	1	1
TSG155	6	0	222	6	11	2	6	1	0	1	0	1	0	1	0	1	0	1	6	1	1
TSG156	6	0	219	6	11	1	6	1	0	1	0	1	0	1	0	1	0	1	6	1	1
TSG157	0	0	106	6	11	1	4	1	0	1	0	1	0	0	0	0	0	5	2	2	1
TSG158	3	0	325	12	17	3	11	2	1	2	0	2	0	1	0	1	0	5	160	2	1
TSG159	1	0	199	6	10	1	6	1	0	1	0	1	0	1	0	0	0	1	6	1	1
TSG160	4,953	0	145	5	10	1	5	1	0	1	0	1	0	0	0	0	0	1	14	1	1
TSG161	0	0	89	5	13	1	4	1	0	1	0	1	0	1	0	1	0	5	8	2	1
TSG162	265	0	315	7	13	2	6	1	0	1	0	1	0	1	0	1	0	2	157	1	1
TSG163	5,907	0	146	5	9	1	5	1	0	1	0	1	0	0	0	0	0	1	57	1	1
TSG164	6	0	294	6	12	2	6	1	0	1	0	1	0	1	0	1	0	2	11	1	1
TSG165	0	0	179	8	16	2	8	1	0	1	0	1	0	1	0	1	0	6	4	2	1
TSG177	0	0	293	7	13	2	7	2	0	1	0	1	0	1	0	1	0	3	7	1	1
TSG178	7,110	0	141	5	9	1	5	1	0	1	0	1	0	0	0	0	0	1	1,996	1	1
TSG180	3,128	0	144	5	9	1	5	1	0	1	0	1	0	0	0	0	0	1	12	1	1
TSG166	84	0	147	5	11	1	6	1	0	1	0	1	0	1	0	1	0	2	29,900	1	1
TSG167	22	0	145	5	9	1	5	1	0	1	0	1	0	0	0	0	0	1	37	1	1
TSG168_turq	51,137	0	186	6	11	1	6	1	0	1	0	1	0	1	0	1	0	1	421	1	2
TSG168_blue	12,060	0	188	6	11	1	6	1	0	1	0	1	0	1	0	1	0	1	594	1	1
TSG169	26	0	148	5	8	1	5	1	0	1	0	1	0	0	0	0	0	1	12	1	3
TSG170	33,057	0	199	5	9	1	5	1	0	1	0	1	0	1	0	0	0	1	6,600	1	2
TSG171	8	0	195	6	11	1	6	1	0	1	0	1	0	1	0	1	0	1	26	1	1
TSG172_blueopq	8,023	0	175	6	11	1	5	1	0	1	0	1	0	1	0	0	0	2	465	1	1
TSG172_grntint	30,333	0	144	7	13	1	6	1	0	1	0	1	0	1	0	1	0	1	1,149	1	1
TSG173	870	0	189	5	10	1	6	1	0	1	0	1	0	1	0	1	0	1	425	1	1
TSG174	29,953	0	196	6	11	1	6	1	0	1	0	1	0	1	0	1	0	1	89	1	1
TSG175_cless	3,417	0	46	2	3	0	2	0	0	0	0	0	0	0	0	0	0	0	149,333	0	0
TSG175_pinkstreak	3,577	0	47	2	3	0	1	0	0	0	0	0	0	0	0	0	0	0	156,533	0	0
TSG175_yell	31,800	0	54	2	4	0	2	0	0	0	0	0	0	0	0	0	0	0	259,033	0	0

TSG176_red	3,207	0	35	1	2	0	1	0	0	0	0	0	0	0	0	185,267	0	0
TSG176_white	209	0	28	1	2	0	1	0	0	0	0	0	0	0	0	262,033	0	0
TSG041	9	0	296	8	13	2	6	1	1	1	1	1	1	0	2	154	2	1
TSG044	25,420	0	90	6	12	1	5	1	0	1	1	0	1	0	3	315,800	2	1
TSG045	535	0	99	7	14	2	5	1	0	1	1	0	1	0	3	827	1	2
TSG051	66	0	130	5	10	1	4	1	0	1	1	0	1	0	2	58,833	1	1
TSG055	11	0	116	5	9	1	4	1	0	1	1	0	1	0	2	4,867	1	1
TSG057	52	0	153	6	11	1	5	1	0	1	1	0	1	0	3	21,800	1	1
TSG058	14	0	146	6	12	1	6	1	0	1	1	0	1	0	2	7,900	1	1
TSG068	3	0	544	9	16	2	7	1	0	1	1	0	1	0	4	17,100	2	1
TSG179	0	0	181	9	18	2	8	2	0	1	1	1	1	0	5	4	3	8
TSG144	0	1	63	16	30	3	13	2	0	2	2	0	1	0	1	6	3	1
TSG145	0	2	381	18	33	4	16	3	1	3	3	1	0	0	2	5	6	1
TSG146	0	0	317	25	44	5	20	4	1	4	4	2	2	0	5	2	6	2
TSG147	0	0	67	18	34	4	15	3	1	2	2	1	1	0	1	0	4	1
TSG148	0	3	720	16	27	4	14	2	1	2	3	1	1	0	1	3	3	1
TSG149	0	1	305	24	43	5	20	4	0	4	4	1	1	0	2	3	6	1
TSG150	0	1	99	15	27	3	13	2	0	2	2	1	1	0	1	3	3	1
TSG151	4,669	0	218	7	12	2	6	1	1	1	1	1	1	0	2	104	1	1
TSG152	2	0	212	7	12	2	6	1	0	1	1	1	1	0	1	16	1	1

References

Alberini, E.S. 1998. *Libyan Jewellery: A Journey through Symbols*. Rome: Araldo de Luca.

Antonaras, A. and Anagnostopoulou-Chatzipolichoroni, E. 2002. Glass finds from ancient Ioron. In G. Kordas (ed.), *Hyalos, Vitrum, Glass: History, Technology and Conservation of Glass and Vitreous Materials in the Hellenic World*, Athens: Glasnet Publications, 113–23.

Boulogne, S. 2007a. Glass bangles from Hubras and Malka excavations. In B.J. Walker (ed.), *The Northern Jordan Project 2006: Village Life in Mamluk and Ottoman Hubras and Sahm, a Preliminary Report, Annual of the Department of Antiquities of Jordan* 52, 429–70.

Boulogne, S. 2007b. *Réflet d'un art populaire: Les bracelets de verre coloré de la période médiévale (1171–1517) et ottoman (1517–1864) du Bilād al-Shām*. Unpublished doctoral thesis, Université Paris IV.

Boulogne, S. and Henderson, J. 2009. Indian glass in the Middle East? Medieval and Ottoman glass bangles from Central Jordan. *Journal of Glass Studies* 51: 53–75.

Bowdich, T.E. 1819. *Mission to Ashanti*. London: John Murray.

Brill, R.H. 1995. Chemical analysis of some glasses from Jenné-Jeno. In S.K. McIntosh (ed.), *Excavations at Jenné-Jeno, Hambarketolo, and Kaniana (Inland Niger Delta, Mali), the 1981 Season*, Berkeley, CA: University of California Press, 252–56.

Brogan, O. and Smith, D.J. 1984. *Ghirza: A Libyan Settlement in the Roman period*. Libyan Antiquities Series. Tripoli: Department of Antiquities.

Carboni, S. 1994. Glass bracelets from the Mamluk period in the Metropolitan Museum of Art. *Journal of Glass Studies* 36: 126–29.

Cissé, M. 2017. The Trans-Saharan trade connection with Gao (Mali) during the first millennium. In Mattingly *et al.* 2017, 101–30.

Cissé, M., McIntosh, S.K., Dussubieux, L., Fenn, T., Gallagher, D. and Chipps Smith, A. 2013. Excavations at Gao Saney: New evidence for settlement growth, trade, and interaction on the Niger Bend in the first millennium CE. *Journal of African Archaeology* 11.1: 9–37.

Cole, F. 2013. Small finds reports. In Mattingly 2013, 455–72.

Davison, C.C., Giauque, R.D. and Clark, J.D. 1971. Two chemical groups of dichroic glass beads from West Africa. *Man* 6.4: 645–59.

De Juan Ares, J. and Schibille, N. 2017. Glass import and production in Hispania during the early Medieval period: The glass from Ciudad de Vascos (Toledo). *PLoS ONE* 12.7: e0182129.

Devulder, V., Vanhaecke, F., Shortland, A., Mattingly, D.J., Jackson, C.M. and Degryse, P. 2014. Boron isotopic composition as a provenance indicator for the flux raw material in Roman natron glass. *Journal of Archaeological Science* 46: 107–13.

Duckworth, C.N., Córdoba de la Llave, R., Faber, E.W. and Govantes-Edwards, D. J. 2015a. Electron microprobe analysis of 9th–12th century Islamic glass from Cordoba, Spain. *Archaeometry* 57.1: 27–50.

Duckworth, C.N., Cuénod, A. and Mattingly, D.J. 2015b. Non-destructive µXRF analysis of glass and metal objects from sites in the Libyan pre-desert and Fazzan. *Libyan Studies*, 46: 15–34.

Duckworth, C.N., Mattingly, D.J., Chenery, S. and Smith, V.C. 2016a. End of the line? Glass bangles, technology, recycling, and trade in Islamic North Africa. *Journal of Glass Studies* 58: 135–69.

Duckworth, C.N., Mattingly, D.J. and Smith, V.C. 2016b. From the Mediterranean to the Libyan Sahara: Chemical analyses of Garamantian glass. *Journal of Archaeological Science: Reports* 7: 633–39.

Dussubieux, L. 2017. Glass beads in the Trans-Saharan trade. In Mattingly *et al.* 2017, 414–32.

Dussubieux, L., Kusimba, C.M., Gogte, V., Kusimba, S.B., Gratuze, B. and Oka, R. 2008. The trading of ancient glass beads: New analytical data from South Asian and East African soda-alumina glass beads. *Archaeometry* 50.5: 797–821.

Dussubieux, L., Robertshaw, P. and Glascock, M.D. 2009. LA-ICP-MS analysis of African glass beads: Laboratory inter-comparison with an emphasis on the impact of corrosion on data interpretation. *International Journal of Mass Spectrometry* 284: 152–61.

Fabri, M. 2013. *Chemische merker voor natron zouten.* Leuven: KU Leuven.

Freestone, I.C. 2006. An indigenous technology? A commentary on Lankton *et al.* 'Early primary glass production in southern Nigeria'. *Journal of African Archaeology* 4.1: 139–41.

Freestone, I.C., Gorin-Rosen, Y. and Hughes, M.J. 2000. Primary glass from Israel and the production of glass in Late Antiquity and the Early Islamic period. In M.-D. Nenna (ed.), *La route du verre: Ateliers primaires et secondaires de verriers du second millénaire av. J.-C. au Moyen-Age*, Lyon: Travaux de la Maison de l'Orient Méditérranean 33, 65–83.

Gliozzo, E., Santagostino Barbone, A. and D'Acapito, F. 2013. Waste glass, vessels and window-panes from Thamusida (Morocco): Grouping natron-based blue-green and colourless Roman glasses. *Archaeometry* 55.4: 609–39.

Henderson, J. 1988. Glass production and Bronze Age Europe. *Antiquity* 62: 435–51.

Hoffmann, B. 2013a. Discussion of the glass from Old Jarma. In Mattingly 2013, 409–19.

Hoffmann, B. 2013b. Catalogue of glass from FP excavations at Jarma. In Mattingly 2013, 707–22.

Insoll, T. 1996. *Islam, Archaeology and History: Gao Region (Mali) ca. AD 900–1250.* Cambridge Monographs in African Archaeology, Volume 39. Oxford: Archaeopress.

Kanungo, A.K. and Brill, R.H. 2009. Kopia, India's first glassmaking site: Dating and chemical analysis. *Journal of Glass Studies* 51: 11–25.

Kock, J. and Sode, T. 2002. Medieval glass mirrors in southern Scandinavia and their technique as still practiced in India. *Journal of Glass Studies* 44: 79–94.

Lancelotti, C. and Madella, M. 2012. The 'invisible' product: Developing markers for identifying dung in archaeological contexts. *Journal of Archaeological Science* 39: 953–63.

Lankton, J.W. and Dussubieux, L. 2006. Early glass in Asian maritime trade: A review and an interpretation of compositional analyses. *Journal of Glass Studies* 48: 121–44.

Lankton, J.W., Ige, A. and Rehren, Th. 2006. Early primary glass production in southern Nigeria. *Journal of African Archaeology* 4.1: 111–38.

Lyon, G.F. 1821. *A Narrative of Travels in Northern Africa in the Years 1818, 1819 and 1820*. London: Frank Cass (1966 reprint).

Magnavita, S. 2017. Track and trace: Archaeometric approaches to the study of early Trans-Saharan trade. In Mattingly *et al.* 2017, 393–413.

Mattingly, D.J. (ed.) 2007. *The Archaeology of Fazzan. Volume 2, Site Gazetteer, Pottery and Other Survey Finds*. London: Society for Libyan Studies, Department of Antiquities.

Mattingly, D.J. (ed.) 2010. *The Archaeology of Fazzan. Volume 3, Excavations of C. M. Daniels*. London: Society for Libyan Studies, Department of Antiquities.

Mattingly, D.J. (ed.) 2013. *The Archaeology of Fazzan. Volume 4, Survey and Excavations at Old Jarma (Ancient Garama) Carried out by C.M. Daniels (1962–69) and the Fazzan Project (1997–2001)*. London: Society for Libyan Studies, Department of Antiquities.

Mattingly, D.J., Leitch, V., Duckworth, C.N., Cuénod, A., Sterry, M. and Cole, F. (eds) 2017. *Trade in the Ancient Sahara and Beyond*. Cambridge: Cambridge University Press.

Mecking, O. 2013. Medieval lead glass in central Europe. *Archaeometry* 55: 640–42.

Meyer, C. 1992. *Glass from Quseir al-Qadim and the Indian Ocean Trade*. Studies in African Civilisation 53. Chicago: The Oriental Institute of the University of Chicago.

Monod, T. 1975. A propos des bracelets de verre sahariens. *Bulletin Institut Fondamental d'Afrique Noire* 37: 702–18.

Monod, T. 1978. Sur un site à bracelets de verre des environs d'Aden. *Raydan* 1: 111–24.

Monod, T. 1982. Bracelets de verre polychromes du Sahara occidental au Népal. In J.P. Digard (ed.), *Le Cuisinier et la Philosophe: Hommage à Maxime Rodinson*, Études d'ethnographie du Proche-Orient, Paris: Maisonneuve et Larose, 55–63.

Mordini, A. 1937. Etnografia e fatti culturali. In *Il Sahara italiano*, Volume 1. Rome, 451–91.

Nesbitt, M. 1993. Archaeobotanical evidence for early Dilmun diet at Saar, Bahrain. *Arabian Archaeology and Epigraphy* 4: 20–47.

Nicholson, P.T. and Jackson, C.M. 2007. The furnace experiment. In P.T. Nicholson (ed.), *Brilliant Things for Akhenaten: The Production of Glass, Vitreous Materials and Pottery at Amarna Site 045.1*, London: Egypt Exploration Society.

Nicolas, N. 2012. Bijoux celtes et romains: Les bracelets en verre. In P. Cattelain, N. Bozet and G. Vincenzo Di Stazio (eds), *La Parure de Cro-Magnon à Clovis, 'Il n'y a pas d'âge(s) pour se faire beau'*, Treignes: Éditions du Cedarc, 71–83.

Pace, B., Sergi, S. and Caputo, G. 1951. Scavi sahariani. *Monumenti Antichi* 41: 150–549.

Pelling, R. 2013. The archaeobotanical remains. In Mattingly 2013, 473–94.

Pollard, A.M. and Heron, C. 1996. *Archaeological Chemistry*. Cambridge: The Royal Society of Chemistry.

Rehren, Th. 2000. Rationales in Old World base glass compositions. *Journal of Archaeological Science* 27: 1225–34.

Rehren, Th. and Nixon, S. 2014. Refining gold with glass: An Early Islamic technology at Tadmekka, Mali. *Journal of Archaeological Science* 49: 33–41.

Robertshaw, P., Magnavita, S., Wood, M., Melchiorre, E., Popelka-Filcoff, R.S. and Glascock, M.D. 2009a. Glass beads from Kissi (Burkina Faso): Chemical analysis and archaeological interpretation. In S. Magnavita, L. Koté, P. Breunig and O.A. Idé (eds), *Crossroads/Carrefour Sahel: Cultural and Technological Developments in First Millennium* BC/AD *West Africa*, Frankfurt: Africa Magna Verlag, 105–118.

Robertshaw, P., Weise, C., Dussubieux, L., Lankton, J.W., Popelka-Filcoff, R.S. and Glascock, M.D. 2009b. Chemical analysis of glass from Nupe, Nigeria. *Tribus* 58: 83–95.

Robertshaw, P., Benco, N., Wood, M., Dussubieux, L., Melchiorre E. and Ettahiri, A. 2010. Chemical analysis of glass beads from Medieval al-Basra (Morocco). *Archaeometry* 52.3: 355–79.

Rolland, J., Le Bechennec, Y., Clesse, J. and Rivoal, S. 2012. Des parures celtiques aux verriers du Népal: Un projet d'expérimentation des techniques de fabrication des bracelets en verre. *Bulletin de l'Association Française pour l'Archéologie du Verre* 2012: 6–10.

Sayre, E.V. and Smith, R.W. 1961. Compositional categories of ancient glass. *Science* 133: 1824–26.

Sayre, E.V. and Smith, R.W. 1967. Some materials of glass manufacturing in antiquity. In M. Levey (ed.), *Archaeological Chemistry, a Symposium*, Philadelphia: University of Philadelphia Press, 279–312.

Shindo, Y. 1996. Islamic glass bracelets found in the Red Sea region. In *Annales du 13e Congrès de l'Association Internationale pour l'Histoire du Verre*, Amsterdam: AIHV, 269–77.

Shindo, Y. 2001. The classification and chronology of the Islamic glass bracelets at Tūr, Sinaï. In *Cultural Change in the Arab World*, Senri Ethnological Studies, Osaka: National Museum of Ethnology, 73–100.

Silvestri, A. 2008. The coloured glass of Iulia Felix. *Journal of Archaeological Science* 35.6: 1489–501.

Spaer, M. 1988. The pre-Islamic glass bracelets of Palestine. *Journal of Glass Studies* 30: 51–61.

Spaer, M. 1992. The Islamic glass bracelets of Palestine: Preliminary findings. *Journal of Glass Studies* 34: 44–62.

Sprague, R. 1985. Glass trade beads: A progress report. *Historical Archaeology* 19.2: 87–105.

Tite, M., Pradell, T. and Shortland, A. 2008. Discovery, production and use of tin-based opacifiers in glasses, enamels and glazes from the Late Iron Age onwards: A reassessment. *Archaeometry* 50.1: 67–84.

Truffa Giachet, M. 2019. *Étude archéométrique des perles en verre d'Afrique de l'Ouest: Vers une meilleure compréhension des dynamiques techniques et commerciales à l'époque des empires précoloniaux.* Unpublished PhD thesis, University of Geneva.

Vellani, S. 1996. La Tène glass bracelets from Emilia Romagna (Italy). *Annales de l'Association Internationale pour l'Histoire du Verre* 13: 33–46.

Verità, M. 2013. Vitreous beads: A scientific investigation by SEM microscopy and X-ray microanalysis. In L. Mori (ed.), *Life and Death of a Rural Village in Garamantian Times: Archaeological Investigations of Fewet (Libyan Sahara)*, Arid Zone Archaeological Monographs 6, Borgo San Lorenzo: All'Insegna del Giglio, 169–76.

11 | Glass Beads in African Society

Beyond Chemistry and Provenience

PETER ROBERTSHAW

Introduction

> Objects accumulate histories and have the ability to tell multiple stories about people.[1]

Glass beads, recovered from many African archaeological sites dating to the first and second millennia AD, are redolent with meaning: tangible evidence of intercontinental trade, perhaps participants in ritual practice, and not only probable markers of wealth and status but also active participants in the production of social differentiation. Often found in small numbers during excavations, sometimes in burials, they can also raise vexing sampling issues revolving around sieve mesh diameters. Safely transported to the lab, they are usually examined by an expert who, the archaeologists hope, will succeed in identifying them – perhaps Indo-Pacific beads, 'Indian-red-on-greens', etc. – and thereby suggest both an origin and perhaps a date. Indeed, beads can be a very valuable dating tool for sites of the last 500 years. The development of minimally destructive and relatively inexpensive chemical analysis of glass during the last 15 years or so, primarily using laser ablation inductively coupled plasma mass spectrometry (LA-ICP-MS), has vastly expanded our ability to discover the region of the world in which a particular piece of glass was originally manufactured from raw materials. Armed with this knowledge, we can then begin to piece together a history of international trade, a history that mixes the material, scientific evidence derived from the analysis of beads, vessel glass, ceramics and metals with more speculative conjectures about the roles played by items that leave

---

[1] Gosselain 2000, 189.

few or no archaeological traces – cloth and slaves in particular – but whose importance is evident from documentary sources.

Despite the allure of glass beads and their importance in long-distance trade, the fact is that most archaeological analyses of this artefact type often succeed only in identifying the probable region where the glass was manufactured and even that may not be the same as where a particular bead was made. But surely there is more that we might learn about the glass beads we so painstakingly recover from our archaeological sites, as even a relatively superficial reading of anthropological literature and historical studies makes clear. Indeed, as Loren has remarked,

> Despite decades of research, the definition of glass beads as a trade good ... is a colonial category constructed by the English that still persists today. Of course glass beads were traded, but it was their lives beyond that moment of exchange that provides deeper insights into lived experience.[2]

Thus, we can set the stage for exploring what we might learn about glass beads by asking several questions: why have glass beads of exotic provenience been found at numerous sites in Africa (and beyond)? Or, perhaps more precisely, why glass beads rather than other kinds of objects? And why were they so often subject to recycling? Some of the answers may seem obvious – for example, glass beads were 'prestige' goods – but the application of such a label raises several questions. What made beads prestigious or valuable, beyond the simple notions that they were small and hence easily transportable and brightly coloured? By analogy to our own Western society, what makes diamonds valuable? What is 'value'? The question of value raises issues of cultural construction and social relations, in addition to narrow economic considerations.[3] Moreover, the value, as well as the function(s), of any particular object varies through space and time, as has been understood by those who have championed the study of the 'cultural biography' of an object.[4] Contemplation of such cultural biographies[5] also involves examination of spheres of both production and consumption, primarily but not exclusively situated at the two fixed points in a bead's life history that archaeologists can identify.

---

[2] Loren 2013, 159.   [3] For example, Graeber 2001.

[4] For example, Kopytoff 1986; Ogundiran 2002.

[5] Rosemary Joyce (2012) prefers the term 'object itinerary' to 'object biography', arguing that the latter implies a linear progression from 'birth' to 'death' while the former emphasises 'things as historicised traces of practices', thereby emphasising the relationships between people, objects and places (see also, Blair 2015).

Who made glass beads and who consumed them? How was production organised? Under what circumstances were they taken in or out of the sphere of economic transactions? How did people use beads? What did they *mean* to different people? All these questions can be asked and addressed, although not necessarily answered to everyone's satisfaction, at both a comparative and theoretical level and also more specifically within the context of Africa in the first and early second millennia AD.

I open consideration with a relatively brief summary of what is known about the archaeology of the bead trade and its context in the Sahara and the Sahel in the first and early second millennia AD.[6] Since this topic has been considered in a previous volume in this series,[7] I confine myself to a few observations particularly salient to the issues of consumption on which I focus later in the chapter. Here insight is aided by a few comparisons with trade and consumption of glass beads elsewhere in Sub-Saharan Africa. Building on the observation that craftspeople quite often reworked beads at Saharan and West African sites, melting down old beads and making new ones to satisfy changing consumer tastes, I explore the social and cultural contexts of bead production, the construction of technical traditions and the relationships between glassworking and other crafts. This leads me to the sphere of consumption, where I discuss the myriad social roles that glass beads play in many societies: in defining and negotiating individual and group identities, including their often intimate connection with the human body; in economic transactions, which are in turn intertwined with their role as sources of power; and in what might be called 'fashion', a topic that cannot easily be separated from the others that I discuss. This discussion of the consumption of beads is cross-cut by an important distinction between beads as goods subject to sumptuary laws and beads as trade items that may or may not have served as monetary equivalents. Any bead in the course of its cultural biography may have been a trade item, sumptuary good, ritual object, body adornment, signifier of ethnic identification and perhaps more. A bead's affect varied across space and time and between owner, wearer and observer. Despite this plenitude of meaning, I hope that archaeologists will be able to investigate the 'meaning' of beads at their sites by careful consideration of their archaeological and cultural-historical contexts, narrowing down the range of interpretive possibilities to shed new light on the past.

---

[6] See also Duckworth, Chapter 10, this volume.   [7] See especially Dussubieux 2017.

The Bead Trade in Northern and Western Africa in the First and Early Second Millennia AD

> It is a three months' journey from Sijilmasa to this country [ancient
> Ghana] and merchants from Sijilmasa go there with great exertion. Their
> stock-in-trade is salt, pine and cedar wood, glass beads, bracelets [of red
> copper] and signet rings of the same, and bangles of brass.[8]

Glass beads are just about ubiquitous on archaeological sites of the first and
early second millennium AD in North Africa, the Sahara and the Sahel,
although they have rarely been discovered at sites in the Senegal River
valley,[9] despite the fact that Arabic sources mention them as trade items
and objects of personal adornment at Takrur.[10] The numbers of glass beads
recovered at each archaeological site vary, which is not a surprise given all
the variables at play in such a determination – the frequency of recycling
and export; depositional processes (accidental loss, ritual deposits, caches);
archaeological contexts investigated (such as burials, public vs. domestic
buildings, elite vs. commoner areas); the extent of excavations; excavation
procedures, including sieve mesh sizes; and standards of reporting – and
thus it would be foolhardy to venture much more than generalities about
the volume of beads in circulation in this part of the world during this
period. Most of these beads were likely to have been imports into Sub-
Saharan Africa from outside the continent,[11] although at least some may
have originated in North Africa.[12] However, one particular type of glass,
probably dating back as far as the last centuries of the first millennium AD,
is probably of West African manufacture,[13] although beads made from this
glass are generally uncommon to rare, even in West Africa itself.

Even generalities may be of interest, however. In this regard, we can
contrast the 'abundant rich imports', including glass, in the Garamantian
period in Fazzan[14] with the relative dearth (but by no means complete
absence) of glass beads found south of the Sahara prior to about the eighth
century AD. However, there is one Sub-Saharan site that is exceptionally rich
in glass beads and other imports in pre-eighth-century contexts, the cemetery site of Kissi in Burkina Faso,[15] while the settlement mound of

---

[8] Mahmud al-Qazwīnī 1275, quoted in Levtzion and Hopkins 2000, 177.
[9] Cissé *et al.* 2013, 32; S. McIntosh, personal communication.
[10] Levtzion and Hopkins 2000, 107, 179.   [11] Dussubieux 2017.
[12] Duckworth *et al.* 2014; Duckworth, Chapter 10, this volume; Rehren and Rosenow, Chapter 12, this volume.
[13] Lankton *et al.* 2006.   [14] Mattingly 2011, 54.
[15] Magnavita 2003; 2009; 2013; Magnavita *et al.* 2002.

Tombouze 1 at Timbuktu is reputed to have yielded 'large amounts of carnelian and glass beads' in a phase dated primarily to the first half of the first millennium AD.[16] The importation of glass beads, as well as other trade goods, to the southern edges of the Sahara and south into the Sahel increased markedly from about the mid-eighth century AD,[17] if not a little earlier. Judging by recent discoveries at Gao Saney;[18] this trade boomed even more in the tenth and eleventh centuries.[19] Relevant to later discussion (below) too is the observation that this trade may have been conducted primarily by members of the Ibadi sect, 'who lived outside the mainstream culture of North African Islam'.[20] However, not all Sahelian trade entrepôts seem to have benefitted equally from this trade expansion: glass beads and copper imports seem to have been far more numerous at towns on the east side of the Niger Bend compared to those on the west side.[21]

In addition to the chronological and geographical distribution pattern of glass beads, what also emerges is the evidence of glassworking at many sites, demonstrated not only by the by-products and activity areas asso-ciated with this industry but also perhaps by the wide variety of chemical glass types present at many sites, particularly in comparison to what has been observed at other sites in Sub-Saharan Africa, notably the southern part of the continent. Table 11.1 shows some sites where either evidence of secondary glass processing has been reported or possible chemical evidence of recycling occurs, although in the latter case we cannot know

Table 11.1 *Evidence for the chemical variability in glass beads and for glassworking at some North and West African sites*

Site	Number of analysed beads	Number of glass types	Evidence for glassworking on site	Chemical compositional evidence of recycling
Al-Basra	30	6	No	Yes
Gao Saney	47	3	Yes	?
Gao Ancien	15	3	No	?
Essouk-Tadmakka	50	4	?	Yes
Igbo-Ukwu	97	7	No	Yes
Kissi	37	3	No (cemetery site)	No

[16] Park 2010, 1081.   [17] MacDonald 2011; Magnavita 2013; Nixon 2009, 247.
[18] Cissé *et al.* 2013, 32.   [19] Nixon 2009, 247–48.   [20] Nixon 2009, 247; see also Savage 1992.
[21] Cissé *et al.* 2013, 32; MacDonald 2011, 79–80.

whether this recycling occurred locally or further afield, even if we suspect that it was a local enterprise; perhaps future compositional and isotopic work will answer this question.[22] In the case of Gao Saney, the evidence of glassworking comprises numerous fragmentary and damaged beads in the form of cut tube remnants of plant ash glass, which in fact comprise the majority of the beads found in two industrial areas of the site, whereas the beads from a residential area were all intact and of many different types.[23] Examination of the damaged beads showed that they had been reheated to 'fairly high' temperatures.[24] Further evidence of reworking was found at Tagdaoust in Mauritania where clay moulds, probably used for glass bead manufacture, as well as glassworking debris, were discovered.[25]

Table 11.1 also shows the number of chemical glass types found at each site where chemical analysis of the glass beads has been undertaken; these numbers should be treated as approximations at best since they are in part the result of sampling considerations (the overall size and heterogeneity of the bead assemblage, the sampling frequency and the selection criteria used).[26] It should also be remembered that evidence of primary glass manufacture from raw materials has been discovered at Ile-Ife in Nigeria in early second millennium AD contexts,[27] while the presence of this remarkable high-lime, high-alumina glass[28] in the late first millennium AD at Igbo-Ukwu[29] indicates its probable earlier manufacture at an as yet unknown location or locations in West Africa. Both primary glass manufacture and recycling may also have occurred in Fazzan in the Garamantian period, as is hinted at by compositional analyses.[30]

Contrasts with Southern Africa

The evidence of glassworking and the substantial variety of glass chemistries identified at some North and West African sites (Table 11.1),[31] as well as at Zuwila in Libya and Sabra in Tunisia,[32] sharply contrasts with the picture in Southern Africa where most sites have yielded only one chemical

---

[22] See Duckworth, Chapter 10, this volume.

[23] Cissé 2011, 119; Wood, personal communication.   [24] Wood 2016.   [25] Vanacker 1984.

[26] Data from Cissé *et al.* 2013; Fenn, Robertshaw *et al.* in preparation; Lankton *et al.* 2017; Robertshaw *et al.* 2009a; Robertshaw *et al.* 2010a.

[27] Lankton *et al.* 2006.   [28] Freestone 2006.   [29] Fenn, Robertshaw *et al.* in preparation.

[30] Duckworth *et al.* 2014; Duckworth, Chapter 10, this volume.

[31] Duckworth *et al.* 2014; Dussubieux 2017; see Rehren and Rosenow, Chapter 12, this volume, for Egypt.

[32] Duckworth, Chapter 10, this volume; Thomas Fenn, personal communication.

glass type present during any particular time period and where evidence of glass reworking is confined to the site of K2 and its environs (K2 being the immediate precursor to the probable capital of the first Southern African state-level society at Mapungubwe).[33]

Why does this contrast exist? There is no simple explanation but we can identify several relevant factors. First, we can infer a continuum of possibilities accounting for the presence of glass beads at a particular site. At one extreme, beads may have been exclusively trade items that were on route to consumers in other places. As such they were strictly 'commodities', items intended for exchange.[34] Their presence in an archaeological site was presumably the result of accidental loss; for example, spillage from a hole in a sack. Perhaps some Saharan and Sahelian sites accumulated their glass bead assemblages in this manner. At the other extreme, glass beads were 'ex-commodities', 'things retrieved, either temporarily or permanently, from the commodity state and placed in some other state'.[35] This other state was primarily as 'luxury goods'[36] 'consumed' in social and cultural practices at the sites where they were later discovered by archaeologists, commonly, for example, as grave goods. The identification of beads as 'luxury goods' would seem to fit the bill for many, if not most, Southern African sites.

However, the occurrence of glass beads at any particular site is rarely explained solely by their presence as either commodities or luxury goods. At many or most sites, some beads were commodities and others luxury goods; indeed, the same bead at different times would have been a commodity and a luxury good, hence the importance of provenance (as opposed to provenience) studies and recognition of the fact that beads have cultural biographies for archaeologists to investigate. An example of this middle ground between commodities and luxury goods is represented by the archaeology of Fazzan during the Garamantian period: on the one hand the Garamantes traded southwards 'a mass of beadwork – in ostrich eggshell, carnelian, amazonite and glass',[37] an assertion that is, however, difficult to verify, given that the beads themselves have left Fazzan and the fact that any chemical analysis of glass beads from these southern destinations may well not point to glass manufacture in Fazzan. On the other hand the Garamantes also consumed beads in Fazzan, as is evident from the fact that one or more glass beads were noted as present as grave goods in ten tombs[38] and that bead necklaces, including glass beads, 'are common in

---

[33] Robertshaw *et al.* 2010b; Wood 2011a; 2011b, 40.   [34] Appadurai 1986a, 9.
[35] Appadurai 1986a, 16.   [36] Appadurai 1986a, 38.   [37] Mattingly 2011, 57.
[38] Mattingly 2003, 230–31.

many tombs'.[39] Also, the sample of beads recovered from excavations 'would suggest that the town of Old Jarma was in certain phases a very bead-rich site'.[40] A similar mix of beads as commodities and as luxury goods is probably evident too at Gao in Mali. Gao was a trading town and glass beads were almost certainly exported from there; indeed, at least 127 morphologically distinctive beads made from a particular plant ash glass have been identified at Gao[41] and beads of this same chemical type, quite possibly traded from Gao itself,[42] were 'consumed' at Igbo-Ukwu in the forested region of Nigeria,[43] where they were taken out of circulation for a thousand years or so until excavated by Thurstan Shaw.[44] However, it seems that beads were also 'consumed' at Gao itself, for more than 6,000 glass beads were discovered, together with other luxury goods, in a stone building of the late ninth or early tenth century at Gao Ancien.[45]

There is another similarity between Garamantian Fazzan and Gao, despite the chronological difference: both Fazzan and Gao Saney contain chemical or archaeological evidence for glassworking.[46] The presence of glassworking indicates that craftspeople were making objects (beads) of particular types, either directly for local consumers or indirectly through traders with very specific knowledge of the desires of more distant con-sumers. Either way it is clear that local glass workers were knowledgeable of and responsive to consumer preferences, which in turn were dynamic, a reflection of what we might call fashion trends. Probable glassworking at many sites in North and West Africa stands, as mentioned earlier, in sharp contrast to Southern Africa where the clay moulds used for the production of 'garden-roller' beads at K2 constitute the only firm evidence for glassworking in Southern Africa prior to European contact.[47] Two hypoth-eses, not mutually exclusive ones, may be offered to explain this contrast: (1) 'fashions', very broadly defined, were different and less dynamic in Southern Africa, although this raises the question of what precisely is meant by 'fashion', a question that I investigate later in the chapter; and (2) knowledge of glassworking skills in Southern Africa may have been

---

[39] Mattingly 2003, 229; see now Mattingly *et al.* 2019, 94–97, for a fuller discussion of beads in Garamantian burial contexts.

[40] Mattingly *et al.* 2013, 125.   [41] Cissé *et al.* 2013, 27.   [42] Insoll and Shaw 1997.

[43] Fenn, Robertshaw *et al.* in preparation.   [44] Shaw 1970.

[45] Cissé *et al.* 2013, 14; Takezawa and Cissé 2012. Takezawa and Cissé 2012 suggest that this building was a palace, but Cissé *et al.* 2013, 14 point out that the pillared architecture and orientation of this building suggest a mosque lacking a mihrab, the absence of which in turn suggests an Ibadi mosque. Were the glass beads and other items found here in storage as commodities by Ibadi merchants who controlled the trade to the north or were they consumed as luxury goods in a palace?

[46] Duckworth *et al.* 2014; Duckworth, Chapter 10, this volume.   [47] Wood 2011a.

a relatively short-lived phenomenon, covering perhaps a couple of hundred years, when glass workers and their knowledge may have been tightly controlled by ruling elites.[48]

Another contrast between North/West and Southern Africa is the fact that, contrary to the situation in the North/West, only one chemical type of glass is found on most Southern African sites during any particular period. While this might be ascribed to cultural conservatism among the consumers of the beads, it is also possible that very strict monopolies may have been exercised either by the coastal (Swahili) African merchants, who were the middlemen in the trade of beads to the Southern African interior, or by their overseas suppliers. However, it is also worth noting that glass vessels (generally in the form of fragments) are present in coastal sites, but have, to date and to the best of my knowledge, never been found at sites in the Southern African interior. Coastal merchants seem to have kept such vessels for themselves or for customers at the coast and/or deemed them far too fragile for the hazards of transport into the interior, although the latter suggestion is undermined by the Garamantian evidence for the overland transport of glass vessels. An alternative explanation for the absence of glass vessels in the Southern African interior may be that they did not fit with existing cultural logics.[49]

The Production of Glass Beads

Evidence for glassworking has been discovered in Fazzan[50] and elsewhere in North Africa[51] and West Africa, notably at Ile-Ife where evidence exists for the manufacture of glass from raw materials in West Africa, thus indicating an independent invention of glass technology.[52] What do we know about the social and cultural contexts of glass bead production in Africa? While the direct archaeological evidence is relatively sparse, ethnographic and ethnoarchaeological analogies, combined with theoretical

---

[48] David Killick 2009, 201 has drawn attention to the relative lack of technology transfer, particularly knowledge transfer, from the Islamic world to the interior of Southern Africa, noting in particular the lack of transfer to Sub-Saharan Africa of the knowledge of how to make glass from raw materials. However, Marilee Wood (personal communication) remarked that the making of the 'garden-roller' beads found at K2 was a very complex technological process, which she tentatively identifies as an example of technology transfer, though its origin remains a mystery.

[49] See Chirikure 2014 and discussion below.

[50] Duckworth *et al.* 2014; Duckworth, Chapter 10, this volume.

[51] Rehren and Rosenow, Chapter 12, this volume.

[52] Freestone 2006; Lankton *et al.* 2006; Ogundiran and Ige 2015.

considerations, may help to identify new avenues for research. In particular, consideration of 'communities of practice'[53] provides a good starting point for discussion, particularly because it may be possible to identify communities of practitioners based on the glass chemistry of their products.[54] Glassworking is but one of several crafts practised in Africa, so insights may also come from studies of the communities of practice of other crafts and even culinary practice as I touch on below.

Communities of Practice and Identity

> Potters observed in Southern Niger clearly *think* about what they do in daily practice, and do not reproduce mechanically what they were taught when initially socialised into the craft. Moreover, they exploit techniques in order to position themselves socially or economically and, occasionally, build new identities – just as modern westerners do.[55]

The concept of 'community of practice' is part and parcel of a theory of social learning[56] that emphasises participation in communal activities which link 'practice, meaning, identity, and community'.[57] In the case of glassworking, as well as other crafts, the social nature of this work, which serves to integrate newcomers into the community, is not only manifest in its products but those products themselves and their manufacture can be considered as active participants in the production of those communities and identities. Thus intimate and reflexive ties are formed between social action and the material world.[58] Such ideas have been explored further, with particular reference to ceramics, in Olivier Gosselain's paper on 'materialising identities', in which he notes that 'the contexts in which technical behaviours are constructed and reproduced correspond to the same networks of social interaction upon which identities are themselves constructed and reproduced'.[59] Thus, 'Potting traditions are what we could call "sociotechnical aggregates", an intricate mix of inventions, borrowed elements, and manipulations that display an amazing propensity to redefinition by individuals and local groups'.[60] Again, in the case of ceramics, this heterogeneity and dynamism poses a challenge for archaeologists. Indeed, while Gosselain suggested that certain stages of the *chaîne opératoire* of pottery manufacture may be more consistently related to identity,[61] perhaps because they are not consciously manipulated by the

---

[53] Lave and Wenger 1991.   [54] Blair 2015.   [55] Gosselain 2008, 77–78.
[56] Lave and Wenger 1991; Wenger 1998.   [57] Blair 2015.   [58] Blair 2015.
[59] Gosselain 2000, 209.   [60] Gosselain 2000, 190.   [61] Gosselain 2000.

potters, his more recent and more intensive research in Niger[62] has revealed that potters exercise considerable flexibility even in what were previously believed to be relatively conservative forming techniques, as well as in other stages of vessel manufacture such as the decoration of the pot, long thought to have been frequently and consciously played with in order to convey varied social messages.[63]

Extrapolating from ceramics to glassworking, it is possible that some technological practices may have been more conservative and, therefore, better indicators of membership within a community of practice than others. Conservative practices might have included the choice of raw materials and the recipe used for primary glass manufacture, the choice of colouring agents and the tools and structures (furnaces, etc.) used to make both glass and beads, although Gosselain's more recent ceramic ethnoarchaeological research cautions us that even these aspects of glass production could have been manipulated by individuals both consciously and unconsciously as they sought to establish themselves within particular communities of practice that were themselves enmeshed within larger heterogeneous communities of both artisans and non-artisans.[64] However, there are aspects of glass bead technology that *a priori* would be prone to frequent manipulation, at least in part to satisfy consumer tastes: such things as bead colour, shape and size. On the other hand, there were different ways of cutting, rounding, polishing, sorting and stringing beads, all of which would have been products of different communities of practice and many of which leave characteristic traces on the beads produced.[65] Blair, for example, has shown, in the case of European beads exported to the Americas, that chemical and material traces of the technologies of different communities of practice can be linked to different Venetian glassworking guilds.[66]

Turning to our African archaeological evidence, we can recognise that the heterogeneity of glass compositions of the beads found on many North and West African sites is likely a product both of the diverse origins of the glass and the beads,[67] each associated with a different community of practice, since in most if not all instances it is likely that primary glass manufacture and bead manufacture were undertaken in different places by different artisans. If glass was worked on site, as at Saniat Jibril and Gao Saney, then one or more local communities of practice would have contributed their own technological traces to the palimpsest of the material traces of earlier communities of practice in the *chaîne opératoire* of glass

---

[62] Gosselain 2008; 2016.   [63] Gosselain 2000, 189, 209.   [64] Gosselain 2008; 2016.
[65] Blair 2015; 2016.   [66] Blair 2015; 2016.   [67] See also Duckworth, Chapter 10, this volume.

and bead making. An example of this is suggested by recent study of some glass and glass beads from Fazzan.[68] While the chemistry of the vessel glass showed the existence of four well-defined glass types, corresponding presumably to four communities of glass-manufacturing practice of distinct geographical and chronological origins, more interesting are the results of analysis of several pieces of glass waste indicative of either primary or secondary glass production in Fazzan itself during Garamantian times. Although the sample size (n=7) is small, the heterogeneity in glass composition, particularly perhaps in respect to magnesia levels, may indicate more than one local community of practice, an observation that reinforces the importance of tying the chemical data to the archaeological contexts from which the samples were obtained.[69]

If we look to ethnography for inspiration, we find glassworking communities of practice that may have guarded technological secrets and had a strong identity, although not necessarily closed membership. At Bida in the Nupe region of Nigeria, both the primary manufacture of glass from raw materials and the secondary production of beads was the work of a guild, the *masagá*, a group of immigrants who may have come from the Kanem-Bornu region. Their products were said to be in such demand in the late nineteenth and twentieth centuries that they were constantly in need of labour that was supplied by slaves and later by apprentices, both of whom were expected to marry *masagá* women and join the kinship group.[70]

The endogamous *masagá* glassworkers of Nupe with their purported immigrant status are in fact typical of craftspeople in West Africa, as nicely revealed in both historical and ethnographic sources and summarised in a recent book by Anne Haour where she draws attention to the liminal status of both craftspeople and traders.[71] 'Craft specialists, whether despised or not, are often considered to be outside ordinary society' because they have exceptional talents and tools and are engaged in transformative practices.[72] Indeed, 'skilled crafting is in many communities seen as similar to long-distance acquisition of goods, because both involve crossing a cultural threshold from the exotic or mystical into the ordered social heartland'.[73] The trader as stranger is something that Curtin has argued is a global phenomenon.[74] However, craftspeople-as-outsiders is less easily viewed in such a global perspective, since, for example, the smith as king is a common trope in Central Africa. Nevertheless, whether kings or outsiders, craftspeople are commonly feared for their powerful

[68] Duckworth *et al.* 2014.   [69] Compare Blair 2015.
[70] Nadel 1942, 278; Robertshaw *et al.* 2009b; Robertson 1935.   [71] Haour 2013.
[72] Haour 2013, 104.   [73] Haour 2013, 94 citing Helms 1993.   [74] Curtin 1984.

esoteric knowledge. The frequent liminal status of craftspeople is often expressed by spatial segregation; they reside in designated quarters or neighbourhoods.[75] Thus, in the Fazzan case it is tempting to see a village like Saniat Jibril in this light, a community of craftspeople close to but separate from the capital at Garama; the possible outsider status of its inhabitants might be evident from differences in material culture. Indeed, the discovery of rouletted ceramic vessels embedded in floors at Saniat Jibril[76] is perhaps further evidence of the presence of craftworking 'strangers' at this site.[77]

My limited knowledge of craftspeople in the Arab world seems to align with these observations. Hourani reports that, 'craftsmen and small merchants might be regarded as lying outside the tribal system'.[78] However, he also notes that craftspeople do not seem to have been organised into guilds akin to those of Medieval Europe, but 'the fact that the ruler treated them as a single body . . . and that they worked together in the same part of the market, must have given them a certain solidarity',[79] although it seems that in Cairo at least many of the workshops were owned by merchants or religious foundations.[80]

A substantial ethnographic literature on bead manufacture is available for India, thanks in large part to the efforts of Alok Kanungo,[81] who has provided rich descriptions of the great technological variation used for the manufacture of different kinds of beads, including varied styles of furnaces and complex toolkits. He also notes that, 'each production process [for different types of beads] leaves behind debitage unique to its individual manufacturing process'.[82] Also of interest is his observation that at one town (Purdalpur, in Uttar Pradesh), glass bead debitage accumulates not at the location where the beads are actually made but at the house or shop of the trader/middleman who buys the locally produced beads, because this is where the beads are sorted from the debitage, which includes such things as half-moulded beads, cracked beads, beads with closed perforations and beads with air bubbles.[83] As for the organisation of bead production, at Purdalpur, where there are about 200 bead-making furnaces and where raw glass arrives in cake form from elsewhere, all the beadmakers are male and most are Muslim, with 14 to 20 men at work in each glassworks,[84]

---

[75] Haour 2013, 112.　　[76] Mattingly 2010, 176.

[77] See discussion of rouletted pottery and associated communities of practice in Gatto, Chapter 13, this volume.

[78] Hourani 2002, 109.　　[79] Hourani 2002, 135.　　[80] Hourani 2002, 113.

[81] See especially Kanungo 2004a; 2004b; 2014.　　[82] Kanungo 2004a, 94.

[83] Kanungo 2004b, 143.　　[84] Kanungo 2004b, 137.

although there is a division of labour, with individuals specialising in each step of the bead-manufacturing process. While the beadmakers are men, 'girls and their mothers can be found cleaning and stringing the large quantities of beads'.[85] Across the country at Papanaidupat in Andhra Pradesh, not far from the ancient site of Arikamedu, Indo-Pacific beads are still manufactured. Here too there is a strict division of labour, although the beadmakers themselves are of lowly status, being paid by the piece. The industry as a whole is controlled by four families, although the industry employs thousands of people, with the largest number of people being bead stringers, 'spare-time' work done by women and girls.[86]

Glassworking and the Organisation of Other Productive Activities

Glassworking is one of many productive activities, including cooking, that may be undertaken in any community. Thus, the production of glass and glass beads cannot entirely be considered in isolation from those other activities.[87] Indeed, Garamantian villages in Fazzan were not only agricultural settlements but also 'centres of manufacturing or craft activity';[88] for example, at Saniat Jibril a U-shaped arrangement of low platforms may have been reserved for craft working, with 'hearth patches' as evidence of specialised workshops that probably included not only glassworking but also copperworking and 'a range of specialist handicraft workshops making jewellery, including carnelian and amazonite beads'.[89] Moreover, 'industrial production and domestic activity (processing of food and wool) took place broadly within the same spaces'.[90] On the one hand, this suggests the possibility of shared technical knowledge, for example in the realm of pyrotechnology.[91] On the other hand, there is also the possibility of competition for limited resources. Indeed, given the climate and vegetation of Fazzan it seems probable that there may have been competition for scarce fuel-wood resources for these industries. The Indian evidence indicates that the glassworking industry there was a heavy consumer of wood; for example, it was reported that in primary glass production involving the heating of mineral soda (*reh*) at one site in the early twentieth century, 'only green shrubs were used as a fuel, the batch being continuously heated for about 2½ days'.[92] The use of dry, deciduous, quick-burning brushwood, which is also quick growing and can be cut several times a year, has also been reported in a more recent

---

[85] Kanungo 2014, 110.   [86] Francis 1991; 2002, 24–25.   [87] Gokee and Logan 2014.
[88] Mattingly 2003, 133.   [89] Mattingly 2003, 115, 121.   [90] Mattingly 2003, 168.
[91] See also Gatto, Chapter 13, this volume.   [92] Kanungo 2004a, 11.

study in Uttar Pradesh,[93] while Kanungo noted that at the same village, in addition to brushwood, cow-dung cakes for use as fuel were made by women.[94] The archaeobotanical evidence from Fazzan reveals that dung, as well as date palm wood, fronds and date stones, might have been used as fuel.[95]

The observation that food processing and industrial production were spatially connected at Saniat Jibril (see above) suggests two other areas of possible study. The first of these lies in what have been called 'taskscapes', defined as arrays of related activities to be considered as analogous to landscapes but emphasising the temporalities of work.[96] Consideration of the gendered allocation of labour at multiple scales, such as hours of the day, or seasons of the year, encourages us to ponder how glassworking may have been integrated into the lives of men and women in Fazzan. Were some or all glassworking activities seasonal, conducted perhaps in lulls in the agricultural cycle, or were they driven by seasonal variations in the tempo of long-distance trade, itself perhaps linked into annual climatic variations?[97] Did the demands of food preparation structure the activities of glass workers? In the absence of ethnographic and historical data, evidence may be hard to acquire, but perhaps a comparative study of food preparation and consumption in Fazzan households with and without spatially associated industrial activities might be revealing.[98] There may also be a connection between glassworking and cuisine that lies in questions of identity and the frequent liminal status of craft specialists discussed earlier in this chapter. Perhaps crafters ate foods shunned by others or prepared their food in different ways, perhaps rooted in some of their specialised pyrotechnological traditions.[99]

The Consumption of Glass Beads

> It is clear that materials, revered natural objects as well as artefacts, become invested with meaning through social interaction and are capable of accumulating histories that embody the essence of social life.[100]

---

[93] Kock and Sode 1995.   [94] Kanungo 2004b, 131.
[95] Duckworth, Chapter 10, this volume; Pelling 2013.   [96] Ingold 1993, 158.
[97] See Logan and Cruz 2014 for an analogous study in West Africa.
[98] See Stahl 2014a for other suggestions for future study of crafts and cuisine.
[99] See, for example, Lyons 2014.   [100] Wilmsen 2014, 399.

Beads and Value

Why were beads 'consumed'? What made them valuable? The value of an object is not intrinsic, but intimately connected to social and cultural constructs, including economics. Value, in a narrow economic sense, is determined reciprocally in the context of exchange; what are we prepared to surrender in order to acquire an object?[101] In this regard, the available supply or price of an object may often be less important in determining its value than its role in the conveyance of critical social messages.[102] Indeed, such a consideration is the essence of the definition of 'luxury goods': 'those whose principal use is *rhetorical* and *social*, goods that are simply *incarnated signs*'.[103] There are five characteristics by which we can easily recognise luxury goods, all of which would appear to be applicable to glass beads, at least in the context of their final consumption. These characteristics are:

'(1) restriction, by price or by law, to elites;
(2) complexity of acquisition, which may or may not be a function of real 'scarcity';
(3) semiotic virtuosity, that is, the capacity to signal fairly complex social messages . . . ;
(4) specialized knowledge as a prerequisite for their 'appropriate' consumption, that is, regulation by fashion;
(5) a high degree of linkage of their consumption to body, person, and personality.'[104]

However, it should be noted that Appadurai's approach in which the role of material objects is limited to the rather passive conveyance of messages is now outmoded, since we now recognise that material goods are themselves active participants in the production of social identities and distinctions through the fact that they are intimately embedded within the lived experience of people's daily lives.[105]

Glass beads, like precious stones in Europe worn as jewellery in the last few centuries, were exotic, foreign goods that by their very foreignness carried an aura of being difficult to acquire, an aura that was reinforced by the fact that they were produced by the use of complex technologies. Graeber has explored the reasons behind the great value attributed to beads by members of the Iroquois confederacy in seventeenth-century

---

[101] Simmel 1978.   [102] Appadurai 1986a, 33.
[103] Appadurai 1986a, 38; emphases in original.   [104] Appadurai 1986a, 38.
[105] For example, Loren 2013; Ogundiran 2014; Stahl 2002.

North America, where about three million beads may have been in circulation and where the island of Manhattan was supposedly 'bought' from the
local Indians by Europeans for 60 Dutch guilders' worth of beads and
trinkets.[106] While never strictly equivalent to money, beads have often been
used as a currency of trade, objects that can be easily exchanged (since they
can be treated as individual, indivisible objects) between people of different
cultures who have different conceptions of the meaning of beads.

No doubt one reason beads lend themselves so well to this role is that they can be so
easily transformed back and forth from unique forms to generic ones: they can be
bought in bulk, sewn together into elaborate beadwork or onto other forms of
adornment, and then – whenever the need is felt –broken up into individual,
mutually indistinguishable items once again. It makes them ideally suited to pass
back and forth between radically different domains (or, if you really must,
'regimes') of value.[107]

Beads, assembled into wampum belts, became the embodiment of Iroquois
culture: 'the sense of brightness, clarity, expansiveness, of unhindered communication with the cosmos, whose social manifestation was peace and the
unobstructed solidarity of human beings'.[108] Clearly the meaning of beads
among the Iroquois was complex and multifaceted, based on far more than
simply their exotic origin[109] or their use as currency in the fur trade.
Wampum was used in diplomacy, peace making and particularly in the
construction of social identity. Captives were integrated into society by
throwing a wampum around their shoulders, thereby giving each of them
a name.[110] Beads then were instrumental in the construction and maintenance
of identity, perhaps a particularly important characteristic of societies where
an ideology of individualism was absent and social identity was constructed of
such things as titles, ritual paraphernalia and badges of office.[111]

    Moving beyond a narrow economic focus on the value of beads permits
recognition of the fact that in many societies all beads were valuable (*sensu
lato*), not just the imported glass ones; thus it should come as no surprise
that some past cultures, including perhaps the Garamantian, can be
thought of as 'beady cultures', a phrase coined by participants at the
Leicester workshop. However, if we are to investigate such 'beady cultures'
we need to explore not only the different archaeological contexts in which

---

[106] Graeber 2001, 91, 148.   [107] Graeber 2001, 106.   [108] Graeber 2001, 131.
[109] Glass beads were in fact replaced over time by shell beads manufactured in New England; cf.
Turgeon 2004.
[110] Graeber 2001, 148.   [111] Mauss 1938, cited in Graeber 2001, 93.

beads occur, such as the association of particular types of beads with individuals of different ages and sexes in different Garamantian tomb types, but also the combinations in which beads occur, such as the juxtapositions of beads of different colours, shapes and sizes, and, with the aid of such things as figurines depicting the wearing of beads and perhaps very careful excavations of interments, their positioning on the human body (see discussion below).

Beads and Power

We can move away from the Iroquois and back to Africa by drawing attention to the fact that beads are commonly associated with power. Beads are objects that not only produce and signify identity but also participate in the production of the status of their wearer. As objects that can be cached, hidden away from view, beads are emblems of power as well as potential producers of that power. Beads assist in allowing their wearer to define himself or herself so that others are thereby persuaded to act in accordance with the wearer's wishes without necessity of command. Clearly this situation occurs in cultural contexts where beads are viewed primarily as luxury objects rather than commodities. One example of this from West Africa is provided by the Yoruba in Nigeria. Beads became 'the insignia of political and cultural authority' in Yorubaland from perhaps at least as early as the eleventh century. Indeed, Ogundiran even goes so far as to argue that Ile-Ife's emergence as the centre of kingship in the region was at least in part attributable to its near monopoly in the production and distribution of beads.[112] Moreover, stone sculptures of presumably important people that may well date earlier than the eleventh century are embellished with representations of beads.[113] Specific glass bead types, which derived from the Trans-Saharan trade, were associated with royal authority, while beads in general were regarded as signs of good fortune and spiritual well-being.[114] Certain bead types, however, were more than simply symbols of power; they embodied power:

When the right of succession is in dispute, it is the possession of ... the ... beads ... that can determine who ultimately sits on the throne. These beads are not viewed as ornamental, but are considered to have effective power (*ase*), that is,

---

[112] Ogundiran 2002, 434, following Horton 1992.   [113] Ogundiran 2002, 432; 2003.
[114] Ogundiran 2002, 432–37.

the power to cause any vow or curse to come to pass. Wearing these beads is a crucial component of what gives an Oba (monarch) divine powers.[115]

The theme of beads as powerful objects is echoed elsewhere in Africa. Among the Samburu in Kenya, beads are not only worn as personal attire, but 'the green or blue beads worn around the waists and necks of infants and small boys and girls do not merely signify well-being, they *are* a prayer for health, just as blue beads hung at the house door are a prayer for the entire household'.[116] Elsewhere, in southern Zambia a founding myth of Kapembwa origins describes how a daughter of the first couple emigrated to a new land where she defeated the headman because she was 'brilliant . . . with beads on her head and ankles'.[117] This myth (and the associated quotation) is used by Wilmsen to argue for the importance of beads as 'signifiers of status and power' and 'as such, they would be concentrated mainly in the hands of holders of such power and in the places where such power is to be found'.[118] For 'the long-distance movement of beads, marine shells and cloth entailed costs that made their possession in places in the far interior [of Southern Africa] in itself a marker of sumptuary distinction regulated by the expense of their acquisition'.[119] Based on this and the distribution of imported glass beads at different kinds of archaeological sites across the Southern African interior, Wilmsen argues that beads were symbols of power and goods subject to sumptuary laws as early as the mid to late first millennium AD in this part of the world.[120]

This identification of beads as objects of power subject to sumptuary rules is clear from many parts of Sub-Saharan Africa where beads were 'consumed' and in periods ranging from the mid to late first millennium AD to the nineteenth century, when the trade in beads to Africa had been taken over by European merchants. Two further examples will perhaps suffice to document this connection between beads and power (authority). The first derives from the famous site of Igbo-Ukwu in Nigeria where excavations recovered more than 150,000 glass beads as well as a variety of other luxury goods, notably copper and bronze artefacts.[121] Probably dated to the late first millennium AD,[122] the main contexts in which these items occurred

---

[115] Ben-Amos 1999, 124, quoted by Ogundiran 2002, 435.

[116] Straight 2005, 274, emphasis in original.   [117] Willis 1999, 50.   [118] Wilmsen 2014, 408–9.

[119] Wilmsen 2014, 415; also Wilmsen 2009, 270.

[120] Wilmsen 2009, 2014, following, for example, Calabrese 2007; Huffman 1986; but see Chirikure 2014.

[121] Shaw 1970; 1977.

[122] Onwuejeogwu and Onwuejeogwu 1977; Shaw 1975. The large standard deviations of the available radiocarbon dates mean that when calibrated, the dates fall almost anywhere between about the eighth and twelfth centuries. However, the presence at Igbo-Ukwu (Dussubieux

were a burial, which has been convincingly identified ethnohistorically and ethnographically as that of an *eze Nri*, which is usually translated as 'priest-king', and what was probably an *obu* or lineage temple.[123] Glass beads were found in both contexts, perhaps most remarkably in the form of a beaded headdress of at least 30,000 beads in the burial, as well as thousands more beads that were incorporated in sleeves covering the lower arms. The *eze Nri* and the hierarchy of officials beneath him were powerful ritual specialists who were members of a group of people, the Umunri, who claimed a common, foreign origin. The ritual and political activities of the Umunri are presumed to be the reason why they managed to accumulate such material wealth, although what was exported from this forested region to pay for the luxury imports has not yet been satisfactorily determined.[124] Dressed with thousands of glass beads, like the 'brilliant' newcomer in the Zambian myth (see above), the *eze Nri* must have cut an imposing figure in his rare public appearances.[125] Burial of the beads and other luxury items in the *eze Nri*'s tomb would not only take these items entirely out of circulation, thereby augmenting the value of those that remained, but their inclusion in the tomb, as well as the storage of others in the lineage temple, whence they were worn on rare occasions by Nri officials, would have provided 'enduring material markers of the position of their guardians in Nri society and cosmos in a context mediatory between gods, lineage ancestors, and the living community'.[126]

Our final example of the connections between glass beads and power is provided by the ethnohistorical work of Kajsa Ekholm on the Kongo kingdom of Central Africa. 'In Central Africa, power relationships are established, consolidated and maintained through the control of prestige articles [including glass beads] – products which are not necessary for material subsistence but which are absolutely indispensable for the maintenance of social relations.'[127] Thus, in this instance, goods such as beads are not primarily objects of display and symbols of ritual authority but rather are equivalent to money, which is converted into wives and slaves, who in turn produce more food and more local products, items like copper and salt but notably slaves.[128] These local products can then be exchanged for more foreign products in a system where the rich get richer.

2017) of numerous beads of a distinct chemical type of plant-ash glass that in Southern Africa was made into beads of the well-dated Zhizo series (Wood 2011a) firmly points to a date somewhere between the mid-eighth and late tenth centuries AD.
[123] Onwuejeogwu 1981; Ray 1987; Shaw 1977.
[124] Craddock *et al.* 1997; Insoll and Shaw 1997; Sutton 1991; 2001.   [125] Ray 1987, 71.
[126] Ray 1987, 75.   [127] Ekholm 1977, 119.   [128] Ekholm 1977, 120, 123, 129–30.

Extraversion, Sumptuary Rules, and Fashion

> [F]ashion was as dominant among Central African tribes as among the belles of Paris or London. . ... Each tribe must have its own particular class of cotton, and its own chosen tint, colour, and size among beads.[129]

The Kongo system is an example of a larger process termed 'extraversion',[130] which 'refers to strategies of producing power through mediated access to external resources and environments'.[131] Thus, Bayart in arguing about African 'dependence' on Europe and the West in more recent times makes the point that African leaders are active agents in fostering this dependence because it is the source of their success and that this leads to distinctive features of African political, economic and social systems.[132] Clearly 'extraversion' encourages us to think about African links to global economic and political systems in fresh and perhaps more nuanced ways than we may have done previously. Indeed, Ekholm, having discussed how prestige goods are converted into power, goes on to remark:

> If the king's monopoly over external trade is bypassed and his vassals are able to acquire European prestige articles through other channels, which is what happened after the initial phase of contact, the established hierarchy breaks down. As the prestige articles are transmitted to local groups from outside and not via the hierarchy, the basis for this hierarchy disappears.[133]

This important observation has several implications, although it should be noted that it can itself be challenged.[134]

First, it explains the importance of sumptuary rules established by those in power to control the trade and distribution of imports. The restrictiveness of such sumptuary rules is clear, for example, from many parts of West Africa presided over by kings; according to a seventeenth-century Dutch manuscript the Oba of Benin controlled the distribution of various types of beads, and when such beads were awarded to individuals the award was considered temporary since the beads could be reclaimed from people who fell out of the king's favour. Similarly, when a chief died his beads of office had to be returned to the Oba.[135]

While we lack historical evidence relating to sumptuary rules in Southern Africa in pre-European times, the concentration of glass beads at elite

---

[129] Thomson 1881, 35–36; quoted by Prestholdt 2004, 761.   [130] Bayart 2000.
[131] Stahl 2014b, 20.
[132] Bayart 2000; see Stahl 2014b, 21, for further considerations in terms of African history.
[133] Ekholm 1977, 131.   [134] Chirikure 2014.
[135] Ogundiran 2002, 435–36, citing Jones 1995, 54, and Roth 1968, 42.

settlements, such as Mapungubwe and Bosutswe, appears to be indicative of such sumptuary rules. Indeed, when 2,600 glass beads were discovered in a pot at Kgaswe in Botswana, a small cattle-post or farmstead where even the male burials lacked glass beads, it was a notable surprise, requiring their presence to be explained away as 'a hidden hoard of illicit trade'.[136] However, the recent recovery of more than 300 glass beads at Mutamba, a peripheral site of the Mapungubwe culture, has been used as evidence that people at what seem to be commoner sites at some remove (in this case, about 50 miles/80 km) from the capital did have access to glass beads and perhaps to occasional examples of relatively rare types of beads that may therefore have been of greater value than the more common types.[137] In addition, Wood compiled evidence to show that glass beads are in fact frequently encountered in significant numbers on commoner, as well as elite, settlements.[138] However, since it seems highly likely that the elites at the centre of the redistribution system would have rewarded followers with beads or exchanged beads for valued local products, such as ivory for export (see also the Central African case described below), it may not be surprising that significant numbers of beads have been discovered at sites like Mutamba. As Antonites notes, the fact that the density (a sampling measure of overall frequency) of beads varies between peripheral sites suggests complex patterns of exchange that, with more excavated data, might in future be amenable to more detailed analysis.[139] Furthermore, Chirikure has recently drawn attention to the fact that, at least by the time of Portuguese contact in the sixteenth century, the rulers of the Mutapa state, the successor to that of Great Zimbabwe, did not monopolise the trade with the coast that brought glass beads, cowrie shells and cloth into the interior,[140] although they did tax that trade, with glass beads being one acceptable form of payment.[141] Under these circumstances, Chirikure argues for the enduring importance of ancestors, cattle and land as the bases of royal power.[142]

Second, in regard to extraversion, the fact that the import and control of glass beads became crucial to royal power, at least during the early second millennium AD in Southern Africa, meant that glass beads were not the cheap trinkets of European perspective, but highly valued items that were

---

[136] Wilmsen 2014, 416; see also Huffman 2000, 20.   [137] Antonites 2014.

[138] Wood 2011b; see also Chirikure 2014, 718–19.

[139] Antonites 2014. It seems that the recovery of the beads, most of them tiny, found at Mutamba was primarily the result of micro-sampling and flotation, suggesting that beads may well be underrepresented in assemblages from less meticulously sieved and sampled deposits.

[140] Chirikure 2014, citing Mudenge 1974; 1988.   [141] Chirikure 2014, 717.

[142] Chirikure 2014, 721.

part and parcel of the production of royal power and social order and essential to their maintenance. Under those circumstances the merchants who imported the beads (and the cloth with which they were undoubtedly associated) may easily have been able to manipulate the prices of these goods and those of the ivory and gold that they received in exchange, to their benefit and to the detriment of the Africans in the interior, fostering increasing economic dependency.[143] However, such manipulation was only possible in circumstances where the beads were indeed valued by consumers because they conformed with existing 'cultural logics'; other items such as imported ceramics may have held no attraction for people in the Southern African interior even if they were offered them.[144]

Third, the existence of sumptuary rules and royal monopolies on external trade would have fostered particular kinds of relationships with those who conducted the trade. On the one hand, as noted above, merchants may well have manipulated prices in their favour, but this must have been offset by the fact that they may have been restrained from being able to sell their products on an open market. As Appadurai notes, 'This antagonism between "foreign" goods and local sumptuary (and therefore political) structures is probably the fundamental reason for the often remarked tendency of primitive societies to restrict trade to a limited set of commodities and to dealings with strangers rather than with kinsmen or friends'.[145] In this regard it is perhaps no surprise that much of the Trans-Saharan trade was conducted by members of a sect who were outside the Islamic mainstream (see above); in some other parts of the world Jews filled this role. Traders were always treated with suspicion; of necessity they had strong ties to distant, alien communities from or through which the goods they imported passed. Like craftspeople they were feared for their specialised knowledge and their alien connections, but were needed for precisely the same reasons. As with craftspeople, they sometimes lived in separate neighbourhoods or villages from their hosts or they built large storage facilities from which they could conduct trade hidden behind facades that blended in with the architecture of their host communities; each of these arrangements has the potential to leave distinct archaeological signatures.[146]

Finally, the tension between traders and sumptuary rules can also be broadened into the realm of fashion, a term that 'suggests ... rapid turnover, the illusion of total access ..., the assumption of a democracy of

---

[143] Killick 2009; see also Wilmsen 2009, 270–71.   [144] Chirikure 2014.
[145] Appadurai 1986a, 33.   [146] Haour 2013, chapter 3.

consumers and of objects of consumption'.[147] Thus, 'fashion and sumptuary regulation are opposite poles in the social regulation of demand,
particularly for goods with high discriminatory value'.[148] The clash
between fashion and sumptuary rules often occurred historically in the
context of colonialism when indigenous consumers were keen to imitate
the fashions of the new elites and where merchants were keen to create new
and bigger markets for their imports, while traditional rulers strove to
retain old sumptuary laws.[149] This clash of values, amid the attendant
integration into a world economy, often sparked 'remarkable bursts of
cultural creativity' as new resources were shaped to fit existing values
alongside the ongoing negotiation of cultural identity during a period of
major economic and political changes.[150]

Although the historical contexts were not those of the advent of colonialism, it seems reasonable to suggest that analogous contexts may have
existed to spur such bursts of cultural creativity in Fazzan at the time of the
probable immigration of Berber Libyans in the late second or early first
millennium BC and again at the onset of the Classic Garamantian period
when the volume of trade and other connections with the Roman Empire
rose.[151] One might also search for similar creative bursts with the jump in
the volume of Trans-Saharan trade goods arriving at the Niger River and
thence further south in the West African savannah and forests after the
mid-eighth century. Indeed, the development of new glassworking technology at Ile-Ife[152] and the fluorescence of metallurgy at Igbo-Ukwu[153]
might be viewed in this light.

As for the dictates of fashion at the onset of colonialism, we can gain
some impression of fashion's power and the struggle between fashion and
the sumptuary rules of indigenous rulers by invoking the example provided
by East Africa in the nineteenth century, a time when East African consumers' tastes in glass beads and particularly in cloth were so economically
influential as to stimulate both the building of the first steam-powered
textile mill in Salem, Massachusetts, and the industrialisation of Bombay,
India.[154] Prestholdt[155] reminds us of the experience of the Scottish
explorer, Joseph Thomson, in the 1870s who lamented, 'the fashions are
just as changeable [as in England] ... In one year a tribe goes mad for
a particular bead; but the trader having supplied himself with the fashion-
able article, according to latest news, might, if his journey was long, arrive
to find the fashion changed, and his stock just so much unmarketable

---

[147] Appadurai 1986a, 32.   [148] Appadurai 1986a, 38.   [149] Appadurai 1986a, 38.
[150] Graeber 2001, 147.   [151] Mattingly 2003, 234.   [152] Freestone 2006; Lankton *et al.* 2006.
[153] Shaw 1970.   [154] Prestholdt 2004; 2008.   [155] Prestholdt 2004, 761.

rubbish'.[156] Beads, active participants in the establishment, negotiation and expression of identity, encompassed an amazing array of types, such that Richard Burton, during his travels in this part of the world in 1857, reported that there were not less than 400 types of bead in circulation, each with its own name, value and location where it was preferred.[157] As for indigenous rulers, the plenitude and, thus, democratisation of beads forced them to seek out more unusual imports, 'such as music boxes, silk cloth, musical instruments, European or Asian prints, and the latest firearms', which often copied the preferences of elites at the ports of the East African coast.[158] The incredible variety of bead types in circulation in nineteenth-century East Africa stands in marked contrast to the narrow range of types present in earlier centuries in Sub-Saharan Africa. While this contrast can probably be explained in large part by the increase in the volume of trade, together with perhaps one of those 'bursts of cultural creativity' that accompanied the onset of colonialism, the conservatism of earlier centuries must also in part have been maintained by strict enforcement of sumptuary laws, although those laws were probably also in flux in response to the shifting availabilities of goods.

This discussion can be advanced by consideration of the notion of 'taste', an explanatory concept with perhaps more interpretive potential than 'fashion'.[159] People make choices about adopting things, such as items of material culture, that do or do not appeal to their tastes. These choices are rooted in the history of the entanglements that people have had with material culture. It seems feasible to make inferences about past 'tastes' based on contextual and historical studies of material culture in a given region, without necessarily having to identify the 'meaning' of particular goods.[160] From this perspective 'identity' is not a 'thing' that is simply expressed or negotiated, as described above, but rather a process that is both ongoing and has 'moments when the habits of taste are diverted or interrupted'.[161] Whether or not a bead appeals to a person's taste – a phrase which itself illuminates the active role played by material culture in the process of identity formation – will be dependent upon that person's pre-vious entanglements with beads and other objects of adornment within the social and cultural milieu in which s/he lives.[162] Stahl's discussion of the role

---

[156] Thomson 1881, 35–36.   [157] Burton 1860, vol. 2, 396 cited by Prestholdt 2004, 762.

[158] Prestholdt 2004, 765; see also Stahl 2002 for another example from West Africa.

[159] Stahl 2002.   [160] See Stahl 2002 for further discussion.   [161] Stahl 2002, 834.

[162] See also Loren 2013 for another example of the role of beads in the embodiment of identity. 'In southern New England, the Wampanoag and other Native Americans wore glass beads with copper and shell beads . . . to embody allegiance, wealth, gender and status: to honour the living and the dead. Glass beads were also worn to promote health and cure sicknesses' (Loren 2013, 156).

of 'taste' is echoed in a recent paper by Chirikure, who suggests that imports were only embraced if they fitted within the 'cultural logics' of the recipients, arguing, for example, that porcelain and other imported ceramics were rejected by the Shona peoples of interior Southern Africa because, being neither red nor black, colours central to ancestor worship, they could not take the place of local ceramics.[163]

Stahl mapped a 'cartography of taste' in beads in the Banda region of Ghana where both locally produced beads of various raw materials and imported glass beads varied in numbers and in diversity of types through time, prompting changes in both taste and the uses to which beads were put. '[T]he desirability of imported forms was likely predicated on the existing practices of taste for beads, which were subsequently transformed by the incorporation of new bead forms.'[164] These new beads began to be associated with female initiation rituals, but as bead frequencies increased they appeared more widely distributed across Stahl's archaeological site, 'suggesting that their use was increasingly quotidian'.[165] Finally, and perhaps of particular interest in terms of Garamantian material culture, is Stahl's observation that locally produced ceramic and shell beads continued to be produced and consumed, albeit in relatively small quantities, even in the face of plentiful imported glass beads, which she interprets as evidence of the continued relevance within society of earlier practices of taste.[166] Thus, a temporal series of bead assemblages from well-defined archaeological contexts from a region like Fazzan can be interrogated in terms of the changing tastes of the inhabitants; for example, it seems that glass beads became more popular, as well as perhaps more readily available, in Late Garamantian phases at the expense of faience beads.[167]

Beads and Identification

> 'Without beads men laugh at you and you're not a person.' (Turkana woman's response to the question, 'Why are beads so important?')[168]

> Beads and cloth are crucial in making necessary distinctions between men and women, men and boys, women and girls. Beads follow Samburu from birth to death, whether figuring in significant ceremonies or simply forming a part of daily attire.[169]

---

[163] Chirikure 2014.   [164] Stahl 2002, 841.   [165] Stahl 2002, 841.
[166] Stahl 2002, 841; cf. Chirikure 2014; see also the discussion above of 'beady cultures'.
[167] Cole 2013, 458; Martin Sterry, personal communication.   [168] Williams 1987, 33.
[169] Straight 2005, 274.

It seems self-evident that beads, adornments commonly worn on the body, serve to fashion, display and often reinforce identity, in part because, as we have already seen, they are also often intimately bound up with wealth, power and status. We can also readily acknowledge the existence of cross-cultural variation in the ways in which beads create and express identity and in the nature of that identity. Therefore, we are unlikely to generate any useful insights into the connections between glass beads and identity by assembling a database of cross-cultural ethnographic comparisons. A better approach may be to think about the creation and maintenance of identity within particular archaeological, historical or ethnographic contexts. Prior to doing so, however, we may note that the intertwined creation, negotiation and materialisation of identity (be it at the level of the individual, group, faction, class or ethnicity) using glass beads would commonly seem to involve conscious manipulation of societal norms for this process through choices such as the selection of beads of particular sizes and colours, where on the body they are worn and the juxtaposition of particular colours of beads in the fashioning of jewellery, etc.[170] It is also worth noting that this conscious appropriation of material culture for the purpose of creating and negotiating identity is far from universal, with glass beads – being both 'glittering emblems'[171] and foreign objects – particularly apropos for this purpose. In most cases perhaps, '[acts of] appropriation of material culture in the realisation of social strategies ... are so embedded in our cultural values and representations as to remain unnoticed, a part of our habitus'.[172]

In the case of the Turkana, an ethnic group of East African pastoralists and a quotation from whom opened this section of the chapter, beads can be thought of as a component of a performative repertoire through which women create, negotiate and signal their identity, although this performance will not be understood similarly by all observers. For the Turkana themselves,[173] 'beads signify identity, beauty, relationship, context, gender, and wealth; they also heal and protect'.[174] Turkana, for example, recognise that a woman wearing all white beads is a widow.[175] However, what is probably not consciously recognised by most Turkana is that, '[T]he desire for beads and the display of traditional material culture inscribe women as

---

[170] See, for example, Klumpp and Kratz 1993; Straight 2005.   [171] Karlström and Källén 2003.

[172] Gosselain 2000, 189; see also discussion above of beads and identity in cultures lacking an ideology of individualism.

[173] Permit me to assume simplistically here that all Turkana understand the information conveyed by the wearing of particular beads by a Turkana woman.

[174] Williams 1987, 35.   [175] Williams 1987, 34.

staunch supporters of a system in which they are blatantly exploited physically, emotionally, economically, and intellectually . . . . [Women, T] hrough their desire for beads, men, and children, actively create social organisation.'[176] Turkana, however, are not the only people who use beads to negotiate Turkana identity. Turkana beads are seen by Kenyan government officials as symbols of primitive behaviour and of opposition to modernisation, perhaps as a result of which licenses to import beads were not approved at the time of Williams' fieldwork.[177] In a similar vein, the British colonial authorities banned the songs and beads of Samburu warriors and their girlfriends in Kenya, an act that was 'memorialised immediately in songs and stories'.[178]

How might beads have participated in processes of identification and identity in Fazzan during Garamantian times? To answer this question we begin by outlining what has been reconstructed about cultural identity from the archaeology of Fazzan. Several summary statements in volume one of the Fazzan reports suggest that Garamantian cultural identity was multifaceted, negotiable and cross-cut by racial and class distinctions. 'Garamantian culture and society was something that came together in Fazzan, uniting diverse influences and being subsequently affected by contacts between the Garamantes and their neighbours';[179] Garamantes 'probably comprised a great confederation of tribes',[180] with the 'maintenance of discrete tribal identities within the structure of the polity' evident from the variety of tomb types in the Classic Garamantian period.[181] Also, skeletal evidence indicates that more than half of the people were of 'mixed blood or full negro physiognomy', while there was also a 'significant component of light-skinned Libyans'.[182] Moreover, the endurance of these diverse racial traits into later times 'would seem to indicate that intermixing of the races was not completely open and may have been structured within Garamantian society'.[183] Finally, with reference to class, 'the kingdom was never based on a uniform "ethnic" identity, but was a product of military power and centralised organisation of labour and resources by a dominant group', 'who celebrated elite status with images of chariots and horses'.[184] At the other end of the class spectrum, Mattingly argues that literary references to Garamantian raids on

---

[176] Williams 1987, 36. This is, of course, the ethnographer's interpretation!

[177] Government officials explained the refusal of import licenses as part of a ban on luxury imports prompted by foreign exchange deficits (Williams 1987, 35).

[178] Straight 2005, 273.   [179] Mattingly 2003, 234.   [180] Mattingly 2003, 346.

[181] Mattingly 2003, 349.   [182] Mattingly 2003, 233.   [183] Mattingly 2003, 233.

[184] Mattingly 2003, 361–62, 349.

'Ethiopians' supports the notion that some of the negroes were probably slaves and that one of the jobs performed by slaves was the construction of the remarkable underground canals (foggaras) that sustained the agricultural economy.[185]

All of the above indicates that the construction and maintenance of both individual and ethnic identity must have been an important facet of Garamantian society. Beads, as valued objects, are highly likely to have participated as part of a performative repertoire that shaped identification. Moreover, that identification and its overt signalling through beads worn on the body or clothing is likely to have been particularly important when we consider that there were resident slaves, as well as probably slaves passing through in transit across the Sahara, that these slaves may have been primarily negroid and that more than half of the population is estimated to have been of 'mixed blood or full negro physiognomy'. Under such circumstances, one can imagine that many residents of Fazzan would be keen to establish their status as free rather than slaves, despite their appearance. As an example of this process we can point to areas of West Africa during the period of the European slave trade where the adoption by Africans of European styles of dress, furnishings and other imports served to distinguish free residents from the enslaved and enslaveable.[186] Building upon this insight, Stahl has argued that, 'Consumption practices may be a particularly productive way to investigate processes of inclusion and exclusion shaped by slavery'.[187]

'Tribal' identity may also have been important to the maintenance of economic, political and social ties. Hair styles, tattoos and scarification, body adornment, dress, house styles, tomb types and material culture, as well as practices of limited visibility or invisible to archaeologists, such as speech, belief systems and the cultural organisation of space, all had the potential to forge identity and signal aspects of it to others.[188] Indeed, we have already seen that variation in tomb types in Fazzan has been linked to ethnic identity. Glass vessels, as luxury imports, would have signalled wealth and status when displayed or used in houses and when placed in tombs, presumably during the course of well-attended funerary rites. However, when individuals were away from their homes, a strong sense

---

[185] Mattingly 2003, 233, 276.   [186] Lovejoy and Richardson 2003.   [187] Stahl 2008, 41.

[188] Cf. Loren 2013 where she describes how some Native New Englanders' wearing of beads both mimicked and mocked Puritan dress and values, with the beads helping to shape Native values and embody their own identity in the face of Puritan efforts to convert them to Christianity and the Puritan ethos. This itself was a time of culture contact that may be seen perhaps as analogous to what immigrants, free or enslaved, to Fazzan may have encountered during Garamantian and later times.

of identity, embodied in dress and ornament, may have been required to avoid being seized as a slave. Glass beads and bangles could have been important in creating and signalling the status of a free person.

Conclusion

This wide-ranging survey of the production, movement and consumption of beads has drawn on numerous anthropological and archaeological studies to reveal the perhaps remarkable variety of functions performed by beads and hence both their importance in African societies and the numerous ways in which they may enter the archaeological record. Clearly there has been a constant demand for beads in many parts of Africa spanning the entire period of their availability. Such demand led people in some regions to develop or learn from others the technology to make new beads from recycled glass. As we have also seen, beads in different places at different times may have been regarded as commodities or as luxury goods, the latter often subject to sumptuary rules, particularly perhaps in regions at or near the terminus of trade routes in the Sub-Saharan interior.

We are reaching the point where we can be reasonably confident about identifying the provenience of glass manufacture; the value of LA-ICP-MS studies in this regard is now established. Future studies that already seem to be increasingly focused on isotope analyses will further refine, but perhaps not radically alter, the results of provenience studies obtained by LA-ICP-MS. They may, however, move us towards more knowledge of when and where colouring agents may have been added to the base glass, likely as part of bead manufacture. Thus, they hold considerable promise for elucidating the journey of a bead from original glass manufacture to place of deposition and thereby shed light on the several communities of practice through which the bead was probably moved.

In the absence of ethnographic or historical evidence, the interpretation of the function and meaning of beads on an archaeological site poses significant challenges. However, it seems reasonable to suggest that examination of the archaeological context in which the beads are found, together with knowledge of the broader cultural and historical setting in which the site and beads occurred, permits some optimism about the identification of the beads' functions and cultural contexts, even if the subtleties of such topics as colour symbolism may often elude us. It is important to examine beads and particularly bead production within a comparative context that includes other types of artefacts and their associated technologies, as well as linked questions such as those of the social relations of production and the scheduling of labour. By thinking about these issues and by considering them in relation to depositional practices on our archaeological sites,[189] we may be able to have productive discussions about how everyday life, including the making of pots, the cooking and consumption of particular foods, the working of glass and the wearing of beads, *inter alia*, produced and materialised complex, shifting identities that allowed the multicultural milieu of Fazzan to flourish during Garamantian times. Glass beads and other items of material culture do indeed 'accumulate histories and have the ability to tell multiple stories about people'.[190] If we marry recent anthropological insights about material objects with careful consideration of archaeological contexts and depositional practices, as well as use the analytical tools of the hard sciences, we have the potential to explore, with some confidence, the lived experience of the ancient inhabitants of Fazzan.[191]

References

Antonites, A. 2014. Glass beads from Mutamba: Patterns of consumption in thirteenth-century southern Africa. *Azania: Archaeological Research in Africa* 49.3: 411–28.

Appadurai, A. 1986a. Introduction: Commodities and the politics of value. In Appadurai 1986b, 3–63.

Appadurai, A. (ed.) 1986b. *The Social Life of Things: Commodities in Cultural Perspective*. Cambridge: Cambridge University Press.

Bayart, J.-F. 2000. Africa in the world: A history of extraversion. *African Affairs* 99: 217–67.

Ben-Amos, P. 1999. *Art, Innovation, and Politics in Eighteenth-Century Benin*. Bloomington, IN: Indiana University Press.

Blair, E.H. 2015. Glass beads and global itineraries. In R.A. Joyce and S. Gillespie (eds), *Things in Motion: Object Itineraries in Archaeological Practice*, Santa Fe, NM: School for Advanced Research, 81–99.

---

[189] Joyce and Pollard 2010; Ogundiran 2014.   [190] Gosselain 2000, 189.

[191] I am very grateful to Ann Stahl and Marilee Wood for their comments on earlier versions of this chapter; Ann, in particular, served as my guide to a vast literature with which I still have only passing familiarity. I wholeheartedly thank the organisers of the conference at Leicester for the invitation to participate and for their organisational skills and kindness that made the conference such a pleasant experience. I also thank the conference participants for their feedback on my paper. While it may be unwise to single anyone out from what was a team effort, I am particularly grateful to Chloë N. Duckworth for all her support.

Blair, E.H. 2016. Glass beads and constellations of practice. In A.P. Roddick and A. B. Stahl (eds), *Knowledge in Motion: Constellations of Learning across Time and Place*, Tucson: University of Arizona Press, 97–125.

Burton, R. 1860. *The Lake Regions of Central Africa: A Picture Exploration*, Volume 2. London: Longman, Green, Longman and Roberts.

Calabrese, J.A. 2007. *The Emergence of Social and Political Complexity in the Shashi-Limpopo Valley of Southern Africa, AD 900 to 1300: Ethnicity, Class, and Polity*. Oxford: British Archaeological Reports.

Chirikure, S. 2014. Land and sea links: 1500 years of connectivity between southern Africa and the Indian Ocean rim regions, AD 700 to 1700. *African Archaeological Review* 31.4: 705–24.

Cissé, M. 2011. Archaeological Investigations of Early Trade and Urbanism at Gao Saney (Mali). Unpublished PhD thesis, Rice University, Houston (USA).

Cissé, M., McIntosh, S.K., Dussubieux, L., Fenn, T., Gallagher, D. and Chipps Smith, A. 2013. Excavations at Gao Saney: New evidence for settlement growth, trade, and interaction on the Niger Bend in the First Millennium CE. *Journal of African Archaeology* 11.1: 9–37.

Cole, F. 2013. Small finds report. In Mattingly 2013, 455–72.

Craddock, P.T., Ambers, J., Hook, D.R., Farquhar, R.M., Chikwendu, V.E., Umeji, A.C. and Shaw, T. 1997. Metal sources and the bronzes from Igbo-Ukwu, Nigeria. *Journal of Field Archaeology* 24.4: 405–29.

Curtin, P.D. 1984. *Cross-Cultural Trade in World History*. Cambridge: Cambridge University Press.

Dowler, A. and Galvin, E.R. (eds) 2011. *Money, Trade and Trade Routes in Pre-Islamic North Africa*. London: The British Museum.

Duckworth, C.N., Cuénod, A. and Mattingly, D.J. 2014. Non-destructive µXRF analysis of glass and metal objects from sites in the Libyan pre-desert and Fazzan. *Libyan Studies* 45: 1–20.

Dussubieux, L. 2017. Glass beads in the Trans-Saharan trade. In Mattingly *et al.* 2017, 414–32.

Ekholm, K. 1977. External exchange and the transformation of Central African social systems. In J. Friedman and M.J. Rowlands (eds), *The Evolution of Social Systems*, London: Duckworth, 115–36.

Francis, P. Jr. 1991. Beadmaking in Arikamedu and beyond. *World Archaeology* 23.1: 28–43.

Francis, P. Jr. 2002. *Asia's Maritime Bead Trade 300 B.C. to the Present*. Honolulu: University of Hawaii Press.

Freestone, I.C. 2006. An indigenous technology? A commentary on Lankton *et al.* 'Early Primary Glass Production in Southern Nigeria'. *Journal of African Archaeology* 4.1: 139–41.

Gokee, C. and Logan, A.L. 2014. Comparing craft and culinary practices in Africa: Themes and perspectives. *African Archaeological Review* 31.2: 87–104.

Gosselain, O.P. 2000. Materializing identities: An African perspective. *Journal of Archaeological Method and Theory* 7.3: 187–217.

Gosselain, O.P. 2008. Thoughts and adjustments in the potter's backyard. In I. Berg (ed.), *Breaking the Mould: Challenging the Past through Pottery*, Oxford: Archaeopress, 67–79.

Gosselain, O.P. 2016. The world is like a beanstalk: Historicizing potting practice and social relations in the Niger River area. In A.P. Roddick and A.B. Stahl (eds), *Knowledge in Motion: Constellations of Learning across Time and Place*, Tucson: University of Arizona Press, 36–66.

Graeber, D. 2001. *Toward an Anthropological Theory of Value: The False Coin of our own Dreams*. New York: Palgrave.

Haour, A. 2013. *Outsiders and Strangers: An Archaeology of Liminality in West Africa*. Oxford: Oxford University Press.

Helms, M. 1993. *Craft and the Kingly Ideal: Art, Trade and Power*. Austin, TX: University of Texas Press.

Horton, R. 1992. The economy of Ife from c.A.D. 900–c.A.D. 1700. In I. A. Akinjogbin (ed.), *The Cradle of a Race: Ife from the Beginning to 1980*, Port Harcourt: Sunray, 122–47.

Hourani, A. 2002. *A History of the Arab Peoples*. Cambridge, MA: Belknap Press.

Huffman, T.N. 1986. Iron Age settlement patterns and the origins of class distinction in southern Africa. *Advances in World Archaeology* 5: 291–331.

Huffman, T.N. 2000. Mapungubwe and the origins of the Zimbabwe culture. In M. Leslie and T. Maggs (eds), *African Naissance: The Limpopo Valley 1000 Years Ago*, Goodwin Series, Volume 8, Cape Town: South African Archaeological Society, 14–29.

Ingold, T. 1993. The temporality of the landscape. *World Archaeology* 25.2: 152–74.

Insoll, T. and Shaw, T. 1997. Gao and Igbo-Ukwu: Beads, interregional trade, and beyond. *African Archaeological Review* 14.1: 9–23.

Jones, A. 1995. *West Africa in the Mid-Seventeenth Century: An Anonymous Dutch Manuscript*. Atlanta: African Studies Association Press.

Joyce, R.A. 2012. Life with things: Archaeology and materiality. In D. Shankland (ed.), *Archaeology and Anthropology: Past, Present and Future*, Oxford: Berg, 119–32.

Joyce, R.A. and Pollard, J. 2010. Archaeological assemblages and practices of deposition. In D. Hicks and M. C. Beaudry (eds), *The Oxford Handbook of Material Culture Studies*, Oxford: Oxford University Press, 291–309.

Kanungo, A. 2004a. *Glass Beads in Ancient India: An Ethnoarchaeological Approach*. BAR International Series 1242. Oxford: Archaeopress.

Kanungo, A. 2004b. Glass beads in ancient India and furnace-wound beads at Purdalpur: An ethnoarchaeological approach. *Asian Perspectives* 43.1: 130–50.

Kanungo, A. 2014. *Indian Glass Beads: Archaeology to Ethnography*. New Delhi: Research India Press.

Karlström, A. and Källén, A. (eds) 2003. *Fishbones and Glittering Emblems: Southeast Asian Archaeology 2002.* Stockholm: Museum of Far Eastern Antiquities.

Killick, D. 2009. Agency, dependency, and long-distance trade: East Africa and the Islamic World, ca. 700–1500 CE. In S.E. Falconer and C. Redman (eds), *Polities and Power: Archaeological Perspectives on the Landscapes of Early States*, Tucson: University of Arizona Press, 179–207.

Klumpp, D. and Kratz, C. 1993. Aesthetics, expertise, and ethnicity: Okiek and Maasai perspectives on personal ornament. In T. Spear and R. Waller (eds), *Being Maasai: Ethnicity and Identity in East Africa*, London: James Currey, 195–221.

Kock, J. and Sode, T. 1995. *Glass, Glass beads and Glassmakers in Northern India.* Vanlose, Denmark: THOT Press.

Kopytoff, I. 1986. The cultural biography of things: Commoditization as process. In Appadurai 1986b, 64–91.

Lankton, J., Ige, O.A. and Rehren, T. 2006. Early primary glass production in southern Nigeria. *Journal of African Archaeology* 4.1: 111–38.

Lankton, J., Nixon, S., Robertshaw, P. and Dussubieux, L. 2017. Beads. In S. Nixon (ed.), *Essouk-Tadmekka: An Early Islamic Market Town in the Southern Sahara*, Leiden: Brill, JAA Monograph Series in African Archaeology, 160–73.

Lave, J. and Wenger, J. 1991. *Situated Learning: Legitimate Peripheral Participation.* Cambridge: Cambridge University Press.

Levtzion, N. and Hopkins, J.F.P. (eds) 2000. *Corpus of Early Arabic Sources for West African History.* Princeton: Markus Wiener Publishers.

Logan, A.L. and Cruz, M.D. 2014. Gendered taskscapes: Food, farming and craft production in Banda, Ghana in the eighteenth to twenty-first centuries. *African Archaeological Review* 31.2: 203–31.

Loren, D.D. 2013. Considering mimicry and hybridity in early colonial New England: Health, sin and the body 'behung with beades'. *Archaeological Review from Cambridge* 28.1: 151–68.

Lovejoy, P.E. and Richardson, D. 2003. Anglo-Efik relations and protection against illegal enslavement at Old Calabar, 1740–1807. In S.A. Diouf (ed.), *Fighting the Slave Trade: West African Strategies*, Athens, OH: Ohio University Press, 101–18.

Lyons, D. 2014. Perceptions of consumption: Constituting potters, farmers and blacksmiths in the culinary continuum in eastern Tigray, northern highland Ethiopia. *African Archaeological Review* 31.2: 169–201.

MacDonald, K.C. 2011. A view from the south: Sub-Saharan evidence for contacts between North Africa, Mauritania and the Niger, 1000 BC–AD 700. In Dowler and Galvin 2011, 72–82.

Magnavita, S. 2003. The beads of Kissi, Burkina Faso. *Journal of African Archaeology* 1.1: 127–38.

Magnavita, S. 2009. Sahelian crossroads: Some aspects on the Iron Age sites of Kissi, Burkina Faso. In Magnavita *et al.* 2009, 79–104.

Magnavita, S. 2013. Initial encounters: Seeking traces of ancient trade connections between West Africa and the wider world. *Afriques* 4. http://afriques.revues.org /1145.

Magnavita, S., Hallier, M., Pelzer, C., Kahlheber, S. and Linseele, V. 2002. Nobles, guerriers, paysans: Une nécropole de l'Age de Fer et son emplacement dans l'Oudalan pré- et protohistorique. *Beiträge zur Allgemeinen und Vergleichenden Archäologie* 22: 21–64.

Magnavita, S., Koté, L., Breunig, P. and Idé, O.A. (eds) 2009. *Crossroads/Carrefour Sahel: Cultural and Technological Developments in First Millennium* BC/AD *West Africa*. Journal of African Archaeology Monograph Series, Volume 2. Frankfurt am Main: Africa Magna Verlag,

Mattingly, D.J. (ed.) 2003. *The Archaeology of Fazzan. Volume 1, Synthesis*. London: Society for Libyan Studies.

Mattingly, D.J. (ed.) 2010. *The Archaeology of Fazzan. Volume 3, Excavations Carried out by C.M. Daniels*. London: Society for Libyan Studies, Department of Antiquities.

Mattingly, D.J. 2011. The Garamantes of Fezzan: An early Libyan state with Trans-Saharan connections. In Dowler and Galvin 2011, 49–60.

Mattingly, D.J. (ed.) 2013. *The Archaeology of Fazzan. Volume 4, Survey and Excavations at Old Jarma (Ancient Garama) carried out by C.M. Daniels (1962–69) and the Fazzan Project (1997–2001)*. London: Society for Libyan Studies, Department of Antiquities.

Mattingly, D.J., Thomas, D.C., Pelling, R. and Sterry, M. 2013. Explanation of the Fazzan Project work, phasing and AMS dating. In Mattingly 2013, 117–34.

Mattingly, D.J., Leitch, V., Duckworth, C.N., Cuénod, A., Sterry, M. and Cole, F. (eds) 2017. *Trade in the Ancient Sahara and Beyond*. Trans-Saharan Archaeology, Volume 1. Cambridge: Cambridge University Press and the Society for Libyan Studies.

Mattingly, D.J., Gatto, M., Ray, N. and Sterry, M. 2019. Dying to be Garamantian: Burial and migration in Fazzan. In M. Carmelo Gatto, D.J. Mattingly, N. Ray and M. Sterry (eds), *Burials, Migration and Identity in the Ancient Sahara and Beyond*. Trans-Saharan Archaeology, Volume 2. Series editor D.J. Mattingly. Cambridge: Cambridge University Press and the Society for Libyan Studies, 51–107.

Mauss, M. 1938. Une catégorie de l'esprit humain: La notion de personne, celle de 'moi', un plan de travail. *Journal of the Royal Anthropological Institute* 68: 263–81.

Mudenge, S.I. 1974. The role of foreign trade in the Rozvi Empire: A reappraisal. *Journal of African History* 15.3: 445–56.

Mudenge, S.I. 1988. *A Political History of Munhumutapa c.1400–1902*. Harare: Zimbabwe Publishing House.

Nadel, S.F. 1942. *A Black Byzantium: The Kingdom of Nupe in Nigeria*. London: Oxford University Press.

Nixon, S. 2009. Excavating Essouk-Tadmakka (Mali): New archaeological investigations of Early Islamic Trans-Saharan trade. *Azania: Archaeological Research in Africa* 44.2: 217–55.

Ogundiran, A. 2002. Of small things remembered: Beads, cowries, and cultural translations of the Atlantic experience in Yorubaland. *International Journal of African Historical Studies* 35.2–3: 427–57.

Ogundiran, A. 2003. Chronology, material culture, and pathways to the cultural history of Yoruba-Edo region, Nigeria, 10th–19th century. In T. Falola and C. Jennings (eds), *Sources and Methods in African History: Spoken, Written, Unearthed*, Rochester, NY: University of Rochester Press, 33–79.

Ogundiran, A. 2014. Cowries and rituals of self-realization in the Yoruba region, ca. 1600–1860. In A. Ogundiran and P. Saunders (eds), *Materialities of Ritual in the Black Atlantic*, Bloomington and Indianapolis: Indiana University Press, 68–86.

Ogundiran, A. and Ige, O.A. 2015. 'Our ancestors were material scientists': Archaeological and geochemical evidence for indigenous Yoruba glass technology. *Journal of Black Studies* 30 August 2015. doi:10.1177/0021934715600964.

Onwuejeogwu, M. 1981. *An Igbo Civilisation: Nri Kingdom and Hegemony*. London: Ethnographica.

Onwuejeogwu, M. and Onwuejeogwu, O. 1977. The search for the missing links in dating and interpreting the Igbo-Ukwu finds. *Paideuma* 23: 169–88.

Park, D.P. 2010. Prehistoric Timbuktu and its hinterland. *Antiquity* 84.326: 1076–88.

Pelling, R. 2013. The archaeobotanical remains. In Mattingly 2013, 473–94.

Prestholdt, J. 2004. On the global repercussions of East African consumerism. *American Historical Review* 109.3: 755–81.

Prestholdt, J. 2008. *Domesticating the World: African Consumerism and the Genealogies of Globalization*. Berkeley: University of California Press.

Ray, K. 1987. Material metaphor, social interaction and historical reconstructions: Exploring patterns of association and symbolism in the Igbo-Ukwu corpus. In I. Hodder (ed.), *The Archaeology of Contextual Meanings*. Cambridge: Cambridge University Press, 66–77.

Robertshaw, P., Magnavita, S., Wood, M., Melchiorre, E., Popelka-Filcoff, R. and Glascock, M. 2009a. Glass beads from Kissi (Burkina Faso): chemical analysis and archaeological interpretation. In Magnavita *et al.* 2009, 105–118.

Robertshaw, P., Weise, C., Dussubieux, L., Lankton, J., Popelka-Filcoff, R.S. and Glascock, M.D. 2009b. Chemical analysis of glass from Nupe, Nigeria. *Tribus* 58: 83–95.

Robertshaw, P., Benco, N., Wood, M., Dussubieux, L., Melchiorre, E. and Ettahiri, A. 2010a. Chemical analysis of glass beads from Medieval al-Basra (Morocco). *Archaeometry* 52.3: 355–79.

Robertshaw, P., Wood, M., Melchiorre, E., Popelka-Filcoff, R.S. and Glascock, M. D. 2010b. Southern African glass beads: Chemistry, glass sources and patterns of trade. *Journal of Archaeological Science* 37.8: 1898–912.

Robertson, K.R. 1935. Nupe Glassworkers (Masaga), Bida. Unpublished report by the Superintendent of Education, February 1935.

Roth, H.L. 1968. [1903]. *Great Benin: Its Customs, Art and Horrors*. London: Routledge.

Savage, E. 1992. Berbers and Blacks: Ibāḍī slave traffic in eighth-century North Africa. *Journal of African History* 33.3: 351–68.

Shaw, T. 1970. *Igbo-Ukwu: An Account of Archaeological Discoveries in Eastern Nigeria, 2 volumes*. Evanston, IL: Northwestern University Press.

Shaw, T. 1975. Those Igbo-Ukwu radiocarbon dates: Facts, fictions and probabilities. *Journal of African History* 16.4: 503–17.

Shaw, T. 1977. *Unearthing Igbo-Ukwu*. London: Oxford University Press.

Simmel, G. 1978. *The Philosophy of Money*. London: Routledge.

Stahl, A.B. 2002. Colonial entanglements and the practices of taste: An alternative to logocentric approaches. *American Anthropologist* 104.3: 827–45.

Stahl, A.B. 2008. The slave trade as practice and memory: What are the issues for archaeologists? In C.M. Cameron (ed.), *Invisible Citizens: Captives and their Consequences*, Salt Lake City: University of Utah Press, 25–56.

Stahl, A.B. 2014a. Intersections of craft and cuisine: Implications for what and how we study. *African Archaeological Review* 31.2: 383–93.

Stahl, A.B. 2014b. Africa in the world: (Re)centering African history through archaeology. *Journal of Anthropological Research* 70: 5–33.

Straight, B. 2005. Cutting time: Beads, sex and songs in the making of Samburu memory. In W. James and D. Mills (eds), *The Qualities of Time: Anthropological Approaches*, Oxford and New York: Berg, 267–83.

Sutton, J.E.G. 1991. The international factor at Igbo-Ukwu. *African Archaeological Review* 9: 145–60.

Sutton, J.E.G. 2001. Igbo-Ukwu and the Nile. *African Archaeological Review* 18.1: 49–62.

Takezawa, S. and Cissé, M. 2012. Discovery of the earliest royal palace in Gao and its implications for the history of West Africa. *Cahiers d'études africaines* 208: 813–44.

Thomson, J. 1881. *To the Central African Lakes and Back: The Narrative of the Royal Geographical Society's East Central African Expedition, 1878–80*. London: Low, Marston, Searle and Rivington.

Turgeon, L. 2004. Beads, bodies and regimes of value: From France to North America, c.1500–c.1650. In T. Murray (ed.), *The Archaeology of Contact in Settler Societies*, Cambridge: Cambridge University Press, 19–47.

Vanacker, V. 1984. Perles de verre découvertes sur le site de Tegdaoust (Mauritanie orientale). *Journal des Africanistes* 54: 31–52.

Wenger, E. 1998. *Communities of Practice: Learning, Meaning, and Identity*. Cambridge: Cambridge University Press.

Williams, S. 1987. An 'archae-logy' of Turkana beads. In I. Hodder (ed.), *The Archaeology of Contextual Meanings*, Cambridge: Cambridge University Press, 31–38.

Willis, R. 1999. *Some Spirits Heal, Others Only Dance: A Journey into Human Selfhood in an African Village*. Oxford: Berg.

Wilmsen, E.N. 2009. Hills and the brilliance of beads: Myths and the interpretation of Iron Age sites in southern Africa. *Southern African Humanities* 21: 263–74.

Wilmsen, E.N. 2014. Myths, gender, birds, beads: A reading of Iron Age hill sites in interior southern Africa. *Africa* 84.3: 398–423.

Wood, M. 2011a. A glass bead sequence for southern Africa from the 8th to the 16th century AD. *Journal of African Archaeology* 9.1: 67–84.

Wood, M. 2011b. *Interconnections: Glass Beads and Trade in Southern and Eastern Africa and the Indian Ocean – 7th to 16th centuries* AD. Studies in Global Archaeology 17. Uppsala: Department of Archaeology and Ancient History, University of Uppsala.

Wood, M. 2016. Glass beads from pre-European contact Sub-Saharan Africa: Peter Francis's work revisited and updated. *Archaeological Research in Asia* 6: 65–80.

12 | Three Millennia of Egyptian Glassmaking

THILO REHREN AND DANIELA ROSENOW

Glass Production

Primary glassmaking consists of the melting together of raw materials such as finely ground quartz pebbles or sand, with a flux such as plant ash or mineral natron. It is a chemical operation resulting in an artificial material which must then be worked further into usable objects. Locating glass manufacture can be done directly through the discovery of installations and waste material, or indirectly through the interpretation of the composition of particular glass groups in relation to potential raw material characteristics, or their preferential occurrence and use in certain regions (Figs 12.1–12.2).

The Earliest Period of Glassmaking: During the Late Bronze Age

Regular glassmaking in Egypt began in the mid-second millennium BC and flourished for nearly half a millennium, producing intensely coloured glass, simulating precious stones such as turquoise, carnelian, lapis lazuli, amethyst, obsidian and others.[1] It arrived as a seemingly fully fledged industry with little if any evidence for a developmental stage. While it shared its raw materials with Egyptian faience, there is no evidence that would indicate an emergence of glassmaking from faience production; instead, the technology appears to have arrived from further east, together with the glass itself, as well as glass workers.[2] Links to the emergence of metallurgy are often touted[3] but difficult to demonstrate and not universally considered likely.[4]

---

[1] Shortland 2012.   [2] Nicholson and Henderson 2000.
[3] Hauptmann *et al.* 2000; Mass *et al.* 2002.   [4] Rehren 2003.

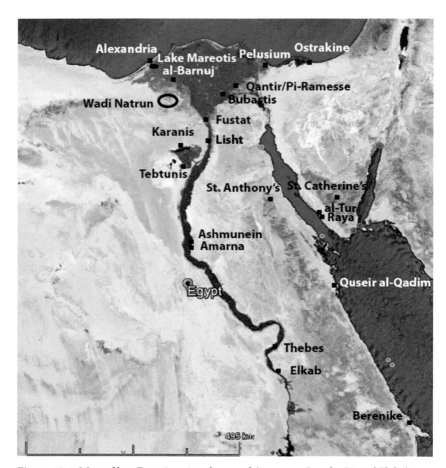

Figure 12.1 Map of key Egyptian sites discussed (imagery: Google, DigitalGlobe).

It is now widely accepted that during this period, soda-rich plant ash with significant lime content, and crushed quartz as a very pure silica source, were the main raw materials used to make glass, both in Egypt and in Mesopotamia. The archaeological evidence for glassmaking during this period has been recognised only recently and remains very limited. At present, production remains are known from Ramesside Qantir-Piramesse in the Nile Delta[5] and from Amarna in Middle Egypt,[6] with some further indications for glassmaking elsewhere in Egypt, such as Lisht near Cairo.[7] No such direct evidence is known from Mesopotamia, even though it is generally recognised that this is the region where glassmaking first

---

[5] Pusch and Rehren 2007; Rehren and Pusch 2005.   [6] Smirniou and Rehren 2011.
[7] Smirniou 2012; Smirniou and Rehren 2016; Smirniou *et al.* 2018.

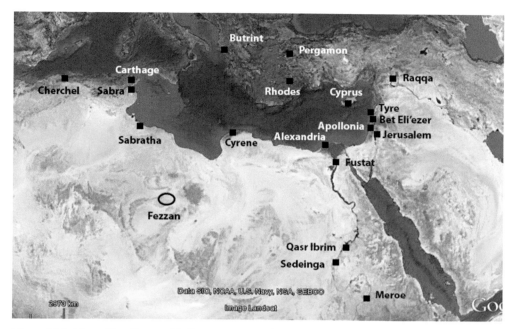

Figure 12.2 Map of key Eastern Mediterranean sites discussed (imagery: Google, DigitalGlobe).

evolved.[8] However, written and iconographic evidence supports the idea that glass was supplied from there to Egypt, and trace element analysis, first developed by Shortland and co-workers,[9] can clearly distinguish between glass found (and most likely made) in Mesopotamia and that from Egypt. This has enabled us to trace the flow of Bronze Age glass across much of the Old World; what we see is that both Mesopotamia and Egypt were exporting glass, mainly to Greece[10] but also as far as Denmark.[11]

The First Millennium BC: The Dark Ages

After half a millennium of glassmaking based on plant ash, in almost exactly 1000 BC the old flux was replaced by mineral natron, with crushed quartz remaining as the silica source. This change in recipe removed the main source of lime from the batch, and resulted in a chemically less stable glass composition, as shown by Schlick-Nolte and Werthmann for a series of objects from the tomb of Nesikhons in

[8] Lilyquist and Brill 1993; Nicholson 2013; Petrie 1926.   [9] Shortland *et al.* 2007.
[10] Walton *et al.* 2009.   [11] Varberg *et al.* 2015.

Thebes,[12] and by Freestone for similar objects such as the 'weeping scarab' from the British Museum.[13]

The use of this chemically unstable glass is, in our view, the main reason that for up to 500 years glass almost completely disappears from the archaeological record in Egypt and the surrounding regions, even though it may well have remained in production. Only those glasses survive which for some reason have stabilisers other than lime, such as very iron-rich black beads imitating obsidian, but none of these are known from first millennium BC Egypt. On the other hand, the political turmoil and economic downturn during this period would also have contributed to the disappearance of glass from the material record. The re-emergence of glass finds in Phoenician contexts, continuing the brightly coloured and figurative glass use of Pharaonic Egypt, and then in Classical Greece and into the Hellenistic periods, suggests an ongoing Egyptian glass industry we just do not see. Remarkably, hardly any glass objects are known from Egypt itself for almost the entire first millennium BC, probably reflecting a lack of research more than an absence of material.[14]

There is some evidence from the Hellenistic period for glassmaking and glassworking on Rhodes, which seems to have been a major centre for these activities,[15] but still nothing from Mesopotamia or Iran which would explain the Iron Age and Sasanian glass use there.[16] Significantly, it appears that at some point in the first millennium BC the dominant glass recipe in the Eastern Mediterranean changed, this time to the use of sand rather than crushed quartz as the main silica source, which reintroduced a source of lime into the batch. As a result, glass became chemically stable again, and from this point on has survived much better in the archaeological record. The exact when, where and why of this change, however, remains a mystery. One explanation could have been the growth in demand for glass as a result of the economic upturn and large building programmes of the Classical period in Greece and the Phoenician world, which may have stimulated a change of silica raw material from the hard-to-source white quartz pebbles to the seemingly inexhaustible white sands of the Eastern Mediterranean, with their lime-bearing shell fragments. Without well-dated evidence for a number of glassmaking installations from this transitional period, however, it is impossible to explore this further, and we are left with a single primary glass workshop (Rhodes) for the entire first millennium BC.

---

[12] Schlick-Nolte and Werthmann 2003.   [13] Fletcher *et al.* 2008.   [14] Nicholson 2013.
[15] Rehren *et al.* 2005; Triantafyllidis 2003, and literature therein.   [16] Simpson 2014.

First Millennium AD: Mineral Natron Industry and Glass Blowing

Glass production increased in the last few centuries of the first millennium BC and took a dramatic upturn when the technique of blowing glass was invented around the middle of the first century BC. Possible evidence for early experimentation came from a sealed deposit of cast and blown dumped workshop material discovered in a bath complex in Jerusalem.[17] Blowing glass allowed a much greater variety of shapes and a higher speed of manufacture, and was coeval with a rapid evolution and expansion of glass vessel styles and types. At the same time the cost of production was reduced, and glass became available for a much wider section of society; by the middle of the first century AD glass vessels had moved from valuable, high-status objects to a material commonly available – glass vessels became even more popular than pottery or metal vessels,[18] being odourless, easy to shape and remeltable if necessary. It is thus unsurprising that Roman glass has been found across the whole empire in domestic, industrial and funerary contexts, including in Egypt.[19] Its aesthetic qualities and unique physical properties were favoured by craftsmen, who used it to make items ranging from storage vessels, tableware, jewellery and mosaics, to window glass.

The organisation of Roman, Late Antique and Byzantine glass production has been a matter of debate over the past 20 years or so. Initially, the discussion had been very much driven by Pliny claiming that there were two ways of making glass, 'the old way' with sand coming from the Belus river in northern modern-day Israel, and 'the new way' using sands from areas in Italy, Gaul and Spain. This led to the development of two competing models of glass production: a more dispersed model,[20] assuming the existence of a range of regional primary glass production centres where every workshop had its own distinctive composition, and a more centralised system, which supports the idea of raw glass production in a few large-scale factories.[21]

From the fourth century AD onwards there is good archaeological and compositional evidence for a strongly centralised production of glass in large-scale factories on the Eastern Mediterranean shores, both in Egypt and the Levant, where the necessary raw ingredients – natron from the Wadi Natrun and chemically suitable sand – were readily available.[22]

[17] Israeli 1991.   [18] Beretta 2009.   [19] Rosenow and Rehren 2014.

[20] Baxter *et al.* 2005; Degryse and Schneider 2008; Wedepohl and Baumann 2000.

[21] Foy and Jezegou 1997; Foy *et al.* 2000; Freestone *et al.* 2000; Nenna 2007; Paynter 2006; Picon and Vichy 2003; Rehren and Brüggler 2020.

[22] Freestone *et al.* 2000; Gorin-Rosen 2000; Nenna 2007; Picon and Vichy 2003.

Contemporary glassmaking installations have been discovered primarily in the Syro-Palestine region, as in Apollonia and Bet Eli'ezer producing the so-called Levantine I[23] and Levantine II glass,[24] which supplied most of the Levant with raw glass. Significantly, little if any of this Levantine glass reached consumers in Egypt.

Glassmaking Evidence from Egypt in the First Millennium AD

Glassmaking in Egypt is attested around the turn of the millennium, with large-scale production evidence from the area around Lake Mareotis west of Alexandria, loosely dating to the Roman period, and in the Wadi Natrun, about 100 km north-west of Cairo, where raw glass batches of up to 25 tonnes in weight were produced in tank furnaces dating to the first two centuries AD.[25] Both regions produced their own distinct compositions: while the naturally coloured glass produced in the Mareotis region is extremely high in lime and alumina, glass from the Wadi Natrun shows rather low levels of lime and high levels of alumina. In the latter region, four different types of glass were produced: a manganese-decoloured glass, three variants of an antimony-decoloured glass, two variants of a naturally coloured glass without any additives and a raw glass group where plant ash instead of mineral natron was used as a flux.

Throughout the first millennium AD, mineral natron from the Wadi Natrun remained the dominant flux, although different alkali sources are known, for example, from al-Barnuj near Damanhur in the Western Delta, Elkab in Upper Egypt and Fazzan. These may have to be taken into consideration as well.[26] This mineral natron was mixed with changing sand sources resulting in discrete and chemically distinct glass groups. Some of these reached almost all corners of the Roman and Byzantine Empires within a few decades, while others remained of merely regional significance.

Based on composition and distribution pattern, several early Roman to Early Islamic primary glass groups can be linked to Egyptian production regions, even though potential production sites for these are yet to be found. The earliest of these groups is probably the antimony-decoloured glass that dominates the assemblage in Bubastis in the western Nile Delta

---

[23] Apollonia, fourth to seventh centuries AD: Freestone *et al.* 2000.
[24] Bet Eli'ezer, eighth/ninth centuries AD: Freestone *et al.* 2000.
[25] Nenna 2010; Nenna *et al.* 2000; 2005; Picon *et al.* 2008.
[26] Jackson *et al.* 2018; Lucas and Harris 1962, 263–67; Nenna 2007; Picon *et al.* 2008; see also Duckworth, Chapter 10, this volume.

for the late Ptolemaic and early Roman period,[27] and is also found widely across the early Roman Empire.[28] A few centuries later, this was replaced by the so-called HIMT glass which is characterised by its 'high iron, manganese and titanium' content. This was probably produced along the north-western coast of the Sinai Peninsula, most likely between Pelusium in the west and Ostrakine in the east.[29] It has been detected as close by as Cyprus, or indeed Fazzan in Libya, and as far away as London.[30] The same may be true for similar glass compositions often linked to HIMT that show slightly lower levels of the eponymous elements iron, manganese and titania, but are slightly higher in their lime content.[31] We believe that this glass, which we have referred to earlier as weak HIMT, is a primary glass group in its own right first defined by Foy and co-workers as série 3.2,[32] using sands similar to, and possibly quarried in close geographical proximity to, the sand used for the HIMT group. Both groups date to the fourth to sixth centuries AD.[33]

The so-called Egypt I glass group is characterised by the same distinct composition detected in the earlier Wadi Natrun glass (low lime, high alumina) and on this basis has been linked to the same production area.[34] It seems to have been manufactured there between the mid-sixth and the seventh century AD. It was succeeded by the so-called Egypt II glass with high levels of lime and low levels of alumina,[35] which was first detected in the Middle Egyptian town of Ashmunein, and may have been produced in that area.[36] This type of glass dates mostly to the eighth and ninth centuries AD.

The Early Second Millennium AD: Resurgence of Plant Ash Glassmaking

Towards the end of the first millennium the use of mineral natron for glassmaking in Egypt and the Levant ceased, and plant ash became once again the main flux used.[37] Despite this, large-scale glassmaking in the

---

[27] Rosenow and Rehren 2014.   [28] For example, Silvestri *et al.* 2008, and literature therein.

[29] Freestone *et al.* 2005; Nenna 2014.

[30] Cyprus: Freestone *et al.* 2002b; Ceglia *et al.* 2016; Fazzan: Duckworth, Chapter 10, this volume; London: Freestone *et al.* 2005.

[31] See Nenna 2014 for a detailed discussion.

[32] Rosenow and Rehren 2014; Foy *et al.* 2003a; see also Rehren and Brüggler 2020.

[33] For an up-to-date summary see Nenna 2014.   [34] Foy *et al.* 2003a; Freestone *et al.* 2008.

[35] Gratuze and Barrandon 1990; unpublished data Gratuze.

[36] Bimson and Freestone 1987; Gratuze and Barrandon 1990; Kato *et al.* 2009.

[37] Whitehouse 2002; Shortland *et al.* 2006; Phelps *et al.* 2016.

Levant continued into the early second millennium, as demonstrated by the tank furnaces from Tyre, in Lebanon.[38] Similar evidence is also documented from Raqqa in Syria.[39] Compositional evidence indicates that glass was also produced in western Turkey, using an as yet unidentified flux probably related to the large boron deposits in that region. This glass has been found from Bulgaria in the west to the Syrian border in the east; it emerged first in the third or fourth centuries AD, when it replaced Egyptian-produced glass in Pergamon, and continued to be produced well into the mid-second millennium AD.[40]

Very little evidence is known for glassmaking in Egypt during this time; Kato *et al.* interpret plant ash-based glass chunks with high titania content from waste dumps in Fustat near modern-day Cairo as probably of Egyptian origin, possibly even from Fustat itself;[41] however, the dating evidence for these finds is rather thin, and they are only very tentatively assigned to the tenth century AD or shortly thereafter.

Glass Use

The Earliest Period of Glass Use During the Late Bronze Age

Throughout Pharaonic Egypt, glass was considered an elite, luxury material. Its use was almost exclusively decorative, for jewellery, as surface adornment of walls, furniture and other large objects, and for small vessels used as containers for precious liquids or powders.[42] Its use alongside natural precious stones, typically mimicking them, indicates that it was not seen as much different from these colourful minerals, at least not by its elite users.[43] The craftsmen producing these objects clearly knew the differences, however, as is evident from the elaborate and sophisticated way they worked the glass; only for the very earliest objects did they use traditional lapidary techniques to work glass.[44] The scale of production, measured in kilograms and restricted to tightly controlled palace workshops, and the way glass was treated in both royal correspondence and in tombs of high-ranking officials, reflects this royal status.[45] There was remarkably little change in technology visible during the *c.*500 years of

---

[38] Aldsworth *et al.* 2002; Freestone 2002.   [39] Henderson *et al.* 2004.

[40] Rehren *et al.* 2015; Swan *et al.* 2018; Rehren *et al.* 2018.   [41] Kato *et al.* 2010b.

[42] Lilyquist and Brill 1993.

[43] See, for example, Broschat and Rehren 2017 for the glass headrests of Tutankhamen, imitating lapis lazuli and turquoise.

[44] Shortland 2012.   [45] Nicholson 2013.

Late Bronze Age glass use, indicating a rather static technology, satisfying the needs of its patrons.

Also remarkable is the near absence of evidence for the use of Mesopotamian glass in Egypt, at least after the first generation or so, despite the repeated and substantial references to glass imports found in the Amarna letters and various tomb paintings. This is a conundrum that needs further research to explain.[46]

The First Millennium BC: The Dark Ages

Very little is known about glass use during most of the first millennium BC from anywhere in Egypt; only with the Ptolemaic period does this picture change again. Some of this may simply reflect the limited number of published analyses of glass from the Third Intermediate period and Late period up to 332 BC, and the possible loss of less chemically stable glass to extensive weathering, discussed above.

The First Millennium AD: Resurgence and Bloom

Until recently, only scattered data on Roman and Late Antique glass existed, from sites such as Karanis and Qasr Ibrim,[47] Elkab[48] and the Northern Sinai,[49] as well as the data from the primary glass furnaces in the Wadi Natrun and the Mareotide. Most analytical data from Egyptian sites were for finds from the Early Islamic period, such as those from Tebtynis and Fustat,[50] as well as Raya and Wadi al-Tur[51] and St Catherine's on the Sinai, and St Anthony's in the Eastern Desert.[52] To address this gap in our knowledge, and as part of a current research project, about 450 glass vessel fragments (together with a few fragments that can be linked to secondary glass production) deriving from about 20 Egyptian sites and dating from the first century BC to the early eighth century AD were selected from various excavation archives and museum collections for typological and chemical analysis. This dataset forms much of the basis of the analysis in this chapter. Glass beads have not been taken into consideration for the following evaluation of Egypt's glass production and trade as, on the one hand, there are barely any analytical data available for

---

[46] Rehren 2014, but see Varberg *et al.* 2016 for the first evidence of some most likely Mesopotamian glass in Amarna.

[47] Brill 1999.   [48] Van der Linden *et al.* 2009.   [49] Freestone *et al.* 2002a.

[50] Brill 1999; Foy *et al.* 2003b; Gratuze and Barrandon 1990; Kato *et al.* 2010b; 2012.

[51] Kato *et al.* 2009.   [52] Brill 1999.

Egyptian glass beads and, on the other hand, glass for bead making often displays a higher degree of compositional variation[53] or might have been heavily recycled.[54] This restriction of our focus should of course not deny the social, cultural, religious and economic importance of glass beads in Ancient Egypt, or indeed the whole of the African continent.[55] As evidenced by archaeological and scientific work on glass beads from North and West Africa,[56] much can be learned by archaeologically and scientifically studying this object group, and it is hoped that future work on beads from Egypt will fill this geographical gap in our understanding of the social and economic role of beads in past societies. The current substantial work by Then-Obłuska on Meroitic and later glass beads in the Red Sea region already goes a long way towards this.[57]

Egyptian glass vessels dating to the Roman period belong to two major and one minor compositional groups, namely manganese-decoloured, antimony-decoloured and a plant ash-based glass. The last two of these groups can be linked to Egyptian production areas and make up altogether about 75 per cent of the material.

The earliest glass vessels, dating to the late Ptolemaic and early Roman periods (first century BC to first century AD), were produced in the earlier technique of cast moulding and are made of glass decoloured by the addition of manganese.[58] The available evidence suggests that manganese-decoloured glass continued to be used in Egypt, as represented by a few fragments from sites in Lower and Upper Egypt that – on typological and archaeological evidence – date to the late first to early third centuries AD. This is paralleled by the more sustained presence of manganese-decoloured glass elsewhere in the Western Mediterranean, North Africa and Roman Britain.[59] This glass is low in titania and iron oxide, a rather atypical composition for Egyptian raw glass. It thus seems reasonable to suggest that this manganese-decoloured glass reached Egypt as an import, most likely coming from the Levant and representing the only glass imported into Egypt during Roman times.

More than half of all sampled glass fragments dating to the Roman period, all of them free-blown, were made of colourless to light green glass decoloured by adding antimony oxide, a primary glass group

---

[53] See Duckworth, Chapter 10, this volume.

[54] See Robertshaw, Chapter 11, this volume; Duckworth, Chapter 10, this volume.

[55] See Robertshaw, Chapter 11, this volume.

[56] For example, Cissé *et al.* 2013; Insoll and Shaw 1997; Robertshaw *et al.* 2010.

[57] Then-Obłuska and Dussubieux 2016; Then-Obłuska and Wagner 2019, and references therein.

[58] Rosenow and Rehren 2014, 174.

[59] For example, Duckworth *et al.* 2015; Foy *et al.* 2003a, série 3.1; Jackson 2005, group 2b.

generally seen as a luxury glass in the Western Mediterranean, northern Africa and the northern provinces.[60] Antimony-decoloured glass has been detected in three different Wadi Natrun furnaces, but there is no chemical match between them and the fragments analysed from Roman Egypt, as the former is significantly higher in natron and lower in lime. The complete absence from the assemblage of glass produced in the Wadi Natrun is noteworthy, especially given the huge amounts of raw glass that were produced there (see above). Still, in view of the relative abundance of the antimony-decoloured glass groups among the analysed finds, an Egyptian origin is likely. This holds particularly true in view of the complete absence in Egypt of Roman blue-green glass, the most common glass group during this time in the Central Mediterranean and the northern provinces which has been connected to a Levantine production site supplying most of the Central Mediterranean and the northern empire.

Rather surprisingly, small-scale, plant ash-based glass production continued in parallel to the mineral natron-based industry, producing dark green, blue/green, brown, olive green, black, purple, blue and light green transparent glass.[61] Plant ash-based glassmaking persisted in the Sasanian Empire (to the east of the Euphrates) from where it may have found its way back into the west following the collapse of natron supply in the eighth or ninth century AD.[62] However, the composition of Roman-period plant ash-based glass discovered in Egypt differs from Sasanian plant ash glasses, which are much higher in magnesia and potash, and therefore are unlikely to be Sasanian imports. Instead, it is compositionally close to plant ash glass produced in Egypt during the Late Bronze Age, and to Early Islamic glass (tenth/eleventh centuries AD) from the monastery of al-Tur on the Sinai, which Kato *et al.* believe to be of Egyptian origin.[63] A production centre in Egypt can therefore be assumed.[64] Again, its composition does not resemble the glass produced in the Wadi Natrun, making a second Egyptian production site most likely. This glass composition persisted beyond the Roman period into late antiquity, as proven by a few finds from sites in the Delta and Upper Egypt.[65]

Enigmatically, the chemical compositions of raw glass groups detected in the Wadi Natrun and around Lake Mareotis are not matched in the composition of any Roman glass objects from Egypt analysed so far – or

---

[60] Duckworth *et al.* 2015; Foster and Jackson 2010; Nenna 2007; Paynter 2006; Silvestri *et al.* 2008.
[61] Talk presented by D. Rosenow during the 20th Congress of the International Association for the History of Glass at Fribourg/Romont, 7–11 September 2015.
[62] Shortland *et al.* 2006; Whitehouse 2002.   [63] Kato *et al.* 2010a, 1390, group PA-1b.
[64] Rosenow and Rehren 2014, 180–81.   [65] Unpublished own data.

indeed the whole Mediterranean – despite the fact that huge amounts of raw glass have apparently been produced in these areas. Thus a consumer site or region outside of Egypt and the Mediterranean world might have to be considered, and perhaps the glass factories in the Wadi Natrun and around Lake Mareotis were feeding into the Indian Ocean trade network in which Egypt, and in particular its harbour cities Berenike and Quseir al-Qadim, played a crucial role, especially between the third century BC and the second century AD.[66] The *Periplus maris Erythraei*,[67] a shipper's guide dating to the middle of the first century AD, lists amphora-borne products, clothing, metal, but also glass (as finished objects and raw material) among the objects exported from Egypt, while the main imports from India included Chinese silk, ivory and black pepper. An exchange of such items has been archaeologically confirmed by the discovery of corresponding finds at Berenike – such as an Indian pottery vessel containing 7.5 kg of black pepper – and Quseir al-Qadim on the Egyptian side,[68] or Pattanam on the Indian side of this network, where over 6,000 sherds of Roman amphorae and *sigillata* have come to light,[69] along with fragments of 'Roman pillar-moulded bowls' and fragments 'of mosaic variety'.[70] Thus, a parallel trade in vessel and/or raw glass from Egypt to the Indo-Pacific region, as stated in the *Periplus*, does not seem entirely unlikely.

Overall, the Roman glass industry appears fluid and complex with multiple separate production and consumption spheres operating simultaneously, possibly indicating specialisation as well as macroeconomic developments. Egypt mainly consumed locally produced glass, and imports are reduced to the manganese-decoloured group, perhaps deriving from the Levant. This glass dominates among the earlier glass, but becomes much less important from the late first century AD onwards. Only minor amounts of the plant ash-based glass have been detected outside Egypt,[71] and to the best of our knowledge the raw glass produced in the Wadi Natrun is not reflected in the archaeological record of the Mediterranean Sea at all. Antimony-decoloured glass seems to be the only Egyptian raw glass group during this period that was circulated in the Mediterranean, but it was considered a luxury product. The predominant glass group used in Roman times, Roman blue-green glass, was probably a Levantine product and is completely absent in Roman Egypt.

[66] Nenna 2007; Stern 1991; Tomber 2012.   [67] Translation: Casson 1989.
[68] Cappers 2006; Tomber 2012.   [69] Cherian *et al.* 2007.   [70] Cherian 2011.
[71] For example, Henderson 1996.

Late Antique/Byzantine Period

Towards the end of the third or early fourth century AD, antimony-decoloured glass was replaced in Egypt by HIMT and série 3.2 glasses which become almost the only compositional glass groups detected in the country throughout the fourth, fifth and early sixth centuries AD. HIMT glass is seen as far west as Carthage, where it was first defined as a compositional glass group.[72] Both groups seem to have been used pretty much simultaneously, and there is no detectable connection between raw glass group and vessel type. Around the middle or end of the sixth century AD, a new Egyptian raw glass group, Egypt I, was gradually introduced, although it has so far only been found in the western Delta and the Fayum region, as well as only a very small number of sites elsewhere in Egypt.

HIMT and série 3.2 glasses are widely attested across the late Roman and Byzantine world. Egypt I glass, on the other hand, is mainly attested in Lower Egypt. Outside the country it has so far only been discovered in Southern Jordan,[73] Jarrow (UK),[74] among the finds of the Serçe Limani shipwreck (Turkey)[75] and at a handful of sites in Israel.[76] This glass group thus seems to be of only regional, if not local, significance and – for reasons we do not know – never became one of Egypt's main exports.

Interestingly, imports of glass into Egypt are virtually non-existent during this period. Less than 2 per cent of the Late Antique glass analysed from Egypt were imports from northern Israel (Levantine I glass), and some of these vessels might have reached the country as finished objects, due to their colour or specific decoration, rather than as a regular trade in raw glass.

This observation neatly illustrates changing trade patterns, with a huge amount of Egyptian glass leaving the country for the Central and Western Mediterranean, as well as North Africa and the northern provinces, during the Byzantine period. On the other hand, even less glass was imported than during the Roman period, and Egypt seems to have relied heavily on its local sources. The same pattern, but in reverse, is visible in the Syro-Palestine region, where almost no Egyptian-made glass has come to light, and in western Turkey where locally produced glass dominates from the mid-first millennium onwards, at least at Pergamon.[77] Each of these regions had their own large production centres. For Egypt and the Levant, this was already the case in the Roman period, although there

---

[72] Freestone 1994.   [73] Rehren *et al.* 2010.   [74] Freestone and Hughes 2006.   [75] Brill 1999.
[76] Phelps *et al.* 2016.   [77] Rehren *et al.* 2015.

was slightly more exchange at that time. This changing pattern might be due to the increasingly regional character of the Byzantine Empire compared to the Roman one, and a changing focus from the Western (Rome) to the Eastern (Constantinople) Mediterranean.

Late First to Early Second Millennium AD: Back to Plant Ash

From the late sixth century AD onwards, the only detectable compositional glass groups circulating in the country seem to have been Egypt I[78] and, from the late seventh or early eighth century AD, Egypt II. The latter glass group may have been made in Middle or Upper Egypt[79] or in Fustat[80] and, in contrast to the first group, was demonstrably exported on a larger scale. Significant amounts have come to light in Raya,[81] a seaport on the southwestern coast of the Sinai, in Israel,[82] and at Butrint,[83] a harbour town in current-day Albania. This glass thus played an important role in the Mediterranean, but increasingly also the Red Sea, trade. Levantine II glass, an import from production sites in Bet Eli'ezer/northern Israel, has so far only been detected in Raya, where it constitutes around 30 per cent of all analysed artefacts. Given that the site was an important harbour city, this does not necessarily reflect on Egypt's overall consumption of Levantine raw glass. The discovery of glass finds made of various mineral/natron-based as well as plant ash-based compositional groups in Raya[84] bears testimony to the city's expansion of commercial activities across the Islamic world, and at the same time exemplifies another shift in trade patterns: from Byzantine trade, concentrated in the Mediterranean with raw glass leaving the country probably via Alexandria towards Constantinople and the Western Mediterranean; towards the Muslim trade area, with Egypt now being part of the Mamluk world and the country's trade focused upon the Red Sea, distributing products via Fustat, and possibly cities in Middle and Upper Egypt, through the Eastern Desert and the Red Sea towards regions to the east of Egypt, the core of the Islamic world.

At some point, most likely during the ninth century AD, Egyptian glassmaking reversed to plant ash as the main flux. Until then, Islamic glass workers had continued using mineral natron glass, and had not developed distinct (stylistic or compositional) characteristics. For about one and a half centuries the new socio-political and religious system does

---

[78] Gratuze and Barrandon 1990.   [79] Bimson and Freestone 1987.   [80] Kato *et al.* 2010b.
[81] Kato *et al.* 2009.   [82] Phelps *et al.* 2016.   [83] Schibille 2011.   [84] Kato *et al.* 2010a.

not seem to have had any serious influence on the glass industry. The reasons for returning to a plant ash-based recipe in glassmaking are unknown.[85] An increased demand for glass objects, in combination with environmental, social and political instability in the Nile Delta region resulting in a shortage of mineral natron supply, have been brought forward by several authors.[86]

It is known that Fustat was a major centre of the glass industry from the Early Islamic period onwards,[87] and significant secondary production remains have come to light at this site.[88] Glass analysed from Fustat, dating from the seventh to the thirteenth centuries AD, proved to be made of both mineral natron glass (dating to the seventh and eighth centuries AD)[89] and plant ash-based glass.[90] A similar picture emerged in Raya, with mineral natron glass in eighth/ninth centuries AD contexts,[91] and glass dating to the ninth–eleventh centuries made of at least three different plant ash-based glass groups with a possible provenance of Egypt (Fustat?), Mesopotamia (Nishapur?) and the Syro-Palestinian region (Raqqa?).[92] All glasses analysed from St Catherine's (uncertain date) and St Anthony's (eleventh century AD) monasteries are made of plant ash-based glass.[93] For now it seems reasonable to pinpoint the late ninth to early tenth century AD as the transitional period from mineral natron to plant ash glass in Egypt, as also evidenced by the analyses of dated (inscribed) glass coin weights from Egypt.[94]

After the Arab conquest of Egypt in the mid-seventh century AD, Islamic glass production then flourished for eight centuries, further exploring established decorative techniques such as mould-blowing, carving, cutting and applied trails, as well as more recent decorative traditions such as enamelling, lustre-painting and gilding. To our knowledge, however, and with a few exceptions (stamped glass coin weights mentioned above, glass from Fustat, St Catherine's and St Anthony's monasteries[95] and enamelled glass from Fustat[96]), no Islamic glass from Egypt has been subjected to chemical analysis, making it difficult to more fully reconstruct Egypt's role in Islamic glass production and trade.

---

[85] See also Duckworth, Chapter 10, this volume.
[86] Picon *et al.* 2008; Shortland *et al.* 2006; Whitehouse 2002.   [87] Carboni 2001.
[88] Kato *et al.* 2010b; Scanlon and Pinder-Wilson 2001.
[89] Brill 1999; Foy *et al.* 2003b; Kato *et al.* 2010b; 2012.   [90] Brill 1999; Kato *et al.* 2010b.
[91] Kato *et al.* 2009.   [92] Kato *et al.* 2010a.   [93] Brill 1999.
[94] Gratuze and Barrandon 1990; Schibille *et al.* 2019.   [95] Brill 1999; Kato *et al.* 2010b.
[96] Henderson and Allen 1990.

Discussion

The Late Bronze Age glass industry has been the subject of several recent publications,[97] and there is little that could be added here that would be relevant to the main topic of this chapter. To our knowledge, no Late Bronze Age glass finds are known from Africa outside Egypt, suggesting that little if any glass left the country during the New Kingdom in this direction.

The Hellenistic period marks the transition from limited to mass production of glass objects, with a greater number of vessels being produced, partly as a result of the introduction of a new glassworking technique that started in the third century BC, often referred to as moulding or slumping, and even casting (although the glass was never poured in the way that metal was cast). Although the older technique of core-forming persisted until the end of the first millennium BC, it only allowed the production of closed vessels such as amphoriskoi or alabastra, while the new technique opened up a market for items such as plates or bowls. These literally found their way onto people's tables, and glass was no longer primarily found in the sphere of royal courts, temples or tombs.

Finally, glass became more accessible for a broader section of Roman society, and by late Roman times had become a material of everyday use. This process was inseparably connected to the invention of glassblowing around the turn of the eras, as this technological innovation meant that less material was needed to produce a glass vessel, and a much shorter amount of time. As a result, around the end of the first century AD – one and a half centuries after the earliest possible evidence for glassblowing – glass objects are archaeologically attested in literally every corner of the Roman Empire, in both funeral and domestic contexts, including all of Roman Africa, as vessel glass, window panes and mosaic tesserae, with the pattern continuing in the Byzantine Empire. It is less clear whether the same holds true for the late first millennium AD – that is, the Early Islamic period – where fewer finds are recorded from northern Africa and particularly Egypt, but this impression may be due to a relative lack of excavations exploring Early Islamic contexts, in an area traditionally connected to research undertaken by Egyptologists or Classical Archaeologists focusing on pre-Islamic eras.

For Roman and Late Antique times, research into Egypt's relationship to its neighbours has so far mainly focused on contextualising the country within the Eastern and Northern Mediterranean trade area (see above),

---

[97] Rehren 2014, and literature therein.

with significantly less data that contribute to our understanding of the country's connection with regions south and west of it. From an analytical point of view, the only data available for glass from Nubia, Egypt's southern neighbour, are Brill's analyses of a few glass objects from Sedeinga,[98] and a handful of glass fragments from Qasr Ibrim.[99] They confirm that Egypt was indeed the major supplier of raw glass consumed south of the country, with the vessels from Sedeinga being mainly made of antimony-decoloured glass and a plant ash-based glass while three out of four Qasr Ibrim fragments are HIMT glass. One glass fragment from each site cannot be ascribed to any of the known compositional groups.

From an archaeological point of view, glass consumption in Nubia seems to have happened at a significantly smaller scale than in Egypt, and compared to the northern part of the country even fewer sites in Middle or Upper Nubia revealed any glass finds,[100] maybe hinting at the fact that glass – at least during the first half of the first millennium AD – did not represent a commodity of everyday life. Accordingly, little is known about glass use south of Egypt. The recent work by Then-Obłuska and co-workers is beginning to shed light on glass use in this area as beads,[101] and current fieldwork by UCL in and around Meroe, and our own ongoing study of glass from museum collections, is aiming to change this also for vessel glass.

For the area west of Egypt, analytical data exist for glass from Carthage,[102] Sabra/Kairouan,[103] Thamusida[104] and several Garamantian sites,[105] as well as the numerous analyses of glass beads from Sub-Saharan Africa. The analysed samples from Carthage belong to various raw glass groups, including antimony-decoloured and manganese-decoloured glass, a glass group with elevated levels of both antimony and manganese, and HIMT glass.[106] A similar pattern was observed at Roman Thamusida (Morocco), which also seems to have imported glass from the Levantine as well as the Egyptian glassmaking centres. A comparably diverse picture emerges for Fazzan, where antimony-decoloured and HIMT glasses from Egypt have been detected alongside glass with elevated levels of manganese, more likely deriving from the Levant[107] and higher amounts of both

---

[98] Brill 1991.   [99] Brill 1999.   [100] Gradel 2012.
[101] Then-Obłuska and Dussubieux 2016; Then-Obłuska and Wagner 2019, and references therein.
[102] Brill 1999; Freestone 1994; Thomas Fenn, personal communication.
[103] Thomas Fenn, personal communication.   [104] Gliozzo *et al.* 2013.
[105] Duckworth *et al.* 2015; Duckworth, Chapter 10, this volume.
[106] Brill 1999; Freestone 1994; Thomas Fenn, personal communication.
[107] Rosenow and Rehren 2014.

manganese and antimony, perhaps a product of recycling.[108] Judging by the current state of the archaeological evidence, glass objects have come to light to a significant degree in at least the coastal towns and areas of northern Africa (for example, Volubilis, Carthage, Sabratha, Cyrene, Tripolitania, Berenike and Cherchel) and the region generally seems to have been well integrated into the Roman and Late Antique glass trade networks. It is hoped that further research on glass from Garamantian sites as well as in Sudan will broaden our dataset and expand our knowledge about the movement of glass in inland North Africa.

Several interesting questions emerge from these observations. One concerns the spread of glass: not just the material itself, which is easily traded both in its raw form and as finished artefacts, but also the spread of the knowledge of how to make and work it. In the early periods in particular, and in its strongly coloured form, the similarity to precious stones (both conceptually and materially) will have influenced the extent to which people far from the main centres of glass use would have perceived and used it. Much more research is still needed before we can begin to build a picture of glassmaking in Africa outside Egypt, especially for the Islamic period;[109] and the spread of glass first from Egypt and later also from Europe, across the continent.

Another key question is: what drove the major changes in glass production? It is easy – perhaps too easy – to link the apparent collapse of the Late Bronze Age glass industry to the collapse of the Late Bronze Age 'world system'. Elsewhere, one of us has argued that the Late Bronze Age glass industry relied on the connections and regular exchange of glass among the main producers of the time, each specialising in one or two colours only, but having access to all colours thanks to the elite network linking the various palace and temple workshops with each other.[110] This, however, is not necessarily the full picture, and a monochrome or at best oligochrome glass industry may well have persisted into the Iron Age. By Phoenician times, at the latest, we are 'back in business', with glass in all colours of the rainbow at the disposal of the artisans. Why there was the change at around 1000 BC from plant ash to mineral natron, and whether it was a universal change or just a partial one, remains enigmatic; but a causal link to major political or economic changes is not immediately obvious.

Beginning in the second half of the first millennium BC we see an increasing use of glass in line with the expansion of the elites of society.

---

[108] Duckworth *et al.* 2015.   [109] See Lankton *et al.* 2006; Babalola *et al.* 2017; 2018.
[110] Rehren 2014.

More work is needed to link glass use to social status, and the expansion of an elite outside the traditional nobility and religious orders; an elite based on wealth created through trade, the ownership of land or wealth derived from industry. So far, it seems that these gradual social changes during the first millennium BC were syncopated, but not interrupted by large-scale shifts in the balance of power, from the Persian rule over Egypt to the Classical Greek influence, the Hellenistic Empire and its successors, the Roman and Byzantine Empires, and finally to the various Islamic caliphates. Major changes in glass production and working patterns occurred during these two millennia – but again, no causal or other link is yet apparent between the socio-political changes and the changes in glass production. Different forces were at work here, and we know far too little about what drove and controlled the glass industry in any of the periods mentioned to really understand the changes happening. The one major link that is becoming increasingly apparent is that between the degree of globalisation of the economy of the time and the range of glass compositions available to the artisans and users. In times of economic fragmentation, we see a greatly reduced diversity of glass compositions being used and vice versa. This is not surprising, but it does confirm that glass was not fundamentally different from other commodities, despite its unique character with regard to tightly focused production regions compared to much wider consumption regions.

It must be stressed that the emerging regional picture of glass production and use does heavily depend on the accessibility of relevant archaeological material for chemical analyses – an issue not limited to Egypt. Future research will thus have to focus on developing methods that allow the characterisation of large glass assemblages non-destructively in the field, as currently tested, for example, by the application of a portable X-ray fluorescence (XRF) device, or optical spectroscopy.[111] It is hoped that this work will stimulate discussions and further research that will be able to complement, develop and correct the picture put forward here.

Conclusion

Evidence for primary glassmaking in Egypt exists first for several Pharaonic sites such as Qantir-Piramesse, Amarna, Lisht and most likely other places, and then again for the early Roman and Roman period, where

---

[111] Portable XRF: Kato *et al.* 2009; Kato *et al.* 2010a; 2010b; optical spectroscopy: Ceglia *et al.* 2012.

glassmaking furnaces have been discovered in the Wadi Natrun and the area around Lake Mareotis, and compositional analyses strongly suggest that several primary glass groups were produced in Egypt, alongside the better known sites in the Levant.

For the consumption of glass in Egypt, the following patterns emerge: in Pharaonic times, use was apparently rather firmly restricted to glass made in Egypt, despite the ample iconographic and textual evidence for the importation of glass from the East. For later periods, the same major glass types known from across the Roman Empire occurred in Egypt too, with a strong – sometimes near-exclusive – dominance of Egyptian-made glass. Similarly, Levantine glass groups greatly dominated glass consumption in the Levant. Elsewhere, however, raw glass from both regions seems to be in competition and can be found in similar amounts at the same sites. This pattern of glass use most likely reflects the changing interregional versus regional character of the Roman and Byzantine economies. Surprisingly, some plant ash-based glass is present at least on a small scale during the period of mineral natron dominance in Egypt, particularly during the first half of the first millennium AD.

During the Early Islamic period, Egypt II glass seems to have been of importance not only in Egypt itself, but also in the wider Islamic world. It is attested in cities involved in the Mediterranean and Red Sea trades. After the reintroduction of plant ash-based glass in Egypt, approximately in the late ninth to early tenth century AD, the picture becomes less straightforward, as plant ash glass groups are compositionally more variable than mineral natron-based glasses, and very few glass analyses from this period have been published to date.

Examining Egypt, and her role as a producer of glass at a regional level, reveals some clear trends. For almost the entire period of interest here, glass production occurred in Egypt as well as farther east, in the Syro-Palestine region and Mesopotamia. Within each of these two main regions, regionally produced glass massively dominated local glassworking and consumption. Only in periods when there is no evidence for contemporary glassmaking in Egypt do we find imported glass from the east arriving in Egypt in significant proportions. Outside these two regions, in a broad sweep from the North African coast to the west, across the Mediterranean and all of Europe, to Anatolia in the east, glass from Egypt coexisted with glass from Mesopotamia (Bronze Age) and the Syro-Palestine coast (Hellenistic to Early Islamic period). The absolute quantities and relative proportions of glass from these two main regions that were reaching individual sites elsewhere fluctuated over time, and differed even among contemporary sites, giving rise to research opportunities into trade and communication networks, and wider economic connections. In contrast, very little information is available so far regarding the origin of glass used in south-western Egypt and its flow into Africa, and Egypt's potential link into the Indian Ocean trade to the south-east.

On a final note, several fragments analysed by us as part of our current project could not be assigned to any of the known primary glass groups, particularly among the material from Middle and Upper Egypt and particularly of post-Roman date. This could indicate that additional primary production sites existed in Egypt, so far unknown to us. These furnaces perhaps produced raw glass from local sands and natron sources other than the Wadi Natrun, however most likely only on a small scale to cover local markets.[112]

References

Aldsworth, F., Haggarty, G., Jennings, S. and Whitehouse, D. 2002. Medieval glass making at Tyre. *Journal of Glass Studies* 44: 49–66.

Babalola, A.B., McIntosh, S.K., Dussubieux, L. and Rehren, Th. 2017. Ife and Igbo Olokun in the history of glass in West Africa. *Antiquity* 91: 732–50.

Babalola, A.B., Rehren, Th., Ige, A. and McIntosh, S. 2018. The glass making crucibles from Ile-Ife, SW Nigeria. *Journal of African Archaeology* 16: 31–59.

Baxter, M.J., Cool, H.E.M. and Jackson, C. 2005. Further studies on the compositional variability of colourless Romano-British vessel glass. *Archaeometry* 47: 47–68.

Beretta, M. 2009. *The Alchemy of Glass: Counterfeit, Imitation and Transmutation in Ancient Glassmaking*. Sagamore Beach: Science History Publications.

Bimson, M. and Freestone, I.C. 1987. The discovery of an Islamic glass-making site in Middle Egypt. In *Annales du 10e Congrès de l'Association International pour l'Histoire du Verre, Madrid-Segovie 1985*, Amsterdam: Association International pour l'Histoire du Verre, 237–44.

Brill, R.H. 1991. Scientific investigations on some glasses from Sedeinga. *Journal of Glass Studies* 33: 11–28.

[112] The research presented here was partly done while one of us (DR) was a Marie-Curie Fellow (Glass in Late Antiquity: Science and Society, project number 298127, FP7-PEOPLE-2011-IEF), based at the UCL Institute of Archaeology. We thank all our colleagues, especially from the British Museum, the Petrie Museum, Harrow School and the Ashmolean Museum, as well as the Egyptian authorities who have made glass samples available to us for analysis, including allowing us to use some unpublished results. We acknowledge support from the NPRP grant 7 – 776 – 6 – 024 from the Qatar National Research Fund (a member of Qatar Foundation). The statements made herein are solely the responsibility of the authors.

Brill, R.H. 1999. *Chemical Analyses of Ancient Glass*. New York: Corning Museum of Glass.

Broschat, K. and Rehren, Th. 2017. The glass headrests of Tutankhamen. *Journal of Glass Studies* 59: 377–80.

Cappers, R.T.J. 2006. *Roman Footprints at Berenike: Archaeobotanical Evidence of Subsistence and Trade in the Eastern Desert of Egypt*. Los Angeles: Cotsen Institute of Archaeology Monograph 55.

Carboni, St. 2001. *Glass from Islamic Lands*. London: Metropolitan Museum of Art.

Casson, L. 1989. *The Periplus Maris Erythraei: Text with Introduction, Translation and Commentary*. Princeton, NJ: Princeton University Press.

Ceglia, A., Meulebroeck, W., Wouters, H., Baert, K., Nys, K., Terryn, H. and Thienpont, H. 2012. Using optical spectroscopy to characterize the material of a 16th c. stained glass window. In H. Thienpont, W. Meulebroeck, K. Nys and D. Vanclooster (eds), *Integrated Approaches to the Study of Historical Glass*, Proceedings of the SPIE Vol. 8422, Bellingham: SPIE, 84220A.

Ceglia, A., Cosyns, P., Nys, K., Terryn, H., Thienpont, H. and Meulebroeck, W. 2016. Light through glass: The spectrum of Late Antique glass from Cyprus. *Journal of Archaeological Science: Reports* 7: 614–24.

Cherian, P.J. 2011. *Pattanam Excavations: Fifth Season Field Report*. Trivandrum: Kerala Historical Research Council.

Cherian, P.J., Selvakumar, V. and Shajan, K.P. 2007. *Interim Report of the Pattanam Excavations/Explorations*. Thiruvananthapuram: KCHR Publication.

Cissé, M., McIntosh, S.K., Dussubieux, L., Fenn, T., Gallagher, D. and Chipps Smith, A. 2013. Excavations at Gao Saney: New evidence for settlement growth, trade, and interaction on the Niger Bend in the first millennium CE. *Journal of African Archaeology* 11.1: 9–37.

Degryse, P. and Schneider, J. 2008. Pliny the Elder and Sr–Nd isotopes: Tracing the provenance of raw materials for Roman glass production. *Journal of Archaeological Science* 35: 1993–2000.

Duckworth, C.N., Mattingly, D.J. and Smith, V. 2015. From the Mediterranean to the Libyan Sahara: Chemical analyses of Garamantian glass. *Journal of Archaeological Science: Reports* 7: 633–39.

Fletcher, P.J., Freestone, I.C. and Geschke, R. 2008. Analysis and conservation of a weeping glass Scarab. *The British Museum Technical Research Bulletin* 2: 45–48.

Foster, H.E. and Jackson, C.M. 2010. The composition of late Romano-British colourless vessel glass: Glass production and consumption. *Journal of Archaeological Science* 37: 3068–80.

Foy, D. and Jezegou, M.P. 1997. Une epave chargée de lingots et de vaisselle de verre, un temoignage exceptionnel du commerce et de la technologie du verre en Méditerranée antique. *Verre* 3.3: 65–70.

Foy, D. and Nenna, M.-D. (eds) 2003. *Échanges et commerce du verre dans le monde antique: Actes du colloque de l'Association française pour l'archéologie du verre, Aix-en-Provence and Marseille, 7–9 June 2001*, Montagnac: Editions Monique Mergoil.

Foy, D., Vichy, M. and Picon, M. 2000. Lingots de verre en Méditerranée occidentale. In *Annales 14ème congrès de l'Association pour l'Histoire du Verre, Amsterdam 1998*, Lochem, Netherlands: Association Internationale pour l'Histoire du Verre, 51–57.

Foy, D., Picon, M., Vichy, M. and Thirion-Merle, V. 2003a. Charactérisation des verres de la fin de l'Antiquité en Méditerranée occidentale: L'émergence de nouveaux courants commerciaux. In Foy and Nenna 2003, 41–85.

Foy, D., Picon, M. and Vichy, M. 2003b. Verres Omeyyades et Abbasides d'origine Egyptienne: Les témoignages de l'archéologie et de l'archéometrie. In *Annales 15ème Congrès de l'Association Internationale pour l' Histoire du Verre, New York-Corning 2001*, Nottingham: Association Internationale pour l'Histoire du Verre, 138–43.

Freestone, I.C. 1994. Chemical analysis of 'raw' glass fragments. In H.R. Hurst (ed.), *Excavations at Carthage, Vol II, 1 The Circular Harbour, North Side*, Oxford: Oxford University Press for the British Academy, 290.

Freestone, I.C. 2002. Composition and affinities of glass from the furnaces on the island site, Tyre. *Journal of Glass Studies* 44: 67–77.

Freestone, I.C. and Hughes, M. 2006. Origins of the Jarrow glass. In R. Cramp (ed.), *Wearmouth and Jarrow Monastic Sites, Vol. 2*, Swindon: English Heritage, 147–55.

Freestone, I.C., Gorin-Rosen, Y. and Hughes, M.J. 2000. Primary glass from Israel and the production of glass in late antiquity and the early Islamic period. In Nenna 2000, 65–83.

Freestone, I.C., Greenwood, R. and Gorin-Rosen, Y. 2002a. Byzantine and Early Islamic glassmaking in the Eastern Mediterranean: Production and distribution of primary glass. In G. Kordas (ed.), *Hyalos – Vitrum – Glass. History Technology and Conservation of Glass and Vitreous Materials in the Hellenic World. 1st International conference Rhodes, Greece 1–4 April 2001*, Athens: Glasnet Publications, 167–74.

Freestone, I.C., Ponting, M. and Hughes, M.J. 2002b. The origins of Byzantine glass from Maroni Petrera, Cyprus. *Archaeometry* 44: 257–72.

Freestone, I.C., Wolf, S. and Thirlwall, M. 2005. The production of HIMT glass: Elemental and isotopic evidence. In M.-D. Nenna (ed.), *Annales du 16ème Congrès de l'Association Internationale pour l'Histoire du Verre, London 2003*, Nottingham: Association Internationale pour l'Histoire du Verre, 153–57.

Freestone, I.C., Hughes, M.J. and Stapleton, C.P. 2008. Composition and production of Anglo Saxon glass. In V.I. Evison (ed.), *Catalogue of Anglo-Saxon Glass Vessels in the British Museum*, London: British Museum, 29–46.

Gliozzo, E., Santagostino Barbone, A. and D'Acapito, F. 2013. Waste glass, vessels and window panes from Thamusida (Morocco): Grouping natron-based blue-green and colourless Roman glasses. *Archaeometry* 55: 609–39.

Gorin-Rosen, Y. 2000. The ancient glass industry in Israel: Summary of the finds and new discoveries. In Nenna 2000, 49–63.

Gradel, C. 2012. Les verres d'époques hellénistique et romaine dans le royaume de Méroé. In Ignatidou and Antonaras 2012, 114–19.

Gratuze, B. and Barrandon, J.-N. 1990. Islamic glass weights and stamps: Analysis using nuclear techniques. *Archaeometry* 32: 155–62.

Hauptmann, A., Busz, R., Klein, S., Vettel, A. and Werthmann, R. 2000. The roots of glazing techniques: Copper metallurgy? *Paléorient* 26: 113–30.

Henderson, J. 1996. Scientific analysis of selected Fishbourne vessel glass and its archaeological implications: Excavations at Fishbourne 1969–1988. In B. Cunliffe, A. Down and D. Rudkin (eds), *Chichester Excavations 9*, Chichester: Chichester District Council, 189–92.

Henderson, J. and Allen, J.W. 1990. Enamels on Ayyubid and Mamluk glass fragments. *Archaeomaterials* 4.2: 167–83.

Henderson, J., McLoughlin, S.D. and McPhail, D.S. 2004. Radical changes in Islamic glass technology: Evidence for conservatism and experimentation with new glass recipes from early and middle Islamic Raqqa, Syria. *Archaeometry* 46: 439–68.

Ignatidou, D. and Antonaras, A. (eds) 2012. *Annales du 18e Congrès de l'Association Internationale pour l'Histoire du Verre, Thessaloniki 2009*. Thessaloniki: Association Internationale pour l'Histoire du Verre.

Insoll, T. and Shaw, T. 1997. Gao and Igbo-Ukwu: Beads, interregional trade, and beyond. *African Archaeological Review* 14.1: 9–23.

Israeli, Y. 1991. The invention of blowing. In M. Newby and K. Painter (eds), *Roman Glass: Two Centuries of Art and Invention*, London: Society of Antiquaries of London, 46–55.

Jackson, C.M. 2005. Making colourless glass in the Roman period. *Archaeometry* 47: 763–80.

Jackson, C.M., Saynter, S., Nenna, M.-D. and Degryse, P. 2018. Glassmaking using natron from el-Barnugi (Egypt); Pliny and the Roman glass industry. *Archaeological and Anthropological Sciences* 10: 1179–91.

Kato, N., Nakai, I. and Shindo, Y. 2009. Change in chemical composition of Early Islamic glass excavated in Raya, Sinai Peninsula, Egypt: On-site analysis using a portable X-ray fluorescence spectrometer. *Journal of Archaeological Science* 36: 1698–707.

Kato, N., Nakai, I. and Shindo, Y. 2010a. Transition in Islamic plant-ash glass vessels: On-site chemical analyses conducted at the Raya/al-Tur area on the Sinai Peninsula in Egypt. *Journal of Archaeological Science* 37: 1381–95.

Kato, N., Nakai, I. and Shindo, Y. 2010b. On-site chemical analysis of raw and waste glass unearthened in al-Fustat using a portable X-ray Flourescence Spectrometer. In M. Kawatoko and Y. Shindo (eds), *Artifacts of the Medieval*

Islamic Period excavated in al-Fustat, Egypt, Tokyo: Waseda University, 17–28.

Kato, N., Nakai, I. and Shindo, Y. 2012. Comparative study of Islamic glass weights and vessel stamps with the glass vessels in Egypt. In Ignatidou and Antonaras 2012, 367–72.

Keller, D., Price, J. and Jackson, C. (eds) 2014. *Neighbours and Successors of Rome: Traditions of Glass Production and Use in Europe and the Middle East in the Later 1st Millennium* AD. Oxford: Oxbow Books.

Lankton, J., Ige, A. and Rehren, Th. 2006. Early primary glass production in southern Nigeria. *Journal of African Archaeology* 4: 111–38.

Lilyquist, C. and Brill, R.H. 1993. *Studies in Early Egyptian Glass*. New York: The Metropolitan Museum of Art.

Lucas, A. and Harris, J.R. 1962. *Ancient Egyptian Materials and Industries*. London: E. Arnold.

Mass, J., Wypyski, M.T. and Stone, R.E. 2002. Malkata and Lisht glassmaking technologies: Towards a specific link between second millennium BC metallurgists and glassmakers. *Archaeometry* 44: 67–82.

Nenna, M.-D. (ed.) 2000. *La route du verre: Ateliers primaires et secondaires de verriers du second millénaire av. J.-C. au Moyen-Age.* Lyon: Travaux de la Maison de l'Orient Méditérranean 33.

Nenna, M.-D. (ed.) 2005. *Annales du 16e Congrès de l'Association Internationale pour l'Histoire du Verre, London 2003.* Nottingham: Association Internationale pour l'Histoire du Verre.

Nenna, M.-D. 2007. Production et commerce du verre à l'époque impériale: Nouvelles découvertes et problématiques. *Facta* 1: 125–47.

Nenna, M.-D. 2010. Les ateliers primaires de l'Égypte gréco-romaine: Campagne de fouilles 2007 sur le site de Beni Salama (Wadi Natrun). *Annales du Service des antiquités de l'Égypte* 84: 259–316.

Nenna, M.-D. 2014. Egyptian glass abroad: HIMT glass and its markets. In Keller *et al.* 2014, 177–93.

Nenna, M.-D., Picon, M. and Vichy, M. 2000. Ateliers primaires et secondaires en Égypte à l'époque gréco-romaine. In Nenna 2000, 97–112.

Nenna, M.-D., Picon, M., Thirion-Merle, V. and Vichy, M. 2005. Ateliers primaires du Wadi Natrun: Nouvelles découvertes. In Nenna 2005, 59–63.

Nicholson, P.T. 2013. Pharaonic glass. In R. Bagnall, K. Brodersen, C.B. Champion, A. Erskine and S.R. Huebner (eds), *The Encyclopedia of Ancient History*, Oxford: Wiley-Blackwell, 5225–30.

Nicholson, P. and Henderson, J. 2000. Glass. In P. Nicholson and I. Shaw (eds), *Ancient Egyptian Materials and Technology*, Cambridge: Cambridge University Press, 195–224.

Paynter, S. 2006. Analyses of colourless Roman glass from Binchester, County Durham. *Journal of Archaeological Science* 33: 1037–57.

Petrie, W.M.F. 1926. Glass in the Early Ages. *Journal of the Society of Glass Technology* 10: 229–34.

Phelps, M., Freestone, I.C. and Rosen, Y. 2016. Natron glass production and supply in the late antique and early medieval Near East: The effect of the Byzantine-Islamic transition. *Journal of Archaeological Science* 75: 57–71.

Picon, M. and Vichy, M. 2003. D'orient en occident: L'origine du verre à l'époque romaine et durant le haut Moyen Age. In Foy and Nenna 2003, 17–32.

Picon, M., Thirion-Merle, V. and Vichy, M. 2008. Les verres au natron et les verres aux cendres du Wadi Natrun (Egypte). *Bulletin de l'Association Francaise pour l'Archeologie du Verre*: 36–41.

Pusch, E. and Rehren, Th. 2007. *Rubinglas für den Pharao: Forschungen in der Ramses-Stadt, Band 6*. Hildesheim: Gerstenberg Verlag.

Rehren, Th. 2003. Comments on J.L. Mass, M.T. Wypyski and R.E. Stone, 'Malkata and Lisht glassmaking technologies: Towards a specific link between second millennium BC metallurgists and glassmakers', Comment I. *Archaeometry* 45: 185–90.

Rehren, Th. 2014. Glass production and consumption between Egypt, Mesopotamia and the Aegean. In P. Pfälzner, H. Niehr, E. Pernicka, S. Lange and T. Köster (eds), *Contextualising Grave Inventories in the Ancient Near East, Qatna Studien*, Supplementa 3, Wiesbaden: Harrassowitz Verlag, 217–23.

Rehren, Th. and Brüggler, M. 2020. The late antique glass furnaces in the Hambach Forest were working glass: Not making it. *Journal of Archaeological Science: Reports* 29: 102072.

Rehren, Th. and Pusch, E. 2005. Late Bronze Age Egyptian glass production at Qantir-Piramesses. *Science* 308: 1756–59.

Rehren, Th., Spencer, L. and Triantafyllidis, P. 2005. The primary production of glass at Hellenistic Rhodes. In Nenna 2005, 39–43.

Rehren, Th., Marii, F., Schibille, N., Stanford, L. and Swan, C. 2010. Glass supply and circulation in early Byzantine southern Jordan. In J. Drauschke and D. Keller (eds), *Glass in Byzantium: Production, Usage, Analyses, RGZM, Mainz*, Regensburg: Schnell and Steiner, 65–81.

Rehren, Th., Connolly, P., Schibille, N. and Schwarzer, H. 2015. Changes in glass consumption in Pergamon (Turkey) from Hellenistic to late Byzantine and Islamic times. *Journal of Archaeological Science* 55: 266–79.

Rehren, Th., Cholakova, A. and Jovanović, S. 2018. Composition and texture of a set of marvered glass vessels from 12th century AD Braničevo, Serbia. *Starinar* 68: 125–49.

Robertshaw, P., Wood, M., Melchiorre, E., Popelka-Filcoff, R.S. and Glascock, M. D. 2010. Southern African glass beads: Chemistry, glass sources and patterns of trade. *Journal of Archaeological Science* 37: 1898–1912.

Rosenow, D. and Rehren, Th. 2014. Herding cats: Roman and Late Antique glass groups from Bubastis, northern Egypt. *Journal of Archaeological Science* 39: 170–84.

Scanlon, G.T. and Pinder-Wilson, R. 2001. *Fustat Glass of the Early Islamic Period: Finds Excavated by the American Research Center in Egypt 1964–1980*. London: Altajir World of Islam Trust.

Schibille, N. 2011. Supply routes and consumption of glass in first millennium CE Butrint (Albania). *Journal of Archaeological Science* 38: 2939–48.

Schibille, N., Gratuze, B., Illivier, E. and Blondeau, E. 2019. Chronology of Early Islamic glass compositions from Egypt. *Journal of Archaeological Science* 104: 10–18.

Schlick-Nolte, B. and Werthmann, R. 2003. Glass vessels from the burial of Nesikhons. *Journal of Glass Studies* 45: 11–34.

Shortland, A.J. 2012. *Lapis Lazuli from the Kiln: Glass and Glassmaking in the Late Bronze Age*. Leuven: University Of Leuven Press.

Shortland, A.J., Schachner, L., Freestone, I.C. and Tite, M. 2006. Natron as a flux in the early vitreous material industry: Sources, beginnings and reasons for decline. *Journal of Archaeological Science* 33: 521–30.

Shortland, A.J., Rogers, N. and Eremin, K. 2007. Trace element discriminants between Egyptian and Mesopotamian Late Bronze Age glasses. *Journal of Archaeological Science* 34: 781–89.

Silvestri, A., Molin, G. and Salviulo, G. 2008. The colourless glass of Iulia Felix. *Journal of Archaeological Science* 35: 331–41.

Simpson, St J. 2014. Sasanian glass: An overview. In Keller *et al.* 2014, 200–31.

Smirniou, M. 2012. *Investigation of Late Bronze Age Primary Glass Production in Egypt and the Eastern Mediterranean*. Unpublished PhD thesis, University College London.

Smirniou, M. and Rehren, Th. 2011. Direct evidence of primary glass production in Late Bronze Age Amarna, Egypt. *Archaeometry* 53: 58–80.

Smirniou, M. and Rehren, Th. 2016. The use of technical ceramics in early Egyptian glass-making. *Journal of Archaeological Science* 67: 52–63.

Smirniou, M., Rehren, Th. and Gratuze, B. 2018. Lisht as a New Kingdom glass-making site with its own chemical signature. *Archaeometry* 60: 502–16.

Stern, M. 1991. Early exports beyond the Empire. In M. Newby and K. Painter (eds), *Roman Glass: Two Centuries of Art and Invention*, Occasional Papers from the Society of Antiquaries of London, Volume 13, London: Society of Antiquaries of London, 141–54.

Swan, C., Rehren, Th., Dussubieux, L. and Eger, A. 2018. High-boron and high-alumina Middle Byzantine (10th–12th century CE) glass bracelets: A Western Anatolian glass industry. *Archaeometry* 60: 207–32.

Then-Obłuska, J. and Dussubieux, L. 2016. Glass bead trade in the early Roman and Mamluk Quseir ports: A view from the Oriental Institute Museum assemblage. *Archaeological Research in Asia* 6: 81–103.

Then-Obłuska, J. and Wagner, B. 2019. *Glass Bead Trade in Northeast Africa: The Evidence from Meroitic and Post-Meroitic Nubia*. PAM Monograph Series 10. Warsaw: University of Warsaw.

Tomber, R. 2012. From the Roman Red Sea to beyond the Empire: Egyptian ports and their trading partners. *British Museum Studies in Ancient Egypt and Sudan* 18: 201–15.

Triantafyllidis, P. 2003. Classical and Hellenistic glass workshops from Rhodes. *Instrumentum Monographies* 24: 131–38.

Van der Linden, V., Cosyns, P., Schalm, O., Cagno, S., Nys, K., Janssens, K., Nowak, A., Wagner, B. and Bulska, E. 2009. Deeply coloured and black glass in the northern provinces of the Roman Empire: Differences and similarities in chemical composition before and after AD 150. *Archaeometry* 51: 822–44.

Varberg, J., Gratuze, B. and Kaul, F. 2015. Between Egypt, Mesopotamia and Scandinavia: Late Bronze Age glass. *Journal of Archaeological Science* 54: 168–81.

Varberg, J., Kaul, F., Gratuze, B., Haslund, A. and Rotea, M. 2016. Mesopotamian glass from Late Bronze Age Egypt, Romania, Germany, and Denmark. *Journal of Archaeological Science* 74: 184–94.

Walton, M.S., Shortland, A., Kirk, S. and Degryse, P. 2009. Evidence for the trade of Mesopotamian and Egyptian glass to Mycenaean Greece. *Journal of Archaeological Science* 36: 1496–503.

Wedepohl, K.H. and Baumann, A. 2000. The use of marine molluskan shells for Roman glass and local raw glass production in the Eifel area (Western Germany). *Naturwissenschaften* 87: 129–32.

Whitehouse, D. 2002. The transition from natron to plant ash in the Levant. *Journal of Glass Studies* 44: 193–96.

PART V

Handmade Pottery

13 | Garamantian Ceramic Technology

Change and Exchange in a Trans-Saharan Perspective

MARIA CARMELA GATTO

Introduction

This contribution aims to use Garamantian ceramic technology as a proxy for exploring the existence of, and establishing the degree of, Trans-Saharan interconnectedness. This approach provides us with two unique standpoints: that of handmade pottery, seldom considered in the frame of enquiries of this type in North Africa, for which wheel-made productions are preferred; and that of 'Trans-Saharan' connectivity, in contrast to traditionally favoured 'extra-Saharan' connections. For the first time, ceramic evidence from both the Wadi al-Ajal and the Wadi Tanzzuft (Fig. 13.1) is used for assessing technological traits of Garamantian pottery through a time span including the first millennia BC and AD. Chronological and spatial variations within the Garamantian pottery, as well as comparisons with previous and contemporary ceramic production from the same region and elsewhere across the Greater Sahara, are discussed, attempting to track the timing and directionality of technological change and exchange and its social meaning.[1]

Setting the Stage

It is only in the past decade that systematic publications on Garamantian pottery have been produced, relating both to the work done by the Fazzan Project of the University of Leicester in the Wadi al-Ajal, and by the Italian

---

[1] This overview relies heavily on the results of a workshop on Saharan and Sub-Saharan handmade pottery organised in 2015 in Leicester, in conjunction with the Trans-SAHARA Project's Mobile Technologies conference, upon which this book is based – see Preface and Chapter 1, this volume.

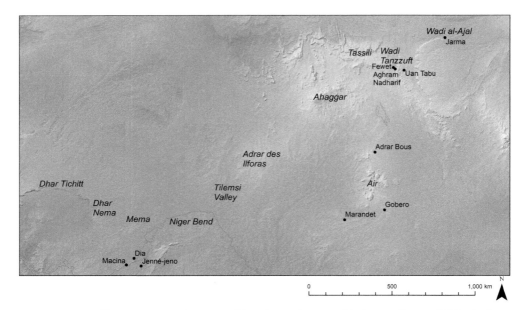

Figure 13.1 Location map of key sites and geographical areas discussed (Martin Sterry for Trans-SAHARA Project).

Mission of Sapienza University of Rome in the Wadi Tanzzuft/Tadrart Akakus region.[2] An important point is that the two projects addressed the archaeological material in very different ways. The British team consisted of Roman pottery specialists who concentrated their efforts upon constructing a full-scale pottery type series including both local productions and imported wares, covering a long chronological span not confined only to the Garamantian period.[3] I was responsible for the Italian team's systematic analytical classification, which covered only the handmade pottery from sites dated to the Garamantian period, leaving aside the relatively limited Roman imports recovered in the area.[4] Being a specialist of prehistoric pottery from north-eastern Africa, my approach in studying the Garamantian pottery focused not only on the description of manufacturing processes,[5] but gave particular attention to the analysis of decorative technologies and tools, following a classification developed by Isabella Caneva and used widely in Africa.[6]

---

[2] Liverani 2006; Mattingly 2003; 2007; 2010; 2013; Mori 2013.
[3] Dore *et al.* 2007; Leone 2013; 2013b; Mattingly 2010.
[4] Castelli *et al.* 2005; Gatto 2006a; 2010; 2013a.   [5] For the latest overview see Roux 2016.
[6] Caneva 1987; 1988; Caneva and Marks 1990; Gallin 2011; Gatto 2002; 2006b; 2006c; 2013b; Livingstone Smith 2010.

The latter has been essential in identifying, for the first time in the Central Sahara, the use of cord twisted roulette implements to obtain simple and rolled impressions on vessels,[7] as well as an important shift towards a higher percentage of painted wares in the local Late and Post-Garamantian ceramic production. These two key changes in Garamantian pottery technology have an impact on a broader scale. In fact, both elements are outliers in terms of the previous Central Sahara ceramic tradition: the roulette technique is a Sub-Saharan phenomenon; while painted wares (with the kind of decoration encountered from the late first millennium AD in Fazzan) have similarities with Berber wares of Mediterranean Africa.[8] The claimed identification of roulette pottery in Fazzan has raised criticism by Sub-Saharan archaeologists, who disputed this definition, perceiving the occurrence as too weak to argue for Trans-Saharan connections.[9] To them, the use of twisted cord roulettes in Sub-Saharan and Central Africa covers too long a time period, and is too widespread to be considered a sensitive diagnostic tool.[10]

In order to justify (or overcome) such scepticism, a group of scholars at the forefront of ceramic analysis in Africa was invited to a workshop organised in Leicester in 2015 as part of the Trans-SAHARA Mobile Technologies conference. They were given the opportunity to handle a selection of Garamantian handmade pottery (from both the Wadi al-Ajal and the Wadi Tanzzuft) and compare it to ceramics from their own regions of expertise, which they kindly brought to the meeting. Three pre-circulated stand-alone papers under the general preliminary title of 'Garamantian handmade pottery: technological change and stylistic exchange in a Trans-Saharan perspective', authored respectively by myself, Anne Haour and Kevin MacDonald, set the agenda for the debate, which was also summarised and presented for discussion by Anne Mayor during the Mobile Technologies conference. A pre-meeting with Haour and MacDonald was organised ahead of the workshop, so they could base their papers on a first-hand analysis of the Garamantian pottery.[11] Results are debated in detail further below. However, two statements must be made at this stage: (1) all scholars agreed that indeed Garamantian pottery is roulette decorated, making it the northernmost

---

[7] Castelli *et al.* 2005; Gatto 2006a; 2010; 2013a.

[8] For roulette ceramics in Africa see Haour *et al.* 2010; Livingstone Smith 2007. For Berber painted wares see Camps 1956; Fili 2011.

[9] See for instance, Haour 2017; Magnavita 2013; 2017; but also S. McIntosh, personal communication.

[10] Mayor *et al.* 2005.   [11] The meeting was held in January 2015.

evidence of the kind; and (2) that this attests to some connection with regions to the south of the Garamantes, although recognising that the meaning, timing and nature of this is, for now, difficult to ascertain.

The current outline of the Garamantian pottery sequence and classification was mainly developed based on data from the Garamantian citadel of Aghram Nadharif, excavated by the Italian team in the Barkat Oasis.[12] Material from the Fewet compounds and necropolis, also investigated by the Italians, and the hilltop citadel of Zinkekra, excavated by Charles Daniels in the 1960s, and more recently by the British team from Leicester (led by Mattingly), were used for comparison.[13] The ceramic evidence from site G4-324, a campsite located to the west of Ghat Oasis, also proved helpful for an understanding of the transition with the Final Pastoral phase.[14] That from Aghram Nadharif, in turn, was essential in understanding the transition to the Post-Garamantian period in the Tanzzuft/Tadrart Akakus region. The available data only made possible the development of a preliminary chrono-typological outline, which needs further improvement from new datasets (currently a distant prospect given the political situation in Libya). In August 2014, I joined the Trans-SAHARA team and, although dealing with handmade pottery was not my primary role, I had the opportunity to access the pottery sample from the Wadi al-Ajal now housed in Leicester. Unfortunately, I did not have the time for a systematic and detailed analysis of the collection, which would require a stand-alone project. Instead, I tried to concentrate on gathering information on key research questions, which resulted from my work on the Tanzzuft pottery, making a quick assessment of the ceramic material and mainly relying on Anna Leone's publication of the pottery from the Garamantian capital Jarma.[15] Thus, for a detailed description of assemblages from the Wadi al-Ajal and the Wadi Tanzzuft please refer to the main publications. Here I shall present a comparative assessment of technological traits of the Garamantian pottery from the two study regions, how they differ chronologically and spatially, and how they are unique compared to previous and later ceramic manufacturing traditions in Fazzan.

The handmade pottery represented the bulk of the ceramic material recovered in Garamantian contexts and was the only locally produced pottery. Any wheel-made vessels found thus far were imported from the Mediterranean. At Jarma, handmade pottery represents 89 per cent of the total; at Aghram Nadharif, 93 per cent; and at Fewet, almost the entire

---

[12] Liverani 2006.   [13] Daniels 1968; Mattingly 2007; 2010; Mori 2013.

[14] Castelli *et al.* 2005; Mori *et al.* 2013.

[15] Leone 2013a; for distribution of pottery from Garamantian sites, see also Leitch *et al.* 2017.

collection, as only a few sherds of imported Roman jars were found.[16] In spite of the difference in percentage occurrence between Jarma and the sites in the Tanzzuft, the numbers clearly show that the Garamantes relied on handmade pottery wares in everyday life. The ratio is different in funerary contexts, where there were either: (1) one or very few vessels, if any, associated with a grave, and they were handmade and placed on or near the grave superstructure; or (2) many vessels, mostly Roman imports, except for local handmade incense burners, which were located inside the grave shaft.[17] The latter case is quite common in the Wadi al-Ajal in Classic and Late Garamantian graves (dated to the first millennium AD), but some of those graves have also been found in the Wadi Tanzzuft.[18]

The next section discusses the technological features of Garamantian pottery.[19]

Technological Features

The technological features of Garamantian pottery production are analysed here following the *chaîne opératoire* approach.[20]

Raw Material Procurement and Processing

Clay sources for Garamantian pottery have been identified in both the Wadi al-Ajal and the Wadi Tanzzuft as locally or regionally derived, with that used to produce pottery in the citadel of Aghram Nadharif, in the southern Tanzzuft valley, being only local, while those used in the capital, Jarma, came from different locations, which could also mean that some of the vessels were imported.[21] At a macro-analysis level, the fabrics usually appear as a mix of sand, crushed minerals, gypsum/kaolinite, organic inclusions and grog. The interpretation given for this mix is that inclusions were naturally present in the clay, being intentionally added only in the coarser variants,[22] although grog, of course, was a deliberate inclusion. It is

---

[16] Gatto 2006a; 2013a; Leone 2013a.

[17] For an overview of Garamantian funerary evidence from the Tanzzuft/Akakus region see Gatto *et al.* 2019a. For Garamantian burials from the Wadi al-Ajal see Mattingly *et al.* 2019.

[18] Gatto *et al.* 2019a; Mattingly *et al.* 2019.

[19] This is a revised version of the paper circulated for the workshop. I particularly thank Anne Haour, Kevin MacDonald, Susan McIntosh, Olivier Gosselain, Sonja Magnavita and Anne Mayor for their invaluable contribution to the discussion and re-evaluation of the Garamantian ceramics.

[20] Roux 2016.   [21] Artioli *et al.* 2006; Leitch *et al.* 2016.   [22] Gatto 2006a.

Figure 13.2 Negative evidence for coiling in a sherd's profile.

important to note that this is the first known occurrence in the Libyan Sahara of grog as tempering agent.

Shaping

The most frequently recorded shaping techniques, often complementary to one another, are pinch-moulding, and coiling (Fig. 13.2).[23] The practice of moulding the vessel by pinching the lump of clay (defined by Gosselain as drawing of a lump)[24] is clearly indicated in most of the body sherds, and was probably used mainly to build up bodies. On the other hand, the use of coiling seems to have been more closely associated with the shaping of shoulders, necks and rims of jars, pointing to the combination of different techniques in the same vessel. Markings associated with the aforementioned techniques are mainly visible on the interiors of small to medium-sized vessels (Fig. 13.3). For large vessels, markings on the interior surface are less visible, suggesting that alternative shaping techniques could have been used.[25] Unfortunately, no systematic observation of traces left by forming techniques was produced by either the Italian or the British team, effectively preventing a full comprehension of fashioning modes and operational sequences. This aspect was highlighted by all workshop participants as a vital avenue for future investigation. An early attempt at properly approaching the reconstruction of the fashioning sequence was made by Alexander Livingstone Smith in his analysis of the pottery from the shelter of Uan Tabu (Tadrart Akakus); however, the fragmentary preservation of that pottery seriously limited his results.[26] This comes as no surprise for those working on prehistoric pottery from the Sahara and

---

[23] Rice 1987.   [24] Gosselain 2000.   [25] See for instance those in Mayor 2011, fig. 3.
[26] Livingstone Smith 2001.

Figure 13.3 (a) Collared cup from Fewet, the irregular shape and wall texture suggests the use of drawing of a lump as shaping technique (image © Italian Mission of Sapienza University of Rome); (b) interior surface of a painted vessel from Jarma with pinching marks visible in the intersection between the body and the neck (image © Fazzan Project of the University of Leicester).

the Nile Valley, and it is the reason why Isabella Caneva developed an analytical mode focused on decorative techniques and tools, which can usually be detected even on smaller sherds.[27] The presence within the

---

[27] Caneva 1987; 1988; Caneva and Marks 1990.

Figure 13.4 Example of a typical Garamantian globular collared pot with roulette and applied decorations from Fewet (image © Italian Mission of Sapienza University of Rome).

Garamantian ceramic assemblage from Fewet of some large vessel parts, as well as of a few complete examples, leaves scope for a future analysis.[28]

Recorded forms include bowls, and jars with unrestricted and restricted contours.[29] Many restricted vessels had a simple contour (built up on two zones), but several others, particularly jars, were collared (built up on three zones). A range of vessel sizes are represented. At Fewet, form variability follows that encountered at Aghram Nadharif, with jars making up the majority of the pottery repertoire, while bowls are under 20 per cent of the total (18 per cent at Fewet and 16 per cent at Aghram Nadharif).[30] Similar ratios are suggested for Jarma, where shapes unknown in the Tanzzuft are also quite common.[31] Most of the recorded shapes are globular, wide-mouthed, everted rim jars, with a restricted, collared, inflected contour (Fig. 13.4), and bowls of both restricted and unrestricted contours.[32] Shapes such as platters and handled pots, as well as incense burners, are

[28] The assemblage is housed at the Museo delle Origini, Sapienza University of Rome.
[29] For detailed typologies, see Gatto 2006a; 2013a; Leone 2013a.   [30] Gatto 2006a; 2013a.
[31] Leone 2013a.   [32] Gatto 2006a.

time sensitive and not present everywhere. Also notable is the larger size of some of the vessels from Jarma.[33]

Surface Treatment

Outer surfaces were mostly smoothed with a spatula or with fibres. Where the fabric was coarse, a clay wash may be added to even the outside. A layer of clay mixed with organic remains is often reported on the inside, or on both surfaces. Slipping and burnishing were rare. Most of the inner surfaces were left rough, with all the pinching impressions clearly visible. Surface colours range from blackish-brown, to brown, to red. Patches of colour on the surface, due to non-uniform firing, are frequent, as is the zonal colouring of fractures. Some examples of restricted contour vessels whose exteriors were blackened by fire can be interpreted as cooking pots.[34]

Decoration

The great majority of the Garamantian pottery is undecorated: at Fewet and Aghram Nadharif it represents 90 per cent of the total handmade pottery. It is difficult to say for Jarma because the number of decorated sherds is not specifically reported. The typical Garamantian decoration was obtained by impressing a twisted cord on the surface when still partially wet, using the roulette or the simple impression techniques (Fig. 13.5).[35] Different patterns are reported and they appear to be time sensitive.[36] At Jarma is quite difficult to count how many sherds with roulette decoration were recovered, because they are not divided out from the rest of the handmade pottery (except for the painted sherds) and because the use of impressions is not always clearly stated. In fact, one of the types reported in the classification refers to painted and incised sherds, specifying that 'incised' also encompassed impressed decoration.[37] My impression is that the percentage may be lower than in the assemblages from the Tanzzuft. As previously stated, this is the first evidence of roulette decoration in the Central Sahara, a conclusion that was initially very much criticised, but finally accepted as such.

Incisions were almost exclusively used to create geometric patterns, such as alternate triangles, open triangles, wavy lines, checker-board designs or

---

[33] Leone 2013a.   [34] Gatto 2006a; 2013a.
[35] For an updated description of African roulette decorations see Haour *et al.* 2010.
[36] Daniels 1968; Dore *et al.* 2007; Gatto 2006a; 2013a.   [37] Leone 2013a.

Figure 13.5 Examples of roulette decorations from the Tanzzuft (image © Italian Mission of Sapienza University of Rome).

vertical lines.[38] These were restricted to the upper part of the vessels. Incisions were significantly less frequent than roulette impressions and were generally applied to jars. Again, it is difficult to say from the publications how many incised sherds were found in Jarma. Applications, such as circular, pyramidal or flat knobs, were sometimes added to the vessel shoulders as the only decoration or as part of composite patterns. At Fewet these were mostly circular or pyramidal knobs, in relief, and were associated with roulette impressions.[39] At Aghram Nadharif, in addition to the knobs, often the

[38] Gatto 2006a.   [39] Gatto 2013a.

Figure 13.6 Jar fragment from Fewet Site 11, showing an applied decoration in the shape of a snake (image © Italian Mission of Sapienza University of Rome).

only decoration applied to the vessel, we also find flat buttons, which were always associated with the roulette decoration, with or without incisions.[40] A single example of a kind of wavy snake from Aghram Nadharif and a snake applied to a jar (Fig. 13.6) found at Site 11 in Fewet are the only examples of the sort.[41] Few examples of applications are present at Jarma, but there is a kind of long, thick application, identified as handles, which may also have some decorative function.[42]

Fragments of painted vessels are generally found in limited numbers in the Tanzzuft region (Fig. 13.7). They present reasonably simple patterns, formed by vertical red or white lines and applied in alternation or in combination. A rare cross-hatched pattern, obtained with alternating white and red oblique lines in horizontal bands, bordered by double red and white lines, was found in Aghram Nadharif.[43] The only painted rim sherds available from the

[40] Gatto 2006a.
[41] For the exact location of Site 11 within the oasis of Fewet, see Mori 2013, Fig. 5.1.
[42] Leone 2013a.   [43] Gatto 2006a.

Figure 13.7 Examples of painted pottery from the Tanzzuft (image © Italian Mission of Sapienza University of Rome).

Tanzzuft thus far are from collared pots. An exception to this is the case of the incense burners, commonly found at Jarma and in the graves of the Wadi al-Ajal, with only one example found at Aghram Nadharif.[44] Painted sherds were absent from the Fewet compound, while only a few are reported from the necropolis. This is clearly related to the chronology of the compound, which was abandoned by the beginning of the first millennium AD when this type of ceramic started to be produced. There are also many examples of composite patterns obtained by using different techniques simultaneously. As a rule, the body is decorated with roulette impressions, while the other decorations, incisions, paintings and applications are located on the rim band

[44] Gatto 2006a; Leone 2013a; Mattingly *et al.* 2019.

Figure 13.8 Painted pottery from Jarma. Bottom right example is the same pot as in Figure 13.3b (image © Fazzan Project of the University of Leicester).

and shoulders.[45] The situation is rather different in the Wadi al-Ajal, where painted pottery is relatively common in the Jarma sequence from the Classic Garamantian period up to Medieval times (Fig. 13.8). As a matter of fact, it corresponds to 5 per cent of the total pottery assemblage at the site. The earliest example is dated to around the beginning of the first century AD; a cross-hatched pattern of painted lines is visible on the neck of a collared jar.[46] For most of the Garamantian period, cross-hatched patterns, simple lines, dots[47] or simple geometric patterns are the most common painted

---

[45] Gatto 2006a; 2010.   [46] Leone 2013a.
[47] A sherd decorated with white dots on a red surface, identical to many from Jarma, was found at Marandet in Niger and brought to the conference by Sonja Magnavita, who suggested it to be an import to Niger (see Magnavita 2017).

decorations, changing into more Berber-esque painted patterns only in the Late Garamantian period. As in the Tanzzuft, there is evidence of combined decorations and painting associated with incisions and/or impressions. The collared globular jar is the most common form of painted vessel; at Jarma there is a larger variability as far as the shape is concerned, including some which have not been found in the Tanzzuft.[48]

Rims were also often decorated with oblique roulette impressions. Most seem to have been produced with single impressions of twisted cord roulette, but some may have been obtained with the roulette technique. Simple impressed notches were also fairly common, while the milled and the zigzag/criss-cross patterns, also obtained with the simple impression technique, were fewer. Oblique, widely spaced notches and dotted oblique lines were again made with a simple impression technique. Finally, wide slashes seem to have been either incised or simply impressed.[49]

Firing

No remains of kilns have been found thus far in Fazzan, which may indicate that temporary structures/bonfires were used for firing pottery. Regrettably, the firing temperature range estimation from archaeometric analysis (*c.*600–800°C)[50] is unhelpful, as it has been well established that this temperature range is common to most categories of firing structure.[51] There is no evidence of specialisation in ceramic manufacturing among the Garamantes, which instead fits the model of what van der Leeuw called a 'household production', ruling out the use of large and complex firing structures.[52]

Chronological and Spatial Variations

Pottery of the Early Garamantian phase (*c.*1000–500 BC) is represented by the material from Zinkekra; that of the Proto-Urban phase (*c.*500–1 BC) by the material from Fewet, Zinkekra and Jarma; while that of the Classic (*c.* AD 1–300) and Late (*c.*AD 300–700) phases is represented by the material from Aghram Nadharif and Jarma.[53]

To date, pottery from the earliest phase is not well known. Among the studied sites, only one (Zinkekra) has an occupational phase dated to the first half of the first millennium BC. It was mainly excavated in the 1960s,

---

[48] Leone 2013a.   [49] For further details see Gatto 2006a.   [50] Artioli *et al.* 2006.
[51] Gosselain 1992; Livingstone Smith 2001.   [52] Van der Leeuw 1984.
[53] The terminology and chronology used here are those in use by the Trans-SAHARA Project.

and good stratigraphic contexts dated to the early phase are limited. One of these is site ZIN001.13 (corresponding to Daniels' site 13), the sequence of which has been radiocarbon dated, and corresponds to the Early Garamantian phase (bottom layers) and to the Proto-Urban phase (upper layers).[54] The pottery recovered, quite limited in number, shows some mixing, as typical late forms, such as platters (the so-called *dokas*) have been found alongside sherds that seem to have been older in date. Some of the latter have decorations obtained by a comb, applied using both simple and rocker stamp impression techniques, reminiscent of the previous Pastoral tradition. The earliest example of roulette decoration, at least from what can be gathered from the publications of Daniels and the Fazzan Project, is pot HM 315,[55] which was found in the bottom layers in ZIN002.013W and is thus dated to the early first millennium BC.[56] A systematic reanalysis of the pottery from Daniels' excavation, now housed at the Libyan Society Archive at Leicester University, is needed to confirm and expand upon this assertion.

Site G4-324, a campsite located in the western fringes of the Ghat Oasis, has provided material evidence of the transitional moment from the Pastoral stylistic tradition to the Garamantian one.[57] Most of the pottery fragments found at the site were in very good condition, and in large pieces, enabling refit (Fig. 13.9). Their fabrics were mainly tempered with crushed quartz. The typical recorded form is a globular bowl with a thick rim band, modelled on the exterior. Both the rim band and the body were decorated. Simple impressed plain or dotted herringbone patterns, obtained using a comb or spatula, and incised criss-cross patterns decorate the rim bands. Rocker dotted zigzags, made with a comb, and roulette or simple impressions made with a twisted cord, forming packed and herringbone patterns, were applied to the bodies. Simple and rocker impressions, as well as incisions, are reminiscent of the Pastoral decorative tradition.[58] By contrast, twisted cord simple or roulette impressions, as already stated, are Garamantian in date, and were new in the Central Sahara at this time. The site has not been securely dated, but it might well be early evidence of the arrival of the new decorative technique and tools, probably around the end of the second/beginning of the first millennium BC (corresponding to the end of the Final Pastoral phase in the Libyan Sahara chronology).[59] Similar pottery has been found in the bottom layers of ZIN002.013W, and in campsites from the Ubari Sand Sea, north of the Wadi al-Ajal, also

[54] Daniels 1968; Hawthorne *et al.* 2010; Mattingly 2010.   [55] Mattingly 2010, fig. 1.55.
[56] Mattingly 2010.   [57] Mori *et al.* 2013.   [58] Livingstone Smith 2001.
[59] di Lernia and Merighi 2006.

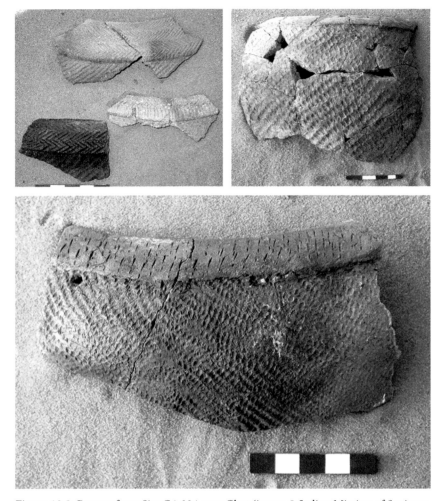

Figure 13.9 Pottery from Site G4-324 near Ghat (image © Italian Mission of Sapienza University of Rome).

tentatively dated to the end of the Pastoral period.[60] Outside of Fazzan, similar vessel shapes are reported from the Adrar Bous and the Gobero area in Niger, with rare examples of roulette technique and implement also described.[61] Both assemblages are dated to the Late Tenerian, roughly contemporary to the Final Pastoral phase in Fazzan, with which it shares many cultural traits.[62] A vessel with a similar shape, rim decoration and a roulette decoration formed of horizontal bands in alternate directions is

[60] See particularly pot n. 12 in Figure 41.52, Dore *et al.* 2007.   [61] Garcea 2008; 2013.
[62] Garcea 2008; 2013.

reported online to be part of Henri Lhote's collection of objects from the Tassili Massif in Algeria, now in Paris.[63] It has the potential to be another example of this transitional (equivalent to Early Garamantian) ceramic type, which would thus include (unsurprisingly) the Tassili as part of a Central Saharan network.

There were thus elements of continuity, and gradual variation, between the Pastoral and the Garamantian ceramic manufacturing processes in Fazzan. These are mainly detectable in the shaping technology, with coiling always in use and a high degree of consistency over time in the vessel forms produced. From the Pastoral to the Garamantian traditions, there was a continual, gradual and apparently uninterrupted move towards undecorated productions, with Early and Middle Pastoral vessels always completely decorated, while Late and Final Pastoral vessels mostly displayed zonal decorations confined to the rim band, and Garamantian productions were predominantly undecorated. But there were also more sudden differences between the two productions, including the number of vessels found at a given site, being higher in Garamantian than in Pastoral times, the use of grog as added material in the fabrics and roulette tool and technique, and later on painting for decoration.[64]

Consistency and continuity is also visible within the manufacturing process of the Garamantian period, with major chronological and spatial variations detected only for roulette and painted decorations and for some vessel shapes.[65] The roulette implement and technique, as already suggested, were introduced by the beginning of – and remained in use until the late – first millennium BC, albeit with less frequency in the Wadi al-Ajal. Painting was added to the repertoire at the beginning of the first millennium AD, and developed mainly in the Garamantian heartlands, remaining the major decorative technique in eastern Fazzan until Medieval times (with Berber-like patterns). Painting was far less common in the Akakus/Tanzzuft region and disappeared soon after the mid-first millennium AD. Combined decorations are attested during the Classic Garamantian phase in both regions.

It is interesting to note that wheel-thrown technology, well known in Mediterranean Africa, was never adopted by local potters, and Punic or Roman vessels, although used by the Garamantes, were never copied locally.

---

[63] www.mnhn.fr/fr/collections/actualites/collection-prehistoire-s-invite-musee-louviers. Unfortunately, the exact provenance of the object is not available online (accessed 7 June 2017).

[64] di Lernia *et al.* 2002; Gatto 2013a; Livingstone Smith 2001. See also the assemblages from Niger, Garcea 2008; 2013.

[65] See Gatto 2006a and Leone 2013a for variability of shape.

Technological Packages in a Trans-Saharan Perspective

Four technological traits of the Garamantian manufacturing process can now be recognised as significant for the detection of technological transfer. They are: grog as temper; drawing out a lump as a shaping technique; roulette as technology and tool; and painted cross-hatching as a decorative pattern. As mentioned previously, further analysis of shaping technology is required. Roulette and grog characterise the Garamantian ceramic technology from its inception at the beginning of the first millennium BC.

As observed by Sonja Magnavita during the workshop, the shaping technique of drawing out a lump is very simple and offers little information about technological transfer. There are more sophisticated techniques, many of which are well known in Sub-Saharan Africa, and future research should investigate if any of those were used by the Garamantes.

The implements that could be used for roulette impressions were varied, the simplest being a twisted cord, obtained by rolling fibres together and then knotting their ends.[66] This is the most widespread roulette implement across Sub-Saharan Africa nowadays, as it was in the past, and one of the earliest in use. It is also the one to have been identified, thus far, in the Garamantian corpus.[67] As highlighted by workshop participants, it is important to note that only this type of implement reached the Central Sahara, and two reasonable explanations for this may be: (1) the early timing of the technological transfer, although even then other roulette implements were already known in the Sub-Saharan zone; and (2) the ease in copying/making the tool, and in learning how to use it. The earliest evidence thus far of twisted cord roulette impression is known from the Lower Tilemsi Valley in eastern Mali, where it is dated to the mid-third millennium BC.[68] By the mid-second millennium BC, roulette decorations were widespread south of the Sahara, in Mauretania, Mali and Burkina Faso, only spreading eastwards along the Sahelian belt much later.[69] The Late Tenerian pottery, found in the Adrar Bous and the Gobero region in Niger, has already been mentioned, and fits in with the Saharan Late/Final Pastoral horizon, in which evidence of roulette decorations are rare, and date (at the earliest) to the end of the second millennium BC, paralleling the proposed timing for their arrival in Fazzan.[70] The scarcity of data, particularly from the Southern Sahara, from key areas such as the Ahaggar

---

[66] For further details on roulette implements and technology, see Haour *et al.* 2010; for twisted cord roulette description see Livingstone Smith *et al.* 2010.

[67] Gatto 2006a.   [68] Arazi and Manning 2010; Manning 2011.

[69] Arazi and Manning 2010; Livingstone Smith 2007.

[70] Arazi and Manning 2010 with references therein; Garcea 2008; 2013.

and the Adrar des Iforas in Mali, prevents any further postulation, and because of this no agreement could be found at the end of the workshop in defining the timing and directionality of this technological transfer. Nevertheless, roulette decorations are unknown in other areas of North Africa, including the Nile Valley, and this – along with the proposed chronology – further supports a correspondence with the Western Sahel for this technological transfer.

The use of grog temper is not a common occurrence among Saharan, Nilotic and Mediterranean African ceramic productions dated before the first millennium BC. Grog is the most common type of inclusion in the Tilemsi pottery of the mid-third millennium BC, however, and was commonly used in the Middle Niger ceramic productions from the second millennium BC, arguing, once more, for a Western Sahel correspondence.[71] MacDonald reminded us during the workshop that grog was not present in the pottery produced in the Tichitt area, where chaff was preferred, but that it *was* present, along with chaff, in pottery of the Tichitt tradition, manufactured in the Dhar Nema and Mema.[72] It is interesting to note that the Dhar Nema and Mema are located east of Tichitt, closer to the Niger Delta and the Tilemsi Valley, from which the earliest examples of grog tempered fabrics are reported. As already mentioned, roulette too is first attested in the Tilemsi Valley and from there moved westwards. The grog may have followed the same trajectory, strengthening the idea developed during the workshop that grog and roulette moved to Fazzan (and apparently elsewhere too) as part of a package.

Katie Manning divides the Tilemsi sites into two groups: the earliest dated to *c.*2500–2300 BC, the youngest to *c.*2000 BC. Fabrics of the earliest group are mainly tempered with grog, but sand/grit is also well attested, while chaff is less present; those of the later group are mainly chaff and grog tempered with much less sand/grit.[73] One might wonder whether sand or grit as a temper were reminiscent of the Pastoral tradition. The earliest Tilemsi pottery was mainly decorated with comb and stylus implements, although twisted cord and cord-wrapped roulettes are also attested, while the youngest pottery has more roulette decorations. Manning suggests the increase in roulette decorations, coupled with an increased use of chaff temper, related to the development of agriculture in the area, and indeed the chaff used as tempering agent is that of domesticated millet.[74] The Tilemsi data may help narrow down the time of the technological knowledge exchange or encounter, or at least

---

[71] MacDonald 1996; Manning 2011.   [72] MacDonald 2011.   [73] Manning 2011.
[74] Manning 2011.

provide a starting date for it. If we take into consideration that what arrived in Fazzan were only the grog and the cord roulettes, then it may be possible that the encounter happened before 2000 BC, which is too early for the dates we have in Fazzan, but we should remember that the evidence currently at our disposal could be those of the farthest extremes within a complex network, and that – should data from the central regions such as the Ahaggar become available – we may discover that there the encounter happened earlier.

Tracking the origin and possible exchange trajectories for the cross-hatched, painted decoration is more difficult, as it indeed is a relatively simple and common pattern that has contemporary and earlier counterparts in many areas of Africa. The earliest evidence of painted wares in the Garamantian corpus are reported from the early first millennium AD, a millennium later than roulette and grog, mainly from the Wadi al-Ajal, and are much less prominent in the Tanzzuft/Akakus region, from where they disappeared after the Garamantian period. In the Wadi al-Ajal, more patterns have been recovered, ranging from simple, vertical lines, to the more complex, cross-hatched patterns, also associated with vessel shapes unknown in the Tanzzuft.[75] In his preliminary contribution for the Handmade Pottery workshop, Kevin MacDonald addressed the presence of a painted cross-hatch motif in a series of sites in the Middle Niger, which are dated from the end of the first millennium BC to the beginning of the first millennium AD, the right timing for a (further) transfer between the two technological traditions.[76] But would the transfer of a single, and quite simple, element make sense after so long? Alternative (possibly northern) avenues of transfer should be taken into consideration, particularly because of the similarities between the Late and Post-Garamantian or Medieval painted patterns in the Wadi al-Ajal and those found in the Berber world.[77] The chronological and geographical distribution of painted wares in Garamantian and Post-Garamantian Fazzan points to a possible northern connection, which would fit well with the evolving relations with Roman Africa established by the Garamantes at that time. Furthermore, one should address the few examples of complex decorations found in the Garamantian corpus, comprising roulette impressions on the vessel's body and painted cross-hatches on the rim band/collar (Fig. 13.10), which have similar counterparts in the Middle Niger region. MacDonald mentioned a Deltaware from Horizon II of Dia-Shoma, Macina, in Mali (dated to 200 BC–AD 200). In my own early work on the Aghram

---

[75] Gatto 2006a; Leone 2013a.
[76] MacDonald 2011; McIntosh 1995; Park 2010; Schmidt *et al.* 2005.
[77] Camps 1961. A very similar painted pattern to that here discussed can be found for instance in Banasa, Morocco, dated to the first millennium BC, Girard 1984.

Figure 13.10 Sherd showing a combination of roulette decoration and chequered painted pattern (image © Italian Mission of Sapienza University of Rome).

Nadharif pottery, I mentioned examples from Phase I/II at Jenné-jeno dated to 100 BC–AD 200.[78] These are not the only combined decorations that share similarities with those of West Africa. Wavy lines incised on the upper body, in association with roulette impressions and applied knobs, again in association with roulette, are also reported. Can they be interpreted as evidence for technological transfer, and if so can it be compared to that of the grog and roulette implement and decorative technique? Probably not in both instances. I must state here that the examples found in Garamantian contexts are locally made, not imports, which could explain their occurrence. As rightly commented by MacDonald in his pre-circulated workshop text, 'these could well be coincidental co-occurrences of common traits among different schools of knowledge'.

In conclusion, both roulette and grog, as implement/technique and tempering agent, arrived as a package, at the same time and likely from the same source. Painting, in contrast, needs further investigation before any statement on origin and directionality of transfer can be made. Unfortunately, the state of research on painted wares, and more generally handmade wares, in Mediterranean Africa is very limited, hampering further analysis. A new avenue of investigation should be devoted to the

---

[78] Gatto 2006a; MacDonald 2011; McIntosh 1995.

subject, and would greatly improve the chances of understanding inter-regional interaction and technological transfer between the Sahara and the northern regions.

A further element to be considered is the great percentage of undecorated vessels in the Garamantian corpus, which has no parallel in the heavily decorated Sub-Saharan assemblages, another feature that the Garamantian ceramic production may share with northern regions.

Social Dimensions of Technological Transfer

Despite the huge biases observed in the data, there is no doubt that technological transfer occurred, somehow and somewhere. One of the main discussions during the workshop, led by the pre-circulated contribution of Anne Haour, focused on the social dimension of technology transfer, and on this the expertise contributed by Olivier Gosselain has been essential. A pivotal point is that the use of both grog as temper and roulette as implement and technique mean that the potters of the Early Garamantian communities made choices that went far beyond the mere copying of something they 'saw'.

Tempering agents used by potters can vary greatly, for different reasons, including availability of raw materials, functionality of the pot produced, traditions and taboos. In the Sahara, naturally available organic and mineral tempers, such as plants, sand and coarse minerals, have always been preferred. The technical properties provided by grog inclusions in the paste could have been easily delivered by any other available agent, as was in fact the case until the Garamantian period in Fazzan. The choice to temper pottery with grog was thus intentional, and likely influenced by cultural factors. The clay preparation stage in pottery production was usually an activity performed in the potter's workshop, and emulation by knowledgeable craftspeople, who happened to be around, could have been a mechanism of knowledge transfer. A discussion between potters, perhaps in a marketplace, on what kind of tempering agents they used could have been an alternative route. Indeed, it is not difficult to understand how to crush a sherd into tiny pieces and use them as temper. A third situation could have been that of new potters arriving in Fazzan and directly participating in the manufacturing process. It would have been highly unlikely for a potter who had never used grog, or did not know of its existence, to notice it inside a pot and decide to use it instead of his/her usual temper.

As for the roulette, Gosselain ruled out the possibility that the transfer happened because pots from the south reached Fazzan as imports of some kind. In fact, if a potter wanted to replicate a roulette decoration without having any previous knowledge of the tool and the technique that have been used to produce it, (s)he would have surely applied a tool and technique already known to her/him. Two possible scenarios were considered. The first is that the potter had some way to discuss with the other potter how the decoration was made, how to use a cord and how to make it, but was not present when it actually happened. In this case, the encounter could have happened, as suggested above for the grog, in a marketplace. For the twisted cord roulette – the only one known in Fazzan and the easiest to make – that discussion could have been enough for the knowledge to be transferred. Alternatively, the potter could have been trained by potters from a different school, learning first-hand how to make the tool and apply the technology to produce the roulette decoration. Alternatively, a potter using those technical features could have moved to Fazzan. Gosselain observed that these last two circumstances would be the only possible means of knowledge transfer when more complex types of roulette tools are used. In other words, the more complicated the tools are, the more they can tell about identity and contacts.[79]

Gosselain also pointed out that those 'transitional' vessels from, for example, Ghat, Zinkekra and the Ubari Sand Sea, which have shapes and rim top decorations reminiscent of those of the previous Pastoral period, could have been made by newcomers. In fact, both globular shapes and decorations made by incisions, and simple impressions, are easy to emulate, and an incoming potter would have been willing to make them if there was a local demand. He also specified that this kind of encounter is better defined as the arrival of another 'learning network', which does not necessarily imply different identities.[80]

Divergences and continuities with both local (Pastoral) and southern traditions would support the arrival in Fazzan of potters from a different learning network. Giving an identity to those potters, however, is a difficult task. Liverani and Mattingly have suggested that the 'new' agents were slaves.[81] An ethnographic parallel for this is provided by Gosselain from the Dendi region in northern Benin, where most of the female potters descend from slaves who remained attached to their owning family.[82] Discussion among the workshop's attendees, however, concluded that this

[79] Gosselain 2011.   [80] Gosselain 1998; 2000; 2008; 2016.   [81] Liverani 2006; Mattingly 2003.
[82] Gosselain 2016.

interpretation was highly unlikely because – as Gosselain pointed out – there is usually no possibility for slaves to maintain their own traditions, for instance in making pottery. In 2006, I suggested that those potters could have been either females entering Garamantian society through marriage, or through being part of groups (castes) associated with crafts-men as wives and daughters, a well-known occurrence nowadays in the Inland Niger Delta.[83] Livingstone Smith suggested the same link for the spread of roulette/rouletting.[84] Both were agreed to be valid possibilities by the attendees of the workshop. If the latter assumption is taken into consideration, the arrival of those potters could be used as a proxy for dating the appearance of metalworking in Fazzan. Metal remains in the region only date as far back as the mid-first millennium BC, with earlier evidence completely lacking, which unfortunately makes the assumption rather difficult to prove.[85]

Ethnographic examples tell us that in family economies, such as those of the Sahara at the inception of the Garamantian era, kinship, friendship and neighbourly relations are the basic structuring forces behind knowledge circulation.[86] Potting technology is usually learned by children as part of their upbringing and by young women who join the family through marriage. Potting is a communal activity in which several people, probably women in this case, are involved, and there is no specific moment at which the knowledge is transferred. Rather, it happens as part of everyday duties, through assisting older relatives. Interest in learning is essential for chil-dren and young wives, as they are living in an environment where potting is a frequent occurrence, and they have the time to practice. On the other hand, a young married woman, even if already a skilled potter, seldom has time to spare as she is burdened with numerous everyday tasks.[87] The interaction between producers and users should be addressed at this point. Users are not necessarily aware of the technological procedures employed to manufacture a pot, and probably do not even care. The outcome, however, should be recognised by them as meaningful, both socially and functionally. Changing learning contexts leads to the reinterpretation of technological traditions and the adoption of new choices, which would become (entangled with traditional ones) meaningful at a social level. If such changes happen within the household, possible social tensions among actors would be better absorbed as part of a single and well-established system of interaction. If, instead, changes occur because of the arrival of

---

[83] Gatto 2006a with reference wherein.   [84] Livingstone Smith 2007.
[85] For a detailed review of metal remains in Fazzan, see Cuénod, Chapter 7, this volume.
[86] Gosselain 2016.   [87] Köhler 2012.

a new social group, perhaps a caste as here hypothesised, social tensions would probably need to be regulated at a higher level, and this would fit with the move towards increasing socio-political complexity that was underway in Fazzan at the time.

Environmental and Archaeological Correlates

A technological change in pottery manufacturing, as occurred in the Central Sahara by the early first millennium BC, is certainly the result of, and the material evidence for, a long-term transformative process that affected all aspects of local society, and as such can be better understood if other archaeological and environmental correlates are taken into consideration.[88]

The end of the second millennium BC marked a climatic crisis that is thought to have caused the collapse of the empire system in the Near East and the Mediterranean, and which also affected North Africa. This crisis must be viewed as the apex in a trend towards aridity that had already begun by the fourth millennium BC. In the Sahara an oasis-dotted landscape developed, which completely changed the lifestyle of local pastoral nomadic populations.[89] Some settled more permanently in confined settings – the oases – inevitably resulting in a higher population density and the need to adopt new forms of subsistence, such as agriculture; domestic architecture, with stone (and later brick) structures; funerary arrangements, with actual burial grounds; and so forth. Others retained their pastoral mobile lifestyle but engaged in seasonal movements involving larger areas and longer and more random routes, becoming fundamental in expanding the superregional sphere of cultural contact. The premises for technological encounter and transfer were thus set in place, and as already suggested the 'space of experience'[90] could have been temporally and geographically different from the Fazzan of the early first millennium BC.

The geographical definition of this sphere of interaction is well documented by the spatial distribution of graves, either isolated or in small clusters, sharing complex stone superstructures with crescent, keyhole and V-like shapes, and which range in date from the fourth to the early first millennium BC.[91] These are found in the section of the Western and Central Sahara that is nowadays part of Morocco, Algeria, Libya,

[88] Santacreu 2014.
[89] Gatto and Zerboni 2015 with references therein; also Sterry and Mattingly 2020.
[90] Gosselain 2016.   [91] Berkani *et al.* 2015; Gauthier and Gauthier 2008.

Mauretania (including the Atlantic coast), Mali and Niger.[92] It is interesting to note that the spatial distribution of rock art with representations of chariots and rock inscriptions in Libyco-Berber, both associated with the broader Garamantian cultural horizon, mostly overlap with that of the tombs.[93]

Conclusion

The aim of this chapter is to establish Trans-Saharan interconnectedness using a technological dataset – handmade pottery – that has seldom been considered for this purpose. Garamantian pottery was chosen as a starting point because it represents the only reasonably well-documented corpus of Central Saharan ceramics, and because of the identification of roulette decorations in the assemblage. Despite the many gaps in the analytical study of the Garamantian corpus, as well as in the documentation of other Saharan and Sub-Saharan assemblages, this chapter illustrates that a special line of connectivity was established between the Central and Western Sahara and the regions of the Western Sahel from the late phase of the Pastoral period, around the fourth millennium BC. It shows that it is from this sphere of interaction that further details in connectivity, timing and directionality of technological encounter and transfer need to be considered.

The major outcome of the 2015 workshop was the collective agreement among the experts present of the presence of roulette and rouletting within Garamantian pottery, the northernmost attestation of the kind known thus far in North Africa. The definition of a technological package, which at the moment can only include the grog temper and the roulette/rouletting decoration, but that in the future might be expanded to include also shaping technologies and painted decorations, represents the other major achievement. The workshop's attendees, who I again acknowledge for their invaluable contribution, remained cautious in defining the timing and directionality of such technological transfer. In my present reconstruction I certainly went beyond what they felt comfortable saying.

There is much scope for further research on Trans-Saharan handmade pottery. A future agenda should include a detailed reassessment of Garamantian ceramics in order to establish their complete set of technological features, particularly as far as shaping techniques are concerned, and a secure chronology for the first roulette and painted decorations.

[92] Gauthier and Gauthier 2008.   [93] Dupuy 2006; Gauthier and Gauthier 2011.

A detailed analysis of prehistoric Saharan ceramics is also needed for a better understanding of the changes encountered in the Garamantian corpus, and, of course, that of contemporary repertoires from Sub-Saharan and Mediterranean Africa, so as to provide a solid framework for the many research questions we want to address. The political instability of most of the North African countries hampers our chance of obtaining fresh data from well-dated contexts. For the time being, we shall focus on already-existing collections, starting by applying novel and cohesive methodology and terminology across the diverse panorama of ceramic studies in Africa.

References

Arazi, N. and Manning, K. 2010. Twisted cord roulette/Roulette de cordelette torsadée. In Haour *et al.* 2010, 134–43.

Artioli, G., Laddaga, L. and Dapiaggi, M. 2006. Archaeometry of pottery: Mineralogical and chemical analyses. In Liverani 2006, 249–57.

Berkani, H., Zazzo, A. and Paris, F. 2015. Les tumulus à couloir et enclos de la Tassili du Fadnoun, Tassili Azger (Algérie): Premières datations par la méthode du radiocarbone. *Journal of African Archaeology* 13.1: 59–70.

Camps, G. 1956. La céramique des sépultures berbères de Tiddis. *Libyca* 4: 155–203.

Camps, G. 1961. *Aux origines de la Berbérie: Monuments et rites funéraires proto-historiques*. Paris: AMG.

Caneva, I. 1987. Pottery decoration in prehistoric Sahara and Upper Nile: A new perspective. In B.E. Barich (ed.), *Archaeology and Environment in the Libyan Sahara*, Oxford: Archaeopress, 231–54.

Caneva, I. 1988. *El Geili: The History of a Middle Nile Environment, 7000* BC–AD *1500*. Oxford: Archaeopress.

Caneva, I. and Marks, A. 1990. More on Shaqadud pottery: Evidence for Saharo-Nilotic connections during the 6th–4th Millennium BC. *Archéologie du Nil Moyen* 6: 65–92.

Castelli, R., Cremaschi, M., Gatto, M.C., Liverani, M. and Mori, L. 2005. A preliminary report of excavations in Fewet (Libyan Sahara). *Journal of African Archaeology* 3.1: 69–102.

Daniels, C.M. 1968. Garamantian excavations: Zinchecra 1965–67. *Libya Antiqua* 5: 113–94.

di Lernia, S. and Merighi, F. 2006. Transitions in the later prehistory of the Libyan Sahara as seen from the Acacus Mountains. In D.J. Mattingly, S. McLaren, E. Savage, Y. al-Fasatwi and K. Gadgood (eds), *The Libyan Desert: Natural Resources and Cultural Heritage*, London: Society for Libyan Studies, 111–21.

di Lernia S., Merighi F., Ricci F., and Sivilli S. 2002. From regions to sites: the excavations. In di Lernia S. and G. Manzi (eds), *Sand, Stones and Bones: The Archaeology of Death in the Wadi Tanezzuft Valley (5000–2000 BP)*, AZA 3, Firenze: All'Insegna del Giglio, 69–156.

Dore, J.N., Leone, A. and Hawthorne, J. 2007. Pottery type series. In Mattingly 2007, 305–431.

Dupuy, C. 2006. L'Adrar des Iforas (Mali) à l'époque des chars: Art, religion, rapports sociaux et relations à grande distance. *Sahara* 17: 29–50.

Fili, A. 2011. La céramique de tradition amazighe. *Asinag* 6: 21–29.

Gallin, A. 2011. *Les styles céramiques de Kobadi. Analyse comparative et implications chronoculturelles au Néolithique récent du Sahel malien*. Frankfurt: Afrika MagnaVerlag.

Garcea, E.A.A. 2008. The ceramics from Adrar Bous and surroundings. In J. D. Clark and D. Gifford-Gonzalez (eds), *Adrar Bous: Archaeology of a Central Saharan Granitic Ring Complex in Niger*, Tervuren: Royal Museum for Central Africa, 245–89.

Garcea, E.A.A. 2013. Manufacturing technology of the ceramic assemblages. In E. A.A. Garcea (ed.), *Gobero: The No-Return Frontier. Archaeology and Landscape at the Saharo-Sahelian Borderland*, Frankfurt am Main: Africa Magna Verlag, 209–40.

Gatto, M.C. 2002. Early Neolithic pottery of the Nabta-Kiseiba area: Stylistic attributes and regional relationships. In K. Nelson and Associates (eds), *Holocene Settlements of the Egyptian Sahara, Vol. II, the Pottery of Nabta Playa*, New York: Kluwer Academic/Plenum Publisher, 65–78.

Gatto, M. 2006a. The local pottery. In Liverani 2006, 201–40.

Gatto, M.C. 2006b. The Khartoum Variant pottery in context: Rethinking the Early and Middle Holocene Nubian sequence. *Archéologie du Nil Moyen* 10: 57–72.

Gatto, M.C. 2006c. The most ancient pottery from the Dongola Reach (Northern Sudan): New data from the SFDAS survey related to the construction of the Merowe Dam. *Archéologie Du Nil Moyen* 10: 73–86.

Gatto, M.C. 2010. The Garamantes of the Fazzan: Imported pottery and local productions. *Bollettino di Archeologia*, special volume: 30–38.

Gatto, M.C. 2013a. Ceramics from Fewet. In Mori 2013, 79–92.

Gatto, M.C. 2013b. Preliminary report on the most ancient pottery from the Kerma region. In M. Honegger, M.C. Gatto, C. Fallet and M. Bundi, *Archaeological Excavation at Kerma (Sudan)*, Kerma, Documents de la mission archéologique Suisse au Soudan 5, Neuchâtel: Université de Neuchâtel, 4–10.

Gatto, M.C. and Zerboni, A. 2015. Holocene supra-regional environmental crises as motor for major socio-cultural changes in Northeastern Africa and the Sahara. *African Archaeological Review* 32: 301–33.

Gatto, M.C., Mori, L. and Zerboni, A. 2019a. Identity markers in south-western Fazzan: Were the people of the Wadi Tanzzuft/Tadrart Akakus region Garamantes? In Gatto *et al.* 2019b, 108–33.

Gatto, M.C., Mattingly, D.J., Ray, N. and Sterry, M. (eds) 2019b. *Burials, Migration and Identity in the Ancient Sahara and Beyond*. Trans-Saharan Archaeology, Volume 2. Series editor D.J. Mattingly. Cambridge: Cambridge University Press, Society for Libyan Studies.

Gauthier, Y. and Gauthier, C. 2008. Monuments en trou de serrure, monuments à alignement, monuments en 'V' et croissants: Contribution à l'étude des populations sahariennes. *Cahiers de l'AARS* 12: 1–20.

Gauthier, Y. and Gauthier, C. 2011. Des chars et des Tifnagh: Étude aréale et corrélations. *Cahiers de l'AARS* 15: 91–118.

Girard, S. 1984. Banasa préromaine: Un état de la question. *Antiquités africaines* 20: 11–93.

Gosselain, O.P. 1992. The bonfire of the enquiries. Pottery firing temperatures: What for? *Journal of Archaeological Science* 19: 243–59.

Gosselain, O.P. 1998. Social and technical identity in a clay crystal ball. In M. Stark (ed.), *The Archaeology of Social Boundaries*, Washington, DC: Smithsonian Institution Press, 78–106.

Gosselain, O.P. 2000. Materializing identities: An African perspective. *Journal of Archaeological Method and Theory* 7.3: 187–217.

Gosselain, O.P. 2008. Thoughts and adjustments in the potter's backyard. In I. Berg (ed.), *Breaking the Mould: Challenging the Past through Pottery*, Oxford: Archaeopress, 67–79.

Gosselain, O.P. 2011. Pourquoi le décorer? Quelques observations sur le décor céramique en Afrique. *Azania: Archaeological Research in Africa* 46.1: 3–19.

Gosselain, O.P. 2016. The world is like a beanstalk: Historicizing potting practice and social relations in the Niger River area. In A. Roddick and A. Brower Stahl (eds), *Knowledge in Motion: Constellations of Learning across Time and Place*, Tucson: University of Arizona Press, 36–66.

Haour, A. 2017. What made Islamic trade distinctive – as compared to Pre-Islamic trade? In Mattingly *et al.* 2017, 80–100.

Haour, A., Manning, K., Arazi, N., Gosselain, O., Guèye, N.S., Keita, D., Livingstone Smith, A., MacDonald, K., Mayor, A., McIntosh, S. and Vernet R. (eds). 2010. *African Pottery Roulettes Past and Present: Techniques, Identification and Distribution*. Oxford and Oakville: Oxbow Books.

Hawthorne, J., Mattingly, D.J. and Daniels, C.M., with contributions by Barnett, T., Dore, J.N. and Leone, A. 2010. Zinkekra: An Early Garamantian escarpment settlement and associated sites (ZIN001–003). In Mattingly 2010, 19–84.

Köhler, I. 2012. Learning and children's work in a pottery making environment in northern Côte d'Ivoire. In G. Spittler and M. Bourdillon (eds), *African Children at Work: Working and Learning in Growing Up for Life*, Berlin: LIT Verlag, 113–41.

Leitch, V., Mattingly, D.J., Williams, M., Norry, M.J., Wilkinson, I.P., Whitbread, I., Stocker, C.P. and Farman, T. 2016. Provenance of clay used in Garamantian ceramics from Jarma, Fazzan region (south-west Libya): A combined geochemical and microfossil analysis. *Journal of Archaeological Science, Reports* 10: 1–14.

Leitch, V., Duckworth, C., Cuénod, A., Mattingly, D.J., Sterry, M. and Cole, F. 2017. Early Saharan trade: The inorganic evidence. In Mattingly *et al.* 2017, 287–340.

Leone, A. 2013a. Pottery from the Fazzan Project excavations at Jarma. In Mattingly 2013, 325–408.

Leone, A. 2013b. Pottery catalogues. In Mattingly 2013, 683–706.

Liverani, M. (ed.) 2006. *Aghram Nadarif: The Barkat Oasis (Sha'abiya of Ghat, Libyan Sahara) in Garamantian Times*. AZA 5. Firenze: All'Insegna del Giglio.

Livingstone Smith, A. 2001. Bonfire II: The return of pottery firing temperatures. *Journal of Archaeological Science* 28: 991–1003.

Livingstone Smith, A. 2007. Histoire du décor à la roulette en Afrique subsaharienne. *Journal of African Archaeology* 5.2: 189–216.

Livingstone Smith. A. 2010. A method of identification for rolled impressed decorations. In Haour *et al.* 2010, 116–30.

Livingstone Smith, A., Gosselain, O., Mayor, A. and Guèye, N.S. 2010. Modern roulettes in Sub-Saharan Africa. In Haour *et al.* 2010, 37–114.

MacDonald, K.C. 1996. Tichitt-Walata and the Middle Niger: Evidence for cultural contact in the second millennium BC. In G. Pwiti and R. Soper (eds), *Aspects of African Archaeology: Papers from the 10th Congress of the Pan-African Association for Prehistory and Related Studies*. Harare: University of Zimbabwe Publications, 429–40.

MacDonald, K.C. 2011. Betwixt Tichitt and the IND: The pottery of the Faïta Facies, Tichitt Tradition. *Azania: Archaeological Research in Africa* 46.1: 49–69.

Magnavita, S. 2013. Initial encounters: Seeking traces of ancient trade connections between West Africa and the wider world. *Afriques: Débats, méthodes et terrains d'histoire*. http://afriques.revues.org/1145.

Magnavita, S. 2017. Track and trace: Archaeometric approaches to the study of early Trans-Saharan trade. In Mattingly *et al.* 2017, 393–413.

Manning, K.M. 2011. Potter communities and technological tradition in the Lower Tilemsi Valley, Mali. *Azania: Archaeological Research in Africa* 46.1: 70–87.

Mattingly, D.J. (ed.) 2003. *The Archaeology of Fazzan. Volume 1, Synthesis*. London: Society for Libyan Studies, Department of Antiquities.

Mattingly, D.J. (ed.) 2007. *The Archaeology of Fazzan. Volume 2, Site Gazetteer, Pottery and Other Survey Finds*. London: Society for Libyan Studies, Department of Antiquities.

Mattingly, D.J. (ed.) 2010. *The Archaeology of Fazzan. Volume 3, Excavations Carried Out by C.M. Daniels*. London: Society for Libyan Studies, Department of Antiquities.

Mattingly, D.J. (ed.) 2013. *The Archaeology of Fazzan. Volume 4, Survey and Excavations at Old Jarma (Ancient Garama) Carried Out by C.M. Daniels (1962–69) and the Fazzan Project (1997–2001)*. London: Society for Libyan Studies, Department of Antiquities.

Mattingly, D.J., Leitch, V., Duckworth, C.N., Cuenod, A., Sterry, M. and Cole, F. (eds) 2017. *Trade in the Ancient Sahara and Beyond.* Trans-Saharan Archaeology, Volume 1. Series Editor D.J. Mattingly. Cambridge: Cambridge University Press, Society for Libyan Studies.

Mattingly, D.J., Sterry, M. and Ray, N. 2019. Dying to be Garamantian: Burial, migration and identity in Fazzan. In Gatto *et al.* 2019b, 53–107.

Mayor, A. 2011. *Traditions céramiques dans la boucle du Niger: Ethnoarchéologie et histoire du peuplement au temps des empires précoloniaux.* Frankfurt am Main: Africa Magna Verlag.

Mayor, A., Huysecom, E., Gallay, A., Rasse, M. and Ballouche, A. 2005. Population dynamics and paleoclimate over the past 3000 years in the Dogon Country, Mali. *Journal of Anthropological Archaeology* 24: 25–61.

McIntosh, S.K. (ed.) 1995. *Excavations at Jenné-Jeno, Hambarketolo, and Kaniana (Inland Niger Delta, Mali), the 1981 Season.* Berkeley: University of California Press.

Mori, L. (ed.) 2013. *Life and Death of a Rural Village in Garamantian Time: Archaeological Investigation in the Oasis of Fewet (Libyan Sahara).* AZA 6. Firenze: All'Insegna del Giglio.

Mori, L., Gatto, M.C., Ricci, F. and Zerboni, A. 2013. Life and death at Fewet. In Mori 2013, 375–87.

Park, D.P. 2010. Prehistoric Timbuktu and its hinterland. *Antiquity* 84: 1076–88.

Rice, P.M. 1987. *Pottery Analysis: A Sourcebook.* Chicago: University of Chicago Press.

Roux, V. 2016. Ceramic manufacture: The chaîne opératoire approach. In A. Hunt (ed.), *The Oxford Handbook of Archaeological Ceramic Analysis*, Oxford: Oxford University Press, 101–13.

Santacreu, D.A. 2014. *Materiality, Techniques and Society in Pottery Production: The Technological Study of Archaeological Ceramics through Paste Analysis.* Warsaw and Berlin: De Gruyter Open.

Schmidt, A., Arazi, N., MacDonald, K.C., Cosme, F. and Bedaux, R. 2005. La poterie. In R. Bedaux, J. Polet, K. Sanogo and A. Schmidt (eds), *Recherches archéologiques á Dia dans le Delta intérieur du Niger (Mali): Bilan des saisons de fouilles 1998–2003*, Leiden: CNWS Publications, 191–256.

Sterry, M. and Mattingly, D.J. (eds) 2020. *Urbanisation and State Formation in the Ancient Sahara and Beyond*, Trans-Saharan Archaeology, Volume 3, series editor D.J. Mattingly, Cambridge: Cambridge University Press and the Society for Libyan Studies.

Van der Leeuw, S.E. 1984. Dust to dust: A transformational view of the ceramic cycle. In S.E. Van der Leeuw and A.C. Pritchard (eds), *The Many Dimensions of Pottery: Ceramics in Archaeology and Anthropology*, Amsterdam: University of Amsterdam, 707–74.

PART VI

Conclusion

14 | Technology in the Sahara and Beyond

Concluding Discussion

CHLOË N. DUCKWORTH, AURÉLIE CUÉNOD AND DAVID J.
MATTINGLY

Introduction

The concluding discussion in this chapter addresses several issues. In
the first place it draws together the threads of discussion that run
through the individual chapters relating to the nature of technology
and technological transfer in the Sahara. Here we reflect on 'what is
a mobile technology', 'how to study technology in the Sahara', 'difficulties and solutions' and 'connections'. In the second half of the
chapter, we broaden the discussion to consider further the implications of Saharan technology transfer in relation to the 'and beyond'
part of our title. Finally, we examine some of the ramifications of the
combined results of the four volumes of the *Trans-Saharan
Archaeology* series for archaeologists, historians and related researchers. We present some ideas about how the conclusions of this series
offer a fresh perspective on the Trans-Saharan region and necessitate
a fundamental reshaping of future agendas of study of the ancient
Sahara and beyond.

What Is a Mobile Technology?

What is a 'mobile' technology? Technologies do not move of their own
accord, of course, so what we have really been discussing in this volume is
the movement of knowledge and skills, linked ultimately to the movement of people. Our conundrum is that we cannot 'see' the movement of
knowledge and skills. Nor can we easily trace the movement of people.
We are left with 'things' – the products of technology and, very occasionally, with whatever people wrote about them. We also need to remember,
as outlined in Chapter 1, that technology can be seen as a web of

knowledge, and skills, as well as the social systems required to support and maintain them.[1]

Geography and environment are significant constraining and enabling factors in technological change, a point that is very easy to appreciate when working in the Sahara, but which is true of any region. Similarly, we are fairly used to considering Saharan technologies as ways of overcoming the *constraints* of the desert, but after reading the chapters in this volume it may be worth pausing to consider what is *enabled* by this environment.

Perhaps the most visible way for a technology to be (geographically) mobile is by being embedded in a fundamentally mobile society. The technologies of nomads and pastoralists – at the heart of this volume – are prime examples.[2] However, the dynamic process of sedentarisation and oasis formation also served to create nodes of connectivity within what had been pastoral rangelands, with these often becoming privileged locations for technological transfers. A key aspect of technology transfers in the Sahara has thus been the interplay between mobile and sedentary groups.

Technologies can be socially mobile, moving horizontally from one group to another, or from nomads to settled groups, or vertically by becoming available to a wider cross-section of a given society. Vertical transition is often downwards, with a technology moving from the higher to the lower classes, but may in some cases work in the opposite direction.

This is the complex, multifaceted picture subsumed by the ideas of technological diffusion and technology/knowledge transfer. These ideas are often considered separately to technological change, but what the chapters in this volume illustrate so clearly is that there can be no technology transfer, or diffusion, without some technological change. This is aptly illustrated by Amraoui, who details the ways in which 'Roman' technologies were adapted to North African environments.[3] Wilson *et al.* show that, for all that there was a basic 'package' of technologies associated with the construction of foggaras, these also required novel solutions and adaptations to the lie of the land.[4] Fothergill *et al.* show evidence for a multitude of micro-innovations and adaptations in the movement of animals to new environments.[5] As well as these clear examples of adaptations to different physical environments, technologies are deeply socially contingent, as

---

[1] We shall not repeat the review of debate presented in Duckworth *et al.*, Chapter 1, this volume, but will focus on the specific contributions of chapters in this book and other volumes in the series to advancing our knowledge and understanding of the issues.

[2] See also the important contribution of Scheele 2017 to another volume in this series.

[3] Amraoui, Chapter 4, this volume.   [4] Wilson *et al.*, Chapter 3, this volume.

[5] Fothergill *et al.*, Chapter 5, this volume.

shown so aptly by Robertshaw and Robion-Brunner (who discusses the social and physical embeddedness of glass bead and iron production).[6] Tracing them blandly from one place or time to another divorces them from all meaning.

Technological change must be explained, but we must also consider the maintenance of technologies and the labour involved in this, as discussed in the introductory chapter to this volume. The maintenance of a foggara requires particular resources, the provision of which is, of course, socially embedded. In other cases, such as the domestic pottery production described by Gatto,[7] the required maintenance may be purely social, depending upon marriage and kinship, apprenticeship and learning, and a whole host of factors that are somewhat more difficult to pick out archaeologically.

Of course, the landscape has also changed over time, and this may have had an effect upon – and in some cases been affected by – technology. Liverani notes that donkeys were better adapted to the climatic conditions of the Pastoral and Late Pastoral periods in the Sahara, when there were much larger stretches of land with permanent or seasonal watercourses; the dromedary, in his view, was a response to aridification, and was only widely adopted once it was 'the most convenient solution'.[8] The availability (or lack thereof) of suitable fuel would have been crucial to the development of pyrotechnologies, and creative solutions may have been sought, as suggested by Duckworth with regard to the potential for the use of animal dung in this capacity (a point which also emphasises the interconnectedness of Saharan technologies).[9] Foggara technology continuously had to adapt to the lowering water table, which partly resulted from the use of foggaras themselves, and which ultimately led to their abandonment.[10] The Sahara Desert is often portrayed as being timeless, but the chapters in this book demonstrate that it is ever shifting, and that environmental, social and technological change are deeply entangled.[11]

How to Study Technology: Lessons From the Sahara

A key research priority is to have more scientific data relating to technology from Saharan sites, including compositional analysis of materials like

[6] Robertshaw, Chapter 11; Robion-Brunner, Chapter 9, this volume
[7] Gatto, Chapter 13, this volume.   [8] Liverani, Chapter 2, this volume.
[9] Duckworth, Chapter 10, this volume.   [10] Wilson *et al.*, Chapter 3, this volume.
[11] See discussion in Duckworth *et al.*, Chapter 1, this volume.

metals and glass, as exemplified in the chapters of Cuénod, Duckworth and Rehren and Rosenow.[12] However, we need to be careful in seeking to move beyond the raw data to a deeper understanding of what they tell us about the invention, use, adaptation and transfer of technology. The interpretation of ancient technology is beset by complex discourses and assumptions about these issues, that all too readily may shape and distort our reading of the data.

For example, it is impossible to escape the spectre of colonialism in the interpretation of the Sahara. From debates around when foggaras were introduced, to analyses of African metallurgy, the tension between colonial and post-colonial perspectives remains at the core of the discipline.[13] On the other hand, as noted by Liverani, much as the old 'diffusionist' model of technological change was a side effect of the colonialist relations of the past centuries, we must be aware that the present focus on technological interaction is a side effect of post-colonialism and neo-capitalist globalisation.[14]

How do we recentre the Sahara and its peoples in the narratives we tell of it? The chapters in this volume demonstrate the importance of moving away from the unilinear, unidirectional picture of technological change that has dominated Western archaeology since its inception. This picture is rooted in the idea of technological change as technological development, which is fundamentally anachronistic because its assumed end point is where we are now. In this model, there is little room for the technological interactions, small-scale innovations or gradual changes in already-established technologies that are described by so many of the chapters in this book. In scholarship more generally, the focus to date has been upon the cutting edge; on innovation as a 'moment' that belongs to a single group or individual, and that continues to belong to them as the technologies travel from one location to another. In short, many historical and archaeological models of past technological change seem to be rooted in an understanding that derives from the modern system of patents. There is a gendered aspect to this, too, as domestic technologies that are recurrently practised by women in a domestic setting, including pottery and textile production (though gender is not explicitly discussed by Magnavita),[15] are too rarely considered in this 'big picture'.

---

[12] Cuénod, Chapter 7; Duckworth, Chapter 10; Rehren and Rosenow, Chapter 12, this volume.

[13] See in particular the presentation of the contentious debate about the origins of African ironworking in Cuénod, Chapter 7; Humphris, Chapter 8; and Robion-Brunner, Chapter 9, this volume.

[14] Liverani, Chapter 2, this volume.   [15] Magnavita, Chapter 6, this volume.

By doing things differently, the chapters in this volume reveal how feeble this way of understanding technology is. Robion-Brunner notes that questions about technological choice and craftsperson identity, with regard to the diversity of West African iron smelting, are often overshadowed by the debate on the origins of ironworking in Africa, which has raged for over 60 years.[16] Fothergill *et al.* highlight that domestication was an ongoing, co-evolutionary process – often involving complex and difficult translocation of livestock to new environments – and not akin to an 'invention' that was introduced once and could subsequently be transferred into new environments.[17]

Variability and local adaptation – often of technologies developed outside the Sahara (domesticated animals, plants, water management systems, grain mills) – may make it more difficult to find patterns in the 'noise', but if we listen to the noise itself, we may find that it is also telling us something important, not only about the Sahara and its peoples but about how we understand technology more broadly. As noted by Humphris, technology must be considered as an interwoven web, and is one of the ways we have of glimpsing the lives of non-elites.[18] The matter of power and control over technology, and even of competing influences over technological development, is one that requires further consideration, although it is touched upon in some of the chapters in this volume.

Understanding the origin point(s) of this technology is an important part of the picture, but it should not become so large an issue as to obscure the rest. It is difficult to do this, looking back as we are from a world with intellectual property, patents and copyright, but it is essential. Even if our primary purpose is to construct a global 'history of technology', local innovations and adaptations (and the lived experience of technology and technological practice) tell us much more about how change was articulated than does the construction of 'points of origin'. As Robertshaw so deftly demonstrates, the values and meanings of materials change as they move from one social sphere to another. So, too, do the values and meanings of technological knowledge.[19] Let us celebrate, investigate and seek to understand these complex, shifting, mobile technologies.

---

[16] Robion-Brunner, Chapter 9, this volume. See also Cuénod, Chapter 7, this volume.
[17] Fothergill *et al.*, Chapter 5, this volume.   [18] Humphris, Chapter 8, this volume.
[19] Robertshaw, Chapter 11, this volume.

Difficulties and Solutions

As much as we may learn from it, the study of the Sahara is fraught with difficulties, which must be acknowledged even as we may attempt to overcome some of them. As noted by Fothergill *et al.* and Amraoui, for example, research and excavation bias towards coastal, North African sites exerts a gravitational pull upon any interpretation of the Sahara: our frameworks of analysis are still largely taken from the Mediterranean and West Asia.[20] In a similar way, the regional focus of many researchers, whether towards the Maghrib, Nile Valley or West Africa, metaphorically leads to a turning of backs on the desert. A prime argument of this book (and indeed the *Trans-Saharan Archaeology* series) is that we need to open out the scale of analysis beyond the insulated local focus and consider the Trans-Saharan region as a connected space.

Archaeological visibility is also significant. It is more difficult to link technologies directly with nomadic groups, by comparison with those practised at a single site that is occupied for a long period of time (such as those in the Wadi al-Ajal). Other factors feed into visibility. As noted by Duckworth, recycling means that much of the potential evidence for glass (and indeed metal) production never makes it into the archaeological record. Small, domestic technologies, or those practised sporadically, may also be less archaeologically visible. In most cases, organic materials are all but completely lost to us.

Variability in recording practices means that large-scale comparisons of the sort attempted here are difficult. Choosing to use fine-meshed sieves during excavation may lead to the recovery of hundreds or even thousands of tiny beads that would otherwise have been missed. Site reports may be hugely variable, as shown in the case of faunal assemblages, in which certain remains (for example, chicken bones) may go unidentified, or be lumped together in a 'single identification category for all avians'.[21]

Magnavita compares the search for evidence of early West African weaving technology to 'fishing in the dark', a phrase that may be extended to many of the technologies discussed in this volume.[22] Yet hope is not lost, for as the chapters (emphatically including Magnavita's) have also demonstrated, we can start to reveal tiny spots of light through innovative means, from the microscopic and chemical analysis of glass, metals and pottery, or the recovery of evidence for a weaving pattern in the imprint it left on

---

[20] Amraoui, Chapter 4; Fothergill *et al.*, Chapter 5, this volume.
[21] Fothergill *et al.*, Chapter 5, this volume.   [22] Magnavita, Chapter 6, this volume.

a corroded bangle, to the employment of sophisticated excavation techniques and total recording in the field. The influence of nomadic pastoralists may be glimpsed in the mobile technologies themselves, from the possible movement of domestic cattle and caprines from North Africa to the Sahara, to the suggestion that weaving on a loom was transferred from one region to another by nomads and pastoralists.

Communication between research specialisms helps to connect some of these dots of light, and the intense academic discussion upon which this volume is based was an important step in this direction. The value of including animals in considerations of technology was illustrated by some of the links drawn. For example, salt-tolerant (halophytic) plants are an important food source for camels, but were also significant in the development of early glass technology, suggesting that a link with nomadic groups may be worthy of future exploration. Similarly, animal dung, date palm wood and fronds may have been valuable fuel resources, and the relative availability of these in different areas would have had a significant impact upon the movement of fuel-hungry pyrotechnologies across a desert environment. These examples highlight the need to consider broader technological landscapes, and to integrate historical data and multiple forms of archaeological data.[23]

Connections

One of the key aims of the *Trans-Saharan Archaeology* series of books was to stimulate debate about the current state of knowledge, and future agendas of study, for a series of important themes. In the four volumes, we have presented and discussed evidence for Trans-Saharan connections, in terms of trade, urbanisation and state formation, funerary practices, migration and identity, and technology. A few last reflections are merited as we come to the end of the final volume in the series, in particular seeking to draw out the chief outcomes of the separate thematic investigations and the areas where, like Venn diagrams, conclusions overlap in significant ways. The *Trans-Saharan Archaeology* series above all highlights the theme of interconnectedness – of places, peoples, things, technologies, social structures, cultures and so on. Yet, as noted at various points and by multiple contributors, there is still a strong body of opinion that the

---

[23] See Duckworth, Chapter 10, this volume for discussion of the fuel issue for Saharan pyrotechnology.

historic-era Sahara was a poorly interconnected region prior to the Islamic conquest of North Africa.[24] Archaeological evidence has been accruing for some time to challenge this view, with a picture emerging of the precocious development of oases in some parts of the Sahara from the first millennium BC, accompanied by the initial stages of the installation of a connective network of trails that facilitated interregional contact and trade. The Mobile Technologies dimension of the Trans-SAHARA Project was designed to explore the extent to which it is possible to track technology transfer and invention within the Saharan world and its environs. Crucial to this analysis is a consideration of the degree to which, at any given point in time, the vast spaces of the Sahara were interconnected.

Connectivity has thus been a key theme of this volume, and at its end it is pertinent to ask whether we have sufficient evidence to argue for Trans-Saharan technology transfer – the 'mobile technologies' of the title. What we can establish securely is that there was a network of connections operating at various scales in different parts of the Sahara and surrounding regions in pre-Islamic times, and that there was some long-distance exchange or transfer of technological expertise prior to the late first millennium AD. Liverani provides a perceptive overview of the traditionally identified east to west flow of innovation and technology transfer, seeing its ultimate origins to the east, not the west of the Nile Valley.[25] Irrigation technologies are a significant component of the eastern package that he discusses, and this was the focus of the contribution by Wilson *et al.*[26] An important conclusion of their work is that the diverse environments and hydrological condition of different parts of the Sahara complicated technological transfer and oasis 'start-up'. It was never a case of a single irrigation technology being rolled out across the desert, but rather a careful selection from the 'technology shelf' of what was most appropriate to exploit the hydrological potential of each ecological niche. Sophisticated knowledge was required for the siting, construction, use and maintenance of the complex foggara irrigation systems.[27]

The agricultural components of oasis farming, including the date palm, figs, wheat and barley, were also externally sourced, at least initially, and there is strong evidence for Liverani's eastern point of origin in some of the key domesticated animals that facilitated the interconnectivity of oasis communities and underpinned the development of trade. Fothergill *et al.*

---

[24] See Austen 2010, for a comparatively recent example of this persistent scholarly tendency to minimise pre-Islamic activity in the Sahara.
[25] Liverani, Chapter 2, this volume.   [26] Wilson *et al.*, Chapter 3, this volume.
[27] Liverani, Chapter 2; Wilson *et al.*, Chapter 3, this volume.

provide a wide-ranging overview of the spread of domesticated animals within the Trans-Saharan zone, revealing not only some interesting patterns of interconnection, but also some of the discontinuities in current knowledge.[28] The oases of Egypt's Western Desert appear to be chronologically earlier than those of the Central Sahara, and support the view of an initial east to west direction of technological transfer.[29] It is significant, however, that by the late first millennium BC, additional components of the Saharan farming package were emerging that can be traced to Sub-Saharan precedents (sorghum, pearl millet, cotton).[30] This suggests different trajectories and vectors of technology transfer to the traditionally emphasised east to west spread, and it is interesting that there is a hint of something similar in the handmade ceramic technologies explored by Gatto.[31]

The *Trans-Saharan Archaeology* Series

The other volumes in the series help to piece together more of this complex, enormous patchwork.[32] Each volume has presented some of the key results of the Trans-SAHARA Project, authored by team members, alongside a series of comparative studies and reflections from other experts. Across 66 chapters and over 2,350 pages in the four volumes a huge amount of new material and new thinking has been presented, alongside a thoroughgoing synthesis and review of the evidence. Individually and collectively the volumes have advanced discussion and, while each volume stands alone, there are also strong cross-cutting themes and discussions between them. Although primarily reflecting the work of archaeologists and anthropologists, the debates encompassed in these volumes are also of the highest relevance for historians. We believe that, cumulatively, the data and ideas presented necessitate some fundamental changes in perspectives and agendas of study for the Trans-Saharan zone.[33]

The volume relating to *trade* has shown that a fundamental problem we face concerns the skewed nature of the archaeological record for past commerce.[34] It is heavily slanted in favour of a few (and probably

---

[28] Fothergill *et al.*, Chapter 5, this volume.   [29] See Liverani, Chapter 2, this volume.

[30] Duckworth *et al.*, Chapter 1, this volume.   [31] Gatto, Chapter 13, this volume.

[32] Gatto *et al.* 2019a; Mattingly *et al.* 2017a; Sterry and Mattingly 2020a.

[33] Although not all contributors fully embraced our views – see the debate between Mattingly and Sterry 2020b and Scheele 2020.

[34] Mattingly *et al.* 2017a.

unrepresentative) durable artefacts,[35] whereas we can surmise that Saharan trade has at all times been heavily dependent on: organic commodities including textiles and slaves; high-value items such as gold and ivory that are in consequence poorly represented in the archaeological record; and recyclable materials including metals and glass. A particular achievement of the volume is to highlight the significance of textiles and garments in Saharan trade – commonly overshadowed or overlooked in conventional accounts that tend to emphasise slaves, gold and salt as the key commodities.[36] The impossibility of *quantifying* the importance of the main commodities of Saharan trade from the archaeological record is a fundamental problem for traditional approaches, but there is hope. As outlined above, new scientific approaches, especially the compositional analyses of metal and glass artefacts, can occasionally provide 'smoking gun' evidence for pre-Islamic trade.[37] For instance, we can now demonstrate the presence of Mediterranean-specific glass items and copper alloys, such as brass, in pre-Islamic contexts in the Central Sahara and West Africa.[38] While there is no doubt that Islamic-era trade developed in new ways, achieving a significant scale of exchanges and giving emphasis to new routes, it built on previously established connections and incipient commercial activities.[39] We must also consider numerous scales of trade as operating in tandem. Investigating the mechanisms by which this took place – and the groups of people involved – is a crucial basis for any understanding. Although much work is still needed to refine knowledge of the precise routes that were first developed, and to trace the wider patterns of pre-Islamic trade, there are significant implications for technology transfer in the recognition of an incipient network of early Trans-Saharan connections.

Burials and identity are themes that we have studied in specific relation to *migration*.[40] Migration needs to be understood as part of a wider pattern of mobility.[41] Identity, expressed most tangibly in burials, is related to technological choices, but also to the mechanisms of technology transfer. One of the major conclusions of the Trans-SAHARA Project burials

---

[35] See Bonifay 2017; Leone 2017 on the rare and unrepresentative evidence of Saharan trade involving Roman pottery.

[36] Bender Jørgensen 2017; Guédon 2017; Mattingly 2017, 24–29; Mattingly and Cole 2017; Mattingly *et al.* 2017b; cf. Magnavita, Chapter 6, this volume.

[37] Compare Cuénod, Chapter 7; Duckworth, Chapter 10, this volume; Dussubieux 2017; Leitch *et al.* 2017; Magnavita 2017.

[38] Cuénod, Chapter 7, this volume.

[39] Cf. Cissé 2017; Haour 2017; Horton *et al.* 2017; MacDonald 2011; Magnavita 2013; Mattingly 2017; Nixon 2017; Wilson 2017.

[40] Gatto *et al.* 2019a.   [41] Mattingly *et al.* 2019a.

workgroup was that there were many cultural commonalities spanning large swathes of the Sahara, and suggestive of a sort of cultural *koine*.[42] Of all ancient peoples of the Sahara, we have far more detailed archaeological information available on the Garamantes of southern Libya. Their funerary structures, rites and beliefs, along with integrated palaeodemographic study of the populations buried in that region were a central focus of the volume.[43] These investigations have revealed significant variations across time and space, some at least attributable to migration, evident in the ancient oasis populations of the Garamantes. There is thus a logical connection between the physical migration of people and technological transfers in the Trans-Saharan zone. For example, we can cite the possibility that has been raised, although not agreed by all experts, of a connection between migrant women (married and/or enslaved) and changes in ceramic technologies in the Central Sahara.[44] Other social factors need to be considered in relation to long-range technology transfers, including kinship links[45] and commercial agents.

The wider comparative studies of funerary practices from other parts of the Trans-Saharan region that we commissioned for that volume revealed significant diversity. The closest links with the Garamantes were manifested by the Western Sahara[46] and Maghrib.[47] Although the Nile Valley is highlighted in some chapters of this volume as an important potential origin point of early technologies, the funerary evidence and the isotopic data so far available mark the Nile Valley as a distinctly separate zone to the Sahara.[48] There seems to be an even less clear connection with the burial traditions of the Sub-Saharan zone, although there are some tantalising hints in burial artefacts of long-range contacts to the north.[49]

The final section of the volume focused on the complementary evidence of linguistics and what it can tell us about the nature of past population migration and when such movements may have taken place.[50] The contribution of Fentress is especially important in that it shows in a clear way how the complex Berber/Amazigh linguistic evidence can be brought into alignment with the archaeological evidence of a Saharan cultural *koine*.[51]

---

[42] Mattingly *et al.* 2019a; Sterry *et al.* 2019.

[43] Mattingly *et al.* 2019b; Gatto *et al.* 2019b; Power *et al.* 2019; Ricci *et al.* 2019.

[44] Gatto *et al.* 2019a.   [45] Robion-Brunner, Chapter 9, this volume.

[46] Bokbot 2019; Clarke and Brooks 2019.   [47] Papi 2019; Sanmartí *et al.* 2019.

[48] Buzon *et al.* 2019; Edwards 2019.

[49] MacEachern 2019; Magnavita 2019; Magnavita, Chapter 6, this volume for the key site of Kissi.

[50] Cf. Blench 2019 and Ehret 2019, who disagree on dates, but who both envisage a similar pattern of pre-Islamic 'Berber' migrations, some at least linked to the process of oasis formation.

[51] Fentress 2019.

This is highly significant because it places the Garamantes in a broader cultural context, with a shared early Amazigh language being present across a large stretch of the Northern, Central and Western Sahara in the first millennium BC, when oasis formation, trade and many technological transfers also seem to have been starting up.

The third volume focused on *urbanisation and state formation*, but also foregrounded this with a discussion about the processes of sedentarisation and oasis formation within the Sahara.[52] The first part focused on a region by region survey and analysis – presenting the known archaeological evidence, a full listing of all radiocarbon dates and new observations based on our satellite image analysis.[53] One of the most important conclusions of the Trans-SAHARA Project is the recognition of extensive oasis development across the Sahara in the pre-Islamic period. This has major historical and archaeological implications, but the evidence now assembled allows us to venture additional arguments. The identification of a degree of settlement hierarchy, involving some higher-level sites of evident urban character, can be related to precocious (and rare) state formation/polity development.[54] It is also important, precisely because such nodes of settlement and communication had the potential to be privileged sites for the reception and transmission of technological innovation.

The wider comparative studies, although by no means exhaustive, covered a range of case studies from areas bordering the Sahara to the east,[55] north[56] and south.[57] Several case studies also had a more specific focus on the Islamic era and revealed some distinctive features of that phase of development, but also emphasised the entangled nature of urbanisation/oasis formation, trade, technological developments and population movements.[58]

The overall impact of the four volumes in the series is to emphasise the interconnectivity of the Trans-Saharan zone. This has profound implications for the technologically focused studies presented in this volume. A joined-up space, no matter how vast a desert and how difficult the transits, offered significant possibilities for technological change and transfer. It is not possible to understand technology across such a zone simply by studying one locality in isolation from the others.

---

[52] Sterry and Mattingly 2020a. See Mattingly and Sterry 2020a for introductory discussion.

[53] Mattingly *et al.* 2020a; 2020b; 2020c; Sterry and Mattingly 2020b; Sterry *et al.* 2020, for the regional surveys; Mattingly and Sterry 2020b; Mattingly *et al.* 2018; Sterry and Mattingly 2020c for overall summary discussions.

[54] Mattingly and Sterry 2020b; Sterry and Mattingly 2020c.

[55] Edwards 2020, with obvious relevance to Humphris, Chapter 8, this volume.

[56] Bokbot 2020; Sanmartí *et al.* 2020; Wilson 2020.

[57] MacDonald 2020; McIntosh 2020; Magnavita 2020.   [58] Capel 2020; Nixon 2020.

Where Do We Go from Here?

In his chapter, Liverani makes some pertinent points about the study of the Sahara.[59] Much of it is likely to be inaccessible to Western scholars for a long time and is difficult and dangerous even for national researchers of the Saharan countries. However, in the meantime work needs to continue. More and more so, responsibility for investigation on the ground must be in the hands of local archaeologists. Foreign archaeologists may have a role to play in skills training and capacity building in Saharan countries, and it is clear that the future of fieldwork will be dependent to some extent on collaborative partnerships with local agencies and researchers. Those of us based in European and other Western nations can also deepen our understanding of these themes, in the absence of fresh evidence from excavations, by applying different approaches or by the scientific study and dating of materials that have been already collected. The recent advancement of scientific analysis is one avenue by which we can continue to study the area, and of course is particularly pertinent to the study of technologies (though the paucity of well-dated, well-contextualised materials in available collections is an obvious drawback). We can also continue to apply archaeology at a distance, for example through the use of satellite imagery. The road ahead will be difficult, with many obstacles to navigate, but for us the agenda of future study is clear from the present volume. There are many important new research questions to address, and new, promising methodologies that can be applied to the study of past technologies. Progress can be made, especially if we embrace the possibility of coming together as archaeologists and historians from different backgrounds and research traditions to reshape the questions we are asking of the Sahara's past.

References

Austen, R.A. 2010. *Trans-Saharan Africa in World History.* Oxford: Oxford University Press.

Bender Jørgensen, L. 2017. Textiles and textile trade in the first millennium AD: Evidence from Egypt. In Mattingly *et al.* 2017a, 231–58.

Blench, R. 2019. The linguistic prehistory of the Sahara. In Gatto *et al.* 2009a, 431–63.

---

[59] Liverani, Chapter 2, this volume.

Bokbot, Y. 2019. Protohistoric and Pre-Islamic funerary archaeology in the Moroccan Pre-Sahara. In Gatto *et al.* 2019a, 315–40.

Bokbot, Y. 2020. The origins of urbanisation and structured political power in Morocco: Indigenous phenomenon or foreign colonisation? In Sterry and Mattingly 2020a, 476–97.

Bonifay, M. 2017. Can we speak of pottery and amphora 'import substitution' in inland regions of Roman Africa? In Mattingly *et al.* 2017a, 341–68.

Buzon, M.R., Schrader, S.A. and Bowen, G.J. 2019. Isotopic approaches to mobility in Northern Africa: Bioarchaeological examination of Egyptian/Nubian interaction in the Nile Valley. In Gatto *et al.* 2019, 223–46.

Capel, C. 2020. At the dawn of Sijilmasa: New historical focus on the process of emergence of a Saharan state and a caravan city. In Sterry and Mattingly 2020a, 594–620.

Cissé, M. 2017. The Trans-Saharan trade connection with Gao (Mali) during the first millennium AD. In Mattingly *et al.* 2017a, 101–30.

Clarke, J. and Brooks, N. 2019. Burial practices in Western Sahara. In Gatto *et al.* 2019a, 341–72.

Dussubieux, L. 2017. Glass beads in Trans-Saharan trade. In Mattingly *et al.* 2017a, 414–32.

Edwards, D. 2019. Between the Nile and the Sahara: Some comparative perspectives. In Gatto *et al.* 2019a, 195–222.

Edwards, D. 2020. Early states and urban forms in the Middle Nile. In Sterry and Mattingly 2020a, 359–95.

Ehret, C. 2019. Berber peoples in the Sahara and North Africa: Linguistic historical proposals. In Gatto *et al.* 2019a, 464–94.

Fentress, E.W.B. 2019. The archaeological and genetic correlates of Amazigh linguistics. In Gatto *et al.* 2019a, 495–524.

Gatto, M., Mattingly, D.J., Ray, N. and Sterry, M. (eds) 2019a. *Burials, Migration and Identity in the Ancient Sahara and Beyond.* Trans-Saharan Archaeology, Volume 2. Series editor D.J. Mattingly. Cambridge: Cambridge University Press and the Society for Libyan Studies.

Gatto, M.C., Mori, L. and Zerboni, A. 2019b. Identity markers in south-western Fazzan: Were the people of the Wadi Tanzzuft/Tadrart Akakus region Garamantes? In Gatto *et al.* 2019a, 108–33.

Guédon, S. 2017. Circulation and trade of textiles in the southern borders of Roman Africa: New hypotheses. In Mattingly *et al.* 2017a, 259–84.

Haour, A. 2017. What made Islamic trade distinctive, as compared to pre-Islamic trade? In Mattingly *et al.* 2017a, 80–100.

Horton, M., Crowther, A. and Boivin, N. 2017. Ships of the desert, camels of the ocean: An Indian Ocean perspective on Trans-Saharan trade. In Mattingly *et al.* 2017a, 131–55.

Leitch, V., Duckworth, C., Cuénod, A., Mattingly, D.J., Sterry, M. and Cole, F. 2017. Early Saharan trade: The inorganic evidence. In Mattingly *et al.* 2017a, 287–340.

Leone, A. 2017. Pottery and trade in North and Sub-Saharan Africa during Late Antiquity. In Mattingly *et al.* 2017a, 369–92.

MacDonald, K. 2011. A view from the south: Sub-Saharan evidence for contacts between North Africa, Mauritania and the Niger 1000 BC–AD 700. In A. Dowler and E.R. Galvin (eds), *Money, Trade and Trade Routes in Pre-Islamic North Africa*, London: British Museum Press, 72–82.

MacDonald, K.C. 2020. Architecture and settlement growth on the southern edge of the Sahara: Timing and possible implications for interactions with the North. In Sterry and Mattingly 2020a, 498–520.

MacEachern, S. 2019. Burial practices, settlement and regional connections around the southern Lake Chad Basin, 1500 BC–AD 1500. In Gatto *et al.* 2019a, 399–428.

McIntosh, S.K. 2020. Long-distance exchange and urban trajectories in the first millennium AD: Case studies from the Middle Niger and Middle Senegal river valleys. In Sterry and Mattingly 2020a, 521–63.

Magnavita, C. 2020. First millennia BC/AD fortified settlements at Lake Chad: Implications for the origins of urbanisation and state formation in Sub-Saharan Africa. In Sterry and Mattingly 2020a, 564–93.

Magnavita, S. 2013. Initial encounters: Seeking traces of ancient trade connections between West Africa and the wider world. *Afriques* 4. http://afriques.revues.org /1145.

Magnavita, S. 2017. Track and trace: Archaeometric approaches to the study of early Saharan trade. In Mattingly *et al.* 2017a, 392–413.

Magnavita, S. 2019. Burial and society at Kissi, Burkina Faso. In Gatto *et al.* 2019a, 375–98.

Mattingly, D.J. 2017. The Garamantes and the origins of Saharan trade: State of the field and future agendas. In Mattingly *et al.* 2017a, 1–52.

Mattingly, D.J. and Cole, F. 2017. Visible and invisible commodities of trade: The significance of organic materials in Saharan trade. In Mattingly *et al.* 2017a, 212–30.

Mattingly, D.J. and Sterry, M. 2020a. Introduction to the themes of urbanisation and state formation in the ancient Sahara and beyond. In Sterry and Mattingly 2020a, 1–50.

Mattingly, D.J. and Sterry, M. 2020b. State formation in the Sahara and beyond. In Sterry and Mattingly 2020a, 695–721.

Mattingly, D.J., Leitch, V., Duckworth, C.N., Cuénod, A., Sterry, M. and Cole, F. (eds) 2017a. *Trade in the Ancient Sahara and Beyond*. Trans-Saharan Archaeology, Volume 1. Series editor D.J. Mattingly. Cambridge: Cambridge University Press and the Society for Libyan Studies.

Mattingly, D.J., Cuénod, A., Duckworth, C., Leitch, V. and Sterry, M. 2017b. Concluding discussion. In Mattingly *et al.* 2017a, 433–40.

Mattingly, D.J., Sterry, M., al-Haddad, M. and Bokbot, Y. 2018. Beyond the Garamantes: The early development of Saharan oases. In L. Purdue,

J. Charbonnier and L. Khalidi (eds), *Des refuges aux oasis: Vivre en milieu aride de la Préhistoire à aujourd'hui. XXXVIIIe rencontres internationales d'archéologie et d'histoire d'Antibes*, Antibes: Éditions APDCA, 205–28.

Mattingly, D.J., Gatto, M., Ray, N. and Sterry, M. 2019a. Introduction: Migration, burial and identity in the Sahara. In Gatto *et al.* 2019a, 1–50.

Mattingly, D.J., Gatto, M., Ray, N. and Sterry, M. 2019b. Dying to be Garamantian: Burial and migration in Fazzan. In Gatto *et al.* 2019a, 51–107.

Mattingly, D.J., Merlo, S., Mori, L. and Sterry, M. 2020a. Garamantian oasis settlements in Fazzan. In Sterry and Mattingly 2020a, 53–111.

Mattingly, D.J., Sterry, M., al-Haddad, M. and Trousset, P. 2020b. Pre-Islamic oasis settlements in the Northern Sahara. In Sterry and Mattingly 2020a, 187–238.

Mattingly, D.J., Sterry, M., Rayne, L. and al-Haddad, M. 2020c. Pre-Islamic oasis settlements in the Eastern Sahara. In Sterry and Mattingly 2020a, 112–46.

Nixon, S. 2017. Trans-Saharan gold trade in pre-modern times: Available evidence and research agendas. In Mattingly *et al.* 2017a, 156–88.

Nixon, S. 2020. The early Islamic Trans-Saharan market towns of West Africa. In Sterry and Mattingly 2020a, 621–66.

Papi, E. 2019. Revisiting first millennium BC graves in north-west Morocco. In Gatto *et al.* 2019a, 281–311.

Power, R., Nikita, E., Mattingly, D.J., Lahr, M.M. and O'Connell, T.C. 2019. Human mobility and identity: variation, diet and migration in relation to the Garamantes of Fazzan. In Gatto *et al.* 2019, 134–61.

Ricci, F., Tafuri, M.A., Castorina, F., di Vincenzo, F., Mori, L. and Manzi, G. 2019. The Garamantes from Fewet (Ghat, Fazzan, Libya): A skeletal perspective. In Gatto *et al.* 2019, 162–92.

Sanmartí, J., Cruz Folch, I., Campilo, J. and Montanero, D. 2019. Numidian burial practices. In Gatto *et al.* 2019a: 249–90.

Sanmartí, J., Kallala, N., Belarte, M.C., Ramon, J., Cantero, F.J., López, L., Portillo, M. and Valenzuela, S. 2020. Numidian state formation in the Tunisian High Tell. In Sterry and Mattingly 2020a, 438–75.

Scheele, J. 2017. The need for nomads: Camel-herding, raiding and Saharan trade. In Mattingly *et al.* 2017a, 55–79.

Scheele, J. 2020. Urbanisation, inequality and political authority in the Sahara. In Sterry and Mattingly 2020a, 667–91.

Sterry, M. and Mattingly, D.J. (eds) 2020a. *Urbanisation and State Formation in the Ancient Sahara and Beyond*, Trans-Saharan Archaeology, Volume 3, series editor D.J. Mattingly, Cambridge: Cambridge University Press and the Society for Libyan Studies.

Sterry, M. and Mattingly, D.J. 2020b. Pre-Islamic oasis settlements in the Southern Sahara. In Sterry and Mattingly 2020a, 277–329.

Sterry, M. and Mattingly, D.J. 2020c. Discussion: Sedentarisation and urbanisation in the Sahara. In Sterry and Mattingly 2020a, 330–55.

Sterry, M., Mattingly, D.J., Gatto, M. and Ray, N. 2019. Concluding discussion. In Gatto *et al.* 2019a, 525–62.

Sterry, M., Mattingly, D.J. and Bokbot, Y. 2020. Pre-Islamic oasis settlements in the Western Sahara. In Sterry and Mattingly 2020a, 239–76.

Wilson, A.I. 2017. Saharan exports to the Roman world. In Mattingly *et al.* 2017a, 189–208.

Wilson, A.I. 2020. Mediterranean urbanisation in North Africa: Greek, Punic and Roman models. In Sterry and Mattingly 2020a, 396–437.

Index

[Page numbers in italics are figures; with 't' are tables; with 'n' are notes].